HOWARD CARTER

Howard Carter, by his brother William Carter, 1924

HOWARD CARTER

The Path to Tutankhamun

T. G. H. James

KEGAN PAUL INTERNATIONAL
London and New York

First published in 1992 by
Kegan Paul International Ltd
PO Box 256, London WC1B 3SW, England

Distributed by
John Wiley & Sons Ltd
Southern Cross Trading Estate
1 Oldlands Way, Bognor Regis
West Sussex, PO22 9SA, England

Routledge, Chapman & Hall Inc
29 West 35th Street
New York, NY 10001, USA

© T. G. H. James 1992

Phototypeset in 10/12pt Baskerville
by Intype, London
Printed in Great Britain by
TJ Press, Padstow, Cornwall

British Library Cataloguing in Publication Data
James, T. G. H. (Thomas Garnet Henry)
Howard Carter : the path to Tutankhamun
1. Egyptology
I. Title
932.0072024
ISBN 0–7103–0425–0

Library of Congress Cataloging-in-Publication Data
James, T. G. H. (Thomas Garnet Henry)
444 pp.   234 cm.
Includes bibliographical references and index.
ISBN 0–7103–0425–0
1. Carter, Howard, 1873–1939. 2. Egyptologists—Great Britain—
Biography. I. Title.
PJ1064.C3J3   1992
941.083′092—dc20
[B]

For
ANNE PEMBERTON

CONTENTS

MAPS

ILLUSTRATIONS

the Mena House Hotel, Giza, with the Great Pyramid in the background, 1905 (*courtesy* John Carter)

18 Castle Carter at Elwat el-Diban, built 1911. Phyllis Walker notes (1930): 'left window, dining room – right, UH's [Uncle Howard's] room, middle window, spare room, extreme left kitchen and servant quarters. The rest is desert!' (*courtesy* John Carter)

Between pages 304 and 305

19 Carter with an unidentified visitor inspects a find at Balamun, 1913 (*courtesy* Griffith Institute)

20 One of Carter's drawings of the Opet Festival reliefs in the Luxor Temple (*courtesy* Griffith Institute)

21 The 5th Earl of Carnarvon and Howard Carter, photographed 18 February 1923 by Queen Élisabeth of the Belgians (*courtesy* Fondation Égyptologique Reine Élisabeth)

22 Carter conducts the Tutankhamun 'mannequin' from the tomb; the Earl of Carnarvon sits on the wall, and to his right, behind, is Arthur Weigall (*courtesy* Griffith Institute)

23 The first Ford 'in the desert', outside Castle Carter, 1923. *From left:* Carter, chauffeur, Mace, Burton, Lucas (*courtesy* Margaret Orr)

24 Blocked entrance to the burial chamber of Tutankhamun's tomb, showing the basket-work concealing the intruder's hole and subsequent reblocking (*courtesy* Griffith Institute)

25 Carter's team prepare for the day's sortie into the Valley: *from left,* Alfred Lucas, Arthur Callender, Carter, Arthur Mace (*courtesy* Margaret Orr)

26 The Press Corps advance to battle up the Valley; Arthur Weigall on the right (*courtesy* Griffith Institute)

27 A convoy of cases containing Tutankhamun objects makes its way to the river *en route* for Cairo (*courtesy* Griffith Institute)

28 Percy White at Ludlow, 1930 (*courtesy* John Carter)

29 Carter with his niece Phyllis Walker, *c.* 1931 (*courtesy* John Carter)

30 The study at 2, Prince's Gate Court, 1934 (*courtesy* John Carter)

31 Studio photograph of Carter, *c.* 1930 (*courtesy* John Carter)

32 Carter at the lectern, *c.* 1934 (*courtesy* John Carter)

33 A formal dinner in Stockholm, May 1930. *From left:* Consul-General J. Sachs, Mrs Helling, Carter, Mrs Boström, Admiral Lindberg (*courtesy* John Carter)

34 Howard Carter with the Crown Prince of Sweden and ADC on board the SS *Ausonia*, bound for Egypt, September 1930 (*courtesy* John Carter)

35 Carter with the Egyptian Queen Mother and entourage in the Valley, *c.* 1932 (*courtesy* John Carter)

36 Carter with King Farouk in the Valley, 1936 (*courtesy* John Carter)

37 Letter of condolence written by Howard Carter's house servants to Phyllis Walker (*courtesy* John Carter)

PREFACE

For someone like myself, who grew up before the Second World War, and became a professional Egyptologist after the war, Tutankhamun and Howard Carter have been constant symbols of the popular appeal of Egypt; although for much of the time it would have been thought slightly *de trop* to show professionally too active an interest in them. The great Tutankhamun exhibition of 1972 in London, masterminded by Dr I. E. S. Edwards, not only stimulated unprecedented curiosity in the tomb, its contents and its discoverers, but also obliged many specialists to reconsider the extraordinary achievement of Howard Carter in the management of the discovery. I did not myself appreciate the extent to which I had become, almost subliminally, engaged in the career of this man, until I was approached by Anne Pemberton about the preparation of a biography. In her I was confronted by a true Carter enthusiast who already had, to a far greater extent than myself, a broad understanding of the many aspects of her hero's accomplishments. She certainly stimulated my interest to the point when a Carter biography seemed the natural task to take up in retirement. It is therefore most proper that this book should be dedicated to her. I am profoundly grateful to her for starting me on a remarkable quest, and for regular support over the years. I am only marginally less indebted to her husband Jeremy Pemberton, whose help in many matters – not least in providing the inspiration for the book's dust-jacket – has been a sustaining factor throughout.

Anne Pemberton's happy approach was but the beginning of several years' search and research of a kind I had never undertaken before, in the course of which I received help and stimulation from a wide range of friends, colleagues, private owners of documents, officials in public and private archives, and others who by personal knowledge or family connections were able to point me in productive directions.

Of those who knew Howard Carter personally, I recall with special affection Cyril Aldred, with whom I spoke on a number of occasions before his sad death in 1991, about his meetings with Carter in the early 1930s and of his life-long interest in the great discovery. Margaret Orr, who entertained Carter at a dolls' tea-party in 1924, entertained me more recently with her memories, and most generously allowed me to see and use the letters and other papers of her father and mother, Arthur and Winifred Mace. Dr Harold Plenderleith shared with me his own recollections of working on specimens from the tomb of Tutankhamun in Thebes and London, and of his many meetings with Carter in the late 1920s.

Mr Terry Eva, with ready liberality, has allowed me to quote from the Amherst letters in his possession. Mrs Stanley Chattey has been equally generous with the surviving volumes of Alicia Amherst's journal. The Earl of Carnarvon has from the outset shown great interest in what I have been doing, and has readily allowed me to quote from the few surviving papers at Highclere.

From the Carter family I am especially indebted to John Carter, who made freely available the considerable papers formerly in the possession of Phyllis Walker. Mr Benjamin Ripper, another cousin by descent and the native historian of Swaffham, readily shared family and local memories and also introduced me to Ivy Wilson who, as a little girl, ran errands for Howard Carter's mother and aunts at the Sporle Road Cottage.

Minnie Burton's diary, providentially brought to my attention by Rosalind Berwald, who acquired it some years ago, provides fascinating information about the social life in Thebes during the years of discovery. I greatly appreciate Mrs Berwald's willingness to allow me to quote from it. To Philippa Moore and Vronwy Hankey I am grateful for the chance to see and make use of some of the letters of Arthur Weigall, Mrs Moore's father. Margaret Gardiner equally generously let me see and reproduce extracts from Sir Alan Gardiner's private letters.

The help I have received in public institutions, museums and archives has invariably been unstinted. In the Department of Egyptian Art in the Metropolitan Museum of Art, Dr Dorothea Arnold has been exceptionally kind in making material available from the rich holdings of Carter and associated papers, and I have also received particular assistance from Dr Christine Lilyquist, Marsha Hill (who has very kindly checked so many quotations) and Dr Catherine Roehrig. In Chicago I was greeted most warmly by the former and present Directors of the Oriental Institute, Dr Janet Johnson and Dr William Sumner, and given most creative help by John Larson, the archivist of the Oriental Institute Museum, whose contributions to this biography are many and various. In the Cleveland Museum of Art the Director, Dr Evan Turner, the Curator of Ancient Art, Dr Arielle Kozloff, and the Archivist, Virginia Krumholz, were more than liberal in their help. In distant Portland, Mr Thomas Vaughan, former Director of the Oregon Historical Society, most generously made the facilities of his remarkably well organized institution available to me, with the assistance of his Associate Director Millard McClung, and Chief Librarian Louis Flannery. From the Detroit Institute of Arts, Dr William Peck readily provided information and copies of documents on request; as did Julie Bledsloe, Registrar of the Biltmore Estate, to which source I was generously directed by the late James Manning. Dr Rita Freed, of the Department of Egyptian and Ancient Near Eastern Art in the Museum of Fine Arts Boston, was characteristically helpful; so too my colleagues at the British Museum, Terence Mitchell and Dr John Curtis, former and present Keepers of Western Asiatic Antiquities, and Marjorie Caygill in the Director's Office.

In my old Department of Egyptian Antiquities the present Keeper, Vivian Davies, and his staff have invariably been welcoming and helpful, making the library and other facilities of the department always available. Nicholas Reeves, formerly of the Egyptian Department, with his deep knowledge of the Valley of the Kings and the whole industry of Tutankhamun studies, has been a constant and willing source of reference, and a sounding-board for ideas. David Butters, Curator of the Swaffham Museum, who organized two very interesting Carter exhibitions in 1989, has been a regularly ally in the provision and checking of Norfolk information.

My very special thanks must be extended to the Committee of Management of the Griffith Institute, Ashmolean Museum, Oxford, where the principal Carter archive is housed; and in the Institute particularly to Dr Jaromir Malek, the Archivist, for so much positive help, for seeming always to be on hand and ready to discuss a matter, to Dr Diana Magee, Fiona Strachan and Elizabeth Miles, for answering so many enquiries and for opening and shutting cupboards and lifting down awkward bundles of drawings on many visits to Oxford. Also in Oxford, I am grateful to Dr Derek Hopwood, Director of the Middle East Centre in St Antony's College, and Diana Ring, its librarian, for giving me access to the journals of Mervyn Herbert. To them and to the present Mervyn Herbert I am grateful for permission to use extracts in this book.

In London, the Committee of the Egypt Exploration Society has allowed me to search the early papers in its archives for Carter material; Dr Patricia Spencer, the Secretary, and her assistant Sylvie Weens, have been invariably helpful. The Directors of News international PLC, through their Deputy Archivist, Eamon Dyas, have generously provided me with photocopies of documents, and allowed me to reproduce the text of the agreement made in 1923 between *The Times* and the Earl of Carnarvon. In Geneva I owe a special debt of gratitude to Professor Michel Valloggia for searching out and obtaining copies of Carter, Naville and Maspero correspondence in the Bibliothèque publique et universitaire in that city, and to that institution for allowing me to quote from these documents; and also to Professor Denis van Berchem, a grandson of Édouard Naville, for showing much interest and encouragement.

To the governing bodies of all the institutions mentioned above, I am grateful for permission to quote from the relevant documents in their possession.

There are many others to whom I owe thanks for additional, occasional, and peripheral material, which has helped to enrich and diversify my narrative: Francis Allen, N. G. Stafford Allen, Mrs Elizabeth Reeves and Antony Allen (for information on Carter and the Allens of Cockley Cley), Margaret S. Drower (for help with Petrie information), Dr Andrew Gordon (for an early Carter letter), Robert Keedick (for a copy of his father's recollections of Carter's American tour), Jean Kennedy (for information on holdings in the Norfolk Record Office), Dr Christopher Lee (for Mace information), Deirdre Le Faye (for Carter's association with the Lucovich family), Arpag Mekhitarian (for copies of documents and photographs on ·Queen Élisabeth of the Belgians, Jean Capart and Carter), Dr Peter Piccione (for investigating bricks at Elwat el-Diban), Julia Rushbury (for memories of William Carter), Dr Gerry Scott (for material on Carter's Yale degree), Professor A. F. Shore (for a letter from Carnarvon to A. M. Blackman), Professor W. T. Stearn (on the botanical activities of Alicia Amherst and P. E. Newberry), Edna S. Weiss (for records of Carters at the Royal Academy Schools, and in the RA Summer Exhibitions), P. M. White (on Bretby bricks), Finbarr Whooley (for background material on the British Empire Exhibition of 1924), Irma Wilkinson (for access to the papers of Charles Wilkinson and for general encouragement).

In an early stage in the writing of this volume I receive invaluable help from Annette Webb, Secretary of the Institute of Egyptian Art and Archaeology at Memphis State University, who performed marvels of decipherment. To my former colleague, Christine Barratt, I am indebted for the maps and plan. To my editor, Carol Gardiner, go special thanks for eliminating so many inconsistencies, removing so many infelicities, and generally for giving this book a professional finish.

Readers should not be disconcerted by variations in the spelling of proper names, particularly ancient royal names. The variations reflect differing traditions of vocalizing the unvocalized ancient forms. In the case of Tutankhamun the variations are many, and are retained in quotations; for most scholars in Britain the form above is commonly used.

The ancient dates used in this volume generally follow those given in J. Baines and J. Malek, *Atlas of Ancient Egypt*.

The kindness I have been shown in so many places has, in my experience, been exceptional, and I have the happiest memories of hospitable stays with friends and colleagues during a search which began simply, and expanded enormously over the years. But no one has been more kind and forbearing than my wife Diana, and my son Stephen, who have at all times helped me with my research, and have latterly endured many months of aggrandizement in the use of space at home, and of time in general.

London, January 1992   T. G. H. James

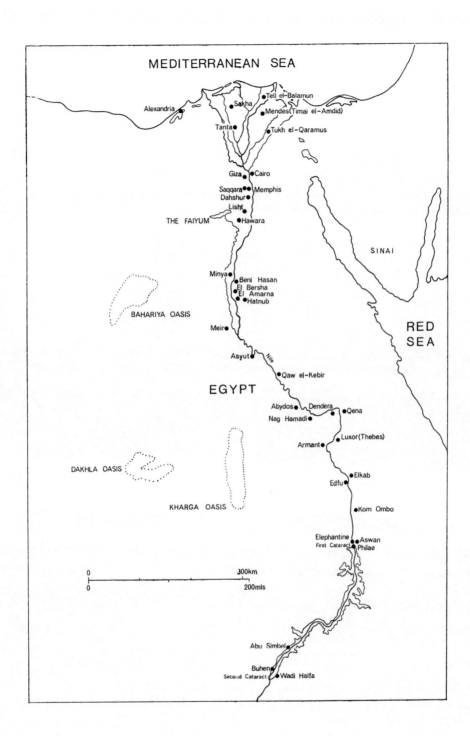

MEDITERRANEAN SEA

Alexandria

Tell el-Balamun
Sakha
Mendes(Timai el-Amdid)
Tanta
Tukh el-Qaramus

Giza Cairo
Saqqara Memphis
Dahshur
Lisht
THE FAIYUM Hawara

SINAI

Minya
Beni Hasan
El Bersha
El Amarna
Hatnub

BAHARIYA OASIS

Meir

RED SEA

Asyut
Nile
Qaw el-Kebir

EGYPT

Abydos Dendera
Qena
Nag Hamadi

Luxor(Thebes)
Armant

DAKHLA OASIS

Elkab
Edfu

KHARGA OASIS

Kom Ombo

Elephantine Aswan
First Cataract Philae

0   300km
0   200mls

Abu Simbel

Buhen
Second Cataract Wadi Halfa

XV

1

EARLY YEARS

A sad, small company gathered at Putney Vale Cemetery in South London on 6 March 1939 to say 'Farewell!' to Howard Carter. It was not the kind of gathering which commonly attends the obsequies of the great and famous, but it yet offered, in modest scale, a fair representation of the various parts of the life of one who had in his time achieved remarkable popular esteem. The 'great Egyptologist', as *The Times* obituary appropriately called him, 'who gained fame for his part in one of the most successful and exciting episodes in the annals of archaeology, the discovery and exploration of the tomb of Tutankhamen', had died in relative obscurity, his ultimate purposes unfulfilled, his real achievements uncrowned by official recognition.[1] He had been born to a life of moderate expectation; he ended his life with none of the pomp and splendour with which he had become familiar in the mortuary ceremonies and paraphernalia of the monarchs of Egypt in the Valley of the Kings at Thebes. And yet his life had been one of greater success than most can expect, and its elements were recognized among the few who listened to the words of the Revd H. C. Kemp, Vicar of Putney, on that grey day. To represent his family there were his brother William, a fine portrait painter, and his nephew Samuel John, an engineer and bearer of traditional Carter names; there was Lady Evelyn Beauchamp, daughter of the fifth Earl of Carnarvon, who had accompanied her father in the early, heady, days of the opening of the famous tomb; there was Gerald Wainwright, a former colleague from the ranks of excavators in Egypt. George Eumorfopoulos, a great collector of oriental and Egyptian works of art, in a sense represented those whom Howard Carter had helped in their collecting in his later years.

If Howard Carter had made preparations well in advance of his death, as the ancient Egyptians had regularly done, he would almost certainly have caused incorrect details to be recorded on his grave-stone. 'It is strange Carter did not know his age – I am all too conscious of mine,'

---

1 *The Times* for 3 March 1939; the obituary almost certainly written by P. E. Newberry. The account of the funeral was in the issue of 7 March.

commented Alan Gardiner to Percy Newberry in 1945.[2] This strange ignorance had been revealed by Carter's niece, Phyllis Walker, who had discovered from a scrutiny of her uncle's birth-certificate that he was born on 9 May 1874, and not in 1873 as he had stated in his annual entries in *Who's Who* since 1924. It was an error perpetuated in the various obituaries which were written after his death, even in those composed by his old friend Percy Newberry. There is no need to think that Carter had any strange motive for falsifying his age – indeed 'falsify' is surely the wrong word to use. What advantage could be achieved by adding one year to one's proper age? Presumably he confused the year at a fairly early stage in his career and the error persisted, fixed in his mind as being correct. He lived, it must be conceded, at a time when form-filling and documentary verification were not as prevalent as they have since become. It would be scarcely worth while drawing attention to Carter's error were it not symptomatic of much that he subsequently wrote, in which precision of detail was not of primary importance. He composed in later life a number of autobiographical sketches of considerable charm, but unfortunately so full of errors and inconsistencies – where precision can be secured from more reliable sources – that they can be taken only as rough guides to his career.[3] They remain, nevertheless, very interesting, if only because they are rightly flavoured with his own brand of personal romance and are studded with comments and reflections which illuminate his attitudes to a wide variety of topics. Some of these were crucial to his whole life – his remarks on drawing and epigraphy, for example – while others preserve his mature views often expressed anachronistically, as if formulated by himself when a youth or young man. His chronological errors tend to be more tiresome than significant, but for a biographer they are very vexing and often time-consuming in their explication. A good example concerns his father's death in 1892. In his late sketch he describes a visit he made with Flinders Petrie to see the recently discovered tomb of Akhenaten at El-Amarna. From Petrie's contemporary diary the visit can be fixed fairly precisely to about 21 January 1892.[4] In his sketch Howard Carter notes that 'the next morning brought one of those sad days which usher in another phase of life'. A cable and a letter arrived announcing his father's death. His father actually died on 1 May 1892. Again the error is of little significance, but it does point to the unreliability of the sketches as primary historical documents.

In one matter, however, the sketch of his early life preserved in the Griffith Institute in Oxford is correct against other published sources. The

2 Letter of Alan Gardiner to Percy Newberry of 1 March 1945; G.I. Newberry Corr. 18/133.
3 A set of versions of the sketches is in the Griffith Institute, Carter Notebooks 15–17; a further set in the possession of John Carter; other versions in the Metropolitan Museum, Egyptian Department. Sketch II, 'An Account of Myself', is in G.I. Carter Notebook 15.
4 See p. 33 below.

Who's Who entries record that Carter was born in Swaffham, Norfolk. This might be described as his 'official' statement, for a *Who's Who* entry is composed by the person concerned. In his sketch he states: 'I was born in the early seventies at my father's town house in Earl's Court.' The mention of Swaffham in *Who's Who* is another harmless error which may represent a kind of inverted snobbism not now easily comprehended. Swaffham was certainly a place of importance, and probably of emotional attachment, for Carter throughout his life. It seems altogether unlikely that he had forgotten his birthplace when he first compiled his *Who's Who* entry, but at the time – not long after the discovery of the tomb of King Tutankhamun – he may have felt it necessary to dignify his origins. Swaffham suggested a good country base; Earl's Court, or Brompton as it might more properly be described, has less comfortable associations. But the reason for the error might have been something quite different; yet it is strange that he allowed it to persist (like that of his birth date) in all entries down to his death.

So, as his birth certificate confirms, Howard Carter was born on 9 May 1874, at 10 Rich Terrace in the sub-district of Brompton in Kensington. Rich Terrace no longer exists. It occupied part of the north side of the Old Brompton Road to the west of the junction with Earl's Court Road, and the site is now filled by Richmond Mansions, 248–250 Old Brompton Road. Rich Lane, originally perhaps a kind of mews or service road for Rich Terrace, still exists to the west of Richmond Mansions. Rich Terrace was demolished in the 1890s, but no. 10 was recorded in the local directory as standing as late as 1892, the year of Howard Carter's father's death.[5] 'My father's town house' is Carter's description of what was certainly a fairly modest terraced house with a garden. It can scarcely have been the property he romantically evokes as 'this quaint old house' with 'a lovely garden with beautiful trees, and for the purpose of study large pens for animals'. The house properly belonged not to his father but to his mother. It is known that it was first rented by the Carter family in 1868 from Miss Elizabeth Hall, who subsequently lived herself in 14 Rich Terrace. On her death some years later, she bequeathed all her property to 'Martha Joyce, wife of Samuel Carter'.[6] For practical purposes, however, Samuel would have acted as the house owner.

Samuel John and Martha Joyce (née Sands), Howard Carter's father and mother, were both natives of Swaffham in north-west Norfolk, a small but thriving market-town on the road from King's Lynn to Norwich. Its appearance in the late twentieth century – at least as far as its heart, the Market Place, and its surrounds, is concerned – differs little from what the Carters would have known a century ago. Like many small country

5 Information on Rich Terrace provided by the Town Clerk of the Royal Borough of Kensington and Chelsea, in a letter to B. Ripper of 20 June 1972.
6 Documents on the ownership of 10 Rich Terrace are with John Carter.

towns in East Anglia, Swaffham presents, architecturally, a mixed face, mostly of stone and brick, and of the eighteenth and nineteenth centuries. The obligatory, but tiny, shopping 'mall' of recent years is discreetly tucked away on the west side of the Square, and most of the remaining additions and modifications of the late twentieth century do little to disturb the settled, comfortable aspect of the whole. Cars have replaced carts, and they fill the Square except on market days when the town reasserts its essential character as a place for buying and selling for the surrounding district, and a centre for general and domestic concourse. As you enter the town from the direction of King's Lynn, a sharp eye will spot the brightly painted carving of the Pedlar of Swaffham, a fifteenth-century local notable, John Chapman, 'who did by a dream find a great treasure'. It is the town sign, one of the many in Norfolk designed and painted by Henry Robert (Harry) Carter, another of the Carters of Swaffham and North Norfolk – mostly interrelated and artistically talented – who was a distant cousin of Howard Carter.[7] Swaffham and its environs, family associations, and art, were to be powerful influences in the development of the young man who would go to Egypt in his late teens and ultimately make the most dramatic archaeological discovery of modern times.

Howard Carter's immediate family has been traced back to a Robert Carter, his great grand-father, who married Susanna Dunger in 1785 at the church of St Andrew, Great Dunham, a village about five miles to the north-east of Swaffham. At that time the Carters lived apparently (the sources are not certain) at Rookery Farm near Great Dunham, a place that earns a mention in Pevsner's *The Buildings of England*.[8] The family has been characterized as being of yeoman stock, and such would certainly apply to Samuel Carter, one of the sons of Robert and Susanna. He was born in 1792, married Frances Spinks of Swaffham in 1832, and became the gamekeeper and agent of Robert Hamond, the local squire and Lord of Swaffham Manor. He lived with his family in the Keeper's Cottage not far from the Manor House.[9] It was here that Samuel John, Howard's father, was born in 1835. From an early age he showed a marked artistic talent which was encouraged by Robert Hamond. A short sketch of the family by Frederick Keeling-Scott, vicar of Swaffham from 1908 to 1928, written shortly after the discovery of King Tutankhamun's tomb,[10] states that at the time of Samuel John's childhood there was a school of drawing in Swaffham supervised by John Sell Cotman, the distinguished water-colour painter and etcher and member of the Norwich School of artists. Samuel John is stated to have won the first prize at the school in 1845

7 For Swaffham generally see B. Ripper, *Ribbons from the Pedlar's Pack* (Swaffham, 1979); for John Chapman see p. 48; for Henry Carter, p. 113. Also, David C. Butters, *Swaffham, In the Pedlar's Footsteps* (North Walsham, 1990), pp. 1–2, 28–31.

8 *North-West and South Norfolk* (1962), p. 176.

9 B. Ripper, *Ribbons from the Pedlar's Pack*, p. 111.

10 *Eastern Daily Press* for 20 February 1923, p. 6.

when he was ten years old. Cotman had died in 1842, but what the Revd Keeling-Scott reported were surely matters as they were remembered by the Carter family, whom he clearly knew well. The school may indeed have been set up by Cotman, and perhaps run after his death by one or both of his sons, Miles Edmund and John Joseph, who were also talented painters. Keeling-Scott further states that Samuel John was sent to the Royal Academy Schools in London, and that he won a silver medal in his first term. Unfortunately this connection with the Royal Academy Schools has not been confirmed from the records of the Schools, and it seems possible that there was some confusion in the family memory in this matter with the early career of Samuel John's most artistically gifted son, William. He certainly attended the R.A. Schools from 1879, winning prizes, including silver medals, on several occasions.[11]

Whatever may be the truth about Samuel John's early career and training, there is no question about his later successful life as an artist, based partly in London and partly in Swaffham. He specialized in painting animals, domestic, agricultural and in the wild. For over twenty years (1867–89) he was the principal animal illustrator for the *Illustrated London News*, contributing excellent drawings of animals in nature, at agricultural shows, and in family circumstances. He developed a considerable practice in the country, painting for the gentry and nobility charming and sometimes dramatic pictures in the high Victorian style perhaps best exemplified in the work of Sir Edwin Landseer. Indeed, another Carter family tradition claims that Samuel John made the original drawings for the great Landseer lion sculptures at the base of Nelson's Column in Trafalgar Square. Sentiment, in harmony with the times and the interests of his patrons, was not avoided, ample confirmation being found in the titles of the paintings shown by him in the annual Royal Academy Summer Exhibitions. He had paintings accepted from 1855 ('A Chase') until 1890 ('The Biter bit'), rarely failing to have one or more canvases included annually. The flavour of his subject-matter is well conveyed by a selection of titles: 'Gelert: "The gallant hound the wolf had slain . . ." ' (1865); 'Rescued from the wolf' (1866); 'A Duel on the Black Mount, N.B. "And 'twere grand sight as the eagles came fighting down the mountains . . ." ' (1874); 'To the rescue: Norfolk coast. "A lifeboat manned with a gallant crew . . ." ' (1882). In 1875 John Ruskin commented most favourably on two of the paintings by Samuel John Carter in the Summer Exhibition.[12] On 'The first taste': 'Altogether enjoyable to me; and I am prepared to maintain (as a true

11 Information provided by Edna S. Weiss of the Information Service of the Royal Academy of Arts.
12 The Samuel John Carter paintings are listed in Algernon Graves, *The Royal Academy of Arts. A Complete Dictionary of Contributors and their Work from its foundation in 1769 to 1904.* For Ruskin's comments see J. Ruskin, *Notes on some of the principal pictures exhibited in the rooms of the Royal Academy* (London, 1875), p. 41. I owe this last reference in the first instance to Antony Griffiths, Keeper of Prints and Drawings in the British Museum.

lover of dogs young and old), . . . that this picture is exemplary in its choice of a moment of supreme puppy felicity as properest time for puppy portraiture'; on 'The Little Wanderers': '. . . a most pathetic and touching group of children in the wood. You may see if you take your opera-glass to it, that the robin is even promising to cover them with leaves, if indeed things are to end, as seems too probable.'

The large animal pens kept in the garden at 10 Rich Terraces housed an unspecified variety of small animals used by Samuel John as models both for his country paintings and for his journalistic sketches. Howard Carter himself was early encouraged to draw animals, using no doubt the residents of those pens to practise on. He retained a very high regard for his father's artistic skills, and in his autobiographical sketch he says of himself and his brothers and sister: 'We all inherited from our father an inborn faculty for drawing: he being an animal painter of no little fame, and one of the most powerful draughtsmen I ever knew. His knowledge of comparative anatomy and memory for form was [sic] matchless. He could depict from memory, accurately, any animal in any action, foreshortened or otherwise, with the greatest ease.'

Samuel John Carter undoubtedly moved easily in the artistic circles of Victorian London, and even if he never reached the highest ranks of fame he yet was sufficiently well acquainted with those who occupied those ranks to be able to secure the sponsorship (or recommendation) of Sir John Everett Millais for the entry into the R.A. Schools in 1874 of his son William, who was then just 16 years old. His familiarity with the artistic life of the capital dated back at least to 1855 when he first exhibited in the Summer Exhibition. He seems to have kept a base in London, mostly in the King's Road, Chelsea, or in Pimlico, until he settled at 10 Rich Terrace in 1868. By then he had been married for 10 years to Martha Joyce, daughter of Mr Sands, a builder of Swaffham. In the meanwhile he had also acquired a house just outside Swaffham, on the road to the village of Sporle. This became the Carter's 'country residence' where some at least of their ten sons and one daughter were born. The Sporle Road cottage remained the Carter Swaffham home until at least the death of Samuel John's surviving sister in 1929. This sister, Fanny, with her younger sister Catherine (Kate), were installed in the Swaffham cottage, maintaining it for the London Carters who might from time to time descend on this country residence for holidays or to pursue painting commissions.

By the time Howard Carter, the baby of the family, was born three of his brothers were already dead, and Howard himself was not thought to be very robust. In consequence he was sent to Swaffham when quite young, to be brought up by his aunts Fanny and Kate. The sketch, quoted from time to time in this chapter, states: '. . . soon after my birth I was taken in charge of a nurse to our house in Swaffham in Norfolk.' His mother, no doubt, was relieved not to have to bring up a weakly baby in a London household with six other children. Howard Carter says little of his mother in his sketch apart from remarking that she was 'a small, kindly woman' who 'loved luxury. A weakness also inherited by her youngest son.' There is no indication from the few surviving letters addressed to her that he felt anything but affection for her, although the ties which commonly bond sons to their mothers were probably less strong than they might have been if he had been brought up conventionally by her from birth. The surviving drawing of her made by William Carter shows her as a most sympathetic person, with a face inclined to humour and understanding, even perhaps indulgence.[13] She might never be quite the confidante of her son; but it was to her that he would address the easiest and most relaxed of the family letters that have survived. He may have been closer to his sister Amy; but the evidence is slight.

It seems likely that the young Howard spent the greater part of his childhood and early teens in Swaffham, but again there is no escaping the fact that the evidence is not substantial. And the same lack of evidence applies to his education. In the Oxford version of his autobiographical sketch he says laconically: 'About education I have next to nothing to say. As I was not strong, I was debarred from public school life and games.' He enlarges on this comment in the version in the possession of John Carter: 'I have next to nothing to say about education. During my younger days I was a bad herniary case, and thus I was unable to go through a regular school training or join in sports such as other lads did and still do.' A search of local Swaffham school records has failed to find Howard's name;[14] and the mention in Who's Who of 'Private education (owing to health)' scarcely advances the matter. The most positive statement comes in the obituary of Carter written by the British Egyptologist Guy Brunton, who knew him well.[15] He talks of education in a dame-school, a fact that he may well have gleaned from Carter in his later life, when he might have been less bothered at revealing the modest nature of his schooling. Dame-schools were in a sense the precursors of nursery and infant schools, run usually by moderately well educated ladies, and offering little more than simple instruction in reading, writing and arithmetic. They lay outside the ambit of the state school system, and could be very poor or very good. Normally they would not retain pupils over the age of about nine or ten. The evidence of Carter's letters written about the time he first went to Egypt suggests that he had received a fair education as far as being able to compose a letter; but his spelling was erratic, and his punctuation rudimentary. Of his mathematics, one can only hazard a favourable estimate from the fact that Flinders Petrie, no mean practical mathematician himself, felt able to entrust surveying and mapping to Carter while they were working together at El-Amarna in the spring of 1892.

13 In the possession of John Carter.
14 The search made by David Butters of the Swaffham Museum.
15 In A.S.A.E. 39 (1939), pp. 49–53.

There remains one unspecific but intriguing clue about education which might have occurred in the years following Howard Carter's attendance at the putative dame-school. The late Mr Nigel Allen, who latterly lived in Guernsey, has written that his father, Mr Francis Allen, 'financed much of Howard Carter's education at Swaffham, and actually sent him on his first expedition to Egypt'.[16] Mr Allen's English home was Cockley Cley Hall in Norfolk, about 3½ miles to the south of Swaffham. From a distance, Cockley Cley Hall today gives the impression of being a mansion of considerable age, red-brick, possibly of the eighteenth century, remodelled in the nineteenth century. It was in fact built in the early 1870s in a kind of Victorian Italianate style, finely conceived for its setting. It would therefore have been brand-new when Howard Carter was young, and it may be wondered how this boy, living in relatively modest circumstances in Swaffham, might have come to the attention of Mr Francis Allen, master of Cockley Cley Hall. It is strange that no mention of the Allens occurs in any Carter papers which have been available for consultation; nowhere, in published or unpublished sources, did Howard Carter give any credit to Mr Allen for his education or for his first visit to Egypt. On the latter point, it will soon be seen that another local county family has always been considered responsible for Carter's first visit to Egypt, a claim for which there is good evidence. Yet, there is some evidence that he at least knew the Allens and may have felt indebted to them. Mr Nigel Allen stated: 'I remember Carter very well, though at the time I was only a boy, as he came to luncheon at Cockley Cley immediately after his return from his discovery in Egypt of Tutankhamen's tomb and reported his find to my father at length and in great detail. This of course is something which nobody could forget, and I remember pretty well every word that Carter said.' Other members of the Allen family have confirmed the essential details of Nigel Allen's letter, emphasizing the strong Egyptian interests of Mr Francis Allen. He had lived, it seems, for most of his working life in Egypt, with a house at Ramla, a fashionable suburb of Alexandria in the late nineteenth century. He left Egypt early in the twentieth century, when he was about 50, but he retained business interests in the country, and, according to members of the family, spoke often of Carter, suggesting that he had at various times helped him. The most specific memory now offered comes from Elizabeth Reeves, a grand-daughter of Francis Allen, who recalls the same luncheon-party: 'I can remember him and his companion arriving rather early and the butler bringing him down to the tennis court where we were playing, and my step grandmother who was with us taking him back into the house. Later we had lunch together and then I saw no more of him.'[17]

16 Letter of 11 April 1972 in the Department of Egyptian Antiquities, British Museum.
17 I owe this information to Mr Francis Allen, and additionally to Mr N. G. Stafford Allen, Mrs Elizabeth Reeves, and Mr Antony Allen.

Without further evidence it is difficult to pursue this connection with the Allens of Cockley Cley, but it could be suggested that Howard Carter may have been brought to Cockley Cley by Samuel John Carter on more than one occasion if his father had been engaged by Francis Allen to paint pictures for him. From other evidence it is clear that the young Carter impressed people with his artistic talent, and even his personality. It was certainly so with the Amhersts of Didlington with whom he retained close relations from childhood onwards. In the relative isolation of Cockley Cley Mr Allen may have engaged tutors for his own children and offered to allow Howard Carter to participate in some of the lessons. He may equally have made some similar arrangement for him in Swaffham itself. Further speculation might be thought unprofitable.

Samuel John Carter divided his time between London where work for the *Illustrated London News* occupied him, and Swaffham, the base for his country practice, where he carried out commissions for the local gentry and land-owners. The Swaffham practice necessitated trips around the countryside, visits to great houses, the painting of prize farm animals, of cherished hunters, of family groups. On such trips he may often have been accompanied by his youngest son, Howard. It might have been seen as a part of his training for the future. In his autobiographical sketch Howard Carter explains that 'the necessity to earn my living from the age of fifteen, made me follow up the study of drawing and painting.' In this study his best instructor was his father, but he was surely able to learn much also from his brothers Samuel, Vernet and William and his sister Amy, all of whom made their professions in painting and the allied arts. It is to his father, however, that he gave the credit for his training as a draughtsman in particular – the skills of eye and pencil – which ultimately led to his going to Egypt. From his earliest years he also fell in love with natural history, the observation of insects and birds, and greatly enjoyed the chance to neglect his studies and make expeditions into the countryside. Among the places which he most probably first visited with his father was Didlington Hall, about eight miles to the south of Swaffham, the country seat of Mr William Amhurst Tyssen-Amherst, and there he came to know the exceptionally talented Amherst family. Samuel John Carter had painted a number of subjects for the family, and among his earliest accepted submissions to the Royal Academy Summer Exhibitions were 'The falconer's lunch, at the Heronry, Didlington Park, Norfolk', and 'An Infant Group; Didlington Hall, Norfolk', both in 1859 when he was at the start of his career. Again, the evidence for Howard Carter's earliest acquaintance with the Amhersts of Didlington is very slight, but as events developed it is clear that he was known sufficiently well to the family that they felt able to recommend him for work in Egypt when the opportunity presented itself in 1891.

A strange concatenation of events and circumstances led up to that occasion in 1891. On the one hand there were the Carters, father and son, visiting Didlington probably for artistic purposes; on the other hand there was Percy Edward Newberry, visiting Didlington for horticultural and Egyptological purposes. In the middle were the Amherts. William Amhurst Tyssen-Amherst projects the image of a typical mid- to late-Victorian gentleman, worthy, high-minded, public spirited, a paterfamilias of solid achievement, a substantial land-owner and a Member of Parliament. He was additionally, and less conventionally, a man of strong antiquarian and literary interests who built up a library notable for its holdings of old Bibles, early printed books (*incunabulae*) and fine bindings; and an Egyptian collection of major importance. In terms of monumental sculpture, the latter was by far the most substantial in Great Britain during the nineteenth century; it also contained important texts on papyri, and a very representative series of small sculptures and minor antiquities. The collection had been founded on Amherst's purchase in the 1860s of the Egyptian holdings of the Revd R. T. Lieder, a Church of England priest of German origin, and of Dr John Lee, a distinguished antiquarian. Amherst continued to collect until the early years of the twentieth century, when a disastrous financial collapse led to the disposal of the most valuable parts of his library and of significant pieces from his Egyptian collection. He had been created Baron Amherst of Hackney in August 1892. Enthusiastically supported by his wife, Margaret, he maintained at Didlington a household of wide artistic, historical and literary attachments. Most of the family (there were five daughters, but no sons) took a lively interest in Egyptian antiquity, and the diary written by Alicia Amherst (their youngest daughter) during the family visit to Egypt in the winter of 1894–5 shows a considerable knowledge of Egyptian history and monuments, and even of hieroglyphs.[18] Lady Amherst herself wrote a *Sketch of Egyptian History from the earliest times to the present day*, published in 1904, which ran to 474 printed pages and was well received as a popular, interestingly illustrated account for general readers. Mary Amherst, their oldest daughter, who married Lord William Cecil, even conducted excavations in Egypt in the early years of the twentieth century when Howard Carter was in a position to be of help. The tombs she uncovered at Aswan are still known in Egyptological literature as the Cecil Tombs.[19]

In visiting a house so oriented towards ancient Egypt, Howard Carter could not fail to have his own interest stimulated, and he later admitted that the Amherst Egyptian collection 'arroused [*sic*] my longing for that country – for the purity of her blue sky, her pale aërial hills, her valleys teeming with accumulated treasures of Age'.[20] If he had indeed shown a real interest in the Egyptian collection, it would not have been surprising

18 See p. 63 below.
19 See pp. 81f. below.
20 In the sketch, 'An Account of Myself', p. 20.

10

to find Mr Amherst taking an interest in him, and even helping him with his education. But again, as with Mr Allen of Cockley Cley, there is no evidence substantially to confirm such benevolent attention.

The Amherst link to Newberry goes back at least to 1890. At that time Percy Newberry was 21, a budding Egyptologist and an accomplished botanist and garden historian. He had already spent some years working on a part-time basis in the office of the Egypt Exploration Fund, building up his knowledge of things Egyptian. In 1888–9 he had contributed a series of articles on the history of English gardens to the *Gardener's Chronicle*. How he came first to visit the Amhersts is not known, but at Didlington he found not only a splendid Egyptian collection, but also a young lady with an incipient interest in the history of gardens. Alicia Amherst was then 25, and Newberry encouraged her to edit and enlarge his articles in the *Gardener's Chronicle* to make a comprehensive work, bringing the story of English gardens down to modern times. Eventually her *History of Gardening in England* was published in 1895, and with revisions it has remained a standard work on the subject.[21] So for Newberry there were two good reasons for maintaining close links with the Amhersts and Didlington.

The Egypt Exploration Fund, for which Newberry worked as a casual helper to begin with, had been founded in 1882.[22] Its primary, but by no means only, begetter was Miss Amelia Edwards, a popular Victorian novelist and writer of travel books. She had been to Egypt in 1873–4 and had been smitten both by the fascination of the ancient civilization and by the need to promote archaeological work in that country. From the beginning the chief purpose of this Egypt Exploration Fund was to conduct excavations in Egypt and to publish the results in annual volumes which would be distributed to the subscribers and sold generally to interested members of the public. Work in the Nile Delta, with some emphasis being placed on biblical connections with Egypt, seemed likely to attract good support, especially from students of the Bible whose interest in ancient Egypt might not otherwise be strong. Throughout the 1880s the Fund thrived, attracting considerable support in financial terms for its campaigns in the Delta. Its excavators were Professor Édouard Naville of Geneva and Mr William Flinders Petrie of London, two very different field-workers: the former an accomplished scholar, essentially a desk Egyptologist with a strong but perhaps misguided wish to excavate; the latter a self-educated, practical excavator who was to transform archaeology in Egypt, establishing standards of observation, recording and analysis which would be far in advance of those practised by any other excavator of that time. The

21 On the respective contributions of Newberry and Alicia Amherst to the history of gardens, see W. T. Stearn in *Garden History* 5, 1 (1977), pp. 42–57. I am indebted to Professor Stearn for this reference.
22 For a good general account of the foundation, see M. S. Drower, 'The Early Years' in T. G. H. James (ed.), *Excavating in Egypt. The Egypt Exploration Society 1882–1982* (London, 1982), pp. 9ff.

styles and abilities of Naville and Petrie differed so markedly that trouble inevitably followed. The rumblings continued for many years, and Howard Carter himself would in due course find his own career strongly influenced by both men in contrasting ways. He would find that sweetness and light are not necessarily to be found in the dig-houses and on the working ground of Egyptology. Jealousy, impatience, scorn, disgust, plain ungentlemanly behaviour, would provide the disagreeable condiments of camp-life. Naville and Petrie would both be somewhat above the cruder manifestations of dislike; but the deep antipathy that existed between them represented fundamental differences of principles and of working practices which erupted in bitter public squabbles from time to time, to the great embarrassment of the Committee of the Fund. Yet Carter was to find very positive advantages in working with both of them; from both he would learn much.

The troubles of the field, however, lay some way ahead, and the event which led to Howard Carter's first going to Egypt was one that scarcely involved controversy. It was the establishment of a new branch of the Egypt Exploration Fund's activities, to be called the Archaeological Survey.[23] For some years a feeling had been growing among people seriously interested in and acquainted at first-hand with the monuments of Egypt that something had to be done about the surviving antiquities before the depradations of time, weather, visitors, vandals and robbers brought about their ultimate fate in destruction. Physical protection on a comprehensive scale was out of the question; even the great, well known monuments in places like Saqqara and Luxor could not properly be guarded by the tiny force of antiquities guards which could be officially maintained. Still, something could be done at least for scientific purposes by recording what was visible throughout the six hundred miles of Nile Valley and Delta. The most eloquent advocate for action was Francis Llewellyn Griffith, a young self-taught Egyptologist, first student of the Egypt Exploration Fund, 28 years old in 1890 and already established as the brightest hope of British scholarship in the Egyptian field. His subsequent contributions to Egyptology were many and formidable, and by a satisfactory circularity of circumstances the Institute which would be founded after his death in his name in Oxford would become the depository of the surviving scholarly archive of Howard Carter, among those of many others. As early as 1889 Griffith had argued strongly for the establishment of an archaeological survey:

> With the countenance and support of the Egyptian Government, we
> might in a few years sweep the whole surface of the country, and
> gather in the harvest which hastens to ruin with every day that

23 On its formation and history, see T. G. H. James, 'The Archaeological Survey', in James, op. cit., pp. 141f.

passes.... What is needed is a sifting of information, an index of
the monuments, a description from a new point of view, taking each
city, its tombs and temples, as a whole, and not merely extracting
scenes, inscriptions, and architectural features.

Contemplating this proposal a century later, one can marvel at the
optimistic expectations of what could be achieved in a relatively short time
– a very few years in Griffith's estimation – but at the same time appreciate
the imaginative intention. In a matter of months after the formal establishment of the Archaeological Survey in 1890, the first recruits for work in
the field had been accepted and preparations were set in hand for a first
season. Two very different workers had been found, and little could have
been guessed at the outset that in their differences lay the seeds of a very
uncomfortable partnership, and ultimately of outright disharmony. George
Willoughby Fraser, an engineer by training, who had worked for some
months with Flinders Petrie in the Faiyum, the lake province of Egypt to
the west of the Nile Valley, had impressed Griffith with copies he had
made of inscriptions in the region of Minya in Middle Egypt. His partner
was to be Percy Newberry, friend of the Amhersts and well acquainted
with the ways of the Egypt Exploration Fund. Although Fraser knew Egypt
better than Newberry, and had real field experience behind him, he found
himself the junior of Newberry in the team, and this apparent subservience
did not suit his naturally ebullient character. Newberry was somewhat on
the sober side; very steady, a trifle plodding, well intentioned and hard-
working, a thoroughly decent person, kind and considerate, but perhaps
not much fun.

When Newberry and Fraser began the first season of the Archaeological
Survey in November 1890 a reasonably realistic target had been set by
agreement between the Committee, Newberry and Griffith, who was to be
the general editor of the Survey's work and its guiding light and chief
support in London. A relatively small stretch of the Nile Valley in Middle
Egypt was chosen for intensive survey and recording; the site of Beni
Hasan became the first focus of attention. At this place was a series of
tombs dated to what are called the First Intermediate period and the
Middle Kingdom (c. 2150–1800 BC). Although the place had been much
visited by early travellers, and some record of the tomb-scenes made, the
monuments there had never been adequately studied or fully published.
The scenes in the larger and better preserved tombs were full of interesting
details, and they required great care in their copying. For this first season
Newberry and Fraser apparently worked well together, and between them
they almost completed the tracing of all the tombs, a decorated area
estimated at 12,000 square feet. It was a long season, extending until May
1891, quite long enough to test the patience and good-will of men better
matched than Newberry and Fraser. They had been joined for the last

months of the season by Marcus W. Blackden, a Royal Academy student whom Newberry had met in London. He happened to be in Egypt on a sketching trip, and he volunteered his services to Newberry. He was engaged to paint details and some of the fine coloured hieroglyphs which make the Beni Hasan tombs of particular interest.

A letter Newberry wrote to Amelia Edwards in February, in which he announces the engagement of Marcus Blackden, contains a revealing account of the regime endured at Beni Hasan:[24]

> We work from about 8 in the morning (for there is not sufficient light in the tombs to begin earlier) till sunset. Then we dine and I generally work on till ten going through and correcting the tracings which I have made during the day or else puzzle out some Coptic inscription or ancient Egyptian painting. This is my round of work for the day and it is seldom altered. Occasionally, once a fortnight or so, I take a walk with Mr. Fraser along the Gebel [mountain], or southward as far as the village of Beni Hassan but as I am *very* anxious to finish here before I return to England I generally prefer to remain in the tombs at my tracing.

It was clearly a tough and unremitting way of life, and a real test of character. The arrival of Blackden undoubtedly eased the situation, and Newberry was pleased with the coloured facsimiles he made. Even so, progress was not as good as had been expected, and by the end of the season Beni Hasan was not completed as Newberry had hoped. Furthermore, there were difficulties over funds. Survey work was not as glamorous as excavation, and although the costs of the operations in the field were not as great as those incurred in digging, there would have to be much follow-up work at the end of the season to be paid for, and, of course, there would be the expenses of publication. Generous donors were not so eager to support this side of the Egypt Exploration Fund's work. But there were a few, and comments by Newberry in the same letter to Amelia Edwards are of particular interest in the light of what was to happen soon after his return to England:

> I received your letter last Wednesday and am very pleased to hear that Sir Francis Grenfell has contributed to our artists fund. The friend you mention in your letter who, I think, is willing to give another £25 is Mrs. Tyssen Amherst. I was staying with them shortly before I left England and she seemed to be enthusiastic about the Survey and said she would help. I will write to her *myself* about it and will immediately I receive her answer let you know her reply.

The subsequent correspondence on this subject has not survived, but it

24 E.E.S. Archives, XII d 31.

certainly was to bear fruit rapidly after Newberry's return to Britain. A letter from Mrs Amherst, dated 29 May 1891, surprisingly states: 'I am so glad that you have been able to get an appointment for Howard Carter. I am very grateful to you and I hope he will prove a useful help in every way. I told his mother that he ought to try and improve himself by study as much as possible during his leisure time. It is a very good start to get £100 a year.'[25]

Carter's appointment may have been in the first instance to help Newberry with the inking-in of his tracings from Beni Hasan; it would have been one way of trying out his capabilities. But from the beginning Newberry may have been thinking of an additional artist for the Survey in Egypt. Quite probably he was considering this possibility when he took up with Mrs Amherst the question of her support for the Archaeological Survey. He no doubt told her of his anxieties over progress and even spoke of the recruitment of another artist to work with him and Fraser in Egypt. Marcus Blackden's commitment to the Survey had been opportunist – in a good sense – and there was little reason at that moment to believe that he would be available for a further season. In fact Blackden did return to Egypt in the autumn of 1891, and worked with Fraser and Newberry on a more formal basis, but it had not been expected earlier in the year. It also happened that the moderate harmony of the first season did not survive the second season, and it was as well that Newberry had Carter to help him when things became difficult. From Mrs Amherst's letter it certainly appears that she had first suggested Howard Carter, her recommendation being based on what she already knew of his artistic skills. It was earlier suggested that the young Carter had probably first visited Didlington Hall with his father; it is certainly likely that it was in Norfolk that the two families, Amhersts and Carters, had opportunities to meet, even if on a non-social level. But both families had 'town' houses, the Carter in Rich Terrace, Brompton, and the Amhersts in Portman Square in St Marylebone, still in the 1890s a handsome, largely eighteenth-century assemblage of town houses. It would not have been out of the question for Mrs Amherst to have called on Mrs Carter in London when she passed on her advice on how Howard should 'improve himself'. She could equally have asked Howard's mother to call on her in London or in the country. It would, however, be wrong to emphasize social niceties in the relationship between the Amhersts and the Carters. All the evidence points to the unconventionality of the Amhersts in their social dealings.

The initial moves which led to this first appointment for Howard Carter were probably rather informal – letters between Newberry, Mrs Amherst and Miss Amelia Edwards, discussions with the various officers of the Egypt Exploration Fund, including Francis Ll. Griffith, negotiations of a

25 G.I. Newberry Corr. 2/9. The sum mentioned by Mrs Amherst does not square with the £50 agreed by the committee of the Fund in October 1891; see below.

kind with the Carter family by the Amhersts. Although Howard Carter's engagement seems to have been effected rather swiftly after Newberry's return to England, the final decision to send him to Egypt was not taken by the Committee of the Fund until October 1891, when his remuneration was fixed at £50, as may be seen in the next chapter. He had presumably given satisfaction by his work during the summer, in which his evident ability would have been revealed. The needs of the Archaeological Survey were pressing, and Mrs Amherst's generosity to the Fund had to be considered. It may be hoped that Carter himself may also have been involved in the decisions, although it would not have been unusual at that time for his future to be decided for him by parents and well-wishers.

Nevertheless, in retrospect Carter always looked back on this change in his situation as the great opportunity of his life – as it turned out to be – and he expressed no regret at abandoning a more conventional career as an artist, if any artistic career may be thought of in terms of conventionality. He had been fired by the Amherst collection of Egyptian antiquities, but it was probably not his enthusiasm for Egypt and Egyptian things that specially commended him to the Amhersts; it was his artistic talent that impressed them and made him a young man worth promoting. He had been well trained by his father in the basic skills of draughtsmanship, and he could draw and paint with more than ordinary skill. He was to remain essentially an artist throughout his life, and his natural instinct was to turn to drawing and painting when he needed mental relaxation. But at the age of 17, as he was in 1891, he may well have had doubts about spending his life as his father had done. He makes a kind of confession of uncertainty in one version of his autobiographical sketch:[26] 'For a living I began by drawing in water colours and coloured chalks portraits of pet parrots, cats and snappy, smelly lap dogs. Although I was always a great lover of birds and animals – in fact I was brought up with them – how I hated that particular species known as lap-dog.' Such evidence of uncertainty should probably not be pressed too hard, but there seems to be no doubt that he welcomed the chance of going to what was a dream-country for him, a land of exotic possibilities, far beyond the expectations of a young man largely country-bred and the member of an untravelled family.

The study needed to prepare him for his great adventure could not be fully pursued in Norfolk. He could spend time at Didlington familiarizing himself with Egyptian antiquities and even talking about Egypt to Mr and Mrs Amherst. He could draw Egyptian objects and work on Newberry's tracings; he could become familiar with Egyptian styles and begin to understand Egyptian artistic conventions. But there was more useful study that he could only carry out in London, as will be seen shortly. All his

26 The John Carter version.

16

preliminary efforts bore good fruit. From the beginning his drawing of Egyptian subjects displays a confidence and grasp of technique which are wholly convincing. Until late in the nineteenth century European artists, trained on classical models, found it difficult to produce stylistically satisfactory drawings of Egyptian material. Howard Carter, by an excellent eye and sure draughtsmanship, never failed to penetrate to the heart of whatever Egyptian subject he might be painting or drawing.

The additional training and study which he carried out in the summer and early autumn of 1891 was conducted in the British Museum. He was able to live in his parents' house at 10 Rich Terrace, from which he could easily reach the Museum by omnibus. At the Museum he worked under the supervision of Francis Ll. Griffith, the architect of the Archaeological Survey. By a bizarre misarrangement Griffith was an Assistant not in the Department of Egyptian and Assyrian Antiquities but in the Department of British and Mediaeval Antiquities and Ethnography. For Carter this apparently strange situation worked to his advantage. From the time of the foundation of the Egypt Exploration Fund there had been a coolness towards its activities from the Department of Oriental Antiquities (soon to be partly reorganized as Egyptian and Assyrian). The distinguished keeper of Oriental Antiquities, Samuel Birch, refused to offer enthusiastic support in the Fund's early years, though he and Miss Amelia Edwards were well acquainted, even friends, as she thought.[27] His opposition may have been due to the fact that he was one of the principal supporters of the Society of Biblical Archaeology, whose *Proceedings* had become the main outlet for published research in Egyptology in Great Britain. From the viewpoint of one hundred years later it can be seen that there was no real threat to Birch's Society from the newly established Fund, but things probably looked rather different in the 1880s. Birch died in 1885 and his successor, Peter Le Page Renouf, maintained the cool attitude, supported by Ernest Wallis Budge, a protégé of Birch who would himself succeed Renouf in 1893. It is not likely that Howard Carter would at this time have been welcomed enthusiastically in the Egyptian and Assyrian Department. Nevertheless, the public galleries, filled with a wealth of Egyptian antiquities far surpassing Mr Amherst's domestic collection, were available for a bright young man to visit at will during the open hours of the Museum. Here with an official sketching permit he could draw to his heart's content. But the main purpose of his visits to the British Museum was to study, under Griffith's supervision, the drawings of Egyptian antiquities, especially paintings and reliefs, made by artists and travellers in the early nineteenth century and preserved in the Department of Manuscripts.

Preeminent among the various collections were the papers of Robert

27 On Birch's attitude, see T. G. H. James, *The British Museum and Ancient Egypt* (London, 1981), pp. 25f.

Hay, a Scottish antiquarian[28] who made several extended visits to Egypt between 1824 and 1838, often accompanied by artists whom he commissioned to help him with the recording of monuments throughout Egypt and the northern Sudan. He was himself no mean artist, and his copies display a remarkable fidelity of observation, even in the drawing of hieroglyphic inscriptions, though he had scant knowledge of the script. There are 49 volumes of Hay material in what is now the British Library, and they engaged most of Howard Carter's attention: 'my principal work was the studying and copying of the MSS of Robert Hay, an explorer, and patron of explorers, who during the first part of the nineteenth century made a collection of detailed drawings, minutely accurate copies of inscriptions and plans of the Egyptian monuments, that put to shame most of the contemporary and later work in that country.' Indeed, Carter could not have had a better model to study, and as Hay's copies included scenes and inscriptions from the tombs at Beni Hasan and El-Bersha, where the Fund's expedition would be working,[29] he received as good a preliminary training as was possible at that time. And so, in a matter of a few months, Howard Carter was transformed from an apprentice animal painter with moderate prospects into a potential archaeological artist, with perhaps even less moderate prospects. He had, however, been offered the opportunity to step out of the rut of conventional illustration, and to enter a new world of unknown possibilities. He was to go to Egypt to exercise his proven talents. His wildest expectations in that autumn of 1891 could scarcely have included what the future would eventually bring some thirty years later.

---

28 Hay's career and achievement are best described in Selwyn Tillett, *Egypt Itself. The Career of Robert Hay of Linplum and Nunraw, 1799–1863* (London, 1984).
29 On the scale and accuracy of Hay's work at Beni Hasan, Tillett, op. cit., pp. 59ff.

2

EGYPT: THE BEGINNINGS

There is an apparent abruptness in the transition of Howard Carter from the protected environment of Swaffham and Brompton in the late autumn of 1891. Carter's own account in his autobiographical sketch is wholly lacking in detail, and simply registers his arrival in Alexandria where he was met by Newberry. Yet this was his first journey out of England, his first separation from family and familiar scenes. He was just seventeen and a half, a youth who had moved little in the world, although with some contacts with leading families in East Anglia. It is tempting to think of him as shy and gauche, a little awkward in human relations, and confident perhaps only when he had a pencil between his fingers. Writing in later life he mentioned both his father and his mother with affection, attributing to the former his artistic talent, and to the latter his taste for the softer side of life. Still, there is no hint in his few surviving letters of these early years of separation that he ever suffered the pains of home-sickness.

It was, of course, a great adventure. He subsequently claimed that he had developed an interest in and a desire to visit Egypt through contact with Amherst's collection, and there seems no reason to doubt this claim. But his going to Egypt was certainly viewed by the Amhersts, and probably by his own family as well, as an excellent opportunity for one whose future otherwise might seem to be that of a jobbing artist. So he was on his way to a new and strange life, one that must have excited him in prospect, even if it threatened uncertainty.

Howard Carter's appointment to work for the Egypt Exploration Fund was not formally approved until a Committee meeting of the Fund on 16 October 1891. It was then resolved 'that Mr. Carter be appointed a Tracer to assist Mr. Newberry at a cost not exceeding £50.'[1] Within a very few days he must have begun his solitary voyage to Egypt, being seen off from Victoria Station in London by his father. It was common practice in those days to proceed, after the Channel crossing, to an Italian port where a passage could be obtained to Alexandria. Newberry had gone ahead of Carter. It

---

1 E.E.F. Committee Minutes.

might have been thought a kindness for him to have taken Carter with him on this first occasion. It did not happen so, and Newberry travelled out in the company of the Revd Greville Chester, who had regularly wintered in Egypt since 1865. In a letter to Griffith written from Brindisi on 25 October he says:[2] 'I had a very jolly time in Venice and saw most of what was to be seen. I also stopped 6 hours at Milan and saw the Cathedral. Yesterday we got to Ancona and G. Chester and I went ashore to see a triumphal arch (fine Roman) and the Byzantine Cathedral. . . . I shall have to stay two or three days at Alexandria to await Carter's arrival and will write from Cairo.'

Within ten days of the writing of that letter Newberry and Carter had arrived at Beni Hasan. Carter had scarcely time to orient himself before he was plunged into the activity for which he had been recruited. In Cairo, however, a few days had been passed in which he was able to spend some time in the Museum, which had at that time been just recently installed in the palace of Ismail Pasha in the suburb of Giza, to which it had been moved in 1889–90 from its original home in Bulaq. Carter also claims in his late sketch that during these days in Cairo he met for the first time Flinders Petrie, and that he had the opportunity of talking to him in the evenings. The great archaeologist, who already had in his eleven years of working in Egypt shown himself to be no ordinary excavator, was on his way to start his season at El-Amarna. Here Carter would, surprisingly, join him in early 1892, but at their first meeting in Cairo there could have been no hint of what was to come within a few months. In retrospect he claimed: 'This meeting of Flinders Petrie, a man of simple tastes, endowed with discernment which gave him confidence and power to solve archaeological problems, remains one of those impressible incidents of my early life. As a son of an artist, what perhaps interested me most, beside the extent and precision of his knowledge, was his recognition and love of fine art.'

Newberry's plans for the 1891–2 season included the completion of the main work of recording the scenes and inscriptions in the tombs at Beni Hasan, and to move on to El-Bersha, a site about 20 miles to the south where a further group of tombs belonging to provincial nobles was located. In addition to himself and Howard Carter, there were two further people in the party, George Willoughby Fraser and later M. W. Blackden, both of whom had taken part in the first season at Beni Hasan. They, with Newberry, were the old hands – of one year's standing – and must have seemed to the young Carter immensely experienced and accomplished in the work and in the ways of the camp. They lived in one of the very substantial tomb-chapels of Beni Hasan, cut into the limestone rock of the escarpment overlooking the Nile Valley from the east. The major tombs at Beni Hasan are reached from a terrace-path of varying width which runs in front of the façades of the tombs, some of which are nobly distinguished

2 E.E.S. Archives XII d 49.

by formal entrances with pillared porticoes, all cut from the living rock. It is a dramatic site, set about 200 feet above the Nile plain which on this eastern side stretches only a few hundred yards from the river before it reaches the rocky hillside. Across the river in the distance the fertile plain extends several miles towards the foothills of the western desert.

In his retrospect Carter waxes lyrical at the site: living was reasonably comfortable, the view from the terrace to the west was glorious, the tombs and their decorations were unique. But he was much less lyrical about the method of work established by Newberry and his other assistants. The tomb-scenes which cover the walls of the best-preserved tomb-chapels provide, in addition to certain ritual and specifically religious representations required by convention, an extraordinary conspectus of Egyptian life in the provinces of Middle Egypt during the late Eleventh and the Twelfth Dynasties: domestic activities in and about the households of the great nobles of the Oryx nome, the varied agricultural processes in field and stockyard, the pleasures and hazards of hunting in the desert – most of the events which were included in the repertoire of the great *mastaba*-chapels of the Old-Kingdom tombs at Saqqara. There were also unusual scenes of young people at play, engaging in extended and elaborate bouts of wrestling, and particular incidents of seemingly historical significance, like the arrival of Asiatics with a consignment of eye-paint. Incidental detail in the scenes was frequently unusual and charming – the harvesting of figs with apes in the fig trees, for example.

The technique of painting directly on the smoothed limestone walls of the tombs, prepared simply with a thin plaster wash, produced a brilliant effect in which much depended on the skill of line of the painter-draughts-man, enhanced by fine added detail. Surfaces were disfigured by occasional hornets' nests made of mud rendered as hard as concrete by the skill of the insects, and by a general patina of dirt, the accumulation of almost four millennia. The Newberry technique of copying could only produce a sad travesty of the originals. Sheets of tracing paper were hung down the length of the decorated surfaces, with some overlap, and the scenes were traced in soft pencil. The same technique was used for those few parts where carved relief replaced straight painting, mostly on the jambs of doorways and some dado inscriptions. These tracings were then rolled up and brought back to London at the end of the season to be inked in, possibly by draughtsmen who had never seen the originals. Figures of men and animals, etc., were filled in solidly in black. The results of this simple, but crude, method of recording may be seen in the volumes published by Newberry on the Beni Hasan tombs.[3] Judged by subsequent standards

3 P. E. Newberry, *Beni Hasan*, vols I and II (London, 1893, 1894) contain the records of the tomb scenes and texts. Vols III and IV (London, 1896, 1900) contain copies of selected hieroglyphs and interesting zoological and other details, with text by F. Ll. Griffith and excellent coloured facsimiles by Carter, Blackden and others.

they are not attractive, and do poor justice to the originals. In extenuation, however, it must be said that Newberry was a true pioneer in the recording of monuments of this kind to a standard of accuracy in other respects never previously achieved. He was, furthermore, not an artist himself, and had not been briefed to record in an 'artistic' manner. The urgency which had characterized the setting up of the Archaeological Survey demanded speed; care in generalities and accuracy in the rendering of hieroglyphic texts, but without the precision that would now be demanded in good facsimile recording, were what was needed. The last thing Newberry required at this point was to have his methods questioned and his techniques changed by a bright youth who already had the eye and the skill to produce something much better.

Again, retrospectively, Howard Carter claimed that he appreciated how much better a copy could be made by working 'as anyone practised in the fine arts would do', and making 'a facsimile from the original with free and understanding hand'. The time would come, and not so far ahead, when he would be able to practise his own method with outstandingly good results. But for the moment he was the new boy and did what he was told. In so doing he pleased Newberry, who wrote to Francis Llewellyn Griffith on 18 November:[4]

> Our time (Carter's and my own) has been spent from 7 morning till sunset entirely on tracing and we now have only a very little more to do here. I never reckoned on getting done so fast. It is astonishing how much can be done by *two* men working hard when the hands are *willing*. I believe that Carter and I could almost trace all the tombs in Egypt in five years!!! On Sunday last I tried Carter at painting and found he could copy things here very well indeed – almost as well as Blackden.

So, after scarcely more than two weeks at Beni Hasan, in his first season in Egypt, Carter had shown himself to be worthy of Amherst recommendation and well worth the £50 voted for him by the Committee of the Egypt Exploration Fund. Now there was to be a change of scene. In the same letter to Griffith, Newberry signalled his intention to leave Beni Hasan for El-Bersha on the following Sunday, and to take Carter with him if Fraser had not completed the work on which he was then engaged. In the event both Fraser and Carter went with Newberry to El-Bersha. In a further letter to Griffith, dated 26 November,[5] Newberry explained how he and Carter had walked much of the way from Beni Hasan, as far as Sheikh Ibada (Antinoupolis), searching the hills for tombs and quarries and finding many, but none inscribed. A rather more chatty letter to Miss Edwards written two days later added some more personal

4 E.E.S. Archives XII d 52.
5 E.E.S. Archives XII d 54.

details.[6] At Sheikh Ibada the two tired walkers had waited hours for their boat to arrive and had taken their tea on 'bread, water and onions (!)'. At El-Bersha they found no tombs suitable as a billet and pitched tents loaned to the expedition by Sir Francis Grenfell (Commander-in-Chief of the Egyptian Army) in the ravine below the tombs. Newberry declared, 'It is my first experience in tenting and I find them very comfortable.' In later years Carter reminisced less fondly about the tents, regretting the coolness of the Beni Hasan tomb, but spoke enthusiastically about the abundant bird and animal life which sustained his interest.

Here, in the tombs of the nomarchs of the Hare nome, the decoration was carved and painted, and in at least one tomb was of a quality superior to that at Beni Hasan. Unhappily, the tombs had suffered serious damage both from the natural slippage of the cliff-face in which the tombs were cut, and from human attack. The most unusual, and famous, scene in the tomb of Djehutihotpe had been grievously damaged since it was first noted and copied by early travellers and their artists in the first decades of the nineteenth century. The scene shows the dragging of a huge seated statue cut from the alabaster quarries called Hatnub. Placed on a sledge, and carefully secured with ropes, the mighty monument is drawn along by a substantial company of men – a scene of exceptional interest and filled with fascinating detail. Carter had the task of tracing this scene, and it is interesting to observe that in the publication of the El-Bersha tombs his plates are presented very differently from those attributed to Newberry.[7] The blocking-in of the figures is abandoned, and the reproduced drawings – even if derived from tracings in the Newberry manner – are of a pleasing clarity and full of visible detail. Carter was certainly employed in the subsequent summer to ink-in the drawings brought back from El-Bersha; he clearly seized the opportunity to show how things could be improved, and the fact that the plates in the Bersha volume completed by him were acceptable to Newberry and Griffith shows how convincingly he had demonstrated the superiority of his methods, in spite of the fact that tracing as the initial stage had not yet been abandoned.

One of the constants of archaeological expeditions is the lack of harmony among the participants. It is not inevitable that personal relations should be strained and that most seasons should end with deep divisions between the individual members of staffs; but it happens far too frequently that differences of temperament, of technical method, of interpretation, bedevil the even course of progress. Discord is often put down to the way of life on an expedition in the field; for months at a time three or four people (and nowadays upwards of twelve to twenty) live on fairly intimate terms

6 E.E.S. Archives XII d 55.
7 The colossus scene is reproduced in P. E. Newberry, *El Bersheh* I (London, 1895), pl. XV. A list if given on p. viii of those plates prepared by Newberry, the remainder all being by Carter.

with little social life and few distractions from the constant presence of the work in hand. Small idiosyncrasies can become major impediments; pedantries become tyrannies; personal preferences in food, in particular, can engender bitter antagonisms. It all looks pretty silly at a distance, but is very real on the ground. Howard Carter, who in later life proved to be one of the less tolerant of field-workers, was early introduced to this particular characteristic of the 'expedition'.

For reasons that are not now wholly clear, a serious division had developed in the camp of the Archaeological Survey. Willoughby Fraser and Blackden ranged themselves against Newberry, and young Carter, Newberry's acolyte, was necessarily ranged along with the last. Things had developed badly after the reopening of the work at Beni Hasan in November 1891, and they were to become so serious that Newberry felt obliged to offer his resignation to the Egypt Exploration Fund. It would seem that Fraser principally had found Newberry's direction of the Survey's activities irksome, and perhaps too restrictive. By training Fraser was an engineer, and he was employed by the Fund as a surveyor as well as a tracer and copier of inscriptions. He had received some earlier field training with Petrie at Hawara and Illahun, had worked in a voluntary capacity for the Irrigation Department in Egypt, and possibly he felt that his experience, if not his competence, was superior to that of Newberry. A certain independence of spirit, and even apparent lack of seriousness, ran counter to Newberry's preferred methods of working; but these tiresome, scarcely insurmountable obstacles to harmony were now to be aggravated by a casual approach to scholarly etiquette which led to a bitter and permanent breach between Fraser and Newberry.

A matter which at this time served as a modest obsession for Newberry and, perhaps to a lesser extent, for Petrie, was the identification of the tomb of Akhenaten. This eccentric king of the late Eighteenth Dynasty, who had established his capital at Akhetaten (El-Amarna) in Middle Egypt, a little to the south of El-Bersha, had only recently been brought seriously to the attention of Egyptologists. The interest in him and his wife Nefertiti, and in the apparently revolutionary ideas they brought to conventional Egyptian religion, was yet to achieve the popular attention which still persists a century later. It was, however, already evident in the last quarter of the nineteenth century that something very unusual, in Egyptian terms, had occurred in Akhenaten's reign, and the idea that his tomb might be in the hills near El-Amarna excited considerable interest and speculation. The focus on the region had recently been intensified by the opening of the first scientific excavation in the Amarna plain by Flinders Petrie in the autumn of 1891.

Subsequently it became apparent that the tomb of Akhenaten had been found by Egyptians some years earlier, and that its precise location was kept secret principally so that it could be cleared and any discoveries of objects exploited unofficially, and perhaps partly by an undisclosed arrangement with Eugène Grébaut, the French Director-General of the Antiquities Service. If there indeed were an arrangement, its purpose has never been satisfactorily explained; but Petrie's ingrained distrust of and antipathy towards Grébaut allowed the latter no credit in the eventual 'discovery' of the tomb at the turn of the year 1891–2.[8] There can be no doubt that in the months running up to the public announcement of the discovery there was abroad in Middle Egypt any number of unsubstantiated and probably deliberately misleading rumours about the tomb's location. And from one series of inaccurate reports came another extremely interesting discovery which Newberry undoubtedly felt he could claim as his own along with Howard Carter.

Late in December Newberry and Carter paid several visits to Petrie, and together they explored outlying parts of the Amarna city area, identifying some of the impressive boundary inscriptions (stelae) set up by Akhenaten to delimit the zone set aside for his new city. On their way back to El-Bersha on Monday 21 December, Newberry and Carter were approached by three men, described by Newberry as 'bedawîn' in the letter he started to write to Griffith from El-Bersha on 23 December.[9] These men told him of a tomb in the desert containing paintings and sculptures and inscriptions. Newberry then 'set to questioning my guide and found that he knew of two stones inscribed as well as the "tomba".' He at once suspected that Akhenaten's tomb was the one in question – he uses the form Chuenaten (alternatively Khuenaten) which was the common reading of the king's name at that time – and he decided to go and have a look. 'So on Tuesday morning Carter and I started off on camels early in the morning for Haggi Kandîl', where Petrie had his camp.'We reached the central ravine at 12 o'clock and then went up over the southern hills.' After an hour's travel they came upon a boundary stela and at that point the camel men wanted to return. Newberry persuaded them to continue to the 'tomba'. 'After about 3½ more hours we at last came in sight of great heaps of limestone chips. You may judge of our excitement when we got quite close to them – and of our disappointment when we found it was only an alabaster quarry!' This disappointment was tempered by the discovery of inscriptions containing the names of kings of the Old Kingdom, and the realization that the quarry was one of greater antiquity than any previously discovered in the region. 'So, on the whole, I think our day has not been quite wasted though I must say that I had great hopes of finding Chuenaten's tomb.'

Later in the same letter, continued on 24 December, Newberry expresses his determination to pursue the search: 'It would be a grand thing if we

8 For Petrie's interest in the tomb and his attitude to Grébaut, see M. S. Drower, *Flinders Petrie* (London, 1985), pp. 192f.
9 E.E.S. Archives XII d 57.

could get hold of it.' But there was first to be a break for Christmas. Newberry was to go to Minya to celebrate the holiday with Major Brown, a Government Irrigation Inspector,[10] and Carter to Petrie. As for Blackden and Fraser, he discovered when it was too late to change that they too would be with Brown in Minya. 'If I had known they were going I most certainly should not have accepted as they both have made it most abominably uncomfortable for me here.' His vexation would shortly be increased immeasurably by behaviour on the part of Blackden and Fraser which Newberry could only see as treachery and very unprofessional conduct.

Two days after Christmas, Blackden and Fraser absented themselves from the Survey's camp and, following up information gleaned from Newberry, made for the quarry. It is not clear whether they had permission to go off on an independent expedition; it is certain that they would not have been given permission if Newberry had known their intentions. They spent two or three days at the quarry and made a much more extensive and leisurely investigation of the place, discovering a number of long and interesting hieratic inscriptions dating from the early Middle Kingdom. The matter that especially excited them was the identification in these inscriptions of several mentions of the name Hatnub, which was already known to them as the quarry site from which had come the colossal alabaster statue represented on the walls of the tomb of Djehutihotpe at El-Bersha. Blackden and Fraser, undoubtedly rightly, but certainly untactfully, claimed the priority of identification and in so doing suggested in effect that they had done a better job in examining the site than Newberry and Carter. Their separate report to the Egypt Exploration Fund was incorporated in a short announcement made by Francis Ll. Griffith in *The Academy* for 23 January 1892.[11] It is entitled 'The Alabaster Quarry of Hat-nub', and states that the discovery of the site had been made by Newberry on 22 December in a day visit. Griffith adds, 'having seen enough only to show its high interest and the probability of its being Hat-nub.' Newberry in his letter of 23–24 December makes no connection with Hatnub. Griffith continues: 'A few days later (December 27–29) Messrs. Blackden and Frazer took leave of absence from the Survey, and leisurely examined the place and its neighbourhood and copies the inscriptions. They found the name Hat-nub five times.'

Subsequently Blackden and Fraser made two more visits to the quarry,

---

10 Robert Hanbury Brown, knighted in 1902; he wrote several books on the Faiyum and Exodus; see W. R. Dawson and E. Uphill, *Who Was Who in Egyptology* (2nd ed., London, 1972), p. 40.

11 Griffith's report was based on Newberry's letter quoted above, on personal conversations with Newberry, who had left El-Bersha for England early in January, and on correspondence with Fraser and Blackden who, reportedly, had sent copies of their notes to him. So they said in a letter to Miss Amelia B. Edwards dated 13 January 1892, in G.I. Newberry Corr. 16/35.

copied many of the hieratic inscriptions, and issued a private publication of their copies in 1894. It was a rather perfunctory publication, lacking any introductory text or descriptive commentary. It was also rather provocatively entitled *Collection of Hieratic Graffiti from the alabaster quarry of Hatnub, situated near Tell El Amarna, found December 28th 1891, copied September, 1892.* An article in the *Proceedings of the Society of Biblical Archaeology* in January 1894 gave Fraser the opportunity to describe the circumstances of his visits with Blackden to the quarry, and to set out his own archaeological findings together with brief discussions of some of the inscriptions.[12]

The Hatnub episode was particularly vexatious for Newberry. He had undoubtedly missed his opportunity, obsessed as he was at the time with the search for the tomb of Akhenaten. He had not made an exhaustive search of the quarry partly because there was little time on his day visit there with Carter, and partly because of his disappointment that it was not The Tomb. By telling Blackden and Fraser of this discovery without presumably indicating any intention to return and to include the copying of the texts there in the programme of the Archaeological Survey, he failed to establish his prior claim for publication, even though this claim should have been recognized by his turbulent assistants. He had, further, missed finding the hieratic texts which now represent the main element of inscriptional interest at Hatnub, containing the personal records of important officials, chiefly of the Hare nome, who report significant details of their careers and of their expeditions to obtain alabaster from the quarry.

Blackden and Fraser for their part secured a rather sour triumph. They had beaten Newberry and unexpectedly discovered more than they had hoped for. But their triumph was based on reprehensible behaviour. They were at El-Bersha as the servants of the Archaeological Survey of the Egypt Exploration Fund, and should have understood the implications of their unauthorized visit to the quarry. In extenuation it should be said that they did make a most interesting discovery, that their copies were thought at the time to be careful and reliable, and that they made these copies available for study and for partial inclusion in the second part of *El Bersheh* (1895). In this volume the difficult hieratic script, little known in the late nineteenth century, was admirably dealt with by Francis Ll. Griffith.

Howard Carter, drawn into this unseemly controversy, received thus an unpleasant initiation into the kinds of quarrel which disfigure scholarship and particularly archaeology. His own allegiance lay naturally with Newberry, and he would have been left in no doubt of the latter's anger. No contemporary record survives in which Carter's feelings were noted, but the incident is described, with a few inaccuracies of detail, in his late autobiographical essay. It is clear that he retained a lively memory of what he felt had been disreputable behaviour by Blackden and Fraser. He

12 *P.S.B.A.* 16 (1894), pp. 73ff.

describes how they returned from their first visit to Hatnub 'when tri-
umphantly they informed us that they had not only succeeded in making
a complete survey of these quarries, but had made careful copies of all the
more important inscriptions ready for publication – dirty dogs!' He later
rather understates the mood in the Survey's camp at El-Bersha: 'Moreover
this unfortunate incident brought about an unpleasant feeling in our camp
– an atmosphere less genial than heretofor.'[13]

The tense situation did not last for more than a few days into the new
year. Newberry left El-Bersha for Cairo and then London on a journey he
had undertaken to make in any case during January in order to advance
the preparation of the first volume of the Beni Hasan publication. But he
left as if for good, furious with Blackden and Fraser, and wholly disen-
chanted with what he thought to be disingenuous behaviour by Grébaut
over the discovery of the tomb of Akhenaten, which was finally 'announced'
in January.[14] At the turn of the year Howard Carter also left the Survey
camp to enter upon yet another, somewhat unexpected, stage in his archaeological initiation. What a first season it was turning out to be!

In the summer of 1891 Flinders Petrie had written to Amelia B.
Edwards, the dynamic joint Secretary of the Egypt Exploration Fund,
offering to take a young potential archaeologist to work with him for a
season. The advantages of such an arrangement, freely offered, were singularly attractive to Miss Edwards, and represented a gesture of exceptional
generosity on Petrie's part. He had ceased to work for the Fund in 1886
after a serious difference of opinion with the Committee over policies and
procedures. Nevertheless he retained a benevolent interest in the work of
the Fund both for its intrinsic importance and also for his affection towards
Miss Edwards. Petrie could see among those working in the field for the
Fund in 1891 nobody who had the talent to become a serious field archaeologist, and he was not so modest as to believe that a nominee with talent,
working under his tutelage, might not become a useful field-worker for the
Fund.[15]

To begin with Miss Edwards had contemplated the detachment of M.
W. Blackden from the Archaeological Survey to work with Petrie at El-
Amarna. Blackden was an artist who had volunteered his services for the
work at Beni Hasan. Newberry was especially pleased with his ability to
make faithful water-colour copies of details of the paintings in the Beni
Hasan tombs, and had conceived the idea, with F. Ll. Griffith, of publish-

13 For a fuller treatment of the Hatnub incident, see T. G. H. James, 'The discovery and
identification of the Alabaster Quarries of Hatnub', in *Mélanges Jacques Jean Clère* (*CRIPEL*
13, 1991), pp. 79ff.
14 For Newberry's annoyance and Petrie's comments on the behaviour of Fraser and Grébaut, see Drower, *Flinders Petrie*, pp. 192f. Newberry's letter of resignation to Miss Edwards,
written from El-Bersha, is dated 4 January 1892; in E.E.S. Archives XVII d 22.
15 For Petrie's offer, see Drower, *Flinders Petrie*, p. 186; for his difficulties in 1886 with the
Committee of the E.E.F., op. cit., pp. 99ff.

ing a collection of copies of the coloured hieroglyphs found in the fine painted tombs of Middle Egypt. Unfortunately the alliance Blackden developed with Willoughby Fraser, and their consequent behaviour in camp, which so much upset Newberry, led to a modification of the plan to take advantage of Petrie's offer. Blackden ceased to be such an attractive possibility to be trained as an excavator for the Fund. Unexpectedly, therefore, Howard Carter found himself being offered to Petrie, although not quite in the role first proposed in the discussions between Petrie and Miss Edwards.

Neither Blackden nor Carter had any experience of excavation; both were artists and were employed by the Egypt Exploration Fund as artists. But excavators just did not grow on trees in the late nineteenth century. To be an Egyptologist was sufficient qualification to be an excavator in Egypt. It did not matter whether the individual scholar's special interest and competence lay in the field of history or in that of the ancient language, and few would have considered that excavation needed special training or technical knowledge. Flinders Petrie understood, long before it was generally accepted, that a good desk-scholar might not necessarily make a good field worker; but potential field-workers had to be found, encouraged and trained. The prospect of having an artist as a field apprentice had at least the attraction of having someone to train who started with an ability to observe; and to be able to draw has never been a drawback to the excavator.

Petrie had looked forward with some expectation to being joined by Blackden. He was alone with his Egyptian workmen at El-Amarna and, while he did not especially mind the solitary state, he could appreciate the possibility of extending his work with a second pair of European hands. As late as 12 December he still hoped that Blackden would come, and on that day was able to discuss the possibility with him and Newberry when they visited his camp. A problem, however, lay in the need for Blackden to obtain permission from the Committee of the Fund for leave of absence from the Archaeological Survey. In his journal of the season Petrie comments:[16] 'There is also the prospect of another digger coming here to work under my permit, but independently of my own work.' This was a clear reference to the possibility of Howard Carter's joining him.

Blackden's uncertainty about going to El-Amarna may, in fact, reflect not so much his inability to secure the Committee's permission at this late date, as his own uncertain future as a member of the Archaeological Survey. It was, after all, by Petrie's and Miss Edwards's initiative that the idea of having someone trained by Petrie had been floated. On 18 November 1891 Amelia Edwards had written to Newberry:[17]

16 The journal for 1891/2 is in the Griffith Institute (I, x); I am grateful to Miss Drower for the loan of a photocopy.
17 G.I. Newberry Corr. 13/24.

I am by no means indifferent to the great advantage it would be to the Fund to have an explorer trained by Mr. Petrie. His pupil would be invaluable to us; but I still hope that some way may be found to procure this advantage without injury to the interests of the Archaeological Survey.

The 'way' by which this advantage might be obtained was to allow Blackden to work first with Petrie and then to complete his Survey work in the summer of 1892. It was not to be.

At about the same time Mr William Tyssen-Amherst indicated an interest in Petrie's work at El-Amarna, and he proposed that he might contribute funds towards the excavations in the expectation that he would receive antiquities for his Egyptian collection at Didlington Hall. The formulation of this idea of co-operation may have sprung naturally from Amherst's wish to enlarge his collections, but it is not unreasonable to suggest that the principal promoter of the plan was Percy Newberry, friend of the Amhersts and near neighbour of Petrie in the field. To what extent Howard Carter figured in the original conception cannot now be determined, but in the end his presence at El-Bersha as part of Newberry's team made him a convenient possible participant.

Petrie saw Amherst's involvement as being rather less than a regular partnership, and the agreement which was quickly and satisfactorily worked out was rather unusual even for the late nineteenth century when informality and even irregularity were characteristic elements in arrangements for working in the field. In his wish to be associated with the work at El-Amarna, Amherst was probably fired more distinctly by a desire to obtain antiquities than a wish to support altruistically Petrie's researches. Support from businessmen and industrialists had regularly helped Petrie to work in Egypt in the years before and after his employment by the Egypt Exploration Fund; and it was his practice to see that his backers were suitably recompensed with some of the fruits of his excavations. There was nothing improper in this practice, although Petrie himself had a clear idea of the priorities in the disposal of his most important finds, after the needs of the Antiquities Service had been met. For Amherst the arrangements were different, and their unusual features may have been influenced by the involvement of Howard Carter. Petrie was undoubtedly dubious about the young man's suitability for excavation, as he made clear later; but he had met him with Newberry on a number of occasions from late November onwards, and saw the two on almost a daily basis from 19 December until the end of the year.[18]

In his journal for the period 21–27 December Petrie records, after noting that Blackden will not join him:

18 Petrie's pocket diary for 1891–2 (in the Petrie Museum, University College London) records meetings on 19–23 December and 26–29 December.

But Mr. Tyssen Amherst wishes to do a little here under my permission [i.e. his excavation permit], and so Mr. Carter is to come
here and work, not exactly with me, but on parts of the ground
which I may assign to him. I having no responsibilities about his
work except to the Government here.

He says further in the journal entry for 3–9 January 1892, after recording
Carter's arrival in his camp:

His position here is to be as agent for Mr. Tyssen Amherst M.P.;
he [i.e. Amherst] takes much interest in Tell Amarna, and had
wished to work here. Hearing of this I offered to him to allow him
to appoint a worker to dig for him under my permission, provided
I controlled the work and had the exhibiting and publishing of what
was found. Thus I expand the amount of ground worked and the
information without any responsibility or expense to myself.

In this same entry Petrie offers his opinion on his new associate in excavation:

Mr. Carter is a good-natured lad, whose interest is entirely in painting and natural history; he only takes up this digging as being on
the spot and convenient to Mr. Amherst, and it is of no use to me
to work him up as an excavator.

This was, to say the least, a premature judgement, written before Carter
had started work on his own, and based presumably on what Petrie had
been able to get out of him during his early encounters in Newberry's
company and on his behaviour during his first few days in camp, when
his time had been engrossed by domestic activities. It would have been
natural for the young man to speak mostly about the things he understood
best – painting and natural history. It would perhaps have been a little
early for him to express opinions on excavations.

On Amherst's side, the proposal for his association with Petrie's work
suited him well enough. He was being offered his own sector at El-Amarna
to be worked on by Howard Carter in whom he could recognize an 'agent'
(as Petrie described him) who would be a diligent representative of his
interests. On 23 December he wrote to Newberry:[19]

Your welcome letter reached me yesterday and I at once sent you a
telegram viz. 'Newberry Der Moës Upper Egypt I accept Petrie's
offer let Howard Carter commence under him' . . .

You are quite right that I wished to help Mr. Petrie in the excavation and to get if I could some fresh monuments of the past for
my museum.

19 G.I. Newberry Corr. 2/72.

I have therefore much pleasure in accepting Mr. Petrie's offer which I think is very clearly stated and if you will kindly arrange that Howard Carter should work for me under him I shall be much obliged. It will save a great deal of delay and expense and under such guidance and the experience he has had with you he should be able to do well.

After stating the procedures for paying £200 to Petrie, Amherst adds:

and now as to Mr. Carter will you kindly make the arrangements with him – if of course Mr. Petrie agrees and let me know what you think he should have and if he agrees to work for it. Is his return passage already arranged by those for whom he went out? How long will he be able to work? I am afraid I am giving you a great deal of trouble but I do not know how else to arrange for my excavation. I shall hope to hear from you shortly.

It is astonishing to see with what speed the Petrie-Amherst agreement was concluded, in view of the fact that Amherst was at Didlington and all the negotiations were carried out by Newberry. In less than a month all was agreed, and on 2 January 1892 Howard Carter joined Petrie from El-Bersha, seeing himself as Amherst's representative on what the latter already chose proprietorily to call 'my excavation'. According to his late autobiographical sketch, Carter was treated by Petrie to begin with not as part of his camp but as a kind of adjunct. He was to live separately from Petrie, prepare his own meals – which in practice meant opening his own tins of food – do his own cleaning and other household chores. And to start with he had to build his own quarters. Petrie describes his own methods of construction at El-Amarna, rather proudly, thus:[20]

Such rooms can be built very quickly; a hut twelve feet by eight taking only a few hours. The bricks can be brought at tenpence a thousand; the boys make a huge mud pie, a line of bricks is laid on the ground, a line of mud poured over them, another line of bricks is slapped down in the mud so as to drive it up the joints, and thus a wall of headers, with an occasional course of stretchers to bind it, is soon run up. The roof is made of boards, covered with durra stalks to protect them from the sun; and the hut is ready for us, with a piece of canvas over the doorway. Such a place is far better than a tent to live in; and on leaving we found that every native was so afraid that we might give away the materials to someone else, that we had offers for all our bricks, boards, and straw, at nearly the new price.

Throughout his lifetime in the field Petrie prided himself on such parsi-

20 W. M. F. Petrie, *Tell el Amarna* (London, 1894), p. 1.

monious activities, which he regarded as pragmatically sensible. Howard Carter was not built of such austere stuff, and could not comprehend the wisdom of spending time on this kind of activity, which could be done far more quickly and more efficiently by local workmen. Equally he marvelled at Petrie's unwillingness to use the local means of transport, the donkey, when walking would suffice. Virtue lay in doing things oneself and in achieving singular feats of physical activity even if they were not really necessary. In a note to Newberry, written on 14 February 1892, Carter acknowledges a letter and adds: 'Please excuse scribble as I am just home from walk with Mr. Petrie from 8 am to 8 pm.'[21] In contemplating the use of a donkey, Carter thought of it as the sensible way of covering the two to three miles' walk daily to and from the site of excavations. For the occasional reconnoitring expeditions which Petrie took in the course of the season, quartering the region and scouring the wadis and hills for inscriptions and signs of ancient occupation, walking was in every respect the better way to go. Such no doubt was the 'walk' reported by Carter, and among others was a visit early in the year to the tomb of Akhenaten.

News of the so-called discovery (it had, as Petrie later determined, been known for several years) was given to Professor A. H. Sayce on about 20 January by Alexandre Barsanti, a technical employee of the Antiquities Service, who had been working at the site apparently since late December 1891.[22] Sayce, an oriental scholar of wide learning who had recently been appointed Professor of Assyriology at Oxford, spent some months in Egypt every year, travelling up the Nile in his own *dahabiya*, visiting the monuments and copying inscriptions. In early 1892 he was at El-Amarna advising Petrie in textual matters, and was invited to visit the tomb; Petrie and Howard Carter accompanied him. In his description of the visit in his journal Petrie makes no mention of Carter, but the account he subsequently sent to the *Daily Graphic* was illustrated by two topographical sketches and a drawing of part of a scene made by Carter.[23] Writing to Newberry some days later Carter commented unfavourably on the discovery:[24] 'The Tomb of Khu-n-aten is a great sell, is very rough and unfinished . . . I have made some drawings for Mr. Petrie of the Valley and the Tomb.' These seemingly were the very first published archaeological drawings from the hand of the young artist-excavator. The impropriety of sending such an unofficial account of the tomb to a newspaper probably never struck Petrie. Now, a century later, it would not be thought at all proper for an unofficial report of an important discovery to be made in this way. The great archaeologist,

21 G.I. Newberry Corr. 8/1.
22 Archibald Henry Sayce was a British Assyriologist who spent much time almost annually in Egypt; see Dawson and Uphill, *Who Was Who in Egyptology*, p. 261. For the discovery of the tomb, see G. T. Martin, *The Royal Tomb at El-'Amarna*, I, (London 1974) pp. 4ff.
23 23 March 1892, pp. 13, 14.
24 Letter of 9 February. I am grateful to Dr Andrew Gordon for allowing me to quote from this letter which is in his possession.

however, surely felt that he had a duty to make the matter known to a wider public, and any implied impropriety could easily be discounted by the bungling manner in which the discovery had been handled by the Antiquities Service. Petrie would certainly not have considered his action as being in any way the equivalent of the behaviour of Blackden and Fraser over Hatnub, which he himself had characterised as not leaving 'a pleasant taste in the mouth'.

So Petrie had already discovered abilities in this 'good-natured' lad which he could exploit in a positive way. In his publication of the Amarna excavation he notes that Carter had completed a survey of the many ancient roads and tracks which criss-crossed and encircled the city and extended into the hills to quarries and to tombs which were mostly unfinished. His statement does not make it clear whether this survey was finished in the following year or at the time of their working together at El-Amarna, but sadly the timing now matters little for 'his map with all his notes was lost in the post'.[25]

Carter's drawings of the tomb of Akhenaten, executed no doubt in less than ideal conditions, reveal his talent clearly, and the accuracy of the copy of the scene is specially commendable if it is compared with the drawing in the first official publication, prepared under the supervision of well qualified Egyptologists.[26] In view of this demonstration of competence, it is sad in retrospect to consider that in one matter in particular Petrie failed to make use of Carter where Carter could have accomplished a far better job than the great man himself. In the early days of his work at El-Amarna Petrie had uncovered in the palace a hall with a very well preserved pavement, painted with remarkable scenes of plants and animals carried out in a naturalistic style which far exceeded in beauty and liveliness most Egyptian painting previously discovered. Petrie held it to be the outstanding find of his season, and he took careful steps to protect the pavement and to provide walk-ways so that it could be viewed by visitors without damage to the surface. All this work he carried out by himself, not trusting the local workmen to do what was needed with sufficient care. He also spent much time making a faithful copy of the whole painting and coloured facsimiles of parts of it. The results, reproduced in his excavation memoir, are good – mercifully so, for the pavement was later wilfully destroyed – but they would have been even better had he entrusted the work to Howard Carter.[27] That he did not make use of Carter's special talent was surely due in the first place to his own belief in his ability to carry out all the functions of a field-worker with more than adequate

25 Petrie, *Tell el Amarna*, p. 4.
26 U. Bouriant, G. Legrain and G. Jéquier, *Monuments pour servir à l'étude du culte d'Atounou en Égypte* (Cairo, 1903), I, pl. 10, reproduced in G. T. Martin, *Royal Tomb*, II, p. 46, also pls 68, 69.
27 See Drower, *Flinders Petrie*, pp. 191–2, 197.

competence. He, after all, had found the pavement, and it was his responsibility to record it. But he probably also felt that he had no right to divert Carter from his principal duty of working separately for Amherst.

The special areas allocated to Carter as Amherst's 'glebe' or portion comprised the great temple and some parts of the town. The responsibility for a youth of seventeen and a half was awesome. From Petrie's diary his programme can be charted in outline: Jan. 2, Carter arrives; Jan. 3, Carter builds house; Jan. 12, Carter begins work. From his own late sketch, Carter makes it clear that he received about one week's instruction from Petrie before he was thrown in at the deep end and expected to get on with it. There is, sadly, neither in Petrie's journal or his published report, nor in Carter's sketch, any indication of how the Amherst side-show was supervised. In the journal Petrie wrote up every few days is an account in varying detail of the progress of his own work, and it is not possible to distinguish at any point whether or not he is talking about something which might have happened, or been turned up, in the Amherst sector. He regularly mentions the expeditions he made with Carter into the desert and the hills encircling the Amarna plain and their identifying the great boundary inscriptions. In the entry for the days 24–30 January he writes at some length about a plaster face brought to him by one of the men. It seems to have been a casual find not an excavated piece, but Petrie was sufficiently intrigued to call in Carter to discuss it; he 'is accustomed to casts. We conclude that without any doubt it is a direct cast from KHUENATEN's [i.e. Akhenaten's] OWN FACE, taken after death.' Petrie would certainly have revised this opinion in the light of subsequent discussions of the plaster faces discovered at El-Amarna by the German excavators before the First World War; but at this point it is interesting to see that he considered Carter's opinions on technique and casting procedures worthy of note. Carter told Newberry that he thought this discovery better than the tomb: 'I don't think they can beat *that*.'[28]

Carter confesses in his autobiographical sketch that his early efforts at excavation were 'wide of the mark and to little or no purpose', but some success attended his later work, in which he was assisted by a few of Petrie's own trained diggers. Of successes he mentions in the sketch there were, in particular, the discovery of Aegean pottery, of considerable importance for comparative dating; the identification of the remains of glass manufactories; the partial contents of a sculptor's workshop; and a deposit of royal sculpture in a ditch by the Great Temple.[29] The last discovery contained fragments of wonderful hard limestone statues of Akhenaten and

28 For a useful summary of later studies, see C. Aldred, *Akhenaten, King of Egypt* (2nd ed., London, 1988), p. 57; id. *Akhenaten and Nefertiti* (London, 1973), p. 43. The face is illustrated as the frontispiece of Petrie, *Tell el Amarna*. Carter's comment is included in the letter mentioned in n. 24 above.

29 All these particular discoveries are properly reported and considered in Petrie, *Tell el Amarna*, pp. 15–17, 25ff., 30–1, 18.

his wife Nefertiti, which were to become important additions to Amherst's collection at Didlington Hall. Everything in fact conspired to intensify Carter's interest in excavation. In his letter to Newberry, partly quoted earlier, he confesses: 'As regards the work I like it very much indeed and find it very exciting. I did not find anything of any great value till yesterday. One of my men found another gold ring' – here he draws the legend on the ring-bezel – 'I have 22 men working for me now and hope to get more this week.'[30]

In his varied discoveries Carter exhibited the kind of luck which often attends the excavator who works broadly, without a precise and well defined purpose on a virgin site, as El-Amarna was at that time. To what extent he was guided in detail by Petrie cannot now be established, but just to have such a man available for consultation and reference was no small advantage for a beginner. There were also many opportunities during the long walks the two took together for the exposition of much wisdom, imparted casually and as such being more easily given and readily absorbed. Carter in later life certainly appreciated the quality of his early instruction: 'Petrie's training during those months of hard work transformed me, I believe, into something of the nature of an investigator – to dig and examine systematically.'

Further opportunities for the acquisition of mature wisdom were provided at El-Amarna by the social contacts with a succession of visitors, learned and grand, who arrived in a sequence to inspect the site and even to visit the royal tomb. The convenient landing point was at the village of El-Hagg Qandil, near which Petrie's camp was established. More or less centrally placed for visits to the city, it was where Sayce and others berthed their *dahabiyas*. Some visitors, like Sayce, the Revd Greville Chester[31] and Charles Edwin Wilbour[32] were knowledgeable and very welcome; others, like Mr Aquila Dodgson,[33] were enthusiastic amateurs who had independent means and had been active in raising funds for Egyptology in England. The Spicers, who spent several days at El-Amarna in Sayce's company, were wealthy sightseers; the Marquis of Waterford with a large party could not be ignored.[34] Most of these visitors distracted Petrie from

30 Petrie's drawing of the design on the ring is published in *Tell el Amarna*, pl. XIV, 31. Squatting figures of Akhenaten and Nefertiti face each other below a sun disc.
31 The Revd Greville Chester wintered regularly during the second half of the nineteenth century in Egypt, collecting and selling antiquities to cover his expenses; see T. G. H. James, *The British Museum and Ancient Egypt* (London, 1981), pp. 20ff.
32 Charles Edwin Wilbour, an American businessman, travelled regularly in Egypt for many years until his death in 1896; see Dawson and Uphill, *Who Was Who in Egyptology*, p. 304.
33 For Aquila Dodgson, an English Congregational Minister with strong Egyptological interests, see Dawson and Uphill, *Who Was Who in Egyptology*, p. 87.
34 The 5th Marquis of Waterford visited Egypt with members of his family in 1891–2 and 1892–3. He was seriously injured in a hunting accident and was accompanied by his doctor. I am grateful to the present Lord Waterford for drawing attention to *Victorian Days* by his great-aunt Lady Clodagh Anson (2nd ed., London, 1957). Chapter VI deals charmingly, but briefly, with the visits to Egypt and life on the Nile.

his work, but some would help in one way or another, and most were
generous with hospitality on their boats. It has been remarked of Petrie
at that time that, 'Never before had he eaten so well and lived so social
a life in the wilderness; never again was he to do so.'[35] Carter was not
omitted from at least some of these entertainments, and he noted that he
was rescued from one particularly nasty bout of illness by the physician
who travelled as part of Lord Waterford's entourage. Dr Bridgeman found
young Carter physically exhausted and mentally depressed, and prescribed
'Valentine's meat-juice, champagne, and a Tonic', items not commonly
found in Petrie's provision boxes.

Carter quickly recovered his health under such careful attention; but
later there was to be one other serious reason for his feeling depressed.
Towards the end of the season news reached him that his father had died.
The cable which Petrie handed him did not come as a complete surprise;
it was a second stroke that his father had suffered. He died on 1 May; he
was only 57, a good but not particularly old age for late Victorian times.
In his letters and in his autobiographical sketches Howard Carter reveals
little of his emotions on hearing the news. It may indeed have been a
psychological weakness on his part that he suppressed his feelings beyond
reason. At severe crises in his life extreme self-control and an apparent
inability to share his sorrow or anger with others resulted in eruptions of
unreasonable temper. On the subject of his father's death he reports his
sadness briefly with only a laconic comment on the transitory nature of life.
He does say, however, that Petrie, when he brought the news, displayed 'a
shade of inexpressible sadness in his utterance'. So may Petrie have been
contemplating the death of his own mother, and that of Amelia Edwards,
his old ally and friend. The former had died early in March, and the latter
in mid-April. Both losses were grievous for him.

Excavation on the Amarna site wound down in early April, although
occasional discoveries continued to be made. Such was reported by Carter
to Newberry on 7 April:[36]

> The work is coming to an end now, and we are hard at work packing.
> I found a very interesting tablet with Khuenaten seated upon a
> throne dancing the Queen upon his knee with the two Princesses
> upon her lap. I am sorry to say that the heads are broken off; Petrie
> says he does not know anything like it in Egypt.

Petrie's assessment remains true today; it was a piece which, even in its
damaged state, would make a valuable addition to the Amherst collection
in due course. For the rest, Petrie and Carter concentrated on tidying up
outstanding matters, completing drawings and other records, and making

35 So Drower, *Flinders Petrie*, p. 194.
36 G. I. Newberry Corr. 8/3. The tablet is now in the Louvre, no. E.11624; see Aldred,
   Akhenatem and Nefertiti, p. 134 (no. 56).

boxes for the transport of the antiquities found during the season. It was characteristic of Petrie to make his own boxes from timber purchased locally, Carter was expected to do the same, and from entries in Petrie's diary it emerges that for many days Carter worked on boxes on his own, as Petrie was unwell with a bad foot. Carpentry and packing occupied much of the last six weeks of the season, interspersed with occasional days spent on drawing and on trips on foot to continue the exploration of the surrounding hills. On 20 May Petrie notes in his diary the dispatch of 125 boxes by boat; a further consignment was sent on 28 May. It was probably this second dispatch about which Carter reported in his sketch, offering a further example of Petrie's practical ingenuity. A group of 36 cases was taken to the local railway station on the west bank of the Nile; permission to dispatch 35 cases had been granted by the Antiquities Service. The station-master refused to accept 36 cases. So Petrie went out and bought some lengths of wood and nailed two cases together, thereby reducing the consignment to the acceptable 35. On the next day, 29 May, they left for Cairo.

So ended Howard Carter's first season in Egypt. It had been, to say the least, eventful. He had been introduced to life in the field, initiated into the currently acceptable techniques of copying for the Archaeological Survey of the Egypt Exploration Fund (and taken an instant dislike to them), spent five months with Flinders Petrie and learned much about excavation methods (and how to rough it unnecessarily); he had participated in interesting discoveries, observed painful controversies, accepted considerable responsibilities.. He was launched on the rising tide of Egyptological activities. But what would happen next? In Cairo he found a letter from Percy Newberry waiting for him, and on 30 May he answered, 'I am much obliged to you for your kind offer and would be very glad to take up the work.'[37]

37 G.I. Newberry Corr. 8/2.

3

CONSOLIDATION AND DIVERSIFICATION

After a few months of anguish at the start of 1892 Percy Newberry found himself once again established as Surveyor, the principal field-officer of the Archaeological Survey, by the late spring of that year. His letter of resignation to Amelia Edwards was never seriously considered, but he had in the meanwhile written petulantly to the newspapers about what he considered to have been unprincipled behaviour by Eugène Grébaut in connection with the discovery of the tomb of Akhenaten and its public announcement. Newberry's behaviour itself was an embarrassment to the Committee of the Egypt Exploration Fund, and a form of reprimand was inflicted on him. But the replacement of Grébaut by Jacques de Morgan, a scholar worthy of much greater respect, obviated a serious difference between the Fund and the Antiquities Service. The death of Amelia Edwards further led to a closing of ranks and a determination on the part of the Fund's officers and workers to ensure that her years of dedication to Egypt should not be dissipated by petty wrangling. In addition, Fraser and Blackden, who had rendered Newberry's last season so miserable, had themselves left the service of the Archaeological Survey, and no longer threatened to disrupt any future work in Middle Egypt. There were to be problems over work left unfinished by Fraser and Blackden, but these were small clouds that had not yet appeared in a sky which for Newberry must have increasingly promised halcyon days.

Plans could now be made for future work, both in Egypt and in England; but a degree of reconstruction was needed. At this moment Howard Carter was again available after his five months of 'training' with Petrie. He was at the end of this period, if not purified by the fire of Petrie's obsessive parsimony and practicality then at least fully tempered in the furnace of the great man's passion and commitment. He had been lucky in enjoying the instruction, even companionship, of the one man working in the field in Egypt who had a conception of archaeological purpose far beyond that of any of his contemporaries. His experience on the staff of the Archaeological Survey had been less intensive, less edifying, and less productive. Nevertheless, it was to that staff that he had first been appointed, and he had more than adequately demonstrated to Newberry that he was capable of doing a good job. What Newberry now had it in mind for him – presumably set out in the letter which Carter had answered from Cairo in late May – may have been his being kept on for the summer to complete and ink in the drawings from Beni Hasan and El-Bersha, and his engagement for the next winter season.

There had been no commitment by the Egypt Exploration Fund to continue Carter's employment in any capacity after the end of the first season. In fact, however, the Fund had received only a partial fulfilment of Carter's obligation because of his detachment to Petrie at El-Amarna, and its officers, as well as Newberry, may have felt that a balance of time was owed by Carter. It was not the practice of the Fund, as indeed it has not commonly been of its linear successor, the Egypt Exploration Society, to employ field-workers on long-term contracts. All appointments were temporary, but renewable. And so with Carter; the Committee at a meeting on 26 July resolved that he should be employed at a remuneration of £1 per week to assist Newberry in the inking-in of his tracings. This decision was in direct response to a letter from Newberry. It would be dull and uncongenial work for the young Carter, but at least it kept him in touch with the Fund and reinforced his claims for future employment. In effect it secured his attachment to the Fund for the next seven years, during which time his annually renewed engagement amounted almost to regular employment on a permanent basis. Still, as a very young man he was regarded as the 'boy' of the Fund's field-workers, and capable of being treated in a rather informal way, as was indeed commonly the case with juniors at that time.

The staff of the Archaeological Survey returned to Egypt in December 1892, with rather ambitious plans to extend the work from El-Bersha to the rock-tombs at El-Amarna, to those at El-Sheikh Said, an intermediate site also on the east bank of the Nile, and even further south to tombs in the more mountainous region of the Gebel Abu Foda, about 30 miles upstream from El-Amarna.[1] The staff members for this season were very different from the mutinous crew of the previous year. Newberry's brother John, a qualified architect, was to work with the Survey for some weeks before moving on to Deir el-Bahri at Thebes, the new Fund excavation to be directed by Édouard Naville. Howard Carter travelled out with the Newberrys from Naples; at Cairo they were joined by Percy Buckman, a topographical artist who was to take the place of Blackden. It was a strong, although over all less experienced, team, with the potential abilities to accomplish much in a single season. Poor organization unfortunately frustrated good intention, and one side-show involving Howard Carter went badly wrong. A casual attitude towards the announcing of plans, and to

1 See generally, Newberry's report on the Archaeological Survey for the season 1892–3, E.E.S. Archives I a 2.

the application for permissions to work, lay at the heart of the matter; perhaps also insufficient secretarial preparation in London following the death of the admirably active Amelia Edwards. She had been succeeded for practical purposes by her friend Emily Paterson, who had been her own secretary for a number of years.

When Newberry presented himself at the Cairo Museum to receive his licence to work for the season, he found that a new rule, previously unannounced, required him to obtain the formal authority of the new Director-General before any work could be started. In those relatively early days of field activities by foreign organizations, there seemed to be no formal set of procedures that had to be followed as a regular practice. Rules were changed and modified almost at the whim of the authorities of the Antiquities Service. Petrie had complained bitterly of the unacceptably changing requirements laid down by Grébaut, the lately superseded Director-General. Unfortunately, things had been much more casual during the régime of Gaston Maspero (1881–6), and now a tightening of controls – almost certainly necessary – was seen to be not only deliberately obstructive, but also typical of French so-called intransigence. The running of a state antiquities organization, the first of its kind, became inevitability an uncertain process as the work of foreign expeditions developed. So many differing expectations had to be satisfied; and if the personalities involved were as varied (to consider only those working for the Egypt Exploration Fund) as the prickly, idiosyncratic Petrie, the mild but touchy Newberry, or the scholarly and superficially undemanding Naville, there was small hope of achieving a consensus of views from which a set of rules acceptable to all could be derived. Successive Directors-General were obliged both to unpick the more unreasonable of existing practices, and to devise new regulations to stabilize procedures. The pattern of change and uncertainty was to continue, and many excavators would claim still one hundred years later that the often unpredictable requirements of the Egyptian Antiquities Organization (successor of the old Antiquities Service) represent a serious impediment to regular field-work in Egypt.

The thought that permission to work on the planned sites might be refused had never entered Newberry's mind. So, after setting out his plans in writing for de Morgan, who was on tour of inspection at Aswan, he moved south and established the Survey's camp at Beni Hasan, a site for which the previous season's permit remained valid. Almost three weeks were spent preparing colour facsimiles of scene-details and of coloured hieroglyphs – work for which Howard Carter was ideally suited. Then, still without formal permission, the camp was transferred to the village of El-Till in the Amarna plain and close to the northern group of tombs which had been prepared for great officials who had served Akhenaten during the brief existence of the ancient city of Akhetaten. Newberry with Carter began copying the scenes and inscriptions in these tombs on 25

January 1893, and on the 28th they received at last de Morgan's reply: permission was refused on the grounds that he had provisionally promised a permit to another scholar. Already, however, to quote Newberry's report on the season, 'we had measured and planned several of the tombs, copied many of the inscriptions and reproduced in colour some of the fresco paintings.' This small initial work would in due course be used when finally, eight years later, the Fund received permission to work on the Amarna tombs and boundary inscriptions. By then Maspero would again be Director-General, and the work would be carried out by Norman de Garis Davies, Newberry's successor as Surveyor to the Fund.[2]

Thus was Newberry frustrated in his hope of working at El-Amarna, and on 4 February he moved camp to El-Sheikh Said. His vexation was then further increased by a development which would again deny him the services of Howard Carter for several months. On 6 February Newberry travelled to Cairo to see if anything could be done to reverse the decision on El-Amarna. *En route*, at the railway station of Mallawi, the largest provincial town close to El-Amarna, he received a letter from H. A. Grueber, the Fund's Honorary Treasurer, requesting him to arrange for Carter to leave El-Sheikh Said at once to join Guthrie Roger in Cairo. It is not clear from surviving evidence whether Newberry had earlier received any hint of what was being decided in London. Sadly, it must be said, the Egypt Exploration Fund's field-workers were frequently treated in a somewhat arbitrary manner by the Committee in London; many of its members had never been to Egypt and seemed to think that their deliberations were absolute, and that communication with their representatives in the field was as simple as writing to Scotland or Cornwall. It is true that for the most part letters travelled from London to the remotest places in Middle Egypt in a very few days, and were delivered with great reliability; but losses undoubtedly occurred from time to time. Little allowance was made for such eventualities. The instructions involving Carter certainly seem to have come as a surprise to Newberry, whose plans for the season were in consequence thrown into disarray. As for Howard Carter, he was being transferred as the Fund's 'reserve' archaeologist to carry out a piece of work in the Delta for which he was scarcely prepared, and concerning which no adequate arrangements had been made from London.

The story goes back to the spring of 1892 when Édouard Naville was engaged in his last campaign of survey and excavation in the Delta. Among the sites which occupied his attention was that of Mendes, the ancient capital of the XVIth nome of Lower Egypt, and the centre of worship of the great ram god Banebded. Of the two great mounds which together

2 The six volumes of *The Rock-Tombs at El Amarna* by Norman de Garis Davies were published between 1903 and 1908. Two further volumes in the series, *The Royal Tomb at El-'Amarna* by G. T. Martin, appeared in 1974 and 1989.

may be characterized as the metropolitan district of the nome capital, Tell el-Ruba is more precisely to be identified as Mendes (the classical name for the site), while Tell Timai el-Amdid is the classical Thmuis. Naville's work was largely confined to the latter mound, and he paid some attention to a series of subterranean chambers containing huge quantities of papyri, mostly in a carbonized, very friable condition, due possibly to deliberate burning in antiquity. From his report on these chambers, which he chose to call the 'library of Mendes', it seems clear that he did not discover them, but did consider clearing what remained of their contents:[3]

> They are most difficult to take out, they crumble to pieces when they are loosened from the earth which covers them, but by looking sideways the characters are still discernible; they generally are Greek in good handwriting . . . I tried to see whether some of the carbonised papyri, well packed in cotton, would stand a journey, but the contents of the five boxes which I sent to London are nothing but crumbs of charcoal and ashes.

The impression given by Naville's brief account is that he lacked the practical abilities, and almost certainly the courage, to proceed with a comprehensive clearance of the chambers. Attempts had already been made to remove portions of the extraordinary archive in the preceding few years, with very little success, and there seems to have been a continuing plundering of the pitiful remains both by scholarly visitors and by the representatives of antiquities dealers. The outlook for the papyri was bleak, possibly hopeless, but Naville, inspired perhaps by his own inadequate efforts, and certainly reacting to taunts from Petrie, suggested to the Egypt Exploration Fund that something further should be done.

The minutes of a committee meeting on 12 January 1893 record a letter from Naville about the papyrus chambers. It was proposed that a sub-committee 'be authorised to settle what should be done in the matter', and it was further suggested that Mr Howard Carter should be instructed to meet Mr Hunt at Timai el-Amdid. Arthur Surridge Hunt, a recently graduated classical scholar of Oxford University, was at this time at the very beginning of his career as a palaeographer. He and Bernard Grenfell were to become the founders of modern studies in Greek papyrology in Britain, and the outstanding publishers of Greek papyri, particularly in the Fund's series *Oxyrhynchus Papyri*.[4] Hunt was 21 in early 1893, three years older than Howard Carter; but the latter knew Egypt from one season, and had earned his excavation spurs with Petrie; he had also acquired an adequate speaking knowledge of Arabic. The deliberations of the Fund's Committee may be imagined: Naville's letter was an embarrass-

---

3 *E.E.F. Arch. Rep. 1892–1893*, p. 4.
4 Volume 1 of *Oxyrhynchus Papyri* was published in 1898. The series continues; vol. 58 appeared in 1991.

ment, raising a piece of unfinished business which, if left unfinished, would surely result in the eventual loss of the remaining papyri. What could be done? Someone with experience should deal with the organization and supervision of the work; someone who knew something about Greek papyri should be there to examine the papyrus rolls as they were extracted and even copy what could be made out before any were again subjected to the hazards of transport, leading probably to disintegration. For the excavator, Howard Carter seemed just right; for the palaeographer, Hunt seemed ideal – he was already known to be a more than competent reader of Greek texts on papyrus, and he was, temporarily, working in the Department of Manuscripts in the British Museum. There is no indication that either of the proposed 'rescuers' had been approached, and it is almost certain that Carter was never asked whether he wished to be detached from the Archaeological Survey. He was, after all, young enough to be told what to do. As for Hunt, it turned out that he was not able to go. Grueber reported so to the Committee on 1 February, and stated at the same time that the sub-committee had decided that Mr Roger 'should receive instructions from Mr. Hunt on the handling and packing of the papyri and that he should join Mr. Carter at Tmei el Amdid as soon as possible. Mr. Roger left England on the 24th Jan. for Egypt.'

Thus began a kind of sad pantomime, a travesty of an expedition – Carter's first 'command' in the field – which reflected little credit on the Egypt Exploration Fund beyond a few moderate marks for good intentions. Not least among the uncertainties of the scheme was Mr Roger himself. Guthrie Roger is one of the shadowy characters of early field-work in Egypt. From his behaviour at Mendes it would seem that he was not well chosen, and that he was ill-fitted for the trials of the camp.[5] It would, however, be singularly unfair to pillory him for his disinclinations and short-comings, because he certainly appears to have been a victim of those circumstances that attended the beginning of the enterprise. He arrived in Cairo on 2 February 1893, on what was presumably his first visit to Egypt, to find, as so many of his successors have found, that there was no room at the inn (the Royal Hotel) to which he had been instructed to proceed. So, with some show of initiative, he took up lodgings at the Hôtel de l'Orient and wrote to Newberry, still in Middle Egypt, announcing his arrival and declaring that he would wait until Carter arrived before doing anything substantive for the expedition.[6] All these preliminaries had taken place perhaps before Newberry and Carter were even aware of what the Committee had decided.

5 Although Carter's later comment (in the version of his autobiographical sketch in MMA, Department of Egyptian Art, Carter files) that Roger's 'archeological attributes . . . comprised athletics and dealing with heavy weights' should have indicated someone ideally suited for roughing it in camp.
6 G.I. Newberry Corr. 38/97.

The episode has the bizarre quality of the old army deception: musical volunteers are called for; the volunteers find themselves moving a piano. Howard Carter had not volunteered, but he was assigned a task which was not lacking in responsibility. He could not have refused. He may even have welcomed the transfer from the regime of tracing maintained by Newberry to an independent and superficially important excavating commission three hundred miles to the north, in the mid-Delta where he had never previously been. It could have been a piece of work which would have brought him great credit. On the other hand, he could have had few illusions about his suitability. He was later to write:[7] 'My touch, my fingers and thumbs, were considered apparently sufficiently delicate to handle such material, about which I knew little.' So, courageously he left El-Sheikh Said and travelled straight to Cairo to join Guthrie Roger. The details of what happened then are only clear in the most general way. After obtaining the necessary stores and equipment, Carter and Roger went to El-Simbillawein, the nearest town to Mendes with a railway station. From there they carried out reconnaissances at Tell Timai el-Amdid. Unfortunately, they had been inadequately briefed, and Carter was soon obliged to write to the Fund's secretary in London informing her that he had not been able to find the papyrus chambers 'owing to insufficient information'.[8] He also told her that he was seeking to obtain the necessary permit to work from the Antiquities Service. Nothing had been done from London to prepare the ground for this hastily arranged enterprise. The secretary advised Carter to find out more about the chambers from Naville who was by that time working at Deir el-Bahri.

Although Naville was the obvious person to contact about the location of the 'library' vaults, notes from Carter to Newberry suggest that a letter from Petrie, probably addressed to Newberry, contained the most precise details about the site. On 10 February Carter wrote: 'As far as I can see there are 3 or 4 places that might be it, but either of them would take at least 2 or 3 months to excavate.'[9] By the first day of March, however, Carter had progress to report: 'I have found the chambers and they seem very promising. I have not yet received the permit, so I am unable to start work as the Sheikh will not let me start work till I show him it.' He adds, 'This is a very bad place for tenting as there is no guard for the wind and the ground is so soft that the pegs will not hold properly.'[10] A postscript comments unfavourably on his companion: 'Camping out is beginning to open Roger's eyes.' Some elaboration of this remark occurs in Carter's late sketch: he explains that wretchedly wet weather hampered

7 In his sketch, p. 11 in MMA, Department of Egyptian Art, Carter files.
8 E.E.F. Committee minutes for 28 February 1893.
9 G.I. Newberry Corr. 8/5.
10 G.I. Newberry Corr. 8/7.

their activities at Mendes, and culminated in a night of such storms that their tents were blown down, the wretched Roger being reduced to tears.

All in all the expedition was doomed to failure, and Newberry became increasingly vexed that his principal assistant was obliged to pass his time idly in the Delta while much unfinished work awaited him in Middle Egypt. Howard Carter was equally unhappy. His position was weak; he found Roger an uncongenial companion and an unsuitable colleague; he himself carried no weight with the Antiquities Service and could not on his own standing obtain a permit; the weather was terrible and the site was infested with jackals. He also felt that his apparent time-wasting with Guthrie Roger was attracting unfavourable attention in Cairo. Yet there was little he could do apart from reminding Newberry on the one hand, and the Committee on the other, that no progress could be made until his little expedition was formally approved; and no approval would be given until the Fund's secretary went through the proper procedures. At a Committee meeting as late as 7 April letters from both Carter and Roger were read. The former informed the Committee of a communication from de Morgan refusing permission because the request had not come through Mr Poole. Apparently an earlier formal application sent by telegram had not been signed by Poole. Another therefore should be sent, properly signed, to be followed by a letter explaining to the Director-General what the Fund's intentions were. Roger's letter pointed out 'the waste of time and money owing to the delay in obtaining permission to work at Mendes'.

It was by now far too late, and in the end Newberry severed the knot of indecision. On 9 April he wrote to Miss Paterson:[11]

I have been to the Museum to-day and heard from Mon. Brugsch that Carter had not yet got permission to work at Timai el-Amdid and from what I could judge of M. Brugsch's behaviour and what I have heard from other people I do not think that there is the least likelihood of the permission being granted. I therefore telegraphed to Mr. Griffith saying that I am recalling Carter to join the Survey again. It is very important that I should have him back at once to do the water-colour drawings that are needed to complete El-Bersheh: the weather is getting very hot and I do not want to remain out here after the end of this month or beginning of May. Of course if the permission is granted whilst Mr. Carter is with me I will at once send him back to join Mr. Roger at Simballawîn. He has been away now more than two months and not done a stroke of work. He feels this most bitterly as I know he wanted to show how much and what good work he could turn out in one season. For three weeks or more he stayed at this hotel [the Royal] and the remaining time in one of my tents at Timai el-Amdid. A good many people here know of this

11 E.E.S. Archives XII f (Archaeological Survey papers for 1893).

and that two men should be out here doing nothing is really doing untold harm to the Fund. I am sorry to say this but I fear the state of things can hardly be realised in England.

At last someone was showing a sense of urgency. On 13 April Newberry returned to El-Sheikh Said with Howard Carter, and two weeks were spent working on the scenes and inscriptions in the tombs there. Meanwhile in London confusion persisted. It was assumed, quite wrongly as it turned out, that the application for work in the Delta would be granted. Even as early as 11 April, Griffith, the head of the Archaeological Survey, wrote to Carter:[12]

As Newberry will leave Egypt directly you will soon be free again for Tmei el Amdid and I hope by that time the permission will have been granted. . . .
In all probability you will be asked to remain through the summer for work at Tmei el Amdid; in order to remove the blocks at El Bersheh, and to finish some matters connected with the Survey. We shall soon know about this, and I tell you that you may not run away from Egypt till you hear.

It was just as well that Carter had serious work to engage his time after his return south from Mendes. Otherwise he would surely have been allowed to hang around in Cairo waiting for the permission to excavate, which in fact never came. After El-Sheikh Said and Newberry's departure from Egypt, Carter moved camp back to El-Bersha to complete his facsimile paintings and to copy more of the coloured hieroglyphs for the projected volume. Already Newberry could trust him to be there on his own and to work conscientiously. He had written to Miss Paterson in mid-March,[13] 'until he [Carter] comes back I cannot possibly get El Bersheh finished, for Mr. Buckman does not know sufficient Arabic to live there on his own; and too, Carter has the only tent I can spare and it is necessary to camp there in tents for there are no available tombs.' By 6 May Carter could report to Newberry that the work was proceeding 'as fast as I can'. There was a little problem over his permit to work even there 'so I am working on the quiet, at the same time to shut him [the local inspector] up I have written a note to Brugsch, but by the time anything is done I shall have pretty well finished the work.'[14] At the end of the letter, he adds mysteriously: 'Awful joke about Roger, should like to see the fun.' It can only be assumed that the ill-fitted Roger had suffered some calamity in Cairo, or even still at Mendes. Nothing more is heard of him in the archives of the Fund or in other contemporary papers. It

12 Copy in E.E.S. Letter book.
13 G.I. Newberry Corr. 34/70.
14 G.I. Newberry Corr. 8/12.

seems quite wrong that someone who was in all probability a very decent fellow, and possibly a promising scholar, should flit so unsatisfactorily through the wings of the excavation stage in Egypt. The whole episode can have done his reputation little good.[15]

Although the Mendes fiasco can have done little for Carter's reputation either, it did not prevent the consolidation of his position in the Egypt Exploration Fund. He was still seen principally as an artist and not an excavator. At the same committee meeting of 7 April 1893, when the critical letters of Carter and Roger were read, the decision was taken to retain the former's services 'as Fund artist during the ensuing year, commencing on Nov. 1st, 1893, at a salary of £100 a year, all authorised travelling expenses to be defrayed by the Fund, and £2. 2. 0 a week to be paid to him for living expenses while in Egypt.' For the moment his future must have seemed reasonably secure, and there is no indication in the meagre surviving documents that he felt other than pleased at the prospect. But matters beyond his control threatened to disturb this situation.

The Archaeological Survey of the Egypt Exploration Fund had been launched in 1891 as something of a side-line among the Fund's activities. Its purpose was taken with the utmost seriousness, but its activities could not command the popular support which nurtured the Fund's excavations. Already by 1893 expenses had greatly exceeded estimates, and contributions were below expectation. More work was being accomplished in a season in Egypt than could be published within the Survey's budget. A pause was needed for reconsideration and for the reassessment of aims. A halt was called to active field-work. Francis Ll. Griffith, the principal initiator and the editor of the Survey, later reported:[16]

> The Survey must still proceed with a close regard for economy. In England our work has consisted in issuing two volumes of 'El Bersheh', and in preparing for publication a series of coloured facsimiles of hieroglyphs and details of scenes at Beni Hasan. . . . We do not lose sight of the main object of the Survey, and we hope that funds will gradually accumulate, and enable us to send out another expedition, and push the work more actively.

For Howard Carter the decision to suspend field-operations could have marked the end of his career in Egypt. There remained the completion for publication of the Beni Hasan and El-Bersha volumes, work that could in normal circumstances have been carried out during the summer months out of Egypt. But happily the Fund had now embarked on a new project, the excavation and recording of the great temple at Deir el-Bahri, already briefly mentioned, for which more than one artist might be required. In

15 On Greek papyri recovered from Mendes, see H. De Meulenaere and P. MacKay, *Mendes* II (Warminster, 1976), p. 219.
16 *E.E.F. Arch. Rep. 1894–1895*, pp. viif.

this major enterprise Carter would find his fulfilment as an archaeological artist. The work he had already accomplished more than established his credentials.

At Beni Hasan and El-Bersha Carter had been employed on some of the routine work of the Survey, tracing the scenes and inscriptions in tombs, the results of which would eventually be inked in for publication. He was also employed on the much more skilled work of copying well preserved parts of the painted scenes, and making careful coloured facsimiles of hieroglyphs. The first two volumes of *Beni Hasan* appeared in 1893 and 1894; they contained the straight black-and-white copies of the decorations in all the tombs to be published. Carter is credited with none of the work, which no doubt pleased him, because the plates represented a style of reproduction of wonderfully executed and detailed paintings and inscriptions which he found wholly unsatisfactory. He had, no doubt, been obliged to do some of the inking-in of the pencilled tracings, but that mechanical process was not acknowledged in the authorship of the volumes. The next two volumes of the Survey, *El Bersheh* I and II, both published in 1895, contained the full record of the tombs at this rocky, remote site. In these Carter had a substantial hand. Part I contains all his Bersha drawings (the colossus tomb of Djehutihotpe), along with some done by Newberry. A comparison between the work of the two men (which is precisely identified in the volume), shows clearly, without the need of any special pleading, that Carter's drawings are in all respects superior to those of his chief. Newberry retains for his plates the method of reproduction used in the Beni Hasan volumes: inscriptions are shown in solid black, male figures are similarly blocked in, detail is inadequately indicated, line is hesitant. In Carter's plates, however, there is clarity, detail, precision, and above all sureness of draughtsmanship and style. It is not simply a contrast between a careful, mechanical copyist and a well trained artist; here the artist himself shows in addition an understanding of, and feeling for, the spirit of Egyptian art, which Carter had remarkably developed from his earliest days in Egypt. *El Bersheh* II contains, in addition to drawings of the remaining monuments by Newberry, the first serious treatment of the Hatnub graffiti, which had been published in facsimile copies only by Fraser and Blackden in the previous year. In the new volume they were, in a sense, reclaimed for the Archaeological Survey, and dealt with by Griffith and Newberry with a competence beyond the capabilities of their discoverers.

Two further Beni Hasan volumes appeared in 1896 and 1900, and the long-planed collection of hieroglyphs in 1898. All three volumes contained much work by Howard Carter in the form of coloured facsimiles mostly from the Middle-Kingdom tombs at Beni Hasan and El-Bersha. Work by Blackden, Buckman and other artists was also included. *Beni Hasan* IV in particular provides first-class examples of Carter's water-colour paintings, mostly of zoological details from the tomb of Khnumhotpe. In spite of the rather dead, dull-toned colour process used in the printing, his plates represent the very best of early copies of Egyptian painting. The quality of his originals can be studied at the Egypt Exploration Society, where most of them are preserved. Griffith makes a telling comment in his introduction to *Beni Hasan* III, which is mostly devoted to copies of individual hieroglyphs by Carter and Blackden. Griffith mentions the damaged state of the tomb walls and the faded quality of some colours:[17]

> Under the circumstances it is not surprising if modern copyists obtain different results from the same subject. Mr. Blackden aimed at ascertaining the original design in a somewhat diagrammatic style; Mr. Carter and Mr. Brown[18] copy faithfully what they see, and render it in its present condition.

Carter was to be rescued from the temporary demise of the Archaeological Survey by being transferred to work with Édouard Naville at Deir el-Bahri. It must have seemed the best solution for the employment of one whose appointment as the Fund's artist at £100 a year from November 1893 had been agreed by the Committee as recently as April. Carter believed that Newberry had been the principal agent in his secondment. From Deir el-Bahri in December he wrote to Newberry:[19]

> I dare say you will think it rude of me for not writing to you before and also for not thanking you for *your kindness* in recommending me for this work which I am very please [*sic*] with. I think M. Naville is a splendid man and his method of working could not be better for this kind of job. . . .
>
> The copying here is not so cool as in the tombs, but the work is more elaborate and I hope to be able to make some fine plates; at present I am drawing them to scale, as you know your own self one had to apply different methods according to the differculties [*sic*] that occur in copying the paintings.

In this letter Carter alludes to two matters on which he clearly felt the special need to comment. The first was Naville himself, and his competence for the task of excavating the temple at Deir el-Bahri; the second was his chosen method of copying.

The decision of the Committee to allow Naville to work at Deir el-Bahri had been severely and openly criticized by Flinders Petrie. His disdain for Naville's aims and methods in excavation were very well founded. Naville was not an excavator in Petrie's sense, but a site-cleaner whose main aim

17 P. E. Newberry, *Beni Hasan*, III (London 1895), p. 2.
18 Percy Brown was an artist recruited by Carter for work primarily at Deir el-Bahri; see p. 58 below.
19 G.I. Newberry Corr. 49/2.

was to recover large inscribed monuments. Petrie proposed that if the Committee was determined to allow Naville to work in the Theban area, he should be directed to Karnak, where in the great temple of Amon-Re there would be plenty of scope for him to wield his broad brush without serious loss of important archaeological evidence. A late decision by the Committee to follow Petrie's recommendation did not reach Naville before he had succeeded in obtaining his permit from de Morgan (at about the same time as Newberry was failing to get his permit for the tombs at El-Amarna), and he began operations at Deir el-Bahri in February 1893. The controversy did not subside at the end of the first season, and Naville returned to Deir el-Bahri in December to continue his massive earth-shifting activities which were greatly helped by the loan, from the Luxor operations of the Antiquities Service, of a tramway with open trucks (a Décauville railway) for the transport of spoil from the temple site to the dumps well away to the east. After the second season he could claim that his workmen had succeeded in shifting 'nearly 60,000 cubic metres of rubbish and stones'.[20] So when Howard Carter joined the Deir el-Bahri camp in December, the row over Naville and his methods was still at a serious level. Carter may have properly had a view on the matter, and he might surely have felt a kind of allegiance to Petrie after his season with him in early 1892; but now the young man, still only 19, rightly sensed that he should express himself tactfully, and show himself as being whole-heartedly behind Naville. In any case he was not at Deir el-Bahri to excavate, but to copy the wonderful reliefs which were rapidly being brought to light by Naville's energetic methods.

On the question of Carter's procedures for copying at Deir el-Bahri, there are several points of doubt. From the outset he was in charge of the very responsible epigraphic operation;[21] it was clearly crucial to establish at the start the best way to set about what promised to be the largest and most important copying venture by the Egypt Exploration Fund. Let it be said in advance that the methods chosen were highly successful, and that the drawn record of the temple decorations, contained on 174 plates in six large volumes, represents the finest epigraphic achievement of the Fund. The most clearly stated description of Carter's methods to have been published must, however, be questioned. Dr R. A. Caminos, himself the finest of the Egypt Exploration Society's epigraphers of the late twentieth century, comments with admiration on the Deir el-Bahri record:[22] 'I know of few epigraphic drawings which so effectively convey the feeling of the sculptured wall. That is epigraphy at it's best.' Of Carter's procedures he

---

20 *E.E.F. Arch. Rep. 1893–1894*, p. 1.
21 Epigraphy is the study of inscriptions; an epigrapher or epigraphist is one who copies and studies inscriptions.
22 In R. A. Caminos and H. G. Fischer, *Ancient Egyptian Epigraphy and Palaeography* (New York, 1976), p. 7.

reports, from information received from Sir Alan Gardiner and Mrs. Nina M. Davies (in her time the outstanding copyist of painted tomb scenes), as follows:

> He made tracings of the surfaces to be recorded, transferred them to heavy drawing paper on a smaller scale by means of a grid of reducing squares, and finally pencilled or, more often crayoned in his reductions, performing all these operations *in situ* with constant reference to the originals; meanwhile Naville would meticulously check and collate Carter's results with the monument itself at every state of the process.

The finished drawings, from which the published plates were reproduced, are still in existence, and a close inspection has revealed no trace of any grid. Carter did use guide lines and one or two other 'mechanical devices' to assist him in laying out his sheets, but the bulk of the drawing was done freehand. They are all finished in soft pencil at twice the scale of the published plates; each is signed by the artist responsible, and it is quite remarkable how homogeneous the results are no matter which artist was involved. They all carry what may be described as Howard Carter's stylistic stamp.

Carter's dislike of tracing was clearly expressed from the time of his first employment by Newberry at Beni Hasan and El-Bersha, and he makes it clear in the letter he wrote to Newberry quoted above that he was abandoning the accepted method: 'I am drawing them to scale, as you know your own self one has to apply different methods according to the difficulties that occur in copying the paintings.' His excuse for change may seem a little lame, but he surely did not want to suggest that his abandonment of the Newberry method was due to anything other than a difference of material. before he had joined Naville at Deir el-Bahri he had written to him from London with a rather different technique in mind:[23] 'For low relief, dry squeezing with pencil outline I found most pleasing and acurate [*sic*], and as I heard from Mr. John Newberry that the greater part of the work is such, I strongly advise that method. Would you kindly favour me with your opinion on the subject.' In the event he never apparently used the dry squeezing method. He probably found it too ponderous a technique for the huge walls which needed to be copied. It is also likely that the considerable areas of deliberate damage on the walls responded poorly to squeezing – a technique which involved the application of a suitably heavy, but flexible, paper to the wall with gentle beating with a brush, or with finger pressure, to produce an impression of what was carved on the wall. Contemporary confirmation that Carter's method involved essentially the copying by eye and hand of what was on the wall is contained in the report given to the Annual General Meeting of the Egypt Exploration Fund by the Honorary

23 Geneva MS, 2542, 38, letter dated 23 October 1893.

Secretary on 26 October 1894: 'Mr. Howard Carter's pencil drawings are exact copies of the scenes portrayed on the walls of the temple, and are being reproduced in half the original size direct from the pencil drawings.'[24]

Throughout his career Carter exercised his artistic talents in the drawing of scenes and inscriptions for epigraphic purposes, in the production of painted facsimiles of coloured reliefs and scenes, in topographical and imaginative water-colours, and in the reproduction of objects found in the course of excavation. For most of these activities the proper use of the artist's eye and hand were essential; but for the first, the strictly epigraphic process, it had been generally accepted that accuracy was the prime aim, with art entering in only marginally, if at all. For Carter this approach was fatally destructive for Egyptian art. On many occasions during his life he expressed himself strongly on the subject, and one of his longest statements, especially relevant to his work at Deir el-Bahri, is contained in his late autobiographical essay. Here he emphasizes the need to copy for publication in such a way that both the artistic quality and the scale of the original are best conveyed in the final production. In copying 'the same infinite pains and competency to meet the task should be employed as in the case of any other archaeological problem. The more so in this case, for Egyptian art depends so much upon the graceful and understanding line.' After many more reflections on the nature of art and the importance of drawing, he explains his own technique:[25]

My excuse for this somewhat lengthy excursus is simply because I felt, that if I attempted to copy the scenes sculptured upon the walls of Hat.shep.sût's Mortuary Temple by the prevailing system of tracing, the essential charm of those beautiful reliefs would have vanished in my copy. And as Professor Naville had given me a free hand in the matter, I felt bounden to study the problem, to find a means to attain the best results. I tried many expedients; but they resolved in this simple solution: To first observe the fundamental laws of Egyptian Art; how it eliminates the unessentials; to copy that art accurately and intelligently with honest work, a free hand, a good pencil, and suitable paper.

There remains, however, the question of the kind of magic that infected Carter and his assistants in the copying, in a remarkably coherent way, of many hundreds of square metres of carved wall. What Carter would surely have claimed is that the results are successful not because of the skills of the artists, but because of their humility in devoting their skills to the revelation of the linear art of the originals.[26]

---

24 *E.E.F. Report for 1893–4*, p. 13.
25 Griffith Institute version (Carter Notebook, 15), p. 71.
26 Carter's methods are more fully discussed in T. G. H. James, 'The very best artist' in the memorial volume to Cyril Aldred, A. B. Lloyd (ed.), *Greatest of Seers* (London, 1992?).

What then was this great monument that generated such passion, not only on the artistic side, but also through the bitter archaeological wrangle between Petrie and Naville?[27] It was a temple which, from its extraordinarily impressive situation, and its remarkably individual architecture, has become one of the principal goals of visitors to Egypt. It lies at the head of a wide valley extending west-north-westwards from the cultivated plain on the west bank of the Nile at Luxor. It is constructed on an axis which, if extended across the river, coincides almost precisely with that of the great Karnak Temple. The valley ends in craggy limestone cliffs of impressive height, and of a colour ranging from a hard white to a pinkish yellow depending on the time of day and the quality of the light. It is a noble situation, and one that develops its own particular atmosphere of blanketing heat even in the warm, but elsewhere ideal, days of winter. Here Hatshepsut, the great usurping queen of the Eighteenth Dynasty in the first half of the fifteenth century BC had her mortuary temple constructed. It was to be built on the northern side of, and partly over, an earlier temple of similar character designed to an unusual plan for King Nebhepetre Mentuhotpe II of the Eleventh Dynasty, five hundred years earlier. Senenmut, Hatshepsut's high steward, and for a time the most important official of her court, is credited with the design. Instead of a temple of courts and pillared halls, with a complex of rooms surrounding a shrine containing the sacred image of the principal deity of the holy place, it took the form of a series of terraced courts with colonnades, rising from the valley to the cliffs, connected by steep ramps, the whole decorated with scenes carved in the finest low relief. There were important side-chapels dedicated to the deities Hathor and Anubis; the principal sanctuary to Amon-Re, here considered as the natural father of the Queen, centred on the west side of the upper court, led back to the very cliffs. What cannot be appreciated by the casual visitor is that by a remarkable feat of ancient engineering the chamber prepared for the queen's burial in a tomb in the Valley of the Kings, on the other side of the rocky barrier of the Deir el-Bahri cliffs, lies almost beneath the temple sanctuary. There was in this way an intimate, but secret, connection between the queen's sepulchre and her mortuary temple.[28]

In its completion the great temple must have presented a wonderful sight: from a distance, a striking piling-up of terraces and colonnades against the dramatic rocky backdrop of the cliffs; at closer inspection, for those allowed within the sacred precinct, a marvel of fine carving with scenes of unusual interest – an expedition to the tropical land of Punt, the

27 The dispute is well set out by W. V. Davies in T. G. H. James, ed., *Excavating in Egypt: The Egypt Exploration Society 1882–1982* (London, 1982), pp. 51ff; also M. S. Drower, *Flinders Petrie. A Life in Archaeology* (London, 1985), pp. 283ff.
28 On the ownership of tomb no. 20 in the Valley of the Kings, usually attributed to Queen Hatshepsut, see C. N. Reeves, *The Valley of the Kings* (London, 1990), pp. 13.ff.

transport of huge granite obelisks from Aswan to Karnak, the divine conception and birth of the Queen, much more in detail and grandeur. There were groves of incense trees, avenues of sphinxes, unusual many-faceted pillars in the colonnades (not unlike some of much earlier date which Howard Carter would remember from the tombs at Beni Hasan). It was called *Djeser-djeseru*, 'Holy of holies', and it remained a holy site long after the temple of Hatshepsut lost its primary sanctity and significance. Important cults were nurtured there throughout the remaining fifteen centuries of Pharaonic and Ptolemaic Egypt. In Christian times a monastery was built on the upper court, the local focus for a huge population of anchorites, drawn to a kind of collective isolation at Thebes. The monastery gave the name to the place in modern times; it was El-Deir el-Bahri, 'the Monastery of the North'. Substantial mud-brick remains of the monastery buildings, including a tower, survived up to the time of Naville's excavation, and it was evident that much stonework from the Eighteenth-dynasty temple was incorporated in the Christian structures.

When Édouard Naville began his operations at Deir el-Bahri the site was unprepossessing, giving the appearance more of a long abandoned industrial area than of an important temple. Debris from occupations extending over more than two millennia, overburdened by rock and shale fallen from the crumbling cliffs, buried the Hatshepsut temple in places to a depth of many metres. Test diggings, mostly of a random nature, carried out in the preceding fifty years, had revealed parts of the original temple, but had left the site archaeologically so disturbed that Naville saw his task firstly as one of clearance rather than excavation, even in his simple sense of that activity. In the second place, a full record was to be made of the temple decorations, and the plan of the whole complex determined. The reliefs, as already mentioned, were of the highest interest, and executed in the fine, precise, sensitive low relief carving characteristic of royal monuments of the middle reigns of the Eighteenth Dynasty. From earlier probings it also seemed likely that substantial remains of colour had survived on the walls. So much could be established from the parts that had been examined in the past, especially by Auguste Mariette, the founder of the Egyptian Antiquities Service. The clearance of the site to reveal the temple was seen by Naville as a task for two or three seasons, even with the help of the Décauville railway. Copying could start as soon as parts of the temple were sufficiently cleared to allow access to the decorated walls. So Howard Carter joined Naville in December 1893, at the beginning of the second season.

From the moment the arrived at Deir el-Bahri, Carter found himself in much more than simple copying. Apart from his occasional use as a supervisor of large gangs of workmen engaged in moving the huge quantities of debris and decayed occupational remains, he was employed as the photographer of the team. It is not known how or where he acquired his skill as a photographer, but the results he achieved were of very high quality; the surviving archive contains many excellent photographs recording the work in progress, and also many details of the relief decorations in the temple.[29] He was also put, necessarily, to the sorting out of rescued fragments which, in so far as possible, had to be placed back into their original positions in the walls. In some places this reconstruction was essential before copying could be undertaken. Carter was no longer quite the 'boy' he had been at Beni Hasan, but he was still only 19, and clearly the one best suited to do the odd jobs about the dig. But copying was his first duty and he set about it, establishing his *modus operandi* and general strategy with the free hand allowed him by Naville.

Writing to Edward Maunde Thompson, a Vice-President of the Fund who often acted as Chairman of the Committee, on 11 January 1894, Naville stated:[30]

> I believe it is important that another artist should join us as soon as possible. I have been able to judge what Mr. Carter can do. He certainly has much talent, his drawings are very good, and in this respect I do not think we could have a better artist. His copies when reproduced in colour or in black will make very fine plates. But he is rather slow, and at the rate he is going at the end of the season we should not have plates enough for the first number of the work on Deir el Bahari. Therefore I did not hesitate to ask for a second artist, especially as you had told me that the Committee was quite willing to send out another man if necessary.

A strong recommendation to send reinforcements had been made by D. G. Hogarth, the classical archaeologist, who had himself been sent to Deir el-Bahri, ostensibly to assist Naville, but also to provide the Fund with an independent judgement in the dispute between Naville and Petrie.[31] Carter suggested that his older brother Vernet should come out and help him, and in late February 1894 the second Carter artist arrived. Vernet, whose name is occasionally spelled Verney, was ten years older than Howard, had enjoyed a similar training from Samuel Carter, and was employed professionally as an artist. He acquired some reputation as an engraver, and was successful in having his work exhibited in the Royal Academy Summer Exhibition during the 1890s. It is probable that Vernet had already been introduced in a marginal way to the copying of reliefs, or at least to the inking-in of copies. In writing to Miss Paterson, the Fund's secretary, in June 1893, mostly about work at El-Bersha, Carter adds as

29 A selection of Carter's photographs illustrates Naville's introductory volume, *The Temple of Deir el Bahari* (London, 1894).
30 E.E.S. Archives, XVII 16.
31 For Hogarth's report, generally favourable to Naville, see *E.E.F. Report for 1893–4*, pp. 18–22, 23–4.

a postscript a request that £20 of his salary should be sent to his brother,[32] 'as the bad weather of the last winter having destroyed his plates has put him so behind hand'. The reference is obscure, but as the date seems certain (the letter existing in original and in copy), it does suggest that Vernet was working on El-Bersha plates in London in 1893.

Soon after he had started work, Vernet's talents were summed up by Naville in very favourable terms:[33] 'Mr. Verney Carter began work at once. He draws as well as his brother, and certainly for hieroglyphical drawing in colour as well as in black they are first rate artists and I believe the plates which will be made from their copies will give a very good idea of the beauty of the work.' Inspection of the drawings completed by Vernet shows that Howard Carter had very distinctly instructed him in how the drawing should be carried out. The work of the two brothers is practically indistinguishable, and their reproduced plates in *The Temple of Deir el Bahari* I, which appeared in 1895, create a wonderfully uniform effect. The prospect of achieving a record of the whole temple by these two artists must have seemed very promising. In order to push the work forward Naville arranged for the Carters to remain at Deir el-Bahri for a month or so after the excavation had been closed. Digging would be brought to an end in late March by the start of the Moslem month of Ramadan, when, because of the daily fasting, the men could not be expected to work as normal. Naville was cynical about his men's observance of the fast at that time: 'all our workmen eat and drink as in any other month of the year; but they amuse themselves at night [when relief from fasting is properly allowed] and in the morning they are not good for work.' In the event, Naville finished excavating on 15 March, and the Carters were still at Deir el-Bahri and the end of April. Howard Carter wrote to Naville, excusing himself and his brother for not having finished earlier:[34] 'owing to the heat being so intense lately; and my brother failing in health; but we expect to finish in about a fortnight or 3 weeks time.' Mid-day temperatures, at Deir el-Bahri especially, at this time of the year may easily reach 115 degrees F (46 degrees C). In such heat pencils become soft and drawing almost impossible because of damp hands and forearms. There were other hazards:

> I must tell you that I am more than glad that I copied the N.W. Chamber of offerings first, for no sooner had you left, there was a great fall of stones from the hill above, covering the floor of the chamber from one end to the other.

The end of the drawing season also brought the end of Vernet Carter's involvement in the work. A brief mention in the Egypt Exploration Fund's

---

32 E.E.S. Archives, XII d 2.
33 Naville to Maunde Thompson, 2 March 1894, E.E.F. Archives, XVII, 17.
34 Geneva MS. 2542, 40, 41.

Annual Report for 1894–5 (p. 14) states that in November 1894 Naville was accompanied to Deir el-Bahri by 'the artists, Mr. Howard Carter and Mr. Percy Brown. The latter artist was appointed in place of Mr. Verney Carter, who could not stand the climate of Egypt'. It was a sad end to a co-operation which had already achieved so much. It is also extraordinary to observe that the sickly Howard, a weakling from childhood, should now outstrip in stamina his 30-year-old brother Vernet. Still, their joint success, evident to all in the excellence of their completed drawings, established the style and quality for the rest of the temple. When it came to publication, it was decided to reproduce the drawings with the least possible technical intervention. A collotype process was used by the printers, Gilbert and Rivington Ltd, of St John's House, Clerkenwell, London E.C. As Stuart Pool commented:[35] 'By this process much of the delicacy that is unavoidably lost when the originals are inked over, is retained, and all details will be faithfully preserved.'

Naville's clearance of the temple was completed during the season 1895–6, apart from some small areas where additional 'tidying up' had to be done. Already the site looked very differently from when he began. The substantial remains of the Coptic monastery were gone, and, with the mounds of other debris, removed to dumps in nearby quarries and depressions. The plan of the temple was now clear, in general terms at least, if not in all respects. There remained, however, much more to do in the way of making safe unstable areas of construction, of rebuilding parts to incorporate additional fragments, of roofing some colonnades and rooms in shrines to protect fine reliefs and well preserved painting. In particular, there was much drawing still to be done – two or three seasons according to Naville's estimate. He and the Committee of the Egypt Exploration Fund could rightly be pleased with what had been achieved. The campaign had not, however, assuaged the curiosity of other Egyptological investigators; nor had it extracted everything of interest from the site. Subsequent, very careful, excavations by the Egyptian Expedition of the Metropolitan Museum of Art, New York, between 1911 and 1931, extended the limits of the earlier campaign, discovered much – including material of great importance concealed inadvertently by Naville's dumps – and revised the architectural history of the temple.[36] Further reconstruction of parts of the temple was carried out by Émile Baraize for the Antiquities Service from 1910 onwards, and an extensive campaign of excavation and reconstruction was started by the Polish Centre of Mediterranean Archaeology in 1960.[37] This last campaign concentrated attention in the area of the Upper Court and under the cliffs, and in its course a whole new temple, built in the

35 *E.E.F. Report for 1893–4*, p. 13.
36 The annual reports in the museum's *Bulletin* by H. E. Winlock are collected in his *Excavations at Deir el Bahri 1911–1931* (New York, 1942).
37 In general see D. Arnold in *Lexikon der Ägyptologie*, I, col. 1017f.

reign of King Tuthmosis III, Hatshepsut's nephew and successor, was discovered. There is no reason to believe that all the secrets of Deir el-Bahri have now been revealed; but it remains to the credit of Naville and the Fund that the importance of the temple was first properly recognized and that its beauty was first revealed.

The copying of the temple decorations, mostly executed and wholly supervised by Howard Carter, continued with many interruptions, and with changes in assistants, until 1899 when he left the service of the Fund. His task was then done, and his greatest epigraphic achievement contained in the six volumes of *The Temple of Deir el Bahari*. He had been very fortunate in his co-workers. His brother Vernet was succeeded as his assistant by Percy Brown, with whom Carter seems to have got on particularly well. Their partnership, which included some mopping-up at Beni Hasan and El-Bersha, lasted until the summer of 1896 when Brown received the offer of a permanent post in India.[38] Carter informed Naville of this serious loss in early September 1896, but wasted no time in finding a replacement. Writing again on 23 September he reports:[39] 'I have got Mr. C. Sillem to take his place, a man whom I have known a long time, and trust he will be successful.' He was indeed successful and quickly took to the Carter method of working. His first task was to draw the scenes in the important Hathor Chapel, planned for volume IV of the great publication: 'He is progressing well,' says Carter on 26 November. The ease with which replacement artists could be found resulted from Carter's association through his brothers William and Vernet, and his sister Amy, with the artistic community of London, and particularly Chelsea which in the late nineteenth century formed the heart and soul of that community. While he was in England during the summer months he used as his base Stamford House, 428 Fulham Road, in the periphery of Chelsea, where Vernet and Amy lived; together they surely passed many hours in the company of young and aspiring artists. To find someone with real talent who might welcome the opportunity to spend three or four winter months in Egypt, and be paid for it, could not have been difficult.

In addition to the regular assistants, Carter was also helped during two seasons by Miss Rosalind Paget, a very competent artist, especially in water-colour, who had been one of Petrie's earliest students at University College London. For the seasons of 1895–6 and 1896–7 she was able to spend several weeks at Deir el-Bahri before joining an expedition at Elkab, further south from Luxor, where Eighteenth-dynasty tombs were the subject of study and recording by J. J. Tylor and Somers Clarke. She was not used for the principal copying task at Deir el-Bahri, but to make coloured facsimiles of unusual, well painted heiroglyphs and other details.

---

38 He subsequently became a distinguished authority on the architecture of the sub-continent.

39 Geneva MS. 2542, 47, 48.

Her accommodation in an all-male camp, when Naville and his wife were not in residence in the cramped quarters of the expedition house, caused superficial problems before her arrival. The proprieties of the time were not to be ignored. Happily no serious difficulties developed and gentlemanly standards apparently prevailed. Naville, however, was also worried in advance about the austere quality of life in his camp:[40] 'she will have to rough it. She will have to accept many discomforts which frightened even gentlemen. Our house is simple as possible. We do not indulge in any luxury. . . . the beds are hard and the furniture elementary.' Still, things were not actively bleak as with Petrie, with whom Miss Paget had first experienced Egypt. 'If Miss Paget begins with Petrie I daresay our way of living will compare favourably with her first experience of an explorer's life,' Austerity in 'way of living' is very relative. Something of the ameliorations possible at Deir el-Bahri is contained in a letter of Carter to Naville written on 28 January 1898:[41] 'You need not trouble about bringing stores as we have a good supply for the present, plenty of Medoc, Graves, and whisky.' First things first, it would seem.

Although the making of the graphic record of Hatshepsut's temple was completed in 1899, the final volume of the publication did not appear until 1908. The scientific monitoring of the artists' work by Édouard Naville was intermittent and slow; some help was given by Percy Newberry. Proper checking had to be carried out in front of the walls that had been copied; it was painstaking and tedious work, but not to be scrimped. The checker's task was much helped by the developed skills of the copyists whose intensive immersion in the style of decoration, and in the subtleties of the hieroglyphic signs, rendered their involvement in the final result no simple mechanical process of mindless copying by uninformed eye. Naville recorded his appreciation of the work of Carter and Brown on the exceedingly difficult Punt reliefs in a most generous manner:[42]

> Most of the inscriptions copied had been erased [in antiquity], and were difficult to read, but owing to the familiarity which the artists had acquired with hieroglyphs at Deir el Bahari, and to their skill in recognizing a sign from a few broken lines or a small coloured fragment, it has been possible not only to correct the former publications of the Punt Expedition by Mariette and Duemichen,[43] but here and there to add materially to what has been deciphered previously by those scholars. These texts have now been subjected to

40 See W. V. Davies in T. G. H. James, ed., *Excavating in Egypt*, p. 60.
41 Geneva MS. 2542, 62.
42 *E.E.F. Arch. Rep. 1895–1896*, p. 5.
43 Johannes Duemichen was Professor of Egyptology in Strasburg 1872–94. His copies of the Punt reliefs and texts are in *Historische Inschriften altägyptischer Denkmäler*, II (Leipzig, 1869).

several revisions, made at different hours during the day, and often at night by candle-light.

It was one thing, however, to obtain beautiful, accurate drawings; it was another thing to secure their good reproduction in the volumes. The printers of the publication, Gilbert and Rivington, were to a large extent in the hands of the man who prepared the plates, and probably also supervised their printing. He was W. Griggs, otherwise unknown, but yet responsible for the success or failure of the completed work. He was neither prompt not easy to deal with, and Carter spent much time during his summers at home visiting Griggs, correcting plates, incorporating suggestions received from Naville in Switzerland, urging, encouraging and even brow-beating. It has always been said that collotype operators (very few of whom still exist) were more artists than printers, and consequently perhaps a little temperamental. Carter's letters to Naville over the years are peppered with Griggs references and complaints:[44] 'Griggs has not finished the plates for the 1st vol. yet, and I have not seen any proofs of the coloured plates, and as you know he had 15 drawings ready for him last November and the rest in January; I cannot conceive how they can take 8 months and not completed yet' (30 September 1895); 'I found that Griggs had not started on the plates or done anything beyond the silver prints' (11 August 1896); 'I am sorry to say that Griggs has disappointed me and will not have all the proofs done before I leave' (24 September 1896). Naville also was not at all satisfied with the published results. In a progress report to the Egypt Exploration Fund after the appearance of the third volume in the spring of 1899, he complains bitterly:[45]

> I am obliged again to direct the attention of the Committee to the very bad way in which the plates are printed. Vol. III is certainly worse than Vol. II. Anyone looking through those plates will be struck by the fact that they are very unequal: a plate so faint that the signs are hardly discernible is followed by another which is much too dark. . . . I cannot help feeling that it is a great pity that such drawings as those of Mr. Carter which as regards accuracy and artistic value are the very best hieroglyphical drawings ever made, should be so badly reproduced.

It was indeed a great shame that only an indifferent result was being achieved. Eventually the printers were changed, and Vol. VI was produced by William Clowes and Sons Ltd of Duke Street and Stanford Street, London, S.E., and Great Windmill Street, London, W.

If Carter grumbled about W. Griggs and the plates while he was in England, he grumbled while he was in Egypt – at least in letters to Naville

44 Geneva MS. 2542, 68 (30 Sept., 1895), 46 (11 Aug., 1896), 48 (24 Sept., 1896).
45 E.E.S. Archives, XI a 3.

– about not being able to get on with the drawing. He had become, in effect, Naville's deputy in almost all matters and he was very distinctly in charge of the many constructional and small engineering operations which continued season after season. His mentor and point of reference in such matters was Somers Clarke, a British architect who in 1897 became Surveyor of the Fabric of St Paul's Cathedral. He participated in numerous archaeological enterprises in Egypt, and was an outspoken advocate for the conservation of monuments in the country. Each year he made visits to Deir el-Bahri to prepare annual strategies for action, to instruct Howard Carter in technicalities, and to leave him to get on with the work. His advice and practical experience were crucial, and Carter took full advantage of his chances to widen his own experience. So when he complained to Naville,[46] 'the Committee have again stopped my drawing – to put up and build the fallen blocks – I think it is a pity,' it may be thought that he was perhaps a little half-hearted in his grumbling. There is much evidence to suggest that he relished the new challenges and enjoyed solving the practical problems which occurred during the work on the temple. He was very effective, as again Naville testified:[47]

> It is certainly quite remarkable how well that difficult work of rebuilding is done by Mr. Carter. Mr. Somers Clarke was at Deir al Bahari only for a few days during which he was not well, so that he could do no more than give general directions; the whole of the excavation was carried out by Mr. Carter. The most difficult part was the pulling down and raising up again of the supporting walls on the upper terrace. . . . Mr. Carter has done the work admirably. He has a very quick eye for finding the places where the stones belong to; besides as he has a thorough command of Arabic, he can direct and superintend the men, or rather teach them what they are to do.

Carter's extended role at Deir el-Bahri had, satisfactorily if surprisingly, been recognized for some time by the Committee of the Fund. On 12 July 1897 it had been resolved that he should superintend the reconstruction work in the temple during the next season, and that his salary should be increased from £100 to £125. Two weeks later, on 27 July, this salary was further increased to £275 a year 'including all expenses'.[48] There had clearly been some additional thinking – or even grumbling by Carter himself – about the extent and variety of the duties he was being asked to perform.

Howard Carter was now 23, and he had developed substantially in competence and in character. Years of exposure to responsibility in a place much frequented by rich and important visitors had brought maturity and

46 Geneva MS. 2542, 56.
47 E.E.S. Archives, XI a 5.
48 E.E.F. Committee minutes.

possibly a kind of comfortable security which he would not often find again in his archaeological career. At the start of his time at Deir el-Bahri he was young and socially unreliable, at least in the eyes of John Newberry, who then was part of Naville's team. Hogarth had arrived and was recommending a second artist: 'I hope', wrote Newberry to his brother Percy,[49] 'Hogarth's influence will somewhat improve Carter's manners; they continue to be much as they were; he doesn't hesitate to pick his last [sic] hollow tooth with a match stalk during dinner, bite bread that is so hard you can hardly cut it with a chopper, and help himself to whisky in an absent minded fashion, emptying half the bottle into his tumbler, then laugh and say he wasn't thinking and pour it back again into the bottle, spilling a lot.' But his virtues were also recognized by John Newberry: 'However he works well, and has taken a lot of interesting photographs, which are very successful, and on the whole we get on all right.' This letter was written on 31 December, and it seems not unlikely that Carter's display of gaucherie occurred over Christmas and was therefore perhaps a little more excusable. Yet paradoxically Carter was at the same time an acceptable guest at Didlington Hall. The year before, on 10 November, Lady Amherst had written to Newberry from Didlington:[50] 'I sent Howard Carter to stay at Swaffham till Sunday as he could not have done much with the proofs in the house. He has arranged some of the things [probably from the Amarna excavation] but could not do your book.' The Amhersts were again pleased to see him at Deir el-Bahri when the family made an extended tour of Egypt by *dahabiya* in 1894–5. They were first reminded of him when they visited El-Amarna on 10 January 1895. In her journal Alicia Amherst records:[51] 'We saw the place where Howard Carter found our statues just outside the sun temple.' On the 20th they arrived for a one-day stay at Luxor, and Carter came to see them in the afternoon. Then after a visit to Aswan (and a steamer-trip to Wadi Halfa) the party returned to Luxor on 22 February, and stayed until 1 March. They paid at least two visits to Deir el-Bahri during this time, and Howard Carter visited them on their *dahabiya* daily, sleeping on board every night.

Among the influential people Carter met while he was at Deir el-Bahri was the wealthy American Theodore Davis, with whom he would have much to do in the way of excavation in a few years' time. Early in March 1899 Davis spent nine days at Luxor with his party, and the visit is recorded in some detail by Emma Andrews, his companion and relative. Through visiting Newberry they came to meet Carter. In her diary[52] Mrs

49 G.I. Newberry Corr. 33/31.
50 G.I. Newberry Corr. 2/16.
51 Two of four tiny volumes in the possession of Mrs Stanley Chattey, to whom I am indebted for permission to quote. The two final volumes are missing.
52 I quote from the transcript of the diary in the Department of Egyptian Art, in the Metropolitan Museum of Art, by kind permission of Dr Dorothea Arnold. The typescript is numbered separately by year. The present reference is to 1899, p. 29.

Andrews states that they took tea with him on the afternoon before they left Luxor and that she 'chose the subjects of two sketches he is to make for me – Queen Aahmes and Queen Sensenet, Mother of Thothmes I.' And she adds: 'The Buxtons, who are on the Nepthys [a *dahabiya*], and whom we met at Aswan, taking tea with us one afternoon, told me that Mrs. Buxton's (Gurney) grandfather's gamekeeper was this young Carter's father, and that he had great talent (the father) in drawing animals.' It is likely that Mrs Andrews (or the Buxtons) confused Carter's father with his grandfather, who could more suitably be described as a gamekeeper, although his employer was Robert Hamond; but she was certainly correct in reporting that his father could draw animals. In her commissioning two sketches there is much of interest. Carter had prepared many coloured reproductions of painted scenes and details in the temple for the printed volumes, and among them were the two subjects chosen by Mrs Andrews.[53] He often showed his paintings to visitors, but this seems to be the first recorded occasion on which he agreed to make additional copies for sale. It is not unlikely, however, that the possibility of earning a little extra money had occurred to him earlier. It is also known that as early as 1899 he was producing topographical watercolours for sale.[54] His success with Mrs Andrews may even have come as a surprise, for it prompted him to send a short note to Newberry,[55] 'A million thanks,' which Newberry annotated with the information that it was written after he had introduced Carter to Theodore Davis, when the latter had bought two Deir el-Bahri paintings. For the next twenty years at least painting was to be a constant solace to Howard Carter; he would on occasion have much time at his disposal for this restful and contemplative activity. His paintings would be of different kinds according to mood, necessity and commission: landscapes, careful copies of painted tomb-scenes, imaginative work incorporating elements of antiquity; he would draw and paint from nature, much in the Theban area and often in the Cairo Zoo, especially birds. The results would be for sale, or given as gifts to friends and patrons; he would paint to order. It is therefore surprising how very few of his paintings are now known to exist. Most of them surely would have been carried away from Egypt unframed, rolled up, or placed flat in the bottom of a cabin trunk; subsequently, in all probability, valued more as charming souvenirs of an Egyptian visit than as fine examples of an artist's work. Many will have remained undiscovered, put away in drawers or portfolios; but easily identified – he always dated and signed his work with a bold, flourishing hand.

At a Committee meeting of the Egypt Exploration Fund on 7 November 1899, 'telegrams were read from Mr. Howard Carter, stating that he had

53 Queen Aahmes (Ahmose) = Naville, *Deir el Bahari*, III, pl. lxvii; Queen Sensenb = *Deir el Bahari*, I, pl. xiii. Mrs Andrews gives the second queen's name incorrectly.
54 A watercolour of Deir el-Bahri in the possession of Anne Pemberton, is dated 1899.
55 G.I. Newberry Corr. 8/15.

been offered the appointment of Inspector of Antiquities to the Egyptian Government, and asking if the Committee would permit him to resign his employment under the Fund from next January 1. Mr. Carter was congratulated on his new appointment, and the permission asked for was given, it being understood that he would make arrangements for the completion of the work at Deir el-Bahari.' Thus, at the age of 25 Carter had achieved, quite unexpectedly as it would seem, recognition of his varied abilities, and the status of an Egyptologist with a permanent appointment. The matter had not come as a complete surprise, but the decision to appoint two Chief Inspectors had followed the reappointment of Gaston Maspero as Director-General of the Antiquities Service in the summer of 1899.[56] It was to be a significant decision not only for Howard Carter, but also for the progress of field-work in Egypt generally for the next fifteen years.

56 Maspero took over from Victor Loret, who had himself succeeded Jacques de Morgan in 1897.

4

CHIEF INSPECTOR

The Antiquities Service set up in Egypt by Auguste Mariette in 1858 was
the first national organization of its kind in any country, but it had never
been provided with funds enough for the establishment of an adequate
staff to fulfil its many functions. The Director-General was from the outset
responsible for the care and excavation of monuments throughout Egypt,
and for the development of the museum in Cairo. Increasingly, towards
the end of the nineteenth century, he was also responsible for the granting
of permissions to excavate to foreign organizations and individuals, and
for the division and disposition of the antiquities found in such excavations.
The duties were formidable, and were in practice almost impossible to
carry out satisfactorily, especially in a country in which general standards
of administrative efficiency and bureaucratic integrity were as yet not seen
to be ideal. Gaston Maspero, the outstanding French Egyptologist of his
generation, had succeeded Mariette as Director-General in 1881, and in
the five years up to 1886 had begun to build on the modest foundations
of the Service which he had inherited from Mariette. In 1886 he returned
to Paris to carry out his duties as professor at the Collège de France, and
to develop with immense energy his academic reputation. In the interim
the Service suffered severely from a weak and changing directorate. Eugène
Grébaut (1886–92), Jacques de Morgan (1892–7), and Victor Loret
(1897–9) were all Frenchmen, for it had become the accepted convention
that the position of Director-General should always be held by a compatriot
of Mariette: none was adequate for a task that needed an Olympian.
Grébaut and Loret were temperamentally unsuited for the position, and
found it difficult to achieve workable relations either with their Egyptian
colleagues or with the Europeans who increasingly came to Egypt to
excavate, expecting special and sympathetic treatment from the European
head of the Service. De Morgan was essentially a Near-Eastern archaeologist, and his brief years in Egypt were devoted by inclination to active
field-work, to the neglect of administration. Throughout this period conti-
nuity of a kind was provided only by Émile Brugsch, a German Egyptologist, employed as assistant conservator in the Cairo Museum, effectively

the deputy of the Director-General, a position he occupied until his retirement in 1914. He held the fort in Cairo whenever the Director-General was absent, and on his shoulders fell the responsibility of keeping the administrative clock ticking.

It was not ticking very strongly when Maspero returned to Cairo in November 1899. In a letter to Naville, an old friend and trusted colleague, written early in January 1900, he complains of the disorder in the administration:[1]

> it seems that for a long time it has been the principle not to deal with matters a little delicate, but to put them on one side in a corner, doubtless in the hope the they will resolve themselves on their own. Also you cannot imagine to what an examination of papers I have to attend to about which nobody in the department (*chez nous*) or in the ministries any longer understand anything.

Maspero's reappointment was greeted with much pleasure, especially in British Egyptological circles. Petrie, who suspected the purposes of all Frenchmen, suspected Maspero less than the rest. For the Egypt Exploration Fund Francis Ll. Griffith voiced the common view eloquently:[2]

> Upon the efficient and single-minded administration of archaeology in Egypt hang great issues of science; workers of all nationalities, therefore, will consider it a happy event that the reins of government of the Department of Antiquities were last year handed . . . to the ablest of contemporary Egyptologists, Professor Maspero . . . [He] thus enters upon his second administration in some respects under singularly favourable auspices, and it hoped that his new accession to power will mark the beginning of a new epoch in the official Egyptology of Egypt.

When Maspero took up the challenge again in the autumn of 1899, the staff of his department, not including local antiquities guards, amounted to just twenty-four people.[3] It was certainly time for improvement and for expansion. In October it was agreed that two European Chief Inspectors should be appointed, with the responsibilities on the ground for the preservation and conservation of monuments in their areas, for the conducting of excavations on behalf of the Service, and for the supervision in a general sense of excavations carried out by others. One of the Chief Inspectors would be based in Cairo with a territory covering the Delta and the Nile Valley south to Qus; the other from Luxor would supervise the Valley from Qus south to the Sudanese frontier. These were huge districts to oversee, and it was recognized from the first that changes might have to

1 Geneva MS. 2529, 205, dated 5 January 1900. The original is in French.
2 *E.E.F. Report 1899–1900*, pp. 8f.
3 *Rapports sur la marche du Service des Antiquités de 1899 à 1910* (Cairo, 1912), p. xv.

be made in the light of the experiences of the first incumbents in their initial years. They were to receive salaries of £E400 (four hundred Egyptian pounds), rising over four years to £E600, and subsequently to £E800, a very reasonable emolument for the time, and a considerable improvement as far as Howard Carter was concerned. He would also receive accommodation in a house at Luxor at the expense of the department. No similar arrangement was made for the Cairo-based Inspector, a difference in circumstance which would lead to grave dissatisfaction on Carter's part when he was transferred north in 1904, and even more so when his base became Tanta in 1905.[4]

It is more than likely that Carter was surprised to be offered one of the two new Inspectorships. He was surely proud and delighted to receive such official recognition of his merits, although no letters of the time to his English friends have apparently survived to testify to his reaction. There can, however, be little doubt that he owed to his appointment to Édouard Naville who had over six years observed Carter's activity at Deir el-Bahri and been able to delegate more and more of the supervisory work to him. Naville had see Carter develop from a young, inexperienced artist with a little excavating training into a reliable deputy, quick to learn new field techniques, an accomplished manager of Egyptian workmen, a competent speaker of Arabic, and skilled controller of architectural and other works. His accomplishments were essentially practical, and almost precisely those which were required for the new appointment. Naville was also a good friend of Maspero, and his intervention in the choice of Carter may be deduced from a letter written to him by Carter on 14 November 1899:[5]

> You will be glad to hear that the Inspectorship has been offered me and I have accepted it, and shall start Jan 1st – the date that the Committee has let me off the work here . . . When in Cairo a few days back I saw Monsieur Maspero whom I found an exceedingly nice man. I believe will be a pleasure to work with him. I cannot do otherwise than thank you for your kindness – as he said he new [sic] me well through you.

Although the appointment of two Chief Inspectors was generally welcomed, especially by British Egyptologists – for the two preferred candidates were both British – there was some surprise voiced privately by those who found the choice of Carter to be unexpected, to say the least. This surprise is clearly expressed in a letter written to Percy Newberry by J. E. Quibell, the other successful candidate, whose own qualifications for the position were on paper substantially stronger than those of Carter: 32 years old, a graduate of Oxford University, with considerable excavating

4 On the setting up of the inspectorate, its duties and salaries, *ibid.*, pp. xxff.
5 Geneva MS. 2542, 74.

experience with Petrie and Somers Clarke, a man of scholarly inclinations who had already collaborated in a number of excavation memoirs, and was at the time of his appointment employed in the Cairo Museum preparing a catalogue of its holdings of Early-dynastic objects. In what he says to Newberry it may be possible to recognize the opinions of others in the archaeological community:[6]

> Two English inspectorships have been made and offered to Carter and me. I have accepted of course; of Carter I do not yet know, but I think he will. Although I am glad to have Carter as a colleague and shall get on with him first rate, I must say I should have *much preferred* to see you in the job. I had assumed indeed that it was certain you would have it – and I am very sorry you haven't.

Writing a month later, again to Newberry, Quibell gives a few first impressions:[7]

> I am starting very soon for the Fayum; as yet I have only had a short trip to Nag Hamadi, Keneh and Abydos. Did I tell you how the land is divided? Carter has Wady Halfa to Kamoula and Kus. I have Kus-Nagada northwards. We shall both have an enormous amount to do – but I think it will be rather nice. We shall not get very learned over it though – almost always away from books.

One may well speculate on whether Carter ever considered his appointment unusual, or even thought that as a candidate he was superior to his old friend and colleague Percy Newberry, who had been partly responsible for his first coming to Egypt. It is also not known if Newberry had himself entertained hopes of obtaining one of the two positions. There are no letters from Carter written during the winter of 1899–1900 among the Newberry correspondence in Oxford; but it would be wrong to deduce from this gap in a fairly steady, if not frequent, epistolary exchange between the two that a coolness existed at that time. Certainly, in the subsequent October Carter could write in a very friendly way to Newberry, looking forward to the latter's coming to Luxor and offering to put him up.[8] Undoubtedly the offer of an inspectorship would have seriously interested Newberry, although he might not have in the end considered its acceptance a practical option. He did not tolerate readily the summer heat of Egypt, and the expected duties of Chief Inspector included spending some summers without home leave. Still, the kudos of obtaining such an appointment could scarcely have been ignored and Newberry may well have reflected wryly on Carter's extraordinary promotion. It was only eight years since Carter had come out with him to Beni Hasan as a 'tracer'.

6 G.I. Newberry Corr. 38/20, dated 9 November 1899.
7 G.I. Newberry Corr. between 38/20 and 38/21, dated 21 December 1899.
8 G.I. Newberry Corr. 8/17, dated 31 October 1900.

In a consideration of Newberry's scholarly interests and known temperament, there can be little doubt that he would not have made a good Chief
Inspector of Antiquities. Even so, in choosing Carter, Maspero – if it were
specifically his choice, as seems to have been the case – was taking a
chance. There was much that remained untested about Carter. Maspero
took an early opportunity to travel to Upper Egypt, and he spent some
days in Luxor on general inspection, which included a good look at his
new man. His letter to Naville, quoted at the start of this chapter, contains
a measured assessment in which enthusiasm is tempered with at least one
perceptive comment on Carter as a man:[9]

> I have been at Luxor since 26 December and I have installed Carter.
> He is going to shore up the wall of the Ramesseum, which threatens
> collapse, two or three rooms of Qurna, and several other places which
> are in urgent need of repair. I find him very active, a very good
> young man, a little obstinate, but I believe that things will go well
> when he is persuaded of the impossibility of securing all the reforms
> in one go: the only misfortune is that he doesn't understand French,
> but he is learning it. We have already prepared the tombs of
> Tuthmosis III and Amenophis II for visitors; we are waiting for
> Garstin's approval to put up iron gates.

Carter's obstinacy (Maspero uses the word *entêté*) was both a strength
and a weakness; it would throughout his career sustain him at times of
difficult decision; it would also threaten the success of his efforts, and even
bring him close to losing all he had striven for. Maspero would himself meet
the problem in a few years' time over an incident at Saqqara when Carter
stood admirably by principle, but foolishly in almost every other respect.
Later Carter would almost lose control over the great Tutankhamun discovery by failing to understand the necessity of bending in the face of
a storm. Yet from the beginning, Maspero and Carter developed a very
sympathetic relationship, which must indicate in particular the former's
appreciation of those talents which characterized Carter's work: an excellent
artist, a good organizer, an accomplished engineer, a careful excavator, a
firm (if stubborn) representative of the interests of the Antiquities Service;
he understood and got on well with Egyptians, especially the villagers who
lived in and around the archaeological sites, whose co-operation was so
often needed in the daily work of the Chief Inspector. Carter was not an
academic Egyptologist, and could not have joined Maspero in discussing
the kinds of Egyptological problems – philological, literary, historical –
which were his principal interests. His practical abilities more than com-
pensated for his lack of formal training, and Maspero was pleased to have

9 Geneva Ms. 2529, 207, the original in French. In the translation, names of places and
  ancient kings have been converted from French convention of the time to English present-
  day forms.

found someone who could efficiently prosecute the policies of conservation and protection of the monuments which he was instituting.

Carter, for his part, greatly appreciated the interest and support shown him by Maspero, and in spite of the vicissitudes of his career, when Maspero was obliged in his official capacity to go sometimes against the advice or intentions of his young colleague, he could in later life write warmly of his former chief:[10]

> A more distinguished savant, a more charming gentleman, or kinder master could not be found. Maspero's single-hearted devotion to Egyptology and his encouragement and consideration for others occupied in its research – irrespective of nationality – were but one manifestation of his noble and generous nature, which critical colleagues were apt to look upon as weakness.

In the same context he writes briefly about the vagueness of his commission as Chief Inspector, and reports that he was at first required to draw up reports on the Theban Necropolis and its monuments with the intention of organizing a system for their future protection. A move in this direction is mentioned in Maspero's letter to Naville in which he talks of preparing two of the royal tombs for visitors, and of plans to install iron gates. The idea of fitting protective gates on tombs was new, even though it was an obvious first step to preserve these ancient monuments from the destructive actions of visitors, especially antiquities hunters, and from the illegal occupation of tomb-chapels by Egyptian *fellahin* who found the Theban tombs in particular very convenient ready-made dwellings. It seems inconceivable that less than one hundred years ago access to most tombs in the Theban region was unimpeded by anything more than a local guard, who was only on duty from time to time. Even then substantial numbers of visitors trod the archaeological trails to the Valley of the Kings and over the hills of Qurna which were honeycombed with finely decorated tombs.

It was an urgent and very rewarding work, and Howard Carter, with strong encouragement from Maspero, worked steadily, although rather slowly, on the task while he was at Thebes. Money, unfortunately, was short, and Carter was obliged to do what he could when he had funds. Sometimes he might persuade a visitor to contribute something towards costs; such was the donation of £10 (£E9.750) given by a Mrs Goff – described as 'the charming Mrs. Goff' by Emma Andrews in her diary entry for 6 April 1902 – which Carter used to clean out and provide a gate for the tomb of King Sethos II in the Valley of the Kings.[11] Several

10 From a late sketch 'Tomb of the Horse'; the Griffith Institute version in Carter Notebook 16, 92.
11 Carter reports the gift in *A.S.A.E.* 4 (1903), p. 44. A copy of his letter to Mrs Goff acknowledging the gift, dated 21 March 1902, is in the library of the Department of Egyptian Antiquities, the British Museum.

accounts suggest that Howard Carter had very considerable social charm which he was able to use to the advantage of his work. As early as 1895 he had encouraged Mr Frederick Horniman, MP for Falmouth and Penryn, to donate £100 towards the work on the Deir el-Bahri temple. In reporting the matter to the Committee of the Egypt Exploration Fund, Naville emphasized particularly 'that it is to Carter that the Society is indebted for that gift'.[12] His greatest success, however, was to concentrate the interests of Robert Mond, the British industrialist and chemist, in the excavation and preservation of the private tombs at Thebes, a task to which he had been introduced by Percy Newberry in 1902. Tombs excavated by Mond were properly conserved and provided with doors. A few years later Mond more actively supported this particular aspect of work at Thebes, and it was energetically pursued on his behalf by Arthur Weigall, Chief Inspector from 1906, by Alan H. Gardiner, and by Ernest Mackay. In the beginning, many of the doors put up by Carter were of wood,[13] but they proved to be of little use against the determined and wholly unscrupulous activities of those robbers who found a ready market for fragments of tomb-decoration through the antiquities dealers of Luxor and Cairo.

Iron grilles did not fare much better if a truly resolute effort at entry were to be made, as one serious incident proved almost two years after Howard Carter had taken up his appointment. One of the tombs first fitted with iron doors was that of King Amenophis II of the Eighteenth Dynasty (c. 1427–1401 BC). This tomb had only been rediscovered in 1898 in excavations by Victor Loret, Maspero's predecessor as Director-General. It contained, to the great surprise of the discoverer, in addition to the mummy of Amenophis II in its quartzite sarcophagus, a group of royal and non-royal mummies and unwrapped bodies, and some funerary equipment.[14] The tomb had, in fact, been converted some time in the late Twentieth Dynasty into a cache for the reburial of the plundered remains of a number of very important kings of the Eighteenth, Nineteenth and Twentieth Dynasties. After the clearance of the tomb, the bodies were left in their places, and that of Amenophis II himself lay undisturbed in his sarcophagus. When Maspero came to Luxor at the start of his new regime he decided in January 1900 to remove to the Cairo Museum with Carter's help all the royal mummies, with the exception of that of Amenophis II. At the time Theodore Davis with his travelling party were in Luxor in his *dahabiya*, and Maspero suggested that Carter should take the Americans to view the newly ordered tomb of Amenothes – as he called the king.

12 Letter of Naville to Grueber, E.E.S. Archive XI b 2. Frederick John Horniman (1835–1906) made a fortune as a merchant and he collected widely, founding the Horniman Museum at Forest Hill, South London, in 1897.
13 The history of protection is outlined in A. H. Gardiner and A. E. P. Weigall, *Topographical Catalogue of the Private Tombs of Thebes* (London, 1913), pp. 7ff. On Carter's wooden doors, see *Rapports sur la Marche . . .* , p. 58.
14 See C. N. Reeves, *The Valley of the Kings*, (London, 1990), pp. 192ff.

The visit took place on 17 January, a fine hot day, as Mrs Andrews reported in her diary. The descent into the tomb was arduous and dangerous. Those who know the tomb today will recall the steep descents from level to level, the wide deep well-shaft, and the oppressive heat. The present-day luxuries of proper stairs and electric light were not yet installed in early 1900, and Mrs Andrews writes vividly of the difficulties of the visit: gentlemen invited to take off their coats, candles handed around, steep so-called stairs of broken stones with ropes to hold on to, beams across the shaft, another impossible stair with a roof so low they were obliged to bend. But they were struck by the 'chaste' decoration on the walls, and by the king's mummy in the sarcophagus – the body untouched, 'probably protected Mr. Carter told us by the curse pronounced in the band of hieroglyphs around the top of the sarcophagus upon any marauding hands.' There is no such curse on the sarcophagus, and it is piquant to find Carter invoking such here when he would later in life be plagued constantly by the mythical curse of Tutankhamun.

Carter and the Antiquities Service did not, however, have to rely on the supposed curse to protect the tomb and its remaining contents. The iron gate had been installed – noted by Mrs Andrews – and guards were on duty day and night in the Valley of the Kings. Nevertheless, rumour, always a potent factor in and around areas where antiquities are being found, had it that there remained in the tomb bodies covered with jewels in gold and silver. It is impossible to persuade Egyptian villagers who know anything at all about the work of excavators, that the principal aim of all archaeologists is not to find gold and jewels. Surely it would be madness, they would think, to engage in such dirty, uncomfortable activities were there not something special to be found. Of course, the search might not always be successful, but any discovery about which a fuss might be made must certainly incorporate an element of 'Treasure'. So goes the thinking. And unfortunately, gold is found sufficiently frequently for the idea of the treasure-hunt to become part of the myth of archaeology. Unfortunately also, there have been many archaeologists who have measured their success by the precious objects found in their explorations. It is hard wholly to blame them if they receive greater public recognition for the finding of a few precious objects than of, for example, a rich archive of documents. At least the publicity may help in securing more support for the work; and the discovered objects may be beautiful, and fine examples of ancient craftsmanship. At Luxor, especially in the early years of the twentieth century, there has always been considerable archaeological activity, and discoveries, interesting and exciting, were and are not uncommon. There was always, therefore, a stimulus for the inhabitants of the villages on the West Bank of the Nile opposite Luxor town to pursue their traditional activity of tomb-robbing. It had flourished in antiquity, and had been revived in modern times when the search for antiquities became part of the opening-up of Egypt in the wake of the Napoleonic invasion.

The responsibilities of antiquities inspectors naturally include the close surveillance of threatened areas and, when thefts can be identified, the tracking down of stolen objects and the bringing to justice of the thieves. Howard Carter was reckoned to be assiduous and successful in this respect. The chatty Mrs Andrews said of him – reporting no doubt the views of Theodore Davis and his friends – that he 'has proved himself a most efficient officer – is absolutely fearless – carries no arms – and rides about quite unattended at all hours of the night.'[15] He found his information about possible thefts as much by examining the purchases of wealthy tourists, like Theodore Davis, as from talking informally to the villagers of Qurna and the antiquities dealers of Luxor. The whole business was circular, a process of supply and demand. In January 1900 Carter was shown a number of objects purchased by Davis in Luxor, and he expressed his suspicions that 'some rich and important tomb was being robbed and that he was on the scent of it'.[16] It is today surprising to contemplate the ambivalence with which Carter, and others in similar positions, were obliged to act in response to antiquity thieving. A Puritan approach to archaeology and its finds had not yet developed and it was possible, perhaps even necessary, to sit on the fence, on one side condoning the acquisition of antiquities by private persons which must have come 'hot' from illicit excavations, and on the other side attempting to thwart the efforts of the tomb robbers. Somewhere in the middle of this unsatisfactory traffic was to be found the antiquities dealer, untroubled by any qualms of morality; he bought what was offered, often in ignorance of the origin of the finds, and sold for the best price to European and American visitors.

In the autumn of 1901 Carter successfully trapped two bands of illicit diggers at Thebes and brought them to trial. To him, and to every well intentioned person, the outcome was highly unsatisfactory: the culprits were found guilty and fined either 5 or 15 piastres – utterly insignificant sums. As Maspero reported, in such cases 'the robbers are less discouraged than encouraged to continue in their practices'.[17] This fiasco was shortly followed by a well planned robbery of the tomb of King Amenophis II. The report of the theft, published by Carter in the newly established journal of the Antiquities Service in the following year, is both fascinating and scandalous.[18] In parts it reads not unlike the official reports of ancient tomb robbery at Thebes prepared in the late Twentieth Dynasty. The theft took place apparently on the evening of 24 November. Carter was away

15 Diary entry for 17 January 1900, transcript, p. 74
16 Diary entry for 20 January 1900, p. 89.
17 *Rapports sur la marche . . .* , p. 37.
18 'Report on the robbery of the tomb of Amenothes II, Biban el Moluk', in *A.S.A.E.* 3 (1902), pp. 115ff.

from home on a tour of inspection, and heard the news next day while he was at Kom Ombo on his way to Aswan. His investigations, conducted with representatives of the local civil authorities and the police, were inconclusive. It seems that the Valley guards were overpowered, the tomb entered, the royal mummy cut open, another body smashed, and a model boat stolen. The cutting-open of the royal mummy had, according to Carter, been carried out skilfully and clearly by someone who knew where to look for precious objects. None were found. Carter had strong suspicions that the theft was the work of the Abd er-Rasul family, the most accomplished robbers in Qurna, and that the guards had lied about the events. A tell-tale footprint, photographed by Carter, corresponded with one belonging to Mohammed Abd er-Rasul. In due course three Abd er-Rasul brothers were arrested, but the stolen boat was not recovered. Carter was very dissatisfied with the behaviour of the guards: 'I cannot help thinking that the theft was known to them some time before the 24th of November, and that they have made up the tale for some reasons, perhaps to cover their negligence. There are many evidences and witnesses to show that the inspector and the guards were holiday-making in Luxor without leave, during my absence.' Everything about this theft was inconclusive and frustrating. Mohammed Abd er-Rasul alone was eventually brought to trial, but was not convicted; even the evidence of the footprint was rejected, Carter believed because the photograph produced in court was of a small size and the court was unwilling (or unable) to see the correspondence between it and the foot of the accused. In a late sketch which includes an account of the theft, Carter describes the extraordinary sequel.[19] His attempts to find the stolen boat came to nothing until, one day much later, he spotted it in a case in the Cairo Museum. It had, it seems, been purchased from an antiquities dealer by one of the Museum's officials, using state funds. Subsequently it emerged that it had been sold by Mohammed Abd er-Rasul to a dealer in Giza.

Although Howard Carter could in no way be held responsible for what had happened in the tomb of Amenophis II, a certain odium stuck to him in the opinion of those who did not approve of his appointment, or of the way in which he exercised his responsibilities. He might try to be all things to all men, but priorities of duty could only prevent him from being equally well disposed to all. For example, in the supervision of the excavations of others at Thebes and elsewhere in his fief, the division of finds between the excavator and the Cairo Museum was a particularly sensitive procedure. The Chief Inspector could favour those whom he liked to a degree that might incur hostile criticism from elsewhere. It was a kind of tight-rope walk in which a false step might result in the loss of friends, or in the charge of improper behaviour. A letter to Lady Amherst written from

19 G.I. Carter Notebook 17, p. 189.

Thebes on 19 December 1900 is particularly revealing in the matter of the dividing of finds:[20]

> Last week I allowed some excavations to be made in the tombs of the Kings by a native, resulting in the finding of the tomb of Sennefer, Mayor of Thebes during Amenhotep II; there are many antiquities in it mostly inscribed vases of good work. As my agreement was with the native that either half value or half antiquities shall be the finder's property and there are many duplicates, I am advising Newberry to purchase one for you. *Would willingly do so myself* but feel that I ought not to under one's present circumstances.

Later in the same letter he continues:

> Newberry has been most fortunate in finding 3 gold and copper dishes with Hathor cows in them – they are very beautiful and unique – Shall do all I can to let him carry one away for I think two are ample for the Museum.

None of Carter's actions or intentions mentioned in this letter is tainted with impropriety in the context of normal Antiquities Service practice of the times. Straightforward 50:50 division was the common arrangement, except that specially important or unique pieces could always be claimed for the Cairo Museum. Objects from the so-called Sen-nefer tomb divided to the excavator were in due course acquired for the Amherst collection, and others went to Theodore Davis; some of these latter are now in the Metropolitan Museum of Art, New York. Others, by different routes, ended up in museums elsewhere – the Kestner Museum in Hanover and the British Museum.[21] One of the cow dishes was divided to Newberry, whose work had been financed jointly by Theodore Davis and Mrs Andrews; it is now also in the Metropolitan Museum of Art, having come by way of the Davis collection.[22]

Among those who observed Carter's activities with displeasure was J. H. Insinger, a Dutch dealer in antiquities, who lived for most of the year in Luxor, and was well known to European and American visitors. In June 1903 he wrote a virulent letter to the editor of the French-language daily paper *Le Phare d'Alexandrie*, attacking Carter and linking him with E. A. W. Budge, the Keeper of Egyptian and Assyrian Antiquities at the

20 In the Amherst Letters; T. J. Eva Egyptian Collection.
21 On the problems of the identification of the owners of the tomb, thought at first by Carter to be Sen-nefer, see C. N. Reeves, *Valley of the Kings*, pp. 24ff. For the present location of objects from the tomb, *ibid.*, p. 33, notes 121–4.
22 See W. C. Hayes, *Scepter of Egypt*, II (New York, 1959), pp. 205f., with fig. 121. For a full study including details of Newberry's agreement with Theodore Davis, see H. E. Winlock, 'An Egyptian flower bowl', in *Met. Mus. Studies* V (1936), pp. 147f. Mrs Andrews's participation is made clear in letters of 24 August and 18 September to Newberry, G.I. Newberry Corr. 3/2 and 3/3.

British Museum, whose methods of acquiring objects for the Museum were often thought to be less than scrupulous. In publishing the letter (written in French) in the issue of 3 June, the editor of *Le Phare* comments favourably on the standing of his correspondent, and deplores the facts raised in the letter as being seriously damaging to 'la patrimoine historique de l'Égypte', and requiring public airing:[23]

> A lack of supervision, amounting to complicity, allowing the clandestine dispatch to Europe of antiquities taken surreptitiously from poorly guarded excavations, sanctioning the plundering of the royal tombs, defrauding Egypt, to the advantage of 'the most favoured nation', of ancestral documents, those whose rightful ownership can the least be disputed.

Insinger begins by complaining of the number of English officials being appointed, and of the possibility that some are not fitted for their posts, e.g. Monsieur X . . . , i.e. Howard Carter, 'formerly a junior draughtsman [employed] at £5 a month. He worked at Deir el-Bahri for the Egypt Exploration Fund. He has been appointed Inspector-in-Chief to the Antiquities Service at £43 a month.' How could such an insignificant person be so employed? 'Not a year passes without the recording of some disappearance of antiquities or a serious accident, such as the violation of the tomb of Amenophis II, the collapse of the tomb of Sethos I, or some blunder.' He then raises the matter of the despoiling of a late Eleventh or early Twelfth Dynasty tomb about which M. X . . . seemed to know less than anyone. Inscriptions from this tomb have been purchased in Luxor, and fraudulently exported by Monsieur Y . . . , i.e. Budge, for the British Museum. Insinger hints that the blocks from the tomb may have been exported in the diplomatic bag, and should perhaps be returned in the same way. And as for M. X . . . , he ought to be transferred to another division of the public service; he is quite unfitted to look after antiquities: 'Every time somebody of importance visits Upper Egypt, one wonders with fear what calamity will happen to the things entrusted to M. X . . .'s care. You could say that he is pursued by an evil destiny.'

An energetic and very well argued riposte was offered by the *Egyptian Gazette* two days later.[24] In an editorial entitled ' "Antica" Stealing', the writer addresses 'our excellent confrère, *Le Phare d'Alexandrie*', taking him to task in particular for his unjustified comments based on Insinger's letter. The writer does not set out to defend Dr Budge, and he has some very pertinent comments to make on the antiquities trade, which is actively exploited by 'antiquities authorities' of many countries. 'No one nation is

---

23 I am grateful to my friend the late Professor Magdi Wahba for tracking down a copy of this rare publication and for obtaining a photocopy of the relevant page.
24 Files of this paper are to be found in the British Library Newspaper Library at Colindale, North London. The leading article is on p. 2 of the issue of Friday 5 June 1903.

more favoured than another in this respect, though perhaps England and the British Museum may be more actively represented.' He points out that there is a Decree regulating the export of antiquities, but it is difficult to enforce because upwards of 40,000 Egyptians earn a living 'from the disposal of Egypt's ancient records'. He concludes his leader thus: 'The only means of dealing with Dr. Budge is to arouse scientific public opinion in England against him and his methods.'[25] It might just be mentioned here that the specific monument about which Insinger accuses Budge, and by implication Carter, the fine stela of Tjetji, had been available on the antiquities market in Luxor for some time before Budge purchased it for the British Museum, and could therefore have been acquired for the Cairo Museum by purchase or even by confiscation.[26] This would surely have been known to Insinger, of whom the leader-writer of the *Egyptian Gazette* says: 'In view of Mr. Insinger's peculiar position in Luxor we can also understand that an active and energetic Inspector like Mr. Carter is a considerable thorn in the flesh to him, and that such accusations as are brought against the latter, are prompted by a whole-souled desire to see the last of him.'

On Insinger's charges that Carter was in some way responsible for robberies in tombs and the collapse of the tomb of Sethos I (referred to here as Seti I), the *Gazette* editorial comments very sensibly:

> No single case of robbery has taken place at Thebes, Mr. Carter's headquarters, during his presence there. It is impossible to expect a single inspector to look after a stretch of 500 miles of country, containing innumerable tombs and temples, in anything more than a superficial manner. We do not understand why Mr. Insinger should look upon the falling in of the roof of the tomb of Seti I as a reflection upon Mr. Carter's capacity. Perhaps Mr. Insinger is also aware that the roof of the Temple of Edfou has fallen in and also the enclosure walls of the temple of Kom Ombo.

But the hardest hit is against the charge that Carter had acted in complicity with Budge in the so-called theft of the Tjetji stela. The accusation had not been made by Insinger himself, but by the editor of *Le Phare d'Alexandrie* on the strength of Insinger's letter. 'We trust', the editorial thunders, 'that Lord Cromer will take this matter up and call upon our contemporary for a written apology for such an unwarranted aspersion.'

It must be presumed that nothing followed, for there is no mention of

25 Budge comments on the affair in his *By Nile and Tigris*, II (London, 1920), p. 366, and suggests that Carter's later dismissal from the Antiquities Service was due partly to the energetic nature of his exercise of his duties. Carter was not dismissed; see the next chapter.

26 BM 614 (Tjetji's stela) was first seen and the texts copied by G. C. Pier, an American Egyptologist, who published an account of it with help from J. H. Breasted in *A.J.S.L.* 21 (1905), pp. 159ff.

the written apology or of any other reaction in later issues of the *Egyptian Gazette*. Whether the affair damaged Carter's reputation, it is hard to determine. One year later moves were made to transfer Carter to the northern inspectorate, and to bring Quibell to Luxor; but such a change had been envisaged from the time when the inspectorates were first set up. In his report on the progress of the Antiquities Service for 1904, Maspero noted that the change of inspectorates should have taken place at the beginning of 1903, but had been delayed for two seasons at Carter's request so that he could complete certain pieces of work he had in hand at Thebes and elsewhere.[27] Maspero had agreed; then Carter had decided to exercise his option to move in June 1904. Maspero would surely not have allowed him to stay on at Luxor after the scandalous charges had been made if he had felt that there was any truth in them. Equally he would not have tried so hard to prevent Carter from resigning in late 1905, had he not valued his services so highly.[28]

There was, as the editorial in the *Egyptian Gazette* noted, a lot of work for an inspector with 500 miles of country to cover. Many of the duties were routine – the chore of simple but regular inspection, for example – others involved the practical care and repair of monuments. These activities together constituted what might be called the bread-and-butter jobs. There were also other tasks, much more to Carter's liking, which could be characterized as the icing on the cake – exploration and excavation. All in all, however, he relished his new position, as a letter written to his mother in September 1900 shows.[29] It is one of a very few surviving letters to her illustrated with small snap-shots set within the text. Unexpectedly he addresses his mother as 'mater', a usage (with 'pater' for 'father') which was not uncommonly used by those who had received an education with a classical element in it, probably in a public school. It was used, for example, by Percy and John Newberry to refer to their mother, and not only in letters addressed to her. Americans also employed the usage, at least in academic families like that of James Henry Breasted, the great Chicago Egyptologist. In Carter's case it might be put down, perhaps unfairly, as an affectation. His own education had been sketchy, and throughout his life he made up for the deficiencies of schooling and of social training by aping the behaviour of those with whom he worked closely, and whom he regarded as being suitable models to follow. Here in this letter he starts with an account of what he has recently been doing:

> Yesterday I returned from an Inspection up country, at a place called Edfou, with the great pleasure of finding a letter from Mater dated Sept 2nd and also a much needed ½ doz. prs of socks that caused

27 *Rapports sur la marche . . .* , p. 118.
28 *Ibid.*, p. 164; and Chapter 5 below.
29 Letter dated 12 September 1900, in the possession of John Carter.

great joy – to show my pleasure I work hard and developed photos in the evening, and hence the prints. Tomorrow I am off again North, to Esneh and Baliana on Inspection and look into a case between subinspector and guards, either of which having taken palm-oil for settlement of some Antiquity land.

After domestic details of his house (Castle Carter) and garden and some animal news, he ends:

It is only a short time since I wrote my last, so have hardly anything to say. My flying visits to unexpected places make a few days seem weeks ago. It is a curious life – a letter may come in the morning and I go in quite an opposite way, or perhaps must stay where I am – For that is an Inspector's life.

Among the places where Carter carried out essential and important work of conservation and reparation were the Ptolemaic-Roman temples of Kom Ombo and Edfu, to the south of Luxor; at the latter a few huge roofing blocks of the first pillared hall had fallen to the ground and needed to be replaced safely, for the temple was much visited by tourists. In Nubia he was much involved in shoring up the foundations of the temple of Philae, recently partially submerged by the building of the Aswan Dam. Here the work was largely paid for and carried out by central government, but Carter was required to monitor progress and to note the effects of the water which now flooded the temple for most of the year. At Abu Simbel he took steps to minimize damage to the great Ramesses temple where one of the huge colossal statues was regularly clambered over by visitors for the taking of holiday snaps. He also organized the installation of electric light in this temple with the practical and financial help of Messrs Thomas Cook, whose steamers regularly brought groups of eager tourists to view the distant monuments of Nubia.

Most of his work, however, was concentrated in the Theban area, not including the great temples of Karnak and Luxor on the east bank of the Nile, which were the special responsibility of other representatives of the Antiquities Service.[30] Much had to be done at the Ramesseum, the mortuary temple of Ramesses II – an enclosure wall to be built and considerable areas of the temple compound to be cleared of debris accumulated over more than 3000 years. The fitting of iron gates to many of the tombs in the Valley of the Kings has already been mentioned; and he also greatly improved the experience of visiting six of the tombs by installing electric light. He was particularly proud of this achievement, for noticeable disfigurement of the paintings and reliefs in these tombs was caused by the

30 Carter's own published reports on his work during the years 1900–4 are in *A.S.A.E.* 1–4 (1900–3). More general reports by Maspero are in *Rapports sur la marche . . .* , pp. 10f (1900), 31ff. (1901), 58ff. (1902), 92ff. (1903), 119ff. (1904).

soot deposited by candles, torches and magnesium flares used by visitors. Thebes was always archaeologically a hive of activity which needed to be watched closely or superficially, depending on who was in charge of the operations. Robert Mond with Percy Newberry could be trusted to excavate private tombs in the area known as Sheikh Abd el-Qurna. Ernesto Schiaparelli, head of the Italian Archaeological Mission, could equally be supervised lightly in his work in the Valley of the Queens. There remarkable monuments like the wonderfully decorated tomb of Nefertari, principal queen of Ramesses II, was found during Carter's inspectorate. Closer surveillance had to be made, however, on the work of less experienced excavators, like Messrs Chinouda Macarios and Boutros Andraos who were allowed a permit to clear the tomb thought to be that of Sen-nefer.

Casual finds made in unofficial diggings were particularly difficult to track down and control, especially if small, precious, objects were involved. The licensed and unlicensed work of the *sebbakhin* was a constant problem. The *sebbakhin*, small farmers and farm-labourers, retrieved decayed mud-brick and top soil (*sebakh*) from ancient sites, of which town areas were the most productive; the material was spread as fertilizer on the cultivated fields, and its retrieval was in a sense a community right and in some places intensive and very difficult to supervise. Inevitably ancient objects were turned up and rarely would they be handed over to the antiquities authorities, unless the discovery became known before the find was dispersed. Carter was to have a notable success in this tricky area in 1905 when he was already operating in the Delta. But success was rare, and Maspero's reports every year comment on the problem. The practice still continues, with devastating effect on ancient town mounds, especially in the more remote parts of the country, little visited by tourists and difficult to oversee on a regular basis. Casual digging for other purposes might also reveal things of interest, as when Jusef Ahmed el-Neggar (as Carter names him) came across a group of fine sculptures and other large monuments too heavy to spirit away, while enlarging his house in Luxor. On that occasion the house-owner was paid £E5 as compensation for the retrieval of the pieces and for the rehabilitation of his house.

Few excavations took place in other parts of Upper Egypt during Carter's years of duty there, but one, unusually conceived, had a special call on his interest and care. A concession was granted to Lady William Cecil, Mary the eldest daughter of Lord Amherst, who would succeed as Baroness Amherst on her father's death in 1909. She had acquired a love of Egyptian things from her parents, and on a visit to Egypt in 1901, encouraged by the presence of Howard Carter in Upper Egypt, she started excavations at Aswan, at the place called Qubbet el-Hawa. Here a series of very important tombs of the Old and Middle Kingdoms had been found by Sir Francis Grenfell in 1885 while he was Commander-in-Chief of the Egyptian Army. Lady William Cecil records in her journal how the enterprise began.[31] The Cecil party settled at Aswan for a long winter stay, and one day made an excursion to the west bank of the river. Billy (the son) with another member of the party walked to the top of Qubbet el-Hawa to see the view. Here they found that

> all the top of the hill was full of what looked like tombs. He was quite excited about it so next day I went up to look too. And the day after Howard Carter, having arrived at Aswan, we made him come up too. He said it certainly was an ancient cemetery and he knew nothing about it, it is not on any map or guide. He said we might if we cared, have a 'permit' to excavate these tombs and we were delighted with the idea, and he (H. Carter) arranged to send us an inspector and 4 men from Luxor, and we got Nubians to carry baskets, and we began our first excavation on 31st Dec.

In such a casual way could an excavation be started at that time; but it was properly supervised in the general manner of the period, and the Cecils were conscientious. 'The work was intensely interesting and we spent all day out in the desert watching the work.' Maspero visited the site and gave his blessing by enlarging the area covered by the 'permit'. Lady Cecil was punctilious: 'I have kept a daily diary of all the details of our excavation' which would be 'the report which I have to make officially to the government on all our discoveries.' In due course this report appeared in the *Annales du Service des Antiquités de l'Égypte*, in some respects a model publication of its kind and of its time.[32]

Letters from Carter to various members of the Amherst family contain information which sheds light on the informal, relaxed, ways in which such work was conducted.[33] To Lady Amherst on 31 August 1902, from Cairo:

> Do you not think that Lady William Cecil's excavations were most successful and exceedingly interesting. Great credit is due to her in the way they were carried out. Maspero was very pleased. Sorry I had to grab some of the best things but could not do otherwise. . . . I am sure it was a good thing or rather a good way of spending the time – with a pleasant result at the end.

In the spring of 1904 while Lady William was again at Aswan, not having a very successful season, a sensational discovery of papyri with texts written in the Aramaic script was made by *sebakh* workers. Carter wrote almost immediately to Lord Amherst on 24 March:

31 Lady Cecil's journal is kept in Biltmore House, Ashville, North Carolina. I am grateful to the late James Manning for drawing it to my attention, and to Julie Bledsloe, Registrar of the Biltmore Estate, for providing photocopies and transcripts of relevant sections.

32 'Report of work done at Aswan', in *A.S.A.E.* 4 (1903), pp. 51ff; and a second report on work in early 1904 in vol. 6 (1905), pp. 273ff.

33 The Amherst Letters; T. J. Eva Egyptian Collection. Further quotations in *E.E.S. Newsletter* 6 (Oct. 1990), p. 5.

An important find of Aramaic papyri was made this season by some natives at Aswan; either in the sabach works at the south end of the Island of Elephantine, or in the mounds of the ancient town of Aswan between the Railway Station and the Cataract Hotel when a new road was made early in the winter. These documents are apparently of a lady – betrothal deeds – dating in the time of Artaxerxes I to Darius II. They are most important, they being in the original Biblical language, and mentioned the citadel and fortresses of Aswan as well as the mixed courts (the Hebrew court being mentioned). As far as I am able to tell these are the only Aramaic papyri existing, excepting perhaps a few fragments now at Berlin.

Of the find, Lady William was fortunate enough to obtain 4 more or less perfect ones and Billy some pieces. 6 other documents were purchased by Mr. Robert Mond. . . . Mond has very kindly given to me his documents for the Cairo Museum. I am to make facsimiles of the same with his permission for carte-blanche to publish, facsimiles by hand and photos: reproductions for distribution to the scientific world. . . . As most probably all these papyri belong to one another, I cannot help but think that they should be published together – would you kindly allow this, and let yours be published with the others.

This letter was sent along with one from Lady William to her father. She is thrilled by her acquisition and intends to bring them back to Lord Amherst, sealed and unrolled as they are. They could then be unrolled, facsimiled and photographed for publication. She adds: 'He (i.e. Carter) considers them too valuable to be *returned* to Egypt after once in England. . . . Professor Sayce is wildly excited about them.'

In the end the Cecil papyri joined the Mond papyri in the Cairo Museum. Either Carter or Maspero had convinced Lady William that this would be the proper course. But for such a generous act there would be a recompense, a kind of *bonne bouche* for good behaviour. Carter wrote to Lady William on 11 June 1904 as follows:

I came down to Cairo yesterday and Monsieur Maspero told me that he had sent you some photos of statues from the Karnak find for you to chose from in exchange for the papyri that we took from you. He shew [*sic*] me the statues today and suggested that the large standing one was the best – this I certainly agree, and it is really a very good one and personally I advise taking it, but if Lord Amherst does not think he would like it, I will do what I can and getting anything else, though I cannot say that you can [do] much better. The work is good and the figure bears the cartouche of Psamtik.

The work indeed was good, and Lord Amherst did like it. It was a standing figure of Harbes holding an image of Osiris, and dated to the late sixth century BC.[34] It was one of the many hundreds of sculptures retrieved from a vast deposit of mostly votive statuary found in the Karnak Temple in 1903 and subsequent years – so many in fact that Maspero felt able to dispose of some which might be considered duplicates, or, at least, not needed for the Cairo Museum. For its time this was a sensible and practical policy, and could be used, as in the case of the Aramaic papyri, to the advantage of both sides. The papyri of the find were in due course published at Robert Mond's expense in a handsome large volume.[35] The texts were dealt with by Sayce and by A. H. Cowley of the Bodleian Library, Oxford. The quite excellent photographs of the papyri were by Carter who had carried out the delicate task of unrolling the little packets himself. No facsimiles were in the end made.

Carter relished his practical talents and enjoyed exercising them as circumstances allowed. Photography was as much a hobby as a professional aptitude; unrolling papyri was for him new – having missed his special opportunities in the fiasco of the Mendes library in 1893 – but his dexterity with such fragile materials demonstrated his ability to handle delicate objects with professional success. He continued his artistic work, both in the completion of the plates for Naville's great Deir el-Bahri volumes, and in accepting commissions for other archaeological work. He painted a series of watercolours of precious objects for a lavish publication by the German Egyptologist Friedrich Freiherr von Bissing,[36] and was used by Theodore Davis to make coloured illustrations for the volumes resulting from his excavations.[37] And whenever he could, he took his paintbox to monument or landscape in the Theban area. But there was one activity in which he wished above all to engage in, and that was excavation. When he became Chief Inspector his experience in digging was very slight, but he already had something in mind which he quickly obtained permission from Maspero to pursue. It had, like an unspent coin, been burning a hole in his pocket of intention.

It was what came to be known as El-Bab el-Hosan, the Tomb (literally Gate) of the Horse.[38] One day in November 1898, while Howard Carter was working on the reliefs at Deir el-Bahri, there was a very heavy rainstorm which did dreadful damage to the expedition house, and to the

34 Now in the Metropolitan Museum of Art (no. 19.2.2); see The Brooklyn Museum, *Egyptian Sculpture of the Late Period 700 B.C. to A.D. 100* (New York, 1960), p. 55, pls 44, 45.
35 A. H. Sayce and A.E. Cowley, *Aramaic Papyri discovered at Assuan* (London, 1906).
36 F. W. von Bissing, *Ein thebanischer Grabfund aus den Anfang des neuen Reichs* (Berlin, 1900).
37 Of these volumes dealing with tombs on which Carter worked, *The Tomb of Thoutmôsis IV* (London, 1904); *The Tomb of Hâtshopsîtû* (London, 1906). For his paintings in *The Tomb of Iouiya and Touiyou* (London, 1907), see p. 134 below.
38 For Carter's official report see *A.S.A.E.* 2 (1901), pp. 201ff,; the late sketch in G.I. Carter Notebook 16 (sketch III), is less reliable in detail. The date of the discovery, given otherwise as late spring 1898 in the sketch, is confirmed as November 1898 in a letter from Carter to Grueber, Hon. Treasurer of the E.E.F., E.E.S. Archive XI e 18.

ancient paint on the walls of the temple. He went off with his artist-colleague Charles Sillem to see what the effects may have been elsewhere, and on his return to the house his horse stumbled, and both it and rider fell. The small hole which had caused the tumble had traces of stonework in it and Carter concluded that there might be a tomb below. In due course he informed Naville in the hope that the Egypt Exploration Fund might be interested in investigating. The hole, however, lay outside the area allotted to the Fund for its work, and Naville did not follow the matter up. So Carter waited until his opportunity came in January 1900 and he was allowed to begin work with the help of funds provided by a private individual who has not been identified. The operations which followed were huge in scope and rather disappointing in result; but they were his first important piece of independent excavation.

What might have seemed in prospect to be a simple matter of opening up a small shaft and clearing a chamber or two turned into a mammoth task. The small opening led to a vast man-made cleft in the rock of the valley floor, with a sloping descent leading to a blocked-up and sealed entrance at a depth of 17 metres. This apparently unbreached barrier suggested a possibly unrobbed burial. So far the work had taken until 10 March – a wearisome labour with a large number of men. When this cleft was reopened in 1923 by the Egyptian Expedition of the Metropolitan Museum of Art, it took 200 men and boys 'slaving' for 3 weeks to empty it.[39] Beyond the blocked entrance Carter found a sloping shaft 150 metres long, which led down into a large chamber containing a statue wrapped in linen, a wooden coffin inscribed but with no owner's name, and some miscellaneous pots and remains of food offerings. A vertical filled-in shaft in the floor of the chamber promised to lead to the actual burial chamber. Carter put his men to clear it, but by 20 April he felt obliged to discontinue the work for the summer. He began again in early December, shoring up the sides of the shaft and hoping for success. He wrote to Lady Amherst:[40]

> I am hard at work trying to get to the bottom of the tomb I found at Deir el-Bahari last year [i.e. last season]. I trust to manage it soon though under difficulties – the men have now got down 97 metres vertical drop [i.e. from ground-surface level] and still no end, but cannot help but think the end will come soon; then there are chances of perhaps a good find, it being untouched.

Alas! His hopes were to be frustrated. On 31 December, when the shaft itself had reached a depth of about 30 metres below the floor of the chamber, a small blocked room was found. It contained only three rough wooden boats and a few pots. The anticlimax was in itself bad enough, but worse, he had foolishly alerted Lord Cromer, the British Consul-

39 H. E. Winlock, *Excavations at Deir el Bahri 1911–1931* (New York, 1942), p. 85.
40 Letter of 19 December 1900; the Amherst Letters; T. J. Eva Egyptian Collection.

General and virtual ruler of Egypt, suggesting that possibly an intact tomb, even a royal tomb, had been found. As Maspero wrote to Naville:[41]

> He had announced his discovery too soon to Lord Cromer. Lord Cromer came to be present at his success and he is now [in despair?] at not having been able to show him anything of what he had foretold. I console him as best I can, for he truly is a good fellow and he does his duty very well.

One final discovery, a small wooden box, buried in another, but much shorter, shaft, produced at least a good clue to the identification of the person for whom this 'tomb' had been prepared. The texts on it were inscribed for 'the son of Re, Mentuhotpe', undoubtedly one of the kings of that name who ruled as the later Eleventh Dynasty. It would be only a few years later before the identity of this king would be clinched as Nebhepetre Mentuhotpe II (c. 2061–2010 BC), the builder of the great funerary monument in the bay at Deir el-Bahri, 500 years before Hatshepsut's remarkable temple complex was conceived. Again Naville was to excavate it for the Egypt Exploration Fund.

The status of this 'tomb' discovered by Carter remains something of an enigma,[42] as does the precise identification of the extraordinary sculpture that had been found swathed in linen. It is of sandstone, shows a king somewhat larger than life-size, seated on a plain throne, wearing the red crown of Lower Egypt (one of the two regional crowns of royalty), and a short cloak of the kind worn by the king at his *heb-sed*, or festival of renewal.[43] The carving is immensely powerful and gives a strong impression of primitive authority, enhanced by the black colouring of the exposed skin – a colouring associated by the Egyptians with death. This statue alone might now be considered ample return for all the effort of the excavation.

After the discovery of this, perhaps dummy, tomb of Mentuhotpe, what was to come next? Carter's passion to excavate was by no means diminished by his relative disappointment at the outcome of his first substantial operation. It had, however, been a much more arduous and costly piece of work than he had expected, and the prospect of being able to dig again on behalf of the Antiquities Service and at their expense was very remote. All available funds were needed for the rehabilitation of the tombs that were already known, especially the royal sepulchres in the Valley of the Kings. Carter's success in making these tombs more accessible and more agreeable to visitors during his years in Thebes was generally admitted.

---

41 Geneva MS. 2529, 223, of 8 January 1901 (in French).
42 For the alternatives, see I. E. S. Edwards, *The Pyramids of Egypt* (rev. ed., Penguin, 1985), pp. 199f.
43 Much photographed; see K. Lange and M. Hirmer, *Egypt* (4th ed. London, 1968), pls XI and 81.

His improvements included a donkey park for a hundred animals – how much more pleasant than the coach and car parks that have to be provided one hundred years later! But working methodically in the Valley of the Kings did provide Carter with excellent opportunities to survey the main valley and the subsidiary side valleys, to become thoroughly acquainted with the great tombs in which he carried out his work of conservation, and to develop a desire to excavate in the area on his own account.[44] The way out of the financial difficulty was to find an enthusiastic and wealthy private individual who would put up the funds. The choice was Theodore Davis, the American businessman, whose interest in all the work progressing at Thebes had been made apparent in his visits to Egypt over a number of years. He had already in 1900 provided the financial backing for one season of Newberry's work on the private tombs at Thebes, and he, with Mrs Andrews, had benefited by the acquisition of a splendid bronze bowl. Mrs Andrews was his constant companion on his Egyptian trips, and in her diary she records the many meetings they had with Howard Carter from the time of his appointment as Chief Inspector. The references move from the impersonal to the formal, and even to the enthusiastic. On 17 January 1900 Carter took the Davis party to the tomb of Amenophis II, a visit already described; 20 January 1900, 'Mr. Carter came to lunch. . . . He is the Inspector of Antiquities for Upper Egypt'; 11 February, tea at Carter's house; 12 February, 'Mr. Carter to dine, and we had a pleasant evening'; 3 February 1901, the Davis party invited to dine with Carter and to visit the tomb of Sennedjem which was not generally open to the public, 'an excellent dinner . . . brilliant little tomb . . . our ride home was entrancing'; 17 January 1902, 'Carter dined with us – always so pleasant – in spite of his dominant personality.' Earlier on this last day she reports: 'After lunch, Maspero and Carter walked about with Theodore to fix upon the site of an exploration, which Theodore under Carter is to make in the Valley of the Tombs.'[45] It is clear that Carter took some trouble to develop a friendly relationship with Theodore Davis and his party through social activities and by the archaeological indulgences of special visits – always appreciated by those who have seen all the standard tourist sites time and again. If it were a conscious process of softening up the rich American, it worked; and if, as Carter later maintained, he was responsible for proposing Davis's involvement in excavation on behalf of the Antiquities Service,[46] then he could claim substantial credit for having instituted a series of Davis excavations which found more tombs than any previous series. Carter was in charge until 1904; thereafter

44 For brief details of Carter's work in the Valley up to early 1902, see Reeves, *Valley of the Kings*, pp. 289f.
45 Diary entry in transcript 1902, p. 75.
46 G.I. Carter Notebook 16, p. 116.

Davis worked with greater independence, although still nominally for the Antiquities Service.[47]

The first season was something of a trial-run for Carter, as indeed it was for Davis. Several places in the main valley and in one side valley were tested, and some modest discoveries made: a tomb-shaft, possibly the burial place of Userhet, an overseer of the fields of Amun, of Eighteenth-dynasty date, robbed and reused, and its few remaining contents destroyed by rain water; also a box containing two leather loincloths of extremely fine cut-work belonging to the burial of a Maherper, whose tomb, of approximately the same date, had been found a few years earlier by Victor Loret. The results were not spectacular, but they were sufficient to enable Carter to obtain Davis's support for a second season. And so at the start of 1903 he turned his workmen on the mounds of debris cluttering the small valley running roughly eastwards from the tomb of Sethos I, at the head of which was a known tomb, only partly excavated and unidentified. Here within a few days he found indications of the burial of King Tuthmosis IV, eighth monarch of the Eighteenth Dynasty (c. 1401–1391 BC), and shortly afterwards the unmistakeable entrance to a tomb. In front of the entrance two holes dug in the rock contained complete foundation deposits – groups of small vessels and model implements – inscribed with the king's name. Such deposits, invested with magical power, placed at the entrance to or corners of important buildings, inaugurated, marked and sanctified them. With this discovery Carter felt sure that he had found his first royal tomb in the Valley.

Theodore Davis had at this important moment left Thebes for Aswan, and Carter was faced with something of a dilemma. Should he enter the tomb, or should he wait for Davis to return, and for Maspero and perhaps others to come down from Cairo? He sensibly remembered the mistake he had made in inviting Lord Cromer to the opening of the Mentuhotpe tomb, and so he decided to make a preliminary entrance with Mr Robb de Peyster Tytus, an American friend of Theodore Davis. Tytus had spent a number of seasons excavating, with Percy Newberry's assistance, the palace of King Amenophis III at Malkata, a little to the south of Medinet Habu, and was a familiar figure in the excavation camps and the *dahabiya* salons of Luxor. On entry into the new tomb, Carter and Tytus found a sepulchre which had been robbed at least twice in antiquity, with some rooms decorated with splendidly painted reliefs and ritual texts, the main chamber littered with fragments of vessels of many different materials and of other items of funerary furniture, a magnificent but empty quartzite sarcophagus, and the body of a war chariot.[48] Entry was difficult and

47 See Reeves, *Valley of the Kings*, pp. 292ff.
48 Carter's official account is given in H. Carter and P. E. Newberry, *The Tomb of Thoutmôsis IV* (London, 1904); an informal account in his sketch 'Six milk white camels', in G.I. Notebook 16, pp. 131ff.

dangerous, and the way was interrupted, as often, by a deep well – a protective device and also, probably, a sump to catch rain water which might flood into the tomb. It had been a prudent move to enter in advance of a formal opening, and the common sense of it should be remembered and carried forward to the time when Carter returned to the tomb of Tutankhamun by night with the Earl of Carnarvon and surreptitiously entered the burial chamber – an act for which they were subsequently vilified. Now at least he had carried out his reconnaissance, appreciated the hazards, and was in a position to prepare for an 'official' opening at a later date. In any case, he was now Chief Inspector, the man on the spot, and responsible for the affairs of the Antiquities Service locally.

Without much delay he let Theodore Davis know the good news by travelling himself to Aswan and allowing his financial backer to participate proprietorially in the discovery: 'This is a fine success both for Theo and for Carter,' notes Emma Andrews in her entry for 21 January. So Davis, without actually rushing, reduced his party's stay in Aswan to three days, and was back in Luxor by 1 February. Two days later the opening party gathered in the Valley. There were eighteen people altogether, according to Mrs Harriet Cox whose two daughters were included. Mrs Cox wrote from Aswan a few days later to Lady William Cecil including general comments on the tomb and its contents. She remarks:[49]

> It appears that Mr. Carter made the opening arrangements so perfectly that the visitors had electric light along with them as they penetrated into the inner chambers and altogether it was a profoundly interesting experience to be present, for which my girls have to thank Mr. Maspero.

Mrs Andrews's account contains numerous untechnical details which provide something of the flavour of the occasion:[50] 'Carter was not to be seen, he had been down in the tomb since 4 o'clock having slept before it with his guards. . . . he emerged looking like a ghost – his careful man was waiting for him with a thick ulster, which he clapped upon him, and he was given some water and a cigarette.' She went in with Maspero and Davis, descending with difficulty two long inclines, the second of which was so low that 'Maspero being so stout had to actually lie down, with his feet sometimes on Carter's shoulders.' She notes the well over which Carter slung a precarious suspension bridge, the fine decorations, an hieratic graffito indicating that the tomb had been entered, no doubt for purposes of inspection and perhaps rehabilitation, in the eighth year of King Horemheb (c. 1312 BC). The great burial hall had no decoration, but 'was strewn with a mass of beautiful debris. . . . Carter had placed boards along which we walked, and were requested not to step off them.'

49 Letter dated 7 February 1903, in The Amherst Letters; T. J. Eva Egyptian Collection.
50 Diary entry for 3 February; transcript for 1903, pp. 135ff.

They saw the sarcophagus and the 'dash board of a war chariot. . . . Maspero was delighted with this, as it is absolutely unique.' And then out they came – more difficult than getting in – had lunch and were home by 5 o'clock – 'we were glad enough to have tea'. And so another exciting day passed.

The social side of excavation, as exemplified by this occasion, was an inevitable concomitant of having patrons and of having to maintain the interest of senior officials and government servants. The serious side of the work, however, could not be neglected, and Carter was here receiving a further lesson in balancing priorities; it was his responsibility to see that the main purpose of this excavation was carried through without compromise. To this end the electric light, the rope hand-rails, the walkways placed over potentially valuable archaeological material, the limitation of the size of parties viewing the tomb, all contributed to the kind of control which was not so common in excavations of that period, and indeed might not be maintained in later Davis excavations supervised by others. Nevertheless, priorities were not determined in quite the same way in 1903 as they would be in a relatively few years time when a new generation of excavators, many of them Americans, would focus greater effort on the recording of fragmentary material previously considered to be of little interest. Howard Carter with his touch of Petrie training was more aware than most of his contemporaries excavating in Egypt that small and damaged objects had their own stories to tell. So in the final publication of the tomb of Tuthmosis IV, which was written principally by Carter and Newberry and lavishly financed by Theodore Davis, a fair amount of space was devoted to the so-called secondary finds.[51] But most attention was given to the very special chariot body with its leather covering embossed with scenes of the king engaged in war-like activities – scenes which were copied exquisitely by Carter in his confident yet sensitive line.

To open up one royal tomb would now be thought quite sufficient for one season, but for Carter in 1903 Tuthmosis IV was just the beginning. It was followed by the investigation of another smaller tomb in the same side valley, not far from the entrance to the known tomb of Ramesses-Mentuhirkhopshef, a son of Ramesses IX of the Twentieth Dynasty. Here again the discovery was disappointing, and Carter's summary report must reflect his conclusion that time should not be wasted on it.[52] So after making a rather perfunctory record of its contents, and removing one or two objects, he closed the tomb again. It was reopened in 1906 by Edward Ayrton, at that time Theodore Davis's executive archaeologist, who apparently removed a mummy in a coffin before closing it once more. It remained closed, and indeed lost, until 1989 when it was once more investigated by Dr Donald Ryan as part of a campaign to re-examine a

51 See n. 48 above.
52 In *A.S.A.E.* 4 (1903), p. 176.

group of small neglected tombs in the Valley of the Kings. What may have seemed unimportant in 1903 can achieve much greater archaeological significance when the techniques of nearly one hundred years later are applied.[53]

There was yet more to be done. A little way to the north of tomb 19, at the head of the side valley and tucked under the cliff, was the entrance to tomb 20 which had been noted and planned, in so far as it could be entered, in the early nineteenth century. It might have been thought an unpromising prospect, but again Carter, by careful examination, sharpened anticipation of an interesting result by the discovery of two foundation deposits – '(as in the case of Thothmes IV)', as he put it – in front of the tomb-entrance, containing objects inscribed for Queen Hatshepsut;[54] earlier in the season he had found nearby an alabaster saucer and a scarab carrying the queen's name. He was convinced, and wrote to his old chief Naville:

> If you look at the map, you will find that Tomb No. 20 is exactly central with the axis of D. E. B. [Deir el-Bahri]. I have opened the passage and now cleared 170 metres down now working in the Tafl [shale] strata and still no signs of the Tomb chamber, the plan being similar to the rest, only elongated and very rough owing to the bad quality of the rock; the heat is awful and work very slow and cannot continue until I get tubes and fans for air. . . .
>
> I do not hope for an untouched tomb and fear rain water will be a great enemy, but hope for the best. As I shall not continue until next October, it would be awfully nice if you would come and assist in the opening, which I expect will be some time in November. . . .
> I shall not touch anything by myself, or until after somebody has seen it. Of course Maspero will be there.

Predictions are usually wrong in archaeology. When work was resumed in mid-October 1903, progress was pitifully slow. The 'rubbish', as Carter called the blocking material, mostly valley debris, was packed hard by successive floods of rain water. Pickaxes were needed, and in some places it was difficult to distinguish between virgin rock and 'rubbish'. It was scarcely excavation, although sharp eyes were always required to spot the occasional fragments of funerary equipment in the tomb corridors and rooms as the debris was quarried away. Every yard had to be fought for, and the work extended well beyond Christmas and into the New Year. Mrs Andrews reports a visit to the tomb by Theodore Davis on 12 Febru-

53 A useful general account by Dr D. Ryan, 'Who is buried in KV 60?', in *K.M.T.* 1 (Spring 1990), pp. 34ff.
54 So he states in a letter of 2 May 1903 to Naville, Geneva MS. 2542, 79ff. Subsequently, in the final publication, T. Davis, E. Naville and H. Carter, *The Tomb of Hâtshopsîtû* (London, 1906), Carter mentions only 'a foundation deposit' (p. 77). Could 'a deposit' comprise two pits?

ary.[55] At last the entrance to the burial chamber had been reached. Carter and Newberry went in to look beyond the blocking; Newberry could not stand the foul air and retreated 'looking very ill'. Carter made two attempts to investigate and was able to identify a large chamber with rooms opening out of it. 'When Carter emerged from the tomb, he was a horrid object – dripping and wet from the heat, with a black dust over his face and hands – he was very sick too, and had to lie down for sometime.' Final clearance of the burial chamber came on 10 March, and the tomb was 'completed' by the end of the same month.

In spite of the effort and the miserable conditions of work, Carter found time to write a long and informative letter to Lady Amherst on 18 March:[56]

> I fear the paper reports are incorrect as regards it being found intact; contrariwise it is very much plundered and it only contains the Queen's sarcophagus, canopic box, and the sarcophagus of her father Thothmes I. Beside them, among the rubbish many fragments of broken stone vases were found bearing the Queen's names, some of her father, Thothmes II, and Ahmes-Nefertari.

After a very full description of the tomb and of the difficulties of the work, he sums up the discovery:

> I think we have obtained from the sundry inscriptions on the sarcophagi and broken fragments of vases a good [harvest] of historical interest and it is in that way, notwithstanding the discovery itself, that we have been fully repaid.

This assessment of the excavation, which had taken 15 months over all, may appear to be making the best of a disappointing outcome. But Carter would now surely be judged to have assessed correctly. He had found what had to be found; he observed what was to be seen, although not with the precision expected in excavation today; he then published with his associates what had been found, illustrating the most important objects – the fine sarcophagi and the canopic chest in particular – and what he considered to be the best and most informative of the fragments. He offered some interpretation of the tomb: that it was excavated for Queen Hatshepsut, to be used by her and for the burial of her father, King Tuthmosis I, transferred from his original tomb (no. 38) elsewhere in the Valley. This interpretation has been challenged in recent years with good reason,[57] and an alternative, which seems to fit the archaeological facts more reasonably, postulates the cutting of the tomb originally for Tuthmosis I, later extended by Hatshepsut with the intention of making it her tomb also; she was not, however,

55 Diary entry for 12 February; transcript for 1904, p. 24.
56 The Amherst Letters; T. J. Eva Egyptian Collection.
57 See J. Romer; in *J.E.A.* 60 (1974), pp. 119ff.; also C. N. Reeves, *Valley of the Kings*, p. 13, for a useful summary of the arguments.

buried there and subsequently, possibly in the reign of Tuthmosis III, the body of Tuthmosis I with some funerary equipment was moved back to tomb no. 38. It is to Carter's credit that his records of the excavation, published and unpublished, allow significant reinterpretation.

From statements made by Maspero, mentioned earlier,[58] it would appear that in the spring of 1904 Carter still expected to spend at least one more winter season in the southern inspectorate. His projected move to the north was ultimately not to be significantly delayed, and indeed, again according to Maspero, he decided in June to make the move in the autumn of that year. There seems to have been no special reason to prompt this apparent change of plan. He remained on good terms with Theodore Davis, and the maintaining of the latter's support for work in the Valley of the Kings should have offered Carter the prospect of the continuation of his own preferred activity. Yet, strangely, in his letter to Lady Amherst on 18 March he asks:[59] 'I wonder if Lord Amherst would like me to look for the tomb of Amenhotep I; this I spoke about when in England. If so I can do it this summer before I leave for Lower Egypt.' He had, therefore, known as early as March of his move from Thebes. The search for the new royal tomb would be a kind of last Theban fling. It is also fascinating to discover that he had already in 1904 developed a wish to find that particular tomb. It was to become quite an obsession, and would occupy his attention a few years later when he had left the Antiquities Service; and eventually in 1914 he was apparently successful in his search.[60] This letter to Lady Amherst provides the first indication of his interest, predated as he says by talks with Lord Amherst in 1903. The original stimulation may even have come from the discovery of the funerary chapels of Amenophis (Amenhotep) I and his queen Ahmose Nefertari in 1896 and 1898 by Spiegelberg and Newberry. There is, however, no more than a suggestion in the letter that Carter knew where to look. But he would have been conducting the search as Chief Inspector, with Amherst funding any serious work. Progress was disappointing; a further letter to Lady Amherst on 11 June contained no encouraging news; another on 23 July was equally unpromising. Here he outlines his winding-up programme:

> tours of inspection in Upper Egypt until the 15 of August, then to Cairo for Lower Egypt work until the 15th September, then back again until the end of October when Maspero returns and Quibell (who is now in England) and change over. If possible I hope to find Amenhotep I tomb some time in October, or rather what I should like to do. Directly any real and certain promises show I shall request

58 P. 79 above.
59 This and the following letter in The Amherst Letters; T. J. Eva Egyptian Collection.
60 See p. 167 below.

£ – s – d. At present I have been making the investigations on economies.

A letter from Cairo to one of the Miss Amhersts on 2 December 1904 marks the end of the search, at least for the time being: 'In the Amenhotep I tomb I was quite unsuccessful as far as I got but I shall stick to it when next I go there.'

Howard Carter's five years as Chief Inspector at Luxor wound down quietly to the end. Much had happened, much had been achieved. He had lived in many ways a strange, almost unnatural, life, tied to his post with only two summer leaves to England (in 1901 and 1903). His year swung from a winter of feverish activity, professional and social, to a summer of isolation, discomfort and the duties of inspection. For most of his time at Thebes he lived in a house of the Antiquities Service at Medinet Habu. The intention was to provide a properly designed Inspectorate – house and offices – between Karnak and Luxor on the eastern bank of the Nile, but lack of funds delayed its completion until after Carter had moved to Cairo. The Medinet Habu house was apparently reasonably spacious and had a good verandah with an arcade, and a large enclosure in the front. Carter embellished it with a garden and 'peopled' it with unusual tame animals – almost a free-range menagerie of the kind he had known in his childhood at Rich Terrace. All this was to be expected from one of whom Mrs Andrews said:[61] 'His taste for all natural things is so charming to me'; and again: 'We admired the little house, and the pretty garden within the enclosing walls. There was a real avenue of scent [i.e. *sunt* = acacia] trees.' Apart from his horse Sultan, whom it seems found the tomb of Mentuhotpe II for his master, he had a series of pets, many of which fatefully suffered sad ends. A pair of young gazelles was taken in not long after he arrived at Medinet Habu; they were killed in some tragic way. To an enquiry from his mother he answered: 'No my Dear Mater, all that remains of my poor Gazelles are 2 tomb stones on a cairn in the dessert [*sic*]. The story being too sad to repeat.' Later came his young donkey San Toy: 'He used to go through the house looking for Carter, and when he found him he would bray with delight.' Poor San Toy! In the summer of 1902 he was bitten in the mouth by a cobra and died in three hours. He was not the last of Carter's pets to meet a violent death.

As ever, birds, their observation and painting, helped him to survive in the long hot summer months at Thebes. In one of his late sketches, 'Summer Life at Thebes, and the tale of the "Rat and the Snake" ', which is concerned principally with his experiences of Arab story-telling in the villages of the Theban necropolis, he writes briefly of the life he led during these summer months. There was the work of inspection to be done during

61 Diary entry for 11 February; transcript for 1900, p. 100.

the day, but the evenings could be long and trying.[62] He describes how, during the time of the inundation of the Nile, when the flood-waters covered the cultivated fields and approached close to his house, he would in the evening take a small boat out on the shallow basins between the desert and the main stream of the Nile and watch birds, particularly the pelicans. He did not read much. In one version of his autobiographical sketch he admits:[63] 'I work extremely hard when it pleases me, and when it does not, I can be extremely idle. Although I am a lover of books, my regret is that I never read sufficiently.' His natural bent was to things practical; he was a good doer, but not much of a student or writer, particularly at this early stage in his career. He had in fact a good natural talent for expressing himself, and his published material of the time – official reports on excavations – were clearly written and just as adequate in scholarly terms as those written by many of his contemporaries. No doubt these reports had been subjected to some form of editing by friends like Newberry. His private letters reveal serious weaknesses of spelling, grammar and syntax, confirming all that he had said about his inadequate education. Even so, these letters are not illiterate; they have considerable strengths of expression, and seem to reproduce the staccato style of utterance which people later mentioned in talking about his way of speaking. It must be supposed that he was very conscious of his inadequacies of education, for in later life he overcame those that could easily be corrected by the following of good exemplars and by diligent application. He had much help in the preparing of the three volumes of his popular work on Tutankhamun's tomb; but in his late sketches, already much mentioned and quoted, there are no signs of 'editing' by literary friends; he writes fluently and colourfully, even cultivating a grand style with occasional overblown forms of expression.

For all his attachment to the Theban area, and in spite of the plentiful evidence from his later career and life that it was in Thebes that he felt most at home, he did not care for the loneliness and discomfort of the summer months:[64]

> This last month has been most trying in Upper Egypt and I am glad that Maspero has kindly let me come down [to Cairo] for a time. The hermit's life is perhaps even more trying than the heat – during the summer one seldom sees anybody up there [27 May 1902].

Before going on leave:

> This last two years of Upper Egypt has pulled one down and am on the sick list so shall be glad to get away [2 May 1903].

62 Sketch V in G.I. Carter Notebook 16, pp. 114ff. It includes tales told to him over local coffee-hearths; they are somewhat 'literary' and contrived.
63 With John Carter; possibly earlier than that of G.I. Carter Notebook 15.
64 Quotations from letters to Naville, Geneva MS. 2542, 41f., 85, 88.

And again, just before he left for Lower Egypt:

> Being here alone I found too trying and I am suffering from the same complaint as you were when here – cannot sleep at night. I went over to Luxor for a short time but only to return and find the same thing. Thank goodness I am leaving for the North this next Autumn. . . . Egypt in the Winter has its charms, but Egypt in the Summer has its —— [16 May 1904].

Luxor was dead in the summer; the visitors were gone; the hotels closed; the *dahabiyas* were in the Cairo dockyards being overhauled. He missed the lively social activity of the season, the changing company as boats came and went, luncheon parties, dinner parties, even tea parties, nights spent comfortably 'on board' in well appointed cabins. The concomitant duties of conducting official visitors around the principal monuments brought him into contact with important and influential people – the Crown Prince of Siam (February 1902), Princess Henry of Battenberg and Prince Alexander (January 1904), Mr and Mrs Joseph Chamberlain (February 1904).[65] In March 1904 he paid his first visit to the newly discovered tomb of Nefertari, conducting Rider Haggard who was in Egypt collecting information for a series of articles in the *Daily Mail*.[66] Such were only some of the more weighty interruptions to his busy life of inspections and excavations. The Davis party, Professor Sayce, the Cecils, Mond, Robb Tytus, all provided entertainment and diversion, and exacted their toll of special visits and particular attentions. All in all it was a bad discipline for regular work, destructive of concentration, and seductive from a social point of view. On the other hand, it helped Carter to fit more easily into the kinds of society for which he had not been equipped by station or training; it taught him gentle manners and the importance of hospitality, not insignificant lessons in the reign of King Edward VII. In spite of the many distractions he yet completed much notable work during his five years in the southern inspectorate, and he could go north well satisfied with his achievements so far. As Maspero's 'good fellow' (*bon garçon*) he had justified his appointment and not disappointed his chief.

---

65 Mrs Andrew's diary charts the visits of the famous to Luxor. In addition every day had its entertainments, and Carter was often included.
66 The articles were published on 23 April, 30 April, 7 May, 21 May, 4 June, 22 July. That of 4 June, 'The Debris of Majesty' describes the visit. I am grateful to Miss Jean Kennedy, Norfolk County Archivist, for information about the Haggard material in the Norfolk Record Office in Norwich, and to John Larson for first apprising me of the *Daily Mail* articles.

5

THE SAQQARA AFFAIR

In the autumn of 1904 Howard Carter changed places with J. E. Quibell, and became Chief Inspector for Lower Egypt. He exchanged Luxor for Cairo, moving very distinctly from the known to the unknown. His career in Egypt had, up to this point, been spent almost wholly in the Theban area and he had established for himself a position in which his experience not only of this region but also of the inhabitants of the principal towns and ancient sites made him exceptionally well equipped to perform a Chief Inspector's function. He knew the foreign excavators and patrons of excavations who came regularly to this most tempting (at that time) of ancient sites; he knew the antiquities dealers in Luxor, who handled the material filtering from the licit and illicit excavations in Eastern and Western Thebes, and in the rich sites north and south of Luxor; he knew the regular wealthy visitors who wintered in their *dahabiyas* on the Nile, or in the Luxor Hotel, to whom he sold his water-colours; he knew, above all, the dwellers in the Theban Necropolis. These last, from whom the Antiquities Service had regularly drawn its local officials, were the guardians of the tombs in more senses than one; they preserved the intimate knowledge of the ancient places, known and unknown to the Antiquities Service, derived from generations of systematic grubbing about; they were truly the descendants of the ancient Egyptians of Western Thebes who looked after the sacred places for public and private reasons. Carter had increasingly hob-nobbed with them, feeling perhaps more at ease in their company than in that of the grand and the wealthy to whom his instincts for advancement and security irresistibly drew him. In the manner of the times, which in a sense was the manner of the British land-owner to his tenant, Carter could play the part of patron to client, of *bey* to *fellah*, to act *de haut en bas*, but without the feeling of strict dependence which could so easily have turned a kind of intimacy into cringing subservience. He had used his local contacts with some, though not complete, success in trying to solve the mystery of the despoliation of the tomb of King Amenophis II; information about potentially important discoveries was often, but surely not regularly, filtered to him; occasionally inhabitants of Qurna applied officially for permission to excavate where previously they might simply have dug without permission.[1] Howard Carter was clearly 'at home' in Western Thebes, and it may even have been the case that his comfortable intimacy with his Egyptian neighbours contributed to his transference to Lower Egypt. It is certain, however, that the new organization of the Antiquities Service instituted by Maspero needed periodic adjustments, and the switching of Carter and Quibell, together with the establishment of a new chief-inspectorate in Middle Egypt under Lefebvre, represented one stage in the process. Further changes in the refining of responsibility were to come again in the spring of 1905, and again Carter was to be substantially affected. For the moment it looked as if he quite welcomed the change, hinting as much in a letter to Lord Amherst, written from Cairo on 2 December 1904:[2] 'I am now down in Cairo for good in possession of the Lower Egyptian inspectorate. It is a nice change though perhaps not so interesting, but after 11 years of Luxor one can get a little tired and slack.'

Carter's 'for good' was scarcely well expressed, for the move, so full of expectation, turned sour within a few weeks, and one year later he had left the Antiquities Service, this time certainly 'for good', initially in the temporal sense and ultimately in terms of his own career. What happened at Saqqara on 8 January 1905 has been seriously misrepresented both in the facts and in the consequences in later accounts. The generally accepted belief has been that the events of that day led to Carter's resignation, even dismissal, from the Antiquities Service. Percy Newberry, in many ways Carter's oldest and most sympathetically inclined friend and colleague throughout his career, could write in his obituary notice in the *Journal of Egyptian Archaeology*:[3] 'In 1903 Carter was transferred to the Inspectorate of Lower and Middle Egypt and made his headquarters at Sakkarah. Soon after his arrival there an incident occurred which led to his resigning the post that he held under the Egyptian Government.'

The most dramatic account of the incident, reported with characteristic lack of moderation, was given by Sir Flinders Petrie in his memories of an exceptionally long career in the field, scarcely recollected in tranquillity. Writing of the season 1904–5, he speaks of the little expedition at Saqqara led by his wife:[4]

One Sunday some drunken Frenchmen tried to force their way into her huts, and were stoutly resisted by the cook boy. They went on to the official house and began to smash furniture and fight the native

1 See, for example, his reports in *A.S.A.E.* 1 (1900), p. 191; 2 (1901), p. 144; 4 (1903), pp. 47, 177.
2 The Amherst Letters; T. J. Eva Egyptian Collection.
3 *J.E.A.* 25 (1939), p. 68.
4 W. M. F. Petrie, *Seventy Years in Archaeology* (London, 1931), p. 192.

guards. Carter, then inspector, was fetched, and he very rightly allowed the guards to defend themselves till the police could come.

The indignity of letting a native resist a Frenchman weighed more than the indignity of being drunk and disorderly, in the eyes of the French Consul, who demanded an apology from Carter. With proper self-respect, Carter refused to apologize for doing his obvious duty. For this he was, on demand of the French, dismissed from the Service. This was perhaps the dirtiest act of the subservience to French arrogance.

There is more than a germ of truth in Petrie's account of what happened on the Saqqara plateau, but his glosses and conclusions were wildly wrong. What may, however, be said of these inaccurate reports is that they conflate into a single incident the events of Carter's career for almost the whole of 1905 with their eventual consequences. Disastrous as the whole sequence must have seemed to Carter's friends at the time, there can be no doubt that in the long run the outcome was very much to his advantage.

The events of that fateful day in early 1905 were reported officially to Maspero by Carter on 10 January:[5]

About 3 p.m. on the 8th of January, 1905 some 15 visitors, whom I believe to be French, arrived at the Necropolis of Saqqara in a rowdy condition, some of them going to Mrs. Petrie's camp and behaving in an offensive manner. They eventually came to the Service's rest-house (known as Mariette Pasha's House) where they stayed for an hour or so talking in a loud manner and drinking. They afterwards stated a wish to visit the monuments. Upon this the ticket-Inspector Es-Sayid Effendi Mohammed informed them that they must take tickets and he requested the necessary fees. It was not until after some trouble that he was able to collect the money for 11 tickets, the remaining persons refusing to take tickets. The whole party then went to the 'Serapeum' accompanied by a gaffir [guard], who at the entrance of the monument requested to see who had tickets and who had not, knowing that some of the party had not obtained tickets and thus had no right to enter. The party would not wait for this inspection, but rushed the door and forced it open breaking one of the side catches which held the pad-lock. Upon their finding, when they entered, themselves in darkness they returned and demanded candles from the gaffir. The gaffir explained to them that he had not any candles nor did the Service supply visitors with candles. The party then roughly handled the gaffir and demanded their money

5 Two copies in Carter's handwriting are contained in a transcript of materials relevant to the Saqqara affair in the Griffith Institute: G.I. Carter Papers V, 148. There are minor variations between the two copies; in the version given here, what seems to be the better reading has been taken when necessary.

back. The gaffir called for assistance, to which the Inspector Es-Sayid Effendi Mohammed came, and he was treated in even a rougher manner; his tarboush was knocked off his head and trampled upon. Reis Khalifa was called for and was also treated in a similar way. Reis Khalifa, on hearing from the gaffirs that one of the party had taken the pad-lock off the door, demanded it to be given up; this was done after some difficulty. The party still continuing to give trouble, he returned with them to the house, where they entered with Es-Sayid Effendi Mohammed and the gaffirs, and came at once to fetch me.

I was at that time some distance away, near the edge of the desert, with Mr. Weigall and the Misses Kingsford and Hansard;[6] and upon hearing from Reis Khalifa of what had occurred I immediately returned with him to the house.

During the meantime the party had turned out the gaffirs from the house and barricaded the doors and attempted to get the money from Es-Sayid Effendi Mohammed, the ticket Inspector, by force.

I found the East Door of the house to be closed, the gaffirs outside, and had some difficulty in entering. Here I found the whole party in an excited state, and on finding one of them knew English I requested him to give an explaination [sic].[7] He and all of them spoke to me in an exceedingly rough way and I was unable to get from them a proper explaination. I then requested the above Inspector to explain to me what had occurred, and he told me how they had entered the 'Serapeum' by force and of their general behaviour. I then explained to them that they had no right to take such steps or touch the men and that they had no right to be in the house, it being private property, and that they must leave it at once. This they refused to do. I told them that if they did not go out steps would have to be taken to remove them and at the same time I requested their names and addresses. They refused to do both and became more offensive. On my again warning them, and on my telling the gaffirs that the party must go out,[8] one of the party immediately without any reason struck a gaffir with his fist in the face and knocked him down in a savage manner,[9] and on my interfering the same man raised his hand and threatened to strike me. I arrested his striking arm and warned him. The number of gaffirs, then there, being inadequate to remove these people, I commanded Reis Khalifa to send for more and on their entering by the second

6 The two ladies were in Mrs Petrie's party. Arthur Weigall would shortly obtain an appointment as Chief Inspector in the Antiquities Service.
7 Carter has added in pencil in the margin 'Mons Hirsh'.
8 Var. 'must be turned out.'
9 A pencil note identifies him as 'Jouveau'.

door (south door) the whole of the party immediately attacked them with their sticks and chairs belonging to the Service. Seeing that the gaffirs were being very badly knocked about I at once gave them the order to defend themselves and drive the people out. In the affray some of the party were hit, one of them being knocked down. The party fled leaving the injured man which I attended to and during the meantime one of the party returned. From outside stones were hurled at us.

I demanded the names from these two last men – this they gave me on a visiting card – their names given were: – Georges Fabre and Ferdinand Estienne. On their request I gave them my name and official capacity. They left the house threatening prosecution. I sent for the ombdeh [head-man, 'mayor'] of Saqqara and requested the ombdeh of Abou-zeer [Abusir], who was there, to inform the police at once of what had happened and request them to take the necessary steps against these people. The ombdeh of Saqqara came as soon as possible and made a small enquiry and informed the mariquis of Ayat of the same.

Some of the gaffirs were badly hurt. Chairs of the Service broken by the party. Strict instructions were given to the gaffirs not to leave the house while the party was outside – which order was carried out by them and I wish to commend the gaffirs on their behaviour during the whole affray.

Upon the arrival of the police a complete enquiry and procès verbal was made, consisting of some 35 sheets of foolscap.

I beg to request that legal steps should be taken against these people for assaulting the gaffirs, for raising a hand with intent to attack me, and for damaging Government property.

This document, signed and dated by Howard Carter is completed by a note: 'Some of these people understood and spoke Arabic.'

From the other side, Monsieur Jouveau, Chief Book-keeper of the Cairo Gas Company, had already submitted his account of the incident to Maspero, dating it on 9 January 1905.[10] He reports that their party of 14, including 2 ladies and 2 children, arrived at Saqqara and took tickets to visit the Serapeum. Having no candles to see the monument, they asked for their money back, and they were told that the matter would be referred to Carter. In the meanwhile, the dispute got worse and a score of 'beduin' collected in Mariette's House. Carter arrived with about 15 more, armed with sticks (nabouts). He refused their claim for repayment and when they said they would not go without repayment he ordered his subordinate in English 'to drive away these dirty French and to strike us'. The order was repeated in Arabic and a general scuffle began in which about 40 indi-

10 G.I. Carter Papers V, 108. See Appendix I for the full French text.

viduals set upon 7 Frenchmen, the remainder protecting its women and children. Jouveau reports that he was struck on the head with a stone and fell 'bathed in my blood'; that Georges Fabre fell with his forehead cut open by a *nabout*; that M. Baudry fell from a *nabout* blow on his back and the rest were more or less bruised.

With difficulty the party got back to Badrashein, made a report at the police station, returned to Cairo, reported again at the police station at the railway station, and was taken to the Governorate where medical attention was first given.

Jouveau then requested Maspero 'to draw the conclusion of such an act ordered by an English official.'

Maspero was in Nubia on his annual tour of inspection at the time, and Jouveau's letter was received by his deputy, Émile Brugsch, who at once wrote to Carter, sending a copy and requesting a report. Carter's report, given above, was the result of this request.[11] It is surprising that he had not sent his account to Maspero on the day following the incident, but it may be assumed that he felt no urgent necessity to do so as he knew that Maspero was away and that Brugsch would have been able to take no more than formal action. What he did do was to send a telegram to the Earl of Cromer, on the evening of the 8th, announcing briefly what had happened:[12]

> My Lord I am exceedingly sorry to inform you that a bad affray has occurred today here Mariette's House Saqqara 5pm. with 15 French tourists who were here in a drunken state. The cause of the affray was started by their rough handling both my inspector and gaffirs. As both sides have been cut and knocked about I feel it my duty to inform your Lordship immediately and will report the matter to you personally tomorrow morning.

The possible repercussions from the event were surely evident to Carter, and he was well aware that the opposing party would lose little time in making their own official complaint. A rare personal comment on Carter's reaction is given by Ronald Storrs, recently arrived in Cairo as a junior official in Finance.[13] He was initially befriended by Ernest Richmond, who was himself a junior official, but of a little greater seniority than Storrs; he invited the latter to share the flat which he occupied with Howard Carter. 'One evening', Storrs reports,[14] 'Carter came in, unharassed but

11 G.I. Carter Papers V, 109 includes Brugsch's letter to Carter and Carter's covering letter accompanying his report; both dated 10 January.
12 G.I. Carter Papers V, 107.
13 Storrs had recently joined the Egyptian civil service. He later became Oriental Secretary in the Residency and, later again, Governor of Jerusalem. He became a notable oriental specialist.
14 Sir Ronald Storrs, *Orientations* (London, 1937), pp. 23f. I am indebted to John Larson for bringing this passage to my attention.

rather fierce,' telling them of the afternoon's drama at Saqqara. Storrs states, rather anticipating events, that 'Carter was summoned by Lord Cromer for the morrow and was of the opinion (which we shared) that he was For It.' Storrs's description of what subsequently happened between Cromer and Carter is somewhat telescoped, and he, like others in later recollection, attributed Carter's departure from the Service to his recalcitrance. He further points out the ultimate happy consequence of this departure, likening Carter's fate to that of Klindor in Corneille's *Illusion: 'de son bannissement il tire son bonheur.'*

All this, however, is substantially to look beyond the immediate outcome of events. As it turned out Carter was unable to see Lord Cromer on 9 January because of the police enquiry instituted at Saqqara; but he saw him on the following day. Carter noted, in the dossier he compiled on the affair, that after hearing his account of what happened, Cromer instructed him 'to tell Monsieur Brugsch that we must put ourselves in communication with Rocca-Serra of the Contentieux de l'Etat.'[15] The two went to see Rocca-Serra on the next day, and they were instructed to write a letter to the Giza *mudiriya* (administrative district) drawing the attention of the *mudir* (administrative head) to the report made by Carter to the Giza police about the incident, requesting the *mudir* to forward this report to the French Consulate in Cairo so that Carter's demand for damages for injuries and the destruction of government property could be followed up.[16]

Meanwhile news of the affair had become known and had been taken up by the foreign-language newspapers in Cairo. The French participants made much of the scandalous nature of their treatment, and the tone of their version of events is sufficiently conveyed by the report published in the French-language *L'Égypte* on 12 January. This report follows up a notice of the incident published the day before, and it purports to be that of one of the party involved in the events. After outlining the preliminary events of arrival at Saqqara, the buying of tickets, the lack of candles and the request for the return of the ticket-money, the correspondent speaks of the referring of the matter by the chief *ghaffir* to Howard Carter 'who was encamped not far from the spot'. The French party then withdrew from the Serapeum to Mariette's House where they found armed 'beduin'. When Carter arrived, 'one of the party addressed the Inspector in English asking whether there was any reason why the money should not be refunded, and it is stated that the Inspector replied very discourteously by a refusal, and declined to give any explanation.' The party, therefore, remained on the terrace of the house until they obtained satisfaction, 'whereupon the Inspector immediately gave orders to his subordinate in English to eject them. The order was repeated in Arabic to the Bedouins, who proceeded to attack the party with their nabouts and commenced throwing stones.' A

15 The legal department of the State.
16 G.I. Carter Papers V, 111; the text is in French.

bloody fracas followed in which large stones were thrown. 'Finally the wounded were picked up from the terrace and the whole party with great difficulty regained Bedrachein.'

A more sober, not so say sanctimonious, line was taken in the English-language *Egyptian Gazette* on 12 January:[17]

> In regard to the stories about the attack on some tourists by Bedouins at Sakhara which have been appearing in the Cairo newspapers, we hear on high authority that there is a good deal to be said on the other side. An official enquiry is about to be held, and we will refrain from commenting on the affair as it is *sub-judice*. Some of our contemporaries seem to us to have been a little too hasty in assuming that the fault was entirely on one side.

The wrangle in the newspapers was characteristic of the attitudes of the French and British communities towards each other in Egypt at that time. The French resented the administrative near-monopoly exercised by the British in the running of the country; the British took exception to the cultural superiority of the French and the fact that French was the *lingua franca* of the administration and of cultured society. The tensions were largely confined to the ranks of junior officials and to members of the commercial sector, and they welled up from time to time when some apparent insult was suffered by one or other of the two dominant foreign communities. Suspicions of intentions were deep-seated at all levels of society and resentment came to the surface even among senior officials and others who should have known better how to control long-established antipathies. The words used later by Sir Flinders Petrie about 'French arrogance' were sadly all too representative of British prejudices; the tone of Monsieur Jouveau's report to Maspero embodies the contrary French attitude – describing Carter as 'Inspecteur en chef (Anglais)' and 'un fonctionnaire Anglais'. In both cases the implication is clear: how can one expect good treatment from someone from the 'other' community?

Ronald Storrs noted in his brief account of the affair that Monsieur de la Boulinière, the French Consul-General, with whom the complaint of the French party had been lodged 'had no particular sympathy with the complainants, but feared lest reports in the local gutter-press might reach Paris; the Entente Cordiale was hardly a year old, and Lord Cromer must give him some satisfaction.'[18]

Here then were the makings of a first-class inter-community row, one that might easily have been forestalled had a less stubborn person been

17 In the *Egyptian Gazette* of 30 January, p. 3, it is noted that three cases were pending: one lodged by the French against Carter at the British Consulate; one by Carter at the French Consulate; one by the French against the *ghaffir* in the Native Tribunals. To simplify matters a commission had been appointed to look into the affair: 'This solution seems an extremely practical one.'

18 Storrs, *Orientations*, p. 24.

in charge at Saqqara, one that might still be hushed up or at least suppressed if the various involved parties were to behave reasonably and, as some would have said, in a gentlemanly manner. For Carter the issue was quite clear, and he was convinced that his actions would be vindicated. Even so, in view of the passions generated, the supposed insults suffered on both sides, the background of racial animosities, and the involvement of the native Egyptian guards, the outcome of the affair was by no means assured.

As a result of the various steps taken on the simple administrative level, but undoubtedly also through unrecorded contacts between the office of the High Commissioner, the French Consul-General, and the legal authorities, a commission was set up to investigate the incident. Émile Brugsch informed Carter of the details in a letter of 23 January.[19] It was to consist of Monsieur de Hulst, counsellor at the Native Court of Appeal, the Advocate-General of the Native Tribunals,[20] and Monsieur Molteni, deputy at the State Legal Department, and was to meet on the 25 January to hear the depositions of the witnesses on the side of the Antiquities Service. Brugsch instructed Carter to appear on that day at 9.00 a.m. at the Native Court of Appeal, together with members of his staff at Saqqara, including Reis Khalifa Roubi and six *ghaffirs*.

No extended account of the meeting of the commission of enquiry has been found, but notes made by Carter at the time indicate that it extended into a second day and that at least five members of the French party were also examined.[21] It closed at.6.00 p.m. on 26 January. Writing to Maspero on 31 January, Carter said of the enquiry:[22] 'Apparently they were not to make any decision but only sift evidence. I was not at all pleased at the general atmosphere, though I feel sure that they thought I was in the right. I believe their report is to go to the Minister of Foreign Affairs.' From a friendly note of enquiry from Sir William Garstin, Carter notes the same reaction on his part. It may be thought that nothing but a standing ovation by the members of the commission of enquiry would fully have satisfied Carter, indicating the recognition that he had not only been in the right at Saqqara on that fateful Sunday afternoon, but had acted with complete propriety. Although it subsequently emerged that the commission found '*in my favour without doubt*', the triumph was more apparent than actual.

It was most unfortunate that Maspero was in the south throughout the whole of January; his friendly advice, delivered face to face, would surely have moderated Carter's obstinacy and perhaps led him to accept a course of action which he ultimately rejected. The matter had indeed ruffled the

19 G.I. Carter Papers V, 116.
20 Identified elsewhere as Safwat Bey.
21 G.I. Carter Papers V, 148, p. 27.
22 G.I. Carter Papers V, 120.

feathers of Cairo society and sent waves of embarrassed concern through government and diplomatic circles. It was even thought necessary to send the Inspector of the Interior, Major Elgood, to Saqqara on 23 January, two days after the commission met, in order presumably to make a separate examination of Egyptian witnesses on the spot.[23] No channel of enquiry was being neglected. Reis Khalifa Roubi had informed Carter of this visit and the latter was told subsequently by Elgood that he had found fresh evidence from the donkey boys of the French party. The nature of this evidence is not specified; the implication of Carter's note, however, is that it was to the advantage of his case, possibly that the Frenchmen on their arrival at Saqqara were appropriately influenced by the picnic luncheon they had enjoyed in the palm-groves of Mit Rahina, the site of the ancient city of Memphis. On this point it is worth noting that in the French report in *L'Égypte* on 12 January it is stated: 'Les excursionnistes emportaient dans des paniers des provisions de bouche et 12 bouteilles de vin rouge, contenant trois quarts de litre chacune. Sur ces 12 bouteilles, quatre furent rapportées au Caire. . . . A 11h. 30 tous les excursionnistes se trouvèrent réunis à la statue de Ramsès [at Mit Rahina], où ils déjeunèrent joyeusement.'

It says much for postal and other communications in Egypt and Nubia at this time that Maspero was able to follow events not only in the newspapers but also by regular correspondence. Already on 14 January he wrote from Kalabsha noting the fuss in the Arabic newspapers and requesting Carter's report so that he could answer any complaint.[24] He had unerringly estimated the potential bother that might be generated. After receiving the reports of both sides he again wrote to Carter on 19 January from Debod in Nubia: 'I think your case is good: there would be nothing to say against us, and the issue would be certainly in our favour, if your men had not used their nabouts. That is the bad part of the business: policemen may be beaten, they are not allowed to beat except under extremities.' At Esna on 30 January he again writes to Carter asking how the business progresses. He reports correspondence with Sir William Garstin and Monsieur de la Boulinière, noting that the latter will meet him in a few days at Luxor; perhaps something can be arranged. He urges Carter to keep him informed of developments so that 'I may not be taken aback in my conversation with him by something which would be new to me.'

Carter, sadly, had formed his own conclusion, and his adamantine nature, highly tempered by the isolation in which he found himself, stiffened his resolve to yield not an inch in what he saw as the right and proper course of action. It may be supposed that he was offered much friendly advice both by sympathetic officials, even at the highest level, and

23 G.I. Carter Papers V, 148, p. 24.
24 Extracts from Maspero's letters are transcribed in G.I. Carter Papers V, 148, p. 25f.

by such friends as he had in Cairo. Later developments were to show that he did not lack for friends who saw the justice of his actions at Saqqara, but who equally saw the wisdom of a little flexibility. The most eloquent appeal for moderation came, perhaps unexpectedly, from Theodore Davis, as will shortly be seen. But Maspero, French as he was, realized as soon as anyone that Carter had made one serious error at Saqqara in giving the order to his men to protect themselves. The matter now may seem ludicrous; it was otherwise in the Egypt of 1905. In this respect Carter was thoroughly out of step with his countrymen and other well wishers. If his attitude had been due wholly to the necessities of natural justice, his subsequent behaviour would surely have been wholly meritorious. Unfortunately, it must be accepted that stubbornness, untempered by pragmatic common sense, drove him to behave utterly without reason. It was an element in his character which exerted itself from time to time throughout his career, most notably in 1924, the year of crisis, when the completion of the excavation, clearance and recording of the tomb of Tutankhamun was seriously jeopardized by his attitude. This earlier manifestation of obstinacy was not forgotten on the later occasion, when of course far more was at stake.

His position is made quite clear in the letter he wrote to Maspero on 31 January announcing the course of the commission of enquiry, already mentioned. He writes from Mena House, the relatively new and splendidly appointed hotel set in spacious grounds and relative isolation just below the pyramid plateau at Giza. Here he had come 'to get rid of a very bad cold I have taken for a second time this month – After so many years in Upper Egypt I have become a hot-house plant and do not stand the Cairo winter well.' All who know Egypt from multiple visits will be acquainted with the Egyptian cold, infinitely various in its forms and symptoms, ranging from nose to throat, to chest, to nose again, and seemingly resistant to all common medicaments. It is not surprising that he took such a jaundiced view of the turn which events had taken. He takes up in his letter Maspero's complaint about *nabouts*:

> You mention in your letter that you do not like the idea of giving the order to defend – Nobody was more disgusted on the matter than myself – But what was one to do in such a disorderly mob, threatened and one's men knocked about?
>
> I fear unless these men are properly punished I shall have to decline any further responsibility for the protection of the Service's property and at the same time send in my resignation owing to the impossibility of taking any further personal risk under such conditions. Might I remind you that my work requires me to be either 1 mile or a hundred in the desert absolutely single handed with the exception of the natives.

Here is the first hint that he might resign if his position were not totally supported and action taken against the French. What the incident reveals is the extraordinary lack of confidence shown by Howard Carter. He had been seriously shaken by the events at Saqqara, although there is no indication that he himself took an active part in the brawl or was in any way hurt. Could his subsequent anger and determination to have exemplary punishment inflicted on the wretched French be due to some weakness in his own behaviour at Mariette's House? That can never be established; but it is strange that after the apparently successful passage of arms and the routing of the French party, he was unable to show some generosity of spirit. Did he perhaps feel that only by taking such a determined line could he confirm his standing with his Egyptian subordinates in the Service? Again it can never be confirmed or refuted. The suspicion must remain.

It probably never occurred to Lord Cromer, to Sir William Garstin, to Monsieur Gaston Maspero, or to anyone else in Cairo at that time that Carter would fail to toe the official line. Maspero began the attempt to get things back on an even keel as soon as he had returned to Cairo on 3 February and seen Garstin. He writes:[25]

> It is agreed with him, and I may say with Lord Cromer, that you are to come with me tomorrow between nine and ten and pay a call on M. de la Boulinière there to express our regrets that the order you gave brought so strong consequences. That will stop the matter which was becoming irritating, and for the rest we will arrange it together.

He further states that Carter should get the *ghaffirs* to withdraw their complaint and indicates that in this matter Carter had behaved irregularly. His suggestion throughout this letter is that by diplomatic fudging the whole affair will blow over:

> I must add that you are not to take as different what we are going to do tomorrow. M. de la Boulinière, whom I have just seen, will be quite friendly to us and it is to be more of a conversation than of a formal meeting. I am going with you to act as an interpreter, at the same time being head of the Department; and I will take my part of the excuses with you.

It is not clear whether the meeting with the French Consul-General ever took place. Carter could not or, more probably, would not see that he was not being asked to apologize but to express regret, and he notes in his transcript of documents that he 'asked that these people should either be punished in some way or be made to apologize to my Director and that

25 G.I. Carter Papers V, 121.

only under these conditions could I make an apology to the French Consul-General.'[26] He would not comprehend the subtlety of what he had actually been asked to do.

There is much evidence that his intransigence greatly upset his colleagues and friends. What had happened, and Carter's refusal to offer an expression of regret for it, had become well known, at least in Egyptological circles. As early as 5 February a telegram from Theodore Davis urged:[27] 'Sacrifice your rights for the benefit of the Government, don't hesitate.' Quibell on 10 February wrote warmly and sensitively: 'I don't think you care for interference . . . you will damage your career if you continue to refuse to do what your friends urge. . . . Trust Sir William Garstin! He has always been a good friend to you.' Arthur Weigall, apparently, found it difficult to offer true commiseration, unless his approach had been face-to-face and not by letter. He had been at Saqqara on the afternoon of the affray, but had not accompanied Carter when he was summoned to Mariette's House. Still he then was with the ladies of Mrs Petrie's camp, who were no doubt badly shaken by their own experiences with the French, and felt in need of some protection until the rowdy party had left the area. Subsequently Weigall took over temporarily at Saqqara, and two short communications to Carter have survived.[28] The first, undated, but certainly written soon after the events, reports: 'The guards here are very nervous – think they are all going to be imprisoned.' A postcard, dated simply Thursday, but post-marked 13-1-05, and therefore written on 12 January, tells Carter of the sick-leave sought by the injured *ghaffirs*: it ends simply: 'Hope things are going well.' Weigall was shortly to replace Quibell as Chief Inspector at Luxor, and from his subsequent behaviour clearly did not find Carter a congenial colleague. Carter in later years did not conceal his distrust of Weigall. The causes of their mutual antipathy were perhaps already germinating as early as 1905.[29]

The one closely argued appeal to Carter's good sense came from Theodore Davis in an answer to a letter possibly sent by Carter in response to Davis's telegram of 5 February. It is unusually long, but is so well argued that it may be quoted in full as a kind of summing up of the whole affair. Davis wrote it on his *dahabiya Bedawin* at Luxor, and it is dated 10 February:[30]

> I duly received your letter and have in sadness and thoughtfulness considered your attitude. You are so entirely wrong, and in danger of a crushing blow. I cannot help laying before you a statement of

---

26 G.I. Carter Papers V, 148, p. 28 verso.
27 For Davis's telegram, G.I. Carter Papers V, 139; Quibell's letter, V, 123.
28 The two Weigall communications are G. I. Carter Papers V, 143 and 146. He rarely dated a letter.
29 See p. 157 below.
30 G.I. Carter Papers V, 124.

your case which you will honestly consider as coming from your friend.

The row at Sakkara was submitted to a Commission and you were held to be justified in your activities even if you used 'a high hand'. *This* ended your connection with the affair except the police prosecution of the men. And as Lord Cromer told you 'it must be purely a police question etc.'

Now comes your trouble! For some cause unknown the French Minister asked the Gov. to desire you (or rather the 'Inspector Genl.') or the Gov. to apologize for the connection the Insp. Genl. had with the Sakkara row.

It seems that the Gov. concluded that whatever might be the rights and wrongs of the affair it would be a wise and friendly thing to do as between the two Governments, particularly as the French Minister stated that he wanted only an expression of regret of the affair, a shake of the hand etc.

Thereupon you were directed or requested to go through the form as above stated. This you refused to do, in spite of *astounding* fatherly advice of M. Maspero and Sir William (I have heard from M. Maspero why you decline but I confine myself to your letter to me).

As per your letter your reasons are, 1st. 'I have no doubt that the instant that I went to the French Embassy the papers would publish at once.' The natural deduction from this, and certainly that of the public would be, that thereby your pride, vanity, or self love would be wounded. Can you for a moment lay yourself open to such attribution?? 2nd. 'My offer has been that if these people will apologize to my *Director* I will most willingly and heartily express my regrets on the whole affair and especially for the steps taken by me.'

Have your directors asked any one to apologize to them? Have they asked you to secure an apology? No. On the contrary they have asked and almost begged you to make the apology, which you say you are willing and glad to make if etc.

On what ground do you undertake to secure any apology from anyone? Who authorized you to act for your 'directors'? Have not your directors repudiated your assumption that *they* want any apology?

My poor boy don't you see that the public will say that it is not the 'directors' but Carter who want the apology, and for the same reasons enumerated in clause *one*. 3rd. 'I cannot believe that they will allow a gentleman to be treated in such a way while endeavouring to carry out his duty.' Wherein have 'they' (directors I suppose you mean) treated you badly? Doubtless they think you free from blame as per the report of the Commission. They also think that the affair is closed for all time. *But* one entirely new aspect has arisen. Namely the diplomatic side of the affair and they practically say to you, Whatever may be the details of the affair or our rights at the premises [?] let us make the formal apology and end the business, and they simply and kindly ask you to go through the form. Instead of treating you badly they have treated you as a wilful *son*, who would not or could not see but one side of the case, and that the wrong one. Let me say, and pardon me for it, a gentleman will always apologize if thereby peace can be restored and good feeling secured and no fundamental principle violated; the more right you are, and neverthe-less apologize, the more magnanimous you are.

Finally, there is only one manly, upright and gentlemanly thing to do, and that is to express your regrets etc. Pay no attention to whatever the papers or vain and silly people may say! All men whose respect is worth having will praise and approve of your action. Contemplate the harm of being dismissed from the service 'for dis-obedience'. It will stick to you as long as you live, and all your justification will be forgotten. I have written as a true friend should, however much you may dislike it.

always your friend
Theodore Davis

The straight talking of this letter must have touched several raw nerves in Carter's over-sensitive person, not least the references to gentlemanly behaviour. It had no recorded effect; yet Carter kept it with his dossier of papers on the incident, although not including it in the transcript of documents which he made as a record, possibly for later justificatory publication. It is not impossible that Maspero had himself stimulated Theordore Davis to write. His hand certainly seems to be behind a letter in similar vein sent earlier to Carter on 7 February by Naville.[31] Such interventions were requested by Maspero a little later when the likelihood of Carter's resignation from the Service seemed probable. At this distance it may seem remarkable that Maspero persisted in his attempts to prevent Carter's departure. One might think that after all the bother he had caused, his resignation might have been actively sought. This was not so; but Carter was not to escape without further bruising.

Serious blows were struck by two letters written by Maspero from Luxor on 17 February. The first, a formal communications in French, was addressed to 'Monsieur l'inspecteur en chef', informing Carter of a reorganization of the inspectorates resulting from the creation of two new posts.[32] The former inspectorate of Lower Egypt was to be diminished in size, to consist of the six *mudiriyas* of the Delta with the peninsula of Sinai. The *mudiriyas* of Giza, Beni Suef and the Faiyum were to go to others

31 G.I. Carter Papers V, 145.
32 G.I. Carter Papers, V, 127.

(subsequently specified thus: Giza to Quibell; Beni Suef and the Faiyum to Lefebvre); Alexandria to become an autonomous district under the Director of the Museum in that city. Maspero further informed Carter that as a result of recent events, it was thought better that his administrative office should be not in Cairo but in Tanta in the Delta; he should make the move no later than 15 March. Maspero stated: 'However, I am authorised to tell you that this action [i.e. the move to Tanta] is the consequence not of your actual action at Saqqara, but of your attitude after the event.'

This reason was reiterated in the second, less formal, but scarcely more friendly, letter which was written in English.[33] Maspero reports that Sir William Garstin had that day informed him that the matter had been settled between Lord Cromer and Monsieur de la Boulinière. 'The question of excuses is settled, but as you refused to do what was asked from you, you are reprimanded somewhat for it.' The move to Tanta, he explains, was because of his behaviour after the event. 'I have written you an official letter, which, however, is not to be sent to you until it has been seen by Sir William Garstin, and which I have conceived in the most mild way I could; I hope that he will approve of it, and if he can make it milder I will accept his suggestions readily.' Maspero then explains more fully the changes in the inspectorates, and asserts that they had been planned before the Saqqara incident; Carter would in any case have been transferred to Tanta; but the changes were accelerated by what had happened. He further suggests that by making the moves at this time and with the approval of Sir William Garstin, more serious steps could be avoided. His final sentences are significant:

> May I add that I received a letter from M. de la Boulinière saying that, as soon as I am in Cairo, he will send me one of the people who were so outrageous at Sakkarah to make excuses for their conduct. Pray do not let yourself be carried too far by your feelings, but remain with us: you will know that I, for one, will not esteem you less nor be your friend less than I had been up to the present time.

In spite of his exasperation Maspero remained on Carter's side at least to the extent of not wanting to lose him from the Service. Could he ever have recalled at that time the words he wrote to Naville at the very outset of his second tour as Director General of the Service?[34] Among many other activities he had been to Luxor to install Carter as Chief Inspector: 'I find him very active, a very good young man, a little obstinate (entêté)'. It must be concluded that Maspero detected sterling qualities in Carter, and the experiences of five years including the events of recent weeks had not led

33 G.I. Carter Papers V, 125.
34 See p. 70 above.

him to modify his opinion. Still he was to have his work cut out to convince Carter that he should not resign from the Service.

In Carter's dossier of the Saqqara events, there are laconic entries which chart to some extent the battering he received in the way of official disapproval. On 19 February he was asked to see Sir William Garstin at 12 o'clock on the following day.[35] He does not record that this meeting took place, but for 28 January he notes: 'Sir William Garstin repeated the above letter No.38 [Maspero's official letter of 17 February], reprimanding me in a severe manner.' He notes again for 23 February:[36] 'Saw Lord Cromer, who said he considered that I was entirely in the wrong, that I could have prevented the affair when I saw that the people were excited instead of aggravating it, to set natives against Europeans was not a proper thing to do, that he entirely agreed with Sir William Garstin's action in the whole matter, and that he can have nothing more to do with it.'

The wretched Carter could scarcely have known what to do. He was still just 30 years old; his future had seemed secure in the Antiquities Service; he had substantial archaeological achievements behind him; he was respected by his colleagues, trusted by his superior, Maspero. Now he had seriously blotted his copy-book. His judgement, not as a professional archaeologist but as an official and a man, had been seriously tested, and many thought that he had failed the test. Cromer was finished with the matter. Was he equally finished with Carter? Had Carter totally sacrificed the substantial good-will which he had enjoyed up to early January 1905? Could he with dignity continue in the Service? Resignation might be the only honourable course. Yet why should he behave honourably when his friends were telling him that he was not behaving as a gentleman? He was very hurt. 'I may say that I feel the humiliation to an exceeding extent. The treatment I have received after I have carried out my duty which has always been my endeavour and after my services to the department is inconceivable.'[37] He was quite incapable of standing back and viewing the affair with any impartiality. While nothing is known about the company he kept in Cairo at the time, it may be concluded, on the basis of his known way of life at other times, that he had few, if any, intimate friends to whom he could turn and discuss matters. He was a brooder, and the Saqqara affair provided ample material for brooding.

Nevertheless, some spirit of battle remained, and he worried away at the authorities, through Maspero, trying to obtain a copy of the findings of the enquiry. His insistence was again a source of vexation, because the papers of the enquiry did not belong to the Ministry of Public Works of which the Antiquities Service formed a part, but to the Legal Department.

35 G.I. Carter Papers V, 148, p. 31. The note on the actual meeting is written on the verse of p. 31.
36 G.I. Carter Papers V, 148, p. 33 verso.
37 Letter to Maspero of 21 February; G.I. Carter Papers V, 130.

His insistence in this matter implied a wish to take further action, but in none of the surviving documents does he suggest what was in his mind. He probably had not formulated any clear plan of action beyond the idea that if he were to get to England he might be able to engage the interest of well disposed people like Lord Amherst. Such an intention would have horrified Maspero, and certainly convinced the authorities that Carter had rightly been admonished and that he deserved no further support.

Maspero was therefore distinctly worried when Carter, in the middle of considering his move to Tanta, asked for three and a half months' leave of absence from 14 March 'owing to the strain of work during the last 17 months'.[38] The request for leave, irregular for this time of the year, was passed on to the Ministry with Maspero's favourable recommendation, but he felt obliged to write at length to Carter on 24 February, from Balliana in Upper Egypt. It is a remarkable letter from a superior to a junior, from a very serious and respected scholar to one who had yet to produce a substantial piece of scholarly research:[39]

> What I would say to you to-day refers to other matters. It is evident that by going to England now, you intend beginning what you spoke to me about, raising a debate about what happened at Saqqarah and afterwards. You know my opinion about it, and I will repeat it very briefly: you may make trouble for your countrymen in Egypt who have decided about the matter, but you are certain in the end to have the worse of it. I would advise you, not to renounce your way of thinking, but to do nothing before you have taken a certain time for reflection. I have given to Sir William as a reason for granting your demand though it is not usual to grant it at this time of the year, that you have been greatly shaken by the turn events have taken, and that I do not consider you can recover your calmness and balance of mind while you remain in Egypt. I hope that finding yourself at home, far from the scenes of your difficulties, and surrounded by friends who are quite free from prejudice in the matter under consideration, you will come if not completely to my way of thinking, but to a more definite idea of what was the position of the affairs; you will see, perhaps, that what seemed to you a real humiliation was only a form of international courtesy, which we were to accomplish together without more shame for you than for me. For the transfer to Tantah it was intended to take place very soon, and that being so it was considered as being the equivalent of what you did not like to do and a very small mark of displeasure for the trouble you gave to the Egyptian and British Governments. If, even, you do not come to look at the matter with the same eyes I look, at any

38 Letter of 21 February; G. I. Carter Papers V, 129.
39 G.I. Carter Papers V, 132.

rate do not hurry your decision, and take your time; I am pleading
for the whole of your life which is really in the balance and the course
of which may be completely altered by your decision. Whatever that
decision is to be, do not forget that I am only activated by a real
feeling of friendship that I have conceived for you, and even if you
do not remain with us, pray remember that I will try to help you,
as much as I can, without going against my duty as an Egyptian
employé.

Such an impassioned appeal could hardly have failed to make some
impression on Howard Carter's obduracy, and indeed for the time being
he seems to have accepted the need for his transfer to Tanta with a
province of inspection much diminished in size. The order confirming the
changes in inspectorates and setting 8 March as the day when Carter
should take up what was now termed the Inspectorate of the North was
issued by Maspero on 4 March. On the 7th Carter reported that he had
found a house at Tanta suitable for office and home. It belonged to Abdou
Effendi, and could be rented for £E7 per month. As it was still being put
in order he sought permission to delay his move beyond the 8th to the
13th. Émile Brugsch gave the necessary permission, and it was presumably
on that later day that Carter left Cairo for Tanta.[40] His leave of three
months was to begin on 20 March, and it must be assumed that on that
day or shortly afterwards, he left Tanta, Cairo and Egypt for what was
intended to be a period of recuperative holiday.

Maspero, however, could not rest in his efforts to retain Carter in the
Service, and he wrote to several friends of Carter's outside Egypt in the
hope that they too might weigh in with letters of encouragement, urging
him not to resign. The pleas must have had some effect on Carter's
thinking at this time; to know that his troubles were understood must in
itself have encouraged him, even if criticism was interlarded with exhor-
tation. From Florence wrote Jeannette Buttles, a relation of Theodore
Davis, who had known Carter in Luxor and who would later include
Carter paintings in her book *The Queens of Egypt*, something of a best-seller
in its day. Her letter is not dated, but from internal evidence it may be
placed after the initial fuss and crisis, and to a time when his resignation
seemed likely.[41] She certainly had not fully understood what had happened:
'I have just heard with the greatest concern, of the difficulty between you
and the French gov. in Cairo. *Of course* you are in the right – so clearly
so, that you can afford to be generous.' After some remarks about a man's
duty, she continues: 'Now there can be no doubt that your services are of
an unestimable value to the Antiquities department of Egypt. Just now,

40 For transcripts of letters about the move to Tanta, see G. I. Carter Papers, V, 148, pp.
35–7.
41 G.I. Carter Papers V, 144.

you have what it most needs, to develop old Egypt history and protect her treasures for future generations. *You* have above other men the special talents most needed for the work.' The balm of these words was shortly followed by sterner stuff: 'What if you are required to sacrifice the letter of your rights in the matter; that is better than sacrificing the Service itself. Don't be selfish!' The themes and tone are those of Theodore Davis's earlier letter. What did the Amhersts think?

Lady Amherst had also heard at second hand of the troubles. Writing from Valescure in the South of France to Percy Newberry on 5 May 1905, she first congratulates Newberry on the wonderful work he is to do (presumably on the recent finds from Theodore Davis's discovery of the tomb of Yuia and Tjuiu), and then turns to the proper subject of concern:[42]

> I am glad Howard is going to help with the drawing – Lady William had a most pathetic letter from M. Maspero today saying how distressed he was to think of Carter's leaving. He says he does not know what he will do without him and how he trusts us all to try to persuade him to see that there must be some 'giving and taking' and hoping that he will return. I shall get Lady W. to write to him and quote Maspero's own words.

Maspero would have written to Lady William Cecil while Carter was away from Egypt on leave. He had left in a distinctly dispirited mood with resignation on his lips, if not finally in his mind. Would he ever return? That must have been Maspero's concern. His hope that a change of scene and meeting family and friends in England might help to soothe the hurt seems to have been fulfilled, for the immediate future at least. Carter wrote quite positively to Naville on two occasions during his time away from Egypt.[43] He was busy with matters Egyptological. The first letter, from Carter's club, the Constitutional in Northumberland Avenue, with the date '21 Avril 1905' added by Naville, speaks of their collaborative work on the publication of Theodore Davis's *Tomb of Hâtshopsîtû*. Carter talks of returning to Egypt on 5 May: 'I go back so early so as to begin the plates for the new find' – a reference to the tomb of Yuia and Tjuiu. He then says, 'The Sakkara affair seems to be blowing over and things coming to a better prospect – so all's well at present.' Two later letters, both written from the Constitutional Club, on 3 and 4 May, reveal Carter's deep involvement at that time with the Davis publication. In the first of them, after discussing proofs, he tells Naville that he will not be able to look in at Geneva on his way back to Egypt because of his 'wanting to get on with the plates of the new find'. This is not the letter of a man who has lost his enthusiasm for his work, although the work precisely mentioned did not result from any of his own activities as Chief Inspector. He notes

42 G.I. Newberry Corr. 2/40.
43 Geneva MS. 2542, 89f. (21 April), 93f. (3 May), 91f. (4 May).

that his address will be Cairo. In view of the problems connected with his accommodation at Tanta, it was probably a prudent suggestion.

The letter of the next day takes up the point overlooked in the previous letter, that 'Davis does not wish me to say anything about the theory regarding the mummies of the Queen and Thothmes I [Tuthmosis]. So at his request I have cut it out. He evidently does not want to hurt Maspero's feelings in any way – a little diplomacy perhaps. Maspero seemed to me to agree with the idea.' Carter then states his intention of publishing a small paper on the problem in the *Proceedings of the Society of Biblical Archaeology*; he would send it from Cairo to Naville before submitting it for publication.

What was involved here was the problem of the mummified bodies of the queen and her father which were absent from the quartzite sarcophagi found by Carter in the tomb which he had cleared with Davis's financial backing in 1903–4. The difference of opinion between interpretations of the inadequate evidence by, it seems, Maspero on the one hand and Theodore Davis, Carter and Naville on the other is not made explicit. It is, however, interesting to observe that Carter here is taking a kind of initiative in deciding what may or may not be included in this publication. It was no doubt the case that his presence in England made liaison with the printers easier through him than through Davis in the USA or Naville in Switzerland. Archibald and Constable had their offices in the Haymarket in London, scarcely ten minutes' walk from Howard Carter's club in Northumberland Avenue. Nevertheless it is surprising to find him proclaiming his intention to publish a paper on the mummy problem. It never appeared; perhaps it was not written, or suppressed at Naville's suggestion, or at the behest of Theodore Davis. In the final publication Davis in his Introduction has a few words only to say on the matter:[44]

> When the tomb of Thoutmôsis I was discovered in 1899, it contained his sarcophagus; we found in Hâtshopsitû's tomb not only her sarcophagus, but one which she had made for her father Thoutmôsis I, as is told by an inscription thereon. Doubtless she had his body transferred from his tomb to hers, and placed in the new sarcophagus, where it probably remained until about 900 B.C., when, during some great crisis in the affairs of Thebes, the priests, thinking it wise to remove the bodies of many of the kings from their tombs in the valley, and to hide them in a safer repository, moved the contents of Hâtshopsitû's tomb to the tomb sometimes called the 'cachette', near her temple at Deir al Bahari. The great find made by the Museum Authorities in 1881 of the Royal Mummies which had been deposited in the 'cachette', included the body of Thoutmôsis I, an ornamental

44 T. M. Davis and others, *The Tomb of Hâtshopsîtû* (London, 1906), pp. xivf. On the disputed history of this tomb, see p. 92 above.

wooden box bearing the names and titles of Hâtshopsitû, and containing a mummified liver, and also two female bodies stripped of all
covering and without coffins or inscriptions.

Therefore with some timidity, I trespass in the field of Egyptology
to the extent of expressing my conviction that Hâtshopsitû's body
was moved with that of Thoutmôsis I from her tomb to the 'cachette',
and that the logic of the situation justifies the conclusion that one
of the two unidentified female bodies is that of the great Queen
Hâtshopsitû.

Sic transit gloria mundi.

It was, then, with such matters that Carter seems to have been concerned
during the later part of his leave. He had left Egypt on about 20 March,
and he was returning on 5 May, in all – by the time he reached Egypt –
scarcely 7 weeks, far short of the three and a half months he had at first
requested, and the three months he was actually granted. His return was
not that of a man disillusioned and determined to make mischief, but that
of one who was devoted to his work and eager to get on with it. It must
be admitted that the work which drew him back was nothing to do with
the Delta Inspectorate; it was the prospect of painting objects found in
the tomb of Yuia and Tjuiu by Theodore Davis. For such, no doubt, he
would be paid separately by Davis. Yet the attraction of painting fine
material was for Carter a real draw, and the work had undoubtedly been
carried out by Davis for the Antiquities Service.

It is surprising to find that during the troubles of the Saqqara affair,
the duties of the Chief Inspector were properly pursued, if perhaps in a
somewhat moderated way. Maspero in his excursion to Upper Egypt did
not fail to pass on to Carter information which might require executive
action on his part. In his first letter from Kalabsha of 14 January, when
he asks Carter for a report on the affray, he ends:[45] 'Petrie sends me a
report about the doings of the miners in Sinai. Immediately you have a
few days, I want you to go there and make an inspection.' In his letter
of 30 January Maspero is concerned principally with the publication of
the Aramaic papyri found at Aswan, a matter in which, as has earlier
been made clear, Carter was deeply involved along with Lady William
Cecil, Professor Sayce and Robert Mond.[46].

So, a kind of professional life continued, as should indeed have been
proper. It was to this regime of inspection that Carter returned in May
1905. His first purpose was to establish a satisfactory headquarters for the
Delta Inspectorate in Tanta. It will be remembered that he had negotiated,
before his departure on leave, the leasing of the house belonging to Abdou
Effendi, but had not apparently taken up quarters there because redecor-

45 G.I. Carter Papers V, 113.
46 G.I. Carter Papers V, 118. On the papyri, see p. 83 above.

ation and repairs were not complete. Knowing, presumably, that little would have been accomplished during his absence, Carter had planned first to operate from Cairo, perhaps returning to the apartment which he had shared with Ernest Richmond and Ronald Storrs. Tanta was about 80 miles north of Cairo by train, no great distance even in the early years of the twentieth century, for it was on the direct railway between Cairo and Alexandria and served by a reasonable train service. But it was not what Howard Carter was used to.

Tanta was the capital of Gharbiya *mudiriya*, an important provincial city, a centre of the cotton industry, busy with its own affairs, which were certainly not those of immediate interest to Carter. Like so many towns in Egypt that had developed commercially and to a limited extent industrially during the late nineteenth century, it had a superficially European flavour in the business area and in those 'suburbs' where the European officials, managers and businessmen lived. 'French', perhaps, would be a better word to use than 'European', for most of the urban development in Egypt had been greatly influenced by the kind of town planning and domestic architecture transplanted from metropolitan France to the French colonies in North Africa, and to the Eastern Mediterranean, to Syria, to Lebanon and to Egypt. Tanta was a town in which an unambitious small official could live reasonably well, but unstimulated by a foreign community consisting largely of people of similar kind.

Howard Carter must surely have found it dull in the extreme. He was accustomed to the lively archaeological circles of Luxor, the lavish hospitality and intelligent company of the annual 'residents' who settled in their *dahabiyas* or in the Luxor Hotel for weeks or even months every season – high society and learned society. From an early age he had shown a distinct predilection for a style of life far grander than he had enjoyed at home, but which he had certainly tasted in Didlington Hall. It had already been observed that he claimed in later life that he had inherited a taste for luxury from his mother.[47] Equally, in Cairo he had been exposed to a similar kind of social choice, but of far greater variety. In Cairo there were also the intelligent, well educated civil servants like Richmond and Storrs. He had the entrée to society in which he might meet not only the grand and noble visitors whom he had known in Luxor, not just the Egyptologists who passed through the capital, but also politicians and senior administrators whose interest in the ancient world might be minimal or non-existent.

The flavour of a day in Cairo society in which Carter participated may be savoured in an entry – one of many – in the diary of Mrs Andrews, the relative and travelling companion of Theodore Davis[48]

Friday, April 1st [1904] Jean, Carter and I went to the Zoo this

47 So he states in his sketch 'An Account of Myself', in G.I. Carter Notebook 15, p. 19.
48 Metropolitan Museum transcript for 1904, p. 42.

morning – on reaching home found Baron v. Bissing[49] and Mr. Weigall, who stayed to lunch with us. A man from the bazaar brought over some things for us to look at and I bought enough peridotes [*sic*] for a necklace – which I will have mounted some day. Lady Oppenheim and another English lady came up to the sitting room and played bridge with Theo. and Carter.

It was then a kind of exile that had been imposed on Carter, and he must have felt it as such. There is little evidence to suggest that he returned to Egypt in May determined to make a real effort to settle into his new inspectorate. A lively correspondence between him and Maspero in the weeks after his return reveals the difficulties he was having in securing the repairs needed to make his accommodation in Tanta satisfactory. He had in a sense been spoiled in Luxor by having a house provided by the Antiquities Service; in Tanta he had to rent a property and he found himself constrained by the rules governing such matters for others in the government service. He could not spend money on things which were covered by the official lease. On 15 July Maspero wrote reminding him that '§9 of your contract is quite conclusive:[50] "Toutes les réparations nécessaires seront à la charge du propriétaire." ' He must not agree to expensive repairs which might rise to £E20 or £E100, especially as the house might not remain his at the end of the year – a truly prophetic comment. Perhaps a small sum of about £E10 could be allowed; but estimates should be obtained first. The chief problem lay in the plumbing. At the end of this letter Maspero adds a comment after his signature: 'If there is a necessity for altering the *fosse* [pit, possibly septic tank] itself, it may take months before the house is ready: if it is only a *cuvette* [lavatory pan] or a watering apparatus it is quite different and may be made rapidly.' The matter was not quickly solved, but Carter had moved in, perhaps even before receiving Maspero's letter. Writing to Naville on 21 July,[51] Carter gives his address as 'Service des Antiquités. Lower Egypt Office, Tantah'. He comments: 'By the above address you will see I am at last installed in Tantah – but have unfortunately discovered the drains to be out of order so cannot get settled until something is done.'

The situation must have been miserable: an alien environment where most Europeans and many Egyptians in commerce and administration probably spoke French, an absence of friends and acquaintances, no inviting ancient monuments on his doorstep, a strong consciousness of being rusticated and on probation, and, to top it all, bad drains. To make matters worse, 'We are having, and have had, a bad summer, the average temperature being considerably above other years.'

49 A distinguished German Egyptologist for whom Carter had made paintings some years previously; see p. 84 above.
50 The batch of letters dealing with the Tanta house are G.I. Carter Papers V, 142.
51 Geneva MS. 2542, 95.

6

CRISIS AND RESOLUTION

In the exceptional heat of the summer of 1905 Tanta could have offered little to refresh the spirit of a man like Howard Carter who was not given to an optimistic view of life. His naturally depressive nature was never enlivened by the kinds of enthusiastic behaviour which would have been proper for someone in his early thirties. In his biographical sketches he emphasized his sickly childhood, and from his early days in Egypt he rarely enjoyed the buoyant good health which would surely have helped him to overcome his melancholic disposition. His was an embattled spirit, expecting the worst to happen, and when it did not happen, unable or unwilling to enjoy the relief. Even at the time of his greatest triumph, there seems to have been a note of restraint in his euphoria. Even then he was not on the top of form. Minnie Burton, wife of Harry Burton, the photographer of the Metropolitan Museum's Egyptian Expedition, noted in her diary for the 11 December 1922 (written in Cairo):[1] 'After dinner with the Bernards as usual, also Mr. Carter, Mr. Fitzgerald, Mr. Percy White. All of us with bad colds.' The adrenalin was clearly not working as it should have done at such a stimulating time.

The tension imposed by the events of the early months of 1905 had undoubtedly lowered Carter's health as well as his spirits. He had fled to Mena House at the end of January to try to rid himself of the 'very bad cold' he had taken twice in that month. He asked for extended leave of absence because of the strain he had endured. Later in the summer he was to fall ill again. The nature of the illness is not made clear in a letter Maspero wrote to him on 8 October; but Carter's superior was concerned enough to comment:[2] 'I heard from Brugsch that you had been ill. You remember what I told you before I left about your general looks: if, when I come back, that is to say in three weeks, you do not feel better, we will try to arrange matters for a new and serious leave.'

---

1 The Burtons had their home in Florence, where Minnie's parents (Lt-Col. and Mrs William Morton Duckett) also lived in retirement. One volume of her diaries, covering 1922 to 1926, is in the possession of Mrs Rosalind Berwald.
2 In a batch of letters, G.I. Carter Papers V, 142.

Tanta in October could have provided Carter with an entertainment which would surely have interested him, if he had been well enough to attend. Every year in that month the great *moulid* of El-Sayyed Ahmed el-Bedawi took place in and around the mosque in which he was buried, and on a great open space just outside the town. El-Bedawi, the much revered local Muslim saint, who came from Fez in Morocco in the thirteenth century and settled in Tanta after his pilgrimage to Mecca, had acquired in his lifetime an enviable reputation for pious works; after his death and burial in Tanta he had assumed a superior position among the saintly worthies of Islam in Egypt. Huge crowds attended this *moulid* or sacred celebration, said at one time to number even more than made the pilgrimage to Mecca.[3] The *moulids* of local saints or holy men resembled only superficially the celebrations in Catholic countries in honour of the Christian saints of particular localities. There were ceremonies centred around the mosque dedicated to or memorializing the holy individual; but the essence of the *moulid*, certainly as far as the people of the locality were concerned, lay in the fair which coincided with the occasion. Such fairs were 'medieval' in character, essentially religious celebrations, but actually secular circuses, occasions when the drab lives of the Egyptian *fellahin* might be enlivened by spectacle, mystery, entertainment, food and drink; occasions when family ceremonies like circumcisions could be conveniently and expertly carried out. Tents and booths covered the broad area reserved for the event; the place was alive with bustling humanity throughout the night; it was a time for unrestrained enjoyment, a kind of Mardi Gras without the stimulus of strong drink. The *moulid* of El-Sayyed Ahmed el-Bedawi lasted a full week, and could scarcely have been missed by Howard Carter, if he had been in town; but no letter has survived in which he makes mention of the celebrations.

Unhappily October was to be dominated by other considerations which were to lead to his departure from Tanta and from office. Yet at the same time he had the opportunity for professional rehabilitation which would surely have led to stability in his official position and a revival of his injured pride. In August he had been required to exercise his official function in a matter of considerable importance. Early in the month a party of *sebbakhin*, farmers digging the decayed mud-brick detritus of the ancient town-mound of Tukh el-Qaramus about 25 miles north of Cairo, discovered a cache of precious temple equipment, including a large silver Greek bowl, a number of incense-burners in Egyptian style and a bronze royal head. A few days later an even more precious cache of gold jewellery, silver vessels and gold and silver coins was uncovered. The second discovery was made when one of the farmers' donkeys put its hoof through the pottery vessel containing some of the treasure.[4] Swift action by the local civil authorities brought

3 See J. W. McPherson, *The Moulids of Egypt* (Cairo, 1941), pp. 285ff.
4 The find is reported in the *Egyptian Gazette* of 7 August, p. 3. See also Maspero's note in *Rapports sur la marche du Service des Antiquités de 1899 à 1910* (Cairo, 1912), p. 182.

Carter to Tukh, and he was able to retrieve a large part of what had been found. It was a substantial coup for the Antiquities Service and was to provide the Cairo Museum with a notable acquisition. Carter's personal records contain not a hint of this success,[5] yet it was thought by Maspero at least to herald the transition of Carter from recent discomfiture to the promise of a successful inspectorate in the Delta.

Maspero was at the time on leave in France, but Brugsch wrote to tell him of the discovery, sending photographs of the best pieces. He was delighted:[6] 'They are splendid some of them, and the whole is very valuable. I told him [Brugsch] to give £E400 to be distributed among the finders as a reward, and I hope that the prospect of getting money from us will encourage them to be honest.' He asks Carter to send him a report that he can present to the Académie des Inscriptions et Belles-Lettres. 'It is a good thing for you that you were able to prevent it from falling into the hands of the Antiquities dealers. I will insist on it in the Comité d'Archéologie and in conversation with Sir William Garstin. It must give you heart to do in the Delta what you did so well in Upper Egypt. Of course the ways are not the same, nor is the work so interesting, but the results are good, if they are different, and you can enrich the Museum and the Service more than you did when you were in Thebes.'

Maspero's last remark encapsulates a number of points about archaeology in the Delta region which he did not have to explain in detail to Carter: that the area was peppered with archaeological sites of great antiquity and uncertain identification; that these sites were for most part town mounds covering extensive acreages, each consisting of many layers of mud-brick structures with few monumental buildings of stone; that such mounds were open to the ravages of the *sebbakhin*, who mined the mud-brick (*sebakh*) for its fertilizing properties on the land; that there was very little practical surveillance of these sites by representatives of the Antiquities Service. Important finds had been made in the past by the *sebbakhin*, but rarely were the points of discovery known or the extent of the finds established; archaeological information about the exact provenances of such fortuitous treasure-troves could not be retrieved, or even expected. Few archaeologists working in Egypt at this time considered precision in recording a matter of importance. It may be recalled that Howard Carter's own search for the chambers of carbonized papyri at Tell Timai el-Amdid in 1893 was frustrated chiefly by the lack of precise information on their location, even though they had been visited and seen in the previous year by Édouard Naville.

5 Newberry in his Diary (PEN/GI/47) records some of Carter's movements at this time: 16 Aug. he and Newberry met in the Cairo Museum and lunched and dined together; 17 Aug. Newberry went to Tanta and returned on the 18th; on 20th Carter dined with Newberry in Shepheards Hotel.
6 A letter dated 28 August in a batch, G.I. Carter Papers V, 142.

Caches of gold and silver objects were particularly vulnerable to theft and rapid dispersal; such objects were intrinsically valuable and could be recognized as such by simple peasants. Swift action by the authorities as soon as a discovery was signalled (which seems to have been the case at Tukh el-Qaramus), might lead to a successful outcome. It was to happen again a few months later when an even more remarkable group of objects in precious materials was unearthed at Bubastis during work on a railway line.[7] On that occasion again the discovery was in two parts, from the first of which many of the objects were purloined by the workmen; only some were retrieved by C. C. Edgar and his assistants in the Antiquities Service. The second part of the discovery was made by the workmen of the Service.

The task facing the Chief Inspector was impossible to carry out without a broad network of junior inspectors and site guards (*ghaffirs*), and an established system of liaison with local authorities throughout the six *mudiriyas* of the Delta. Maspero could see Howard Carter as the man to set up the network and secure the necessary local contacts. He had good reason to believe that Carter would succeed. His spoken Arabic was good, he had the ability to talk freely and without condescension to villagers – the potential *sebbakhin* – who might never have seen a European before. He had done much the same in a relatively limited area in Luxor; here was his chance to operate on a much lager scale. Sadly there is no evidence that Carter ever contemplated rising to the challenge. It may even have been the case that the success of Tukh el-Qaramus persuaded him of the impossibility of his task in view of the lack of resources in money and man-power at his disposal, the vast area to be covered and the difficulty of travel in a part of Egypt where routes ran fan-wise north from Cairo, but rarely east-to-west. In Upper Egypt you travelled up the Nile or down the Nile, by river or by train; no site was distant from these highways more than a few miles. It was very different in the Delta, much of which remained archaeologically *terra incognita*. Further, there was also the peninsula of Sinai in which a small army could disappear without trace.

The Tukh treasure seems not to have sparked in Carter any flame of interest. There is no evidence that he ever sent Maspero the report that had been requested. In his letter to Carter of 8 October, written from Paris, and partly quoted earlier, Maspero states: 'Edgar sent me notes which enabled me to give the Académie informations about the various pieces of plate and jewellery you found at Tukh. I had the great pleasure to be able to tell how much we owe to your activity and energy.' It was C. C. Edgar, Carter's successor in the Lower Egyptian inspectorate, who would investigate the site further and find some additional, but less striking, objects in the area of the chance discoveries of the *sebbakhin*.

Anticipating Maspero's suggestion of a 'new and serious leave', Carter

7 See note in *E.E.F. Arch. Rep. 1906–1907*, pp. 29f.

had taken a four weeks' holiday from 12 September and travelled to Cyprus with an acquaintance, Colonel Griffith, who wanted to visit the island to purchase mules for the Sudan. This break clearly did much to enable Carter to get over his summer's illness and the unpleasantness of the humid conditions which characterized the months of July to September in the Delta. Cyprus was new to him and he wrote with real pleasure of all that he saw and did while he was there. For once (at least as far as surviving documents reveal) he addressed a really long letter to his mother, illustrated with his own photographs, and couched in the somewhat self-consciously overblown style that he affected when he wrote at ease and without hurry.[8] The flavour is well conveyed by this account of his impressions on walking on his first day at a rest camp on Mount Troödos:

> The following morning I awoke to find in Troödos a glorious peace – the camp dotted under the pine trees with magnificent scenery. The whole island stretched below surrounded by the sea: both skye [sic] and sea seemed to be one, the horizon lost in mist. The atmosphere reeking with the scent of pines and tiny wild pinks. Amongst the trees chaffinches, tits, jays, and many other birds filling the air with their chatter and only broken by the caw of the raven. Buzzing around the tents the humming-bee moth as common as the white butterfly at home.

This letter was written from Tanta on 6 October (a Friday), and he remarks that he 'came back to harness on Monday'. There is no hint here that he was about to tender his resignation from the Service.

Maspero was still in Paris on 8 October, and he wrote in his letter of that day that he would be in Egypt in three weeks, that is about the end of the month. He must have changed his plans soon afterwards, perhaps on hearing what Carter might be intending to do. On 21 October the Chief Inspector of Lower Egypt wrote formally from Tanta to the Director-General in Cairo[9]

> Sir
>
> Owing to the late treatment I have received and the difficulties I now find while endeavouring to carry out my duties as Inspector in Chief in Lower Egypt in the Service des Antiquités, I beg herewith to submit my resignation.
>
> Believe me
Sir
Yours faithfully
Howard Carter

8 This letter is in the possession of John Carter.
9 Carter's fair copy in G.I. Carter Papers, V, 147.

N.B.

Will you kindly delegate a representative of the Service des Antiquités to whom I can hand over all the papers, archives, office and office materials, and working materials that have been placed under my charge by the Service des Antiquités.

H.C.

The crisis seems to have come to a head with the renewal of problems over his Tanta quarters, not the drains on this occasion but the terms on which the leasing of the property had to be effected. From the very outset of his move to Tanta the matter of the lease and the rent had caused difficulties. Carter seemed incapable of agreeing terms which were in fact far more favourable than those commonly accepted by other government servants. In an attempt to persuade him to withdraw the notice of resignation, Maspero saw him on Thursday 26 October. He had perhaps found the notice waiting for his return from France a few days earlier. From a letter which followed up this meeting it may be concluded that little progress was made. Once again Maspero wrote to Carter persuasively and at length:[10]

I saw M. Webb and spoke with him. There is no possibility of doing anything more than what has been done already. It is only by a special forbearance that our Chief Inspectors are permitted to have houses at the expense of the Service and he quoted me a case in the Irrigation department where the Inspector has been recently charged with the frais [expenses] incurred for his lodging. Of course I have no time to look closely into the details, but it appears to me that we could not do any good by insisting on it and that the only result would an intimation from the Finances to cease giving the Chief Inspectors indemnities for lodgings, which would be a real loss for you and for Lefebvre, Weigall having the house we built last year.

The question remains therefore in the same position it had when I saw you on Thursday. I think it would be better for you to accept the facts as they are and to make the best of a bad bargain. Whatever your final decision turns out to be, there is no hurry about it and you may take time to consider it quietly. Do not be rash, since there is no necessity for you to decide one day in preference to all other days. I can understand that you wish to leave us, since your heart is no more in the business as it was when we began to work together, but it seems to me that you might remain as long as [=until] you have found another post which would give you more satisfaction. You know that I am speaking to you my impression of the matter

10 In the batch of letters, G.I. Carter Papers V, 142.

as to a friend and I would like you to act accordingly, for we would be really sorry to lose you after so many years of common activity.

Why did Maspero take such trouble over someone who had so clearly lost sympathy with government service and interest in his job? He undoubtedly saw in Carter a man of unusual talent who unfortunately would not allow his humours to submit to his intelligence; a man possessed of the ability to achieve the kinds of goal that Maspero had set for the Service he had nurtured over two terms of appointment. Carter loved Egypt, respected its people, understood the purposes of the foreigners who wished to work archaeologically there, was competent in excavation, excellent in caring for the monuments, a first-class artist, a practical engineer, seemingly a good administrator. He was quicksilver to the stolid Quibell; a tower of strength against the uncertain Weigall. Lefebvre was a better scholar, as was Edgar, but the former lacked the personality and the latter the field ability which distinguished Carter. He was worth the £E400 which the Chief Inspectors were paid. How could he not be sensible and stay? To attempt to divert Carter from resigning was the least that Maspero could do. But in Carter's cussed mood there could be no diverting him.

On Saturday 4 November 1905 the *Egyptian Gazette* announced:[11] 'Mr. Howard Carter has resigned his inspectorship under the Antiquities Service.'

On Thursday 14 December 1905 the *Egyptian Gazette* announced: 'The Earl and Countess of Carnarvon are to spend a few weeks in Egypt in the New Year, and will leave Marseilles on January 12.'

On Thursday 21 December 1905 the same newspaper announced Edgar's appointment as Inspector in Chief to the Antiquities Department at £E400 a year from 1 December.

It would be quite improper to speculate on Carter's feelings at this turning point in his life. He was not one given to pouring out his emotions in letters to such friends as he had. His style was essentially laconic; in personal matters he was restrained and terse to the point of seeming to be unmoved. Both in enthusiasms and in disappointments he appeared, on paper at least, to be wholly contained. His bitter comments to Maspero about his treatment over the Saqqara affair were exceptional, and certainly were brought about by what he would have considered to be extreme provocation. His departure now from the Antiquities Service was at his own instigation. It was presumably what he wanted, unless he had cherished the hope of complete surrender to his demands over his conditions of work and accommodation at Tanta. This last, however, seems very unlikely. Nevertheless, his departure brought brutally to an end the career in the

11 The three announcements are all placed under 'Personal and Social', in each case on p. 3 of the issue.

Antiquities Service which he had probably seen as containing the promise of a lifetime's practice of archaeology.

He had come north from Luxor with such expectations. Highly regarded by Maspero, he may even have been selected for a task which might have seemed of unusual responsibility for an official of relatively small experience. Writing to Miss Amherst a year earlier, just as he was taking up his northern inspectorate, he confided to her some surprising information:[12] 'Would you tell Lord Amherst a *secret* – the Government has entrusted to me to make the solution of the Antiquity Law for this country – I am so proud, but it must not be known at present.' The truth of this 'secret' cannot now be established. It could have represented a touch of that romancing to which Carter was inclined throughout his life; it might just have been the case that he had been invited with the other Chief Inspectors to submit his views concerning a review of the law. Presumably he forfeited this opportunity after the events of Saqqara on Sunday 8 January 1905.

It is from more certain ground that some speculation may be entertained on what he envisaged for the future. His financial assets were probably minimal. Although his annual salary was £E400, a reasonably substantial emolument for the early twentieth century, he may have saved little; subsequent events suggest that he had little in the way of a cushion to protect him from adversities. He had, on the other hand, considerable personal talents on which better prospects could be built. He was an experienced excavator with notable successes to his credit; he was an artist of recognized merit whose work was sought by discriminating visitors to Egypt. He had also a wide acquaintance with influential people who might use his services as a superior guide to the monuments, or recommend him to others for the same purpose – he could be expected to behave in a gentlemanly way, displaying none of the importunate habits of most local dragomans.

First, however, he must leave Tanta and make the break with his former way of life. On Friday 24 November 1905 Emma Andrews wrote:[13] 'Saw much of Mr. Carter – who has at last resigned from the Service des Antiquités. I was very glad to hear it. Jean and I drove out to the country to the pretty house he has taken, and had tea with him. He is going to devote himself to painting – a thing he should have done years ago.' Her remarks on Carter are strange but interesting. They almost certainly reflect the views of Theodore Davis, with whom she had travelled in Egypt for many seasons. They may also reflect the views of others in the transient foreign community which came to Egypt every winter, resuming among themselves a kind of social activity which would not necessarily have extended to Europe and America in the summer. In such society Howard Carter may well have been thought to have let the side down. Excellent

12 Letter of 2 December 1904, The Amherst Letters; T. J. Eva Egyptian Collection.
13 Metropolitan Museum transcript, 1905, p. 109.

though he might be in helping to organize an excavation for someone like Theodore Davis in the Valley of the Kings, he was not one to allow the man who paid the piper to call the tune. That he might be Chief Inspector of Antiquities in Upper Egypt was one thing; that he should in effect dictate how the work might be carried out was quite another thing.

Theodore Davis was not a man willingly to be directed in the way he should act, and there were undoubtedly times when he found Carter's general overseeing of his activities in Thebes interfering and irksome. Things became much easier with Carter's move to the north, when supervision at Thebes passed to Quibell, and from late 1905 to Arthur Weigall. It remained for Davis to discover that one Chief Inspector of the Antiquities Service might be just as tiresome as any other. Carter, of course, was exceptionally stubborn, and in matters archaeological not one to defer to a rich amateur. It is not unlikely, therefore, that in the after-dinner talk on the *Bedawin*, Davis's *dahabiya*, and at the polite tables of Cairo, Carter's move to the Delta was at first greeted as a happy removal of an awkward agent of authority. His subsequent behaviour in the Saqqara affair revealed him as not quite the gentleman he had hoped to be. Perhaps, after all, he was not the right person to be a Chief Inspector. On the other hand, he did paint well. Did he not come to Egypt first as an artist? Were not his water-colours eagerly sought? Was he not an ideal archaeological artist who need never be lacking for a job? Was it not quite proper, therefore, that he should now turn to painting to make his living?

It is difficult to reconstruct the course of Carter's life in the months that followed his resignation. He did not, apparently, remain long in his 'pretty little house' not far from Cairo. By February he was back temporarily in Luxor, undoubtedly the place where he felt most at home. Here he could more easily see the Europeans and Americans from whom he could expect best to make some kind of a living. From the Turf Club in Cairo he wrote on 23 February 1906 to Lady Amherst.[14] Beginning with suggestions on how her book *A Sketch of Egyptian History* might be promoted in Cairo, he continues: 'I am having a very crowded winter, but not many nice people in proportion. I have just come from Luxor after a sojourn of two weeks.' By happy chance, entries in the Visitors Book kept at Deir el-Bahri by the Egypt Exploration Fund expedition give some idea of the kind of person whom Carter accompanied at Thebes at this time. Under the date Feb. 5, 1905 (clearly an error for 1906, as adjacent entries make certain), the following names are written in autograph[15]

14 The Amherst Letters; T. J. Eva Egyptian Collection. Lady Amherst's book had been published by Methuen in 1904; its full title was *Sketch of Egyptian History, from the earliest times to the present day*. Carter had helped with the illustrative material, and felt an obligation towards Lady Amherst to help in promoting the book.

15 The vistors' book is preserved in the Egyptian Department of the Royal Ontario Museum, Toronto; it was brought to my attention by John Larson. I am grateful to Dr Nicholas Millett of the Museum for permission to publish this extract.

M. Thornburgh Cropper
  5 Gloucester Terrace
  Regent Park, London
Ian Whyte, 7 Charlotte Sq. Edinburgh
Helen K. Gould, New York
Howard Carter, Cairo
Frank Jay Gould, N. York
Percy Newberry, Liverpool University
Prince Louis de'Orléans
Prince Antoine d'Orléans
(and two others whose names are not clear, but who probably belonged to the entourage of Prince Louis)

It seems very probable that Carter, perhaps with Newberry as well, was acting the superior dragoman to some or all of the others whose names occur for that day.

The mythology of Egyptology preserves a story that during his time in the uncertain life of the free-lance Howard Carter returned to Luxor with very little money and in no position to set himself up in a suitable home either in Luxor town or on the West Bank where he had always lived. In this state of penury he was, it is said, taken in by an Egyptian of Qurna, a former associate in the Antiquities Service. In 1940 Professor John Wilson, Director of the Oriental Institute of the University of Chicago, in answering a series of questions from Charles Breasted, son of James H. Breasted, reported what could be remembered in this matter by Dr Harold Nelson, the Director of Chicago House in Luxor.[16] Nelson recalled that James Breasted had said that the Egyptian who had sheltered Carter was not a member of the notorious tomb-robbing family of Abd er-Rasul (as Charles Breasted had suggested), but 'the former sheikh of the guards at the Valley of the Tombs of the Kings who had held that post at the time when the tomb of Amenhotep II was robbed in 1901 . . . and although this man had been on his weekly holiday when the tomb was allegedly rifled, Carter held that he had been responsible and had him dismissed. This man's name does not appear clearly in any written material known to me.'

A similar tale was told by Charles Wilkinson who had come to work in Luxor for the Metropolitan Museum's Egyptian Expedition in 1920.[17] He knew Carter in the quieter times before the discovery of Tutankhamun's tomb, and became an associate of his subsequently through their common links with the Metropolitan Museum. Beyond this reported memory of Charles Wilkinson, and that of James Breasted (by way of Harold Nelson),

16 O.I. Director's Office Archives. Letter of John Wilson to Charles Breasted of 28 November 1940. The words quoted are as reported by Wilson and not a direct quotation of Nelson. For the episode of the robbing of the tomb of Amenophis II, see above, pp. 74f.
17 Personal communication by Cyril Aldred.

there is very little else that is known of this low point in Howard Carter's life. It is possible that a very temporary billet was provided in the generous and typically Egyptian manner by the former chief *ghaffir* until Carter could find somewhere convenient and inexpensive to live. It is unlikely that such an interlude lasted long, for there was work for Carter to do and he would need space to paint and draw. Furthermore, it is not at all likely that his acquaintances would have tolerated indefinitely such an arrangement for an Englishman and former respected government official. Carter's acceptance of such hospitality would have been seen as 'going native'. Even if it had lasted but a month, or even a few days, it would have shocked, and would have remained in the memories of the foreign community as strongly as if he had lived thus for the whole period of his free-lance activity.

This interlude of informal employment was to last, it seems, until the early months of 1909, a full three years – by no means as long as some have claimed, but certainly a tedious period for Carter. His principal activity, if one may judge from published archaeological works begun or completed in these years, was painting, and his services seem to have been in regular demand. The most enduring work was carried out for Theodore Davis who undoubtedly did his best to put commissions in Carter's way, even when the response from Carter may have been slow and even ungracious.

Whether Davis could be classified as a patron is difficult to determine. His association with Carter went back to the days when he first obtained permission to excavate in the Valley of the Kings. From the outset the relationship was seen differently from the two sides. It should not have been so, because Carter, who supervised the early excavations, was the representative of the Antiquities Service and distinctly the specialist in charge. Davis, the man who paid the bills and took most of the credit, no doubt regarded Carter as working for him. There could scarcely be a harmonious partnership while roles were observed so differently, and the tensions, misunderstandings and awkwardness that occurred have already been described. The position would become even more complicated after Carter's move to the Delta and return to Thebes.

It is surprising that there was no greater coolness between Carter and Davis after the very forthright letter the latter had written in the painful days of the Saqqara affair; yet Carter in this matter saw, no doubt, that he could expect work from Davis and had therefore to keep on reasonably good terms. Mrs. Andrews notes in her diary for 17 February 1907:[18]

Theo. was in Luxor this A.M. and Carter told him of various small and precious things which had been shown him by a native which had been stolen from Tyi's tomb. The man had told Carter that Mr.

18 Metropolitan Museum transcript, 1907, p. 29.

Davis could have them all for £400 . . . provided no attempt at arrest was made! These fellows are difficult to deal with. Theo. told Carter if the men would produce everything they had, and would show them, he might consider a price and promise no arrest to be made. Their practice is to mass together a lot of valuable things on such an occasion, with what has been stolen from a late find, and try to get a big price for all. Later in the day Theo. went into Abd el-Hamed's and Ali's shops on the river, and the latter handed him several small objects from the tomb – some gold 'neferts' from the necklace, carnelian lotus flowers, and a lovely bit of gold and enamel from a necklace – only one of which we have – and it is marked No. 17 in hieroglyphic characters. Ali would not take anything for these – among them one bearing Aten's cartouche. It is humiliating to find that thieves have been among your trusted workmen – they have such chance in sifting débris, to hide a valuable thing in their loose clothes.

The naïvety of attitude displayed in this entry is characteristic of those who believe fondly that one's own employees, if treated reasonably well, will respond generously and honestly. The Egyptian workmen used by Davis – probably engaged by his foreman (*reis*) – came from the villages in and around the Theban Necropolis on the western side of the Nile at Luxor. Tomb-robbing was part of their heritage, and they felt – not without some primitive justice – that the fruits of the earth – their earth – the antiquities in the tombs, were there for their taking. From the early years of the nineteenth century, when the first European travellers came to Egypt and began to collect antiquities, it had become clear to the Qurnawis (the name used rather generally for the modern inhabitants of the Theban Necropolis) that the products of the tombs, among which they lived, were more valuable than they had ever formerly conceived. Why, therefore, should a poor workman on Theodore Davis's excavations, paid a few piastres a day, neglect the opportunity to share in the good fortune of a discovery; small portable objects were made for slipping into the folds of one's head-scarf or *galabiya*?

Informal trade in antiquities had always in modern times been a surreptitious activity, even before the establishment of the Antiquities Service and the official regulation of antiquities dealing. Belzoni had found it so in the early days:[19] things had not changed. A man with something good to sell might belong to a syndicate of informal excavators with some agreement to share costs and profits; if he found some good pieces on his own he would at first attempt to find a buyer without informing his fellows.

19 See G.-B. Belzoni, *Narrative of the Operations and Recent Discoveries . . . in Egypt and Nubia* (London, 1820), I, pp. 288ff.; also, T. G. H. James, *Ancient Egypt. The Land and its Legacy* (London, 1988), p. 150.

Secrecy at the individual and at the syndicate level was very important, for the well established dealers with businesses in Luxor town had ways of persuading the small operators to pass on their discoveries at low prices.

Theodore Davis was a prime victim for exploitation. His excavations in the Valley of the Kings had become extensions of the social round on his *dahabiya*. Arthur Weigall, the Chief Inspector at Luxor, kept only a very general eye on the work which was ostensibly in the charge of Edward Ayrton.[20] The situation had changed since Howard Carter was Chief Inspector and in charge of the Davis excavations. Weigall, whose style and interests were distinctive, and unlike those of Carter, felt unable to exercise as much control over Davis's work as he might have wished. In a letter to Francis Ll. Griffith, written from Lancing in Sussex and dated only 'October 1' (probably in 1908 on internal evidence), he follows up a diatribe on Carnarvon with an only slightly more restrained attack on Davis:[21]

> With regard to Horemheb I purposely did not say much about it, because my position is such a very delicate one in regard to Davis. I insist on the formality of supervising his work on behalf of the Govt., simply to prevent him thinking himself an ordinary digger, which would lead to obvious abuse. Davis materially dislikes this, and though we are good friends, I find it very difficult to prevent him running the Tombs of the Kings as a social affair. Ayrton behaves as badly as he could while there, being entirely under Davis's thumb; and also on his own account resenting my appearances on what he considered his own field. I so sympathize with him in this that I need not say any more!

Weigall had good reason to feel disgruntled. Davis had received the concession to work in the Valley of the Kings on special terms. He was effectively working on behalf of the Antiquities Service, and therefore not, in Weigall's words, 'an ordinary digger'. But his years of activity had proved to be unusually successful, with the discovery of increasingly important tombs, most notably that of Yuia and Tjuiu, and the one known as the tomb of Queen Tiye. Success of this kind breeds confidence in one's own capacities and judgements, and it is not surprising that Davis felt himself to be independently competent, and unwilling to suffer easily the interventions of a patently contemptuous Weigall.

Howard Carter, however, was a man of a very different temper, and he was still in a position to be helpful when it came to the matter of thefts

20 Edward Russell Ayrton had worked with Petrie at Abydos and with Naville and Hall at Deir el-Bahri. His promising archaeological career was cut short by his accidental death in Ceylon in 1914.

21 G. I. Griffith letter 362; see further p. 138 below; also A. E. P. Weigall, *The Life and Times of Akhnaton, Pharaoh of Egypt*, (London, 1922), p. xivf. The tomb of Horemheb was found on 25 February 1908.

from excavations. Throughout his career he took trouble to get to know the inhabitants of the Theban Necropolis, and indeed of anywhere else his work might take him. Thebes was his old familiar field, and he clearly retained access to sources of information unavailable to the grand, like Davis, or even the supercilious, like Weigall. The excavation of the so-called tomb of Tiye had been a notably mismanaged operation from the start, and the inadequacy of the work, compounded by a very indifferent publication, has provided archaeologists with ample scope for interpretation and reinterpretation ever since.[22] It is not surprising that material from the tomb passed into the hands of Luxor dealers, or that Carter was the one to hear about them.

Earlier, in 1905, Carter had been asked by Davis to make paintings of some of the finest objects found in the tomb of Yuia and Tjuiu, the parents of Queen Tiye, favourite wife of King Amenophis III. The discovery had been spectacular, and the objects from this virtually undisturbed sepulchre represented easily the finest group of grave-goods to enter the Cairo Museum before the overwhelming paraphernalia of Tutankhamun's tomb. Carter, it will be recalled, returned to Egypt in June 1905, looking forward in particular to executing this commission for Davis. Most of what Davis required was completed satisfactorily in Thebes before the antiquities were taken down to Cairo. There remained, however, the finest of the coffins which had been taken to Cairo. Davis was quite determined to have Carter paint it, and did all he could to ensure that he might have access to it in the galleries of the museum. It would seem that Carter had been unable to carry out the work in the galleries while visitors were allowed into the museum.

During the summer of 1906 Carter was able to return to Britain, and letters to Percy Newberry, addressed from Fyvie Castle in Aberdeenshire, suggest that he was taking advantage of hospitality offered by visitors he had shown around in Egypt.[23] Davis pursued him, from his summer home in Newport, Rhode Island. Writing to Newberry on 21 July, he showed surprise that even he had been unable to get permission for Carter to work.[24] It seems that Carter was reluctant to work because the coffin could not easily be moved. In a further letter to Newberry, Davis encloses a copy of a letter to Carter conveying the bad news about the state of the coffin. Maspero had written to say, 'It is really impossible to move the lid of the coffin and stand it on its feet . . . the wood is so dry that the gold foil and the enamels hardly keep on it. Even in its present position, with

22 The original Davis publication, *The Tomb of Queen Tiyi* (London, 1910), included an historical essay by Maspero. The tomb, known archaeologically as KV 55, has most recently been studied by Martha Bell, 'An Armchair Excavation of KV 55' in *J.A.R.C.E.* 27 (1990), pp. 97ff. See also, C. N. Reeves, *The Valley of the Kings* (London 1990), pp. 42ff.
23 Two letters of 5 and 7 September in G.I. Newberry Corr. 8/23 and 8/24.
24 Two letters to Newberry in G.I. Newberry Corr. 12/7 and 12/8.

the glass-case on, flakes of gold fall from it. If it were taken out, raised in such a manner that the whole weight should bear on the feet, we could not answer for the consequences: perhaps half the ornamentations would be spoilt.' Maspero's solution was to suggest that 'if Carter would agree to paint it laying on its back, we would have only to take away the glass . . .' Davis continues in his letter to Carter, 'can you paint it lying in the box if the glass is taken off? As you know, I must have it painted, as it is quite the most beautiful and impressive of the coffins.

Subsequently a painting of the upper part of the coffin was carried out, and the finished volume, *The Tomb of Iouiya and Touiyou*, was published in the summer of 1907, containing in all 14 plates painted by Carter. He was not at all pleased at the result:[25] 'What has happened! It seems an absolute bungle and minus seemingly the most important points. My plates have been reproduced fearfully and absolutely contrary (in some cases) to my instructions. No proof was ever submitted to me. *Do tell me what you think* of the whole thing . . . Davis has behaved like a bear to me of late, but no matter.' Carter could not afford to be too particular. Davis had been a source of work during his period of difficulty, and should continue to be so. In a letter to Newberry in March 1906, Harold Jones, an artist/archaeologist in the Davis circle, mentioned, 'I believe Howard Carter got about £15 a plate for his drawings.'[26] This would not have been a bad price for those days. Painting was Carter's principal source of income at this time and he could not have afforded to alienate Davis without a truly compelling reason. At £15 a plate he would have made £210 for his work on Yuia and Tjuiu.

Theodore Davis was not the only one to use Carter's talents. For the Earl of Northampton, who had carried out excavations with Newberry and Wilhelm Spielgelberg in the Theban Necropolis in 1898-9, he made a painting of a scene of pig-herding from the tomb of Nebamun. This was published in *Report of some excavations in the Theban Necropolis* (London, 1908). Jeanette Buttles used some Carter water-colours of royal 'portraits' for her popular work *The Queens of Egypt*, based on the sensitively carved reliefs in the Hatshepsut temple at Deir el-Bahri, which Carter had first copied for the Egypt Exploration Fund. This volume was also published in London in 1908. The Deir el-Bahri portraits became standard subjects for his brush, and several copies of his paintings of Queen Ahmose and King Tuthmosis I survive from this period. He also issued in about 1908 a portfolio of coloured reproduction of Deir el-Bahri subjects, a rare publication, possibly issued in a limited edition.

In spite of these commissions, Howard Carter's existence during his period in the wilderness was uncertain and precarious. On the one hand, he maintained a kind of social life, some elements of which can be observed

25 Letter of 29 September, 1907 to Newberry, G.I. Newberry Corr. 8/26.
26 G.I. Newberry Corr. 27/2. Harold Jones, a Welsh artist and excavator who worked for Davis, Carnarvon and the Metropolitan Museum at Lisht, died prematurely in 1911.

in the pages of Emma Andrews's diary – tea in the Luxor Hotel, lunch or tea with the Davis party on the *Bedawin*, visiting the excavations with Lord and Lady Halsbury (10 February 1907). He seems to have had some kind of suitable quarters in Luxor or on the West Bank in early 1907, for on 21 February Mrs. Andrews records a visit to his studio. From inclination and experience Carter would certainly have done his best to maintain appearances, perhaps even to the point of extravagance in his current straightened circumstances. Harold Jones in Cairo in the late autumn of 1906 found that Carter was staying at the Continental Hotel, a place that he could hardly have afforded at the time unless he was the guest of some affluent visitor whom he was accompanying. On that occasion he snubbed Harold Jones:[27] 'it was too much trouble I suppose to worry about me, so I didn't see him tho' the servant told me that he was in! . . . I'll be more careful in the future.'

It is also possible that Carter was able to finance his way of life, with a few extravagances, by selling antiquities. In a few years' time, much encouraged by the Earl of Carnarvon, he carried out many commissions for public and private clients, as will be seen later on. It is difficult to believe that he would have neglected this obvious source of support in earlier years. He was, after all, a free agent now, with no responsibilities owed to the Antiquities Service; and he had the good contacts with dealers in Luxor and Cairo. Still, some economy had to be exercised. His visit to Britain in the summer of 1907 was of much longer duration than would have been normal in earlier years. there would have been little for him to do in the off-season in Egypt, and he could live more modestly by staying with friends or family. On 15 July Harold Jones, writing, interestingly, from Highclere Castle, reports to Percy Newberry,[28] 'Of course you know that Howard Carter is in England. I have seen him a few times, but now I think he is with his mother.' Later during this stay in Britain Carter told Newberry of the chance that he might go to work for Robert Mond in the Theban Necropolis, and that in the meanwhile he would probably return to Swaffham.[29]

There is in this letter of 7 September a sadly wintry note: 'Didlington is in brown paper parcels and Lady Amherst is saving odd bits of string.' The Amhersts had fallen on difficult times, and were having to give up their beloved Didlington.[30] For Carter this must have come as an occasion of great sorrow, especially as it did at a time of crisis in his own life. Didlington had provided him with perhaps the best point of reference and

27 Letter of Jones to Newberry of 27 November 1906, G.I. Newberry Corr. 27/5.
28 G.I. Newberry Corr. 27/6.
29 G.I. Newberry Corr. 8/24.
30 'Owing to the dishonesty of a solicitor entrusted with the administration of estate and trust funds, Lord Amherst found himself in 1906 obliged to announce the sale of the finer portion of the magnificent library at Didlington Hall'; so *Dictionary of National Biography. Supplement 1901–1911*, pp. 40f.

base in Britain after the Carter house in Swaffham where his mother was ever ready to welcome him on his occasional visits. At Didlington there seems always to have been a friendly reception. The Amhersts had provided him with much more than hospitality; they had known him as a young boy, recognized his artistic talent, encouraged his interest, recommended him for work in Egypt, promoted his career, supported him in his fall from grace in 1905, and bought his water-colours. It would not all end with the loss of Didlington, but things would never be the same again. Lord Amherst would die in 1909, and Carter would help in the dispersal of the great collection. He would shortly acquire a new and powerful patron, and his career was on the point of achieving stability once again; yet the warmth of his friendly relationship with the Amhersts would never be fully repeated. Among themselves and with close mutual friends they regularly called him Howard, and his company was sought and enjoyed whenever possible. It was unusual for someone of his undistinguished background to reach this degree of intimacy with a wealthy and influential landed family. It remains astonishing to find Alicia Amherst writing in her journal of the Amherst Nile trip of 1894–5, when their *dahabiya* had reached Luxor on the return from Nubia:[31] 'Howard Carter came to dine and sleep, as he did every night when we were there.' And this was the young man of whose social habits John Newberry had complained so bitterly scarcely more than a year before.[32]

Carter's return to Egypt at the end of the summer in 1907 could scarcely have been an occasion of heightened expectation, and his own uncertain prospects could not have been cheered by the contemplation of the Amhersts' tragedy. On 29 September he wrote to Percy Newberry from Luxor about the preparation of the plate showing pigs from the tomb of Nebamun for the publication of the Northampton excavation on which Newberry was at the time engaged. It was the letter in which Carter complained of the poor reproduction of his plates for Davis's volume, *The Tomb of Iouiya and Touiyou*.[33] The communication is not sanguine. The plate Newberry needs is in Cairo: 'I will send it to you directly I do go down but that moment of my life seems even *farther* away than my next week's grub and lodgings.' Such a lament surely implies a degree of domestic uncertainty which may have manifested itself in the acceptance of charity from whatever source it might come, even the Egyptian inhabitants of Qurna. But some relief was not far away. On 11 January 1908 Harold Jones wrote to Newberry from Matania, near Lisht, where the Metropolitan Museum expedition was working:[34] 'I haven't seen Carter yet – he is

31 Entry for 26 February 1895 (Shrove Tuesday); see p. 63 above.
32 See p. 63 above.
33 G.I. Newberry Corr. 8/26.
34 G.I. Newberry Corr. 27/11. At the time Jones was working with the Metropolitan Museum Egyptian Expedition at the Middle-Kingdom pyramid field at Lisht.

living again in his old house at Medinet Habu – I suppose the Government have lent it to him.' Could this act of generosity have represented a first move in Maspero's scheme to have Carter work with the Earl of Carnarvon?

It may be remembered that the *Egyptian Gazette* announced in its Personal and Social column on 14 December 1905 that the Earl and Countess of Carnarvon were expected shortly to pay a visit of a few weeks to Egypt. The visit, one of a series of Egyptian tours, was essentially to be one of recuperation, for Lord Carnarvon was still suffering from the after-effects of a motor accident in which he had been involved in Germany in 1901. In the course of his visits he had developed a wish to excavate. Good precedents for excavations in Egypt by private persons, as opposed to public institutions, existed: in Thebes alone, Theodore Davis demonstrated exceptional success in the Valley of the Tombs of the Kings, and there were also the Marquis of Northampton and Robert Mond with less spectacular but not negligible results. There is no reason to doubt the seriousness of Carnarvon's intentions, even if he may have viewed himself as entering into competition of a kind with those who were already well established. His position enabled him to persuade Maspero, seemingly through Sir William Garstin, head of Public Works and therefore in charge of antiquities, to grant him permission to work at Thebes. The onus of finding a suitable site was placed on Arthur Weigall, who had only recently taken over the inspectorate of Upper Egypt from Quibell. Weigall undoubtedly disapproved. He was already expected to supervise in a general way the work of Ayrton for Theodore Davis, and his comments on that excavation have been quoted earlier. They were in fact prompted by his reflections on Carnarvon's operations, offered to Francis Ll. Griffith. Writing of the finding of a 'tablet' by Carnarvon, Weigall confesses:[35]

> I am quite ashamed to tell you the tale of its discovery. Two years ago Lord Carnarvon asked Sir William Garstin to obtain him a digging concession. Maspero having approved the application, Sir William wrote to me telling me to find him a site. Fearing that he might do damage to a good site, I placed him on the rubbish mounds of Shêkh abd'el Gurneh, where of course he worked for the season without finding anything, though I had hoped that he might find a good painted tomb, which would have been a useful find, without much to damage in it.

Carnarvon was not put off by his lack of success, but seems to have sensed that he may not have been treated by Weigall as fairly and generously as he would have expected. So he sought advice elsewhere. Weigall continues:

In the following year, however, Lord Carnarvon thought it better to

35 G.I. Griffith letter 362; written probably on 1 October 1907.

arrange the sites for himself, and acting on native information asked for concessions in Dra Abu'l Neggar. These were granted without my having an opportunity of protesting and excavations were carried out under a rough supervision by me. Towards the end of the work I had to go away, and when I returned to Luxor Lord Carnarvon had gone, leaving his antiquities in my office. There was a basket full of odds and ends amongst these, and stuffed anyhow into the mouth of the basket was this tablet in two pieces, and I am sure this rough handling is responsible for some of the flaking. A sadder instance of the sin of allowing amateurs to dig could not be found. Lord Carnarvon does his best, and sits over his work conscientiously; but that is not enough. Next year he is to dig at Dra abu'l Neggar and Aswan, I believe. He is a good sort, but perfectly irresponsible.

It is most unlikely that Weigall failed to pass on his misgivings about Carnarvon's competence to Maspero, insisting in all probability that the concession to dig should be withdrawn or that some other arrangement for supervision should be made. The former of these alternatives would have seemed out of the question to Maspero who had an excessively indulgent attitude to people of influence like Carnarvon; he would in any case not have been able to take such a step without consulting higher authority. On the other hand, to provide Carnarvon with professional help was well within his power. Who could better serve in this capacity than Howard Carter, his erstwhile protégé, for whose present unfortunate plight he no doubt still felt partly responsible? Such a solution was altogether satisfactory for Maspero; and there is no reason to believe that it was not equally satisfactory to Lord Carnarvon who had at about this time written to Weigall about bringing out 'a learned man as I have not time to learn up all the requisite data'.[36] With Carter's professional competence behind him, the scholarly reputation of his enterprise would be established. For Carter the proposal could only have been gratifying; now he would be able once again to do what his whole professional career had equipped him for; he would also receive a regular salary. It is very probable that Carter and Carnarvon would already have met in Luxor; it seems even possible that when Weigall talked of Carnarvon's 'acting on native information' Carter was behind the advice. His was the ear into which a Qurnawi would have entrusted significant intelligence about promising sites and finds.

The proposed association may have been first suggested by Maspero at the end of Carnarvon's 1908 season before Carnarvon returned to England. It may have been later in the year. No matter what the preliminaries were, they resulted in Carter's joining Carnarvon for his third season in Thebes

36 The letter, which is among the Weigall Papers, is quoted in N. Reeves, *The Complete Tutankhamun* (London, 1990), pp. 44, 218.

in 1909. The omens were good. That the partnership would lead after many years and the interruption of a World War to the most dramatic archaeological discovery of the twentieth century, could hardly have been foreseen. But for Carter it at once brought to an end a singularly unhappy and difficult period. The memory of the sad events of 1905 and his resignation from the Antiquities Service could not easily be forgotten. His return to painting – 'a thing he should have done years ago', as Mrs Andrews confided to her diary – had not worked out as he had hoped. Living a kind of hand-to-mouth existence did not suit his temperament. Now, to work with the Earl of Carnarvon held a promise of much better things. Carter aspired to grand company, and could expect social advantages of the kind he had enjoyed with the Amhersts. He never subsequently suggested that his departure from the Antiquities Service provided him in due course with the chance to work for Carnarvon; but he would surely have thought in later years that in his earlier misfortune lay the seed of his later success. Truly *de son bannissement il tire son bonheur.*

7

FIVE YEARS' EXPLORATIONS AT THEBES

A mummified cat in a case represented the sum total of the finds from the Earl of Carnarvon's first Theban season. It was one object more than Arthur Weigall credited to him in his letter to Francis Ll. Griffith, and in his more considered report which Griffith included in the *Archaeological Report 1906–1907*,[1] he puts the outcome starkly: 'his labours were fruitless.' Subsequent contributions about Carnarvon's work to later *Archaeological Reports* were equally terse, and generally uninformative. In the *Report* for 1907–8: 'Lord Carnarvon conducted some small excavations at Gurneh, and obtained a few valuable antiquities, including the tablet of which I send you the photos. An interesting tomb of Dynasty XIV-XVII was uncovered.' Here a note by Griffith gives a short but useful account of this tablet, which, as will appear, was one of the objects for which the Carnarvon excavations are best remembered. In the *Report* for 1908–9 he covers Carnarvon's season in two lines, adding, 'I hope that next year will see the successful completion of this bit of work.' At the same time, he separately devoted a whole paragraph to reporting a theft from a tomb previously excavated by Carnarvon, with some tendentious comments on dealers and 'better-class Egyptians'. At last in the *Report* for 1909–10, Carter is included with Carnarvon in Weigall's three-line note on their discoveries. For 1910–11, two lines suffice. No further annual dispatches on excavations were sent by Weigall, but in the *Report* for 1911–12 there was a good notice of *Five Years' Explorations at Thebes*.[2] It was written by Griffith, always the most sympathetic and generous of scholars, whose judgements, briefly expressed, contained more wisdom than the lengthy commentaries of most of his contemporary colleagues.

The annual *Archaeological Reports* of the Egypt Exploration Fund, edited and largely written by Griffith, represented the first serious attempt to

---

1 Weigall's short reports on Carnarvon's work are included in the *E.E.F. Arch, Reps*, as follows: 1906–7, p. 18; 1907–8, p. 7; 1908–9, pp. 12f.; 1909–10, p. 18; 1910–11, p. 20. The cat coffin of the first season is illustrated in N. Reeves, *The Complete Tutankhamun* (London, 1990), p. 23.

2 *E.E.F. Arch. Rep. 1911–1912*, p. 23.

offer to professional scholars and interested amateurs a conspectus of what
was happening universally in the world of Egyptology. It might, therefore,
be thought that Weigall's modest annual comments on the Carnarvon
excavations at Thebes were exceptionally ungenerous, inspired perhaps by
hostility towards Carnarvon and, later, Carter. This view, however, may
give insufficient credit to Weigall's own deeply felt ideas on excavation, its
methods and purposes, on professionals and amateurs, and on priorities
in archaeological work generally. It has already been made clear that he
did not give Carnarvon much of a chance to carry out a good excavation,
even though he admitted to finding him 'a good sort'. He did not like the
way he had obtained his concession, and he distinctly objected to Carnarvon's exploitation of personal standing with the British officials in Egypt.
As Chief Inspector of Upper Egypt, based in Luxor, Weigall no doubt felt
that he had been outmanoeuvred in his own parish, and practically ignored
in his official capacity; and this feeling was surely intensified when Howard
Carter joined Carnarvon as his expert.

For the early years of Weigall's inspectorship Carter had lived mostly
at Thebes during the winter months, scratching a living, trying to keep
up appearances, with no archaeological pretensions, acting occasionally as
a superior dragoman for parties of grand tourists or as personal guide for
individuals of wealth and importance. He was a former colleague, six years
older, from whose fall Weigall had perhaps benefited – although the latter
would surely have received an official appointment sooner or later. He was
no threat, might even be mocked in his indigent state, and could be the
recipient of charitable attentions. The Chief Inspector could put work
unofficially in his way – painting or guiding – but there is no evidence for
any such helpful interventions. And then, in 1908–9 Howard Carter became
redivivus, quite unexpectedly one must assume, and given a position which
rendered him independent from those who might previously have been
able to patronize him. He had been promoted to be Carnarvon's man by
Maspero, who was delighted to be able to bring him back into the archaeological field. In his report on the progress of the Antiquities Service for
1909 Maspero, for the first time since 1905, mentions his old protégé.
Referring to Carnarvon's work, he adds:[3] 'He had entrusted the supervision
of his working site to our former inspector Mr. Howard Carter, whom we
have been happy to see return to archaeology at least for a time.' It is
not likely that Maspero would have consulted Weigall before putting Carter's name before Carnarvon. Any surprise on Weigall's part, however, may
have been diminished by Maspero's allowing Carter as early as the spring
of 1908 to move back into the old Antiquities Service house at Medinet
Habu – the first Castle Carter. This was apparently a real act of charity

---

3 *Rapports sur la marche du Service des Antiquités de 1899 à 1910* (Cairo, 1912), p. 293; original
in French.

on Maspero's part, but perhaps anticipating his intention to recommend Carter to Carnarvon.

If there was a serious possibility of a clash of personalities and interests between Weigall and Carter, it may not have been imminent in the early years. Weigall appears to have thought that Carnarvon's patience in excavating would not survive many seasons of indifferent results. He may even have formed the opinion from hints dropped by Carnarvon himself, who in about 1908 was thinking of applying for a concession to excavate at Aswan. He believed that some diversification might bring a better chance of success, and there was the evidence of the good results achieved at Aswan by Lady William Cecil a few years earlier. But this idea was dropped after Carter joined him, and by his own skills turned a modest enterprise at Thebes into a very interesting and successful campaign. The improvement in Carnarvon's operations may then have led to a hardening of Weigall's attitude, and some element of jealousy might be detected. It is likely, however, that dislike of what was being effected by Carnarvon and Carter was prompted more by a strong, almost ideological, antipathy on Weigall's part to the nature of the Carnarvon dig. Weigall was a man of considerable intelligence, with a quick mind, a sharp pen, and a scornful attitude towards amateurism. He also developed firm views about the ethics of excavation, incorporating a somewhat puritanical approach for the time. He saw in Carnarvon's excavation much to object to in principle: Carnarvon, the rich man, playing at excavation; Carter, the new man, with imperfect training, and a distinct interest in the comfortable life which went with hobnobbing with the great; and Maspero himself, a great scholar, but too inclined to be well disposed towards persons of position, and exercising the wrong priorities in his attitudes to field-work generally. The differences would simmer, and to some extent fester, in the years leading up to the First World War, and Weigall would become more positive and outspoken in his views. It will be seen, when the matter is discussed later, that Weigall's opinion was not unique to himself, and it was in a sense anticipating what would develop politically within the Antiquities Service after Maspero's resignation in 1914 (at the age of 68) and the appointment of Pierre Lacau as his successor, and in the changed circumstances after the war. Then a momentum, fuelled by the rise of nationalism in Egypt and a new realism in regard to archaeological work there, would lead inexorably towards drastic changes in the exercise of the antiquities laws and practices. It would be not only the privileged digs of rich amateurs that would be threatened, but all excavation work, and the most dramatic withdrawal from working in Egypt would be that of the most dedicated excavator of them all, Flinders Petrie.[4]

Those developments, which may trace their embryonic stirrings to the

4 See M. S. Drower, *Flinders Petrie. A Life in Archaeology* (London, 1985), pp. 356ff.

views of Arthur Weigall, sharpened on his dislike of Carnarvon's excavations and all that went with them, lay some years ahead. Nevertheless
it is worth bearing them in mind when the actual work paid for by
Carnarvon and directed by Carter is considered. Was it as 'irresponsible'
as Weigall at first suggested? Was it conducted badly and supervised
inadequately? Was it, in the end, profitable archaeologically, and reasonably published? On the evidence of Carter's surviving field-notes, preserved
in the Griffith Institute in Oxford, and of the volume *Five Years' Explorations
at Thebes*,[5] no one could deny the value of the information provided by the
discoveries made in the course of the whole enterprise, or the very decent
standard reached in the publication of the results. There is good evidence,
further, from private letters and independent accounts of the work in
progress, that both Carnarvon and Carter were deeply committed to the
excavations, and conducted them with close supervision on a regular basis.
The dig lacked entirely the social element that characterized the Theodore
Davis excavation in the Valley of the Kings.

The area in which Carnarvon and Carter worked at Thebes lay in
what might have been described then – though quite wrongly – as the
'unfashionable' district of the Necropolis. It was in part of what was named
the Asasif, extending from in front of the enclosure of the great Deir el-
Bahri temple of Queen Hatshepsut, eastwards along the line but to the
north of the temple causeway, and taking in the southern slopes of the
region known as Dra Abu el-Naga. It was known to be a place where
tombs had been excavated and constructed in antiquity, and one which
from its appearance had already been worked over by the diligent inhabitants of the neighbouring villages. It was a challenge for Carnarvon, and
it says much for his serious intentions that he chose to excavate in this
somewhat unpromising concession. The time was one of relative quiet in
the Theban Necropolis. The Egypt Exploration Fund had recently completed their major excavation of the earlier temple at Deir el-Bahri, that
of King Nebhepetre Mentuhotpe II of the Eleventh Dynasty. The Egyptian
Expedition of the Metropolitan Museum of Art was yet to settle down in
a fine new excavation house – a Ritz among dig-houses – to work in the
area to the south of the Carnarvon concession. Yet there was still a fair
amount of Theban field-work in hand, with Theodore Davis in the Valley
of the Kings and Ernesto Schiaparelli in the Valley of the Queens. A
welcome newcomer to the West Bank was Norman de Garis Davies who,
with his wife Nina, was to make the recording of Theban tombs his life-
work. He had succeeded Percy Newberry as the principal field-worker of
the Archaeological Survey of the Egypt Exploration Fund, completing in
the early years of the century many of the tasks which Newberry had once
planned for himself and Howard Carter. Now he had been offered a

5 The Earl of Carnarvon and H. Carter, *Five Years' Explorations at Thebes. A Record of work
   done 1907–1911*, (London, 1912).

144

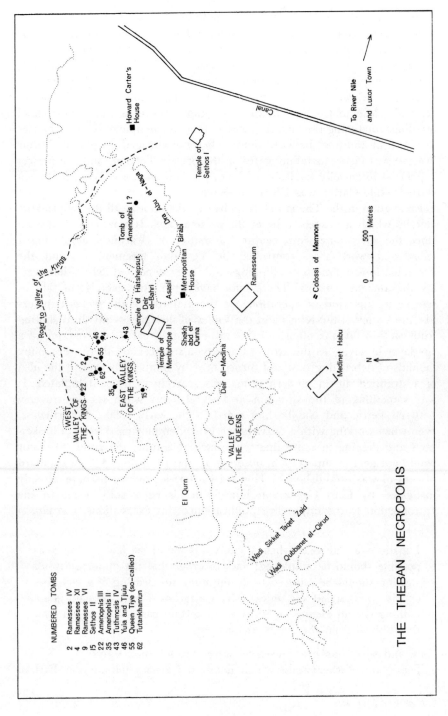

NUMBERED TOMBS

2   Ramesses IV
4   Ramesses XI
9   Ramesses VI
15 Sethos II
22 Amenophis III
35 Amenophis II
43 Tuthmosis IV
46 Yuia and Tjuiu
55 Queen Tiye (so-called)
62 Tutankhamun

THE THEBAN NECROPOLIS

permanent appointment by the Metropolitan Museum and, with a secure future ahead, could settle with his wife at Thebes for six to eight months every year, establishing a congenial domestic environment where Carter in particular could find sympathetic company. Émile Baraize, a French architect employed by the Antiquities Service, was busily engaged in conservation work at the Ramesseum, the funerary temple of King Ramesses II, and, close to Carter's house at Medinet Habu, a huge complex of buildings, including the almost complete funerary temple of King Ramesses III. And in addition, between times, when not engaged elsewhere, Arthur Weigall was busily installing gates on the private Theban tombs, a project supported financially by Robert Mond, in continuation of what had been started while Carter was Chief Inspector.

Excavation in the Theban Necropolis was then not at all the painstaking activity which it is seen to be at the present time. It was, as it had been since the early nineteenth century, a matter of clearance, employing a substantial work-force, controlled by Egyptian foremen, to shift the accumulations of limestone chippings and water-deposited debris that overlay the ancient remains. There may have been little exercise of skill or science in this kind of operation, for the majority of the work in places like the Valley of the Kings and the Valley of the Queens involved shifting 'rubbish' – as it was often called – rather than a careful uncovering of a site layer by layer. In the area of Carnarvon's concession there were many mounds of debris dug into and turned over by tomb-robbers, and the idea of a stratified dig in modern terms was scarcely to be contemplated. It was something of the situation at Deir el-Bahri when the controversy between Petrie and Naville had raged in the early 1890s. Nevertheless, even when working with a fairly broad brush, employing dozens of basket-boys and digging in more than one place at a time, the good excavator would not neglect supervision, observation and recording. A high standard of control was established by Howard Carter, a practice perhaps already instigated by Lord Carnarvon himself in his early solo years. In the Introduction to the impressive publication of his excavations, Carnarvon explains:[6]

> I made it a rule that when a tomb was found, as few workmen as possible should be employed; and, in order that the opportunity for stealing should be reduced to a minimum, no clearing of a chamber or pit was carried on unless Mr. Carter or I was present. That nothing should escape us, we also, in certain cases, had to sift over the rubbish from the tombs three times.

Care and surveillance at this level were rare for such times.

The years of excavation which followed Carter's joining the Earl of

6 *Fives Years'*, pp. 1f.

Carnarvon provided him with more sustained serious digging than he had ever practised before. It was a period of consolidation, in which he was obliged to develop his techniques of field-work far beyond what he had been accustomed to do in his earlier years at Thebes when he worked on the Tomb of the Horse and on the first operations for Theodore Davis in the Valley of the Kings. Excavation was generally becoming very much more professional, and Carter must himself have appreciated that the standards now expected were higher than those that had passed for good practice even with Flinders Petrie in the season at El-Amarna in 1892. Nevertheless, he was much more a Petrie man in the way he worked than a Naville man; but above all he was his own man, relying on a patient persistent temperament, supported by his ability to record superbly well whatever he found in drawings, plans and photographs. He also had for the first time the opportunity to prepare a fuller and more professional publication of the results of his work than had ever been possible for him to do previously. Although the volumes sponsored by Theodore Davis on the various tombs found in the excavations he had financed in the Valley of the Kings were lavishly produced, they were disappointingly thin and rather imperfect records of what had been found. The volumes in which Carter himself had been involved, dealing with the tombs of Tuthmosis IV and Tomb 20, described as the tomb of Queen Hatshepsut,[7] are archaeologically more satisfactory than those that followed, but even so they fall short of what he was able to prepare for Carnarvon's work.

Five Years' Explorations at Thebes, subtitled *A Record of work done 1907–1911*, appeared commendably quickly in 1912. It covered the early years of Carnarvon's excavations, after his first trial season, as well as the years of co-operation with Carter, and it is instructive to perform a kind of excavation on its contents themselves to see what represents the results of Carnarvon's first two seasons, and to examine the way in which his discoveries are presented compared with that dealing with the finds made with Howard Carter. The distinction is not explicitly made because the book is written as if all the results stem from the co-operative efforts of Carnarvon and Carter; and there can be little doubt that Carter's hand was involved in the book as a whole, except in those chapters written by specialist scholars dealing with particular finds. Among the earliest of the important finds made by Carnarvon was the tomb of Tetiky, a mayor of Thebes who lived in the early Eighteenth Dynasty (c. 1525 BC). It had been discovered in early 1908 before Carter had joined him; the photographic record of the painted scenes on the walls of the tomb was made by Carter perhaps before his formal engagement by Carnarvon. The volume contains a very brief note on the excavation of the tomb written

7 H. Carter and P. E. Newberry, *The Tomb of Thoutmôsis IV* (London, 1904); T. M. Davis with contributions by É. Naville and H. Carter, *The Tomb of Hâtshopsîtû* (London, 1906).

by Carter, but singularly thin in detail.[8] The tomb scenes and inscriptions, and the very interesting early *shabtis* (funerary deputies) found in it, are described by two other scholars, Georges Legrain and Percy Newberry. It is this tomb about which Weigall had reported thefts in the notes he had written for Griffith's *Archaeological Report 1908–1909*. The tomb of Tetiky was sealed by Weigall to prevent further thefts of parts of the painted walls, and it was generally thought, presumably on the basis of Weigall's inspection, that there was little left to see, in Legrain's words, 'The tomb . . . having unfortunately been mostly destroyed.' So it was not readily available for Carter to study when the time came to write it up for the publication. Subsequently, in 1924, it was reopened for Newberry, and the opportunity was taken by Norman de Garis Davies to copy what was left of the painted scenes. He was surprised to find that the damage done since the excavation was relatively slight, and he was able, with his assistant Charles Wilkinson, to make a good record of the scenes;[9] this record could presumably have been made by Carter years before if the tomb had not been sealed.

The tomb of Tetiky, historically and artistically important, was essentially a robbed sepulchre, quite the most common state for the majority of tombs found at Thebes. Some better luck came with the tomb numbered 9 in the excavation sequence. It again was found early in 1908 before Carter joined Carnarvon,[10] but he was able to complete its clearance and study in 1909. Apart from a huge quantity of pottery and of poorly preserved mummies, two damaged writing boards were found. One of these, known as the Carnarvon Tablet I, bears on one side the beginning of a very important historical text.[11] It relates the start of the campaign which led to the expulsion from Egypt of the Asiatic Hyksos rulers who had usurped royal authority in Egypt during what is usually termed the Second Intermediate Period, between the Middle and New Kingdoms. The text, which is written in the cursive hieratic script on the gesso-plastered surface of the writing board, is dated to the reign of Kamose, the last king of the Seventeenth Dynasty (*c*. 1555 BC). As soon as it was discovered and made known to scholars, it excited great interest and considerable controversy, the debate hinging on whether the text was a true historical document or part of a fictional account of the expulsion of the Hyksos. Persuasive arguments in favour of the historical interpretation were provided by Alan H. Gardiner in a classic article written in 1916.[12] Yet, when

8 *Five Years'*, pp. 12f. The Legrain and Newberry chapters follow, pp. 14ff. and 19ff.
9 In *J.E.A.* 11 (1925), pp. 10ff.
10 So N. de G. Davies, *ibid.*, p. 10.
11 See F. Ll. Griffith in *Five Years'*, pp. 36f. The text on the reverse is part of a well known Middle-Kingdom composition, 'The Instruction of Ptah-hotpe', on which generally, see M. Lichtheim, *Ancient Egyptian Literature*, I (Berkeley, Los Angeles, London, 1973), pp. 61ff.
12 In *J.E.A.* 3 (1915), pp. 95ff. The discovery in Karnak in 1954 of a large stela of King Kamose virtually clinched the historical credentials of the text on Carnarvon Tablet I, see L. Habachi, *The Second Stela of Kamose* (Glückstadt, 1972).

it was found, it was understandably not recognized by Lord Carnarvon as an object of great importance. He had no competence in reading the hieroglyphic script, and no possibility of penetrating the hieratic signs of the ink text on the tablet. Had he already been supported by Howard Carter, he would not have been better informed at the time of discovery about the nature of the text; but Carter would surely have divined the possibility of its importance, and sought an opinion from some scholar passing through Thebes who might have been able to give at least some idea of what the text was about. As it was, and according to Weigall's letter to Griffith of October 1908,[13] the tablet in two pieces was stuffed into a basket and left with the other antiquities in the Chief Inspector's office when Carnarvon left Thebes at the end of his season.

Enhanced rigour, system and control were to characterize the Carnarvon operations after Carter's arrival, and the effects of the change are clearly reflected in the detail and authority to be found in the chapters of *Five Years' Explorations at Thebes* which report what was accomplished in the three years of his improved supervision. In his Introduction, summing up the achievements of the five seasons, Carnarvon lists the three parts of his concession to which he confined his attention.[14] The first was a spot near the old village mosque where there was said to be a hidden tomb; it was the tomb of Tetiky. Second, there was the part of the lower slope of Dra Abu el-Naga, known as the Birabi, a name explained in the publication as meaning locally 'vaulted tombs', of which there were many in the district. Strictly the word is the plural form of *birba*, meaning 'temple ruin'. Tomb no. 9 was an early example of the kind of discovery which awaited the attention of Carnarvon and Carter. The third part included a segment of the area on the north side of the Deir el-Bahri valley, containing burials of the Eleventh Dynasty. Working at times with a force of as many as 275 men and boys – by no means an unusually large number by the standards of the times – they uncovered many tombs in both of the main parts, and, additionally, structures which were both archaeologically important and also difficult to interpret. From the excavator's point of view, the least profitable part of the work was that listed as third by Carnarvon. The day-to-day work was supervised by a young Welshman, Cyril Jones, who had come to Luxor in the steps of his brother Harold, a talented artist who was employed both by Theodore Davis and, latterly, by the Metropolitan Museum Egyptian Expedition at Lisht in Middle Egypt. The area was much worked over, yet the discoveries were not negligible, including several early tombs which had been re-used in the later dynasties of the Pharaonic Period (after about 1100 BC) for multiple burials. Cyril Jones also discovered two virtually intact foundation deposits[15] associated with the

13 See p. 139 above.
14 *Five Years'*, p. 2.
15 *Five Years'*, pp. 30ff.

dromos, or causeway, leading from Hatshepsut's temple to the edge of the Nile plain where one would hope to find a temple to be used in the funeral services of the queen, and subsequently for ceremonies connected with the royal funerary cult.

As happens so frequently in excavation, the unexpected led to what might have been expected – part of a well-constructed wall, found by chance during the clearance of tomb no. 9, turned out to be a trace of the so-called Valley Temple of Hatshepsut. What remained of the temple was uncovered by Carter in 1910–11, at first unidentified but later firmly dated to the queen's reign by ink inscriptions on some of the blocks naming the architect of the structure, Puyemre. A foundation deposit with objects inscribed with the queen's name, and stamped mud-bricks, further confirmed the identification, but there was little to be made of the building itself: it was either never completed, or fairly comprehensively destroyed, quarried away probably for its fine stone-work.[16] The remains of another destroyed royal building was found near by, a colonnaded temple of King Ramesses IV of the Twentieth Dynasty (*c.* 1160 BC). Its traces were concealed by a range of vaulted tombs which extended also over part of the Hatshepsut Valley Temple. These tombs, the source of the locality's name, Birabi, contained the remains of burials of the Ptolemaic Period and yielded few objects of interest at the time, apart from two well preserved papyri with texts written in the demotic script, the very cursive form of Egyptian writing used mostly for secular purposes in the late periods of Egyptian antiquity. These two documents, found in a sealed pottery amphora, could be dated to the early second century BC, and contained legal contracts for the sale of temple land. Carter arranged for them to be studied by Wilhelm Speigelberg, a leading demotic scholar and professor of Egyptology in the University of Strassburg. He contributed a brief account for the great Carnarvon volume, and published a scholarly article on the documents in a specialist journal in 1913.[17]

The most striking finds in the way of objects were made by Carter in earlier tombs in the Birabi, tombs of the late Middle Kingdom re-used in the Second Intermediate Period and early Eighteenth Dynasty (*c.* 1700–1500 BC), which had in some cases been made repositories for multiple burials. What would have been rich early burials were, however, sadly diminished in content by vandalism, theft and natural causes. Writing to Percy Newberry sometime in 1910–11 (the letter is just dated 'Saturday'), Carter laments:[18]

What treasure there would have been had not the early plunderers done so much damage and the white ants too. But still quite a nice

16 For the valley temple, see Carter's chapter, *Five Years'*, pp. 38ff. For the building of Ramesses IV, p. 48.
17 *Five Years'*, p. 46f.; for the full publication see *Rec. Trav.* 35 (1913), pp. 150ff.
18 G.I. Newberry Corr. 8/79.

lot of things turn up. Lord Carnarvon has still two more tombs to clear, making now 8 in all and there must be many more yet to be uncovered.

Three tombs in particular (nos 25, 27, 37) produced a huge amount of funerary equipment in the form of painted coffins, many in the style peculiar to the late Second Intermediate Period, known as *rishi* coffins because of their feathered decoration.[19] There were also excellent individual finds of small statuary, cosmetic equipment, including from one tomb a fine toilet box splendidly fitted out with mirror and alabaster vessels, made for an official of King Ammenemes IV of the Twelfth Dynasty, named Kemen. The same tomb (no. 25) produced a wood and ivory object which at first was not recognized for what it was, as a letter from Carter to Mrs Newberry makes clear:[20]

> another small ivory box in the form of an axe on four bull's legs. This had a cornelian and gold brooch and 10 most beautiful ivory hair pins – 5 with jackal heads and 5 with slughis (hunting dogs) heads.

Carter subsequently identified it as a board game, the ivory pins being the pieces; he called it 'Hounds contra jackals', and in the excavation volume provided a set of rules for play.[21] Extracting damaged, delicate objects under the working conditions of a large Theban dig was a chancy matter, and success depended greatly on the vigilance of those in charge. Carter's account of the first encounter with promising pieces in tomb no. 25 is instructive:[22]

> At first this grave seemed to be a great disappointment. But when, in Lord Carnarvon's presence, the men found in the lower filling of the shaft an ivory pin and a piece of a box with silver binding, our hopes were raised. Lord Carnarvon at once stopped the workmen until a time when full surveillance of the clearing could be made. It was a difficult job, most careful work had to be done with trowel, bellows, and sometimes a spoon, extricating fragile objects while stones and sand poured down from the overhanging masonry above in a menacing manner at every gust of wind.

One may be sure that it was Carter himself who wielded the trowel, bellows and spoon.

Tomb no. 37, cut into the rock, with a frontage having 18 openings, was considered by Carter to be one of the largest private tombs in the Theban Necropolis. There were only a few material traces of the original

19 Descriptions and inventories of finds are given by Carter in *Five Years'*, pp. 51ff.
20 G.I. Newberry Corr. 8/33, of 16 March 1910.
21 *Five Years'*, pp. 58ff.
22 *Ibid.*, p. 54.

burial, and nothing by which the first owner could be identified. It had, however, been made a repository for many later burials, including 64 coffins, some domestic furniture, unusual instruments, a splendid 'working' scribal outfit, toilet equipment, and much ordinary jewellery, pottery and basketwork. There was also, in one coffin, a beautiful silver-bronze statuette of a boy called Amenemhab, 13 cm high, standing on a wooden base; also a larger wooden figure of his brother, Huwebenef.

So the excavations that the Earl of Carnarvon began in 1907 had, in the end, turned out not at all badly. He could be well pleased with the results, both historical and archaeological; the return in good objects had also been very satisfactory. It seemed a good moment, therefore, at the end of the 1911 season, to take stock and publish the results so far. For him it had been the full five years of the subsequent volume's title. For Carter it had been just three seasons, and it was as such that he estimated his own contribution. Writing to Spiegelberg on 1 July 1911 he says:[23] 'I left the burning Theban hills, now three weeks ago, and I am getting Lord Carnarvon's Report of the last three years work ready for publication.' In the writing he incorporated the results of the first two seasons, and Lord Carnarvon in his very informative Introduction sets out the course of the whole campaign, crediting Carter, as much as himself, with the totality of the five years' work. This kind, but misleading, extension of Carter's association with him back to 1907, was well-intentioned and generous; it would not have confused those who were about in Thebes during the first decade of the century. Yet Percy Newberry in his obituary notice of Howard Carter[24] indicates that the association began in 1908, while Carter himself stated that he 'began to excavate for Lord Carnarvon in 1907'.[25] He did not recall dates with precision, even when they marked significant moments in his life and career.

The three years of collaboration between Carnarvon and Carter had established more than a working bond for this disparate couple. Lord Carnarvon, the undoubted grandee in the tradition of the late nineteenth century, but complicated by a characteristically informal Edwardian element, had taken enthusiastically to Carter, the talented artist, who could command respect from Europeans and Egyptians by his authoritative presence when at work in the field. Carnarvon was prepared to join in the rough and tumble of excavation, as much as his health allowed; he did not direct from a *dahabiya* or his suite at the Winter Palace Hotel. Carter found in Carnarvon someone he could truly respect, and not just because he paid the bills and had rescued him from a rather miserable and undignified existence. They had one further special interest in common, which helped to increase their affectionate interdependence. This was a passion

23 O.I. Spiegelberg-Carnarvon papers.
24 *J.E.A.* 25 (1939), p. 68.
25 H. Carter and A. C. Mace, *The Tomb of Tut.ankh.Amen*, I (London, 1923), p. 75.

for fine antiquities. Nothing that is known about the beginnings of Carnarvon's work in Egypt suggests that he took to excavation in order to build up a collection. But an interest developed, presumably as soon as he found enough antiquities to be entitled to a share. The opportunities increased dramatically once he was joined by Carter, who had much experience already in helping wealthy collectors to acquire material. His capacity for getting to know the dealers of Luxor has already been mentioned. The years of enforced archaeological idleness had sharpened this capacity, and enabled him, without official ties to the Antiquities Service, to engage freely in acquiring objects for collectors, private and institutional. The nature of the market in Egypt, at Luxor and at Cairo, depended both on the random discoveries made by farmers and labourers working as *seb-bakhin*, and on illicit excavations carried out by experienced villagers like the Abd er-Rasul family in the Theban Necropolis. A trickle of objects also came from the regular pilfering that went on in most excavations; such were the pieces of jewellery and other precious objects lifted from the Theodore Davis excavation of the tomb of Yuia and Tjuiu, which Carter found in the hands of dealers in 1906.[26]

In the time when he was Chief Inspector, Carter built up his knowledge of the dealer network in Luxor, and he used his contacts to obtain advance information of important, but unofficial, discoveries. As a private person, acting as an agent for private clients, he could exploit his experience, profitably combing the commercial sources for likely purchases. He might also be approached by free-lance diggers who would know that he was in the habit of buying, and that he would usually offer a seller a fairer price than any dealer would. In acting thus, buying for himself and on behalf of others, he was not acting improperly according to the law or to the usual practices of the time. Authorized dealers in antiquities had official licences; they maintained, in principle, registers of their stock, and were subject to inspection by representatives of the Antiquities Service. Inspection was not regular, or common, and it cannot be doubted that many important antiquities passed through the hands of dealers without the knowledge of the Cairo Museum. Again, in principle, antiquities for export from Egypt were to be shown to the authorities at the Cairo Museum and passed, or confiscated with compensation. Unfortunately the system was not rigorously maintained, and even when inspections took place many things escaped the process and passed out of Egypt by way of the abundant loopholes. The scandal of Wallis Budge's buccaneering approach to the acquisition and export of antiquities, with which Carter had been wrongly linked in the newspaper campaign of 1903,[27] was but one example of what went on commonly in Egypt in the early part of the twentieth century. Howard Carter certainly claimed that in arranging the export of items

26 See p. 131 above.
27 See p. 77 above.

purchased on behalf of institutions he did submit objects to the Cairo Museum for licences; but it cannot be asserted that he was regularly punctilious in all his other transactions. There is, however, no evidence that in the many purchases he made on behalf of Lord Carnarvon he ever behaved in such a way as to attract serious criticism.

Generally speaking, the Carnarvon collection of Egyptian antiquities consisted of small, beautiful, pieces – sculptures, objects of precious metal, glass, jewellery – the emphasis being on fine quality.[28] Such were the kinds of thing Carter sought out and Carnarvon was pleased to buy. In addition there were the objects from the excavator's share of the results of the work at Thebes. Not everything acquired from this source could fit easily into the company of fine pieces; but many were worthy, and all helped to provide the collection with an authentic archaeological base against which the purchased objects could be judged. Not all the pieces from the excavator's share were retained for Highclere Castle; some were presented as gifts to institutions like the British Museum and the Metropolitan Museum, and even the local museum in Newbury, Berkshire; others, particularly larger items like the splendid coffins found in the Birabi tombs, were sold to interested museums. Sales of material found in excavations were not at all unusual, and could be justified as a way of recouping some of the heavy expenses of the field-work. Flinders Petrie was himself accustomed to do this occasionally,[29] and the practice is not so very different from the persisting method of financing field-work, whereby contributing institutions receive shares of the objects from divisions.

There was no secrecy about Carnarvon's collecting, and he was delighted to show visitors his latest acquisitions. When Carter wrote to Wilhelm Spiegelberg on 9 July 1911, chiefly, about the demotic papyri he was publishing, he adds at the end:[30]

> I have shown your MS. to Lord Carnarvon and he is immensely pleased and he trusts that whenever you should come to England that you will not fail to let him know. The little collection 'Specimens of Egyptian fine Art' is gradually growing and beginning to become most interesting, and I am sure you will like to see it.

The quality of the objects Carnarvon delighted in acquiring is typified by the three bracelet plaques of the reign of King Amenophis III (c. 1360 BC) which were purchased by Carter from a Luxor dealer towards the end of 1912, in a minor coup by which he just beat the Berlin Museum

---

28 On Carnarvon as collector, see N. Reeves, *The Complete Tutankhamun*, p. 47.

29 The comments by T. Hoving in *Tutankhamun. The Untold Story* (New York, 1978), pp. 136f., about antiquities sales by excavators are badly misjudged, and as far as Petrie's transactions over the Lahun Treasure are concerned, far from the mark.

30 O.I. Spiegelberg-Carnarvon Papers.

through prompt action.[31] Two of the plaques were made of carnelian and carried finely carved miniature representations of royal ceremonies; the third was of purplish-brown sard and showed in open-work a female sphinx, probably an imaginative depiction of the king's principal wife, Tiye, holding a cartouche with the prenomen of Amenophis III. In Carter's stated opinion, enthusiastically adopted by Carnarvon, these precious objects probably came from the tomb of the king in the Valley of the Kings. Some work had been carried out in the mounds of debris near the entrance to this tomb in early 1912 by Theodore Davis's team,[32] and it was a reasonable assumption that these plaques were stolen in the course of this investigation. Carnarvon was delighted with their acquisition, and wrote enthusiastically to Percy Newberry inviting him to Highclere Castle, using the plaques as an inducement.[33]

Like most collectors of works of art, Carnarvon was not averse to doing a little bit of trading in the course of the hunt for new acquisitions. It is not clear whether he visited dealers along with Carter, or followed up leads offered by Carter after he had himself made preliminary sorties. There was probably no regular pattern in their searching; but there was certainly encouragement from both sides, and some eagerness on Carnarvon's part that Carter should take advantage of his opportunities to purchase and then sell on his own behalf. He also did the same for Carnarvon, and Carnarvon himself occasionally shows himself to be an eager trader. Letters from him to Wallis Budge in the British Museum in 1911–13[34] suggest that he took some of the initiative himself, offering one or two Seventeenth-dynasty coffins found in the Birabi and even, extraordinarily, suggesting that he might be able to buy for the Museum the sarcophagus of Tuthmosis III. He reports, 'Carter seems to think that Maspero would sell it for 1000£.' Such transactions were proposed, and in some cases carried through, with a great deal of practicality, but always spiced with a show of real interest in the objects discussed; they were not just commodities to be bought and sold.

One person who did not approve of this kind of commerce was Arthur Weigall, and his presence at Thebes remained a source of discomfort, especially to Howard Carter. From his earliest days as Chief Inspector in Upper Egypt, Weigall had devoted much of his energies at Thebes to the

31 See the editorial article (unattributed) by Alan Gardiner in *J.E.A.* 3 (1916), pp. 73ff., and letters from Carter to Lord Carnarvon at Highclere. The plaques are now in the Metropolitan Museum of Art.

32 An unpublished piece of work, see N. Reeves, *The Complete Tutankhamun*, p. 320 under Site 39; the royal tomb is WV 22.

33 G.I. Newberry Corr. 7/107, dated 10 November 1912.

34 The old correspondence files of the Department of Egyptian and Assyrian Antiquities are kept in the present Department of Western Asiatic Antiquities. I am grateful to the Trustees of the Museum and to Mr. T. C. Mitchell, former Keeper of Western Asiatic Antiquities, for permission to consult and quote from them. The letters quoted here are dated 25 February 1911, 4 February 1912, 14 March 1913.

cleaning and protection of the private tombs. In 1909 he began a systematic cataloguing and numbering of these tombs, and was fortunate in obtaining the co-operation of Alan H. Gardiner, the outstanding British Egyptological scholar of the younger generation, who at that time was 30. For three years Gardiner spent several months annually working with Weigall on this Theban tomb enterprise.[35] Together they spent much time discussing the problems afflicting Egyptian archaeology, particularly in the Theban scene. Weigall was comprehensively dismissive of his colleagues, immensely confident in the rightness of his own views, and desperately eager to retain the support of Gardiner. He was to leave Thebes for health reasons for some months in 1912, and some time afterwards he sent Gardiner a long letter including proposals for the regulation of excavations, divisions, and the export of antiquities.[36] In it he declares, before explaining his scheme:

> it is absolutely essential to me that I should in every case have your approval, for your opinion is the only one I care a damn about, and you are the only Egyptologist whose views I regard as sane. (That is perhaps putting it rather too strongly, but you will know what I mean).

In the course of the letter he takes swipes at many targets. He is eager to reform the practice of the division of antiquities; to reduce the quantities of antiquities in the Cairo Museum by sales to foreign museums, but never to private persons; to use the money from such sales to purchase antiquities in the hands of dealers. On the last he declares, 'It is hateful to me always to see the splendid things in dealers shops all going into private hands or into distant American museums.' He castigates Maspero and 'K'[37] as Philistines, and is sure that the former will be totally opposed to what he, Weigall, might propose.

Gardiner, it seems, was not wholly in agreement; he could foresee problems with the international Egyptological community. But there was much of Weigall's exasperation that had rubbed off on him. In a letter of 4 October 1911, written from the Theban Necropolis to his wife, he praises extravagantly the work Weigall has been doing to protect the tombs, and compares his activity most favourably with what happened previously.[38] 'How terribly culpable Maspero and Carter and Newberry have been!'

---

35 *A Topographical Catalogue of the Private Tombs at Thebes*, by Gardiner and Weigall, was published in London in 1913. A *Supplement* by R. Engelbach was issued by the Antiquities Service in 1924.
36 G.I. Gardiner Corr. AHG/42.355.14.
37 I. e. Lord Kitchener, who had succeeded Sir Eldon Gorst as Diplomatic Agent in 1911. Other evidence, including one reference in this same letter of Weigall, suggests that Kitchener was by no means an ally of Maspero's.
38 Letters from Thebes to Gardiner's wife, now in the possession of their daughter, Margaret Gardiner, who has generously allowed me to see and to quote from them.

After a long discussion with Weigall, 'We went to bed with rather gloomy and despairing thoughts!'

It is not surprising, therefore, to find that Carter felt uncomfortable when visiting Weigall and Gardiner. Problems seem to have started soon after Carter began working with Carnarvon and was living in his old Castle Carter I at Medinet Habu. He complained to Newberry in the late summer of 1909, while he was on holiday in Swaffham:[39]

> Just had a most unpleasant letter from Weigall wherein he accuses me of negligence, acting against the interests of the Dept. and has put a man into the M. H. house. Isn't it beastly – I shall have to make a fuss and I don't like it on account of having to distance [?] from old Maspero who has been so kind and generous to me – It spoils the whole pleasure of my returning to Luxor.

In a much longer letter to Newberry, written after his return to Egypt, Carter continues:[40]

> Weigall has behaved stupidly. My existence I fear will always be an irritation to him. Why I do not know for my intentions towards him have, I may say, always been to his welfare than otherwise. I shew [sic] his letter to Maspero when in Paris. He was disgusted and ever so kind. Maspero had nothing whatsoever to do with the placing of the man [name uncertain] or rather boy (not a bad little chap) in the house here. However I have made the matter right and have now taken him in as a guest, which in some ways is a bore but on the other hand I wish to show Maspero my full appreciation for his lending me the house and not in any way put him in a false position with Weigall.
>
> Weigall I had over here to lunch with Gardiner (who by the way I am as a man much disappointed with). I gave Weigall a good quiet talking to in regard to his insinuations and accusations and I think his private feelings were somewhat uncomfortable. I have acted and shall act friendly to him and I told him any time that he had a grievance against me to come direct and tell me before he came to any conclusions and I hope he will though I rather fear not.

This unfortunate tension, in which Gardiner was involved, continued until after Weigall's final departure from Thebes. Gardiner, although generally sympathetic to many of Weigall's views, was a very different kind of person. Throughout his life he never shirked declaring his position in a matter, never hesitating to express his views strongly, even if personal relationships might suffer. His priorities scientifically were always stated vigorously; he much objected to the explosion of excavation in Egypt in

39 G.I. Newberry Corr. 8/31, dated 6 September 1909.
40 G.I. Newberry Corr. 8/32, of 2 October 1909.

the period before the First World War, believing that ill-considered or unnecessary excavation was positively harmful. His training and inclinations led him to place emphasis on the recording and conservation of those monuments already above ground and in danger of destruction. It can well be thought that he was not as tactful in his dealings with Carter as good diplomacy might require:[41]

> Citoyen Gardiner is still here – the more I see of him the less I like him, and am even more sure that as far as any real friendship goes he is not to be trusted. Certainly, living alone as I do often is inducive one letting the 'milk curdle', but for real friends I have never had this occur. Ever forgive me if I warn you against him. I have already nearly punched his head for nasty insinuations against my friends.

In this outburst a strong hint of the kind of malaise that affects members of excavation teams may be detected, even though Carter and Gardiner did not meet on a daily basis. In a sense Thebes was one excavation site, widely spread and not at all coherent, but with much coming and going between the members of the various component missions. It is, therefore, good to be able to anticipate the considerable scholarly co-operation which developed between Carter and Gardiner in the years to come and, later, Carter's turning to Gardiner for specialized help when Tutankhamun's tomb was found.

The difficulty over the Medinet Habu house, whatever it might have been, was resolved in the winter of 1910–11. Carter had by then been working for Carnarvon for two seasons, and it must have become clear to both that there was to be a future in their association. It has been commonly stated, by Carter himself initially,[42] that from the start of this association the ultimate aim was to obtain the concession to work in the Valley of the Kings. A gesture in the direction of putting down roots in Thebes, presumably with an eye to future work, was the building by Carter of Castle Carter II. It was designed by himself along vernacular lines – solid, roomy, four-square, with a central hall with a dome. Its situation was unusual and striking, set on a hill named Elwat el-Diban, to the north end of Dra Abu el-Naga and at the entrance to the rocky wadi leading to the Valley of the Kings. It was conspicuously sited, and may have derived some of its inspiration in design from the house which Somers Clarke had built for himself, close to the Nile at Elkab. In this new house was a visible commitment for the future, even a hostage to fortune, and in its building he was encouraged by Carnarvon and significantly helped, possibly financially but certainly practically. At that time the Carnarvon family owned an estate and mansion at Bretby in Derbyshire, and at

41 Letter to Newberry of 27 October 1911, G.I. Newberry Corr. 8/35.
42 E.g. *The Tomb of Tut.ankh.Amen*, I, p. 75.

Newhall, near Burton-on-Trent, a brickworks. In 1910 a large number of bricks was made with the impressed inscription:[43]

MADE AT BRETBY
ENGLAND
FOR HOWARD CARTER
A.D. THEBES 1910

These bricks, survivng examples of which show that they were of a red fabric, but with a blackened surface, were surely used in the construction of the house Elwat e'Dibān, as Carter called it on his letter heading. It must be supposed that they represented a donation towards the building; Carter could have used locally made bricks – in those days most probably sun-dried only, not baked – but the house could not have been so solidly constructed. In a sense also Carter was aping his Pharaonic predecessors at Thebes who built their structures of bricks stamped with their names.

Established in his new home early in 1911, Carter could at last feel that he was firmly based, and this state he largely owed to the Earl of Carnarvon. In no time he would be receiving guests; there was much to be admired. 'Carter has built himself a delightful house at north end of the necropolis and moves into it soon' (Weigall);[44] 'Theo and I had a charming afternoon with Mr. Carter in his new house – so well built and arranged and pretty – it looked like the abode of an artist and a scholar' (Mrs Andrews);[45] 'By noon we had reached the new house that Carter had built for himself . . . and, it being very warm, we determined to call upon Carter and take drinks off him. I was glad to have an opportunity of looking over his house, which is quite delightful; simple mud walls, not rendered conspicuous by any plaster; very little furniture, but what there is artistic. In the middle is a little domed hall quite in the ancient Arabic style. Carter seems well, but has a dreadful greenish colour; he is quite sociable and decent towards us, and in a way I am always quite pleased to have his company' (Gardiner).[46]

After the publication of *Five Years' Explorations at Thebes*, the spirit to continue excavating in the Theban concession dimmed somewhat. Work in the Birabi district of the Asasif involved large numbers of men and a great deal of hard work, the results from which tended to be repeated – Ptolemaic vault tombs on top, and pit and corridor tombs of the late

---

43 I am grateful to Mr P. M. White of the Church Cresly Historical Record Group for first drawing my attention to these bricks, and for pointing out the Carnarvon connection. Examples of the bricks survive in Staffordshire and at Highclere Castle. Extensive investigations in the winter of 1990–1 by Dr Peter Piccione of the Oriental Institute Expedition at Chicago House, Luxor, failed to discover any certain evidence that such bricks were used in Carter's house; but he was not able to make a full examination of the walls and the foundations of the house. I am grateful to him for his efforts.

44 G.I. Gardiner Corr. AHG/42.355.21, dated 10 January 1911.

45 Metropolitan Museum transcript, for 19 February 1911.

46 Gardiner letter of 4 October 1911, in the possession of Margaret Gardiner.

Middle Kingdom to early Eighteenth Dynasty below. The latter were filled with coffins of the Second Intermediate Period and later periods, with only a little additional material of interest. As in the tombs discovered earlier in the area, destruction by robbers and by white ants rendered much of what was found irrecoverable. It was very frustrating work, yielding progressively less in the way of material dividends on Lord Carnarvon's investment. Still, the concession could not be abandoned, for if it were to be left, the chances for a switch to the Valley of the Kings would be less than promising. Tenacity in sticking to an unexciting excavation is always though to be meritorious, and may sometimes result in an unexpectedly good outcome – as Carter himself was to demonstrate ten years later.

There was, however, the possibility of diversification. Now that the employment of Carter seemed to be on a firm footing, and he was well settled as a man of property at Thebes, excavation need not be limited to the two or three months in the early part of the year when conditions at Thebes were thought to be best. In considering a second concession, Carnarvon hoped for a site that would be likely to produce material of a kind more distinguished than he had been finding at Thebes. His first choice, based on Carter's advice, was Dahshur, a place at the southern end of the great desert necropolis of Memphis, where there were two great pyramids of the Fourth Dynasty, and others, less dramatic in size, of the Twelfth Dynasty. Jacques de Morgan had dug there in 1894–5, while he was Director-General of the Antiquities Service, and had made spectacular discoveries. It was commonly understood that the site was reserved for official excavations, but Carnarvon was convinced that he could persuade Maspero to allow him to work there. There was no shifting Maspero, however, and Carnarvon's assault on his opposition continued until 1913. Maspero's objections rested on a supposed law, suggested by Lord Cromer in 1904–5, reserving the pyramid fields of Dahshur, Saqqara and Abusir for official excavation. Maspero had further claimed that if Carnarvon were allowed a concession at Dahshur he could not refuse permission to other applicants. Carnarvon and Carter were not impressed by the arguments:[47] the 'law' had never been promulgated, but was used by the Antiquities Service as a reason for applying for extra funds to work on these sites. In addition they maintained that the Service would never have enough money to excavate adequately there. The matter resulted in a serious deterioration in the previously good relations that had existed between Maspero and Carnarvon. It is piquant to find Carnarvon (but perhaps not Carter) lining up in a sense behind Weigall in opposition to Maspero. In a letter to Budge, he even seems to suggest a possible high-level intrigue against Maspero:[48]

47 Carnarvon's and Carter's views are set out in a draft memorandum in MMA, Department of Egyptian Art, Carter Papers.
48 Letter of 20 March 1913 in Department of Western Asiatic Antiquities, British Museum.

At the present moment the Daschur business is in a very unpleasant state as far as regards (this is entirely between ourselves) [something missing, perhaps 'Maspero'] but I am pretty sure that if I don't get it Maspero will be more or less forced to resign by indirect methods – Please do not mention all this. I had a great passage of arms with the Professor [i.e. Maspero] yesterday. I was pretending to be very angry. Old Brugsch came to the door lifted his hands to Heaven and bolted . . . K [i.e. Kitchener] is very set against Maspero.

It was a sad thing that after many years of devoted and inspiring service in the management of Egypt's antiquities, Maspero and his regime were attracting so much diverse criticism. Even Alan Gardiner, a one-time pupil of his in Paris, someone who no doubt had been affected in his views by too much talk with Arthur Weigall, but who was more than capable of judging an issue and of making up his own mind independently, now found it hard even to mix socially with Maspero. Writing to his wife, he explains how he felt:[49]

Maspero has been here for a few days and I felt I must come over to pay him a call. As a matter of fact I met him just as I arrived at the Nile, so turned back with him and rode with him as far as the temple of Gurna. He was very kind as usual, but as usual I felt the utter hopelessness of ever persuading him to do anything from enthusiasm for the science. Not he! He belongs to those who believe that to do anything at all for any other reasons than 1) self-interest 2) pleasing people of influence or 3) a general courtesy is the sign of a fool. Well, it may be so, but I'd rather be a fool in that case.

The Director-General of the Antiquities Service, to be any kind of success, had always to balance and trim, to please the politicians, satisfy the needs of the employees of the Service, content foreign colleagues, wheedle dealers, and, above all, protect the monuments. Maspero had been immensely successful for his first term (1881–6), and for most of his second term (from 1899). In 1913 he was 67, and the next year he resigned, ostensibly for health reasons, and returned to France. He died in 1916. His successor as Director-General of the Antiquities Service was Pierre Lacau, Director of the French Institute in Cairo, a very sound scholar. The appointment was generally welcomed, and for his first years, which coincided with the First World War, his task was not complicated by conflicting demands from excavators. He was also on war service for part of the time. The pleasure at having a new Director-General who was scrupulous, courteous and less partial to blandishment survived into the post-war period; but things were to change, and ultimately the great catalyst of change was to be the discovery of the tomb of Tutankhamun. The disillusion which would

49 Letter of 20 January 1913 in the possession of Margaret Gardiner.

then envelop Lacau, and for many years discredit him in the eyes of many of his colleagues, was not quite the same as that which afflicted Maspero in his last years. Yet the essential difficulty for both Lacau and Maspero was the reconciling of the various requirements of the job of Director-General. It is a theme to be followed again later in the history of Howard Carter's career in Egypt.

While the struggle for Dahshur continued, there were other possibilities, and on Carter's advice Carnarvon decided to test a Delta site. In so doing he would again, consciously or by chance, be following the view expressed to Gardiner by Weigall. The many huge and neglected town-sites in Lower Egypt were in grave danger from indiscriminate illicit digging, and from the activities of the *sebbakhin*. Carter had met and locally dealt with some of the problems when he was briefly Chief Inspector there in 1905; but it was a surprise to find him recommending work in that region. Experience had shown that digging conditions might be difficult, and that returns could be disappointing. But it was necessary to convince the Antiquities Service that the intentions and practices of the Carnarvon operations, directed by Carter, were honourable, serious and efficient. The bait of the concession for the Valley of the Kings still dangled before them.

The choice of site for excavation in 1912 was the ancient city of Xois in the central Delta, identified as the capital of the sixth Lower Egyptian nome (province); its Arabic name is Sakha.[50] The reasons for the choice are not known, but it may be supposed that Percy Newberry had an important hand in suggesting it. At this time he was engaged in writing a series of articles on early cults, many of which had Delta connections. At Xois there might be a chance of striking early strata and finding much new information. The place was also known to have been the centre of the minor royalties classified traditionally as the Fourteenth Dynasty (very approximately 1750–1600 BC), of whom no archaeological traces had survived. The mound at Sakha was huge and apparently promising. Carnarvon applied for a permit in the autumn of 1911 and hoped that work could start in late March 1912. A good description of the site was sent to Carnarvon by Carter rather later when it was clear that nothing could be done until April-May:[51]

It is a mound about 80ft in height and covering some 80 feddans [the *feddan* being a little larger than an acre]. It has been considerably dug into for Sabakh more especially the north part, and in the centre within what appears to be a large square enclosure or temenos wall of mud brick. To the S. the private dwellings have not been so much touched and S. of them again, is a large area partially cleared to the Older Egyptian level. On a smaller portion of this area (S-E) is a

50 For a recent account of Xois, see P. Vernus in *Lexikon der Ägyptologie*, 6, col. 1302ff.
51 G.I. Newberry Corr. 49/3.

modern Arab cemetery and mosque – the latter standing on a slightly higher level and built upon a fine Graeco-Roman mosaic floor. This end appears to be the more interesting and where results would be, I think, more easily obtainable.

After further notes on other parts of the site, he concludes:

Sakha though a heavy site to work certainly looks promising and from its geographical position should be an important one. To obtain any fair result a good months work should be at least required.

Of all the places dug by Carter for Carnarvon, Sakha/Xois was the least well recorded, and very disappointing in results. It was the kind of place to which Carnarvon and his entourage were not immediately drawn. At Sakha he would not be able to install himself in a comfortable hotel from which he could issue at a respectable hour in the morning, and to which he could return in the evening with the prospect of a bath and a good dinner in pleasing surroundings. In planning the Sakha dig he outlined some of his requirements to Newberry.[52] There would be seven people in the main party: Lady Carnarvon, Lord Carnarvon, Newberry, Carter, Lady Carnarvon's maid, Lord Carnarvon's servant, Dr Johnson (his personal physician). Each of these would need a tent. Then there would be two living tents, and WC tents, a bathroom, kitchen, etc.; also Egyptian domestic servants, cook, washer-up. It would cost a fair amount of money; 'you must remember I pay Carter £200 per mensem'. On the last point one must assume that this rate of pay would probably only apply when Carter was 'on duty' in the field; nevertheless, in a full year that might amount to four or five months, in all near £1000 per annum – not an insignificant salary for 1911. It is not clear whether the whole of the proposed party in the end went to Sakha. What is clear is that the conditions on the site were so disagreeable, with large numbers of snakes supplementing the general physical difficulties, that only about two weeks' work was carried out, apparently inconclusive and unproductive.

It might be thought that the idea of digging a large Delta site for a short period would have been discredited by the Sakha experience. On the contrary; with the possibility of Dahshur virtually abandoned, Carter chose to investigate another huge town mound, that of Tell el-Balamun, a remote place in the northern Delta, not far from the Mediterranean Sea. With fewer exceptions than in the previous years, Carter managed a much more successful season. Carnarvon certainly planned to join him for a part of the time, but it is not certain whether he felt fit enough to make another foray into the Delta. Writing to Budge on 14 March he catalogues his troubles:[53] 'I finished up at Luxor yesterday in a blaze of disaster, found

52 Letter of 13 December 1911, G.I. Newberry Corr. 7/97.
53 Letter in Department of Western Asiatic Antiquities, British Museum.

really nothing and was in bed for the last week a sort of influenza bronchitis altogether a dreadful fiasco.' And later in the same letter, 'I think I go to Diospolis next week or so but the weather is icy so far.' From an account of the work at Balamun which Carter sent to Mrs Newberry, there is no hint that Carnarvon was with him;[54] but photographs in Oxford indicate a large excavation camp and Carnarvon's presence, for a short time at least:

> Here at Ballamān I am making an experimental dig to endeavour to find out something about it. It certainly must have been an exceedingly important place. Certainly the largest in the neighbourhood. And I think there can be little doubt that it was 'Diospolis Parva'. The modern name suggests that it is a contraction of Bellad Amon (town of Amon) which seems in favour of the conjecture.[55] But up to the present I have been able to find but little the ground being so hard and difficult to work. Still, from the fact of it being untouched, one is able to get a good idea of the place and general formation of the ancient town and temple buildings. At present I am making investigations in what I believe to be the Palace. The Temple unfortunately is so low that almost at once we reach water and slimy mud.
>
> For camping it is very nice. We are in among the reeds and bullrushes where it swarms with warblers and other small birds. But bad for mosquitoes. It is beautifully [sic] and cool even though at Cairo and still more in Upper Egypt there is great heat.
>
> I shall remain here unless great finds encourage one to remain longer, until the end of the month. Then I shall return to Luxor for May and trust to return to England by the first week of June.

Another letter to Mrs Newberry, written from Elwat el-Diban on 17 May, gives more concrete news:[56] 'We were on the whole most fortunate in Balamān. And I have I think been able to identify the town as Pa-khen-n-Amen. We also got some jewellery.'

Results at Tell el-Balamun were indeed better than at Sakha; the jewellery, of rather low-grade silver with a fairly intricate design, was found in a large pottery jar. There were also a few other small objects and a fragment of a statue which until 1987 was only known from Carter's notes and a drawing in his record of the excavation preserved in the archives of

54 Letter of 18 April 1913, G.I. Newberry Corr. 8/43.
55 The classical name for this place was in fact Diospolis Inferior. Diospolis Parva was in Upper Egypt at modern Hu, between Luxor and Dendera. The name Balamun most probably derives from the ancient Pa-iu-en-Amun, 'The island of Amun', see J. Malek in *Lexikon der Ägyptologie*, 6, col. 319f. The false etymology 'Town of Amun' was a reasonable idea when Carter was at the place.
56 G.I. Newberry Corr. 8/44. The name used by Carter, Pa-khen-n-Amen, is an old misreading of the name Pa-iu-en-Amun: see last note, and J. Malek in *Rev. d'Ég.* 36 (1985), pp. 181ff.

the Griffith Institute, Oxford. Many of the Balamun objects, including the statue fragment, were among the antiquities which were rediscovered at Highclere Castle in that year. The inscription on the statue provides the alternative name for the site, Sambehdet – an important piece of confirmatory evidence. Carnarvon had taken the fragment to show Budge in the British Museum, possibly with the intention of leaving it there. Subsequently he had second thoughts, and wrote to Budge:[57] 'Amongst the things I gave you the other day is a small piece of broken stone. I don't think it is of any use to you but it is my chief record of Balamân. Would you put it by – there are some hieroglyphs on it I think.' It was worth recovering, as the only piece of textual evidence found that year at Tell el-Balamun.

There would be no return to the Delta after the close of the short Balamun season. Developments in other directions were to determine the future of Carnarvon's operations with Carter. Although work continued for one more season in the Theban concession, it was not pursued with much enthusiasm, and thereafter excavation in the Asasif district would be carried out entirely by the Egyptian Expedition of the Metropolitan Museum of Art. Howard Carter gladly handed over to Ambrose Lansing, the director of the Metropolitan's Theban dig, the sketched-out report he had written on his work there since 1911 – a kind of continuation in the same style of the narrative of *Five Years' Explorations at Thebes*.[58] There was, no doubt, relief in disengaging from the somewhat irksome, repetitive, excavation of the Birabi, especially as the far brighter prospect of the Valley of the Kings now lay ahead. The concession for the Valley had been held by Theodore Davis, in formal fashion, since 1905, although he had financed work there since 1902.[59] His success had been remarkable, marked regularly by the discovery of nine royal tombs, and one non-royal, but virtually intact, burial – that of Yuia and Tjuiu, parents of Queen Tiye, the wife of King Amenophis III. In his later seasons, however, no tomb of major importance had been found, and Davis believed that the Valley in this respect was exhausted. Maspero also believed the same to be the case. Carter was not convinced, and he was able to persuade Lord Carnarvon that there were possibilities of further undiscovered royal tombs, just waiting for the excavator with the right eye, the right instincts, and sufficient persistence. It is not clear for how long he had cherished the wish to work again in the Valley. In the first volume of his Tutankhamun publication he briefly outlined his early work in Thebes with Lord Carnar-

---

57 Undated letter filed in the 1913 correspondence in Department of Western Asiatic Antiquities, British Museum; from its position in the file, probably late November or early December.

58 A file containing this 'report' is now in the Metropolitan Museum.

59 An outline of the Davis excavations from 1902 to 1914 is conveniently given in C. N. Reeves, *The Valley of the Kings* (London, 1990), Appendix B, pp. 292ff. A copy of his first contract of work in 1905 is reproduced on pp. 331ff.

von, claiming that from the outset they had hoped for a concession in the Valley.[60] That may indeed be so. Carter had achieved some good success in the Valley working with Davis's financial backing in 1902–4. But while Davis continued working, with other professional collaborators, there was no chance for Carnarvon and Carter. The best they could do was to make their wishes known clearly to Maspero, so that they could step in and take over when Davis surrendered his rights. This Davis was to do after his unprofitable season in the spring of 1914; he was then 77 and a sick man.

In June of 1914 at last Carnarvon was granted the concession. It was possibly not quite as exciting a moment for him as for Carter. He was surrendering one concession which for him had ceased to yield results enough to maintain his interest; he was taking over a concession which had been relinquished by Davis for much the same reason. It would be many years before the success of a great discovery would come; but in the meanwhile there would be some minor excitements, and some useful discoveries made within the constraints of war-time conditions. There had already been a start to their 'royal' campaign in the spring of 1914.

60 Carter and Mace, *The Tomb of Tut.ankh.Amen*, I, pp. 75f. See also p. 215 below.

8

ROYAL TOMBS AND THE GREAT WAR

Carter returned to Thebes in the autumn of 1913 after a busy leave in England. It was now for him a pleasure to travel south from Cairo with the comfortable assurance of having decent employment and a fine house to come back to. One may, perhaps, vicariously enjoy with him the gradual approach to Castle Carter II: the drive from Luxor railway station to the river, accompanied no doubt by some faithful servant, perhaps Abd el-Aal Ahmed, who would in advance have arranged for a ferry boat to take his master and his baggage across the Nile to the west bank; then by horse or donkey, a journey of about two miles through the lush cultivation, to the stony foothills of the Theban Necropolis; finally, along the road beside the remains of the royal funerary temples, past the entrance to the Asasif, the Deir el-Bahri valley, scene of Carter's most recent Theban excavations, and the hill of Dra Abu el-Naga, to the wide rocky wadi leading to the Valley of the Kings. Here, almost immediately, on the hill of Elwat el-Diban, on the east side of the wadi, rises the domed house, waiting for its owner, with his dog Gaggia straining to greet him. The sight of Gaggia would have been a special pleasure, for terrible things could happen to one's pets, necessarily left behind during the long, hot, summer months. Carter did not, as was earlier indicated, have much luck with his animals. In 1909 he had come back to 'Soggy (my little dog)', who sent love by letter to the Newberrys' Timmy.[1] Soggy had gone to an unrecorded fate by 1913, and Gaggia, her replacement, was in good fettle at first. Unfortunately, as Carter reported,[2] 'now she is suffering from mange caught from a fox she slayed a week or so back. I am having a lot of trouble trying to cure her – I find paraffin the only thing of use.'

The excitement of the coming season was to be one which Howard Carter had been saving up for a suitable time in the programme of the Carnarvon excavations. It was to be the clearing and investigation of the tomb which Carter was convinced had been made for King Amenophis I of the early Eighteenth Dynasty (c. 1525–1504 BC), and his mother, Queen

1 G.I. Newberry Corr. 8/32, letter of 2 October 1909.
2 G.I. Newberry Corr. 8/50, of 15 December 1913.

Ahmose-Nefertari. From ancient records, especially the official report of the investigation of tomb-robberies contained in the Abbott Papyrus in the British Museum, it was highly likely that the tomb of this king lay outside the Valley of the Kings. When it had been examined in about 1116 BC, the sixteenth year of King Ramasses IX of the Twentieth Dynasty, it was found intact, or at least reported as such, although it had been stated to have been violated. Carter had been interested in trying to find this tomb after his early work in the Valley of the Kings on the somewhat later Eighteenth-Dynasty tomb of Tuthmosis IV, and the one which contained the sarcophagi inscribed for Tuthmosis I and Hatshepsut. After the clearance of the second of these tombs – an exceptionally laborious task – in the spring of 1904, he had interested Lord Amherst in the search for the tomb of Amenophis I.[3] It may be recalled that he had spoken to Amherst in 1903 about his intentions, and he made a firm proposal in a letter to Lady Amherst in March 1904. No positive indications at that time seem to have provided the stimulus for his investigation, but it would be a mistake to discount the possibility that he had been shown something – an inscribed fragment of an antiquity, perhaps – or been told of some suggestive discovery by the squirrel-like free-lancers of the Necropolis villages. Nothing came of that early attempt, and it ended when he was transferred north in the fall of the year.

A few years later, Arthur Weigall confidently identified an empty tomb high in the hills at the deepest, southern, end of the Valley of the Kings, as the tomb of Amenophis I.[4] His evidence was chiefly geographical and circumstantial, based on the indications in the Abbott Papyrus. He found no ancient fragments with confirmatory texts upon them. Although some scholars have subsequently accepted Weigall's identification, most recent studies have rejected it, and it is certain that Howard Carter was unconvinced.[5] As far as he was concerned, his scepticism was to be fully justified within two years of Weigall's publication of his chosen tomb. Carter describes the events leading to his own discovery in one of his autobiographical sketches preserved in the Griffith Institute in Oxford.[6] It all began one evening in the late spring of 1912, while he was taking the air, seated on a bench in front of his new house. He paints a characteristically colourful, somewhat overblown, word picture of the setting:

> I was giving myself up to pleasant fits of musing while watching the serenity of nature. It was one of those beautiful warm evenings when everything seems to sink into repose. The setting sun had shed its rich yellow beams over the landscape. In the distance the tips of white lateen sails slowly winding down the river were visible through

3 See p. 93 above.
4 *Guide to the Antiquities of Upper Egypt* (London, 1910), p. 223; *A.S.A.E.* 11 (1911), p. 174.
5 C. N. Reeves, *The Valley of the Kings* (London, 1990), pp. 3ff.
6 G.I. Carter Notebook 17, Sketch XI.

the palm-trees amid an expanse of green. The Arabian desert opposite, beyond the fertile valley, had assumed opalescent tints. Her distant hills vested in purple and tipped with a mellow tinge of gold were gradually melting into space. The evening was fast closing. From behind one was beginning to be conscious of a faint quivering breeze that was stealing down from the hills of the Libyan Range; when far away across the broken tract of desert between my house and the fertile plain, the figure of a man was slowly approaching.

Carter recognized his visitor as Gad Hassan, who lived in one of the villages nearby, and 'who had taken up the profession of tomb-plundering'. He had brought Carter a basketful of fragments of alabaster vessels, some of which bore the names of Amenophis I and of his mother Ahmose-Nefertari. Carter was reminded of two similar fragments he had acquired some years before, which he had either given or sold to Theodore Davis. These earlier fragments might have provided the spur for his 1904 attempt to find the tomb for Lord Amherst; the temporal indications given by Carter suggest that he obtained his two pieces rather later than 1904, but in matters of this kind, Carter's indications tend to be unreliable.[7] With some skill he persuaded Gad Hassan to produce a few more fragments and, after offering to purchase them, he further persuaded him to take him to the source. On the following day the negotiations for the purchase of the fragments, and for some initial compensation for revealing the site of the tomb, were completed. Carter's account is long and colourful, and perhaps a little elaborated in hindsight to make his narrative more 'literary'; but there is no reason to doubt that he knew exactly how to negotiate with the essentially distrustful and suspicious villager of the Theban Necropolis, and how to exploit such confidences as he might inspire, using promises, cajolery and just enough money to achieve his purpose.

Gad Hassan led him down from his house, across the little valley to the hill of Dra Abu el-Naga, and by way of a small and rocky wadi known as Khawi el-Alamat, to a deserted high point well above the Deir el-Bahri valley. There he showed Carter the entrance to a tomb beneath a great over-hanging rock. In the afternoon of the same day Carter returned to the spot with a few men and tackle, and began a preliminary investigation. What he found was both exciting and depressing – a tomb consisting of an entrance shaft, a corridor with two side-chambers, a protective well (choked with debris), and a further corridor leading to a large burial chamber with two pillars. It was, to his mind, very much what could be expected for an early Eighteenth-dynasty sepulchre. Very little remained of identifiable funerary equipment:

Every remnant of old grandeur and divinity had gone. Woefully

7 Said to be 1907 in Carter Notebook 17, p. 200; see also *J.E.A.* 3 (1916), p. 151, n. 1

gnawed by time and in parts shattered by violence, it now served as a haunt for owls and bats. The walls were sullen and black from fires lit by its dynastic desecrators. The charred remains of its equipment were but evidence of base minds that had wrought revenge upon the illustrious dead.

From this provisional investigation Carter could see that the tomb had suffered comprehensive destruction in antiquity, many centuries before the modern sifting of the debris by Gad Hassan and his collaborators. If it had been the tomb prepared for King Amenophis I and his mother, then its modern condition could hardly have been other than what had been found. The Abbott Papyrus reported it as being intact, but the inspection in the reign of Ramesses IX might have been rather cursory. Certainly the mummy of Amenophis and possibly that of Ahmose-Nefertari, were included in the assemblage of royal bodies found in the Deir el-Bahri cache in 1881.[8] Nevertheless, a tomb pillaged for precious items in antiquity, but cluttered with rubble and rain-washed silt, was always worth careful clearance, and this is what Carter determined to carry out at some later date after he had consulted the Earl of Carnarvon.

The occasion came in the spring of 1914, and the clearance of the tomb became the last piece of work undertaken by Carnarvon and Carter before the outbreak of the First World War in August of that year. It was also, in a sense, a trial run for the taking over of Theodore Davis's concession to excavate in the Valley of the Kings. The tomb identified by Carter as that of Amenophis I and Ahmose-Nefertari lay some distance from the royal valley, and just marginally within Carnarvon's old concessionary area, which included the hill of Dra Abu el-Naga. The site was situated higher on the hill than the slopes where the earlier kings of the Seventeenth Dynasty had been buried – tombs that had been thoroughly robbed in ancient times for the most part. One collection of splendid jewellery had been found many years earlier by the agents of Auguste Mariette, founder of the Antiquities Service. It had belonged to Queen Ahhotpe, the mother of Amosis, first king of the Eighteenth Dynasty, and mother-in-law of Ahmose-Nefertari. Carter had become very familiar with this collection of jewellery at the turn of the century when he had been asked to make the illustrations of many of the precious objects for the splendid publication put out in 1900 by the German Egyptologist Friedrich Freiherr von Bissing.[9] He was therefore well aware that fine things could be overlooked by the diligent tomb robbers, ancient and modern; by implication the clearance of even a well robbed tomb might yield material of great interest.

Operations began in late February after Carnarvon had joined Carter

8 See now J. E. Harris and E. F. Wente, *An X-Ray Atlas of the Royal Mummies* (Chicago, 1980), pp. 239f., and passim.
9 See p. 84 above.

in Thebes. Carter still had some doubts about whether the tomb was just that of the queen, and not of both king and queen. A difficulty was presented by the location of the tomb, stated fairly specifically in the Abbott Papyrus. Carnarvon wrote to Budge in the British Museum where the papyrus was preserved.[10] The letter is interesting in that it shows a degree of care and a tendency to research which may surprise some students of excavation practice of the time. The letter was written from the Savoy Hotel in Cairo, which had been recommended to Carnarvon by Carter for his 1913 stay as being a little more economical than other, more usual haunts.[11] Carnarvon claims the discovery of the tomb for himself, maintaining the convention that any find of Carter's was a find of his own:

> I believe I really have found the Tomb of Amenhotep I, at all events a great deal of inscribed stone and as its being a Royal Tomb there is no possible doubt. Could you get one of your underlings to copy the passage in the Abbott Papyrus (about A Ist) in the hieroglyph and if you could just add the translation it would be very kind, I imagine it is only a few lines, but I want very particularly the various signs such as the determinative of a the [sic] tomb (is it Δ or 𓊃?).[12] All this will help a good deal. It will take a month to work out so I shall not finish it off just at once.

The problem of reconciling the actual position of the tomb under excavation with the indications in the papyrus is not one to be seriously considered here. It should, however, be said that Carter did not avoid the issue, and produced a solution for the article he wrote on the clearance of the tomb which is ingenious, but not very persuasive.[13] He thought initially that the tomb might have been only for the queen, and this view has certainly been more acceptable to many scholars than his later, preferred, idea of the double tomb. The problem continues to interest students of the Theban Necropolis, and there is no doubt that further views will be suggested from time to time, and will continue to do so until the unequivocal discovery of a tomb cut for Amenophis himself is made.[14] That could be never; for Carter's identification remains highly likely.

The yield of objects from the excavation was disappointing. Carter's later account sums up his conclusion very succinctly:[15]

The results were small, but sufficient, I think, to reconstruct the

10 Letter of Carnarvon to Budge of 13 March 1914, in Department of Western Asiatic Antiquities, British Museum.
11 Letter of Carter to Carnarvon of 6 December 1912, at Highclere Castle.
12 The question is not quite properly framed. The signs in question are 𓈖𓉐𓏤𓊃 'horizon of eternity', a synonym for a royal tomb. Carnarvon's second option is closer to the mark. The reference is to BM 10221, page 2, 1. 2.
13 *J.E.A.* 3 (1916), pp. 147ff.
14 C. N. Reeves, *Valley of the Kings*, p. 5.
15 G.I. Carter Notebook 17, p. 315ff.

main outline of its history. . . . Indeed the disproportion between the
work and the results was singularly disconcerting. So let it suffice me
to say that there was no waste of time. The clearance was systematic:
beginning from outside the entrance-shaft and ending in the innermost chamber. Each basket of rubbish as it came up was sifted for
what it might contain. . . . All that was left of the original equipment
were debris of stone-vessels and statuettes wrought in alabaster (calcite), green felspar, white and yellow limestone, a red conglomerate,
serpentine and basalt.

The few and small fragmentary antiquities, some of which pointed to a
possible usage of the tomb in the late New Kingdom (Third Intermediate
Period), are now to be found in the Carnarvon Collection in Highclere
Castle. They were not thought to be distinguished enough to be included
by Carter in the main collection which was purchased by the Metropolitan
Museum of Art after the fifth Earl's death in 1923.[16] Although the material
returns from the clearance of the tomb of Amenophis I and Ahmose-
Nefertari were slight, the actual discovery and reasonably certain identification of the owners were of considerable importance, and could rightly
be regarded by Carnarvon and Carter as well worth the effort and expense.
The operations were also, as has been suggested, a preliminary run for
the possibly imminent campaign in the Valley of the Kings proper.

At the end of the 1914 season, however, there was no sure sign that
Theodore Davis was about to give up his rights in the Valley. A plan for
the future had already been discussed between Carnarvon and Carter, and
the immediate intention was to move north to Hawara near the point
where the Bahr Yusuf offshoot of the Nile passed into the Faiyum
depression. Here Ammenemes III, one of the most influential kings of the
Twelfth Dynasty (c. 1844–1797 BC), had been buried in a great pyramid
attached to which was a vast complex of funerary buildings, known and
wondered at by visitors to Egypt in the Graeco-Roman Period.[17] It was at
that time known as the Labyrinth on account of the size and complexity
of its structure. Here Flinders Petrie had excavated in 1888–9, and again
in 1910–11, but he had by no means exhausted the site, or even tested
comprehensively its whole area. The Americans of the Metropolitan
Museum were meanwhile demonstrating amply what care and persistence
could achieve at the almost contemporary pyramid site at El-Lisht about
30 miles to the north of Hawara. Carter felt confident that there was much
more to be found and he prepared to apply for the site for the coming
season. In a letter written to Percy Newberry on 30 April 1914, the Earl
of Carnarvon suggested that the recent excavation at Thebes had been
'somewhat of a disappointment' for Carter, who had, however, found an

16 C. N. Reeves, *Ancient Egypt at Highclere Castle* (Highclere, 1989), p. 27.
17 *Lexikon der Ägyptologie*, 2, col. 1072f.

assistant for the next season. 'I hear Steindorff is giving up Hawara, so I think we shall take it.'[18] Georg Steindorff, Professor of Egyptology at Leipzig, and an active field-worker as well as an outstanding Coptic scholar, had been working for some years in Nubia, and had presumably applied to work at Hawara subsequently. With his surrendering his claim on the site the way was clear for the British team to step in.

There would be some caution in Carter's negotiations to secure Hawara. It was not so long since Dahshur had been refused, and it would not have done to suffer another rejection. Things were changing, however: 1914 saw Maspero's departure from the office of Director-General. In spite of Carnarvon's extreme displeasure at failing to get Dahshur, there is no reason to think that he played any significant part in Maspero's departure. He had done his best to persuade Kitchener that Maspero needed to be pushed into compliance with his wishes, but Kitchener seemed unwilling to use his influence. There was probably serious misjudgement on Carnarvon's part of what could be achieved by pulling strings. Carter had written to Carnarvon in November 1912:[19] 'If K. of K. [i.e. Kitchener of Khartoum] is keen on your having the site, I think there can be little danger from Maspero beyond a splutter of fire at first.' A month later he wrote: 'I think perhaps it best to let it stand until you come – See Kitchener and if you can interest him then go for Maspero.' Already, however, there was a doubt about Kitchener's support, for Carter had written in late November of the same year:[20] 'Greg of the Embassy is staying for a time at the Winter Palace. He tells me that Kitchener is not very keen on Egyptian stuff.'

In the case of Hawara they might not have to suffer the same set-back – a real humiliation for Carnarvon; but a slow approach to the in-coming Director-General, Pierre Lacau, might be advisable. Ultimately tactics were of no account, for the outbreak of the Great War (as it used to be called) in August 1914 put paid to any serious activity for British expeditions in Egypt. In any case the Valley of the Kings was now the cherished prize, recently won. The future was without a doubt very uncertain. It should be remembered, on the other hand, that at the outset of the war expectations were highly optimistic – 'home by Christmas!' was the common cry. There are no known letters of Carter's covering the early months of hostilities, but he had returned to Egypt some time in the autumn of 1914, after a last pre-war leave in England, with a clear objective for a first piece of work in the Valley. At this moment he was 40 years old, and there could have been no immediate pressure on him to find some war-

18 G.I. Newberry Corr. 7/108.
19 Letter at Highclere Castle.
20 Letter at Highclere Castle. Robert Greg was at the time Second Secretary at the British Agency in Cairo. Subsequently he was in charge of the Ministry of Foreign Affairs, and in 1929 became the British Commissioner for the Eygptian Debt. He was President of the Egypt Exploration Society from 1949 until his death in 1953.

time activity. He could therefore continue as normally as possible under the circumstances and start with a relatively easy task, the clearing of the tomb of King Amenophis III.

Carter's interest in this tomb had been aroused especially by his purchase of the three bracelet plaques for Lord Carnarvon in 1912. He had concluded that they must have come from the recent work carried out by Harry Burton on behalf of Theodore Davis. The tomb, which lay not in the main (or East) Valley of the Kings, but in the more remote West Valley, had been open at least since the time of Napoleon's expedition to Egypt.[21] It had never been properly cleared, and the work which Burton had done was limited to waste-heaps around the entrance. He had found a few damaged remnants of tomb equipment. Carter pointed out:[22] 'The fact that Burton found outside the tomb last spring the parts of Amenhotep III's [i.e. Amenophis III] harness with heavy gold bosses shows there must be stuff still there and he in no way exhausted the heaps nor did he touch the interior, which is full of rubbish.' He hoped that by doing a little poking around unofficially he might be able to test the prospects for further work. Two weeks later he writes:[23] 'I have not yet gone to the tomb (Amenhetep III), but will do so.' Whatever trips of reconnaissance he might have made subsequently, it was not until after the season of 1914 and the acquisition of the Valley concession that Carter could seriously consider tackling the clearance of the tomb.

Work began on 8 February 1915, and continued for precisely one month, finishing on 8 March.[24] It is not clear under what authorization Carter carried out this work. Although the concession for the Valley of the Kings had been surrendered by Theodore Davis in 1914, and been passed over to the Earl of Carnarvon, there seems to have been no official document issued at that time which would have permitted Carter to work in the following spring. The actual written permission under which Carter received his authorization to dig in the Valley on behalf of Carnarvon was not signed until 18 April 1915.[25] It was executed by Lacau's deputy, Georges Daressy and, renewed annually from 1917, remained the document by which they continued to work up to the time when the tomb of Tutankhamun was found. One must presume that Carter received some kind of temporary permit to carry out clearance rather than excavation in February 1915, in advance of the preparation of the full document of authorization.

Within a few days of starting work, while clearing the debris-strewn area in front of the tomb entrance, he found a series of five foundation deposits, one of which was badly damaged by water infiltration. The

---

21 See C. N. Reeves, *Valley of the Kings*, pp. 38ff.
22 Letter of 7 November 1912, from Carter to Carnarvon, at Highclere Castle.
23 Letter of 20 November, at Highclere Castle.
24 G.I. Carter Papers I A, 123ff., I. J, 386f.
25 The text of the permit is printed in Appendix II.

inscribed objects in these deposits carried the names of Tuthmosis IV, the father and predecessor of Amenophis III. Carter rightly deduced that this evidence suggested that the tomb had been started for Tuthmosis, but had then been abandoned for the tomb in the main Valley which he had excavated for Theodore Davis in 1903. There was no doubt that the tomb had finally been prepared for Amenophis III; confirmation came from the poorly preserved mural decorations and inscriptions, and from the many fragments of royal tomb paraphernalia recovered from the entrance passage and the debris in the protective well, bearing the king's name. There was also some evidence that it may have contained the burial of Tiye, the king's greatest and favourite consort. A large number of the damaged objects, including a series of interesting wooden faces from *shabti*-figures, and one fine *shabti*-head in calcite, were among the pieces rediscovered in recent years in Highclere Castle.[26]

This month-long campaign by no means exhausted the possibilities of the tomb, although Carter later claimed to have 'made a complete clearance of the interior of the tomb of Amenhetep III'.[27] From his brief field-notes he seems to have retrieved no objects from beyond the protective well and its associated chamber, although a considerable series of corridors and rooms lay within, including the pillared burial chamber containing the broken lid of the royal sarcophagus. It must be concluded that Carter decided on the basis of general inspection that very little would result from comprehensive clearance. It is, however, also possible that his permit to work had been limited to one month, or that other calls on his time brought this short campaign to a close. Further work, if thought likely to be profitable, could always be carried out in the future.

Some time in the late spring or early summer of 1915, Howard Carter became attached to the Intelligence Department of the War Office in Cairo. It was not a military appointment, and he carried no military rank. There is no positive evidence that this was the case, but it is noticeable that in any references to him during the war years, he is assigned no military rank – a matter which was practised with great punctiliousness in those times of patriotic fervour. He may have been considered too unfit generally to be commissioned, but there would have been no difficulty in his being employed as a civilian. In fact, with his excellent knowledge of Egypt and his command of Arabic (even if it were an unacademic command), he could be usefully employed in many directions. Writing to Albert M. Lythgoe, Curator of the Egyptian Department of the Metropolitan Museum, on 4 June 1915, using official Intelligence Department writing paper, he says:[28] 'I am a fixture here for the summer and possibly longer – We all must do the best in the terrible struggle – to win we shall even

26 C. N. Reeves, *Ancient Egypt at Highclere Castle*, pp. 27ff.
27 In H. Carter and A. C. Mace, *Tomb of Tut.ankh.Amen* I, (London, 1923), p. 79.
28 MMA, Department of Egyptian Art, Carter files.

if the last drop of blood is necessary. Mace I hear is doing great things in England.[29] I am glad as it is up to us all to do something.' The precise nature of Carter's war-work is a mystery. In a late autobiographical essay he talks of being 'tired of war-work and secret ciphers',[30] and there is a suggestion that he was from time to time employed as a King's Messenger, i.e. an official courier for important communications. The suggestion is, however, most unlikely, for the King's Messenger Service was composed of 'a limited number of men who have been properly trained as such and are regular Servants of the Crown.'[31] That he was later dropped from such employment is also unconfirmed, although he does say in a letter to Mrs Newberry in October 1917:[32] 'at present I am nearly dotty. They don't or won't give me any more war work in Cairo, So here I am [in Luxor]. Glad to say well occupied with drawing and painting.' It would not have been surprising if he had not crossed swords from time to time with those who ran the department in Cairo. Blimps and office-wallahs had a poor profile in the Great War; Carter was never one to endure inefficiency patiently, and would surely not have listened to official humbug without making his feelings felt. The few indications of his war-work suggest that it was intermittent and undemanding. It gave him ample opportunity to slip down to Luxor, often for extended periods, to potter around archaeologically, to do a little excavation, to paint, and to keep an eye on what was turning up in the antiquities dealers' shops.

He may also have organized, or participated in, an incident which smacked more of T. E. Lawrence's escapades in the Arabian Desert than of the normally rather cautious Norfolk 'dumpling'.[33] On 4 November 1915 Somers Clarke, Carter's old architectural and engineering mentor of their Deir el-Bahri days wrote from Luxor to Budge in the British Museum:[34]

In these doleful days there is not often to be told news even of a slightly satisfactory nature but I have learnt one little bit that may please you. Possibly you may know it already. You remember that ugly ridiculous red abomination emblematical of German pushful

---

29 Arthur Cruttenden Mace would become Carter's principal collaborator after the discovery of the tomb of Tutankhamun. He had been working with the Metropolitan Museum Egyptian Expedition at Lisht in Middle Egypt up to the war. At the outbreak of hostilities he was enrolled as a special constable; then in September 1915 he enlisted in the 5th Batallion, the 28th London Territorial Regiment, which came to be known as the Artists Rifles. For his war career, see C. C. Lee, ... *The Grand Piano came by Camel* (Renfrew, 1990), pp. 27f.

30 G.I. Carter Notebook 17, p. 227 (sketch XII).

31 I owe the suggestion that he was employed as a King's Messenger to Cyril Aldred. The unlikelihood of such an appointment is confirmed by V. Wheeler-Holohan, *The History of the King's Messengers* (London, 1935), p. viii.

32 G.I. Newberry Corr. 8.56, dated 20 October.

33 So described by the Revd F. Keeling Scott, vicar of Swaffham, in an article on Carter and his family in the *Eastern Daily Press* for 20 February 1923, p. 6. The traditional Norfolk dumpling is not, as might be supposed, heavy and solid, but light and appetizing.

34 In Department of Western Asiatic Antiquities, British Museum.

vulgarity which stands – stood – behind the Ramesseum at Thebes. It stands no more. I arrived at Luxor last week and stayed there a day or two whilst the house at El Kab was being dusted. Then I heard that the thing had vanished, but did not take the trouble to go across and see what was not to be seen.

The building in question was the German House at Qurna, the Luxor base of the German Archaeological Institute. It had been designed by Ludwig Borchardt, the distinguished German Egyptologist, who had carried out important excavations at El-Amarna in the years before the war. The house plan was based on a conjectural reconstruction of an Amarna villa, and was thought to be imaginative or pretentious, according to individual sympathies and taste. After the war Borchardt claimed that the destruction was ordered by the Commander of Allied forces in Egypt, 'because it was found to be a centre of illicit antiquities trade and otherwise undesirable'.[35] It is said that he was convinced that Howard Carter was responsible for blowing up the house, and the tradition has persisted in Egyptological memories. The matter is by no means certain, but it is known that Borchardt and Carter were not well disposed towards each other. It was a long-standing antipathy, which had certainly been aggravated when Carter acquired the bracelet plaques of Amenophis III for Lord Carnarvon. In his letter of 12 October 1912, announcing his purchase to Carnarvon, Carter mentions specifically that he had beaten the German consul who had been put on to the matter by Borchardt.

The perpetrators of this act of vandalism – certainly not seen as such by non-Germans at the time – were almost surely acting on official orders. The blowing-up of a building was not likely to have been the act of the villagers of Qurna; straightforward robbery was much more their style. But in the countryside generally they were troublous times, and there was a constant threat to property and to ancient monuments. Ernest Mackay, who had taken over the Theban tomb conservation operation from Arthur Weigall in 1913, wrote to Alan Gardiner on 23 July 1915 explaining why he was staying on at Thebes and not joining up for war-work. There were then no European inspectors between Cairo and Wadi Halfa on the Sudanese border:[36]

Thefts are now very numerous, the favourite articles being cattle and corn. Three nights ago a party of four men were discovered digging a shaft behind some houses in Drah. A. N. [Dra Abu el-Naga]. One was caught but in the process damaged badly under Sheikh el Gaffir. I also hear that some statues have been stolen from Legrain's maga-

35 Doubt is thrown on Carter's involvement in the incident by Dr Rainer Stadelmann, Director of the Deutsches Archäologisches Institut Abteilung Kairo, to Anne Pemberton, of 22 March 1988. He quotes from the Guest Book of the German House.
36 G.I. Mackay Papers in the Gardiner Papers, 19.

zine [at Karnak] but do not know any particulars yet. You will see by this that it would not be nice for me to go away to Cairo for the present. The bright side of the picture is that none of the dealers are buying antiquities with the exception of very good stuff, as they have been very badly hit by this season, and are likely to be worse off next season.

The Theban conditions described by Mackay were reiterated by Howard Carter in various letters. To Lythgoe in the letter of 4 June 1915, quoted earlier, he reports, 'I picked up one or two wonderful specimens this spring. In the Highclere Collection. But on the whole there has not been much about. The natives are having good crops and thus hoarding for better times.' He was well placed, with war-work in Cairo and leaves in Luxor, to keep an eye on the market and to exploit his contacts. There would be extraordinary developments in 1916, which resulted from his ability to follow up tips more or less at his leisure.

In the meanwhile, however, having time on his hands in Cairo, he began to follow a more systematic approach to his archaeological interests, as opposed to his opportunistic pursuit of good antiquities. In the same letter to Lythgoe he makes an unusual, but significant request:

White is here at the Continental working on his publication on the 'Sayings of Christ'. I wonder if you will mind my asking him to help me later on the Classical stuff re Valley of the Kings. Among other reports of our work there which I trust will be exhaustive to the end – or as far as we can go – I aim want [sic] to publish in parts a kind of 'Record of the Royal Theban Necropolis'.

I think it will be of interest and too of value as you well known [sic]. The mass of the material from that origin has been grossly muddled. And, too, to have all such material in one publication will save a lot of time and expense to students.

The White mentioned here was Hugh G. Evelyn-White, a British classical scholar and archaeologist who had been employed by the Metropolitan Museum for some years up to the war, and was in 1915 on service in Egypt.[37] It is interesting to note that Howard Carter felt it necessary to clear with Lythgoe his projected work with Evelyn-White, and one may presume that it was punctiliousness on the part of the latter which required him to do so. It is further interesting to see that even at this early date the strategy of Carter and Carnarvon to their future work in the Valley was to be 'exhaustive'.

The substantial notes compiled by Carter during the war years for this

37 On Evelyn-White see W. R. Dawson and E. P. Uphill, *Who Was Who in Egyptology* (London, 1972), pp. 101f. His *The Sayings of Jesus from Oxyrhynchus* was published in 1920 (Cambridge). He died in 1924.

comprehensive work on the Valley are now lodged in the Griffith Institute in Oxford.[38] They represent only the preliminary stage in the collecting of material from ancient and modern sources, and never reached a state fit to be published. There was, however, other work to be done, and he was actively encouraged to publish by Alan Gardiner, and to be a partner in publication with him. This was a strange development, for only a few years earlier Carter had expressed such distrust of Gardiner. The co-operation between Gardiner and Weigall, and the poor relationship between Weigall and Carter, had no doubt been mitigated by Weigall's departure from Thebes. More significant, perhaps, were the close relations established by Gardiner with Carnarvon. There had been a coolness between the two, also probably induced by Gardiner's friendship with Weigall; but the real issue between them, according to Gardiner, was Carnarvon's refusal to allow him to publish the important historical text on the Carnarvon Tablet I.[39] After a lengthy period of mutual disapproval, lasting possibly several years, a confrontation in the bar of the Winter Palace Hotel, engineered by a cousin of Gardiner's, led to some plain speaking and a clearing of the air. Gardiner wrote to his wife, not long after this incident:[40] 'This morning I went over to call on Lord Carnarvon at his excavation. He was very friendly and pleasant, quite different from what I had anticipated.' Thereafter close relations were established, although Gardiner was nervous of exploiting the kindness of one whom he considered to belong to a different social world. 'But he deliberately sought me out, invited me to Highclere Castle again and again where I got to know well his magnificent collection of Egyptian antiquities.' Carnarvon and, following in his footsteps, Carter, could not have failed to appreciate Gardiner's total commitment to Egyptology and his exceptional ability as a textual scholar. To have him work with them could only have been advantageous to the quality of their own publications, and beneficial to Egyptology in general.

Alan Gardiner's scholarly interests were primarily linguistic and histori-cal, although they covered many other fields also in so far as the require-ments of the explication of ancient texts were concerned. He was by 1916 the new editor of the recently established *Journal of Egyptian Archaeology*, the scholarly organ of the Egypt Exploration Fund, and he felt it incumbent on himself to sustain the fledgling publication during the war years, even if it meant writing more for it himself than he would have contemplated in less strained circumstances. As it appeared four times annually in those days, the strain of finding sufficient material for its pages was a continuous burden. In the course of the years 1916–18 Gardiner contributed a number

38 G.I. Carter Papers I K, 1–21.
39 The differences and the reconciliation between Carnarvon and Gardiner are explained in Gardiner, *My Working Years* (1963), pp. 37f.
40 Letter of 5 February 1913, written from Qurna, in the possession of Margaret Gardiner.

of long articles of lasting importance, using material found by Carnarvon and Carter, involving Carter with him in the preparation of one important study, and encouraging Carter to provide long reports of some of the most interesting discoveries in Thebes. Gardiner was a careful editor, a master of clear English, and an ideal partner who could bring order, rigour and style into Carter's somewhat undisciplined writing. The co-operation first flowered in 1916, with a long study by Gardiner of the Carnarvon Tablet I, and a short note with a colour plate (always rare in scholarly publications until recent years, and quite exceptional in wartime) making known the three plaques of Amenophis III which Carter had acquired for Carnarvon in 1915.[41]

In the summer of 1916 Carter was able to return to England for some weeks, possibly carrying out some official courier duty. He had the opportunity of renewing Egyptological contacts and of getting to know Gardiner better. So, in early August he was taken by Carnarvon see Budge in the British Museum, surely to discuss the possibilities for the acquisition of antiquities during the war.[42] He had already been in Britain for some time, for as early as May Alan Gardiner wrote to him with some suggestions for the improvement of the article that Carter had written for the *Journal of Egyptian Archaeology* (usually abbreviated to *J.E.A.*) on his discovery of the tomb of Amenophis I.[43] The extraordinary improvement in their relations is indicated by Gardiner's invitation to dinner: 'Let me know whether *Thursday* next here 7 o'clock would suit you. We would then go to some show. Have you seen the Bing Boys? And what do you want to see? I should like to get tickets early, so please let me know as soon as you can.'[44]

There were more serious things to discuss, apart from the article on the tomb of Amenophis I. Gardiner was eager to publish a pair of very interesting inscriptions found in the tomb of Akhtoy (or Khety), no. 65 in the numbering of the Carnarvon-Carter excavations in the Birabi at Thebes in 1913–14. Percy Newberry had been expected to make the publication, but progress had been so slow that Carter needed little persuasion from Gardiner to convince Newberry to give up his rights.[45] The resulting article in *J.E.A.*, 'The tomb of a much-travelled Theban official', was put together by Gardiner from Carter's field-notes on the excavation of the tomb, combined with his own translations and commentaries on the textual material.[46] It was a characteristic piece of forceful initiative by Gardiner.

41 In *J.E.A.* 3 (196), pp. 73f. (plaques); pp. 95ff. (Carnarvon Tablet I).
42 Letter of 14 August 1916 from Carnarvon to Budge in Department of Western Asiatic Antiquities, British Museum.
43 *J.E.A.* 3 (1916), pp. 147ff.
44 G.I. Carter Papers I A 212. The musical revue *The Bing Boys are Here* was the 'hit' of the 1916 season at the Alhambra Theatre; written by George Grossmith Jr and starring George Robey and Violet Loraine. Its best known song was 'If you were the only girl in the world'.
45 G.I. Newberry Corr. 18/22; letter of 1 July 1916 from Gardiner to Newberry.
46 *J.E.A.* 4 (1917), pp. 28ff.

He appreciated that the interest of the texts, and of the whole tomb with its damaged wall-paintings, was such that some friendly pressure was needed to secure their publication, and so his article incorporated all of Carter's written descriptions and interpretations, as well as his own substantial contributions. More was extracted from the shattered remains of Akhtoy's tomb than Carter could otherwise have hoped to include in any sequel to *Five Years' Explorations at Thebes* – a volume he would in any case never write.

For the future there should be more co-operation. Throughout his long career in Egyptology, Alan Gardiner was a great promoter of scholarly activity by others, as separate and independent operations, with or without his participation. He had a keen eye for special talents, and sufficient private resources to subsidize pieces of work which might stand on their own or supplement his own researches. In this respect he was innovative, ingenious, indefatigable and far-sighted, and through his distinctly entrepreneurial initiatives he promoted the interests of many colleagues, and distinctly advanced the progress of Egyptology. In the summer of 1916 he had two further enterprises in mind which would capitalize on Howard Carter's artistic and draughting abilities, and utilize the time he might have available for archaeological activities in Thebes in between his tours of duty in Cairo. The first was an investigation of the archaeological background and textual detail of a plan on a papyrus of a royal tomb at Thebes in the Egyptian Museum in Turin. Superficially it seemed a fairly simple task. The ancient plan had been identified many years earlier as being of the tomb of King Ramesses IV of the Twentieth Dynasty, but the various dimensions of the actual tomb did not seem to agree with those given on the papyrus. Carter was just the man to take his tape-measure into the Valley of the Kings, obtain a careful set of new measurements, armed with those extracted by Gardiner from the papyrus, and then produce new, reliable, plans and sections. Carter readily agreed, and shortly after his return to Egypt in October 1916 Gardiner wrote to him:[47]

> I hope your journey was a good one and not too unpleasant. Here is the translation of the Turin papyrus, with as full comments as I can give. I hope you will be able to clear up every point. It would be very valuable anyhow to have a final and exhaustive plan of the tomb.

In the course of the next few months Carter did his part in the joint enterprise, and on 4 March 1917 Gardiner was able to report:[48] 'Your work on the tomb of Ramesses IV just received with your perfectly deliciously drawn plan and section. I am delighted, and as soon as I have a moment of leisure shall settle down to the article.' He asks Carter to

47 MMA, Department of Egyptian Art, Carter files.
48 G.I. Carter Papers V, 99.

convert all measurements from yards to metres: 'If you did it straight off I should have it in time, if the submarines weren't unkind!'

Co-operation at such a distance and in war-time was slow, very uncertain and vexing for both sides. Gardiner in his eagerness to move forward and complete articles for *J.E.A.* was inclined to make substantial editorial changes in what Carter wrote. Carter, understandably, found Gardiner's rather arbitrary procedures very tiresome. A letter of 3 May 1917 hints at the stresses.[49] Gardiner begins with a spoonful of oil to calm Carter's objections: '*Au contraire!* I did not find your letter disagreeable. It contained some perfectly just answers to my rather finnicking demands, and if I cant accept those, so much the worse for me.' Later in the same letter he elaborates his difficulties as editor:

> You know it is a considerable responsibility to me as editor to write up your articles, but at present a closer collaboration seems unpracticable. I hope you will be lenient with me in the free hand I am taking. At all events I spare no trouble to bring out your results in the very best form.

Gardiner's last remark was fully justified. The article was finally published under both their names in the late summer of 1917.[50]

The second, and much more important, undertaking that Gardiner and Carter discussed in the summer of 1916 was the drawing by Carter of the important series of reliefs and inscriptions in the colonnade of the temple of Luxor. The sequence of scenes depicts the procession by river and land from the great temple of Karnak, two miles upstream, in which the Theban deities Amun, Mut and Khonsu travel during the Opet festival to the Luxor temple. The scenes are rich in detail – divine boats, priests, singers, attendants, musicians, soldiers, offerings – carved in the wonderfully sensitive style of the high Eighteenth Dynasty, and executed with a mastery of technical skill. They were probably begun in the reign of Amenophis III and completed by King Tutankhamun, a name which was not yet quite one to conjure with in 1916. Gardiner in his early references always calls them the Horemheb (Haremhab) reliefs; that king, a near successor of Tutankhamun, completed the colonnade and usurped much of his young predecessor's work. To draw such scenes was a task to delight Howard Carter, and to work on them one to excite Gardiner. For Carter it would be the first extended piece of serious epigraphic work he had engaged in since the completion of the Deir el-Bahri reliefs in 1899; for Gardiner it would represent the achievement of yet one more permanent record of historical and artistic importance, enshrined in a fine publication. After some preliminary discussion, Gardiner summed up his views in a letter to Carter in August:[51]

49 G.I. Carter Papers V, 100.
50 *J.E.A.* 4 (1917), pp. 130ff.
51 G.I. Carter Papers V, 97, dated 24 August 1916.

With regard to the Haremhab procession my idea, since I have got the very best artist to help me, is to reproduce the scenes in the very best way possible; and since the book will not have to form one of a series my proposal is that the size of the book should be made to suit firstly, the nature of the scenes copied, and secondly general consideration of convenience. . . . I should like the book to be an artistic one. I don't mind a little expense.

Carter was to be paid a good, but not excessive, fee for his work:

my recollection is that your suggestion was £75 down and £100 on completion of the job. Or was it the other way round? Anyhow, I send you now a cheque for £75 and will send another if I have made a mistake.

By the spring of 1917, Carter had completed drawings enough for 15 plates of the projected volume, which, he estimated, would contain between 30 and 40 plates. It really did seem that the undertaking would be brought to a successful conclusion before too long:[52] 'It is good news that the Haremhab scenes are going well. In case you come back to England in the summer I should suggest you leave the drawings behind in Egypt. There is every chance of safety for passengers but considerably less for luggage nowadays, and it would be terrible if all that work went to the bottom.' On 1 May Carter sent Gardiner his proposals for the plate arrangements in the book, reiterates that he has completed 15, reckons he has done enough to justify the original agreed payment of £175, and looks forward to being commissioned to complete the further 15, or more, plates needed. Gardiner took up this, or a subsequent, letter on 17 June enthusiastically:[53]

So far as economy goes in publication I want this once to do your admirable drawings real justice and to show the Americans that they have not the monopoly of making *éditions de luxe*. . . . I want our publication to be just perfect, and unless I am ruined by the war I am prepared to remunerate you to whatever you consider the right and proper extent.

So certain did it then seem that the Luxor enterprise would soon be finished that Gardiner began to think up other tasks for Carter to do. It seemed too good an opportunity to have a tame artist in Thebes at a time when most scholars were unable to travel in Egypt. Gardiner probably also thought that he was doing Carter a favour in suggesting new tasks 'to fill out the time until the war ends'.[54] There were new discoveries by

52 G.I. Carter Papers V, 99, letter of 4 March 1917.
53 The Carter letter is preserved in draft only; for it and Gardiner's subsequent letter, G. I. Carter Papers V, 105 and 101.
54 G.I. Carter Papers V, 102, letter dated 24 August 1918.

Carter himself which could be written up for the *J.E.A.*; there later would be the possibility of a co-operation in the publication of inscribed ostraca (limestone flakes, used for casual jottings in antiquity); and Carter could recopy for him the inscriptions on a remarkable early Middle-Kingdom shrine from Dendera which had recently been badly dealt with in the journal of the Antiquities Service.[55]

There can be little doubt that Carter could read the danger signs. If he were not careful he would become Gardiner's man in Luxor, expected more and more to execute his commissions and requests. Carter was still Carnarvon's man, and he was surely not prepared to compromise his principal professional relationship by spending too much time on work for Gardiner, who, although increasingly friendly with Carnarvon, may not have kept him fully informed of the use he was making of Carter. It must be said that it was never unprofitable, in a scholarly sense, to work for and with Gardiner, but he was inclined to regard willing co-operation by another scholar as ready submission to all scholarly demands. Although there are no documents mentioning Carter's backing away from Gardiner's persistent demands, it is noticeable that work on the drawings of the Luxor reliefs ground to a halt during the summer of 1917. There are no letters from Gardiner complaining of the suspension and urging Carter to continue. They were never subsequently taken up again, and the end of the war, resumption of full-scale work for Carnarvon, and other commitments, provided Carter with insufficient time to return with his drawing board to the east bank of the Nile and the processional colonnade of Horemheb in the Luxor temple. Tragically, the work was never completed. The finished drawings were in due course handed over to Gardiner, and they now lie unpublished in the archives of the Griffith Institute in Oxford,[56] a sad and substantial token of what would certainly have been that 'perfect' publication that Alan Gardiner had desired.

During the summer of 1916, while Carter was in England, a most remarkable discovery was made in a remote spot at the southern end of the hilly district of the Theban Necropolis.[57] There had been a heavy rain-storm in the hills, resulting in tumultuous floods pouring down from the western mountains to the Theban plain. On such rare occasions huge quantities of loose debris were moved about by the water, and it was not uncommon for ancient remains, or the indications of tombs, to be revealed. The professional tomb-robbers of Qurna were well aware of these periodic natural, and very effective, scourings, and following this summer downpour they discovered a tomb in the Wadi Qubbanet el-Qirud, 'Valley of the

55 G.I. Carter Papers V, 103, letter of 12 June 1918.
56 G.I. Gardiner Papers AHG/11, 1–13.
57 Account in H. E. Winlock, *The Treasure of three Egyptian Princesses* (New York, 1948). A fuller account of the discovery and study of the treasure is under preparation by Dr C. Lilyquist.

tombs of the monkeys'. It contained the remains of the burials of three Asiatic wives of King Tuthmosis III (*c.* 1479–1425 BC), much devastated by water, but still rich in objects of precious metals and inscribed stone vessels. The find could not be kept wholly quiet, and it was not long before Ernest Mackay heard in broad outline the story of the pillaging of the contents, the 'banking' of the antiquities with the Luxor dealer Mohammed Mohassib, the antics of the robbers in their disputes over the discovery, and in their behaviour after receiving from the dealer a sum reported later by Carter as amounting to £E1100 – a fortune even for reasonably success-ful tomb robbers.[58] When Carter returned to Thebes in October 1916 the stories of the discovery and of subsequent events were in the process of being elaborated in the repeated tellings in the gossip shops of Luxor. Carter believed that he finally determined the broad outlines of what had happened, but his informal account, written down many years later, has never been published.[59] His interest in the objects that had ended up with Mohammed Mohassib was naturally intense, and his negotiations in acquiring most of what had been found will be discussed briefly in the next chapter. Archaeologically, however, he was alerted to the possibility of further discoveries in the region of the Wadi Qubbanet el-Qirud, just as the original finders of the tomb had been alerted by the providential cloud-burst.

Before the end of October, Howard Carter found himself engaged in a further 'cloak-and-dagger' operation in the very same region of the Theban Necropolis.[60] News of another discovery broke in the villages of the west bank one afternoon, and there followed a skirmishing between rival bands of tomb robbers. Carter was asked to intervene to prevent further trouble. He happened to be spending a short holiday in Luxor at the time, and was the most 'experienced and trusted' of the few Europeans still in the area. With a party of his former workmen and accompanied by Sheikh Mansour, one of the influential locals, he set out as soon as possible, and approached the scene of the discovery over the hills to the lip of the small ravine Wadi Sikket Taqet Zaid, which ran northwards out of the Wadi Qubbanet el-Qirud. Here they found a rope dangling over the edge of the cliff, leading down to a cleft from which voices could be heard. Carter severed the robbers' rope and descended on his own. 'Shinning down a rope at midnight, into a nestful of industrious tomb-robbers, is a pastime which at least does not lack excitement.' The eight surprised Qurnawis, understanding the situation, were persuaded to leave without making any trouble, and Carter was left with the duty, initially full of anticipation, of clearing and investigating what had been discovered. It was, and remains,

---

58 A copy of Mackay's report is kept in G.I. Gardiner Papers AGH/42. 196.
59 G.I. Carter Notebook 17, pp. 218ff (Sketch XII).
60 Dealt with briefly in *The Tomb of Tut.ankh.Amen*, I, pp. 79f., an account repeated almost verbatim, but with much added detail, in his Sketch XII, pp. 276ff.

a puzzle how the tomb had ever been spotted. Its entrance in the cleft was invisible both from the top of the cliff 130 feet above, and from the floor of the ravine 220 feet below. But the cleft had not escaped the periodic deluges of flood water and debris, and the whole tomb – as it turned out to be – was choked with impacted rubbish through which the robbers had cut a tunnel over 90 feet long, just large enough to allow the passage of a crawling man.

The eventual clearance of the tomb brought interesting, although unspectacular finds, and the scientific results of an operation lasting 20 days could be scarcely regarded as dramatic as the tomb's situation had promised, or as exciting as its discovery had been. The work was laborious; the daily descent into the cleft was hazardous, Carter himself always making it in a net. Because of the difficulty of access the clearance went on day and night, with relays of workmen, the rubbish being tossed from the cleft down to the floor of the ravine. A passage of about 55 feet in length led down to a square-shaped antechamber from which a shorter corridor descended gently at right-angles to a larger chamber in which Carter found a yellow quartzite sarcophagus, placed on the edge of a further descending corridor leading to what was to have been the sarcophagus chamber. This last room was small but fairly well cut out; the whole tomb was in an unfinished state. The sarcophagus, with its great lid leaning against it, was inscribed for Hatshepsut as royal consort, before, that is, she adopted the full power, panoply and titulary of kingship. Otherwise the tomb contained only a few fragments of pottery vessels. Nevertheless, the sarcophagus was a magnificent monument with finely carved texts, although lacking the required divine representations on its side panels. Every indication pointed to the conclusion that the tomb had been abandoned in favour of a new and more 'royal' sepulchre in the Valley of the Kings, one which Carter had himself cleared for Theodore Davis in 1904.

Following the clearance of this unusual and tantalizing tomb, Carter had it in mind to search the neighbourhood for further hidden tombs, but nature intervened:[61]

the fury of the elements was let loose. Heavy clouds that had been gathering on the summit of the mountain broke. Flashes of lightning quivered from those clouds. Peals of thunder echoed from hill to hill – a storm had let loose its fury. The swifts whirled screaming to their crags. In a few moments the whole mountain-side foamed with innumerable cascades. The tomb in the cleft was filled to its brim with rainwater, and we had but a few minutes to strike camp for higher ground, clear of the boulder-strewn valley which soon became a roaring torrent.

61 In Sketch XII, p. 233.

When the weather cleared Carter decided to grasp the opportunity to follow the local practice of searching the hills for signs of tombs after a torrential downpour. He spent ten useful days on this survey without finding anything as dramatic as the two tombs already discovered earlier in the year. He noted short ancient texts in the hieratic script scribbled on the rocks (graffiti), remains of stone huts, and a number of empty tomb-pits. At Gardiner's insistence he allowed two reports he had sent to Lord Carnarvon to be compiled into an article for *J.E.A.*; it contained his survey and incorporated a brief description of the tomb of the three wives of Tuthmosis III, and a fuller account of the tomb in the cleft.[62] A shorter report on the latter discovery was written up for the journal of the Antiquities Service, with the interesting title 'A tomb prepared for Queen Hatshepsuit discovered by the Earl of Carnarvon (October, 1916)'.[63] It was important that Carter was seen to be acting, in investigating the tomb in the cleft, not independently, but as the agent of Lord Carnarvon, to whom the concession in the Valley of the Kings was assigned.

The time had not yet arrived when Carter could safely embark on the work in the Valley for which he had been so long waiting, and so diligently preparing himself. For the time being he was still working for the Intelligence Department at Headquarters in Cairo. His occasional spells of leave allowed him to go up-river to Luxor and do a little, generally unsystematic archaeological work, continue his Luxor Temple drawing for Gardiner, and paint a little on his own account. A series of lively, rather gossipy, letters to Essie, wife of Percy Newberry, provide rare glimpses of the private Howard Carter, who was not in the habit of unburdening himself to more than a very few intimate friends.[64] Writing on 10 February, still in Luxor, he had some rather unexciting news and gossip to convey. By 31 May he was back in Cairo and living in the Continental Hotel; after writing about work on the Newberry's *dahabiya*, on which he was keeping an eye, and various Cairo acquaintances, he adds:

In many ways I don't think Egypt was ever so prosperous, and excepting rate of living having greatly risen little of the toils of Greater Europe are felt, especially as now the news is so satisfactory.

I may go to the Gaza front, but it is not yet certain. In the meantime I have been fortunate and am keeping afloat.

It is hard to know what he meant by that last remark, unless he was referring to financial matters. He had received some money from Gardiner in the recent months, and he may have been paid a small retainer by Carnarvon, especially as he continued to purchase antiquities on his behalf.

62 *J.E.A.* 4 (1917), pp. 107ff.
63 *A.S.A.E.* 16 (1917), pp. 179ff.
64 Letters to Mrs Newberry in G. I. Newberry Corr. 8/50 (10 Feb., 1917), 8/51 (9 July), 8/55 (31 May), 8/56 (20 Oct.).

He probably received no regular payment for his work for the Intelligence Department, but smallish sums for individual commissions. Sales of paintings were probably slow; but in the following year he was pleased to be able to report to Mrs Newberry,[65] 'You will be glad to hear that I got rid of a nice fat drawing – I believe a good one – this spring in Cairo – most satisfactory.' In general, life in Cairo could be pretty dull, and made more tiresome by the loss of letters from home. He complains so to Essie Newberry on 9 July:

> Here one is muddling along – sometimes depressed and sometimes gay – but as I read the other day – human life – happiness and unhappiness – are far more equally balanced than usually credited. They exist in more or less proportionate quantities and give place to each other at regular intervals. The pessimist counts the one and is unhappy, the optimist the other and [is] more or less joyous.

A letter in October indicates that he had been back in Luxor for two months. It includes the news that he was no longer getting war-work in Cairo; so it must be assumed that he never went to the Gaza front, as he had expected in May. He found life in Upper Egypt lonely, and was in consequence 'nearly dotty':

> I may do a little excavating later. I offered the Service to do what I could until they were able to replace poor Legrain but as I have received no answer in any form I expect I ain't wanted. (Rather glad). . . .
>
> I have a cat, of half wild and half domestic extract. I can't say I like cats, and this one in particular, especially when she cat calls in the middle of the night.

In one area of activity, however, Carter was busy and flourishing during the war, and particularly from 1917; this was the purchasing and placing of antiquities for private and public interests. As he reported on more than one occasion, there was not much of a market for good material during the war, and anything of quality was likely to be put away to mature, to await the return of the big-spending tourists and museum representatives after the war. For someone like Carter the conditions were ideal for picking up bargains, and for having the run of the stocks of the dealers without serious competition. His purchases for Lord Carnarvon were, it seems, straight transactions without commission. Similarly he helped to arrange, in 1915, with the direct assistance of Carnarvon, the sale of seven large granite statues of the lioness deity Sakhmet formerly in the Amherst Collection, to the Metropolitan Museum of Art.[66] Again it appears that in this

65 G.I. Newberry Corr. 8/53, letter of 13 April 1918.
66 Letters between Carter and Albert Lythgoe, May-June 1915, in M.M.A., Department of Egyptian Art, Carter files.

transaction, as in others he had carried through for the Americans, he had not sought, or been offered, a commission. It is not impossible – in fact highly likely – that when he sold something he had purchased privately, the price was adjusted to include some profit. But as an agent he acted 'as a friend *of the family* and of ours as well', as Lythgoe put it in a letter of 1919.[67] It was in the same letter that Lythgoe proposed that Carter should receive commissions for purchases for the Metropolitan. In offering such – which Carter in answer gratefully accepted – Lythgoe had taken a lead from the agreement which he and others had helped Carter to conclude with the Cleveland Museum of Art in 1917. That recently established but already vigorous institution wished to build on its small core collection of Egyptian antiquities, and Carter was recommended as the best available agent.[68] Henry W. Kent, Secretary of the Metropolitan Museum, wrote to Judge William Sanders, Chairman of the Cleveland Board of Trustees: 'he will produce results for you which will give the Cleveland Museum an enviable place among museums of Egyptian Art.'

Howard Carter sent his terms of agreement on 16 September 1917. They were detailed and comprehensive and suggest earlier arrangements made with other institutions, although none have clearly been identified. He was to receive 15 per cent commission on purchases; would obtain best prices; would guarantee the authenticity of pieces. All costs of transport, packing and insurance would be met by the Museum. He would want in general a free hand, but would send photographs of all purchases in advance of dispatch. He also says, significantly, 'from time to time I acquire Egyptian antiquities myself for the purpose of sale. Should at any time your Museum wish to make a purchase from me, I would ask that it be done through a third party accepted or appointed by you.' He also speaks of 'the numerous and considerable purchases I have made for both public and private collections.' It took a little time before Carter began to purchase for Cleveland, but between spring 1918 and the Amherst Sale at Sothebys in June 1921 he acquired a good series of antiquities for the Museum. The results were not perhaps as striking as Kent had predicted, but in those early days Cleveland could not put at Carter's disposal the kind of funds which would have allowed him to buy widely and well. The one good piece of Late-Period sculpture that he bought in 1920 induced an extraordinary and unfortunate controversy with James H. Breasted, which will be examined later. Nevertheless, Carter greatly improved the Cleveland collection with good examples of standard categories of antiquities and a fair number of interesting pieces, the full scientific and artistic potentials of which were not fully appreciated until many years later.

67 Letter dated 26 February, in M.M.A., Department of Egyptian Art, Carter files.
68 An account of the arrangement and its results is given in T. G. H. James, 'Howard Carter and the Cleveland Museum of Art' in *Object Lessons. Cleveland creats an Art Museum*, ed. Evan Turner (Cleveland, 1991), pp. 66ff.

So, in autumn 1917, Howard Carter had reached a modest staging-point in his career. He was, for the moment, unemployed with war-work; he was active, collecting antiquities for his various friends and clients; he was in Luxor and rather bored. It was in fact a time to look to the future. Although the war still raged, there were distinct signs of an end in sight. When it came a degree of normality might be expected; it could be a return to pre-war conditions, with the advantages of excavation heavily weighted in favour of European and American excavators. On the other hand there might be significant changes. Egypt would no longer be the rather subservient state it had previously been, even though a British protectorate had been declared in December 1914. Within Egypt the Antiquities Service would no longer be run by the indulgent and partial Gaston Maspero, but by Pierre Lacau. There had been no real opportunity to assess the temper of the new regime, but initial impressions were favourable. Somers Clarke had written to Budge in the British Museum in September 1916, saying that he saw Lacau as 'a gentleman and man of affairs.[69] I believe the change is immensely for the good; we may look forward in process of time to sundry improvements.' Carter, initially uncertain, was later rather more confident: 'In regard to Lacau – I think that I ought to recall a good deal[70] I said in my letter of last month. He is on the whole friendly – certainly a gentleman – but a stickler and narrow in what he calls "L'idéal au point de vue scientifique".' These remarks followed a visit by Lacau to see Carter's work in the Valley in February 1918, to be considered in the next chapter. By early February Carter had carried out a two-month season of regular work in the Valley of the Kings. He had at last launched Carnarvon's campaign to 'exhaust' the royal site. The life Carter had led for almost three years, chopped up and unsettled – yet so much more 'normal' than that endured by most men during the Great War – was coming to an end. Some residual uncertainties of war-time service would persist, and there would be difficulties in planning a regular life; but now there was real hope.

69 Letter in Department of Western Asiatic Antiquities, British Museum.
70 Letter to Lord Carnarvon of 29 March, 1918 in M.M.A., Department of Egyptian Art, Carter files.

190

9

THE VALLEY OF THE KINGS
AND DISCOVERY

In the late months of 1917, with better news from the war fronts presaging an end to conflict, Howard Carter had good reason to look forward to a serious return to the work for which he was best equipped. The future, however, was fraught with uncertainty. As far as Carter was concerned, the key figure in his plans was the Earl of Carnarvon. He had not seen him since the summer of 1916, and his health was very unpredictable, as indeed it had been throughout the years of their association. Would there be a future for their work in Egypt? In the coming months an almost fatal crisis gave a strong indication of how tenuous that future might be. Writing to Lythgoe in New York in early 1918, Carter remarks:[1]

> Poor Lord Carnarvon, as no doubt you have heard, has had a very poor time. He nearly died this spring – saved only by an immediate operation for septic appendix. He is now in a state of convalence [sic], exceedingly weak, and I am thankful to say daily improving.

Uncertainty resided not only in Carnarvon's health, but also in his commitment to digging in the Valley of the Kings – a matter never explicitly stated in the first years of work in that hope-inspiring, but equally hope-dashing, site, but one to be inferred from Carnarvon's renewed search for another concession away from Thebes. There was, in addition, a new problem, hints of which had been detected earlier; this was the attitude of Pierre Lacau, Maspero's successor as Director-General of the Antiquities Service. In the same letter to Lythgoe, quoted above, Carter voices the doubts he had raised on earlier occasions: 'Lacau as you may already know is back and has taken up the reins of command. He is a gentleman and good workman, but somewhat a stickler when it comes to divisions. I think a certain combination among concessionaires would be of use in the sence [sic] of justice and fair play.'

When Carter wrote this letter he had recently suffered a set-back in

---

1 Letter of 28 May, 1918 (a duplicate of one written 12 April) in M.M.A., Department of Egyptian Art, Carter files. See also H. Carter and A. C. Mace, *The Tomb of Tut.ankh.Amen*, I, p. 34.

plans for the sale to the Metropolitan Museum of an object from the Carnarvon excavations – an act of unwarranted meanness, as he saw it, and suggestive of what might be in store for excavators at the hands of the new administration. The object in question was none other than the quartzite sarcophagus of Hatshepsut that had been found in the cleft tomb in 1916. The excavation/clearance of this tomb had been officially approved in Lord Carnarvon's name, and the excavators had some reason to expect that a find like the sarcophagus might be ceded to them on the grounds that it was not really needed for the Cairo Museum. Need, however, was scarcely the criterion to be used in this case; the sarcophagus was the only considerable object recovered from the tomb and it was royal. In the event the plan foundered on the rocks of official refusal, presumably with the knowledge, if not at the instigation of Lacau:[2]

> Though Lord Carnarvon was agreable [sic] in the matter of the sarcophagus I have been unable to get the museum to meet our views and let us have the monument – thus it has fallen through. It certainly seems like the 'dog in the manger' as the monument has been left neglected ever since the day of its discovery, nor has anyone been to see it excepting myself – but that is not an uncommon trait on the part of the department by which explorer and object suffer.

Carter, very shortly before writing to Lythgoe, had sent a long letter to Carnarvon about excavating prospects elsewhere in the Nile Valley, and had included the telling comment:[3]

> In regard to the sarcophagus – after careful consideration – the subject being a delicate one, and one that might possibly injure your future interests in this country – I think that it is best left alone!

Carter's judgement in the matter was sound, and it was made at a significant moment, after the completion of his first serious season in the Valley, during which he had received a visit from Lacau – his first inspection by the new man. It had not been much of a season. Work had started on 1 December 1917 'in the small lateral valley situated between the tomb of Ramses II and Ramses VI.' Here he first put into practice his intention to clear down to bed-rock, considering this method to be the only one certain to uncover any undiscovered tomb. It would be expensive in terms of labour and of time, but essential if he were to disprove Theodore Davis's claim that the Valley was exhausted. The season's work continued until 2 February 1918. The results in terms of objects were meagre, consisting mostly of inscribed ostraca, which were to arouse the interest of Alan

---

2 In the same letter to Lythgoe of 28 May.
3 In M.M.A., Department of Egyptian Art, Carter files. The Hatshepsut sarcophagus is now in the Cairo Museum, no. 47032.

Gardiner, in expectation of further collaboration between himself and Carter.[4]

Although the two-month campaign had not produced encouraging finds, or given hopeful indications for future seasons, it represented for Carter a real achievement under what were still war conditions. There were distinct worries for him, however, and two in particular, mentioned earlier, needed prompt attention. They were not unrelated to each other. First, there was the need to find another site for Lord Carnarvon; second, what would be their future relations with, and expectations from, Lacau and the Antiquities Service. Soon after the end of his work in the Valley, he began a reconnaissance trip to inspect possible sites between Luxor and Cairo. It took place between 7 and 28 March, by river in a *dahabiya* belonging to the American archeologist Clarence S. Fisher, who had recently been excavating for the University of Pennsylvania at Dendera, and was about to reopen work for a summer season at Memphis, just south of Cairo. Such a trip was more than a novelty for Carter. It was almost a holiday and certainly a huge pleasure. To Mrs Newberry he wrote on 13 April from the Turf Club in Cairo: [5]

I have just come down from the South – a floating trip down stream, seeing various old places along the river . . . it was so nice to see old places again. Tel el Amarna especially, where I had not been for 25 years. I enjoyed it immensely and I felt quite touched in seeing what I call old friends again.

El-Amarna, in fact, was the place he most favoured as a new site for Lord Carnarvon. He wrote a long report to him on 29 March, in which he detailed those places where prospects were good.[6] Akhmim was one; the modern town occupied the site of the ancient capital of the ninth Upper Egyptian nome, the centre of the worship of the fertility god Min. Here he was impressed and disgusted by the state of the relatively modern cemetery 'where domed tombs not more than a century old lie open exposing in each some ten or more ghastly corpses . . . The natives invite you to dig among these horrible human remains and shrouds,' He comments favourably on Meir, an ancient necropolis site further north where there could be 'interesting and profitable results'. But for him El-Amarna was 'the pearl of sites after Saqqara, Dashur and Thebes'. His advocacy was very persuasive:

For you it is an ideal site, convenient in every way, besides being comparatively near Cairo; with a dahabeyeh you would never be

4 The finds of the season are listed in C. N. Reeves, *The Valley of the Kings* (London, 1990), pp. 352ff. For Gardiner's interest in the ostraca, see letter to Carter, dated 12 June 1918, G. I. Carter Papers, V, 103.
5 G.I. Newberry Corr. 8/53.
6 Letter of 29 March, see n. 3 above.

more than a mile from the scene of operations, beautiful desert, light and clean digging and one need hardly say with luck the chance of beautiful things. At risk of all I am fighting for it and sincerely trust to be successful . . . Though only a few hours there my heart I found was there the whole time.

He adds that Mervyn Herbert, Carnarvon's half-brother, who was at the time serving in Egypt as a First Secretary and who accompanied him for part of the trip, 'was much struck by place and surroundings'.

Carter's distinct preference for El-Amarna contained a clear element of nostalgia. It was here that he had first excavated in 1892, under the stern tutelage of Flinders Petrie. In retrospect it had all the attraction one commonly assigns to a place or occasion remembered as much for its disagreeable aspects as for its sentimental ties. He also considered it in terms of Carnarvon's own physical condition and convenience. The 'chance of beautiful things' was not exaggerated. The Germans, under Borchardt, had been exceptionally fortunate in their finds of fine sculpture there before the war. Among their prizes was the famous head of Queen Nefertiti; although the public revelation of this piece did not occur until some years after the war, it may well have been known to archaeologists from the time of its discovery. Yet Carter realized that there might be difficulties over securing the concession. While he was in Cairo after his river reconnaissance he made preliminary soundings about concessions, and about the divisions of antiquities, with Lacau and with Sir Murdoch Macdonald who was the Under-Secretary of State in the Ministry of Public Works in Cairo, and officially in charge of the Antiquities Service. Notes on these conversations, undated, make it clear that the Amarna concession was not likely to be granted. He got the impression that the German pre-war concession was still strangely respected, but that in any case Lacau wished to reserve the site for official excavation by the Service.[7]

This opinion was reiterated by Lacau in a fairly formal letter he sent to Carter on 8 April. It was the result of the visit he had made to the Valley in February, which has already been mentioned. He had several positive comments to make on what Carter was doing, beginning with a friendly enough commendation: 'I entirely approve your plan for work in the Valley of the Kings. By laying bare the rock in large areas, no tomb entrance can escape you . . . Your project for a *complete plan* is naturally essential, and will be an important result of your work.' He requires Carter to remove a retaining wall and the great mounds of debris, which should be dispersed neatly over the walls of the Valley – a task which will, he recognizes, be expensive: 'It is advisable to alert Lord Carnarvon about this without delay.' After giving permission for various minor requests

7 Memoranda and Lacau letters (in French) on the search for new sites in M.M.A., Department of Egyptian Art, Carter files.

submitted by Carter, he restated the position he proposed to take on *partage* – a position in dividing finds between excavators and the Cairo Museum which had been formulated many years earlier under Maspero, but never fully implemented. There would no longer be an automatic right to 50 per cent of finds for the excavator, but an absolute right for the ceding to Cairo of anything deemed necessary for the national collection. He complained of Carter's making a separate approach behind his back to Sir Murdoch Macdonald: 'What if all excavators did the same? . . . But there is one law that I must observe *and make observed*.' Finally, Lacau repeated his position on El-Amarna; it was to be reserved for the Antiquities Service. He added, rather unnecessarily: 'In any case, if we are not able to take it up ourselves in the future, we should grant it to a scientific institution and not to a private individual.'

Clearly annoyed by this last statement, Carter replied promptly on 10 April, challenging Lacau's view of what kind of institution or person might qualify for El-Amarna:

> I fully realize that if this decision is final, I have no alternative but to accept it – but I am sure you will forgive me if I ask what better guarantee can be given by a scientific institution than by an individual . . . is it not a new departure to differentiate between individuals and institutions in matter of this kind?

Unfortunately this was not a debate Carter could win. Lacau answered three days later, saying that there were already two other applicants for El-Amarna in front of Lord Carnarvon – the American George Reisner, and Georges Foucart, Lacau's successor as Director of the French Institute in Cairo. Once more he insisted that in the future, for important excavations, preference would be given to learned bodies. This decision was partly determined by the consideration of the fate of objects found. There should be proper publication of finds, which should also be accessible to students. There was much sound thinking in Lacau's views, but he had a way of presenting them which showed little consideration for the other points of view and was often rather offensive. A draft of a letter prepared by Carter, but possibly never sent to Lacau, pointed out that much of the excavation carried out by the British in Egypt had been under private auspices, including the work of Petrie and Garstang. No work had actually been promoted by museums.

In the end the bid for El-Amarna was dropped. There was no shortage of alternatives. Writing to Carnarvon on 7 June 1918, Carter concentrated on sites in Middle Egypt, the region containing El-Amarna, but rich in other possibilities, as he pointed out. He was interested in Balansura, a necropolis area near the western desert across the Nile from Beni Hasan, and still not properly investigated; there was Tuna, a most important burial ground for the ancient city of Hermopolis (El-Ashmunein); then also Meir again, and El-Bersha where he had worked in his first season in Egypt. Recently Reisner had obtained there, apparently (and, as it later became clear, truly), some success with good finds of objects. Sentiment attracted Carter to consider El-Bersha a place with serious prospects:

> The meeting of old native acquaintances after 25 years was most touching, and I have hardly yet recovered from the reception I received, more especially the sour camels milk that was stuffed down my throat – a beduin luxury.

Sentiment, however, could not contend with practicalities and good prospects, and the decision was taken during the summer of 1918 to do a short season at Meir (or Mir, as Carter called it). It was, like the other favoured sites, a necropolis of rock-cut tombs dating from the late Old Kingdom and the Middle Kingdom, a span of about 2300–1875 BC. The tombs belonged to the provincial nobles of the fourteenth Upper Egyptian nome, and some were decorated with extremely interesting carved and painted scenes. A record of many of the known tombs was made by Aylward Blackman for the Archaeological Survey of the Egypt Exploration Fund in 1912–14 – he was to return there later in 1920–21 and in 1949–50 – and excavations had been carried out privately in the years before the war for Sayed Khashaba, a wealthy landowner of Asyut. These excavations, which had not been conducted in accordance with even the moderate standards of field-work in Egypt at the time, were badly supervised and poorly recorded. On the other hand, they produced good results, and many of the best finds were subsequently purchased for, and may now be seen in, the Metropolitan Museum of Art, New York. In Carter's mind there was surely the idea that the lax methods of Khashaba's workmen would have left much to be retrieved by more systematic methods.

In the meanwhile, with the war still continuing, Howard Carter remained not entirely a free agent. Writing to Lythgoe in New York in September of the previous year he had stated,[8] 'my sundry war jobs seemingly come to an end'. But by the early summer of 1918, he was again involved in unspecified duties, certainly war-work. In a letter to Mrs Newberry, written from Alexandria, where he was on holiday with 'Jack Gordon of the Residency',[9] he says that he would then 'return to Cairo to finish work that I have on hand there. I may and I hope to go to Palestine later on, but that is for the moment in the skyes [sic].' By this time hostilities had ceased in Palestine, and there were clear attractions to a visit to that country, even if undertaken in the course of duty. It did not, apparently, ever take place. In July he was still in Cairo, finding things 'tedious', but enlivened by the news of occasional finds of antiquities, like

8 Dated 16 September, in M.M.A., Department of Egyptian Art, Carter files.
9 Letter of 11 June in G.I. Newberry Corr. 8/57.

a hoard of 'silver gilt stuff at Dendera which the Museum got – very late and horribly ugly.' Reporting to Percy Newberry, he comments:[10]

> Antiquities like everything else have gone up in price – the natives have become so rich, farm produce being threble [*sic*] what it was in value. Too such large sums are brought in through the Army contracts etc. – most of which absorbed by the natives and hoarded for future times. So much so that they are now issuing five piastre notes, the whole of the silver being hidden underground.

Following and negotiating in the antiquities market were now established activities for Carter whether he was in Cairo or Luxor. Already by the summer of 1918 he was engaged in the arrangements under which the bulk of the precious treasure found in the tomb of the three Asiatic wives of Tuthmosis III was purchased by him and later acquired by the Metropolitan Museum.

A sometimes erroneous account of this acquisition has been given elsewhere, in which a partial and very unsympathetic position was taken; a more balanced history of the affair remains to be written, included in a new study of the rich contents of the tomb.[11] It seems clear that in organizing the purchase of the objects from the Luxor dealer Mohammed Mohassib, Carter was encouraged by Lord Carnarvon, who himself put up much of the money needed to secure them. The details of the various transactions remain obscure, but it is clear that Carter found a ready buyer in the Metropolitan Museum. The matter is one in which a balanced judgement is hard to reach, especially so as the attitude of the Antiquities Service at the time seems to have been one of disinterest. When the tomb was first found, and its discovery reported by Mackay,[12] the local Egyptian Inspector carried out a prompt investigation but the authorities in Cairo showed no interest in following up his recommendations. At some point in 1918 or 1919 Ambrose Lansing, representing the Metropolitan Museum's Egyptian Expedition in Egypt, acquired with the help of Carter, and exported in due course with proper documentation and the full knowledge of the Cairo Museum, the canopic jars and silver vessels, along with some of the stone vessels from the tomb equipment.[13] As late as 1924 Rex Engelbach, Chief Inspector of Antiquities in Upper Egypt, could write concerning the tomb and its reported contents:[14]

There were rumours of a great treasure having been discovered there,

10 G.I. Newberry Corr. 8/58, of 5 July.
11 See T. Hoving, *Tutankhamun. The Untold Story* (New York, 1978), pp. 127ff. The new study is in preparation by Dr C. Lilyquist of the Department of Egyptian Art of the Metropolitan Museum.
12 For the story of the discovery, see p. 184 above.
13 H. E. Winlock, *The Treasure of Three Egyptian Princesses*, p. 11ff.
14 In his *Supplement to the Topographical Catalogue of the Private Tombs of Thebes* (Cairo, 1924), p. 6.

which included gold sandals, bracelets, necklaces and beads, a gold head-dress and belt and numerous alabaster vases. Whether a treasure was indeed found will probably never be known. One thing, however, is fairly certain, and that is that the various museum agents and collectors buying in Luxor since my arrival [in 1920] have never acquired any considerable quantity of gold ornaments, neither has any treasure been on the market here or abroad which might have come from this tomb.

Engelbach's statement as a whole, published in an official report, indicates either an inability on the part of the officials of the Antiquities Service to put two and two together, or a deliberate ignoring of the facts of the case. It must, of course, be remembered that the discovery was made in 1916, a time when Mackay had stated that there was no European Inspector between Cairo and Wadi Halfa. Nevertheless, the find was well known in Luxor at the time. Under the circumstances it is rather more understandable that Carter, encouraged by Carnarvon and with a purchaser in mind, was prepared to buy items from the Luxor dealer, probably take them out of Egypt in batches without clearing them through the Cairo Museum, and sell them to the Metropolitan Museum. In a letter to Newberry in 1941, Herbert Winlock said:[15]

> The rest of the summer was spent on trying to write a paper on those things which Howard Carter brought down in his little tin box to your house [in Ightham, Kent] when he and I stayed with you in 1919. We already had a certain number of vases which Lansing had bought, and that lot of Carter's was the first of some six lots of stuff which I bought from Carter in the next three years. You remember well, but some of the things really are gorgeous.

There is much that can be said in mitigation. The Antiquities Service had taken few steps to investigate the discovery when they were first alerted, and none, as far as can now be determined, to track down the objects subsequently. Carter was not in Egypt at the time of the illicit, but very thorough, clearance of the tomb; he had no hand in the acquisition of the tomb's contents by the Luxor dealer Mohammed Mohassib. Carter's faults may have lain in the undeclared export of part of the material from Egypt, and – which was much less open to criticism – his making money out of the transactions. On the former, it must be said that the evidence available is not conclusive, and it is certain that he commonly did show to the authorities in the Cairo Museum objects that he was exporting for museums abroad. On the latter, his personal circumstances have to be

---

15 It is not difficult to see Carter's involvement from what H. E. Winlock says in *The Treasure of Three Egyptian Princesses* (New York, 1948), pp. 11, 23, 24, 61 (objects in Carnarvon's possession); Winlock's letter of 21 November 1941 in G.I. Newberry Corr. 46/45.

considered. It is easy for those who enjoy secure employment and a certain future to disdain someone who behaves in a venal manner. One thing is sure: but for Carter's intervention, the great part of the objects from this tomb of three Asiatic wives of Tuthmosis III would never have been brought together to be reassembled, supplemented, studied and enjoyed with such profit and pleasure; as has in fact happened.

These adventures in the world of collecting gave Howard Carter a kind of standing in museum circles which in these years was exploited and appreciated by those who had dealings with him. A bizarre circumstance occurred in 1919 when he purchased for the Cleveland Museum of Art a sculpture of the Late Period on which James Henry Breasted, Director of the Oriental Institute of the University of Chicago, thought he had first refusal.[16] The purchase was made from the Cairo dealer Nicolas Tano, and there seems to be little doubt that there had been a genuine misunderstanding. Breasted was exceedingly vexed that he had missed a piece which he considered to be particularly fine. Carter had succeeded not only in making the purchase, but in doing so at a price below that which Breasted was prepared to pay. In a long campaign of letter-writing, extending over nearly two years, Breasted did his best to persuade Cleveland to give up the piece, so that it might go not, as might have been expected, to his own Oriental Institute, but to the Art Institute of Chicago, for which he was acting in the matter. In the end the claim was dropped. In the course of a generally very unedifying exchange of letters, the following testimonial for Carter was offered by Henry Kent, the Secretary of the Metropolitan Museum, writing to Frederic Whiting, Director of the Cleveland Museum of Art: 'You should remember that he [i.e. Carter] is a practical buyer, which means more when dealing with the natives in Egypt than many would suppose.' Shortly afterwards he wrote again:[17]

> I am still of the opinion which I expressed to you before Carter was engaged as your agent, that he is probably the most desirable ally you can have in Egypt. He is acknowledged to be the most skilful trader with the natives, he is a gentleman, and I doubt very much whether he would be found lacking in courtesy or fairness to one of his own class.

Although detailed figures are not available, it cannot be doubted that Carter had established a flourishing antiquities practice apart from his strictly professional archaeological work. Private collectors as well as public institutions were pleased to make use of his services. Alan Gardiner, for

16 The piece is a kneeling statue of Horudja of Twenty-seventh-Dynasty date, Cleveland no. 3455.20. For the purchase in the context of Carter's activities on behalf of the Cleveland Museum, see E. H. Turner, ed., *Object Lessons. Cleveland creates an Art Museum* (Cleveland, 1991), pp. 71f.
17 *Ibid.*, p. 72.

example, was in 1918 on the track of a papyrus brought to his attention perhaps by Carter himself. The details are not clear, but in a letter to Carter, dated 13 July, he refers to a cable of earlier date asking Carter 'to purchase the papyrus for me.'[18] He continues, 'I am very grateful for your help, and as soon as I hear that the papyrus is mine I will pay the £100 into your bank. Please keep the papyrus there for me without unrolling it. I shall be full of expectancy to see what it is all about.' Nothing further is known about this papyrus, but it must be assumed that Carter effected the purchase, and perhaps even cleared its export through the Cairo Museum.

There can be little doubt that in making purchases of antiquities for institutional and private clients, Carter operated with great tact and considerable skill, and usually succeeded in his efforts without arousing conflict. The episode involving James Breasted and the Cleveland Museum seems to have been exceptional. Carter was not acting for Breasted; yet it is surprising to find that in spite of the acrimony engendered by the affair, and even before the resolution of the case of the Late-Period sculpture, Breasted himself had enlisted the aid of Carter in acquiring pieces for the Oriental Institute.[19] But skill in buying does not surely induce respect or affection. Carter's general standing had grown during the war years; he now found himself being consulted and taken into the plans of influential people more frequently than formerly. His long sojourn in Egypt during the war, and his helpful attitude to many archaeological projects and problems during those years, and immediately afterwards, rendered him someone to be involved in matters of general archaeological importance. The beginnings of a campaign to counter the new thinking in the Antiquities Service have already been noticed. He was also, as the man on the spot, consulted over the possible establishment of a British archaeological institute in Egypt.

The idea for a British School seems to have started in the mind of Alan Gardiner.[20] He speaks of having plotted with Lord Carnarvon 'to create a British School of Egyptology in Cairo. Through Carnarvon I had a talk with Arthur Balfour on the latter topic, but though the great politician showed the interest and the courtesy for which he was renowned nothing came of this after-dinner meeting.'[21] The possibility of setting up an institute of some kind seemed a sensible development following the establishment of the British protectorate in Egypt in 1914, and the likelihood of an expansion of British archaeological activity in Egypt after the war.

18 G.I. Carter Papers V, 104.
19 E.g. a scribe's paletee; see letter of Breasted to Carter of 1 December 1920; copy in O.I. Director's Office Correspondence 1920.
20 In A. H. Gardiner, *My Working Years* (privately published, 1963), p. 30.
21 Arthur James Balfour was Foreign Secretary from 1916 to 1919.

Carter could make soundings in Egypt. Writing to Lord Carnarvon in November 1918, he says:[22]

> Just before leaving Cairo I had another long conversation [he does not say with whom] in regard to the Service, the institution of a school etc, and by your letters I [i.e. it] seems that we have been working much in the same line and ends. I think you will find good and proper advice accepted.

Gardiner's experience with Balfour represented the negative response that has up to the present day been granted officially to attempts to set up an Institute in Cairo. The lack of one centrally based organization to promote the idea, coupled with an unwillingness by governmental agencies to consider seriously the need for such an institute, has made it impossible to proceed with a plan acceptable to all interested parties. In the period covering the end of the war and the first years after, the efforts by Gardiner and Carnarvon, strongly supported by the eloquent voices of Sir John Evans, Lord Grenfell and Sir John Maxwell, were seriously and effectively countered by the opposition of Flinders Petrie, whose own British School of Archaeology in Egypt – itself no school in the ordinary sense, and with no physical base in Egypt – had for many years usurped the idea in name if not in actual purpose.[23]

Howard Carter was not a diplomat, and would not in normal circumstances have been used to negotiate in a matter of importance requiring tact and patience. In the summer of 1918, however, there was nobody else in Egypt who had the knowledge and experience to pursue an archaeological matter, or the opportunity to engage in discussions on a familiar level with the appropriate authorities. They were indeed strange times, and Carter shows signs in his few surviving letters of suffering from a wholly understandable weariness – not the weariness of the long-serving soldier, but that of one who had spent too long a time with not enough to do, yet constantly on the edge of being called to service. A long letter which he wrote to his mother from Luxor in October 1918 is remarkable for its almost total lack of news.[24] He starts by apologizing for not haven written for some time; his 'occasional silence' is 'no less than "the nature of the beast" ':

> And, here, too, perhaps not un-influenced by the ever rolling desert – silent as if prepared for eternal duration. With it, too, the ancient remains, wherein one dwells; they also may have tendency of dulling the present, obliterating future, and only enlighten the very far past.

He then invokes the antiquities of Western Thebes, and the natural gran-

22 Letter of 21 November in M.M.A., Department of Egyptian Art, Carter files.
23 See M. S. Drower, *Flinders Petrie* (London, 1985), p. 345.
24 Letter of 20 October, in the possession of John Carter.

deurs of hills and desert, contrasting with the 'verdant plains, palm-groves and cool Nile waters':

> Ones ideas wander beyond their usual sphere – everything around is calm and motionless – the sence [sic] of magnitude, time, both past and future, and everlasting space, creeps in through all this stationary, fixed, immutable illustration. And, the one thing of all, 'Beautiful tranquillity'. Such is the influence, and such is the waft from the desert, her [? here] Western Thebes, as far as I am able to convey.

There is something rather pathetic in this essay in fine writing. It seems as if Carter were unable to write familiarly and comfortably about the daily business of living in this most fascinating of lands. He surely did not have to impress his mother and those relations and family friends who might have read this letter in Swaffham. He continues then with a long account of a thunder-storm – 'for three consecutive Octobers we have had heavy downpours, and this time a peculiar phenomenon occurred. While we as dry as a bone, the larger valleys suddenly became seething rivers.' Here his attempts at painting a word picture of the storm are rather more successful. It was indeed difficult for him to find words adequate to describe the fury of the event:

> The Valley of the Tombs of the Kings, joined by the Great Western valley, in a few moments became little short of mountain rivers . . . the torrent cutting out wide furows [sic] in the valley bed and rolling before it stones some two feet in diametre – natives returning home with their animals were unable to ford it, and thus were cut off from their homes.

Further descriptions of the results of the desert storm and of the subsequent valley storm (of far less intensity), lead him to an awkward, uncomfortable, final passage:

> Well dear Mater enough of oneself, local colour and our troubles. How are you welfaring? – And the rest? I trust all well and flourishing as times allow. The telegrams are certainly good [about the progress of the war], things seem to be ripping along nicely – hurrah! Though the peace, what shall I say 'SCARE' one must for the moment take with a pinch of salt.

These words are so unlike anything in the easily written, chatty, letters he sent to those with whom he now felt himself to be in greater intimacy – Lord Carnarvon, the Newberrys, even Alan Gardiner. It is as if he had lost the ability to communicate easily with his mother, perhaps felt guilt of neglecting her, and found it difficult to express true affection. Because of the war he had not been home for over two years, had written rarely, and so, in a kind of embarrassment, substituted pretentiousness for intimate communication in his writing. He ends the letter with 'let me know all the news, and accept every kind thought and wish from your loving son Howard.'

Shortly after this letter was written the war came to an end – a momentous event that is not marked by any weighty comment in any of Carter's surviving correspondence. He was already well advanced with preparations to open work at Carnarvon's new concession at Meir. The decision to dig at this site was taken in the summer. By September Carter had asked Lord Carnarvon to send out to Egypt the three volumes of Blackman's *The Rock Tombs of Meir*, which had been published in the early years of the war. Carnarvon took the opportunity of writing to Blackman for advice:[25]

> What I am writing to you now is to ask you if you could let me have any notes on promising ground, ground that has been dug, best places to camp, in fact anything you think useful. It would be most kind of you if you could help me in this matter. I fancy the district is large naturally we shall not interfere with your work.

Blackman may well have felt that Carnarvon and Carter were trespassing on his own patch of ground, to which he certainly hoped to return when conditions were more normal. Carnarvon should have been well informed about the future intentions of the Egypt Exploration Society (as the Fund was shortly to be known), and his plans to work at Meir did not apparently raise any doubts or opposition in London. Blackman, however, was a sensitive, touchy person, not generally popular in Egyptological circles, although highly respected for his scholarship; he might easily have considered the new excavation an intrusion, repeating the disturbance caused by the Khashaba excavations pre-war. Carter was to express shortly some unspecific comments about Blackman's activities at Meir, which suggest that there may not have been much of an exchange of ideas about the site between the two sides. It may also be recorded that when Blackman published his fourth volume in his Meir series in 1924, he made no mention of the Carnarvon excavation.

Blackman may have had a better reason for not mentioning the work that Howard Carter had carried out in the winter of 1918–19, namely that the results were so disappointing that even to mention them might have seemed a tactless and even provocative act; especially as Carnarvon had only recently died when the volume was ready for printing.[26] Carter never intended, initially at least, to do more than test the site for possible future work. That this was his plan is inherent in the financial provisions he

25 Letter of 20 September in the School of Archaeology and Oriental Studies in the University of Liverpool; kindly brought to my attention by Professor A. F. Shore.
26 Blackman's Preface to his *Rock Tombs of Meir*, IV, is dated 4 December 1923.

made in advance. It was to be a modest, economical, operation. Writing to Carnarvon on 21 November, he provides estimates which form fascinating reading:[27] 12 men and boy (brought in, presumably from Thebes), 25 local boys and 2 men; costing £E3.150 for labour and £E.701 for camp expenses: total £E3.851 *per diem*, i.e. £E115.500 *per mensem*; plus £E86.000 for initial costs. At that moment he had in hand a balance of £E110.125, and he asks for an additional £250. With these funds he could dig for two months. He would revise this budget after work had started, as will be seen shortly.

The prospect of working in a new and rather remote place presented logistical and other problems; in the same letter, Carter told Carnarvon:

> Callender, in the Eg. State Rail., if he can get leave, will join me for a few weeks – he being an engineer with long experience in this country, especially in the provinces, will be of great help, besides companionship.

It is the first mention of Arthur J. Callender, who was to be Carter's right-hand man for technical purposes at the beginning of the Tutankhamun excavation. Little is known about his history and background, but by the time of the great discovery he had retired and was living in a house he had built for himself at Armant, a few miles to the south of Luxor.[28] The season at Meir opened on 1 December, and Carter did not find things at all easy at the outset. Describing the setting up of the camp[29] and the problems locally over supplies, he refers to the

> antagonistic temperament of the neighbouring population. Wages are high. The natives most grabbing. Former excavators have not improved these conditions, and I regret to say that I fear I must blame Blackman for the distinct familiar element noticeable particularly among the better local classes and antiquity gaffirs. They seem to think that we are here for their pleasure – to gallivant upon their firy [sic] steeds, and eat gorgeous but horrible repasts; while a favour such as selling a few eggs, or milk, or bread causes great demurrings – the local workmen to be pampered to the utmost degree. A dog's snarl is not without its uses!!!

What seemed high wages to Carter were by present-day standards extremely modest. They could only represent a reaction to the inflation that had overtaken Egypt towards the end of the war. Even with the revised budget that he submitted to Carnarvon in mid-December, the season's expenditure could not be described as excessive.[30] Now he reckoned on employing 15 men with *turias* (the common hoe/spade, a kind

27 M.M.A., Department of Egyptian Art, Carter files.
28 See W. R. Dawson and E. P. Uphill, *Who Was Who in Egyptology* (London, 1972), p. 50.
29 Letter of 3 December in M.M.A., Department of Egyptian Art, Carter files.
30 Letter of 16 December in M.M.A., Department of Egyptian Art, Carter files.

of mattock, used by Egyptian farmers, and the traditional excavation tool), 30 basket boys, 2 foreman, a scribe, a man and a boy. The daily bill would amount to almost £E5.000, made up of £E3.610 for wages, and £E1.343 for camp expenses; his initial expenses came to £E66.560, and a similar sum might be necessary for winding up. He had enough funds for one and a half months from 30 November. At Meir they lived in uninscribed tombs, as he had done in his first season at Beni Hasan in 1891.

At the end of December Carter could report only disappointing results.[31] Nothing of real interest had been found in the way of objects, and this was the pattern until he closed down the work on 15 January 1919. Carter's notes and a meticulous plan of the site, with the locations of all the rock tombs and indications of the areas excavated by him, are preserved in the Griffith Institute in Oxford. The Meir adventure had been even less successful than the Delta excavations at Sakha and Balamun before the war. It was as if the Fates were determined to thwart any expansion beyond the Theban field. Yet Thebes was not proving to be particularly fruitful. There was very little that Carter could tell Lord Carnarvon to encourage him. It says much for the latter's determination, and confidence in Carter, that he continued to finance the work in the Valley of the Kings. On the other hand, success or disappointment in his excavations made little difference to the interest and undoubted therapy he found in his visits to Egypt. He had been unable to leave England throughout the war years, and his health had in no way been improved by the denial of the months of winter warmth he had previously been able to enjoy regularly. So the prospect of a respectable activity to engage him mentally and, to a moderate extent, physically was much to be welcomed. Meir had in a sense been a long shot at something different, and possibly profitable in the way of finds. It was to be Carnarvon's last excursion elsewhere in the Nile Valley. The serious business of his main concession could now be undertaken. Apart from other considerations, the war had ended while the Meir expedition was in the planning, and a regular programme of work at Thebes could now surely be expected.

For the immediate future, after the unsatisfactory six weeks at Meir, there was no possibility of a full season's work in Thebes. But something needed to be done to mark the return to peace, and to signal Carnarvon's intention to take up his permit for the Valley of the Kings. A very short campaign was therefore carried out between 19 and 24 February, a bare week, clearing the area in front of the tomb of Tuthmosis I, deep in the main valley, and a considerable distance from the workings of the 1917–18

---

31 Letter of early January 1919, to Carnarvon in M.M.A., Department of Egyptian Art, Carter files. His work specifically involved the clearance of one tomb in Group B of Blackman's classification; and the documentation of eleven tomb chapels, i.e. seven undecorated examples to be added to Blackman's four decorated chapels.

season in the East Valley.[32] Very little was found apart from the remains of foundation deposits, probably uncovered and 'destroyed by periodical rains when quantities of water poured over the cliffs above the tomb'. It was not a serious campaign, but a tidying up of a part of the Valley floor, a small contribution towards the general clearance down to bed-rock.

The shortness of the season may, however, have been determined by political reasons. There was considerable civil unrest in Egypt during the winter of 1918–19 and the subsequent spring. Soon after the Armistice in November 1918 a delegation of nationalist politicians, led by Saad Zaghlul to the High Commissioner, Sir Reginald Wingate, demanded autonomy for Egypt and declared an intention to send representatives to London to petition the British government. Refusal and the arrest of Zaghlul led to rioting throughout the country, and under the circumstances Carter may have thought it prudent to close down his dig. His records do not suggest that this was in fact the case, but from a letter to Frederic Whiting in Cleveland it emerges that he was from 22 April, to use his own words, 'commandeered by the Military authorities as political officer for Nag Hamadi district, and was thus unable to continue further research before taking any leave for home.'[33] A strange survival from this time shows that Carter was still in the Nag Hamadi district on 29 May 1919. It is an entry in the autograph album of Anne-Marie-Paule Lucovich, daughter of Gino Antonio Lucovich, a director of the Egyptian Irrigation Company, and manager of the sugar factory at Nag Hamadi.[34] The entry, signed by Howard Carter and dated 29 May, includes a line of hieroglyphs incorporating a standard offering formula from Egyptian funerary inscriptions, and reading 'A boon which the King gives that funerary offerings be granted to the souls of the house of Lucovitch. Done by Carter.'

32 Notes in G.I. Carter Papers I A, 233–4; I. J, 366–7.
33 Letter written from Swaffham on 17 August 1918, in the archives of the Cleveland Museum of Art.
34 I am grateful to Miss Deirdre Le Faye, a former colleague in the British Museum, daughter of Anne-Marie-Paule Lucovich, for permission to reproduce the autograph, and for information on the Lucovich family. Her mother would have been 16 years old in 1919.

It is a rare example of Carter in relaxed mood and demonstrating an unexpected knowledge of hieroglyphs, he even spells Lucovich with an intrusive, but possibly pronounced (or heard), t (the sign ◠, 3rd from right end in the main line). The sugar factory at Nag Hamadi has always been a centre of social life in the part of Egypt between Abydos and Dendera, and would naturally have attracted Carter during his period of enforced duty in the neighbourhood.

He at last managed to get away from Egypt on 25 June. It was his first home leave in three years, and he surely had many calls to make, many relations, old colleagues and friends to see. Details of his movements are almost wholly lacking, and this absence of information is much the same for subsequent annual home leaves up to 1922. He was not entirely idle from the Egyptological point of view. There are in the Griffith Institute, and also in the Egyptian Department of the Metropolitan Museum, substantial notes on the history of Egyptian glass – a general account based on the many pieces in the Carnarvon collection. From internal evidence in these papers it is clear that he spent considerable periods of time during his leaves at Highclere Castle, working closely with Lord Carnarvon on the collection in general and on the preparation of a detailed catalogue. The section on glass seems to have been the most advanced part. There were also plans to transfer at least part of the collection to Carnarvon's Town house at 1 Seamore Place, W.1. Again Carter was involved in making the necessary preparations for new vitrines to accommodate the selected pieces. Life at Highclere during these stays was certainly not without diversions of a more conventional country-house kind. The incidental entertainments are neatly encapsulated in a few remarks to Percy Newberry, written from Highclere in September 1921:[35] 'Have been here practically the whole time – shooting and arranging antiqs. Today we shot again and Friday and Saturday racing at Newbury.' This way of life suited Carter perfectly. He was now very much at ease in these rather grand surroundings; more so than he would have been in the simpler circumstances of the Sporle Road cottage in Swaffham. His visits to Norfolk were brief, especially as his mother died in December 1920; but he did spend longer periods with his brother Samuel, who lived at 10B Collingham Gardens (and later at no. 19), just north of the Brompton Road and within a few hundred yards of Rich Terrace, the Carter London home until the mid-1890s. He used Samuel's address for many years as one of convenience in London, although he also made use of the Constitutional Club in Northumberland Avenue, close to Trafalgar Square. Later in the 1920s he changed from the Constitutional Club to the Savile, then in Piccadilly, but now at 69 Brook Street, near Grosvenor Square. It was a kind of superior gipsy existence that he lived when he was on leave. His true home had

35 G.I. Newberry Corr. 8/63.

now become the house at Elwat el-Diban in western Thebes, and so it remained until the end of his life. In due time, however, he found it necessary to have something more permanent for himself in London, a need that was intensified after Carnarvon's death, which effectively closed Highclere Castle to him. Also after his mother's death Swaffham was not so compelling a place to visit. A note in his diary for 25 April 1922 states that he took possession of the flat no.12 at 11 King Street, St James's, but this was probably only a short-term occupation of a furnished flat for the summer leave of that year for in the immediate subsequent summers he used the Collingham Gardens address.

A new activity took up some of his time in London during the summers following the war. This was acting as the occasional adviser in Egyptian antiquities to Sotheby's, the Bond Street auctioneers. It may have arisen out of the assistance he had given to the Amhersts in the disposal of parts of the Didlington collection. Mention has already been made of the help he gave in 1915 to Lady Amherst (Lady William Cecil) to sell the seven great Sakhmet statues to the Metropolitan Museum. In 1919 his services were again used by the Metropolitan for the negotiation of the purchase from the Cecils of a seated pair-statue of the scribe Nebwau and his wife Tenethat. This piece had been noted by Lythgoe even before the war, and Carter, writing to him in June 1915 said:[36] 'In regard to the statue at Norwich it is best left until, as you suggest, later, the more so as there are lots of other things I think you ought to see.' The acquisition was finally clinched in 1919, and it was followed shortly after by the decision to sell the remaining objects from the Amherst collection at Sotheby's. It was very sensible to commission Carter to make the sale catalogue. He had known the Amherst collection since the 1880s, and had in his early years spent much time working on it for Lord Amherst. Already in February 1920 Carter had written to Frederic Whiting in Cleveland warning him of the forthcoming sale, and suggesting that he might be able to help Cleveland to acquire good pieces.[37] He was in a position to let Cleveland see proofs of the catalogue in the winter of 1920–1, some months in advance of the sale.[38] Unfortunately Cleveland had relatively small funds for purchase at this time, although a great effort was made to raise a sum sufficient to meet the expected costs of the Carter proposals. At the sale, which lasted at Sotheby's from 13 to 17 June 1921, rather higher prices than Carter had expected prevailed, and only a few of his selected pieces fell

36 The relevant letters are in M.M.A., Department of Egyptian Art, Carter files; Lythgoe to Carter of 4 May 1915; Carter to Lythgoe of 4 June 1915; Lythgoe to Carter of 26 February 1919. For the pair statue see W. C. Hayes *The Scepter of Egypt* (New York, 1953, 1959), II, pp. 158f.; now numbered 19.2.3.
37 Letter of 18 February 1920 in the archives of the Cleveland Museum of Art.
38 See T. G. H. James in E. H. Turner, *Object Lessons*, p. 74. Carter also offered to act for Chicago, but funds were not readily available; see letters of Carter to Breasted (12 March 1921) and Breasted to Carter (14 June 1921) in O.I. Director's Office Corr. 1921.

1 Samuel John Carter

2 Martha Joyce Carter, drawn by
William Carter, 1884

3 William Carter, a self-portrait when
young

4 Howard Carter, drawn by William
Carter, c. 1884

5   The Sporle Road cottage, Swaffham

6   Howard Carter as a young man

7   Howard Carter supervises work at Deir el-Bahri, *c.* 1893-4

8 Howard Carter, Percy Newberry, Édouard Naville and servants in
front of the expedition house, Deir el-Bahri, *c.* 1896

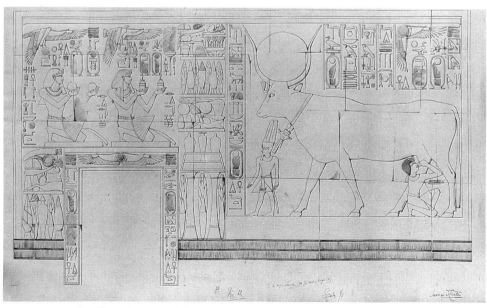

9 Carter's original drawing of a scene in the Deir el-Bahri temple
showing the cow of Hathor suckling Hatshepsut

10 Tea on the terrace of the Luxor Hotel, 1903-4

11 Studio portrait of Howard Carter, 1902-4

12 Castle Carter at Medinet Habu, Western Thebes. Carter relaxes
with a friend, his horse Sultan and one of his pet gazelles

Lofor. 12·9·900.

My Dear Mater

    Yesterday I returned from an inspection up country. At a place
Called Edfou   with the great pleasure of finding
a letter from   mater dated Sept 2nd & also
a much needed   ½ doz. prs of socks That
Caused great   joy — to show my pleasure
I work hard   I developed photos in the evening
& hence the prints.   To morrow I am off again
both, to Lynch   & Baliana on inspection

(Entrance to Sanctuary Edfou) case between Sub-inspector
Guards, either of which having taken palm-oil for settlement of some
antiquity land.

    Leaving other negatives I printed these others both carry
on the 2nd Chapter of "Castle Carter"
Now that the inundation comes up to the
desert, beside the garden, the water
is carried to it by "Shadoof" &
channels that run to each separate
basin, the ground being divided into basins
to receive the water. But to the kitchen
it goes in pails, as here below photo.   (method of watering the garden.)
                                   Called "Shadoof".

The Sheikh & Sultan here below
send you "neighs" & salaams & prosperous
life, with   whinnies
& licks to   the aunts
& all —   The Stones
behind are   parts. of
a large   Colossal
Statue at a Temple called   The Ramesseum
built by Rameses II in Thebes   to appear
the Gods & give life to his soul,

                & may it be so   P.T.o.

13   A letter to Carter's mother. The inserted photographs show the
Edfu Temple and scenes in and around Castle Carter

14, 15 On holiday in 1902: *left:* with his sister Amy Walker and family members on a picnic; *right:* in braces on a bicycle

16 Howard Carter, Chief Inspector of Upper Egypt, with Percy Newberry and Robb de Peyster Tytus at the Palace of Amenophis III, 1902

17 Howard Carter, Chief Inspector of Lower Egypt, in the
stable-yard of the Mena House Hotel, Giza, with the Great
Pyramid in the background, 1905

18 Castle Carter at Elwat el-Diban, built 1911. Phyllis Walker
notes (1930): 'left window, dining room - right, UH's [Uncle
Howard's] room, middle window, spare room, extreme left kitchen
and servant quarters. The rest is desert!'

19   Carter with an unidentified visitor inspects a find at Balamun,
1913

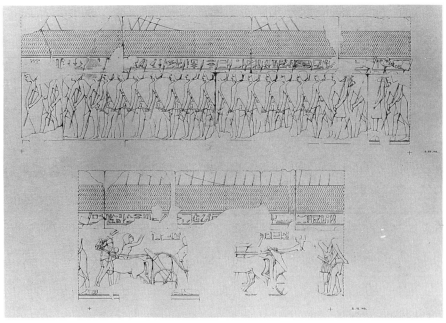

20   One of Carter's drawings of the Opet Festival reliefs in the
Luxor Temple

to Cleveland. The Metropolitan Museum, with greater resources, was more successful; advised by Mace, who bid on the Museum's behalf in London, it acquired, among other things, many of the objects from El-Amarna which Carter himself had excavated under Petrie's guidance in 1892.

In the following year, 1922, he was again engaged by Sotheby's to catalogue antiquities which he described in his diary entry for 8 May as 'Sir Frederick Frankland's papyri'. Frankland, a baronet in his own right, had married into the Curzon family, his wife being the seventeenth Baroness Zouche. The antiquities were remnants of the collection formed by Robert Curzon, fourteenth Baron Zouche, whose travels in Egypt and the Near East are memorably recorded in his *Visits to the Monasteries in the Levant*, first published in 1849. This small collection of about 30 lots was sold in Bond Street on 2 November 1922. A much more important sale of Egyptian antiquities had taken place, again at Sotheby's, over nine days in June of the same year. It involved the remarkable collection of the Revd William MacGregor of Tamworth, at the time far larger in number, and more important, than the much reduced Amherst collection. The MacGregor sale yielded a total of £34,000 compared with the 1921 sum of £14,533 for the Amherst, by no means negligible, residue.[39] Howard Carter was not involved in the cataloguing of the MacGregor objects for Sotheby's, although he may well have been engaged in some of the negotiations which led to MacGregor's decision to place his collection in the hands of the auctioneers. From a few surviving letters it emerges that Carter and Newberry suffered a severe rupture in their friendship over the sale, a disagreement that also involved the Hon. Richard Bethell, a collector of Egyptian antiquities and a mutual friend of the others. Retrospectively the row can be seen as both a cautionary event and as a fiasco. It offers an object lesson in how the secretive negotiations which seem inevitably to attend transactions in the world of fine art and antiquities sales can lead to complications and misunderstandings. It seems that MacGregor, deciding to sell his collection – in 1921 he was 73 years old – placed the matter at first in the hands of Messrs Spink and Son, the reputable dealers of King Street, St James's. Percy Newberry, on the one hand, was consulted and undertook negotiations with possible purchasers. Howard Carter and Richard Bethell, on the other hand, and separately, were interested, and perhaps actively involved, in securing the sale of the whole collection to a single unspecified client. Neither side apparently knew precisely what was happening, but by September 1921 Newberry and Carter had exchanged petulant letters, and were distinctly out of sympathy with each other.[40] The problem between them is made generally, but not precisely, clear, in a letter of mollification written by Bethell to Newberry on 30 September.

39 The total sums are recorded in Dawson and Uphill, *Who Was Who in Egyptology*, p. 190. (MacGregor), and 8 (Amherst).
40 G.I. Newberry Corr. 4/98–100.

It followed up another of a few days (unspecified) earlier in which Bethell had said: 'It seems a great pity that we didn't all work together from the beginning. I should hate you and Carter to really seriously quarrel.' The following letter is more informative:

Now let me explain things as I see them.

Carter and I quite understood that McG [MacGregor] had approached Spink (like a fool) in the first place and that Spink had called you in and that therefore you were unable to tell us the amount of Spink's option etc, but we were under the impression that you stood in with Spink anyhow, whether our buyer *or anyone else* bought the collection.

Therefore, hoping as he did up to the last moment that he would pull it off, Carter did not think it necessary to tell either you or Spink that he had failed, as the option definitely ceased on the 3rd Sept.

That is to say we thought that if we pulled off the deal, we should make a bit for ourselves and also for you, and that if we did not, you still stood a chance if another buyer came along. I am sure that nothing was farther from our thoughts than any idea of doing you out of your chance, and I am dreadfully sorry to hear that we have unwittingly done so, at any rate temporarily. I am sure you will see that this puts a different complexion on our actions . . .

Please have a quiet talk with him over things, and I am sure everything can be explained.

Bethell's intervention appears to have worked, for friendly letters were passing between Carter and Newberry before the end of the year. But the expectations of all parties to make something out of the private sale of the MacGregor collection were frustrated. On 24 October 1921 Newberry cabled to Breasted in Chicago: 'MacGregor's entire Egyptian collection in market; price thirty-five thousand pounds. Could Chicago buy. Would come over about it if you think advisable.' Breasted asked for more information, but was not hopeful, and tried to prevent Newberry's making a futile visit.[41] At the end of November Newberry travelled to Chicago, but was unsuccessful. Subsequently the collection was placed with Sotheby's; Newberry compiled the catalogue and wrote an introduction; and the result of the sale, as noted earlier, was within one thousand pounds of the sum suggested by Newberry to Breasted.

Howard Carter had more to worry him in the autumn of 1921 than the future of the MacGregor collection. The first surviving hint of his trouble comes in a letter to Whiting in Cleveland on 12 October:[42]

41 Letters of J. H. Breasted to Newberry in G.I. Newberry Corr. 5/105–8.
42 The two letters to Whiting are in the archives of the Cleveland Museum of Art.

It was my intention, and I had made all arrangements to leave for Egypt on the 20th of this month, but unfortunately I have been indisposed this last few weeks and I am now obliged to undergo a serious abdominal operation. Thus under the most favourable conditions I cannot expect to be able to return until well into December next.

It was, it seems, an operation for the removal of his gall bladder and it was carried out in Leeds, apparently by the famous abdominal surgeon Sir Berkeley Moynihan, who had operated on Lord Carnarvon for the removal of his appendix in 1918.[43] Carter could not have been in better hands, and he was able to write to Whiting again on 2 December:

I returned this week after 6 weeks in hospital in Leeds and am at last able to attend business matters ... As I shall have to remain convalescent in England for another 6 weeks I shall not be able to return to Egypt until well into January next – in fact, I have booked my passage for 19 Jan. 1922.

His recuperation took place in Carnarvon's house in Seamore Place, and it was from there that he wrote to Mrs Newberry on 22 December:[44] 'My wound healed last week, am now free of nurses and look forward to returning to Egypt in January.' From the same address he wrote to Newberry himself on 17 January, chiefly about proofs of the catalogue of an exhibition organized by the Burlington Fine Arts Club (of which he was a member for most of his life).[45] but adding, 'I'm off on Thursday for Egypt'. That was 19 January, the very day he had mentioned to Whiting in early December.

Carter's diary entries for 1922 show that as soon as he arrived in Egypt on 25 January he launched himself into an active programme of visits to the antiquities dealers of Cairo and (after 2 February) Luxor. He records many purchases for Lord Carnarvon, for himself, and for Joseph J. Acworth, a British collector of choice small antiquities who intensified his collecting after his retirement in 1919. On 7 February Lord Carnarvon arrived, and the following day the excavations were resumed in the Valley of the Kings. Work for the season was concentrated in the upper part of

43 Sir Berkeley Moynihan (later Baron Moynihan) was on close terms with the Carnarvons, and in the 1920s, when he first began operating regularly in London, he made use of a nursing home run by Lady Carnarvon; see Geoffrey Keynes, *The Gates of Memory* (Oxford, 1981), p. 362, and Donald Bateman, *Berkeley Moynihan. Surgeon* (London, 1940), p. 286. Bateman also mentions Moynihan's deep interest in ancient Egypt, and meetings with Carter, pp. 245, 325. I am grateful to Dr Anne Savage for bringing these volumes to my attention.

44 G.I. Newberry Corr. 8/64 and 65.

45 The exhibition was held in 1921, but the catalogue, edited (anonymously) by P. E. Newberry and H. R. H. Hall, did not appear until 1922: *Burlington Fine Arts Club. Catalogue of an Exhibition of Ancient Egyptian Art.*

the main valley leading to the tomb of Tuthmosis III, and more specifically in the region of the tomb of Siptah, a king of the Nineteenth Dynasty (*c.* 1204–1198 B.C.). This last tomb had been first excavated by Ayrton for Theodore Davis in 1905, and its environs were cluttered with 'large mounds of rubbish thrown out during the excavation . . . Its removal took 10 days with 40 men and 120 boys.' It was a short and unproductive season, ending early in March. Carter, who was still recovering from his surgery, left Thebes for Cairo on 13 March, Carnarvon staying on in Luxor. On 28 March Carter returned south and on the following day Carnarvon left for Europe. Carter followed from Luxor on 5 April, and from Cairo on 10 April. Busy buying had gone on at the end of the digging season in Cairo and Luxor, and it may be thought that much consideration was given to the future of the Theban operations.

The unsatisfactory results of the 1922 season largely repeated the outcome of the two preceding seasons.[46] In 1920 Carter had worked from 5 January to 16 March clearing areas near the entrance to the main valley, from the tomb of Ramesses IV to that of Ramesses II. In mid-February Carter was joined by Lord Carnarvon and his small party. Carnarvon himself stayed with Carter on the hill at Elwat el-Diban, an arrangement which made his daily journeys to the site much less laborious than if he had lived across the river, as had been his custom. The rest of his party stayed in the Winter Palace. Commenting on the presence of Lady Carnarvon and their daughter Evelyn Herbert, and on Carnarvon's ever-presence, Carter told Newberry, 'What with the men in the Valley my hands are well full'.[47] For once, a small success attended their work. On 26 February a cache of thirteen fine alabaster vessels was found in a deposit in the debris at the entrance to the tomb of King Merenptah. It was a modest discovery, but in the context of discoveries during the seasons of the Carnarvon campaign, it was, as Carter later said,[48] 'the nearest approach to a real find that we had yet made in The Valley . . . Lady Carnarvon, I remember, insisted on digging out these jars – beautiful specimens they were – with her own hands.' The jars, clearly connected with the burial of Merenptah, and inscribed with his names and with those of his father Ramesses II, were reused to contain oils and other materials for the embalming and burial of Merenptah.

In the following winter an early start was made. On 1 December 1920 Carter continued clearing the small lateral valley leading from the main valley at a point a little to the north-east of the tomb of Ramesses VI to that of Merenptah. His next intention was to clear the area near the entrance to the tomb of Ramesses VI where workmen's huts had been

---

46 The details of the sites dug and objects found in the seasons 1920–2 are given in C. N. Reeves, *Valley of the Kings*, pp. 326ff.
47 G.I. Newberry Corr. 8/61.
48 Carter and Mace, *The Tomb of Tut.ankh.Amen*, I, p. 83.

found in earlier work. Here, however, his progress was limited, as he explained in his entry for 2 January 1921: 'As one is unable to cut away the path in front of T9 (R VI) [i.e. tomb no.9 of Ramesses VI] during the tourist season and the coming visit of the Sultan, have removed men for the time being to another portion of the valley.' Most of the remainder of the season was spent in the end of the Valley towards the tomb of Tuthmosis III. Work came to an end on 3 March. It was in the same area that he worked in the short season of early 1922.

Apart from the disheartening results of their excavations in the Valley of the Kings, Carnarvon and Carter were also anxious about the changed policy with regard to excavations and divisions pursued by Pierre Lacau since the war. The dispute over the granting of a permit to dig at El-Amarna was engaged and lost in 1918; the problem of *partage* had not seriously affected them in the intervening years. In the case of the cache of alabaster vessels found in 1920, a very equitable division had been made: of the thirteen jars, six were allotted to the excavators.[49] It was, perhaps, not a great act of generosity on the part of the Antiquities Service, and it could not have been seen as a measure of what might be expected if finds of greater diversity and value were to be made in the future. As far as the Carnarvon work was concerned, it was still controlled by the licence first issued and signed by Daressy on 18 April 1915, and most recently renewed on 26 January 1921. The significant Articles of the permit were 8,9 and 10 (see p. 414), by which the Antiquities Service undertook, after reserving royal mummies and coffins, and other objects of capital importance, to 'share the remainder with the Permittee', and agreeing 'that the Permittee's share will sufficiently recompense him for the pains and labour of the undertaking'. So much depended on the interpretation of these statements. There was little, from the experience of others, to inspire confidence in what would happen if there were good finds to be divided.

The possible results of Lacau's new policy were bitterly resented by foreign archaeologists, especially those from Britain and the USA, most of whom represented institutions which were only prepared to finance expensive excavations if there was an expectation of good returns of objects. Alan Gardiner, both as a representative of the Egypt Exploration Society, and as a friend of Carnarvon, felt it his duty to pursue the argument directly with Lacau on a personal level. From 1920 onwards he wrote numerous letters and put together with others a series of memoranda on the subject.[50] His own concern lay more with the outcome of excavations and the need to publish results; but he appreciated the special interest in *partage* which was the particular stumbling block for excavators. A little

49 The division certificate is preserved in G.I. Carter Papers I C, 213.
50 Documents on the subject are to be found in G.I. Gardiner Papers; his letter to Lacau, AHG/42, 176. 16; also AHG/39. 37–49.

leniency in the last matter might persuade the excavators to accept more easily the other conditions proposed by Lacau.

Among foreign missions, the one most likely to suffer seriously was the Egyptian Expedition of the Metropolitan Museum of Art. Concern permeated all levels of the staff of their expedition. Lindsley Hall, an artist-draughtsman, who worked principally at Lisht, but also in Luxor, noted in his diary for 8 April 1920:[51]

> M. Lacau and Mr. Engelbach teaed with us this P.M. E. is new antiquities inspector in this district. Mons. L. came to see about the 'division' of our finds. He is inclined to want all the 'pièces capitales' for the Cairo Museum.

Next year, on 4 April at Lisht, he comments:

> Mace had a wire 'No division' from Winlock today, whereby we knew that Lacau has seen the sarcophagus and wants it for Cairo. As he wants a great deal of our other material, too, it has been decided to wait till next year for the division, as we should come out so badly this year if we accepted Lacau's division.

Albert Lythgoe, the head of the Egyptian Expedition, prepared in early 1922 a general briefing statement for the benefit of the American diplomatic representative in Egypt, Dr J. Morton Howell, and for the Director of the Museum, setting out the stark possibilities of the situation as he saw it.[52] In a concluding paragraph he drew attention to the universal opposition of all British and American Egyptologists, who feared that the changes would mean 'the ruination of what we have all been endeavouring to accomplish in scientific results during the past twenty-five years.' But, as with Carter over El-Amarna in 1918, the argument was one which the foreign excavators could scarcely win. The archaeologists of other countries – for the most part not having the same pressures to satisfy museum trustees and other expectant individuals and institutions – were prepared to go on working under the modified conditions. The new political climate in Egypt was not favourable to the privileged requirements of foreigners; and the administrative authorities were not inclined to interfere with the detailed running of the Antiquities Service. The problem, however, was one of real concern to the British and American excavators, and it would very shortly result in a crisis of major severity after the discovery of the tomb of Tutankhamun. Here it may be added that the expectations of excavators in the matter of divisions have continued to cause difficulties

51 Lindsley Hall, a native of Portland Oregon, spent his career with the Metropolitan Museum, returning to Portland after retirement. His diaries and other papers are in the archives of the Oregon Historical Society, Portland. I am indebted to Thomas Vaughan, formerly Director of the Society, and his staff for making my visit to Portland so profitable.

52 M.M.A., Department of Egyptian Art, file on Antiquities Law 1922–3; the full text in Hoving, *Tutankhamun. The Untold Stody*, pp. 68f.

in Egypt. Yet the reduction in the percentage of objects allotted to foreign missions, although continuous and always regretted, has rarely halted the increase in the number of institutions wishing to excavate in the country.

At this point it would be opportune to consider what precisely Howard Carter was hoping to find in the Valley of the Kings during the years of generally fruitless activity since 1917. A chapter, 'Our prefatory work at Thebes' in the first volume of *The Tomb of Tut.ankh.Amen*, written by Carter and Arthur Mace and published within a year of the tomb's discovery, sets out Carter's own interest in Valley excavation, and also charts the course of the work conducted for Lord Carnarvon from 1914 onwards. At the outset, in spite of Theodore Davis's stated belief that the site was exhausted, a view supported by Maspero, 'We [Carnarvon and Carter] . . . were quite sure that there were areas, covered by dumps of previous excavators, which had not properly been examined.' Carter further declared, '. . . at the risk of being accused of *post actum* prescience, I will state that we had definite hopes of finding the tomb of one particular king, and that king Tut.ankh.Amen.' (page 76). He then reviews the reasons for this expectation. First, there had been the discovery by Theodore Davis in 1909 of a few objects bearing that king's name. Davis was convinced that he had found his tomb, badly plundered, and he published it as such in his last volume, *The Tombs of Harmhabi and Touatânkhamanou* in 1912. Carter rightly dismissed the identification, noting that the tomb in which fragments of gold foil and an uninscribed alabaster statuette had been found was too insignificant to have been royal; the objects had clearly been placed there at a later date, but had in all probability come from the proper tomb of Tutankhamun.[53] This deposit was close to the tomb of Horemheb, and the indications were that any tomb of Tutankhamun should be not very far away. A small faience pot, bearing the king's name, was also found not very far away. Additionally Davis had found, in 1907, an extraordinary deposit of vessels which was of so little interest to him that it was passed unstudied to the Metropolitan Museum in 1909, at the request of Herbert Winlock. In a fascinating essay of 1941, Winlock identified the contents of the vessels as some of the embalming materials, and part of the funerary feast, of Tutankhamun.[54] Although he did not publish his findings until after Carter's death, he makes it clear in his description that his conclusions were of some years' standing.[55] 'In the early 1920's . . . I began to realize what Theodore Davis had discovered – obviously fragments of embalming materials and scraps from the funeral meal of King Tūt-'ankh-Amūn.' (Page 7 and note 6). He also notes, 'Eventually I gave Howard Carter further information about the find and he used it in *The*

53 See also, C. N. Reeves, *Valley of the Kings*, pp. 72f.
54 H. E. Winlock, *Materials used at the Embalming of King Tūt-'ankh-Amūn* (New York, 1941).
55 Doubts about the history of the objects before they were deposited in the cache are voiced in C. N. Reeves, *Valley of the Kings*, p. 69.

Tomb of Tut.ankh.Amen (London 1923–33), I, p. 77 and II, p. 97.' Finally, Carter drew attention to the presence of mud-sealings bearing the name of Tutankhamun in the remarkable collection of funerary material published by Davis as the tomb of Queen Tiye, wife of Amenophis III. Carter, probably rightly, considered much of the contents of this cache to have been brought from El-Amarna for reburial at Thebes, in the reign of Tutankhamun (page 78). He claimed:

> With all this evidence before us we were thoroughly convinced in our own minds that the Tomb of Tut.ankh.Amen was still to find, and that it ought to be situated not far from the centre of The Valley.

It may be questioned whether Carter's thinking about what might be found followed precisely the line of clues set out in *The Tomb of Tut.ankh. Amen*, vol. I. When Winlock wrote to him in 1915[56] with a list of the Metropolitan Museum holdings of objects from the Valley of the Kings, he drew special attention to the cache materials found by Davis, but he did not then present his idea about the embalming nature of these materials. Indeed it is not clear when Winlock's interpretation was propounded, but probably not until a late stage in Carter's campaign. There is no mention of Tutankhamun in any of his excavation documentation right up to 1922. Nevertheless, it should be remembered that he had undertaken a study of the history of the Valley of the Kings during the war, and that from the records of ancient robberies and of modern discoveries there was no indication that Tutankhamun's tomb had ever been found or robbed. It is hard to believe that Carter had not placed the name of that seemingly unimportant, late Eighteenth-dynasty king high on his list of possibilities. Furthermore, Alan Gardiner records:[57]

> On November 6th 1922 Carnarvon telephoned me at Lansdowne Road saying that he had just received a cable from Carter, in Luxor, saying that he had made a wonderful discovery . . . and Carnarvon asked me whether it could possibly be the tomb of Tut'ankhamun. I replied that I was not well up in the history of the Valley and that we should have to wait and see.

At that moment Carter had still not found the impressions of the tell-tale seals with Tutankhamun's names on the plastered blocking of the tomb entrance. Yet Carnarvon had the king's name in mind – a sure indication that his tomb was a prime candidate for discovery. It must be concluded that towards the end of his Valley campaign, Carter's own belief was that if he found a royal tomb in the area where he was working, it would most probably be that of Tutankhamun. Carnarvon would have known this, but

56 I am grateful to Marsha Hill for drawing my attention to Winlock's letter of 15 June 1915, to Carter, in M.M.A., Department of Egyptian Art, Carter files.
57 Gardiner, *My Working Years*, p. 37.

possibly few others. Carter was ever one to play his cards close to his chest; early misjudgements over discoveries had undoubtedly made him cautious. That he could subsequently bring together the various clues pointing to the likelihood of the existence of a tomb – possibly intact – of Tutankhamun, and claim that it had been the subject of his search from the beginning, was only moderately disingenuous. Under the circumstances he could well be excused for what he wrote about '*post actum* prescience.'

In the end it was the tomb's discovery that mattered, and it remains the stuff of high drama, even romance, that the discovery was ever made under Carter's direction. The story goes that Carnarvon had come to the sad conclusion that no further work should be done in the Valley. Carter himself records[58] that 'it became a much debated question whether we should continue to work or try for a more profitable site elsewhere. After these barren years were we justified in going on with it? My own feeling was that so long as a single area of untouched ground remained the risk was worth taking.' During the summer of 1922 – the precise date appears to be unrecorded in the parts of Carter's diary for the year which have survived – Carnarvon invited Carter down to Highclere to discuss the future.[59] He was for giving up the Valley, and he put the matter starkly to Carter. The latter had come prepared with arguments in support of at least one more season. He could point on the map to that small area still uncleared to bed-rock, and encumbered with the remains of ancient huts, just below the entrance to the tomb of Ramesses VI. It had been left undisturbed because work in the neighbourhood of that much-visited tomb would have been singularly unpopular during the tourist season. Carter's proposal was that a last season, starting earlier than usual, should be devoted to this area, and he offered to meet the costs himself if Carnarvon felt unable to continue. Inevitably, Carnarvon was persuaded by Carter's devotion and generosity, and agreed. In the course of this crucial meeting, it is said, Tutankhamun's name was specifically mentioned.

It has been suggested that what Carter had offered to do in guaranteeing the expenses of the last season was exceptionally generous. 'A prodigious sum' has been mentioned.[60] It is unlikely, however, that the kind of season Carter had in mind would have cost much more than a few hundred pounds. To remove the stone huts and to clear a relatively small area down to bed-rock would need a small staff of skilled workmen and basket boys – scarcely as many as he had used at Meir, at a total cost of about £E5.000 per day. The overhead expenses of a dig away from Luxor would be avoided; he could live at home; so too most of his workmen. There is

---

58 Carter and Mace, *The Tomb of Tut.ankh.Amen*, I, p. 85.
59 An account of what happened at Highclere is given by Charles Breasted in his biography of his father James Henry Breasted, *Pioneer of the Past* (New York, 1943), pp. 327ff., on the basis of what Carter himself told him.
60 So Hoving, in *Tutankhamun. The Untold Story*, p. 73.

no doubt, therefore, that a limited season could be conducted economically, and that he would be able to fund it himself, probably from his profits from lucrative antiquities dealing. It would be a mistake to think that if he had paid the bills he would have been seriously damaged financially.

So, with a season's work guaranteed, Howard Carter left England to take a boat from Marseilles on 5 October. On 11 October he arrived in Cairo and spent the next two weeks visiting the antiquities dealers, Nahman, Tano, Abemayor, Mansur, and possibly others, purchasing on behalf of Lord Carnarvon and himself. When he arrived in Luxor on 27 October he brought with him a new and, for him, original pet, but very appropriate in view of his great love for birds. Winlock later wrote to Edward Robinson, his Director:[61]

> When Carter came out last November [sic], alone, he got a canary bird, in Cairo, in a gilded cage to cheer up what he figured was going to be a lonely and deserted house. Carter comes over to his house with his servant Abdel Al carrying the canary behind him and the guards and the reises greet him and right off, when they see a golden bird they say, 'Mabrook – it's a bird of gold that will bring luck. This year we will find, inshallah, a tomb full of gold.' Within a week they had made the most fabulous find of all time and at first the tomb was called 'The tomb of the Golden Bird' by the natives. That canary almost had a halo around its cage.[62]

On 28 October Carter went to Armant to visit his friend Arthur Callender, presumably a social visit only, for the events that would cause Carter to summon Callender to Luxor still lay, unsuspected, a few days ahead.

Work began on 1 November in front of the tomb of Ramesses VI. In his work diary, his first entry, after noting the start of excavations, is listed 'item 433'; the numbering resumes his series of excavated finds in the Valley,[63] which had begun in February 1915 with the fragment of an alabaster *shabti* figure of Queen Tiye, found near the entrance to the tomb of King Amenophis III. Item 433 is given as 'Entrance of tomb of '; on the opposite page he adds, 'in bed rock floor of water course (below entrance of R VI). Discovered 4th Nov. 1922'. On 6 November Carnarvon received the cable about which he telephoned Alan Gardiner:

AT LAST HAVE MADE WONDERFUL DISCOVERY IN THE VALLEY. A MAGNIFICENT TOMB WITH SEALS INTACT. RE-COVERED SAME FOR YOUR ARRIVAL. CONGRATU-LATIONS. CARTER

---

61 Letter of 28 March 1923 in M.M.A., Department of Egyptian Art, Carter Files.
62 On the sad fate of this bird, and on its apparent replacement, see p. 305 below.
63 G.I. Carter Papers I J, 387; for the first find, see I. A, 123 and I J, 386.

10

THE ANTECHAMBER

One of the most thrilling and moving comments in the history of archaeological discovery is that which Howard Carter made to Lord Carnarvon when the latter enquired about what could be seen through the small hole cut into the newly discovered tomb on the afternoon of 26 November 1922. 'Can you see anything?'[1] asked Carnarvon. 'Yes, wonderful things,' answered Carter. These three words are enough to conjure up for many the image of the gorgeous, but tumbled, treasures that made the first chamber of the tomb, to be called the Antechamber, look rather like a superior box-room. 'Yes, wonderful things' is now firmly part of the story of the discovery, part, it may rightly be said, of the mythology of the discovery. Carter's more immediate journal account, on which the later, published, narrative (prepared by Arthur Mace) was based, gives his reply as 'Yes, it is wonderful.'[2] Carnarvon himself, in a short, unpublished report on the discovery, has Carter saying, 'There are some marvellous objects here.'[3] It may be supposed that none of the accounts is precise in this one small matter. 'So much', it may be said, 'for verbatim reporting.' It does not much matter, for now the evocative 'Yes, wonderful things' is so clearly the best expression of what was felt by Carter on that momentous occasion, that any attempt to put the record straight would seem to be mean-minded and pointless, and would probably be by no means invested with certainty.

From time to time in this account of Carter's life, it has been pointed out that he was often guilty of apparent untruthfulness whenever he wrote about his past, whether it was distant or recent. When variant accounts of an event exist, judgement supported by independent evidence needs to be exercised. In most cases where error can be detected the faults are of little concern; Carter had what may be termed a careless memory, and lacked the true scholar's impelling need to check his references. In the case of the discovery of the tomb of Tutankhamun, his own uncertain regard for precision was compounded by the intervention of others who,

1 H. Carter and A. C. Mace, *The Tomb of Tut.ankh.Amen* (London, 1923–33), I, p. 96.
2 In G.I. Carter Notebook 1.
3 M.M.A., Department of Egyptian Art, Carter files; reproduced in Appendix III.

in writing at the time and later, provided the ingredients for a rich mixture of myth and imagination. It is not the intention of this narrative to consider every divergence and variant in the many accounts of the discovery, but to rely principally on the outline of the story set out in the first volume of *The Tomb of Tut.ankh.Amen*, which, as mentioned above, was composed by Mace, of whom Carter said in his Preface, 'I should add that the preparation of this book has fallen largely on his shoulders.' This Preface is dated in August 1923, and the book itself appeared in the autumn, within a year of the discovery. It does therefore represent an account of very considerable immediacy, written by someone who, from the evidence of his other archaeological publications, had a superior devotion to precision – it would be unfair to say 'truth' – than Howard Carter. In the same Preface Carter pays tribute also to 'my dear friend Mr. Percy White, the novelist, Professor of English Literature in the Egyptian University, for his ungrudging literary help.' An old friend of Carter's, White was to play an increasingly important part in the preparation of the second volume on the tomb, which came out in 1926. His help is acknowledged in the Preface to that volume but from what Carter says, no mention would have pleased White more. He had no hand in the writing of volume three.

The bare outline of the early days of the discovery can be extracted with confidence from the vivid narrative contained in the initial volume of Carter's popular account. Work in the Valley of the Kings had reopened on 1 November 1922, and by the evening of the 3rd the ancient workmen's huts lying close to the entrance of the tomb of King Ramesses VI had been planned and removed in readiness for the clearance of that part of the Valley down to bed-rock. It is perhaps idle to speculate about Carter's expectations at this juncture. He knew that he was at the start of what would be his last season; experience of recent years could provide little encouragement for his efforts; but his original strategy had aimed at systematic clearance, and at this point he had the opportunity to clear a triangular area which had been deliberately left so as not to impede tourist entry into the popular tomb of Ramesses VI. So matters could proceed according to plan. His workmen were experienced; they knew what to do. Here the clearance of flood-deposited debris was scarcely excavation, and work could begin in the morning of 4 November under the supervision of his long-serving foreman, Reis Ahmed Gerigar. By the time Carter turned up, the first portentous step leading down to the tomb had been found. Whether it was discovered not beneath the site of one of the huts, as the volume states, but elsewhere, and by a water-boy, the junior member of Carter's gang, as Lee Keedick later recorded,[4] is not a matter to be worried about. Something significant had at last been discovered, and Carter, well experienced and backed by intimate knowledge of the archaeology of the

4 I am grateful to Mr Robert Keedick for sending me copies of those parts of his father's unpublished memoirs concerned with Howard Carter.

royal tombs, could at once move into top gear, hoping for a useful find but probably not expecting more than the disappointment of a rifled sepulchre.

Then followed the well charted course that led to the revelations of 26 November. Enough of the stairway was cleared by the afternoon of the day after the discovery to reveal a blocked entrance stamped with the Necropolis seal, showing a device of the jackal of Anubis, divine protector of the Necropolis, set above nine bound captives, the representative enemies of the Egyptian king. Here then, it seemed, was the portal to a very important tomb. After discovering that a corridor packed with debris lay beyond this blocked entrance, Carter, with remarkable self-control, refilled the stairway, sent his telegram to Carnarvon, and made preparations for what he hoped might lie ahead. His restraint and deliberate planning at this point reveal not only the strength of purpose which would in the years ahead both sustain him and bring him close to destruction,[5] but also the caution born of so many disappointments in his excavating career. He spoke of 'nearly three weeks of uncertainty' that followed. In a sense he may even have masochistically enjoyed the delay. At the very least he was saved from the need to take immediate action, and could divert his energies into systematic planning. He was obliged not to rush, and this imposed discipline formed the pattern of his future work on the tomb. No move should be made in a precipitate manner. It was a strategy which confounded those who were eager for results, but it ensured that the work on the tomb would be carried out in an exemplary manner.

Among his earliest actions was to bring his friend Arthur Callender from Armant, a practical move which would quickly prove its worth. Lord Carnarvon was expected to arrive in Alexandria on the 20th, and on the 18th Carter travelled to Cairo to meet his patron. Already there was anticipation in the air; his discovery, which so far remained one of promise only, excited his acquaintances. By some extraordinary expectation people understood that something was up. Carter began to be welcomed in circles which might otherwise have treated him with little more than indifference. He figures in a series of entries in the diary of Minnie Burton,[6] the rather snobbish wife of Harry Burton, photographer for the Egyptian Expedition of the Metropolitan Museum, whose record of the excavation and contents of the tomb was to form such an important part of the archive of Carter's discovery. The Burtons had arrived from Florence, where their home was, in early November, and were still in Cairo on the 18th. Minnie Burton notes for that day, 'Mr. Carter arrives'; on the 20th, 'Mr. Carter at our table' . . . 'Lord Carnarvon arrived, with Lady Evelyn'; on the 21st, 'I to Greek grocer about Mr. Carter's whisky. He left for Luxor.' Her diary for the whole of the period of the excavation, up to the end of October 1926,

5 *The Tomb of Tut.ankh.Amen*, I, p. 90.
6 The diary for 1922–6 is in the possession of Mrs Rosalind Berwald.

has miraculously survived, and while it does not contain much in the way of archaeological evidence, it provides useful tit-bits of information on the progress of the work as part of the social life of the Metropolitan House in the Asasif at Luxor, written by one who was immensely sensitive to the gradations of British, American and Continental society. Carter's potential discovery, and his association with the Earl of Carnarvon, qualified him at this early stage for preferential treatment. There would be times later when their relations would be less than cordial; then he could have done his own shopping.

By the time Carnarvon and his daughter had reached Luxor on the 23rd, Callender had everything ready for the reclearance of the stairway. When this was completed on the afternoon of the following day, seal impressions with the name of Tutankhamun were revealed – the very same king who had been Carter's chosen candidate for discovery. Less encouraging were the signs of forced entry into the tomb; although the clear resealing of the entrance showed that there had been no apparent additional entry since antiquity, a fact reinforced by the existence of the workmen's huts of the reign of Ramesses VI which had effectively protected the stairs since the late second millennium. The removal of the entrance blocking on the 24th was followed by two days clearing the descending passageway leading to a second blocked doorway, similar in form and in its sealing to the first. The rubble and chippings filling the passage showed definite signs of having been burrowed through on at least two occasions; fragments of wood, pottery, stone vessels, and mud sealings with a variety of royal names from Tutankhamun back to Tuthmosis III, suggested that the excavators were on the verge of discovering a cache of reburied royal material, possibly not unlike that found by Theodore Davis in 1907, and identified then as the tomb of Queen Tiye.[7]

Now followed the drama of the breaking of the blocked entrance and the revelation of the contents of the room beyond. The published description of the moment has become established as a classic in the modest literature of archaeological discovery:[8]

Slowly, desperately slowly it seemed to us as we watched, the remains of the passage debris that encumbered the lower part of the doorway were removed until at last we had the whole door clear before us. The decisive moment had arrived. With trembling hands I made a tiny breach in the upper left hand corner. Darkness and blank space, as far as an iron testing-rod could reach, showed that whatever lay beyond was empty, and not filled like the passage we had just cleared. Candle tests were applied as a precaution against possible foul gases,

7 See T. M. Davis et al., The Tomb of Queen Tiyi (London, 1910); for Carter's finding objects stolen from the tomb, see p. 131 above.
8 The Tomb of Tut.ankh.Amen, I, pp. 95f.

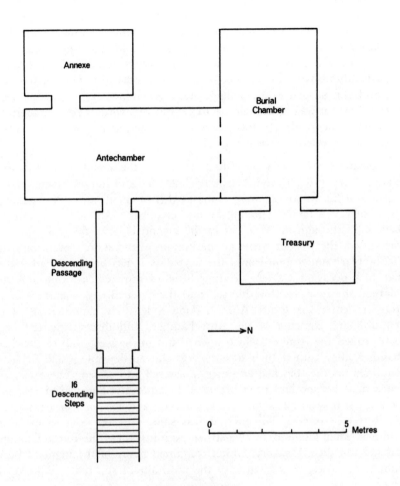

TOMB OF TUTANKHAMUN

and then, widening the hole a little, I inserted the candle and peered in, Lord Carnarvon, Lady Evelyn, and Callender standing anxiously beside me to hear the verdict. At first I could see nothing, the hot air escaping from the chamber causing the candle flame to flicker, but presently, as my eyes grew accustomed to the light, details of the room within emerged slowly from the mist, strange animals, statues and gold – everywhere the glint of gold. For the moment – an eternity it must have seemed to the others standing by – I was struck dumb with amazement, and when Lord Carnarvon, unable to stand the suspense any longer, inquired anxiously, 'Can you see anything?' it was all I could do to get out the words, 'Yes, wonderful things.' Then widening the hole a little further, so that we both could see, we inserted an electric torch.

According to Carter's published narrative, the members of the small party – Carnarvon, Evelyn Herbert, Callender and himself, together with a group of his workmen, were alone at this moment, and after making a visual survey of the contents of the first chamber of the tomb, in so far as they could through the hole cut in the second blocked doorway, the hole was sealed, the wooden grille at the bottom of the stairs closed, and they left the place under guard until the next day. It has been asserted that on that first occasion Carter, needing little encouragement from the rest, enlarged the hole to allow himself and the three British members of the group to enter the tomb. After making a leisurely examination of the extraordinary contents of the Antechamber, and discovering the small room, called the Annexe, which opened out of the west wall of the Ante-chamber, they turned their attention to the north wall, which evidently contained another blocked entrance, plastered and sealed. There was evidence that this too had been breached in antiquity, and Carter reopened the ancient hole to allow himself, Carnarvon and Evelyn Herbert to enter the Burial Chamber; Callender, it was said, was too stout to make the entrance. Then followed an awe-struck examination of the Burial Chamber and the so-called Treasury, which contained many of the items of burial equipment closely connected with the posthumous spiritual welfare of the king.[9]

Much has been made of the supposed irregularity of what Carnarvon and Carter did in so entering the tomb in advance of any official inspection, and in surreptitiously penetrating the Burial Chamber. It has further been alleged that on this occasion a number of small objects were removed from the tomb in the pockets of the *soi-disant* clandestine visitors.[10] What is the truth in all these assertions and allegations? A complete account of what

9 The episode is related with imaginative detail added by T. Hoving, *Tutankhamun. The Untold Story* (New York, 1975), pp. 90ff.
10 E.g. Hoving, *ibid.*, pp. 350ff. The question of the removal of objects from the tomb by Howard Carter and Lord Carnarvon is discussed further, pp. 356, 388 below.

actually happened cannot be compiled from the existing evidence; but it is certain that there was an undisclosed entry of the Burial Chamber at least. The charge that the excavators entered the tomb on the very day when Carter first breached the second blocked doorway is hard to substantiate. The unpublished account written by Carnarvon, and now held in the Department of Egyptian Art in the Metropolitan Museum, does not contain any reference to it. The likelihood that the first entry took place on the 26th is highly uncertain, for it would have been extremely difficult to disguise a hole big enough for the four principals to pass through, only Lady Evelyn being of slight build. It was expected that the Chief Inspector, Rex Engelbach, might be present when the blocking was demolished and a breach larger than one necessary to inspect the first chamber visually from outside would not have escaped his attention. That his local inspector Ibrahim deputized for him made little difference in this respect.

There seems no doubt, however, that at some time after the formal entry into the Antechamber on the 27th the excavators did return to the tomb, probably at night, enlarged or reopened a robber's hole in the blocking between the Antechamber and the Burial Chamber, and spent some time taking stock of what lay beyond that sealed barrier. The only acceptable published evidence on the matter can be found in two short mentions made by Alfred Lucas, the government chemist and authority on ancient materials and technology, who worked hand-in-glove with Carter throughout the clearance of the tomb and the subsequent conservation of its contents.[11] Lucas makes it clear that the entry was made and that the hole was blocked up and sealed by Carter afterwards, the area of reblocking being covered up with basketry and reeds. Confirmation of the secret entry is found in a few private sources, one of which is in a letter written to Carter by Evelyn Herbert on Boxing Day 1922.[12] She talks of her father's continuing excitement, 'and when slightly weary [he] calls me in to tell him again and again of the "Holy of Holies", which always acts like a magnum of champagne!'

Mervyn Herbert also records in his journal that when he drove with his half-brother, Carnarvon, and Lady Evelyn to the Valley for the official opening of the Burial Chamber, Evelyn was urged to tell him something:[13]

> This she did under the strictest promise of secrecy. It is a thing I would never give away in any case, and it is one which I think ought not to be known, at any rate, not at the present. Here is the secret. They had both been into the Second Chamber! After the discovery

11 In *A.S.A.E.* 41 (1942), p. 136; 45 (1947), pp. 133f.
12 In M.M.A., Department of Egyptian Art, Carter files; the full text is given on p. 403 below. Boxing Day, a British public holiday, is the first working day after Christmas Day, usually 26 December.
13 The Mervyn Herbert Journal is partly preserved in the library of the Middle East Centre, St Antony's College, Oxford. The incident is recorded on fol. 369f.

they had not been able to resist it – they had made a small hole in the wall (which they afterwards filled up again) – and climbed through. She described to me very shortly some of the extraordinary wonders I was soon to see. It was a most exciting drive, I cannot remember anything like it. The only others who know anything about it are the workmen, none of which would ever breathe a word to a soul about it.

It is noticeable in this account that Mervyn Herbert does not mention Carter; but his presence as Carnarvon's 'man' was taken for granted. In her letter Evelyn Herbert makes his participation quite clear: 'I can never thank you sufficiently for allowing me to enter its precincts. It was the *Great Moment* of my life.'

Lucas suggested that Carter's behaviour after the event in sealing up the entry hole and disguising it with basketwork was 'most reasonable', and prompted by the wish to avoid being 'pestered constantly by people wanting to go in', and this reason seems still to be the best as justification for action which has been used to castigate Carter for improper behaviour. It must be remembered, however, that from an archaeological point of view, acceptable behaviour in 1922 was very different from what is expected today. Carnarvon and Carter were old hands in Theban excavation, and the concession for work in the Valley of the Kings, which was still valid in 1922, had first been signed by Daressy for Lacau on 18 April 1915; its most recent renewal was dated 16 November 1922. The excavators' Theban experience went back much further than 1915, and Carter, in particular, was in more senses than one 'at home' in the Theban Necropolis. It is reasonable to assume that the excavators were well aware of what they should do on the discovery of a tomb, and a reference to the terms of their permit would have reminded them, first, that any discovery should be announced to the Chief Inspector of Upper Egypt (clause 3); second, that they had the right to open any tomb and be first to enter (clause 4); third, that any intact tomb should with its objects be surrendered without division (clause 9); and fourth, that in the case of a tomb already searched, the excavators could expect a share of the contents, the Antiquities Service reserving for itself 'all objects of capital importance' (clause 10).

In formal respects it is difficult to fault the reported actions of the excavators. The Chief Inspector, Rex Engelbach, had visited the tomb on the 24th, and should therefore have known that a monument of some potential importance had been found. On the 26th he was sent a note informing him that the second blocking would be removed on the following day. He was out of Luxor at that time and so was represented at the entry by his Inspector. It will now seem extraordinary that Engelbach had not been sufficiently infected by the expectation of a great discovery to postpone his trip to Qena, or to ask Carter to delay any opening until his return.

It is a small indication that he was either not as yet aware of the possibility of a substantial find – the Valley was notorious for disappointments – or sufficiently confident in Carter's competence and integrity as an excavator to behave responsibly and within the terms of the concession.

Lucas's justification for Carter's concealment of the early entry into the Burial Chamber, the 'Holy of Holies', is eminently sensible. If he had announced the existence of what was probably an intact royal burial chamber, it would have been extremely difficult, surely impossible, to prevent premature inspection by Lacau and other senior officials of the Antiquities Service, followed by a procession of important people from the King downwards. Systematic work on the recording and clearance of the Antechamber would have been continually interrupted, and much archaeological evidence possibly lost. Nevertheless, even after the Burial Chamber had finally been revealed to the world, it suited the excavators to continue to conceal what they had done. They could never have convinced the authorities or, more especially, the disaffected Press, that they had not helped themselves to objects from the unrevealed parts of the tomb. So the matter was kept quiet, although it was certainly known to more than the intimate circle of the excavators and Arthur Lucas. In 1945 Alan Gardiner wrote to Percy Newberry on matters concerning the Carter material about to be presented to the Griffith Institute, and in a post-script added: 'By the bye, did you see Lucas's article in Ann. Serv. where he – to use a bit of slang – "spilt the beans"? I am quite glad it has been done, though I couldn't have done it myself!'[14]

Here Gardiner could have been referring obliquely to the entry into the Burial Chamber, or to the removal of objects from the Burial Chamber at the time of the 'secret' entry (or even later), for Lucas in his earlier article of 1942 also draws attention to the exquisite and elaborate double ointment box which Carter published as having been found in the sarcophagus, but which Lucas claims to have seen in Carter's house before the official opening of the Burial Chamber.[15] The question of the possibly illicit removal of objects from the tomb will require some further consideration later in this volume. Here it may be remarked, first, that removal did not necessarily imply theft (the ointment box is in the Cairo Museum),[16] and second, that the excavators, aware from the outset that the tomb was not intact, had every reason to expect a share in the contents in due course; a few pieces taken 'on account', although highly improper, and distinctly contrary to good archaeological practice, could be marginally condoned according to the somewhat laxer attitudes of early twentieth-century excavators.

14 G.I. Newberry Corr. 49/10; letter of 21 March 1945.
15 A.S.A.E. 41 (1942), p. 137. Minnie Burton described seeing it along with the jewels from the body of the king in December, 1925, see p. 347 below.
16 Illustrated and noted in N. Reeves, The Complete Tutankhamun (London, 1990), p. 158.

It would be very wrong to concentrate attention on the supposed misde-
meanours of the excavators in the early stages of the tomb's discovery.
Consider rather the steps taken by Carter in organizing the opening of the
tomb and in preparing for the serious campaign of study and clearance
which would follow. From the moment when the excavators realized what
they had found, they were overwhelmingly conscious of the dangers ahead.
The Valley of the Kings would become the magnet to draw unprecedented
crowds of official visitors, notable foreigners including royalty, persistent
members of the Press, and ordinary tourists. Security would be of para-
mount importance, not only to protect the tomb's contents from damage
and theft, but also to ensure the progress of the work, a principal concern
for Carter. What followed was quite exemplary; within a very short time
Carter organized matters in Luxor, with the sterling assistance of Callender, obtained stores necessary to support an extended campaign of work,
and set up, partly by seizing the good offers of help made by established
scholars, and partly by seeking specialist support in the appropriate quarters, an unparalleled team of experienced archaeologists. His prescience
and energy were well rewarded, and when times became difficult he was
much supported by the colleagues and institutions he had so assiduously
involved in his work. How rightly did Petrie comment to Newberry, even
as early as 17 January 1923: 'Why people should now rush to Egypt when
nothing can be shown for weeks or months is a piece of "hard" psychology.
We can only say how lucky it is all in the hands of Carter and Lucas.'[17]

On the morning of the 27th the blocking of the entrance to the tomb
was removed and, with electric lights connected up to the main Valley
system, first installed by Carter himself twenty years earlier, he for the first
time, officially at least, stepped into the Antechamber with the Carnarvons,
Callender, and, it may be presumed, the Egyptian Inspector Ibrahim.
With good light they could at last survey the jumbled contents of the
room, the great beds and dismantled chariots, the thrones and boxes
overflowing with objects like the treasure-chests of romance. There was
gold everywhere, mostly in the form of gold-leaf gilding on plastered wood;
there were intricate alabaster vessels, fine pieces of furniture inlaid with
ivory, faience, glass and semi-precious stones. Beneath one of the great
couches they could see into a further room, even more closely packed,
where the emptying of boxes by robbers had left a state of utter confusion;
no serious attempt had been made to tidy it up as had happened in the
Antechamber. And then, at the north end of the first chamber was the
further blocked entrance guarded by two life-sized figures of the king, black
painted and gilded, and in front the remarkable box painted with exquisite
miniatures of Tutankhamun in fanciful scenes of hunting and warfare.
According to the published account,[18] the excavators were sorely tempted

17 G.I. Newberry Corr. 37/85.
18 *The Tomb of Tut.ankh.Amen*, I, p. 102.

to proceed at once to take down the blocking to what would emerge as the Burial Chamber – perhaps already entered, but if not, then certainly to be so on the next night. Practical considerations dictated otherwise, the immediate necessity being to make a 'complete scientific record of the outer chamber'. They did, however, note that there were again traces indicating that the third blocked entrance had been cut through in antiquity. The evidence for ancient robbery, on probably at least two occasions, seemed incontrovertible, and although the opinion has been expressed that there was no break-in as the excavators had concluded, most scholars would find it difficult to agree.[19]

Carter and Carnarvon now had several important decisions to take. In the first place it was sure that what had already been *publicly* revealed in the Antechamber and glimpsed in the adjacent room, now to be called the Annexe, would create substantial problems of recording, clearance and conservation; careful planning and help would be needed. Second, there was the business of making the find properly known to the authorities and to the Press of the world, representatives of which were already showing what Carter would not have regarded as a healthy interest in the find. Third, there were the problems of security; gold was the most emotive word to the clever tomb-robbers of the Theban Necropolis, and every precaution would be required to guard against robbery. Carter, as excavator, had never been faced with a piece of work of such magnitude and complexity; but he had from the time of his own responsibility for work in the Theban area as Chief Inspector, and later in his fallow years, and later still in the time of his association with the Earl of Carnarvon, observed, and been marginally involved in, several spectacular finds containing material similar to, if not quite as grand as, what now waited his attentions in the tomb of Tutankhamun. Over the years he had developed dextrous skills in handling delicate materials, and he had an eye to detect the problems that so often lurked beneath the outwardly satisfactory appearance of an antiquity. He had also learned the virtue of patience, and developed the attribute of toughness, the second of which in his case readily showed itself as stubbornness. He had not, unfortunately, learned at the same time the necessity of bending sometimes with the wind when it blew from an important quarter; he was jealous of his achievement, too proprietorial ostensibly on behalf of Lord Carnarvon's interests (and later, those of the Countess of Carnarvon), but always of his own. To begin with, however, he made all the right moves, following no doubt the conclusions reached in discussions with Carnarvon before he left Luxor for England with his daughter on 4 December.

An official viewing of the tomb was made on 29 November. The notice was short, and most of those who attended were important provincial

19 See C. N. Reeves, *The Valley of the Kings* (London, 1990), p. 82, n. 34.

Egyptian officials, but included Lady Allenby, her husband being unable to leave Cairo at the time. A second viewing was arranged for the following day when Pierre Lacau, Director-General of the Antiquities Service, attended and also Paul Tottenham, Adviser to the Ministry of Public Works, the civil servant responsible for Lacau's Service. Mr Arthur Merton, representative of *The Times*, who had arrived in Luxor in expectation of the find, was allowed to be present. He subsequently, with much information supplied by Carter, wrote the first dispatch to his newspaper which was published in the issue of 30 November, thereby alerting a world-wide readership to the great discovery, and, in a sense, establishing a pattern of reporting in the public prints which should have been a boon rather than a serious impediment to Carter. Even more significantly for the future was the letter written by Lacau to Carnarvon on 13 December, two weeks after his visit to the tomb:[20]

I have made known to the Committee of Egyptology, at its meeting of 6 December inst., the full importance of the wonderful discovery you have just made in the Valley of the Kings. All my colleagues have been keenly struck, not only by the extraordinary results that have been obtained, but also by the means which have led to these same results. Further, they wished unanimously to associate themselves with their President [i.e. Lacau himself] in conveying to you their congratulations and all their thanks.

Your have placed your name on one of the greatest discoveries ever made not only in Egypt but in all the fields of archaeology.

As for your associate, Mr. H. Carter, who has conducted the work for so many years, it is for him the finest crowning of his career, and the most striking reward that an archaeologist has ever had. Such a reward was truly deserved, for he has given a fine example of system and of patience, the rarest virtue of an excavator, without doubt. May be be copied often.

In addition, the Committee has been especially struck and touched by the conditions of utter unselfishness that have attended the work. Here is the ideal kind of excavation that needs to be carried out in the future. You have demonstrated, to the great surprise of many, that, in a higher scientific interest, it is possible to agree to unselfish conditions for excavation. Further, Egypt and our discipline owe you every thanks. That of Egypt is still only to be seen in newspaper articles which are determined to be unpleasant both for you and for me. That doesn't matter. The King and Council of Ministers know precisely what has happened, and Egyptian opinion, when it understands (it has all the facts before it) will thank you, I am sure, as is proper.

20 M.M.A. Department of Egyptian Art, Carter files; the original in French.

It is a great pleasure for me to repeat to you in my name and in that of the Committee, all the thanks and congratulations of the Antiquities Service.

Any satisfaction that this letter may have given to Lord Carnarvon may be questioned. His distrust of Lacau was well established, and in accord with the feelings of many who were concerned with field-work in Egypt. He could scarcely have forgotten the dismissive way in which Lacau had refused to consider his application for the El-Amarna concession. He had not yet received this fulsome letter of congratulation when he sent Carter his Christmas greetings for 1922, from on board ship off Stromboli *en route* for Marseilles, on 16 December.[21] Among various comments – the unlikelihood of 'this year . . . making a little out of N. York', the inclusion of a cheque, as it seems ('I know that you know that thanks are unnecessary'), and a description of Stromboli ('an enormous perpetual rocket going up') – he writes of Gardiner's coming out, and reflects: 'I must say I hope everything will go off pleasantly, but I fear that with the present Director that is more than we can hope. By the way, the Plum Pudding is I believe addressed to you at the Continental.' Here it may be understood that Carnarvon had in mind the uncertainty over the future division of the finds; there was as yet no hint that the work on the tomb would be jeopardized by Lacau's future actions. Lacau, who was not a Jesuit, or a priest of any other kind, as has sometimes been stated[22] – as if somehow to excuse any devious business on his part – had never interfered with the conduct of Carter's work on the ground, except in marginal matters. *Partage* was another matter altogether.

Carnarvon was on his way home with his daughter to a reception of unexpected proportions, to an audience with King George V and Queen Mary ('both very interested'), to discussions of major significance for the work in Egypt, with Alan Gardiner and Albert Lythgoe of the Metropolitan Museum and with *The Times*.[23] In the meanwhile Carter had much to do. The tomb entrance was closed with heavy timbers, and the stairs once again filled in. On 6 December he travelled up to Cairo with a long shopping list, at the top of which was the steel gate for the tomb – promised for six days ahead. There were also the essential supplies for the care and conservation and eventual packing of the tomb's contents, some photographic equipment (Carnarvon having promised to send out a supply of glass plates by way of Gardiner), and a motor-car. The last, a Ford, would be quite a novelty for an archaeological expedition in Egypt, where boats, donkeys and railway trains were still the most common means of transport, with camels representing heavy haulage over short distances.

21 M.M.A., Department of Egyptian Art, Carter files.
22 Hoving, *Tutankhamun. The Untold Story*, p. 64.
23 All reported in a letter to Howard Carter, dated 24 December, in M.M.A., Department of Egyptian Art, Carter files.

Not the least impressive part of his planning for future work was Carter's assembling of a remarkable group of helpers; for it had been apparent to him from the moment he entered the tomb that he was faced with problems of such enormity that he could not hope to deal satisfactorily with everything himself, assisted only by the practical but archaeologically inexperienced Callender. Luck and opportunity helped him, but one should not underestimate, on the one hand, his own standing with colleagues which allowed them to find it proper to join the Carnarvon-Carter team, and on the other hand, the readiness among such colleagues, and indeed many other scholars and eager amateurs, to be associated with the work on this most remarkable discovery. Carter was well placed in Cairo to talk to some likely helpers, among whom two in particular were to be his first recruits and the longest serving associates, Alfred Lucas and Harry Burton. The former, who had first come to Egypt for health reasons in 1897, was a government chemist in the Survey Department and Assay Office, and, as Carter notes, about to retire. He was 55 years old, and he offered to do what he could as a chemist to help Carter with conservation, and with the scientific examination of the tomb's contents. He had already shown a deep interest in the scientific and technological sides of archaeology, and the small volume he published in 1926, *Ancient Egyptian Materials*, represented a first distillation of his extensive researches. From 1923 until 1932 he was advisory chemist to the Antiquities Service, and remained in technical matters Carter's right-hand man throughout the thrilling and painful years of the tomb's clearance. Ultimately his little book of 1926 developed into a work of magisterial authority and remains, as *Ancient Egyptian Materials and Industries*, one of the most reliable reference works in the small library or archaeological scientific classics.[24]

Although Carter was himself no mean photographer, he never thought of himself as anything but a good jobbing shooter of better-class snaps. Harry Burton, however, was a man of archaeological experience who had been employed almost exclusively as a photographer by the Egyptian Expedition of the Metropolitan Museum; he possessed all the skills that Carter would need. Carter was on good terms with Burton and, for the moment, his wife, Minnie; they were both still in Cairo when Carter came up from Luxor on 6 December. Minnie was thrilled to be on more than nodding acquaintance with the discoverer of the new tomb. On 5 December she records, 'Talk with Ld. Carnarvon about wonderful find'; on the 8th, 'Mr. Carter lunched at our table'. If there were to be any doubt in Burton's mind about helping Carter, Minnie surely would have weighed the scales in favour of acceptance. But the matter was probably already settled. Carter had provisionally agreed with Carnarvon on the necessity to enlarge the expedition's staff, and took the opportunity of a cable from Lythgoe

24 The fourth edition, edited and supplemented by J. R. Harris, appeared in 1962. Lucas died in 1945.

to press the case for co-operation. Lythgoe, in London on affairs of the Metropolitan Museum Expedition, wired Carter, congratulating him on his success. Carter then sent a reply, thanking Lythgoe and asking, 'Could you consider loan of Burton.' Lythgoe's immediate answer was perhaps even more encouraging than Carter had expected: 'Only too delighted to assist in every possible way. Please call on Burton and any other members of our staff.' This cable had arrived before the Carnarvons had left Egypt, and Lythgoe reported in a letter he wrote to Edward Robinson, Director of the Metropolitan Museum on 20 December, that Lady Evelyn Herbert described to him how her father with Carter had brought the cable to her hotel room as soon as it reached Cairo, and how they were 'deeply touched and greatly relieved'.[25]

Lythgoe displayed great energy in prosecuting the policy of help. There was undoubtedly a substantial awareness of the Museum's interests behind what he proposed, but his scientific principles were very strong, and were pursued with equivalent disinterestedness. In talks with Carnarvon in London he pressed the necessity of involving Arthur Mace in the work. Mace, a cousin of Flinders Petrie and an excavator of twenty-five years standing, had been on the staff of the Metropolitan Museum since 1906. He had achieved a reputation as a careful field-worker and remarkable conservator of fragile and intricate antiquities; he seemed not only ideal for Carter, but even essential. In the same letter to Robinson, Lythgoe reported that he had been able to 'discuss thoroughly with Mace our best lines of procedure before he started out [i.e. for Egypt]'; and further, that Carnarvon 'realizes now that Mace is the key to the whole situation and that he is without a rival in the patience and painstaking skill necessary in such an emergency as the present one. It is a case of Senebtisi multiplied to the Nth degree!'[26] Lythgoe did not overstate Mace's capabilities, but even he could not have realized the part Mace was to play in the first two years of the Tutankhamun campaign, as archaeologist, conservator, maintainer of morale, keeper of the peace, unwavering supporter, and literary mastermind behind the written output of the official team. And how impressive this team now looked! Carter and Callender, Lucas and Burton, and Mace; and also two others who were additionally loaned to Carter for a few weeks to prepare a detailed plan of the Antechamber, with everything plotted in place. These two were Walter Hauser and Lindsley Hall, both employed as architectural draughtsmen by the Metropolitan Egyptian Expedition, the former strong-headed and excitable, the

---

25 Cables mentioned in Lythgoe's letter to Edward Robinson of 20 December 1922, in M.M.A., Department of Egyptian Art, Carter files; see also *The Tomb of Tut.ankh.Amen*, I, pp. 107f.

26 Mace had in recent years performed a remarkable piece of restoration on material from the tomb of the princess Senebtisi at Lisht. For bibliography, see *Lexikon der Ägyptologie*, 5, col. 848.

latter fussy and hypochondriac. And in addition Alan Gardiner would keep an eye on the inscriptional material.

Lythgoe's letter to Robinson of 20 December, and another dated 23 December, make it clear that he hoped that advantages other than kudos would accrue to his museum. Carnarvon seemed to be sure that Lacau would 'deal generously with him in giving him a selection of objects'. Lythgoe very honestly commented:

> Strictly in the family circle, I think you can see what I am hoping for in all this – aside from what I know would be the Museum's desire in extending every assistance to Carnarvon in this tremendous emergency. He is certain, in return for all we are doing, to give us some of the things he receives, nor could he be in any way criticised by people here for doing so, for our part in the matter has been publicly recognized in the press.

Changes already planned by Lythgoe for the new season included the suspension of work at Lisht and the moving of Mace to Thebes to work with Winlock on the Eleventh-Dynasty tombs. As it now transpired, it was possible to divert Mace to Carter without seriously interfering with the Museum's Theban operations.[27] Further, Lythgoe pointed out that anything the Museum might get as a return from Tutankhamun would greatly outweigh what might come from more Eleventh-Dynasty tombs. Lythgoe continued:

> I am confident that you and the Trustees will agree with me, and for that reason I know you would be glad to confirm our action by cable to Carnarvon, as I asked this morning, and I know how much Carnarvon will appreciate such a direct message from you.

On 23 December Lythgoe reported to Robinson a further meeting with Carnarvon. Both had received cables from Carter, Lythgoe's informing him of the success of Burton's first photographs, and Carnarvon's containing 'splendid news' about assurances on divisions. Lythgoe then says:[28]

> Carnarvon then asked me to tell *noone* of what he was going to say – 'not even Carter when you see him' – and then said 'I'm going to give you a part of the things which I receive'. He then continued: 'Of course, I shall have to give something to the British Museum,[29]

27 The Metropolitan Museum excavated mainly at Lisht and Thebes between 1906 and 1936. Yearly reports were published in the Museum's *Bulletin*, and the Theban reports were collected in H. E. Winlock, *Excavations at Deir el Bahri 1911–1931* (New York, 1942). The work at both sites is being published fully in continuing series.

28 Letter in M.M.A., Department of Egyptian Art, Carter files.

29 A letter from Carnarvon to Sir Frederick Kenyon, Director of the British Museum, on 29 December 1922, talks of the possibility of a division of objects; but it contains no specific promise of objects for the Museum. I am grateful to Miss Marjorie Caygill for tracing this letter in the Kenyon Papers in the B. M. Central Archive.

but I intend to see that the Metropolitan is *well taken care of.*' He was simply *splendid,* and you can imagine that I met him more than half-way in the assurances I gave him as to the gratitude of the Museum for all he was doing.

Lythgoe then advises Robinson to keep this news very confidential; he would suggest when he might properly let Carnarvon know that he was aware of his intentions. He had further discussed with Carnarvon other possible participants in the work, and in particular had talked of Elliot Smith, an anatomist and physical anthropologist, of Australian origin, who had made a corner for himself in the examination of Egyptian mummies, especially royal mummies. He was, they felt, 'the *only* one who should have responsibility of the evidence on that side', if mummies were found. This agreement, unfortunately made known to Smith, was later to cause some embarrassment to Carter who had his own, and different, preferences in the matter.[30]

In considering the possible future acquisition of objects from the tomb of Tutankhamun by the Metropolitan Museum, and the British Museum, it should be borne in mind that museums are in the business of building up and maintaining specialized collections, and the acquisition of pieces through co-operation, even partnership, is a well established, continuing and proper practice. Even today, many museums participate in the field-work of excavating institutions like the Egypt Exploration Society, partly for scientific reasons, and partly in the expectation of acquiring antiquities when divisions are made with the Egyptian Antiquities Organization, the modern successor of the Antiquities Service. Albert Lythgoe was understandably thrilled about the advantage the Metropolitan had achieved through its offer of help. He may have been worried that the complex of motives might be misread, but he never lost sight of the necessity to ensure that Carnarvon and Carter did a worthy job. He said in the same letter of 23 December to Robinson:

I have impressed on Carnarvon that the eyes of the world (scientific as well as otherwise) were upon him and that in the case of every other royal tomb that has ever been found the major part of the evidence has been wantonly disregarded and lost – but, through the organization which is now assembled and carrying out the work for him and Carter, they have got a *perfect* working-machine and they will be credited with having taken the fullest advantage of this greatest of opportunities and with having furnished a record of the evidence on every side, uniquely complete in every detail.

30 A letter from Dr Douglas Derry to Carter on 12 December 1922 (also in M.M.A., Department of Egyptian Art, Carter files) offered his assistance for the examination of the mummy, if found. For the difficulties with Elliot Smith, see p. 266 below.

Howard Carter had in the meanwhile wasted little time in consolidating his team and completing his arrangements for the commencement of serious work in the tomb. By 15 December he was back in Luxor, the steel gate and other supplies had been delivered, and on the very next day the tomb was re-excavated. On the 17th the gate was fitted and later in the day 'After tea H [Harry] and I to Mr. Carter's and saw the King's cup. Mr Callender there. After dinner Mr. Carter came here.' So reported Minnie Burton; and on the next day she records a *quid pro quo*: 'Mr. C. sent over curtains for me to sew.' On the 19th Carter sent his donkey to convey Mrs. Burton to see the tomb: 'Wonderful' – on the whole her diary comments are economical. She notes that the Breasteds were there. While he was at Aswan James Henry Breasted had received a letter from Carnarvon announcing the discovery, and he had just arrived in Luxor with his family.[31] His recent disagreement with Carter over the Cleveland sculpture was now, it seems, a thing of the past, and he eagerly offered to help Carter with the decipherment of the seal impressions on the entrance blocking – an offer Carter gladly accepted, although he knew that Carnarvon was arranging for Alan Gardiner to take responsibility for any inscriptional material found in the tomb. According to Breasted's own diary entry for the period (actually written up considerably in retrospect on 16 March 1925),[32] he was apparently able to correct several erroneous conclusions already drawn by Carter from the evidence so far discovered, and had subsequently been surprised to find his views incorporated without acknowledgement in the 'official' version of the probable history of the tomb's robberies, published soon after by Carnarvon in *The Times*. Breasted clearly retained misgivings about Carter, but it is possible that at this point he felt somewhat aggrieved because he had been wholly forestalled by the Metropolitan men, and had rather missed the boat. He could not, however, resist the extraordinary find, and did his best in the following years to exploit the tomb both for his own interests and for those of his creation and justifiable obsession, the Oriental Institute of the University of Chicago. His support for Carter in 1924, as will be seen, was distinctly two-sided.

For the moment there was massive suppressed excitement in Thebes. Carter's staff was assembling, he had started Burton on his photography, he had secured permission from the Antiquities Service to use the now empty tomb no. 55 (the so-called tomb of Queen Tiye) as a dark-room for Burton, and the little visited tomb of King Sethos II (no. 15) as a conservation work-room and store for antiquities. The latter was several hundred yards away, but easily protected and quiet; it would become

31 The early days of his involvement with the tomb are described by Breasted in a very long letter to John D. Rockefeller Jr, dated 29 December 1922, in O.I. Director's Office Corr. 1922–3.
32 In O.I. Director's Office archive.

known as the laboratory. Walter Hauser and Lindsley Hall had been started on their task of planning the contents of the Antechamber. They did not begin work quite as early as the published volume states.[33] Hall's diary is fairly specific on the matter. For 20 December he notes:[34] 'This aft. Walter and I climbed over to the Valley of the Kings to see Carter, as we are to make drawings for him of the tomb'; on the 21st: 'We again visited the Valley and this A.M. saw the tomb, the first chamber filled with the most remarkable objects.' He records their first session of planning on 23 December; 'We are placing objects on a 1:10 scale plan of the first chamber' (28 Dec.). Hall had literary as well as artistic interests, and was an inveterate amateur photographer; he did not miss his opportunity: 'I started writing story about Carnarvon-Carter find which I am going to submit to Mr. Stow' (30 Dec.). He subsequently notes the publication of his story and photographs, but does not specify in what journal or magazine (entry for 24 March); it was but one among many hundreds of stories and reports which were to flood the pages of the world's newspapers and periodicals in the months to come.

The arrival of Arthur Mace on Christmas Day signalled the start of the serious work of clearance and conservation. But first a celebration at the Metropolitan House. Mace's letters to his wife, Winifred, record this occasion and chart the progress of his work on the tomb:[35]

> We had a Christmas dinner here last night – the Davies, Wilkinson, Carter and Lucas. . . . We had crackers and all wore caps, and Hall's most appropriately was a Granny cap with ribbons to tie under the chin. What the Berbers [the Nubian servants] thought of us I dont know.

The festive atmosphere also extended to the work at the outset, and Mace's earliest comments suggest a considerable lack of precision over his own role and future. Things were being worked out on the ground as they went along. That is not surprising, for events had moved so fast since the first indication of the tomb; it was remarkable that so much had been organized in such a short time. Mace had worked for the Metropolitan Museum mostly in its excavations at Lisht in Middle Egypt, and was not therefore as well acquainted with Carter as were the regular members of the Luxor camp – Lythgoe, Winlock, Burton, Hall, Hauser, with the Davieses and Charles Wilkinson (the epigraphic wing). He was almost a stranger:

33 *The Tomb of Tut.ankh.Amen*, I, p. 109, gives 18 December.
34 Hall's diary records very selectively the events of each day; health entries take precedence over professional activities.
35 The letters are in the possession of Mace's daughter, Margaret Orr, who has very kindly allowed me to consult and to quote from them. The Mace papers formed the basis for two exhibitions, both entitled '. . . the Grand Piano came by Camel', organized by Dr Christopher Lee at the Lochwinnoch Community Museum (Nov. 1989 to Feb. 1990), and later in 1990 in the Paisley Museum.

I lunched with Carter today [26th], and am to start on the tomb tomorrow. It is a simply stupendous thing, so much so that it takes one's breath away, and leaves one reeling. Carter was extremely friendly, and seems to take for granted that I am assigned to the job for the duration, which might mean two or three seasons in the field to say nothing of further work on restoration and publication. I find my name has already been given to the Press as definitely engaged. They say reporters are thick in the valley, and pop out from behind rocks to photograph and interview, so I seem to be in for an exciting time.

The first object to be removed from the tomb (not counting the King's cup and perhaps a few others which Carter had earlier taken to his house), was the painted chest which had so impressed him with its remarkable miniature paintings. It contained mostly children's clothes, in a poor and delicate condition; it took Mace three weeks off and on to clear it. In many ways the boxes presented the greatest problems to the team in tomb no. 15. All had been ransacked by the robbers and then carelessly repacked by the officials who had attempted to restore order in the tomb. Bead-work, of which there were many pieces, was particularly tricky. Mace's daily bulletins to his wife are full of comments which can only inadequately suggest the difficulties he and Lucas faced:

[6 Jan.] Just now we are working on a box which contains garments and shoes all covered with beadwork. The cloth is so rotten you can hardly touch it, and the beads drop off the shoes if you look at them. Moreover resin has run out and glued all the shoes together, so you can imagine what a job it is.

[6 Feb.] I embarked gaily yesterday on a new box, thinking it was going to be a very simple matter, but on removing the top cloth, I found all sorts of wonderful beadwork underneath, which will take me a very long time to clean and note.

[7 Feb.] The new box is revealing all sorts of unexpected treasures, but they take an infinity of time to work out, especially with the interruptions we get.

[9 Feb.] I finished clearing my third box today, and it was just like a Christmas stocking with oddments of all sorts of things, including a long glass scarab, a perfectly exquisite statuette of the king in dark blue glass, and another, almost equally beautiful, in limestone. By the way keep the details absolutely to yourself. I haven't finished the box yet, however, by any matter of means, for I've got a tapestry woven robe to try and straighten out, and a wonderful upper garment, made up of hundreds of feather shaped pendants of glaze and gold.

It will be a nice problem to fit it all together, as I wasn't able to get the exact shape from the position in which it lay.

Apart from visitors, there were many interruptions when Mace and Lucas were summoned to the tomb to carry out emergency treatment before an object was removed, or to help in the extrication of an awkwardly placed piece. Again Mace provides the feeling of the work:

[8 Jan.] I spent most of the morning in the tomb melting wax and treating a footstool covered with beadwork that was in a very bad condition, and a shoe composed entirely of beads. I think I'll get them up all right, but the amount of restoration work ahead of us is appalling. . . . I am lucky to have such a nice chap as Lucas to work with, as we spend almost all our time together in our tomb workshop.

[22 Jan.] Spent the whole day in the tomb treating the great bed steads with wax. Then this afternoon we took one of them to pieces, and an anxious job it was. It had been too big to be taken into the tomb whole, so had been put together in the tomb itself.

Conditions in the Antechamber were always difficult throughout the two months it took to clear it. Apart from Carter himself, supervising, and at times interfering with, the work of his colleagues, there were Burton, photographing generally and in detail at every stage in the clearance, Hauser and Hall, desperately trying to plot, plan and draw everything *in situ* while objects were being removed from beneath their drawing boards, and Lucas and Mace periodically turning up with their primus stove and paraffin wax to carry out first aid. The difficulties are well described by Carter and Mace in the first volume of the popular publication.[36] What are not there recorded are the tensions, outbursts of temper and sulking that inevitably occurred. Hauser was the first to explode. Hall's diary noted for 7 February: 'Walter rowed with Carter and ended his work with him.' Hall himself, fussy but less explosive than Hauser, stayed the course better, but he too found things difficult: [20 Jan.] 'I worked in the Valley this A.M. Carter took measurements for me until his extraordinary notions about projections caused such a violent disagreement between us that he refused (fortunately) to continue his "assistance".' Hall continued to work on the drawing after the Antechamber was empty, using notes and photographs; his progress was slow, and the drawings were not completed, as he records, until 25 April; he had spent five weeks at Mena House Hotel by the Giza pyramids after a bout of fever and a stay in hospital in Cairo.

Howard Carter was by nature a solitary worker, and for most of his career he had been able to conduct his field operations with a minimum of interference from others, and without having to pay much regard for

36 *The Tomb of Tut.ankh.Amen*, I, Chapters 7 and 8.

external matters. Tutankhamun changed all that, and there must have been many occasions when he lost patience with his fellow-workers because their ways of doing things were different from his own. It needed much understanding on the part of his colleagues to endure the times of stress and irritability. William C. Hayes, who did not join the Metropolitan Egyptian Expedition until 1927, once recalled that Burton, long-suffering and faithful, stormed into the Metropolitan House, bitterly complaining, 'That man Carter is quite impossible!' and then on reflection, 'But I must admit he showed me how to take a photograph I thought impossible.'[37] It was in the end Carter's professionalism that mitigated the trials and tribulations of his team. Still, he had heavy burdens to carry, most especially those of the Press and of distinguished visitors. With the Press his natural impatience was singularly aggravated by the intense interest engendered by the discovery, and hopelessly complicated by the arrangements Lord Carnarvon had negotiated with *The Times*.

It could be said that nothing could have been done fully to quench the thirst of those who had been sent to Egypt to obtain, if possible, exclusive stories from the source, the spring of information, in Western Thebes. Carter had allowed a first press view of the Antechamber on 22 December. Thereafter, when serious work began, Carter found it almost impossible to handle the distribution of information. Carnarvon, after discussion with Carter, had realised that there were extraordinary opportunities for making money from the discovery, to recoup much of his expenditure over the years, and he showed an understandable reluctance to make material available for publication in any form. While he was in England he was greatly exercised by the difficulty of doing the 'right thing' and at the same time protecting his investment. Alan Gardiner, who saw much of Carnarvon in the weeks before Christmas, retells how, one day, while the two lunched together in Carnarvon's Town house in Seamore Place, they were interrupted by the arrival of Geoffrey Dawson, the editor of *The Times*, with a proposal that the newspaper be granted a monopoly of news on the discovery.[38] An arrangement of the same kind had been negotiated with the Royal Geographical Society for the coverage of the Everest Expedition of 1921, and it had worked well and much to the advantage of the R.G.S. Carnarvon and Gardiner went to see the Secretary of the R.G.S. who confirmed the success of the arrangement, and Carnarvon was left to ponder the matter while Gardiner journeyed to Egypt, carrying a long letter from Carnarvon to Carter in which he outlined what had been happening in recent weeks.[39]

In this letter Carnarvon touched on the possibility of the agreement with *The Times*. He had seen Sir Harry Perry Robinson, the newspaper's

37 Reported by Cyril Aldred, to whom the story was told by W. C. Hayes.
38 A. H. Gardiner, *My Working Years* (privately published, 1963), pp. 37ff.
39 Letter of 24 December in M.M.A., Department of Egyptian Art, Carter files.

chief foreign correspondent, and had explained 'that I could *not* give all news first to Times. He is writing to me about it after thinking it over.' Then there was the possibility of a contract with Pathé and others for a film: 'There is I imagine a good deal of money in this what I don't know possibly 10–20 thousand – but there are difficulties.' He advises Carter to reserve the best object for himself to paint; the result would be worth a lot. He writes of possible helpers, professional and amateur, of procedures for dealing with requests for photographs: 'Neither of us having much if any experience of Press sharks one is rather at a loss how to act for the best.' He already looks forward to publication, in which Gardiner would help. He returns finally to the problem of a *Times* monopoly. The R.G.S. had received £1000 for 15 long cables and there had been, according to the R.G.S., much Press grumbling: 'I think the Daily Mail would give more, but the Times is after all the first Newspaper in the world.'

It did not take long for Carnarvon to decide in favour of *The Times*, and an agreement was signed on 9 January 1923. He wrote to inform Carter on the next day, justifying his decision.[40] Any less tight an arrangement 'would make the matter too common and commercial.' Indeed, some sort of agreement seemed essential both to Carnarvon and Carter, not only for financial reasons, but also for practical purposes. Sadly it turned out to be a major blunder, alienating much of the world Press, and particularly the native Egyptian Press which at the time was sensitively jealous of the Egyptian nature of the find and the fact that it was being handled in all respects by foreigners. A taste of what might be in prospect was offered in a letter sent to Carter on 24 January by Engelbach, the Chief Inspector:[41]

I seem in this play to be between the upper and nether millstones. The journalists are asking for a definite statement as to whether they are to be admitted on the date arranged by Lacau and I have not been able to give a reply beyond general evasion – at which I am becoming tolerably expert.

I shall be therefore very grateful if you will let me have an early reply to the official letter as otherwise naturally the pressmen will turn up en masse on the day appointed.

In the meanwhile I am making a corner in all blunderbusses and rifles, etc. in the district, in case I have orders to storm the position and seriously think of asking for some high explosive to demolish that disgustingly strong door by means of which you have locked up the treasures of Egypt's ancestors.

If you see a ray of sunshine in this affair you might let me know, as I – like the hyaena in the old story, haven't much to laugh at.

40 In M.M.A., Department of Egyptian Art, Carter files. The text of *The Times* agreement is reproduced in Appendix IV.
41 In M.M.A., Department of Egyptian Art, Carter files.

This light-hearted attempt to solve one problem did not apparently go down well with Carter, and there is some evidence that he, with Carnarvon's help and possibly that of others like Gardiner and Breasted, tried to have Engelbach replaced by Tewfik Boulos.[42] Carter attempted to regularize a shaky situation by making Arthur Merton, the resident correspondent of *The Times*, an official member of his team; but matters did not improve, and press relations were to remain abysmally low for the whole season and subsequently.

The arrival of Arthur Weigall, Carter's former colleague and neighbour in Thebes, as special correspondent of the *Daily Mail*, led to a serious deterioration in general relations with the Press. Weigall may have expected a modest welcome in the Valley, but he found the opposite to be the case, and he entered whole-heartedly into the guerilla warfare practised by foreign reporters in their efforts to obtain 'copy' free from *The Times* embargo. He felt utterly frustrated, prevented, on what was once his territory, from doing what he considered to be a legitimate job. He had been ever ready to offer advice at length; he did not now hesitate to do so again. He wrote to Carter from the Winter Palace Hotel on 25 January,[43] claiming, probably disingenuously, that he wished:

> to keep out of this warfare which is going on and which looks like becoming a matter big enough seriously to damage British interests in Egypt. . . .
> The situation is this. You and Lord Carnarvon made the initial error when you discovered the tomb of thinking that the old British prestige in this country is still maintained and that you could do more or less what you liked, just as we all used to do in the old days. You have found this tomb, however, at a moment when the least spark may send the whole magazine sky-high, when the utmost diplomacy is needed, when Egyptians have to be considered in a way to which you and I are not accustomed, and when the slightest false step may do the utmost disservice to our own country. You opened the tomb before you notified the Government representative, and the natives all say that you may therefore have had the opportunity of stealing some of the millions of pounds' worth of gold of which you talked. (I give this as an instance of native gossip about you.) They say you have insulted their country, etc. etc., as you doubtless know. You two are being held up to execration of the most bitter kind and already before I left London I was told of the intense feeling which you had both aroused.

Weigall then attacks Carnarvon's sale of rights to *The Times*, and continues:

42 See an undated letter from Carnarvon to Carter in M.M.A., Department of Egyptian Art, Carter files, of late January 1923. Lacau found great difficulty in the proposal.
43 In M.M.A., Department of Egyptian Art, Carter files.

I do most earnestly beg you to do two things. Firstly, persuade Lord Carnarvon to declare publicly that he will not profit financially out of the contract with the 'Times', his expenses in the cause of science being so enormous. Next, show your workshop and its contents, as far as possible, to journalists so that they may tell the public what splendid work Lord Carnarvon is doing in preserving the objects found. And, thirdly, persuade him to give to every journalist, and particularly to native journalists, the bare facts, at least, on the day of the opening of the inner chamber, and *not* one day after the 'Times', which, from a newspaper point of view, would be the same as not at all.

He ends with a warning of what damage could be done to British standing in Egypt.

The group of international journalists which formed a cell of grumbling discontent behaved outrageously in bombarding the excavators with complaints and demands, in canvassing Lacau and the Antiquities Service to circumvent Carnarvon's arrangement with *The Times*, and in stimulating the Egyptian Press to feelings of outrage. There was certainly much justification for their attitude and behaviour, and it cannot be denied that a serious miscalculation had been made by Carnarvon. Little consideration, however, seems to have been given to the unreasonable nature of what the Press demanded, or to the priorities which determined the work in and around the tomb. It is not uncommon for people who are inexperienced in matters archaeological to misinterpret silence and caution for secrecy and inactivity. It is not in the nature of steady scientific work that those involved can readily satisfy the daily requirements of journalists. Weigall could casually talk of one-day-old news being no news at all, but he should have known better, and it was he who especially attracted the displeasure of Carter and his team. He too may have been largely responsible for the deterioration in relations between Carter and the World Press, and perhaps even with Lord Carnarvon, who had made the arrangement with *The Times* without seriously consulting Carter, and certainly without proper consideration of what the effects might be on the work. How easy now it is to see the faults in the arrangements, and the personal weaknesses of the individuals! No one could have foreseen what immense interest would be generated by the find. The comparison with the Everest Expedition provided, as it turned out, no guide at all to what in fact happened. And yet there had been a time when the Press seemed to have some comprehension of Carter's difficulties. On 19 January the report in the *Morning Post* by its own correspondent,[44] discussing life in Luxor around the discovery, states:

44 This report, on page 8 of the issue, was probably written by the American reporter A. H. Bradstreet, who principally represented the *New York Times*. He was to become the most vociferous of the critics of Carnarvon's *Times* agreement, and a serious opponent of the pro-Carter faction in 1924.

Let it be recorded that if there is any prize for patience and unfailing courtesy in the face of overwhelming aggravation it belongs to Mr. Howard Carter. . . . In spite of many approaches by friends and the famous, throughout it all he is merely politely firm. He has the happy faculty of being able to say 'No' without leaving a trace of ill-feeling.

Such sympathetic understanding did not survive the announcement of the monopoly agreement and Carnarvon's return to Luxor in late January. Arthur Mace notes developments as they were observed from within the excavators' camp:

[23 Jan.] The whole newspaper world is agog with our arrangement with the Times about news service, and all sorts of things are threatened. . . . It's a funny business on the whole, this. Weigall has arrived, to represent the Daily Mail, and is going to have rather an uncomfortable time, as noone is prepared to be cordial. Carter I know does'nt intend to let him see anything.

[26 Jan.] Things have got rather lively the last few days owing to Lord Carnarvon's agreement with The Times, which is much more drastic, now we have seen it, than we ever imagined. It has caused a perfect storm among the other newspapers and made complications of various sorts. . . . the atmosphere of Luxor is rather nerve-racking at present. The Winter Palace is a scream. Noone talks of anything but the tomb, newspaper men swarm, and you dare'nt say a word without looking around everywhere to see if anyone is listening. . . . However it is amusing. I can hold my tongue with anyone, and the reporters who tackled me did'nt get much for their pains. Among them was Weigall if you please – very fat and oily, and pretending to be a journalist only by accident so to speak.

Scarcely in second place as a source of aggravation to Carter and his team was the pressure from those who, from influence, position or social connection, felt they could qualify for a special visit to the tomb, or to the laboratory in the tomb of Sethos II, or even to both. The official visitors sent by the Government or Antiquities Service could not be turned away; those with introductions from the Earl of Carnarvon were equally well placed for special attention; there were those closely connected with the Metropolitan Museum who for good reasons were given favourable treatment. The diaries of Minnie Burton and Lindsley Hall are full of the names of important Americans, drawn to Luxor by the lure of Tutankhamun – the Mayor of New York (McClellan), Dr Morton Howell, American Minister to Egypt, Mr and Mrs Everett Macy, wealthy supporters of the museum. After Carnarvon's return to Luxor in late January the pace of social activity increased, and additional strain was put on Carter, who was in grave doubt over the wisdom of the agreement with *The Times*, and possibly also with Carnarvon's determination to pursue his claim for a share of the antiquities in the tomb. Again Mace is a sympathetic observer of the deterioration in relations:

[28 Jan., on the eve of Carnarvon's departure from Cairo]. . . . I fear from now on we shan't have so much quiet in our work tomb. It will take us all we know to restrain Carnarvon from plunging into things. Carter talks to him just like a naughty child.

[31 Jan.] Relations were a little strained today between Carnarvon and Carter, so I hope all will go well.

[2 Feb.] The Carnarvons are rather a nuisance. He potters about all day, and will talk and ask questions and waste one's time. Lady Carnarvon is not coming out. Lady Evelyn is rather an empty headed little thing I should think. She and Carter seem very thick.

[3 Feb.] Relations are much less strained now and we all lunch together.

[7 Feb.] Carter's nerves are giving out with all the worry, and he'll have a breakdown if he isn't careful, Carnarvon makes all sorts of complications by doing things without thinking of the consequences. The Times contract has landed us in all sorts of trouble.

[14 Feb.] This afternoon I had standing around watching me work an earl, a lady, a sir and two honourables. A beastly nuisance they are too, and I wish they'd keep away.

Tensions increased as the day approached when, with the Antechamber cleared, they could turn to the removal of the blocking between the two life-size figures guarding, as Carter and Carnarvon already knew, the entrance to the Burial Chamber. Remarkable results had been achieved by Carter and his exceptional team since the entry of the Antechamber on 27 November. After the closing of the tomb on 3 December to allow for the assembling of staff and materials, there was a break of two weeks before serious work could begin. And now, just a little less than two calendar months later, the tangled mass of material in the first chamber of the tomb had been unravelled and taken to the tomb of Sethos II. A careful plan of the chamber's lay-out had been started, and a comprehensive photographic record completed. In the laboratory tomb, many of the larger objects had been treated and prepared for transport to Cairo; many of the boxes had been unpacked and their contents unpicked and conserved. Much entertainment had been provided to the patient crowds which thronged the Valley, as plums were removed from the rich mixture of the tomb's contents, and carried carefully on open wooden trays to the Sethos tomb. Much frustration had been inflicted on the members of the

Press, and on those whose positions were substantial but influence insufficient to obtain them entry to the tomb. But much information had been published on a regular basis, and it was known by mid-February that soon the blocking would be breached. What would lie behind it? The public was full of anticipation; the Press representatives with anxiety lest they might not be the first with the news; the favoured great waited for the 'off', as if it were to be the 3.30 at Newbury; the excavators were highly charged. On 15 February Mace wrote to his wife:

> I hope tomorrow will go off all right, for everybody's nerves are on edge, and Carter is on the verge of a nervous breakdown I should say. He and Carnarvon are on edge with each other all the time. I shall be glad when it's over. It does seem funny to think that the whole world is on tip toe of excitement over what we are going to find when we take down the sealed door tomorrow,[45] and what a number of people in every country will be talking about it. I think the least excited people are ourselves, but that's I expect because there has been such a fuss and worry about everything that we're getting a bit tired of it. It is funny as you say to have a great fuss made all of a sudden over what one has been doing as a matter of course for twenty years.

Mace wrote in advance of the day of opening, and adopted the acceptably casual, even *blasé*, attitude which would at the time have been thought proper for one of his background and country. His next entry, written on the 17th, reveals the release of tension:

> Yesterday was the great day, and I was so dead with excitement and fatigue and talk that I hadn't time to write. I just rolled into bed and dropped straight off to sleep. It was a day and no mistake. . . .

45 In *The Tomb of Tut.ankh.Amen*, I, the date of the opening is given as Friday the 17th. This is a simple error; see p. 186 where the 17th is described as 'a day set apart for . . . Egyptologists'. The 16th is confirmed as the opening day by the diary entries of Minnie Burton and Lindsley Hall, as well as this quoted letter by Mace.

11

THE BURIAL CHAMBER AND DEATH

The excavation and clearance of Tutankhamun's tomb had developed, in the season of 1922–3, into a programme of set performances, almost theatrical in their staging, with previews and 'first nights', special performances and even 'command' performances. The viewings of the Antechamber after the initial opening in late November and after the reopening in late December were but trial runs for the entry into the Burial Chamber scheduled for 16 February. By now Luxor was crowded, the Valley of the Kings teemed with tourists, and the journalists, whipped into a frenzy of competitive enterprise by the demands of their editors and their disgust at the agreement with *The Times*, haunted the environs of the tomb, the laboratory tomb, Carter's house, the Metropolitan House, and the halls and corridors of the Winter Palace Hotel. It was generally known that once the Antechamber had been cleared, the blocked entrance between the guardian statues of the king would be breached. Speculation on what lay beyond was lively and uninformed; but all felt sure that whatever was there would not prove to be an anticlimax. The official account of the opening by Carter and Mace in the first volume of *The Tomb of Tut.ankh.A-men* is well known, and much quoted – the select gathering on 16 February, the preliminary speeches, the removal of the first blocks by Carter and Mace, the first glimpse of the outermost gilded shrine with blue faience plaques, the enlargement of the hole, and the viewing of the Burial Chamber and of the Treasury leading out of it, the wonder and glory of it all. Arthur Mace wrote another account, less formal and full of incidental details, a few days after the opening while he rested in the Cataract Hotel at Aswan. An extract may colourfully supplement what he later wrote for the volume:[1]

> In the first place, we scored a great triumph over the newspaper men. They for some reason had got it into their heads that we were going to make a secret opening without any representative of the Government being present, so for three or four days they hardly left

1 In the Mace Papers in the possession of Margaret Orr.

the tomb. On the Friday they had no idea anything was up. We fixed it for the afternoon so that the tourists would be out of the way. Sir William Garstin and two or three others came to join our lunch party, but they came straight, so were not seen arriving. After lunch we met by appointment Lacau, Engelbach, Lythgoe, Winlock and two or three native officials, and then we all went in a party to the tomb. The correspondents keeping their vigil above the tomb saw all of a sudden the procession arrive from nowhere, and of course realized what it meant, but too late to make any special arrangements for sending messages off . . . The tomb looked as though set for a stage scene. We had put up boarding to protect the statues which stood on either side of the sealed doorway, and made a small stage to enable us to attack the upper part of the sealing, thinking it was safest to work from the top downwards. A little way back was a barrier, and behind that chairs for the visitors, as it was likely to be a long job . . . Carter mounted the stage, stripped to trousers and vest and struck the first blow with hammer and chisel . . . At this point he asked me to come up and help him, and the rest of the clearing we did together. It was an odd sensation standing on the stage and gradually widening the hole, you could feel the spectators behind the barrier just tingling with excitement . . . I don't seem to have shown much excitement myself, for I heard Lacau say to some-one 'M. Mace est toujours calme'. The order of proceedings was this. Carter with chisel and crowbar eased the stones loose one by one: I held them as he did so to prevent their falling in, and then lifted them out and passed them back to Callender, who passed them on to a native, and then up a chain of men in the passage to get them clear of the tomb. It took nearly two hours altogether, and we must have been sights by the time it was over, dirty, dishevelled and perspiring.

When the hole was large enough Carter entered the Burial Chamber for a preliminary inspection, and then the assembled guests went in, Carnarvon and Lacau first, then Lady Evelyn Herbert and Sir William Garstin, then the others two by two. They could just squeeze between the wall and the side of the great outer shrine, look through its open doors at the second, sealed, shrine within; see the alabaster vessels and other objects on the floor and the linen pall, 'spangled with gold stars', drooping above. They could see into the further room, and marvel at the wonderful gilded Canopic shrine with the figures of the four protective goddesses: 'For modelling I really think they beat anything I have ever seen from any country.' As people came out, 'It was curious to watch them . . . With hardly an exception each person "threw up his hands and gasped".'

Mervyn Herbert, usually rather dismissive in his comments on things, was bowled over:[2]

> It is difficult after five minutes to remember details clearly – all the same I think I kept a pretty definite picture of what I saw. The jackal at the entrance the marvellous gold shrine the figures at the sides opposite the door in between boxes, boats and every sort of thing – I have got the picture in my mind very well, tho' I could not draw it – and after one went out people kept asking, did you see so and so? No, it was maddening, somehow one had just missed *that* detail – However I suppose this sort of thing happens to everybody.

The party left the tomb after five o'clock. 'I think we were all fairly dazed, too dazed to realize what we had found,' said Mace. Carter took the Carnarvon party off to his house for tea, and in the evening he dined at the Metropolitan House. Mace commented:

> We were all more or less like crazy people. The excitement had been too much for us, and I'm sure anyone coming in would have said we had all been taking too much to drink.

Minnie Burton also remarked, 'Very interesting talk.' She was in her element with the influx of the great, the powerful, and, especially, the royalty and the quality. She had a private view of the Burial Chamber on the following day along with others from the Metropolitan House, and then on Sunday she was included in the group invited for what was considered the official opening. pride of place was taken by Élisabeth, Queen of the Belgians, who had travelled to Egypt particularly to visit the tomb. She was accompanied by her son Prince Léopold, and attended on this occasion by Lord Allenby, the High Commissioner. Her visit was grandly arranged by the authorities, and attended by considerable cere-mony. Minnie Burton writes one of her longest entries for the day:

> Lunch at 11.30. The Macys here. Afterwards I walked to the Valley for the official opening with Mr. Hauser, Mr. Hall and Mr. Bull. Very hot with fresh breeze. Long wait for the Allenbys and the Queen of the Belgians and Prince Leopold. The Macys went after the Allenbys. Cold buffet up near Seti II. Lady Evelyn received. The Maudseleys, Thomases, Miss Putnam, Thompsons, Hetheringtons, Drs. Breasted, Capart, Allan [sic] Gardiner, the Daviesas, Mertons etc. Drove home with the Macys. Everybody dead tired.

It was on this occasion that General Sir John Maxwell, an old friend of Carnarvon's, and subsequently President of the Egypt Exploration Society, ran into difficulties. Mervyn Herbert described how 'he got stuck, poor

2 Mervyn Herbert Journal, fol. 373f.

old fellow, and it took four men pushing and pulling to get him out again, which was eventually done with a noise like a champagne cork and with injury to what he wrongly described as his chest.'[3]

Three days later Minnie Burton took her special friend the Contessa to see the tomb. 'Had a row with Mr. Carter! He was very rude.' It may be suspected that she had been over-taxing Carter's readiness to spend time with people introduced by someone like her, wife of his most useful photographer, Harry Burton, whom he would not normally have wished to offend. The day had its compensations for her later:

> Got back in time to change for lunch. The Queen of the Belgians, Prince Leopold ... lunched here. Afterwards the Queen and Ctess C. lay down for an hour and then all went off to the Valley. Mr. Hauser, Hall, Wilkinson, Bull and Frances [Winlock] lunched on the sunporch and came in afterwards to be presented.

This rather more informal, but necessarily demanding, visit by the Queen was the second of four she was to make to the Valley, visits which became increasingly irksome for Carter and his staff. Mace noted the occasions:

> [21 Feb.] The Queen of the Belgians came and spent a long time going over everything in our laboratory, She's embarrassingly keen on everything, proposes to come over again on Sunday to see us open a box. The prince is rather bored with the proceedings, and glad to get away for a quiet chat and a cigarette.

> [25 Feb.] I dodged the Queen this afternoon. She wanted to see a box unpacked, and that I simply would not do for anyone.

> [9 March] Queen of the Belgians today to see a box opened [persistence clearly paid]. We picked out a very dull one in which no harm could possibly be done. To tell you the truth we are all getting very bored with her. This was her fourth visit to us, and she stayed till twenty past five. Royalties haven't much consideration for other folk.

Boring it may have been, but Mace and his colleagues were not to know that the discovery and no doubt their courtesy to the Queen helped towards the establishment later in 1923 of the Fondation Égyptologique Reine Élisabeth.[4] It was the conception of Jean Capart, the distinguished Belgian Egyptologist, who accompanied the Queen on her Egyptian travels and who in 1925 became Director of the Musées Royaux du Cinquantenaire in Brussels. The Fondation with its splendid library, subsequently became one of the leading centres of Egyptological research in Europe, and con-

3 *Ibid.*, fol. 372.
4 See A. Mekhitarian, in *Liber Memorialis 1835–1985* (Brussels, 1985), p. 187ff.

tinues to occupy an important position in the world-wide organization of Egyptian studies.

By the time of the Queen's fourth visit the tomb itself had been closed for the season. It was high time for a break. Since the discovery in November, Carter had been under constant pressure, a pressure which had intensified as time went on. The archaeological work alone would have been more than enough to tax the endurance of any ordinary excavator; but added to that unavoidable responsibility had been the problems caused by visitors and the Press. Delicate work on fragile objects requires conditions of calm with extended periods of time uninterrupted by distractions from outside. To a substantial extent such conditions had been secured for Lucas and Mace in the tomb of Sethos II, but even there they were not free from the importunities of well intentioned visitors, eager to obtain that closer look at a treasure than might be possible in the tomb itself. Carter, on the other hand, bore the brunt of the public assaults and at the same time had to satisfy the constant requirements of his patron. Carnarvon was just about helpless; he had no apparent role to play in the clearing of the Antechamber. He was exposed to the attentions and expectancies of many friends and acquaintances, of important visitors with introductions, and of others who were prepared to impose on his good nature. The tomb of Tutankhamun had become in a sense his estate in Egypt, and his duty was to conduct people around it. He and his daughter were trapped by their social upbringing. Additionally, he was burdened with the difficulties resulting from his contract with *The Times*; he might brush these off on to Carter and Merton, but he could not wholly escape them himself. Mervyn Herbert writes a characteristically impatient account of the atmosphere engendered by the hunt for news:[5]

> Porch [i.e. Porchester], I think, had a very worrying time at Luxor – not that he disliked it all; some of it amused him quite a lot – *But* the journalists were beyond belief. The prince of swine was of course Weigall – who is only satisfactory in one way; he looks as complete a cad as he is – in the hotel where we all stayed there were the 2 groups of journalists, the sheep and the goats. The principal of the sheep was physically like one – Sir H. Robinson – who was sent by the Times to do their will and to help Porch – a good old fellow but not very competent. Weigall and the rest were unutterable – they spied and lied and calumniated as I have not seen it done yet . . .
>
> The last I saw of the old fellow was in the hall of the Winter Palace Hotel talking to Maxwell and Merton, the Times correspondent and others. I had said goodbye more than once. Maxwell said to me that

5 Mervyn Herbert Journal, fol. 376f. The familiar Porch (short for Porchester) had remained the name by which the Earl of Carnarvon had been best known since he had become Lord Porchester, as the son and heir of his father, the 4th Earl.

Porch ought to go to Assouan, as he needed a rest. I agreed that he was tired altho' I don't think more so than was reasonably to be expected – poor old fellow.

Arthur Weigall was for many the one who had let down the side. His position was wretched. He had returned to Luxor unloved and unwanted. Any credit he might have expected for his work in the past in the Theban Necropolis was negated by what was seen as desertion to the ranks of the unprincipled Press. It would not have been impossible for him to have carried out a perfectly decent campaign of reporting, at second hand it must be admitted, but possessing so much more specialist background and archaeological flair than any other journalist. Sadly he felt rebuffed, and he exacted his revenge on former colleagues (even friends) by participating in, if not actually initiating, a campaign of hostile reporting in which scant credit was given to the excavators. It was a sour sequel to what had been a career of considerable achievement and even greater promise. The letter he had written to Alan Gardiner in the heady days of Theban activity[6] expressed his views on the capabilities of his Egyptological colleagues; he liked Carnarvon, as he had once said to Griffith, but disdained his intentions and methods;[7] he probably at that time did not even consider Carter to be more than a competent field-worker, but with little intellectual capacity. And here Weigall now was, in Thebes again, with Carnarvon and Carter in the ascendancy. He knew better than most how chancy archaeological discovery was; he also knew how chancy was the public success resulting from such discovery. That Carter was making such a good show of his achievement may have come as a surprise to him. Nevertheless, the situation Weigall found himself in was false, and his sharp, inquiring intelligence reacted poorly. He was obliged to ally himself with the hostile representatives of the newspapers, with whom he could take some malicious pleasure in discomforting the excavators.

The dramatic opening of the Burial Chamber, and the many visits which followed, provided a suitable climax to the 1922–3 season. It also offered an excellent moment to stop the work in the tomb itself. The strains of life in the field have been mentioned earlier. Even in good conditions, with a comfortable base and with successful work, the tensions develop after a couple of months of daily field intercourse. Normally in the past Carter had dug from January to March, following up with time spent closing down, arranging the consequences of the season, visiting dealers, etc. This year had been very different. He had started early to escape the crowds of tourists in the Valley of the Kings; he had found success immediately, and had been in the field, with only short breaks for essential visits to Cairo, for almost four months. There remained much to do, but everyone

6 See p. 156 above.
7 See p. 139 above.

was ready for a break. Mace caught the spirit well, writing on 22 February to his wife. It happened to be his daughter Margaret's birthday:

> Things are impossible in the Valley these days. It is one constant stream of visitors from morning to night. We have come to the conclusion the only thing to do is to fill up the tomb, lock up our laboratory, and simply all run away for three or four days. That will make a break, and then perhaps we shall be able to start fresh. So next week I may get in my long talked of visit to Assouan after all. Its quite time Carter got away; he's a nervous wreck.

The tomb was shut and filled in on 26 February and the laboratory closed up the next day. On the 28th Arthur Mace went off to Aswan as Carnarvon's guest. He had hoped that others might have joined the holiday party, but there were different priorities:[8]

> Lucas has gone off to Cairo tonight, and Callender is going to Armant to see how his farm is getting on. Carter is going to shut himself into his house and get rest and quiet that way.

It was wise that they all went their different ways. Mace in advance of his holiday felt slightly trapped at the thought of being 'tête-a-tête with Carnarvon' for several days. In the event he greatly enjoyed the break, and was not too dominated by Carnarvon, who had his daughter and Sir Charles Cust, an equerry of King George V and an old friend, with him. They sailed on the river, visited the tombs at Qubbet el-Hawa, the unfinished obelisk, and the Aswan Dam. Mace had an opportunity of assessing Carnarvon away from the bustle of Luxor: 'a queer fish, but in spite of his oddities very lovable. He and Lady Evelyn are devoted to each other. She is somewhat spoilt and a bit slangy, but there is a lot of good stuff in her.'[9]

Mace, whose health was at this time always uncertain, told his wife, Winifred, after he returned to Luxor: 'They all say I look ever so much better for my holiday, and I certainly feel so.' One may hope that Carnarvon also came back refreshed to continue the trials over the tomb. Much had been made of the difficulties which occurred in his relations with Carter, and there is no doubt that the problems of the season upset their close and good friendship, and tested their loyalties to breaking point. Charles Breasted, who had been in Luxor for the opening of the Burial Chamber with his father, James Henry Breasted, retells to his biography of his father[10] how the strain between Carnarvon and Carter developed to such an extent that 'bitter words were exchanged, and in anger Carter requested his old friend to leave his house and never to enter it again.'

8 Letter to his wife, dated 27 February.
9 Letter to his wife of 4 March.
10 C. Breasted, *Pioneer of the Past* (London, 1948), p. 347.

He supports his account by quoting, as it is presented, what his father had written on 12 March. The letter of that date, from James Breasted to Charles, which presumably was his source, is not so explicit. James Breasted wrote:[11]

> While I was there after the opening, Carter asked me to his house were we had a long talk. He then formally asked me to do the historical work on the tomb for the final publication, promising to write me a letter covering the arrangement in a few days. It would take far too long to try to tell you of the painful situation which then developed, resulting in such strained relations between Carter and Carnarvon that a complete break seemed inevitable. Gardiner and I however, succeeded in pouring oil on the waters, but we both fell from Carter's good grace. He is not by any means wholly or even in a great degree to blame. The man has made a marvellous discovery and then been obliged to carry on the most difficult archaeological work and run a ceaseless social function at the same time, and it has broken him down.

There is nothing in this letter about the row which led to Carter's denying his house to Carnarvon and, indeed, there are many verbal differences between the original text and the parts quoted by Charles Breasted. There is no hint of such a serious row in the daily reports written by Arthur Mace, or in the gossipy diaries of Minnie Burton and Lindsley Hall. Carnarvon had, however, written Carter a mollifying letter dated only 'Friday evening', but probably to be fixed as 23 February, that is one week after the opening of the Burial Chamber:[12]

> I have been feeling very unhappy today, and I did not know what to think or do, and then I saw Eve and she told me everything. I have no doubt that I have done many foolish things and I am very sorry. I suppose the fuss and worry have affected me but there is only one thing I want to say to you which I hope you will always remember – whatever your feelings are or will be for me in the future my affection for you will never change.
>
> I'm a man with few friends and whatever happens nothing will ever alter my feelings for you. There is always so much noise and lack of quiet and privacy in the Valley that I felt I should never see you alone altho' I should like to very much and have a good talk because of that I could not rest until I had written you.

Here is no letter written by someone who felt that he had a genuine grievance against the man who was essentially his employee. It is magnanimous in tone, and at the same time somewhat shame-faced. The mention

11 The letter is filed in O.I. Archives, Breasted Papers, Source Materials 1921–4.
12 M.M.A., Department of Egyptian Art, Carter files.

of Evelyn has suggested to some that the cause of the difference was a supposed 'affair' between her and Carter.[13] For such there is no real evidence, even if Mace had thought the two to be 'very thick'. Lady Evelyn had known Carter, presumably, since his first association with her father. There had been regular visits to Highclere over the years. Apart from her father, Carter was her principal point of contact in Luxor, and she would have naturally turned to him when she had nothing better to do. Their relationship was surely as close as one would expect between old friends, but not therefore necessarily to be taken as intimate. A clue to the matter of Lady Evelyn's being mentioned in Carnarvon's letter may be found in a note of Evelyn herself written to Carter on the 22nd, probably the day before. It confirms the close relationship between her and Carter, although its affectionate tone should not be mistaken for more than the natural effusion of a young lady, a 'bit slangy' in Mace's words, concerned for the health of her father's close associate:[14]

I am so terribly sorry to hear that you have been taken seedy with your tummy out of order. I wish I had been with you to look after you dear – for you know how I fancy myself at nursing!

Anyhow I am popping over tomorrow just to have a glimpse of you and shall come very early so as to avoid all the 'ducks' and shall call at your house lest you shouldn't have already gone up.

Poor Marcelle [her maid] has been very seedy but I pray the worst is over now,

Bless you dearest Howard

Eve

It may be presumed that she called on Carter on the 23rd and subsequently spoke to her father about Carter's sickness – a case probably of 'Gippy tummy' – and of his problems which had made difficulties between him and Carnarvon. There was quite enough in Luxor in 1923 to upset the mutual regard which had for so long existed between Carnarvon and Carter. In response to Eve's intervention Carnarvon wrote his generous letter. There is no surviving answer from Carter, and indeed, being a man of such uncertain temper and generally unforgiving nature, he may not have felt it possible to answer equally generously at this time. It is not surprising that he did not choose to take his holiday in Aswan with Mace and Carnarvon, but preferred to shut himself up at home to lick his wounds and contemplate the future.

After the holiday, Carter's plan agreed with Carnarvon was to continue work on the objects from the Antechamber which were in the store-room and in the laboratory. The tomb of Sethos II was the power-house of the

13 T. Hoving, *Tutankhamun. The Untold Story* (New York, 1978), p. 222.
14 M.M.A., Department of Egyptian Art, Carter files.

excavation, the place about which, after a good day, Mace could write,[15] 'for the first time for weeks we had a clear day without any visitors, so I got through a nice lot of work.' Here the objects were brought after they had been numbered, photographed, and initial record cards written. The numbering was quite a problem because of the packed boxes and other groups of objects which could not easily be disentangled before removal. The system devised by Carter seems complicated, and indeed is confusing for those who do not try to understand the reasons behind the use of figures and letters.[16] It has nevertheless proved invaluable as a scheme of identification and reference, and it demonstrates in one more way Carter's remarkable organizational ability. The practical documentation of the tomb and its contents represents a triumph of archaeological percipience and, ultimately, of dedication. The records, in various categories of detail and emphasis – purely Egyptological, epigraphic, physical, scientific, technical, artistic – remain a massive compilation of information ready for mining by interested scholars, and waiting to be used for serious publication. The record cards and associated papers contain innumerable sketches by Carter illustrating details and elucidating points of construction and arrangement. There are Mace's notes on his delicate conservation work, the painstaking results of Lucas's scientific work on material and technical matters. The initial considerations and comments of an excavator and his team are always valuable; things are seen in the course of excavation which, if not noted at the time, are lost for ever. One of the greatest merits of the Tutankhamun documentation is its immediacy.

Most of the noting and commenting took place in the tomb itself and in the laboratory, and it was in the laboratory that Carter hoped that much of the groundwork of cleaning, conservation and preparation for scientific publication would take place in the weeks after the closing of the tomb. And there also the objects, after going through the various stages of study, were to be packed ready for transport to Cairo and the Egyptian Museum. At this point there had been no serious consideration of any ultimate division of the material between the Museum and Carnarvon. It is almost certainly the case that Carter himself favoured the retention of everything, apart from clear duplicates, by the Museum, but his opinion could not take precedence over that of the Earl of Carnarvon. Whatever were to happen, however, there would be no escaping the sending of everything that was ready for dispatch to Cairo.

For the moment Carnarvon and his daughter remained in Luxor. Lady Evelyn was much taken up with the health of her maid who had been operated on suddenly for appendicitis a day or two after the opening of the Burial Chamber.[17] When Marcelle was fit to travel on about 11 March,

15 Letter to his wife dated 7 March.
16 Conveniently explained in N. Reeves, *The Complete Tutankhamun* (London, 1990), pp. 60f.
17 Reported by Mace in his letters of 20 February and 10 March.

Evelyn took her down to Cairo and shipped her off to England, she herself staying in Cairo to wait for her father. He continued to haunt the activities of the team. On 8 March commented: 'Carnarvon and Bethell kind of moon around, so I gave the latter a job today, arranging the pendants of a collar, which will keep him out of mischief for a long time.' The Hon. Richard Bethell, son of the 3rd Baron Westbury, was actively interested in Egyptology, had a collection of antiquities, and was at the time a member of the committee of the Egypt Exploration Society. It may be remembered that he was involved with Carter and Newberry in the fiasco over the sale of the MacGregor collection in 1921.[18] He had offered his services to the Earl of Carnarvon and had joined him in early February, ostensibly to act as his secretary. At this point he was principally a useful companion, a kind of aide-de-camp for the Tutankhamun campaign.

Very shortly Richard Bethell would find himself sadly in a position from which his support for Carnarvon, and even more for Lady Evelyn Herbert, would be crucial. On 14 March he and Carnarvon left Luxor for Cairo, with a first intention of taking up with Lacau matters concerning future work on the tomb and the question of division. Those left at Luxor were rather relieved. Not only was a cause of irritation removed but also, as Mace explained to his wife:[19] 'we have the use of the car again – rather a good thing now it is getting warmer, as the road to the valley is a regular sun trap.' Events moved forward with the slow inevitability of a Greek tragedy, to be viewed from the distance of nearly seventy years as forming a proper and inexorable dénouement to a season of high drama and sour comedy. Alan Gardiner spoke of the sad beginnings of Carnarvon's illness:[20]

> He might, perhaps have recovered from the mosquito bite which he got in Luxor if he had taken better care of himself. Disregarding the doctor's advice he came down to Cairo and invited me to dine with him at the Mohammed Ali Club. He expressed himself very tired and despondent but insisted on going to a film. There he said that his face was hurting him and I begged him to go back to his hotel, the Continental. But no, he would see the film to a finish and he was never out of doors again.

The first inkling of the seriousness of his condition reached Luxor in a letter written by Lady Evelyn Herbert to Carter on 18 March:[21]

> Pups asked me to write you to say that Lacau is laid up with influenza so is hors de combat and what is much more important is the old Man is very *very* seedy himself and incapable of doing any-

18 See p. 209 above.
19 Letter to his wife of 15 March.
20 A. H. Gardiner, *My Working Yers* (privately published, 1963), p. 40.
21 In M.M.A., Department of Egyptian Art, Carter files.

thing. You know that mosquito bite on his cheek that was worrying him at Luxor, well yesterday quite suddenly all the glands in his neck started swelling and last night he had a high temperature and still has today. He feels just *too* rotten for words. I have got Fletcher Barrett looking after him and I think he is very competent, but oh! the worry of it all and I just can't bear seeing him really seedy. However there it is. I've made a point of making rather light of it to most people as I don't want an exaggerated account in the papers. Of course they may never get hold of it at all but since you've all become celebrities I feel there is nothing one does or think that they don't know! But I like *you* knowing exactly what's happening to us. We miss you and I wish Dear you were here.

I will let you know how he goes on

with our fond love

Eve

Even before he could have received this letter Evelyn sent a telegram (on the 19th) saying that her father was very ill, that she was seriously alarmed, and had wired for Lady Carnarvon. Mace noted in his daily bulletin:

Carter is going down to Cairo tomorrow to be of any assistance he can. I hope it's not really serious for I like the man. Moreover, it would make rather a serious complication in our work. It's a nuisance Carter having to go too, for we were really getting ahead with the work with four of us plugging at it.

It is interesting to note how everyone close to Carnarvon felt it necessary to keep Carter informed, which reinforces the idea that relations between him and Carnarvon were not as critical as has sometimes been claimed. Richard Bethell wrote to him also on the 19th from Shepheard's Hotel with the bad news, and adding,[22] 'My wife and I are moving to the Continental to be near Eve and if he does not get better we will cancel our passage for she must have someone to look after her.' Albert Lythgoe similarly wrote on 20 March, the very day when Carter left Luxor for Cairo. The course of Carnarvon's illness – which progressed from blood poisoning to pneumonia – did, as Lady Evelyn feared, become known, and daily bulletins were reported in the newspapers. There were times when it looked as if he might pull through, but his constitution had no recuperative reserves. Alan Gardiner, who was still in Cairo working on Middle-Kingdom Coffin Texts in the Cairo Museum, saw much of Carnarvon during the days of trial and false hope. On 1 April he wrote to his wife:[23]

22 Bethell's letter in M.M.A., Department of Egyptian Art, Carter files, is dated 'Monday' only. Hoving in *Tutankhamun. The Untold Story*, p. 224, erroneously makes this the 26th, but by that date Carter had already been in Cairo nearly a week.
23 Quoted by Margaret Gardiner in her *A Scatter of Memories* (London, 1988), pp. 107f.

I saw him on Tuesday for five minutes, and on Wednesday came his relapse. I have just come back from seeing Evelyn; it has been a bad day and he had a terrible crisis just before six o'clock this evening, I was quite miserable about it . . . why am I so fond of him? And that poor little girl nearly breaks my heart with her devotion. There she sits, day and night, tired out and waits ready to run to him. And in just an agony of apprehension and anxiety. The crisis must come in a short time now. . . . He wanted to see me last night, but of course they wouldn't let me. I do so want him to pull through.

Death came in the early hours of 5 April. Carter had been in Cairo throughout the time of crisis. He had hoped to have been able to return to Luxor after Lady Carnarvon's arrival on 26 March, but Carnarvon's variable condition and Lady Carnarvon's distracted behaviour had obliged him to stay to the end, and even until after the body left Cairo on 14 April for burial at Highclere. In the meanwhile he spent some of his time visiting Lindsley Hall at the Mena House Hotel where he was completing the drawing of the Antechamber on which he and Walter Hauser had worked in January.[24] Carter also pursued his occasional activity as antiquities agent, noting in his diary on 31 March that he received £E200 in commission for the sale of two papyri to the Metropolitan Museum.[25] No expression of what he felt on the death of his patron has survived. When he returned to Luxor on 16 April Mace noted that he was 'looking rather tired and washed out. He must have had an awful time.' For him the return to work was the tonic he needed. He was astonished at how much had been accomplished since he left; but he had been away for almost four weeks.

Howard Carter's partnership with the Earl of Carnarvon – for so their relationship by the end could be described – had lasted for fourteen years. It had developed from a beginning of employer-employee nature, through the more relaxed stage of patron-client, in which mutual respect sustained the connection, to one of true friendship. Carnarvon himself had declared that he had few friends, and the same was certainly the case with Carter. It would be a mistake to pretend that this friendship had not been put under truly testing strains during the preceding months, but the indications seem to have been that both had come to appreciate their mutual dependence, and that the lessons of the many differences that had arisen in the hot-house conditions of the Valley of the Kings had been learned. Carnarvon's death removed the most stable prop of the few that supported Carter in the greatest triumph and most serious crisis of his life. His personal loss would be especially felt in the coming year. For the moment he must

24 The meetings are recorded in Hall's diary on 23 and 31 March, 3, 6 and 10 April.
25 This diary is in G.I. Carter archive.

have thought that all the burdens of the expedition and its related activities now rested firmly and solely on his shoulders.

It would emerge that he was not truly on his own. In principle Lord Carnarvon's widow, Almina, would assume responsibility for the work in Egypt, and she had strong and knowledgeable support from Sir John Maxwell, one of Carnarvon's executors. But Carter would no longer enjoy the close association with one who was not only employer but real partner in interests, one who was prepared to engage in the daily problems of excavation (often, it must be admitted, to Carter's chagrin), who enjoyed the hunt after and acquisition of beautiful antiquities, one of the few with whom he felt at ease. In practical terms Carter would lose the material advantages of close association with an old-fashioned British grandee, the entrée to a level of society which he had come to enjoy, even to accept as his favoured milieu. As it happened, the fame he had now acquired from the discovery of Tutankhamun's tomb would make even more doors open for him. But most of the new relationships would be occasional and without meaning. The extended visits to Highclere Castle, where for a time he would still be needed, would never again be of the same quality. Mace and Gardiner had both used the word 'lovable' about Carnarvon; and others who knew him on more than a casual basis found great attraction beneath the grand manner. It can only be supposed that Carter must have felt even more strongly attached to his old patron and friend; his personal loss was almost beyond measure.

For the weeks following his return to Thebes Carter was fully occupied with the concluding work of the season, the completion of conservation on objects to be sent to Cairo, the preparation for closing down, the arrangements for security – all activities which came naturally to him; they represented the common end-of-season archaeological tasks, but now the degree of intensity was far greater. Mistakes could not be made. He still had with him Mace, Burton, Lucas and Callender. The Egyptian workmen were paid off within a few days.[26] Most of the other members of the Metropolitan Museum Egyptian Expedition left the house that had been such a centre of excitement and social activity throughout the winter. Burton, with difficulty it seems, persuaded his wife Minnie to leave by 23 April, much to Arthur Mace's relief. After a relatively cool spell of weather great heat had returned to Luxor, and determined Carter not to try to complete all outstanding work before finally closing down. Mace commented on 26 April, 'today it must have been well over 100 in the shade. One thing is it is making Carter modify his ideas. His one wish now is to get away as soon as possible.' In early May Lucas left, and shortly afterwards, on the 6th, Burton. They all missed the memorial service to Carnar-

26 The details of the end of season activities are mostly recorded in Mace's letters to his wife.

von which was held in Cairo on 30 April,[27] two days after his burial on Beacon Hill on the Highclere estate. Mace moved into Carter's house for the last few weeks, and there could more easily continue to work on the writing of the first volume of *The Tomb of Tut.ankh.Amen*. Mace first noted their plans, writing to Winifred on 24 April:

> Spent the morning at Carter's house working on publication matters with him. He and I are trying to get a small popular book written to hand in to the publishers when we get home. I've done the first chapter and most of the second, and today he was dictating to me his account of the actual discovery of the tomb. I think it should make an interesting little book with plenty of illustrations, and if we get it out quick enough ought to sell like anything.

And on the 28th, contemplating his move into Castle Carter:

> It is about five degrees cooler than this [the Metropolitan House], as it is on open desert just near the entrance to the Valley. It will be convenient too, as we can get on with the book in the evenings. I have got about five thousand words of it done now, out of about thirty thousand that I have in mind.

Packing continued until mid-May. It was not an easy task; cases had to be built to accommodate awkward and fragile objects. The actual packing was a nerve-racking process, although two more experienced and accomplished handlers of delicate antiquities than Carter and Mace would have been difficult to find. A steamer was to take the cases to Cairo, and the cases were to be transported to the river on Décauville-rail trucks – possibly some of the very trucks used in the clearance of the Deir el-Bahri temple during the 1890s when Carter worked with Naville. The little railway would provide a smoother ride over the rocky trail out of the Valley, as it was in those days. But with insufficient track for the distance of several miles it was necessary to move the laden trucks in stages, transferring track from back to front as the slow convoy advanced. On 14 May, as Carter records in his diary, '34 cases containing 89 boxes started at sunrise and arrived midway of Canal bank 6 pm'; on 15th, 'Restarted sunrise and placed boxes on board boat at 10am in the presence of mamour, Engelbach and others ready for down river trip to Cairo – to start following morning.' Carter himself left Luxor on 19 May in time to meet the steamer when it berthed at Cooks wharf in Cairo on the 21st. On the following three days the cases were transported to the Museum, unpacked, and the objects placed on display. One may now wonder at the apparent simplicity of the operation.

Towards the end of the season in Luxor Carter had other things on his

27 So noted by Minnie Burton in her diary.

mind, in particular the future of the work on the tomb. On 1 May he wrote to Lady Carnarvon:[28]

> I have been thinking of you and all, these days and I do so hope for your dear sake such sad and trying ordeals which you must have suffered are now fast diminishing, and too, I trust all went well [i.e. the funeral].
>
> The call of the work here still to be got through – the heat appalling these last days – made me decide not to go down to Cairo for the memorial service. I felt that under the conditions that if we had a restful and tranquil day to ourselves we should be doing our real duty – I arranged that we were represented in Cairo. . . .
>
> I found Lacau in Luxor when I returned from Cairo. He called here (18th inst.) and we had a long conversation. His visit and conversation was to the effect that he was in perfect agreement and harmony as to the continuation of the work of the tomb of Tut.ankh.-amen – hence my letter to him, copy enclosed,[29] written in accordance with his wish. But in regard to the concession itself i.e. further exploration in the valley, he said the Egyptian Government would look upon that part of the concession as ceasing with poor Lord C's death. This point of view with regard to the actual continuance of the permit for further exploration in the site beyond the completion of the present discovery is in harmony, I think, with all your views, and it is normal under such circumstances, especially as the permit was given in virtue of Lord C. himself, even though the condition was that I carried out the actual work. I should add that I also asked him if there would be an objection on the part of the Government in the event of my wishing to carry on the excavation. He assured me that there would be none provided I attached myself for the purpose to some scientific body. He further added that in any case he would take no action in such a matter without first consulting me – in other words reserve the concession.

He wrote in similar vein to Albert Lythgoe on 6 May, adding comments on the excellent work his colleagues were performing on the objects.[30] He particularly praised Burton who had left that day,

> having completed his section of the recording in a splendid and admirable manner. In fact I do not know how to praise his work sufficiently. He had a colossal task which he carried out to the end

28 A rough draft of this letter is in M.M.A., Department of Egyptian Art, Carter files; there is also a copy of the final version starting from the paragraph beginning 'I found Lacau . . .'.

29 A letter which is almost certainly the one referred to here, is mentioned on p. 272 below.

30 In M.M.A., Department of Egyptian Art, Carter files.

in the most efficient manner possible, and I should like to convey
through you my most sincere gratitude to your trustees and Director
for his good aid.

A letter from Sir John Maxwell, who as Carnarvon's executor was giving
much help and advice to the family, informed Carter of recent developments in England, some of which would require Carter's attention on his
return:[31] 'Everything since Her Ladyship returned has, I believe gone off
without a hitch. She is quite calm and collected and there has been no
contretemps.' He describes an unfortunate brush with a press photographer
on Beacon Hill and continues on Carnarvon's collection: 'The collection
at Highclere passes to Almina and I think she intends to move it to
Seamore Place, but not yet.' After mentioning potential difficulties over
the estate generally, he informs Carter: 'I am urging that the arrangement
with the Times should not be renewed until you have had your say, and
this view will I think be accepted.'

As the time approached for his return to England, Carter was faced
with problems and potential problems of such a diversity as he had never
previously encountered. The exceptional discovery had generated exceptional expectations, and he was exposed to a variety of duties and demands
which would not cease with his leaving Egypt. Apart from the organizational, archaeological and bureaucratic necessities of his work, he had
become the target of an increasing deluge of mail from well-wishers, oppor-
tunists, scroungers, and even a few legitimate enquirers. Arthur Mace
helped him with the sifting of the daily flood, but there was no way in
which most of the letters could even be acknowledged.[32] Miss Christine
Walls of Sydney, Australia, sent one shilling for a 'relic of ancient times';
Louis Silverstein of New York wanted his autograph; Miss Fred Etter of
Alamosa, Colorado, offered to sell him a piece of the first Atlantic cable;
Mrs M. Piper of Liverpool more modestly asked for a little sand from near
the tomb, or a photograph; Miss Lilian Pharaoh of Southsea wondered
about her name; Kh. Nizam el-Moulk from Paris revealed himself as
having formerly been the Emperor Tut-ank-Hamon; Luke Mahon, aged 6,
of Ahascragh, Ireland, sent best wishes in a home-made card with Egyptian
motifs; Mohammed Nour Mohammed Baba of Cairo placed himself in
readiness for his service. These and many other letters form a pathetic,
strangely touching testimony of the profound interest the discovery had
generated. On a rather better informed level, James Breasted, writing just
before Carnarvon's illness developed to congratulate Carter on all he had
done in this first season, put the matter well:[33]

31 Dated 5 May, in M.M.A., Department of Egyptian Art, Carter files.
32 A group of these occasional letters, formerly among the Mace Papers with Margaret Orr,
   is now in the Griffith Institute, Carter archive.
33 Copy of this letter of 6 March in O.I. Director's Office Corr. 1923.

Lest I should not have another opportunity, let me say here that among those who know and whose opinion is worth having, there is universal admiration of what you have accomplished since last October. Without a secretary, without a stenographer or clerical assistance, under crushing pressure from all sides, staggering under responsibilities enough to break down a dozen men, you have quietly and persistently pressed on, with the sole purpose of being true to your scientific obligations. Obliged by circumstances to carry on one ceaseless social function, while at the same time salvaging with brilliant success the greatest body of archaeological material ever found, – that is an achievement absolutely without parallel, and it has aroused in us all the deepest sympathy with you as you have daily met and overcome these unprecedented difficulties.

Breasted had ulterior motives in writing so, especially in a letter dealing otherwise with Carter's publication prospects and his own work on the seal impressions in the tomb. He saw in the discovery wonderful opportunities for the promotion of Egyptology in the United States, and particularly in the further stimulation of the interest of John D. Rockefeller Jr. The latter was the financial backer of much of Breasted's work in the University of Chicago, in the establishment of the Oriental Institute in that university, and in the launching of the Egyptian expedition to be based in Chicago House at Luxor – the last a project about to be realized on the ground. From the outset Breasted had kept Rockefeller well informed of the progress of the discovery, writing huge letters to him with much background information about the stages of the excavation.[34] He had hoped that the Rockefeller family would come out to Egypt in the following season, and might be in Luxor when the royal sarcophagus was opened. In preparation for such a visit, and generally in the hope of further Egyptological propaganda in America, he was eager to obtain slides of the discovery so that he, and others, could give lectures. His requests for slides and for photographs to illustrate specially written articles were highly embarrassing for Carter who was constrained both by the agreement with *The Times* and by his own reluctance to allow others to exploit his discovery in ways which he might be able to follow himself.

The prospect of lecturing was something new for Howard Carter. The matter began to be urgent during his stay in Cairo at the time of Lord Carnarvon's death. After his return to Luxor he told Mace about offers he had received to lecture in Paris and Madrid on his way home:[35] 'The question of lectures is going to be rather a serious one. I don't think Carter has ever given one in his life, and he doesn't in the least know how to set about it. Someone wrote and proposed that he should take the Queen's

34 In particular the letter of 29 December 1922 mentioned on p. 236 above.
35 In his letter to Mrs Mace of 16 April.

Hall for so many afternoons a week!' The following day Mace returned to the subject:

> He wanted to talk on all sorts of future plans, and was most generous in his ideas that I should kind of come into partnership with the firm, and share in all the benefits that may accrue therefrom. He also wanted to know if I would share a kind of lecturing programme with him. I dont know what to think. He has been approached by various agencies, and has had telegrams from Paris and Madrid offering him £50 in cash and travelling expenses from Marseilles to deliver lectures there on his way home. That of course is impossible as there are no slides at present.

The threat of having to lecture may not have pleased Carter, but he surely knew that the demands would come and that he would scarcely be able to avoid his distinct obligation. He had a little earlier been put under some pressure by Breasted over another possible lecture. Breasted had been asked to speak about the tomb of Tutankhamun to the British Association for the Advancement of Science in Liverpool in the following September. He told Carter of the invitation, saying that 'it would be inappropriate for me to do so'. He continued:[36]

> In declining the invitation, I would like also to add, that in any judgement, *you* are the one who should report on the tomb on this important occasion, before the assembled scientists of Great Britain, and to urge you as strongly and tactfully as I can that you be invited to do so. I can hardly do this without first asking your consent, I hope you will concur. . . . I assure you it would give me the sincerest pleasure to know that you were to appear before this greatest scientific body in the world, to tell there, in company with Lord Carnarvon, who has already been invited, the story of your great discovery. . . .
> I think this address ought to be given by an Englishman and I think it ought to be given by the discoverer of the tomb.

Breasted ended the letter with the further appeal for material to use in his own lectures: 'On the *American* side of the water however, an opportunity to speak of the tomb *would* be of the greatest assistance for the future of my work. If I could show to Mr. John D. Rockefeller Jr. on a curtain in his home, a series of slides exhibiting your great discovery, it would immensely aid me in enlisting his further support of my enterprises, especially the work of the Oriental Institute.' No answer from Carter has been preserved; the time was bad for him. It is known, however, that Breasted turned down the British Association invitation and that it was then offered and taken up by Professor Grafton Elliot Smith of University

36 A draft of this letter in O.I. Director's Office Corr. 1923. It is dated 21 March.

College London, the anatomist and author of the standard publication on the royal mummies in the Cairo Museum. He had expectations that he would be asked in due course to carry out the examination of Tutankhamun's mummy. Carter had already decided that the autopsy would be put in the hands of Dr Douglas Derry, a pupil of Elliot Smith, and at the time the professor of Anatomy in the Faculty of Medicine in the Egyptian University. An acrimonious and unpleasant pair of letters[37] from Elliot Smith to Carter made it clear that he thought little of Derry's competence, and informed Carter that he would be speaking to the British Association, without suggesting that Carter would have been the most appropriate lecturer. It is not known if Carter had allowed Breasted to put his name forward, and if so, had received an invitation to speak. In the event, Elliot Smith did not take Tutankhamun as his subject in Liverpool. He gave an evening lecture, 'The Study of Man', concerning the interrelation of Physical and Cultural Anthropology.[38]

The difficulties mounted as Carter left Egypt on 25 May. He was going home, he must have known, to a hero's welcome. But the route was bordered with hazards, and the triumph at the end could be ruined by the problems needing resolution. If he had thought of what lay ahead in an imaginative way, he might have likened his path to that followed by a New-Kingdom Egyptian king passing to his ultimate glory through the gateways of the underworld, harassed by terrible demons and protected by benevolent genii, all so vividly portrayed – and so familiar to him – on the walls of the tombs in the Valley of the Kings. In the event, he slipped quietly into England, arriving in London on 30 May. He notes in his diary that he saw Lady Evelyn Herbert on the same day and Lady Carnarvon on the following day, both probably at the Carnarvon Town house in Seamore Place, at the Park Lane end of Curzon Street. There was much that he needed to discuss with Lady Carnarvon for the future of the work in Egypt, and the resolution of problems concerning Lord Carnarvon's estate. According to his will, the collection of antiquities was left to his wife with certain conditions:[39]

> I would like her to give one object to the British Museum, one object to the Ashmolean, and a fragment cup of blue glass (Thothmes III) to the Metropolitan Museum, New York. The first two bequests need not be capital objects.
>
> Should she find it necessary to sell the collection, I suggest that the nation – i.e., the British Museum, be given the first refusal at £20,000, far below its value, such sum, however, to be absolutely hers, free of all duties. Otherwise I would suggest that the collection

37 Letters of Elliot Smith of 13 and 23 June, and Carter's reply to the first of these, in M.M.A., Department of Egyptian Art, Carter files.
38 See *Nature* for 22 September 1923.
39 The details of Carnarvon's will were published in *The Times* of 18 May 1923.

be offered to the Metropolitan, New York, Mr. Carter to have charge of the negotiations and to fix the price.

Should my wife decide to keep the collection, I leave it absolutely to her whether she leaves it to my son or to the nation or to Evelyn Herbert. I suggest, however, that she consult Dr. Gardiner and Mr. Carter on the subject.

General Sir John Maxwell, in his letter to Carter on 5 May, had mentioned that Lady Carnarvon might move the collection to London 'but not yet'. He also told Carter with a degree of frankness which confirms Carter's intimate relationship with the Carnarvon family, 'that practically everything he [Carnarvon] could dispose of by Will has been left to her Ladyship and I think this will prove all for the best though for the moment Porchester resents it – If he will only play the game, and I think he will, all will be well but he must be nice and tactful to his Mother.' He goes on to point out that after death duties had been paid, 'Porchy will only be able to live at Highclere if he exercises considerable economy and care.' He also mentions deposits in the Bank of England, to be left until Carter returned, and a 'sealed envelope for you "to be handed you [sic] in case of my death".'

The Carnarvon collection had been built up largely with the advice and assistance of Howard Carter, and it was he certainly who could best deal with it. The deposits in the Bank of England might well have been antiquities as yet unincorporated into the collection, but were more probably monies set aside for work in Egypt. The envelope may have contained either particular instructions for the future of the collection, or even an additional undeclared legacy; by the will he had been formally left £500 by Lord Carnarvon. It would not be until 1926 that he would be required to deal finally with the Carnarvon collection, but there were other reasons to take him to Highclere during the summer of 1923, not least to help in the settling of Lord Carnarvon's affairs generally.[40] Carter in all probability knew as well as anyone what his old patron would have wanted in many matters. He was there briefly on 16 June, and then for a longer stay between 23 June and 2 July.

His diary entries for the summer are of the briefest kind, revealing little of what he was actually doing; it was a busy time, spent mostly in London, with many appointments and numerous engagements for luncheon and dinner. Among those who saw and entertained him were Percy White, Alan Gardiner, General Sir John Maxwell, Geoffrey Dawson (editor of *The Times*), the Earl of Northampton, Sir William Garstin, Sir Joseph Duveen (the art dealer), R. H. Molony (Carnarvon's solicitor), James Henry Breasted, Edward Robinson (Director of the Metropolitan Museum), Arthur Mace, Richard Bethell, Calouste Gulbenkian (the oil magnate and

---

40 So Carter states in a letter to Breasted of 22 June, in O.I. Director's Office Corr. 1923.

art collector). It was not all business and tactical planning for the future, although it may be supposed that many axes were ground in the course of the various 'entertainments' he attended. He could not expect to escape Tutankhamun, and he sang for his supper, no doubt, when he spent a weekend at Carisbrooke on the Isle of Wight as a guest of Princess Beatrice, the youngest daughter of Queen Victoria and widow of Prince Henry of Battenberg. Less formal would have been his few days with the Amhersts at Foulden Hall, not far from the old Amherst seat at Didlington and close to Swaffham. He may have visited his aunts in the Sporle Road cottage during these few days, and even paid the visit to the Allens at Cockley Cley, remembered in that family as a special occasion; but these possible incidental visits are not recorded in his diary. He was also a guest at one of the royal Garden Parties at Buckingham Palace on 26 July. He adds to his usual laconic entry for the occasion the note, 'H.M. the King does not want the mummy removed from tomb.' It is not clear whether he actually received this comment from King George V on that day; it is not uncommon at royal Garden Parties for particular guests to be selected from the many hundreds attending for presentation to members of the royal family. He may, however, have been reporting what had been said to Carnarvon when he was received by the King and Queen Mary in December 1922.

Carter's round of engagements, practical and social, was demanding, and gave him little opportunity to recuperate from the trials of the season in Egypt. In a letter to Breasted, written after his return to Egypt in the autumn of 1923, he apologized for failing to answer an earlier letter from the rather importunate professor:[41] 'I was so terribly rushed before returning that I hardly knew which way to turn. In fact during the whole time I was in England I didn't get one week's holiday.' Breasted had again raised strongly the matter of slides for use in the USA, and of Carter's own possibilities of lecturing. In the late summer Carter had himself taken the plunge. His first formal public lecture was given on 10 September at the invitation of the Royal Scottish Geographical Society. It was presented in the Usher Hall, Edinburgh, before an audience estimated at over 3000, with the Lord Provost of Edinburgh, Sir Thomas Hutchinson, presiding. Carter showed 145 slides, both black and white and coloured, and his lecture was well received, although the newspaper reports do not say much about his delivery or presentation. Later in the month came three lectures given in the New Oxford Theatre; the first was on 21 September, before an audience invited by Almina, Countess of Carnarvon, and presided over by Sir John Maxwell. It was a glittering company of society notables, according to the report in *The Times*; among his professional supporters were Petrie, Newberry, Gardiner and Mace. On this occasion moving pictures were shown as well as slides, and 'Again and again the audience

41 Written in Luxor on 23 October 1923, in O.I. Director's Office Corr. 1923.

broke into enthusiastic applause.' Two further comments are of interest: 'Mr. Carter is a good lecturer and spoke gracefully and with ease', and 'Mr. Carter speaks on this subject with an authority which no one else can approach.' On the 25th, with Maxwell again presiding, he spoke for two hours: 'he kept this large audience so intensely interested by a delightful combination of narrative, description, and pictures that they never broke silence for any purpose but to applaud.' A hint of a slightly more critical response to his first essays in public speaking comes in a letter written by Breasted to Gardiner in 1924 after Carter's visit to lecture in Chicago:[42] 'He had dropped the note of high tragedy to which you referred in commenting on his London lectures.'

It may be supposed that in his London lectures, particularly that sponsored by Lady Carnarvon, he had spoken movingly and dramatically about the tragic death of Lord Carnarvon. It may also be suggested that if he had just stood in front of his audience and shown his slides with an occasional comment he would still have been deemed a great success. Nevertheless, the first experiences were sufficiently encouraging to persuade Carter to follow up the negotiations he had started during the summer with an agency to manage a lecture tour for himself in America in 1924. Two entries in his diary indicate approaches by (or to) the Keedick Lecture Bureau Inc. It is not clear whether he met Mr Lee Keedick himself, or a representative, but the outcome was an agreement with the Bureau for a tour to be undertaken in the following year after the winter season in the Valley had ended.

A further persuasive reason which may have driven Carter to make the agreement may have been provided by a long letter which Breasted had written to him in London on 1 July.[43] It was an extraordinary piece of special pleading, masquerading under a rather transparent cloak of disinterestedness. He wrote of the development of the specialized popular lecture in the States; how a distinct category of well trained speakers had evolved; and how he himself had both helped and profited from such professionals. If Carter were to come to America he would need to be properly equipped: 'This kind of experience, which lies so far away from the path of any one living in Europe, I should be very glad to put at your disposal. . . . I have had a long *business* experience with this kind of thing in America.' The letter contained much good advice, but was distinctly overdone, and more than a little disingenuous. Whoever later wrote at the top of the letter 'Ass Carter knew where he was going', put his finger on the right spot.

Breasted pointed out further that 'lectures on the tomb have been given all over the United States and continue to be given at present.' After his return to America he wrote disgustedly to Gardiner:[44]

42 Letter dated 12 June, in G.I. Gardiner Corr. AHG/42.37.13.
43 In M.M.A., Department of Egyptian Art, Carter files.
44 G.I. Gardiner Corr. AHG/42.37.14.

You will be interested to know that Weigall is about to make a tour in America lecturing on the tomb. After his disgraceful defamation of Lord Carnarvon as a man who was debasing archaeology for mercenary ends it is highly edifying to see Weigall lecturing in America with, of course, no other purpose in view than beneficially enlightening the American public on Egyptian Archaeology.

He also included a mention of Weigall's forthcoming tour in a letter he sent to Carter, the principal purpose of which was to inform him of a small ancient astronomical instrument bearing the name of Tutankhamun, formerly in the MacGregor collection, which he had acquired in London for the museum of the Oriental Institute.[45] It was undoubtedly an object *not* from Carter's tomb, but probably from that of King Tuthmosis IV on which Carter had worked in 1902–3. Giving Carter full details of this small but interesting and pertinent piece, Breasted further fostered what he hoped would be the improving relationship which would lead to some fruitful outcome through Carter's lectures in the States. There can be no doubt that he was shocked by Weigall's behaviour, although on cool reflection he might have recognized that Weigall had as much right to lecture on the tomb as many perhaps more academically respectable people who had attempted to satisfy the public demand in Britain, America and Europe. Capart in Belgium was thought to have behaved a little improperly in trying to obtain photographic material from *The Times* for his own lectures and presentations to the Belgian royal family.[46] Griffith and Newberry had both spoken on the tomb, and both had contributions of a useful kind to offer. Public interest could not be assuaged by a reluctant Carter, who in the summer of 1923 had many important things on his mind. Weigall too could make a useful contribution from his particular knowledge of the Theban Necropolis, and his months of surreptitious activity after the discovery of the tomb; but his behaviour in those months had seriously diminished his reputation as a good Egyptologist. For Breasted Weigall's American tour seemed like a gratuitous insult to Carnarvon's memory. He himself had been urged to lecture in the University of Chicago but, mindful of Carter's sensitivities, had reluctantly refused all approaches. In a postscript to a letter to Dr Edgar J. Goodspeed, Secretary to the President of the University,[47] he wrote:

I have just received information to the effect that the Pond Bureau is advertising Weigall as the discoverer of the tomb. Under these

45 Copy in O.I. Director's Office Corr. 1923. The object is numbered 12144 and 10648.
46 A disagreeable exchange of letters between Capart, *The Times* and Carter caused much pain in Brussels. Material at first sent to Carpart was later recalled to London. Letters are in the Fondation Égyptologique Reine Élisabeth, Brussels, and were brought to my attention by M. Arpag Mekhitarian. Carter was almost pathological in his opposition to having his discovery exploited by others.
47Goodspeed was himself a distinguished classical scholar and Greek papyrologist.

circumstances you can understand how reluctant I am to be involved in any way in premature competition with Carter's coming lectures.

One task that took up some of Carter's time during the summer of 1923 was the completion and printing of the first volume of the popular book on the discovery. He worked closely with Arthur Mace on the text, and the work benefited immensely from Mace's greater skill as a writer of decent English prose. Much of the text is composed in the first person as if by Carter himself, and his own voice does come clearly through. Parts had been dictated to Mace in the evenings they had spent together in Carter's house at Elwat el-Diban towards the end of the season. Some help, both stylistically and in matters of general book production, was also received from Percy White, an author of considerable experience. But the principal labour of writing had fallen on Mace, and it is likely that he too was principally responsible for seeing the book through the press. The volume also contained a memoir on the Earl of Carnarvon by his sister Lady Burghclere – a model of affectionate and perceptive writing – and a generous series of illustrations from Harry Burton's photographs. Carter himself was surely involved closely in the form and appearance of the book – matters in which he had always shown particular interest in the past. It was to be a good, if not lavish, production, and finally few complaints could be raised against the printing of the text or the reproduction of Burton's photographs. Its assembly and binding were perhaps not as sturdy as a fairly thick volume required, and many surviving copies display broken spines, loose plates, and a general tendency to disintegration. But these weaknesses – not uncommon in book production of the period – would not have been immediately noticeable, and in the absence of distinct complaints from Carter (and in the fact that the two later volumes were similarly produced), it is reasonable to assume that he was satisfied. Cassell and Co., the publishers, had done well to get it out in a matter of months.

The Tomb of Tut.ankh.Amen, vol I, in spite of having been produced with such expedition, had stiff opposition to contend with. S. R. K. Glanville, reviewing it in the *Journal of Egyptian Archaeology*, vol. II, in the following year, noted that in issuing what was intended as a popular account, Carter and Mace were pitching themselves against all those who had written the innumerable articles in journals, newspapers and periodicals. He did not mention the books that had been rushed into print by authors, some of them distinguished scholars, eager, as they might have said, to satisfy the passionate interest of the general public. In the course of 1923 the prolific Sir Ernest Wallis Budge published *Tutānkhamen, Amenism, Atenism and Egyptian Monotheism*; a series of articles by Jean Capart was translated posthaste into English by Warren R. Dawson, and published as *The Tomb of Tutankhamen*; Grafton Elliot Smith produced, rather provocatively and insensitively, *Tutankhamen and the Discovery of his Tomb by the late Earl of*

Carnarvon and Mr. Howard Carter; and the indefatigable Arthur Weigall cobbled together *Tutankhamen and other essays*. All these books were opportunist and inadequate as far as the discovery itself was concerned, but as a group they tended to spoil the field for the more authoritative work of Carter and Mace.

Carter himself missed the actual day of publication and the initial press reactions, for he left London for Egypt on 3 October; but he may have seen an advance copy before leaving. He recorded the arrival of the first copies in Luxor on 17 November. On 15 November Lady Burghclere wrote enquiring after the presentation copies she had expected, and she comments,[48] 'I hope you are pleased with the reviews? Those I have seen are very benedictory.' She mentions also another event – a family matter which Carter had missed: 'Evelyn Herbert's marriage was very pretty and she looked very happy – the delicious bridesmaids were like a group of Botticelli babes. Your salver quite magnificent and beautiful beyond everything there.' So much then for the supposed affair of less than a year before! She married Bograve Beauchamp, son of Sir Edward Beauchamp the Chairman of Lloyds, to whose baronetcy he would succeed in a very few years.

If Carter received letters of congratulations on the book, they have not survived, but he did keep a letter from Sir Clive Wigram, Assistant Private Secretary to King George V:

> I am desired by the King to thank you for the book which you have been so good as to send to his Majesty and which the King is much pleased to possess.
>
> Your daily progress at Luxor is followed with the closest interest by the King.

When he arrived in Egypt in October, Howard Carter had every reason to think that he would have a relatively trouble-free season. The future of his own work at Luxor had seemingly been settled formally by an exchange between himself and Lacau.[49] In his letter to Lady Carnarvon of 1 May he had enclosed a copy of the note he had written to Lacau confirming the points they had agreed on in conversation after Lord Carnarvon's death: 'I beg to state formally that the family of the late Earl of Carnarvon have every desire to continue in his memory that undertaking. In other words, they wish me to represent them in that particular undertaking.' Lacau sent his authorization 'pour achever la déblaiement de la tombe de Tout.Ankh.Amon (to complete the clearance of the tomb of Tutankhamun)', on 12 July, and asked for it to be signed by Lady Carnarvon.[50]

48 Letter in M.M.A., Department of Egyptian Art, Carter files.
49 See p. 262 above.
50 Carter's letter to Lacau, and the authorization documents are reprodouced in the *Statement*, p. 6. This compilation was put together by Carter, probably with the help of Mace, as background material in his dispute with the Egyptian government in the winter of 1923–4. See p. 274 below.

The authorization made it clear that it was confined to the tomb, that it remained valid firstly until 1 November 1923, and then secondly until 1 November 1924. It could be renewed if the work remained unfinished, and the conditions of the concession would be as before. The Antiquities Service undertook to exercise its rights of control on the site to avoid the Press comments of the preceding year, and to protect the excavators as far as possible from pointless visits. Lady Carnarvon had signed her approval.

The principal differences between the old and new concessions lay in the territorial limitation of the work to the tomb of Tutankhamun, and in the characterization of the work as *déblaiement* instead of *fouilles*, i.e. 'clearance' as opposed to 'excavation'. Carter could not have hoped for a more satisfactory settlement, and as the separate but crucial question of *partage*, 'division', had not been mentioned, he had some reason to think that the expectations of the Carnarvon family might yet be partially fulfilled. In the course of 1923 Lacau and the government had agreed that the controversial new law concerning *partage* would not be implemented for at least one more season; by that time some decision on the Tutankhamun objects should have been reached. And so, by way of the Simplon Express, Trieste, and the S.S. *Helouan*, Carter reached Cairo on 8 October. A few days settling details for the season's work with James Quibell in the Cairo Museum should be sufficient before he could start work in Luxor. It would not turn out so simply.

12

THE SPIRIT OF MISCHIEF

The season which was planned to start as promptly as possible in October 1923 was prefaced by encouraging meetings in Cairo and Alexandria within a few days of Howard Carter's arrival in Egypt on 8 October. The promise at the outset was fulfilled in small part only, and contained no hint of the desperately unhappy events which were to lead to the closure of his work and, as it seemed, the total disintegration of his plans for the proper completion of the clearance of the tomb of Tutankhamun, and the servicing of the objects remaining in three chambers and in the laboratory tomb of Sethos II.

It would be good to pass over these trying months, noting only the positive archaeological work which was accomplished. Unfortunately, much of what happened between October 1923 and April 1924 concerned not only the progress of Carter's enterprise, but also the future of archaeological work in Egypt generally. The behaviour of the principals in the troubles – Carter and his colleagues, especially Arthur Mace; Pierre Lacau and his assistants in the Antiquities Service; members of the Egyptian and British administrations; the Egyptologists who were deeply concerned with the work in Thebes; the legal representatives of Carter and the Carnarvon estate; and some press-men – needs more than passing consideration. The course of events has been exhaustively tracked elsewhere,[1] and may be studied in detail (for the period up to February 1924) in a dossier compiled by Carter, helped probably by Mace.[2] Here only the general lines of the inexorable march of events will be set out with the purpose of illustrating how foolishly intelligent men can behave when the pressure of incidental, even trivial, factors causes the suspension of common sense, and the neglect of the general interests and the requirements of science.

1 See T. Hoving, *Tutankhamun. The Untold Story* (New York, 1978), chapters 25–32.
2 *The Tomb of Tut.ankh.Amen. Statement with Documents as to the Events which occurred in Egypt in the Winter of 1923–4, leading to the ultimate break with the Egyptian Government* (London, 1924), Marked '[*For Private Circulation only*]' and printed by Cassell and Company Ltd, the publishers of Carter and Mace's first volume. The distribution of copies was limited and probably small. The copy used for reference here belonged to Newberry and is in the Griffith Institute, Oxford, Carter Papers VI, 13.

When volume two of *The Tomb of Tut.ankh.Amen* appeared its Preface, dated November 1926, shows Carter in unusually subdued and unvindictive mood (probably under the editorial influence of Percy White), recalling tranquilly what took place in the winter of 1923–4:[3]

> Gradually troubles began to arise. Newspapers were competing for 'copy', tourists were leaving no efforts untried to obtain permits to visit the tomb; endless jealousies were let loose; days, which should have been devoted to scientific work, were wasted in negotiations too often futile, whilst the claims of archaeology were thrust into the background. But this is no place for weighing the merits of a controversy now ended, and it would serve no good purpose to relate in detail the long series of unpleasant incidents which harassed our work. No man is wise at all times – perhaps least of all the archaeologist who finds his efforts to carry out an all-absorbing task frustrated by a thousand pin-pricks and irritations without end. It is not for me to affix the blame for what occurred, not yet to bear responsibility for a dispute in which at one moment the interest of archaeology in Egypt seemed menaced.
>
> How such storms arise is never quite clear. In such conflicts there always enter causes which are intangible, while the spirit of mischief is active in most human affairs. To expect at such times complete fairness and impartiality is to ask too much. Moreover, a man may inherit obligations which it is his obvious duty to carry out, although he personally has not incurred them, and he is certainly not responsible for the acrimony that may be imported by varying sentiments, political and otherwise.

This eminently sensible assessment of the troubled period through which Carter had with little adroitness, but with much help and advice, attempted to guide the progress of his work to an unexpectedly happy outcome, places little if any importance on the one factor which above all had seriously destabilized most administrative procedures in Egypt. Politics, directly or indirectly, were at last significantly affecting the running of the country, which had seemed so well organized and competently carried out under the British Protectorate.

In March 1922 the Sultan Ahmed Fuad had been proclaimed king as Fuad I, and in April 1923 a new constitution for Egypt was promulgated. There was to be universal male suffrage, with a Senate and House of Deputies, the membership of which would be partly elected and partly appointed. Suddenly Egypt had the possibility of becoming a modern democratically run country, a situation which its politicians were ill prepared to exploit judiciously. The administration was still dominated by

---

3 H. Carter, *The Tomb of Tut.ankh.Amen*, II (London, 1927), p. xiii.

British officials headed by the High Commissioner, Lord Allenby. The Protectorate was formally abolished, but in matters of international relations, imperial communications, and the Sudan, control remained in British hands until their transfer could be negotiated. In domestic matters the new Egyptian administration could exercise far greater influence than formerly, and could act without the careful regard for British and foreign interests generally which had characterized internal government under the Protectorate, and earlier this century. The main Egyptian political party, with a strong popular following, was known as the Wafd, a word which means delegation, having been appropriated by the group of nationalists who claimed to represent the majority of Egyptians demanding complete autonomy for Egypt in 1918 at the end of the Great War. The principal leader of the Wafd in 1923 was Saad Zaghlul Pasha, who had recently been allowed to return to Egypt after a short period of political exile. A lawyer by training, Zaghlul was a man of vision but was not very astute in negotiation, and in the autumn of 1923 he was preparing the ground for the first general election planned for early 1924. There was every expectation that the Wafd would gain most seats, and that Zaghlul would become Prime Minister. Nationalists and nationalistic politics were very much in the ascendance.[4]

Howard Carter would certainly have been aware of political developments in the country, but he, no more probably than most foreign archaeologists who knew Egypt well – as they would have claimed – may not have comprehended the consequences of what was happening. A greater appreciation of political reality had undoubtedly penetrated the Antiquities Service, the head of which, Pierre Lacau, had from the beginning of his administration sensed how things were changing, and how possibly the control of archaeological matters in Egypt would have to be accommodated to the requirements of politicians who would not be brow-beaten by the British officials who ostensibly served them. It is now very hard to determine whether Lacau was prompted in his moves to limit the rights of foreign excavators in the country by a sincere desire to protect the interests of Egypt itself, to trim his activities to curry favour with the nationalist politicians, or to act in such a way as to please the politicians in order to protect the particular interests of the Antiquities Service.

If he were playing a clever waiting game, Lacau certainly concealed his motives so successfully that in the course of the winter 1923–4 he managed to alienate many foreign Egyptologists who were otherwise predisposed to admire him as an excellent scholar. Unfortunately, the accessible surviving documentation is substantially anti-Lacau, and it provides a seriously

4 The historical background outlined here can be studied in many good histories of modern Egypt. I have consulted J. Marlow, *Anglo-Egyptian Relations 1800–1953* (London, 1954), chapters 9, 11; also the excellent summary by P. M. Holt in *The Encyclopaedia Britannica*, 15th ed. (1974), vol. 6, pp. 498f.

unfavourable impression of his activities and motives. To judge his behaviour impartially is difficult in the face of so much adverse opinion; and yet there are some indications which suggest that he was a man trapped into false positions by his own well-intentioned but ill-judged purposes.[5] It was inevitable, in the stress of events, that Lacau was compared unfavourably with Maspero, whose indulgence towards foreign excavators became a source of serious criticism towards the end of his second term of duty as Director-General. Memories can be short when it is convenient to forget the inconvenient.

In the outline of events which took place between Carter and Lacau and other members of the Antiquities Service and members of the government and their senior officials, it should be remembered that Carter was already saddled with the reputation of being a difficult, stubborn, unreasonable, person – someone who had already in his career caused much trouble in governmental circles and to his indulgent chief Maspero over the Saqqara incident of 1905. Here memory worked to his disadvantage. Although his earlier behaviour is only once invoked in surviving documents and correspondence, his difficult temperament is often referred to, particularly by his supporters like Gardiner and Breasted. It is certain that the events of 1905 will not have been forgotten by J. E. Quibell and C. C. Edgar. The former had been Carter's fellow Chief Inspector in those early days, and now was Lacau's deputy as Secretary-General of the Antiquities Service. Edgar had taken over as Chief Inspector in the Delta when Carter resigned in 1905, and had tidied up the Tukh el-Qaramus find of treasure; he too was now an assistant keeper in the Cairo Museum, and worked closely with Quibell.

On 11 October 1923 Carter went to see Quibell to discuss matters concerning the coming season. The two substantive problems requiring settlement were the dissemination of news and the admittance of visitors to the tomb. On the first it was agreed provisionally that Arthur Merton, formerly the representative of *The Times* but now taken on as a part of Carter's staff, should give daily bulletins, first to *The Times* in the evening and then to the Egyptian Press early the following day, so that 'the news would reach the public in London and Cairo practically at the same time'. On the question of visitors Carter proposed that there should be no regular admittance on a weekly or fortnightly basis, but that whenever a convenient moment arrived, work should be suspended 'for a week if necessary, while parties of visitors pass through. They should be admitted by tickets obtained at the Public Works Ministry.' The following day Carter took his proposals to Alexandria to obtain the approval of Abd el-Hamid Pasha Suleiman, the Minister of Public Works, and was advised that all would be acceptable if the Residency (High Commission) agreed. R. A. Furness,

5 See further on Lacau's standing with foreign archaeologists, p. 297 below.

the second secretary in the High Commission who dealt with matters concerning the Antiquities Service, also agreed with what was proposed, although in a note written subsequently to Carter on 17 October, he passed on a warning that 'the proposals about visitors would cause disappointment to many tourists'.[6]

In some confidence that prospects for the season were promising, Carter travelled down to Luxor on 16 October, and arrangements were made to reopen work in the Valley of the Kings on 22 October. Carter's confidence would shortly be severely tested, but for the moment he could comment grandly, but rashly, in his diary on the warning in Furness's letter:[7] 'As I do not work for tourists nor am I a tourist agent I have taken no notice of this futile remark.' The grand manner, however, belonged to the past, and no longer would produce the desired effect either with Egyptian politicians or even at the Residency. Still, now all seemed settled and he set about the preliminaries of his work with customary system and orderliness. The environs and approach to the tomb of Sethos II were tidied up, and the deposits covering the entrance to the tomb of Tutankhamun removed. It was a tedious process necessitating the rehabilitation of the walls surrounding the excavation down to the entrance of the tomb, the reinstallation of the electric light supply, and the repair of the roads leading from the tomb of Tutankhamun to the various other tombs used for dark-room, storage and, of course, the laboratory.

Before he had reached the point when he could reopen the tomb itself, Carter received a number of worrying communications from Quibell signalling trouble, particularly over the press arrangements, and a new demand that Egyptian inspectors should be assigned to exercise surveillance over Carter's work.[8] A. H. Bradstreet, the combative reporter of the *Morning Post* had returned to Egypt and had already registered objections to the proposed arrangements for the daily distribution of news, to Quibell and possibly also to the minister and his under-secretary in the Ministry of Public Works, Paul Tottenham. Bradstreet's principal ally now was Valentine Williams, Reuters correspondent in Luxor. Memories of the troubles earlier in the year did not encourage Carter to show any wish to compromise. On 1 November his diary records: 'Bradstreet appeared in the Valley. Refused to converse with him owing to his disgraceful behaviour and action of last season.' On 4 November he then made the first of several trips to Cairo in which the apparently settled agreement was taken apart, argued over, added to, and generally transformed in such ways as to alienate Carter and his staff increasingly from the representatives of the Antiquities Service and the Egyptian politicians. The British officials were unable to reconcile the various sides, and no doubt found the Tutankhamun affair

6 On these negotiations, see Carter's dossier, *Statement*, pp. 10f.
7 Diary in G.I. Carter Notebook 1, entry for 12 October.
8 *Statement*, p. 11.

an exceptionally tiresome side-show at a time when the political situation in Egypt was highly sensitive.[9]

'Shilly-shallying' was the term used by Carter to describe the vexing changes of direction pursued by the people in Cairo, and it is difficult to find a more favourable description of the behaviour which drove the excavators to distraction in the course of that winter. The dossier compiled by Carter with the knowledge and probable help of Mace contains a progressively damaging case against the Antiquities Service and the government, but it must be admitted that the case is presented from Carter's side and could therefore be charged with partiality. However, the documentation from both sides is such that it is hard to accuse Carter of being unfair to the opposition. On 12 November he had apparently reached the brink of a settlement and he returned to Luxor to force matters forward. On the 14th Arthur Mace and Richard Bethell arrived from Cairo to join the camp, and they brought a new agreement which was fairly satisfactory in detail, but unfortunately hedged with reservations. Carter felt obliged to return to Cairo to consult Lord Allenby, the High Commissioner, and to offer to Tottenham his own hedged acceptance. Back in Luxor on 17 November he and Mace set about the serious archaeological business of the season.

At last it looked as if work could proceed without further interruptions, and Carter with evident satisfaction recorded in his diary for the 19th, 'Mace commenced preservation of the couch No. 35 – lion-headed. Lunched in magazine for first time this season, with Bethell, Merton, Mace, Burton and Callender.' Lucas would join them early in December, and so too Dr Alexander Scott, the distinguished archaeological chemist, Keeper of the recently established Research Laboratory in the British Museum. The issue of a public communiqué about the tomb in Cairo on 21 November set out plans for the season and explained the reason for the limitation of visitors and the procedures by which permits to visit the tomb could from time to time be obtained.[10] But, as Carter commented in his dossier, the suggested visitor arrangements were in time negated by the number of permits issued by the Government. 'At the same time there were certain visitors for diplomatic and political reasons Mr. Carter could not well refuse; and, moreover, whenever it was possible without causing serious delay to the work, he extended all courtesy to Egyptian notables and their families, considering that they, of all people, had most right to visit the Tomb.' Imprecision in the agreement, and Carter's own readiness to breach it when circumstances demanded it or seemed otherwise suitable, rendered the superficially calm situation very uncertain. At Luxor they felt rightly that problems could again arise. Mace wrote to Lythgoe on 26 November:[11]

9 *Statement*, pp. 12ff.
10 *Statement*, pp. 22f.
11 M.M.A., Department of Egyptian Art, Carter files.

More than a fortnight's time has been wasted owing to a recrud-
escence of the politico-journalistic trouble. . . . This year Bradstreet
and Valentine Williams of Reuters got busy again, and the Government have let them lead them about by the nose. All the trouble
started up afresh, and impossible restrictions were being put upon
Carter. The matter was fought out for a fortnight and finally a
compromise was agreed on, which may or may not work. Carter was
within an ace of closing up the tomb and refusing to go on with it.
Lacau was all up in the air, agreed to a thing one day and contradicted it the next. Quibell, who, as you know, doesn't like Carter,
was very aggressive, and threatened that the Government would take
over the tomb and work it themselves, and Edgar was impossible.
The whole Department seems to have clean gone off their heads.

In a further letter to Lythgoe on 1 December Mace reiterates the same
points, and Carter adds a piece of his own:[12]

Should anyone of the Eg. Gov. question you about whether you
would withdraw your men [i.e. Burton and Mace] on the staff, please
say yes. As I told them as much if they gave trouble. I had a lot of
trouble with Q and Lacau, far more than I expected. Both Tottenham
and the minister were far easier to deal with.

The next stage in the dispute marked by the Government's demand,
forwarded by Quibell on 1 December, that Carter submit a full list of all
the members of his staff.[13] Such a demand, which has now been regular
for many years and a condition of the issuing of any concession, was at
the time exceptional. The Government claimed the right to exclude anyone
if saw fit to object to, and Carter understood clearly that Arthur Merton,
the ostensible representative of *The Times*, was the immediate target. Bradstreet and Valentine Williams had particularly objected to Merton's privileged position, and found Lacau and Quibell sympathetic to their point of
view.[14] It is not likely that the Egyptian minister or his British officials
would have cared to make an issue of the matter without encouragement
from the Cairo Museum. Carter chose to combat this demand, and drew
in due course from the Government by way of Lacau a more peremptory
demand and a statement setting out the Government's right to manage

12 *Ibid.*
13 *Statement*, p. 24.
14 Arthur Weigall was not sent out by the *Daily Mail* this winter, it was thought because
he had behaved so outrageously in the previous season, see p. 000 below. Valentine
Williams describes his time in Egypt in his *The World of Action* (London, 1938), chapters
XXVI and XXVIII. He had first travelled to Egypt on the same boat as Carnarvon in
January 1923, became acquainted with him, and remained on reasonable terms until the
end of the first season. Of his activities in the autumn of 1923 he writes discreetly. He
left Egypt in the spring of 1924.

the matter as it thought proper.[15] In the course of this statement Lacau voiced the Government's position in a way that particularly angered Carter: 'Ces discussions nous ont prit ainsi qu'à vous-mêmes beaucoup plus de temps qu'il était nécessaire, et le Gouvernement ne discute plus mais vous transmet sa décision.' (These discussions have taken for us, just as for yourself, much more time than was necessary, and the Government no longer discusses, but conveys to you its decision.) The words 'Le Governement ne discute plus mais vous transmet sa décision' were objectionable and ominous. Equally ominous was the draft of the new form of concession sent by Lacau at the same time.

For the moment Carter felt protected in the essentials of his work by the existing permit which had been received in Lady Carnarvon's name in July 1923, but very vulnerable in matters marginal which for that moment seemed to be attracting the attention of the Government. He rightly felt that he was being given no support by the Antiquities Service, and he chose to delay any reply until he could confront Lacau on his next visit to Luxor. This took place on 12 December.[16] On that day Carter was, as he said in his diary 'seedy', and it was not until the next day that he was able to discuss the contentious matters with Lacau. He could not accept the official position and told the Director-General that he now proposed to conduct his work under the legal rights conferred by his original concession. The interview, he noted, was made in the presence of Lythgoe, Harkness, Mace and Callender, and was followed by an inspection of recent discoveries from the tomb; 'though grave as the whole matter was, the whole incident was not without amusing aspects.' One may presume that there was much loss of dignity and general confusion, offset by the formality of the subsequent inspection. It was not, however, a laughing matter, and any momentary satisfaction Carter may have derived from apparently discomforting Lacau was dispersed by a summons to Cairo and a further tiresome exchange of views with Tottenham and the Minister of Public Works.[17] It was now made clear that Arthur Merton was the principal target for attack, and Carter was asked by the minister to exclude him from the tomb except on normal press days. Instructed to put his refusal to comply into writing, on the advice of Tottenham, Carter sent a very strong letter to Lacau on 20 December in which he also complained about the publication of information on Tutankhamun objects in the Cairo Museum *Guide*; he even threatened legal action. Tottenham attempted to retrieve the situation by stopping the letter, but Carter declared that it was too late. He had already wired for support in London, and sent copies of all the correspondence on the dispute to *The Times*. In

15 *Statement*, pp. 26f.
16 *Ibid.*, p. 30.
17 *Ibid.*, pp. 31f.

a sense the die was now cast, and the irrevocable march of events in the New Year may be said to have its precise beginning in this act of defiance.

He arrived back in Luxor on 21 December and noted in his diary, 'Recommenced work. Mace having already started in Lab.' In the tomb the principal task was the dismantling of the series of shrines enclosing what was expected to be the royal sarcophagus. It was a difficult and slow process: there was little room to work in; the parts of the shrines were hard to separate; false moves would damage the plastered and gilded surfaces of the shrine walls; there were objects placed between the shrines; and especially risky was the removal of the linen pall with gilded rosettes which covered the second shrine. In spite of the many interruptions and constant worry over the future, Carter doggedly pressed on with the work, heroically aided by Mace and Callender. Indeed the therapy provided by the practical activities in the tomb was one of the few comforting aspects of the situation. Carter seemed to have the ability to switch his concentration totally to the problems of the removal of the shrines, and the continuing treatment of the objects taken from the tomb.[18]

It is noticeable, from the entries in Minnie Burton's diary in particular, that Carter visited the Metropolitan House very frequently in the evenings at this time. There he could avoid the loneliness of his own house, and also discuss matters archaeological and political with his friends and colleagues. Just before Christmas Arthur Mace was joined by his wife Winifred and their daughter Margaret who was eleven; she had been brought to Egypt to recuperate from a bad bout of typhoid. In the Maces in particular Carter found sympathetic support. Winfred's letters to her mother are full of angry comments on what she, and certainly her husband, considered to be the insufferable treatment Carter was receiving.[19] In a letter of 21 December she reported: 'Mr. Carter told me that Arthur's advice behind him and fighting instincts had helped him through.' On 23 December she describes her first visit to Tutankhamun's tomb:

> Today Mr. Carter sent for Margaret and me to go to the Valley. . . .
> An impressive, awesome Valley. . . . Tutenkhamen Tomb is nearly
> the first, hardly anyone goes there now . . . work has been so delayed
> and there are so many troubles Mr. Carter may even close the work
> down, then who knows what will happen. All the correspondence
> will be published; everyone trusts that this will not happen.

She describes first impressions in the tomb, and then:

> I climbed three steps and with a torch looked between the cover and
> the shrine which is bolstered up by beams and there lay the palls of
> linen, dark brown with age studded with gold buttons as were on

18 *The Tomb of Tut.ankh.Amen*, II, pp. 42ff.
19 Winifred Mace's letters are in the possession of her daughter Margaret Orr.

the wig of little Senebtisi fifteen years ago, in front of the great doors the pall fell to pieces but the ingenious man has a plan to save the rest.

A visit to the laboratory followed, to see where Arthur Mace worked, and she adds, 'Margaret and Frances have an excavation and Margaret said it gave her many ideas for their work, so the time was not wasted.'[20]
Christmas Day saw a great evening party in the Metropolitan House. Minnie Burton had much to put down:

Xmas Day. Busy all day. With Harry and Miss Stillman up the Gurn[21] after breakfast and back for 1 o'clock lunch. Mr. Seager and M. de Bildt for tea. Arranging Xmas tree between lunch and tea. Had all candles going for tea. Mr. Carter and Mr. Lucas for dinner and also Mr. Wilkinson. 17 at dinner, counting the children. Gave Frances a Tyrolese dress in which she looked very well, and Margaret a necklace. Ellis dressed up as a suffragi [Egyptian butler] and took us all in. Games after and to bed at 1.

Winifred said a little more about the games in her letter to her mother on 26 December:

many toasts were drunk and the children had a good time; the games, including dumb crambo[22] by the children, it was quaint seeing the assemblage playing the most childish games. One was very amusing, we sat around and Mr. Carter drew line by line, each one copied their neighbour and the result was very funny.

Work in the tomb resumed immediately after Christmas and by early January enough progress had been made for Carter to decide that the moment had arrived when the doors of the remaining shrines could be opened to see what lay within. Everything took longer than had been expected, and no part of the multiple protective screens surrounding the burial had proved so difficult as the pall. A solution was devised by Dr Alexander Scott[23] who had been given leave by the Trustees of the British Museum to spend some weeks in Luxor. For much of his time, unfortunately, he was unable to work because of a painful carbuncle which kept him in his hotel in Luxor. Mrs Mace noted on 16 January that he had been able to do only one week's work. Nevertheless he proposed a method of strengthening the fabric so that it could be wound on to a wooden roller

20 Margaret Orr says that Carter gave her and Frances Winlock help in setting out their excavation. He got on well with the young inhabitants of the Metropolitan House, and on one occasion, as Margaret Orr recalls, accepted an invitation to a dolls' tea-party.
21 The Gurn or Qurn is the pyramid-shaped peak overlooking the Valley of the Kings.
22 Dumb crambo is a game in which one side guesses a word suggested in mime by the other side.
23 *The Tomb of Tut.ankh.Amen*, II, p. 43.

and removed for further treatment and lining. On 3 January Carter informed Engelbach that he should come that afternoon to the Valley:[24] 'I find that I shall be able to make an interesting experiment which I think would interest you to see.' And so, at about 3.00 p.m. that afternoon in the presence of his staff, Engelbach, and a few chosen scholars who happened to be available – Lythgoe, Winlock and Newberry among them – the doors of the third and fourth shrines were opened to reveal within, and almost wholly filling the available space, the great quartzite sarcophagus, wonderfully embellished with high relief carvings of the four protective goddesses Isis, Nephthys, Neith and Selkis at the corners with wings outstretched guarding the sacred royal contents within. This further confirmation of the intact nature of the burial was highly satisfactory, and Carter went through the polite ritual of informing Lacau about the sarcophagus by telegram. Lacau replied on the 5th with 'cordiales félicitations', and asked to be informed when it might be opened. Carter wired agreement.

At this point it might have seemed that work could now proceed without further interruption, according to Carter's plan for the season; but any confidence in this prospect was shattered on the same day – the 5th – by a visit from Tottenham bringing a complaint from the minister on two counts; first, that Carter had without official permission allowed another representative of *The Times* to enter the tomb; and second, that no Egyptian inspector had been present when the shrines were opened. The first complaint, easily denied by Carter, was based on a malicious telegram sent to the minister by Bradstreet; the second was equally malicious in that Engelbach, the Chief Inspector, had been present and had himself chosen not to be accompanied by one of the Egyptian inspectors. It was a simple matter for Tottenham to advise the minister to take no further action,[25] but it did not prevent Lacau from sending Carter a strongly worded letter dated 10 January. On close and calm examination it is clear that some of Carter's objections to the Government's position on visitors (and that of the Antiquities Service) and the submission of a list of his collaborators were accepted, but the tone of the letter was unusually severe and unfortunate in expression. It also claimed the right for the Museum to publish descriptions of the Tutankhamun objects on display, and it implicitly stated that the tomb and its contents were the property of Egypt. It prejudged, therefore, the question of any division of the contents, a matter which Carter had hoped would remain undecided until after the total clearance of the tomb.

Carter was seriously depressed by this letter, which was studied in detail by his Egyptological collaborators and colleagues and on which he took

24 *Statement*, p. 33.
25 *Ibid.*, p. 34.

legal advice.[26] His answer, sent on 3 February, was not composed before there had been other developments in Luxor. Th processes of complaint and opposition to Lacau and the Government were greatly and perhaps foolishly stimulated by the arrival in Luxor of Gardiner and Breasted, both of whom were heavily encumbered by feelings of responsibility and by inclinations to interfere. Breasted also brought with him his son Charles, formally acting as his secretary but also hoping to exploit his privileged position by securing 'scoops' for the *Chicago Daily News*. The arrangements made with this newspaper are contained in a letter from Charles Breasted to Mr C. H. Dennis, the managing editor in Chicago, dated 12 December 1923 and written from London.[27] Breasted's purpose was to circumvent the arrangement with *The Times*:

> I must again emphasize the great importance of refraining from the use of my name in any way in connection with the publication of any news I may be able to gather. It is only by working in the strictest secrecy that I shall be able to elude the unjust copyright cordon which the TIMES has thrown round the whole story. In order not to compromise my father's position of confidence with those concerned with the work. I shall show him none of my dispatches. Should Mr. Howard Carter learn of this arrangement, my peculiar position of vantage with relation to THE CHICAGO DAILY NEWS will be at once killed. You understand, of course, that I shall not include in my dispatches any items which Mr. Carter may give me or Dr. Breasted in confidence, honor-bound; but this does not preclude my getting hold of 'inside' stuff not available to any other Pressman but the TIMES, and often even not to them.

He then requests that all dispatches be printed 'from our Special Correspondent'; and he outlines how he would send material to avoid the surveillance of *The Times*.

His comments on the 'unjust copyright cordon' of *The Times* did not prevent him from taking a stance against Bradstreet and others who were stirring up so much trouble. Charles Breasted was rather disingenuous in stating to Carter after his arrival in Luxor that, at the suggestion of his father, he might be able to help him 'in the interests of the work you are doing in the face of such unfair opposition.'[28] He said that the 'opportunity had offered itself of employing the aid of two leading American journals in combatting the elements which are so wrongly arraying themselves against your work.' Both the *Chicago Daily News* and the *Christian Science Monitor* would be prepared to publish, anonymously, 'any airing you might

26 The lawyer he engaged was F. M. Maxwell, a man of considerable experience in the Egyptian courts.
27 O.I. Director's Office Corr. 1923–4.
28 In a letter of 27 January 1924 in O.I. Director's Office Corr. 1923–4.

desire yourself or me to give to the efforts being put forth to hamper and retard your work.' He pointed out that *The Times* itself could not in good taste defend itself – why indeed not? – and the American papers could be seen as 'disinterested parties of his standing'. They could, moreover, provide useful publicity for his projected American lecture tour.

Charles Breasted then had the nerve to add that if Carter would agree, it would not infringe his *Times* contract or 'in any way lend to my father or me the aspect of newspaper correspondents'. Howard Carter was very prudent in his reply.[29] He thanked Charles Breasted and his father, thought the suggestion admirable, but advised caution because of the recent change of government in Cairo. He 'might communicate later upon the subject.' Breasted conveyed Carter's response a day or two later to P. S. Mowrer of the Paris Bureau of the *Chicago Daily News*; for the moment they should wait, but Carter 'feels that a fight is almost inevitable. In such event I shall be right on the inside, and the story, which will at once take on an important political aspect, ought to be a good one.' He would use the name Mecham for filing his dispatches. A letter dated 7 March, at the height of the subsequent troubles, shows that Breasted had regularly been filing dispatches 'with perfect smoothness'. There is no reason to believe that he had any other motive than self-interest in acting in this way, and there is no evidence that he seriously took advantage of his special position to make reports to Carter's disadvantage. Equally there is nothing to show that Breasted 'pater' (as he called himself to Charles) was aware of this little piece of enterprise on the side by his son.

Considerable caution needs to be exercised in dealing with the events involving Carter and Carnarvon interests on the one hand and the Antiquities Service and Egyptian Government on the other during the next few weeks. It will become clearer shortly that what happened in Luxor did not represent in microcosm what was happening, or was likely to happen, in archaeological expeditions elsewhere in Egypt. The extraordinary nature of Carter's discovery, the intense public interest, the press controversy with its machinating agents, the sensitive reactions of Egyptians to what seemed to be foreign archaeological monopolies, all lubricated by the perfervid passions generated by Carter and Lacau in particular, engendered a quite unparalleled turbulence in Luxor. It almost unhinged Carter mentally, and it rendered the judgement of most of the principals involved on both sides unreliable and increasingly partial. It seemed certain to the senior members of the Egyptian Expedition of the Metropolitan Museum of Art that a point of crisis had arrived which needed drastic action. On 23 January Albert Lythgoe wrote a strong letter to Edward Robinson, his Director, indicating the threatening signs in what was happening:[30]

29 This and the following letters in the same archive.
30 M.M.A., Department of Egyptian Art, Carter files.

A very serious situation is developing here between M. Lacau . . . and Howard Carter . . . with regard to the work in Tutankhamen, in which M. Lacau is clearly seeking to oust Carter and our Expedition from the tomb in order that they may take the work over themselves.

He mentions the 'unending series of "pin-pricks" ' of recent weeks and reports the disgust at Lacau's attitude expressed by disinterested scientists. He refers to the offensive letter of 10 January, and reports that Carter has called in a lawyer and that a case may shortly be brought in the Mixed Tribunal in Cairo. The American expedition should not be involved in the court proceedings, but their work will be affected by the new form of concession which Lacau intends to introduce and make retroactive. The proposed changes will seriously affect the prospects of the Metropolitan Museum in Egypt, and he urges Robinson to get the Museum Trustees to make representations to the Egyptian minister in Washington, and to approach the French Ambassador 'with friendly representations as to the *united opinion* of the Egyptological world as to the complete inefficiency of France's present official appointee as Director-General of Antiquities at Cairo.' He sums up his opinion in stark manner:

In plain words it has become increasingly apparent to us all during this season that if we don't put an end to M. Lacau, or effectively stop his activities, he will unquestionably put an end to all archaeological work here such as ours, and that in the very near future.

With Gardiner and Breasted now in Luxor as well as Newberry, and all deeply involved in the work at the tomb, the possibilities for extended discussion, even plotting, were greatly increased. Lythgoe and Gardiner together drafted a letter to Lacau which they hoped would be signed by Breasted and Newberry, in which they made clear their opinions on recent events, on the treatment meted out to Carter, and on Lacau's failings as Director-General. Gardiner wrote personally to Breasted on 27 January,[31] sending Lythgoe's draft and requesting Breasted, if he agreed with it, to get Charles to type it out so that Gardiner himself could take it to Cairo on 30 January, signed by them all including Newberry. It was an uncompromising document. It drew attention to the danger to the scientific record of the tomb from the many acts of interference that had taken place; it reminded Lacau of the excellence of the work carried out by Carter and his co-workers; it pointed out how the Egyptian Government had benefited from the work of this and other foreign enterprises:

We feel obliged, therefore, to put ourselves on record at this time, as calling your attention to the serious nature of the present interrup-

31 O.I. Director's Office Corr. 1924.

tions and to the further fact that unless the unnecessary difficulties now obstructing the work in the Tomb of Tutankhamen are moderated, we can only hold one opinion, namely, that you, as Director General of Antiquities, are failing completely to carry out the obligations of your high office to protect the scientific procedure of this all-important task. It is hardly necessary for us to call attention to the unfortunate effect of such failure of your administration upon the public and the great scientific world now so eagerly following the progress of the task.

It is not certain that Carter knew anything about this letter until after it was sent, but he inevitably became associated with it and with the general activities of his well intentioned colleagues. Of these Gardiner, now being in Cairo, was initially the most active. On 2 February he wrote to the new Minister of Public Works, Morcos Bey Hanna, requesting an interview,[32] and he was subsequently able to report to Carter on the morning of 7 February that the minister would be friendly and was 'willing to let bygones by bygones'. Noting this in his diary, Carter added: 'He (Gardiner) seemed to have medled [sic], with the affair rather much, but with obviously good intention.' Gardiner had also written to the new Prime Minister in London, Ramsay Macdonald, who was also acting as Foreign Secretary, to the British Academy (with a copy of the jointly signed letter); and shortly he would write at length to Sir Frederick Kenyon, Director of the British Museum, and Chairman of the Joint Archaeological Committee in Great Britain. When Gardiner decided to espouse a cause, he did not act by half measures; but his good intentions were often frustrated by a failure to consult others before acting, and by over-reaction. He was not, however, the only one who seemed to know best in this wretched controversy. The one who suffered the consequences of the unwise interventions was always Howard Carter.

He had come to Cairo following exchanges with Tottenham over the timing for the opening of the sarcophagus and the admission of journalists, and also to pay his respects to the new minister. His visit had been preceded by the long reply he had written on 3 February in answer to Lacau's objectionable communication of 10 January.[33] It was carefully argued, covering all the points raised by Lacau, rehearsing all the recent interferences to the work, and drawing attention to the arbitrary tone of the Director-General's approach, noting in particular *Le Gouvernement ne discute plus, mais vous transmet sa décision.* The letter ends on a pained, puzzled note:

The work on which I am engaged has been done not for gain, but

32 A draft of this letter and of the others written by Gardiner, mentioned here, are in G.I. Carter Papers VI, 13A.
33 *Statement*, pp. 36ff.

in the interest of science. The discovery of the tomb has produced great benefits for Egypt, and for the Egyptian Antiquities Department in particular. It has also produced rights in the Earl of Carnarvon, the author of these benefits. It is a matter of surprise and regret to me, that whereas every other Department of the Egyptian Government has shown only goodwill, kindness, and eagerness to help, your Department has ever since the death of the late Lord Carnarvon not only been endeavouring to frustrate the rights of the Carnarvon family, but also to impede, hinder, and delay the scientific work without which the fruits of the discovery would be wasted. I am at a loss to find the motives for this action, but I have no doubt as to what will be the verdict of the World of Science on the issue between us.

Before seeing the minister on the 7th, Carter was advised by Tottenham to confine his remarks to the timing of the sarcophagus opening.[34] He hoped that all the tiresome earlier negotiations might be forgotten and the papers destroyed. Carter, it seems, tried to follow Tottenham's advice, but the minister, who received him cordially, raised several old problems, and complained in particular of Gardiner's visit, which he assumed had been proposed by Carter himself. Lacau joined the meeting 'armed with complete dossiers', but apart from one exchange over visitors to the tomb, the discussions were confined to the arrangements for the sarcophagus opening and press visits. An agreement on these and related matters was drawn up by Carter, Lacau and Tottenham on the following day, and on 9 February Carter was able to return to Luxor. The day for the official opening was fixed for 12 February, so there was not much time to get things ready, erect the necessary tackle to lift the great (and cracked) granite lid, and ensure that electric light would be available, for there had been problems over its supply.

On the morning of the 12th Carter met Lacau and Mohammed Pasha Zaghlul, Under-Secretary of State in the Ministry of Public Works and representing Morcos Bey Hanna at the opening.[35] The list of those who were to attend the opening was agreed, and Carter mentioned that he proposed to allow the wives of his colleagues to view the sarcophagus on the following day, after the Press visit. Zaghlul expressed surprise at this, for him, unexpected development and said he would have to refer the matter to the minister; no immediate objection was raised. And so the opening ceremony was ready to go ahead. Carter, in the second volume of his work on the tomb, lists the names of those who were present from both sides.[36] Archaeologically it was very impressive, including in addition

34 *Ibid.*, pp. 44ff.
35 *Ibid.*, pp. 49ff.
36 *The Tomb of Tut.ankh.Amen*, II, pp. 50f. for list and Carter's account of the opening.

to those who might be considered 'regular' at such ceremonies in the tomb, others like Robert Mond, Georges Foucart, Director of the French Institute, Bernard Bruyère, the excavator of the remarkable workmen's village at Deir el-Medina; also the Hon. J. J. Astor MP proprietor of *The Times*. Gardiner and Breasted were there, and the latter sent, two days later, a long account of the proceedings to John D. Rockefeller Jr.[37] In it he describes events before the opening, when he and Gardiner went over the river from Luxor to have lunch with Carter and his staff. There was huge tension in the air, and there were few signs of the happy expectancy that had characterized the day when a similar gathering viewed the entry into the Burial Chamber:

> We sat down and rested in the shade and quiet of the little sunken area at the head of the entrance stairway where we had so often sat with Carnarvon but one short year before. . . . At one o'clock he and Callender came out, tired and dusty. Carter looked ill and said he felt so. We walked down to Number 41[38] and sat down to lunch. I looked around. There we were sitting, the same group in the same order as when we lunched with Carnarvon on the memorable day almost exactly a year before – the day when the burial-chamber was opened. But now Carnarvon's chair at the head of the table was occupied by Carter who pulled out a roll of papers. It was a communication from Morcos Hanna, Minister of Public Works, decreeing in needlessly autocratic and offensive terms the tomb program for the next few days. We talked of nothing else throughout the lunch, and Carter told me the whole thing had made him ill.

Just after 3 o'clock the whole group gathered in the tomb, and shortly after, with a few pauses to adjust the tackle, the great lid was raised and slung clear to about two feet above the sarcophagus. Breasted makes much of the occasion, embellishing his description with imaginative comments. He considered the figures of Tutankhamun's successor, King Ay, shown on the far wall supervising the original burial:

> To me at that moment the painted Pharaoh on the wall seemed to take on a strange though ghostly reality; why did I feel a sense of unworthiness as I looked up at him? Why did he seem so calmly superior? . . . [There] stood Eye [Ay] still calmly extending his censor and still burning the last incense to the soul of his dead predecessor.

When the ropes of the tackle had been secured, Carter and Mace began to unroll the discoloured, brittle, linen shrouds covering the coffin which could clearly be discerned beneath the wrappings:

37 O.I. Director's Office Corr. 1924.
38 Tomb no. 4 (Ramesses XI) was the lunch tomb.

Complete silence ensued. It had in it something of the oppressiveness of those silent intervals in funerals of our own day. At the same time, reminding for all the world of the routine efficiency of modern undertaker's assistants, Carter and Mace stepped quietly forward to the head of the mute figure.

After several pages of reflections on the last days of the youthful king, on the fate of his wife, and on the political moves of those who were to succeed him, Breasted describes the moment of revelation as the last layers of shroud were rolled back from the coffin:

> we suddenly saw the gleaming gold of the vulture head and the upreared cobra on the King's forehead; we saw his eyes seeming to look out upon us as if in life itself, and as the shroud rolled downward the King's whole figure burst upon us in all the splendour of shining gold.

None of the Egyptologists present would have doubted that a nest of coffins would be found in the sarcophagus, but none could have known how the burial would have been furnished for a king, and none could have expected to see such remarkable beauty in such excellent condition:

> What we saw, as we had dimly known from the first moment, was the lid of the outer coffin, cunningly wrought by the portrait sculptor, with the aid of the lapidary and the goldsmith, into a magnificent portrait figure of the king lying as if stretched out on the lid of the coffin, like a crusader on his tomb slab in some European cathedral. . . . As a work of art, no known anthropoid coffin lid can approach it.

The whole operation had taken barely one hour. It was a moment of great triumph for Carter, and he was sufficiently buoyed up to take the whole party for a small celebration in Tomb no. 4, that of Ramesses XI, the luncheon tomb which had witnessed many joyful toasts in the last fifteen months. Carter then seems to have gone home as soon as he could, to rest and prepare for the Press viewing on the following day. Minnie Burton does not put him down for dinner on the 12th. Any feelings of triumph, or even satisfaction, were quickly dispersed on the following morning.

Lacau had been blamed for what happened next, although it seems certain from surviving documents that he only became involved in the tragic sequence of events when decisions had been taken in Cairo without his advice.[39] Late on the 12th, Mohammed Pasha Zaghlul received a communication from his minister forbidding the visit by the wives of Carter's collaborators to the tomb after the Press visit. Carter was not

39 *Statement*, pp. 50ff.

informed until early on the 13th, but the information was passed to Lacau earlier. In a pencil note, undated, unplaced and untimed, Richard Bethell wrote to Newberry:[40]

> Have you heard the latest? A wire came last night from the Minister forbidding the visit of the ladies today. Lacau was wringing his hands and his beard to me up to 12.30 last night. 'Mon Dieu, Mon Dieu, que faire!' I don't know what H.C.'s action will be, very likely to start filling in the tomb at once.

Carter received the information in a note from Mohammed Zaghlul at 6.40 in the morning; it came 'as a thunderclap'. What right had he in the tomb? Off he went, first to the Metropolitan House. Winifred Mace described to her mother what happened:[41]

> Mr. Carter has had one indignity after another heaped upon him, and the climax was when the dispatch was sent to the papers, saying it was opened in the presence of certain native Ministers, secretaries and moudirs and at the end Mr. Lucas and Mr. Carter – then Mons. Lacau said the wives could not go today without a permit from Cairo, this so infuriated the man, such an insult that a note came at eight o'clock this morning to say Mr. Carter was coming over; he arrived looking desperately ill and in a fury. Arthur and Mr. Lythgoe were to go over with him to Luxor and he would tell the Minister he would shut down the tomb and Messrs Mace and Burton had resigned.

On his way to the river to cross to Luxor Carter was shown two documents signed by Lacau, the first signalling the refusal to allow the ladies to visit the tomb and instructing the three Egyptian inspectors to keep a guard at the tomb to prevent any unauthorized entry 'avec toute la courtoisie désirable'.[42] The second, a note to Carter, expressed Lacau's unhappiness at the turn of events, but pointing out that he had no option but to act on the minister's instructions. The impression is certainly given that Lacau had made no attempt to modify the action, no matter what his personal feelings were.

Carter, Mace and Lythgoe then joined Newberry, Merton, Bethell and Gardiner in Breasted's room in the Winter Palace Hotel, and the day was spent in discussing moves, drawing up statements, attempting to moderate Carter's understandable fury. At 12.30, after failing to see Mohammed Zaghlul, Carter posted the following notice in the hotel:[43]

40 G.I. Newberry Corr. 4/104.
41 Letter of 13 February 1924.
42 *Statement*, p. 51.
43 For the meeting in Breasted's room, see Breasted's letter to Rockefeller of 14 February, cited in n. 37 above. For Carter's notice, see *Statement*, p. 51.

Owing to impossible restrictions and discourtesies on the part of the Public Works Department and its Antiquities Service, all my collaborators in protest have refused to work any further upon the scientific investigations of the discovery of the tomb of Tut.ankh.-amen.

I therefore am obliged to make known to the public that, immediately after the Press view of the tomb this morning, between 10 A.M. and noon, the tomb will be closed, and no further work can be carried out.

This closure was seen by the authorities as being contrary to the agreement drawn up with Carter regulating procedures for visitors and continuing work on the tomb, and it was thought to be unjustified. It also gave the authorities the opening they seemed to be seeking to take even more drastic action. Carter on his part would almost certainly have filled in the tomb, had he not been dissuaded by his collaborators. He was himself dumbfounded, deeply aggrieved, furious and ill; he felt that the whole of his staff had been insulted by the gratuitous refusal to allow the ladies into the tomb, and that by implication the insult extended to Almina, the Countess of Carnarvon. Utter despair pervaded those who were affected. Winifred Mace, again voicing partly the views of her husband, conveys the general pessimism:

> [Feb. 21] The whole is a disagreeable business and Carter is such an autocrat that to be thwarted at every turn takes all reason from him; Arthur is writing out the statement for the lawyer and he is often in despair to avoid Mr. Carter making wrong statements.

> [Feb. ?] We feel very low tonight, things look bad and it is greatly on the cards that Mr. Carter will not win his case, for of course in the concession no one ever thought of all this possibility. The Egyptian Government find this the right moment to get rid of a well known Englishman of thirty years standing, who has had power with the natives. I fear that it may end very badly and Carter will be forced to give the whole thing up. . . . Mr. Carter said sadly today to Arthur 'I am a nuisance to myself and my friends'.

A lively exchange of notes and letters between Carter, various government ministers, Lacau and Engelbach did nothing to cool tempers, instil good sense, or in any way to ameliorate the situation.[44] Carter made much of the fact that the sarcophagus lid was suspended on devices which had been intended to be only temporary; the minister rebuked him for not having made the lid safe before arbitrarily closing the tomb. Carter instigated legal proceedings in the Mixed Courts, writing on 18 February to

44 *Statement*, pp. 52ff.

instruct his lawyer F. M. Maxwell, who had much experience of the Egyptian courts and had an office in Alexandria. It has rightly been pointed out that the choice of Maxwell as his lawyer turned out to be a tactical blunder, for it was Maxwell who had prosecuted Morcos Hanna some years earlier in a treason trial, demanding the death sentence. Morcos Hanna was found guilty and sentenced to a relatively short prison term; but he would remember Maxwell with little affection. In mitigation of Carter's choice it must be pointed out that he had first engaged Maxwell in January before the change in government which had led to Morcos Hanna's becoming Minister for Public works. Carter's purpose in instituting legal proceedings was initially to secure a judgement concerning his rights in respect of the tomb, as specified in the renewed concession permit under which he had been working. The hearing was to take place on 23 February. He was in no mind to compromise with the Government until the hearing had taken place. He also required an apology from the Government and Lacau for the disrespect they had shown to the wives of his collaborators. Here was a sadly piquant stance which did not escape his supporters. Gardiner in Cairo wrote (as he did almost every day) to Breasted who was laid up with illness in Luxor:[45]

> I heard from Delaney, Reuter's agent here news of Carter's reply to the Minister. If what I hear is true, that *inter alia* Carter demands an apology from Lacau. I am incredibly shocked. That Carter, the man who himself retired from the Eg. Service because he would not give an apology, should now stand on his dignity and demand an apology from others, is I feel the silliest thing he could do.

That Carter requested an apology on behalf of the ladies made little difference.[46] The memory of the events of 1905 clearly lingered on in the minds of many who had been about in archaeological circles in Egypt in the early years of the century. Although Gardiner himself had not been in Egypt at the precise time of Carter's leaving the Service, he would have heard much from Weigall during their months of working in the Theban Necropolis, while Carter was still in the wilderness but about to start his association with Lord Carnarvon. Quibell and Edgar, however, as noted earlier, were both involved marginally in 1905, and now centrally in 1924. Quibell no doubt felt obliged to support Lacau, in being his deputy; but he need not have written to the Lythgoes some days earlier defending his Director so strongly:[47]

> I have an impression, from a few sentences from Gardiner, from something Firth said, from other odd words from I forget whom, that

45 Letter of 20 February in O.I. Director's Office Corr. 1924. Gerald Delany (spelt so), was in charge of Reuters, Cairo.
46 Text of the telegram demanding an apology, *Statement*, p. 55.
47 Letter of 9 February in M.M.A., Department of Egyptian Art, Carter files.

some of you have an idea that Lacau has shown and is showing hostility to the diggers, and particularly to Carter. Now, I want you and your lady wife to know that my firm conviction is that anyone who harbours such an idea is very, very unjust to Lacau. . . . I have been much struck by his patience and loyalty and the firmness with which he has defended the diggers' interests when they have been threatened, as they repeatedly have been. . . .

It is not Lacau who worries Carter with this surveillance by native inspectors, but the native Minister who is terrified by the native journalists who are stirred up by these sweet-scented geraniums from the garden of newspapers whose names you might guess in three shots.

Lacau's personal justification at this time was included in the letter he addressed to Breasted and Gardiner on 19 February in answer, at last, to their open letter (also signed by Lythgoe and Newberry) of 30 January.[48] He expresses great regret that differences should have come between them, and that he had been unable to convince one of them (presumably Gardiner) of the reasons for his actions. He remains firm in his belief that the official decisions had been taken justly, and he ends:

As for the tomb of Tout-Ankh-Amon, no difficulty on a scientific level has ever been raised. The work merits only praise. But it so happens that the work is carried out in a land in which we are the guests, which I represent in archaeological matters, and which believes it necessary to remind excavators of its rights. I reckon that it has clearly had the right to do so. From now on the dispute has been put on a legal basis and the legal side will deal with Carter. I think that the rights of the State and the interests of science are perfectly compatible in this circumstance, and I shall endeavour to sacrifice neither the former nor the latter.

Lacau bends little in this letter, and he shows little understanding of the strength of feeling held by Carter's associates and supporters. He may have had good reasons to believe that his first duty was to support science in the name of the Egyptian state. The Carter camp certainly believed that Lacau had a duty, apparently unrecognized by him, to support and represent the interests of the archaeologists working in Egypt, as the result of whose activities the Egyptian Museum was greatly enriched and the reputation of the country enhanced. Lacau, however, may have realized that the view taken in Luxor was not universally supported by Egyptologists elsewhere. The lines of opposition and support were not clearly drawn. Apart from Carter, Gardiner, Breasted and the members of the Metropolitan Museum Egyptian Expedition, the most vociferous anti-Lacau cham-

48 G.I. Carter Papers VI, 13A; the original in French.

pion was Percy Newberry. Later, in May, he wrote to T. E. Peet who had succeeded him as Professor of Egyptology in Liverpool in 1920, lamenting the decline of British prestige in Egypt, putting it down to, among other things, 'French intrigue':[49]

> The Carter incident is I believe the direct result of the latter. Lacau and unluckily two or three Englishmen in the Service des Antiquités have deliberately tried to down Carter and get the tomb into their own hands. . . . I have definitely decided never to have any further intercourse with Lacau, Quibell, or that impossible little cad Engelbach. I know well that Carter is difficult but when I think of the mean tricks that have been played on him this winter it fairly makes my blood boil.

Newberry was certainly off mark in talking of 'French intrigue'. Gardiner told Breasted that he had been talking to Gustave Lefebvre, the distinguished director of studies at the École Pratique des Hautes Études in Paris, 'who takes a most reasonable and fair-minded view.'[50] Georges Foucart, Director of the French Institute in Cairo, seems to have offered no support to Lacau at this time, and he certainly appeared distinctly hostile to his countryman, as Carter himself observed in the following winter when he happened to be in the office of the new Prime Minister Ziwar Pasha, where Foucart was also waiting for an audience. Carter reported that he 'conversed freely on Tut.ankh.amen and his (Foucart's) feud with Lacau, which struck me at the time as being somewhat inopportune.' Later, when both were with the Prime Minister, 'We discussed the Tomb question in Foucart's presence, Foucart intriguing against Lacau the whole time.'[51] So if there were French intrigues they were not necessarily aimed at Carter.

On the other side there were those who were not prepared to come out clearly in support of Carter, even some who might have been thought of as natural allies. Francis Llewellyn Griffith, who was still the Editor of the Archaeological Survey of Egypt, under whose auspices Carter had first come to Egypt in 1891, was in early 1924 directing the Egypt Exploration Society's excavations at El-Amarna – the site denied to Carnarvon and Carter some years before by Lacau. Lythgoe wrote to enlist Griffith's support and had, it seems, initially obtained his signature to an appeal to be made against Lacau. On 21 February Griffith wrote apologetically, withdrawing his signature:[52]

> We are here [i.e. in El-Amarna] in absolute darkness except for

49 Letter of 4 May, G. I. Newberry Corr. 36/78.
50 Letter of 17 February in O.I. Director's Office Corr. 1924.
51 Letter of Carter to Molony of 16 January 1925 outlining developments, in G. I. Carter Papers VI, 13A.
52 Griffith's and Petrie's letters in M.M.A., Department of Egyptian Art, Carter files.

glimpses in the Egyptian Gazette or a chance reference in a private letter, as to everything going on outside our work. Under these circumstances it is improper to join in strife that is very serious but as yet has not touched us, and for all I know it might be disastrous to the Egypt Exploration Society which I represent here to join in before knowing the history of the affair.

Flinders Petrie wrote in similar terms, but more fully, from Qau in Middle Egypt on 24 February. He was in considerable sympathy, but again claimed ignorance of the facts. He was not well disposed to Lacau, and greatly resented the proposed changes in the antiquities law. Still, to introduce the Carter case and Tutankhamun into the argument was bad tactics: 'It is most desirable to keep all Tut. questions entirely clear of general antiquity law. 'Hard cases make bad law', and gold always maddens people.'

Both Griffith and Petrie were being prudent, in spite of their sympathy for Carter. It is also the case that George Reisner, the very successful American archaeologist, who was excavating for Harvard University and the Museum of Fine Arts, Boston, in the pyramid field at Giza, was well satisfied with the treatment of his expedition by the Antiquities Service. It seems that he claimed to be indebted to Lacau for generous *partages*, for the acquisition by Boston of several outstanding pieces of Old-Kingdom sculpture found in the course of his work at Giza. Reisner had no respect for Carter as an excavator or as a man; he wrote a letter of unusual savagery in October 1924 to Mr Hawes, the Assistant Director of the Museum of Fine Arts, concerning the circumstances surrounding the Tutankhamun discovery. He had this to say about Carter's principal advocates:[53]

> Last winter, Dr. Gardiner, Mr. Percy Newberry, Prof. Breasted, and Mr. Lythgoe formed a little coterie of archaeologists who identified themselves fully with Carter's work and Carter's contentions in his controversy with the Egyptian. Government. . . . all of them were interested to some extent in the matter, and they all, talking together, worked themselves up into an unnatural frame of mind in which they saw all things with a distorted vision.

It seems to have been the case that excavators working away from Thebes had better experiences with the Antiquities Service, and their reactions to the troubles in the Valley of the Kings were determined equally by a degree of self-interest. Less well disposed to Carter on other

---

53 I quote from this letter by courtesy of the Department of Egyptian and Ancient Near Eastern Art in the Museum of Fine Arts Boston, and am grateful to Dr Rita Freed, the departmental curator, for her help. Reisner's view of Lacau's generosity in *partage* was explained to B. V. Bothmer by Dows Dunham who had worked with Reisner in Egypt in the 1920s.

grounds was Jean Capart. Gardiner had written to him on 7 March, when events, as will be seen, had taken an even worse turn.[54] He sought the support both of Capart and of his Queen, who had been so well entertained by Lord Carnarvon and Carter the year before. He readily admitted, 'Carter is a difficult man and by no means tactful', but his work is good. Lacau, however, 'has dishonoured himself and dishonoured the science of which he is here the trustee'; he has harassed Carter in so many small ways that 'Carter has been driven into errors of judgement which we all deplore. But on Lacau falls the guilt of not having defended him and made his work possible.' Capart in reply said little about Gardiner's charges against Lacau, but wrote at length about his own grievances against Carter. He had behaved badly over the photographs Capart had needed; he had never acknowledged Capart's book of collected articles on the Tomb; he had, worst of all, failed to be helpful to Mademoiselle Marcelle Werbrouck who had visited Egypt as an emissary of the Fondation Égyptologique Reine Élisabeth. The Queen had not been pleased. In short, Capart reckoned that Carter had 'shown a rare clumsiness and . . . been badly advised; or rather, and I believe this to be more accurate, that he has chosen not to listen to good advice.' Towards the end of his letter he tells Gardiner that he found that the 'collective letter to Lacau was somewhat unfortunate, not the fact of having written it, but to have publicized it immediately in The Times. There was no better way to inflame again the questions of prestige, those terrible questions of prestige, and to entrench the parties in their various positions.' He was in effect adopting the classic position of sitting on the fence, and would not help: 'As for myself I have publicly taken the stance of saying nothing and sending away all journalists who ask for my comments. By his attitude towards me, Carter prevented me from acting in any other way.'

There were, no doubt, others like Capart, who could not bring themselves to support Carter actively; it is surprising that Capart could not see that in the context of troubles in Egypt, his own grievances were trivial and even petty. There remained enough supporters to sustain Carter, although he was about to lose Mace and even Callender. Mace fell ill towards the end of February and left Egypt with Winifred and Margaret on 6 March. The strain of the season, the constant disputes, the need to keep things going in Luxor while Carter was in Cairo, all contributed to the steady deterioration in his condition. On the night before the family left Egypt, Winifred Mace dined with Howard Carter: 'He was a pathetic person, and he really felt Arthur's going so much.'[55] Carter was indeed losing his best collaborator and truest supporter. It is difficult to over-

54 Gardiner's letter and Capart's reply in G.I. Carter Papers VI, 13A. I am grateful to Anne Pemberton for establishing the French text of Capart's difficult handwriting, and for providing a translation.
55 Letter to her mother of 4 March, written on board ship *en route* for Italy.

estimate Arthur Mace's contribution to the first two seasons on the tomb of Tutankhamun. Apart from his practical skills, his ability to write and to think clearly, to keep a cool head, and to moderate Carter's passions, he helped to set up the systems for conservation and documentation which were to carry Carter through to the end of the task. Carter saw him occasionally in subsequent years during his summer visits to England, but Mace himself was sadly finished. He never returned to Egypt, and after four years of continual ill-health and the search for a cure in Switzerland, the Riviera, and the USA, he died in Sussex on 6 April 1928.[56]

Arthur Callender left in some discontent shortly after the closure of the tomb on 13 February. He and Carter had not enjoyed easy relations for some time. There is no precise evidence for the differences between the two. Callender was Carter's principal assistant in matters of practical engineering, and his constant helper in the tomb itself. It is very probable that they saw too much of each other on a daily basis, and any problems would be carried back at night to Carter's house at Elwat el-Diban, where Callender apparently lived during the season. Everyone who worked closely with Carter was from time to time contradicted, obliged to conform with Carter's own ideas of how things should be done, made the target of his contrary temper and unreasonable moods. Walter Hauser and Lindsley Hall had troubles early on; Burton would complain; even Carnarvon felt the effects of the claustrophobic conditions in the tomb within which Carter's poor humours were nourished. Mace, by equal professionalism and by self-control and understanding, survived the difficult times. Callender is thought to have been reasonably phlegmatic and capable of enduring the regular verbal abuse, but perhaps only because he alone of the staff was paid from Carnarvon funds. Yet on 25 January Carter had noted in his dig diary, 'Callender sent in his resignation, blaming my action towards him.' This laconic entry is not further explained, and Callender was certainly still with the team until the tomb was closed. He was then paid off for the season, prematurely as he seems to have seen it. Writing from his house at Armant on 19 February, principally to report the favourable reactions of various non-archaeologists to Carter's actions, he comes to the real point:[57]

> I hate troubling you, and had I only myself to think about, I would not care, but this Season's work ending in February, whereas last Season it ended in May, it is a serious pecuniary loss to me, but I leave it to you.

The problem, as it emerged over a year later, was that he claimed to have joined the Carnarvon team 'on the verbal understanding of 7 months work

56 On his last years, see C. Lee, . . . the Grand Piano came by Camel, (Reufrew, 1990), pp. 49f.
57 In M.M.A., Department of Egyptian Art, Carter Files, along with other letters about his claim for loss of earnings, see p. 338 below.

a year at a monthly salary of £E50 (increased the second season to £E60), and all found board and lodging etc.' At the time, in 1924, he received no satisfactory reply from Carter, and relations were so strained that when Callender wrote to Newberry in Luxor on 16 March he felt obliged to state:[58]

> I have been thinking over about my coming down to Luxor tomorrow and have come to the conclusion I had better not, yet I will be sorry at not being able to wish you all goodbye.
>
> You see, had Carter wished to see me, he would have dropped me a line, and as he will be about, I would be forced to go to see him, or to meet him in Luxor or the American house, so I have decided it is better not.

Things had now got to the point between Carter and the Government that he could no longer handle matters with any confidence. He was also constrained by the arrangements he had made to travel to America for his lecture tour, due to start in New York in mid-April. The row over the closure of the tomb, and the need to reopen it to secure the sarcophagus and the personal materials of the staff of the expedition, developed by a series of acrimonious communications from both sides.[59] On 20 February Morcos Hanna, the minister, had issued a ministerial decree cancelling Lady Carnarvon's permit, and instructing Lacau to open the tomb and other associated stores and the laboratory, and to take urgently all necessary measures for the safety and the conservation of the antiquities found in them. Lacau informed Carter that he would be in Luxor on 22 February and would hope that they could together supervise the opening of the various tombs. Carter tried to temporize on the grounds that action should be delayed at least until after his case had come to court on 23 February. Lacau had his orders, and proceeded to carry them out. In his dossier on the whole unhappy sequence of events, Carter quotes as his final entry in the main text the report on what happened, presented to him by his *reis*, Ahmed Gerigar [pp. 58f.]:

> M. Lacau, Mr. Engelbach, M. Barazie, Chaban Eff., Ibrahim Eff., the Sheikh of the Antiquity guards, and their smith, arrived in the Valley accompanied by the Governor of the Province, the Commandant of the Police, the Mamour and Molais of Merqis Luxor, and thirty-three armed police – camel- and horse-mounted and foot. There was also another Government representative (?) of judicial side.[60] They proceeded to cut the padlocks on the steel gates of both the tomb and the laboratory. Entered therein. Made a 'procès-verbal'

58 G.I. Newberry Corr. 7/7.
59 *Statement*, pp. 56ff.
60 A footnote in *Statement*, p. 59, specifies him as 'Mohammed Riad Bey, Director of the Legal Department, P.W.M.', i.e Public Works Department.

and made certain dispositions within the tomb, using materials belonging to the expedition both within and without the tomb. The Antiquity officials ordered me and my three assistants to leave our respective posts. We were prevented guarding even the photographic laboratory, so we retired to the magazine, where we were left unhindered. I understand they are continuing their procedure in the laboratory today.

The action was in part observed by Charles Breasted, who sent next day a lively account to the *Chicago Daily News*. He began dramatically:[61]

It is well known that King Tutankhamen's tomb was broken into in ancient times, but yesterday was the first time that an official breaking in sponsored and abetted by the Egyptian government, took place.

After outlining the events of the day, he recounts that he called on Carter in his house:

I found him a sorrow-stricken man, deprived by a strange series of episodes of completing the greatest archaeological discovery ever made in the orient.

Minnie Burton noted nothing of these dramatic happenings in her diary, but she does record the 22 February as Margaret Mace's eleventh birthday: 'Gave her an elephant tail mounted in gold bangle.'

Carter may have been 'sorrow-stricken', but he retained a grim capacity to fight. He began a second law-suit to secure his right to resume work, and went down in a few days to Cairo so that he could keep in touch with his lawyer, F. M. Maxwell. The subsequent legal actions and separate negotiations form a wearisome narrative which at long distance seems to be characterized by stubbornness, *parti pris*, bruised dignity, feelings of revulsion, and plain dislike. The outline of the legal stages is set out in a long memorandum dated 29th March sent by Maxwell to R. H. Molony of the Carnarvon Estate solicitors Frere, Cholmeley and Co. of Lincoln's Inn Fields, who also did business for Carter in England.[62] First writs were issued on 21 February and a hearing took place on the 23rd. After an adjournment an offer of a new concession was made, and on 29 February Breasted was invited by the Egyptian Government to draw up the new terms. Breasted then, with Carter, Mace and Maxwell, agreed terms which they thought could be discussed with the Government. At once Carter saw problems and raised difficulties. Maxwell reported to Breasted on 2 March,[63] 'Carter is in a very obstinate mood which has been aggravated

61 Copy in M.M.A., Department of Egyptian Art, Carter files.
62 M.M.A., Department of Egyptian Art, Carter files.
63 In O.I. Director's Office Corr. 1924.

by the fact of Mace falling ill. . . . Nevertheless I think it is important that Zaghlul Pasha should be told . . . that the action will be stopped if a new concession is granted on conditions approved by a representative of the scientific world such as yourself.' Maxwell thought that Carter might gain more from such a move than by persisting in his case, although Carter seemed to him 'very unwilling to take any step at all. In fact he said that he would rather lose his action than do anything more to accommodate the Government.' Breasted was inclined to agree with Maxwell's proposal, and felt that he might be able to secure some agreement, but not before the renewal of the court hearing on Saturday 8 March.[64] For on the 6th there was to be a great governmental visitation of the tomb with celebrations to which many ministers planned to go, including Morcos Hanna; but not Zaghlul, who was ill.

Both sides were again trapped by their intransigence. Carter refused to allow a further adjournment, let alone the dropping of his case; the Government in return considered, according to Breasted, 'the continuance of the fight in Court next Saturday as evidence that Carter does not want a peaceable settlement.' The *fantasiya* at the tomb was particularly worrying to the Carter camp; as Maxwell reported to Molony, there had been little control, and moreover, further entertainments were planned. There had been special trains from Cairo, bands and banquets; while nothing untoward seemed to have occurred on the first occasion, there was a real chance of damage if the event were to be repeated. Mace in a letter to Newberry, written on 9 March on board ship for Italy,[65] called it 'this infernal beanfeast', and he told of his worries that Breasted might, in his eagerness to achieve a settlement, 'give anything away in the interests of peace, and was quite confident. Carter and I were sceptical because we had been through the same programme several times already in the course of the Winter.' Breasted wanted Carter to postpone the hearing, but Carter had refused as it 'seemed to us like throwing away all your weapons before going into a fight.' Maxwell had agreed, but Breasted 'was very angry, said that Carter's action was a deadly blow to science and that he should tell everyone that it was he (Carter) who had wrecked the whole thing.'

It did not come to that, fortunately. The hearing went ahead on 8 March, and certain exceptions raised by the Government were discussed; then a further adjournment. The minister indicated to Breasted that if Carter signed a renunciation covering the objects from the tomb, he would offer concessions. With some difficulty Carter was persuaded to sign the following on 9 March:[66]

I hereby declare that I for myself never have made, do not now

64 Letters of Breasted to Maxwell on 4 and 5 March in O.I. Director's Office Corr. 1924.
65 G.I. Newberry Corr. 30/13.
66 In M.M.A., Department of Egyptian Art, Carter files.

make, and never intend to make any claim against the Egyptian Government or against anyone else to any of the objects found in the Tomb of Tutankhamen.

Apparently by chance, although in fact at the urgent request of F. M. Maxwell, General Sir John Maxwell, representing the Countess of Carnarvon, turned up in Cairo at this point, and on her behalf signed a similar renunciation. The complete accord between both sides, which Breasted hoped could be achieved on the basis of a draft agreement he had worked out with the Egyptians, now seemed clinched. It was frustrated by one word spoken by F. M. Maxwell in court on the 10th. Maxwell explained what happened to Molony:[67]

> In the course of my argument the Judge asked why Mr. Carter had abandoned possession of the tomb before issuing his writ, because he said it was one thing to confirm a possession by appointing a sequestrator, and another to transfer it. I was somewhat horrified at the Judge having overlooked so material a part of our case. I therefore said that Mr. Carter was in possession when he issued his writ but that the Government had since come like a bandit and forced him out of possession by violence. Maître Rosetti protested. The judged [sic] asked me whether the bandit was necessary to my case. I replied that any word would suit me which expressed the violence and illegality of which I complained. There is no word for bandit in Arabic, and the native papers used the word for thieves. This annoyed the Ministers who like to think that they are unusually honest.

F. M. Maxwell should undoubtedly have appreciated that under the circumstances, with passions running high and the Egyptian ministers, at this early stage in constitutional government in the country, particularly sensitive about their status and dignity, the use of a word like 'bandit' could be explosive. It provided the Government with the ideal excuse to break off all negotiations in the matter of the new concession.

In an attempt to rescue the situation before it deteriorated beyond recovery, Breasted decided to write to Morcos Hanna dissociating himself from the use of the word. He discussed the form of his letter with Sir John Maxwell and F. M. Maxwell in the Semiramis Hotel, and in due course signed the shorter and less strong of two letters. It was abject in tone, and unnecessarily obsequious; the crucial sentences read:[68]

> I wish to dissociate myself absolutely from this regrettable utterance and to express my profound disapproval of such language. I ask your Excellency to accept my assurance of deepest regret that such an

---

67 In M.M.A., Department of Egyptian Art, Carter files.
68 Dated 11 March. This and other documentation on this episode in O.I. Director's Office Corr. 1924.

expression should have furnished the just occasion for the termination of our negotiations.

He thought that the lawyer Maxwell approved. The opposite was the case, and Maxwell later objected in the strongest terms that such a letter, impugning his professional competence, had been allowed to be made public.[69] In any case, the letter did not mollify Morcos Hanna to whom Breasted had taken it personally the same night. The Minister was 'in a state of intense indignation', as Breasted wrote to Carter on the following day.[70] 'The assurance of the Minister that the negotiations were ended was final and every effort to bring about a more conciliatory attitude completely failed.' Breasted therefore announced the termination of his mediatorship. In spite of the reservations expressed on his own and on Carter's behalf by Mace to Newberry, Breasted had laboured hard and had come within an ace of success. Whether there was ever a real chance of a settlement with the Zaghlul administration in power cannot be claimed with confidence. Carter seemed prepared to be grateful. He had written to Breasted on 6 March expressing his appreciation;[71] 'Nobody realises more than I the difficulties you have had to contend with. . . . Whether successful or otherwise the *good intention* can never be obliterated.'

Although he thus bowed out formally as mediator in the negotiations between Carter and the Government, Breasted did not, indeed could not, wholly disengage from the matter. In the first place the Egyptians had got used to him and had established a kind of understanding – even if an uneasy one – with him; second, his inclination obliged him to continue negotiations, especially as a new official American interest began to be taken in the affair. Dr J. Morton Howell, the American Minister in Cairo, now intervened, and he found it appropriate to work with Breasted. There is good evidence that this development was due to Breasted himself. He had earlier written to Dr George E. Hale, a most distinguished American astronomer who had organized, and was until 1923 the first director of, the Mt Wilson Observatory. He was a good friend of Breasted who had hoped that he would get him to Egypt during the time of the momentous discovery. In 1924 he was Director of the National Research Council, and had been sent a copy of the letter to Lacau signed by Breasted, Gardiner and the others.[72] Direct intervention on the official level was ruled out by the State Department in Washington because Carter was British, and the relevance of the dispute to American interests had to be argued. A communication on the same subject from Edward Robinson, pointing out the damage that could be done to the interests of the Metropolitan Museum

69 Letter of 17 March to Breasted, see last note.
70 Breasted to Carter on 12 March; copy in O. I. Director's Office Corr. 1924.
71 Also in O.I., see last note.
72 The Hale to Breasted correspondence is in O.I. Breasted Papers; especially Hale to Breasted of 23 February 1924, and Breasted to Hale of 22 March 1924.

21 The 5th Earl of Carnarvon and Howard Carter, photographed
18 February 1923 by Queen Élisabeth of the Belgians

22 Carter conducts the Tutankhamun 'mannequin' from the tomb; the
Earl of Carnarvon sits on the wall, and to his right, behind, is
Arthur Weigall

23 The First Ford 'in the desert', outside Castle Carter, 1923.
From left: Carter, chauffeur, Mace, Burton, Lucas

24 Blocked entrance to the burial chamber of Tutankhamun's tomb,
showing the basket-work concealing the intruder's hole and
subsequent reblocking

25 Carter's team prepare for the day's sortie into the Valley: *from left*, Alfred Lucas, Arthur Callender, Carter, Arthur Mace

26 The Press Corps advance to battle up the Valley; Arthur Weigall on the right

27 A convoy of cases containing Tutankhamun objects makes its way
to the river *en route* for Cairo

28 Percy White at Ludlow, 1930

29 Carter with his niece Phyllis Walker, *c.* 1931

30 The study at 2, Prince's Gate Court, 1934

31 Studio photograph of Carter, *c.* 1930

32 Carter at the lectern, *c.* 1934

33　A formal dinner in Stockholm, May 1930. *From left:*
Consul-General J. Sachs, Mrs Helling, Carter, Mrs Boström,
Admiral Lindberg

34　Howard Carter with the Crown Prince of Sweden and ADC on board
the SS *Ausonia*, bound for Egypt, September 1930

35 Carter with the Egyptian Queen Mother and entourage in the Valley, *c.* 1932

36 Carter with King Farouk in the Valley, 1936

El-Korna Luxor Upper
Egypt 19/3/1939.

He

Sir Miss Phyllis Walker Nutfield House
Nutfield Place Marble
Arch London

Respectifully we have heard with illness by
the death of our Head Dr. H. Carter we & our
famillies & all the native of our country &
Egypt ill. I have sarved Dr. H. Carter 42 years
pass well. This notice ill us much specially
about us your most obbedient servants.
Sir Mr Bartin gave us this notice we are
gun content we are write this letter hoping
that you Miss shall be well & in a good
health & you shall be in the service of the Dr
H. Carter. we hope that you shall be well
& good health - we are waiting your notice
& about health & All.

we remain.

Your most obbedient servants
Abd-El-Aal Ahmad Sayed & Hosein
Ibraheem Sayed El-Korna Luxor
Upper Egypt... Egypt.
19/3/1939.

37 Letter of condolence written by Howard Carter's house servants
to Phyllis Walker

by the proposed changes in excavation permits, and further arguments from Hale led, as Breasted reported, to 'instructions from Washington to bring personal and informal pressure on the Egyptian Government.'

Breasted was in something of a quandary. He had resigned as mediator, he would shortly be leaving Egypt; yet it was he who had apparently stimulated Washington to act, and Howell naturally turned to him for background information and specialist support. Then, on 21 March, Breasted wrote to Howell informing him that he had just heard that Carter, at the moment of leaving Egypt, had on the previous day appointed H. E. Winlock 'as his agent in the matter of the tomb, with power of attorney.' He felt obliged therefore to end his involvement: 'the new information of Mr. Winlock's appointment, makes it impossible for me to reenter the case.'[73] That, however, was not to be the end of the matter as far as Breasted was concerned.

In the meanwhile, since the breakdown of the negotiations and Breasted's letter of withdrawal on 12 March, Carter had returned to Luxor to consider his position and to make arrangements for some kind of supervision of the closing of the tomb. He would leave Egypt on 21 March. Recently he had not taken much part in the negotiations with the Egyptian government after the closure of the tomb, but had left matters in the hands of Breasted and F. M. Maxwell, intervening only to exercise his stubbornness and to object to concessions. After Breasted it would be Winlock, but his involvement would not seriously begin until after Carter had left Egypt. The report that during this period Carter went to see Allenby and threatened to publish papyrus texts from the tomb giving the Egyptian side of the events surrounding the departure of the Jews from Egypt in antiquity represents an unjustifiable interpretation of an implausible story said to have been told to Mr Lee Keedick by Carter himself during his lecture tour in America. The report, included in Mr Keedick's notes on Carter, is quite unspecific as to place, time and even the person involved. There is no independent witness for the event, and it may best be treated as apocryphal.[74]

Minnie Burton charts some of Carter's movements in Luxor in the days before his departure. On 7 March he came to dinner at the Metropolitan House – the last time for the season. On the 18th she records: 'Mr. Carter came to say goodbye and brought me his canary.' This canary presents a problem. It may be remembered that when he came to Luxor on November 1922 he brought a 'golden bird' to keep him company.[75] This canary did not last long. Winlock recorded how, when Carter was up in Cairo collecting Carnarvon, Callender found a cobra in the cage 'just in the act of

73 The Breasted to Howell correspondence also in O.I. Director's Office Corr. 1924.
74 See Hoving, *Tutankhamun. The Untold Story*, p. 310. His interpretation of the Keedick account goes far beyond the facts as recorded by Keedick, and is too specific.
75 See p. 218 above.

gulping the canary down, halo and all.' It was a strange story, for it is hard to imagine how a cobra could have got through the bars of the cage. If they were so spaced that the snake could get in, surely the canary could have got out. At the time the good omens, assigned initially to the bird, were transformed into forebodings. It is surprising therefore to find that Carter had later replaced the bird with another. And here it was being placed in the hands of Minnie Burton, who was not very well disposed to Carter. She was, however, just an intermediary, and eventually on 16 April, the day before the Burtons' own departure, she took the bird across to Luxor and put it in the charge of Mr Parissis, the bank manager. She also notes in her entry for 19 March that she took various friends and Frances Winlock to the Valley of the Kings, 'and got Mr. Engelbach to let them into the Tomb.' She would scarcely have dared to do that if Carter had been in Luxor. And one wonders what Harry Burton thought about it. He may not have been told.

When Carter left Luxor he had much to worry him; the future of his work in Egypt was in grave doubt; he would not be returning to England to a hero's welcome; he had the uncertainties of his first lecture tour in the unknown lands of North America before him. Would he ever return to complete the tomb? He still had his house at Elwat el-Diban to come back to, whether he would work or not. So life on one level, if not on another, would continue. So, on his last day he methodically checked his stores and noted the results in his diary. The list is very much that of an expatriate Englishman wishing to maintain a certain style of life in foreign parts. Much was in tins: marmalade, strawberry, apricot and blackcurrant jam; mock turtle, gravy and julienne soups; tinned pineapple, peaches, fruit salad, figs and pears. There were tins of sardines, of tongues and sausages; quantities of Brand's Essence, beef and chicken, about which Winifred Mace had remarked, 'At times Mr. Carter seems to live on it';[76] and pâté de foie gras. There was a great deal of sugar and, more prosaically, candles, Yardley's soap, Sunlight soap, Scrubbs ammonia, and 6 packets of Bromo toilet paper. He had laid in plenty of biscuits – 12 three-pound tins of water biscuits, 5 similar tins of Marie biscuits, and 6 tins of cheese-assorted biscuits. There were bottles of vinegar and tins of oil. Also a small, limited cellar: 12 bottles of Fortnum and Masons 10-year-old brandy, 2 bottles of Sandemans 50-year-old brandy, 18 bottles of Fortnum and Masons 10-year-old whisky, 12 bottles of Gordon's gin and 3 bottles of crème-de-menthe. He would be able to survive for a time, if he were to return. He took ship from Alexandria to Venice on 21 March, and arrived at Victoria Station, London, on the 25th.

76 Letter in January 1924.

13

AMERICA AND IMPROVING PROSPECTS

The approach of his lecture tour in North America offered Howard Carter at least a change of scene, and the possibility of some relief from the burden of negotiations with the Antiquities Service and the Egyptian Minister of Public Works. Unfortunately, soon after his return to England his prickly antennae picked up information about a quite separate and potentially vexing matter which seemed to merit rapid attention. The great national event of 1924 was the British Empire Exhibition, a celebration of the peoples of the Empire and their achievements. It was to be opened by King George V and Queen Mary on 23 April in an impressive ceremony at the exhibition site at Wembley in north-west London. In the extensive exhibition grounds, apart from the grandiose pavilions of the dominions and colonies, lay the Amusement Park within which, close to the Safety Racer, the Wheel of the World, and Flying Machines, was the Tomb of Tut-Ankh-Amen, entry price 1/3 (one shilling and threepence). Excavated in the sand of Wembley, and contained within a long white building purporting to represent the cliffs of the Valley of the Kings, the chambers were filled with replicas of objects found in the tomb – the great gilded beds, the thrones, a chariot, the king's mannequin, the guardian figures of the king, stools and boxes and the gilded shrines and the sarcophagus of the Burial Chamber.[1]

A particularly disagreeable feature of this 'side-show' was the fact that Messrs William Aumonier and Son, the firm responsible for the replicas, had been advised by Arthur Weigall. His welcome absence from Thebes during the preceding winter had been put down, no doubt rightly, to the reluctance of the *Daily Mail* to employ him as their correspondent after his behaviour in the previous season.[2] He had certainly not been idle in the meanwhile, and much of what he had been doing was irksome for

1 I am grateful to the staff of the Grange Museum of Community History, Neasden, London N.10, and especially the Curator, Mr Finbarr Whooley, for their help and for providing access to a copy of the Official Guide to the exhibition from the collections of the Wembley Historical Society housed in the Museum. See also, Donald R. Knight and Alan D. Sobey, *The Lion roars at Wembley* (London, 1984), passim.
2 So according to Winifred Mace in her letter to her mother of 17 March 1924.

Carter. Weigall, as a free-lance author, had to make a living as best he could, by writing, by journalism, by lecturing, and in recent months by providing Aumonier and the contractors for the construction of the tomb with detailed information on the form and contents of the tomb. Carter did not see the Wembley show until after his visit to America, but he did what he could in advance of his departure, and before the opening of the exhibition, to scotch the enterprise. He therefore instructed his solicitors to issue a writ against the Directors of the British Empire Exhibition. His objection was that the making and showing of replicas represented a violation of copyrights. He assumed that the work had been carried out using photographs, and possibly other materials, which were the property of the Carnarvon-Carter expedition. The writ was issued on 21 April, and reported in the *Daily Express* on the following day as 'Mr. Carter's Wembley Bombshell'. The newspaper report included a denial by Aumonier and Weigall that Carter photographs had been used; they claimed that they had worked from photographs taken in Egypt by many different people. In the event, the writ was withdrawn after the exhibition organizers were able to satisfy Carter's solicitors that their claim was valid. One may wonder whether Carter would have given up so easily if he had been in the country.

The Wembley replica tomb was much visited, and was said to be very like the real tomb. Photographs of the wood and plaster copies of the objects suggest that they were no more than approximate representations of the originals, some being much better than others. Nevertheless, a great deal of care had been taken to ensure that, from the front at least, a fair idea of the originals could be obtained. It was claimed that almost £1000-worth of gold was used to embellish the shrines, and that 'the smallest hieroglyphs were reproduced so faithfully that they could be read by Egyptologists.' The little folder prepared for the visitors describes the tomb replica and its contents as if the actual objects were on display in Wembley:[3] 'From the entrance, down 16 steps, a passage leads to the first of three chambers, only two of which have so far been opened. . . .' One page of description is accompanied by two pages containing a poem of 125 lines, 'The Seeker' by C. E. Briggs. It scarcely merits reprinting, but one stanza may convey the flavour of the whole:

> From the wings of evening a gentle wind did blow,
> Harbinger of death, for the King was stricken low,
> And as Ra descended behind a bank of cloud,
> Ominous, forbidding, as though it were a shroud,
> Journeyed had the King to a land he did not know.

It is unlikely that Carter himself knew much about what was planned

3 A copy of this folder in the collection of the Wembley Historical Society in the Grange Museum.

for Wembley, but he quite understandably felt that a gross liberty was being taken with his discovery. The law may not have been broken, but proprieties had been neglected. He may also have suspected that Aumonier would not go out of his way to deny that the show was organized with the knowledge and permission of Carter and the Carnarvon estate. There is nothing to suggest that at the time such a claim was made; Weigall was always credited with the specialized advice. But memories and impressions are liable to imprecision. A report in the *Eastern Daily Press* of Norwich on 6 May 1969 describes a figure of the Egyptian goddess Sakhmet still to be seen at that time in the offices of Crotch and Son in Norwich. This firm, it was claimed, had carried out the excavation and building of the Wembley replica, and the Sakhmet statue 'with certainty . . . emanated from the Wembley 1924 Exhibition . . . and is a replica of the actual statue that was placed in the tomb of the weak and vacillating teenage ruler 3300 years ago.' That there was no Sakhmet statue in the tomb is just one misconception in the report. Another is the claim that Carnarvon and Carter 'were invited to erect and furnish a replica of the Luxor tomb and Crotch received the contract.' Howard Carter would not have appreciated the long survival of such a myth in his own Norfolk heartland.

The Wembley problem could be left in the hands of his solicitors. He himself had a different adventure before him, and on 12 April he had left Southampton on the SS *Berengaria* for New York.[4] He was accompanied on the voyage by the Lythgoes and Edward Harkness and also, according to the report in the *New York Times*, by Percy White, described as 'an authority on Egypt and a professor of history in the Egyptian university in Cairo, who will also lecture on Tut-ankh-Amen.' Carter makes no mention of White in his brief diary notes of the American tour, and it is probable that he did not keep Carter company throughout the tour. Minnie Burton mentions White's presence at a showing of Harry Burton's 'movies' in New York on 10 June, when Carter himself was in Canada. Although Carter would stand up to the stresses of the tour with remarkable resilience, he might have appreciated having Percy White to talk to in the few times of relaxation from the inexorable travel, public speaking and socializing. His sole companion seems to have been Mr Lee Keedick of the Keedick Lecture Bureau, who, as will be seen, had his hands full managing his lucrative client's movements and appearances.[5]

Howard Carter had received much advice from Breasted about the business of lecturing in the United States, but he may not have been properly warned of the probable interest of the public and the newspapers. About the latter he knew something (and that not especially good) from

---

4 Carter's movements in America are breifly noted in his Pocket Diary for 1924 in the G.I. Carter Papers.

5 Notes on the Carter tour have been made available to me by Mr Robert Keedick, son of Mr Lee Keedick.

his recent experiences in Egypt. In America he would be met at every point by eager news-hounds requiring interviews and statements, and as the tour progressed he would witness the extravagance of public enthusiasm and the inaccuracies of the published reports. The account of his first interview, published in the *New York Times* on 19 April, runs to about 50 column inches (128cm), and ranges widely over his discovery, his life and career, his views on a broad range of Egyptological matters, especially those concerning Tutankhamun. The report scarcely warrants close scrutiny. The inaccuracies – which are many – may be due to his own lack of precision, to bad reporting, or to the invention of the interviewer. The most engaging prediction Carter is claimed to have made concerned the probable discovery of 'literary relics' in the burial of Tutankhamun:

> there was a chance, he said, of finding 'a novel of travel' which some literary man of the time had written to entertain Tut-ankh-Amen on his pilgrimage through the lower world.

He also hoped that in the future:

> He could undertake the expedition into Somaliland and Abyssinia where he will seek corroboration of his theory that civilization originated there and traveled down the Nile to Egypt and east to Mesopotamia.

For the first time he denied that he was American – 'a widespread mistaken belief'; he would have to do so frequently in the coming weeks. He also paid generous tribute to the help and support he had received from the Metropolitan Museum.

In spite of its length, this first newspaper interview in America was surprisingly free from the weaknesses that are commonly found when enthusiasm unbalances the natural scepticism of the hardened journalist. It did not, apparently, raise Carter's hackles, and Ludlow Bull could write to Breasted after its appearance[6] that Carter 'seemed in good health and spirits' and, specifically on the interview, 'I see that he referred to you as the greatest historian of Egypt. I was glad to see that.'

If anything could have restored Carter's self-confidence and removed some of the shadows persisting from the unhappy events in Luxor, it was surely the reception he received in New York. It is known that he was more than adequately lionized, but the full list of his engagements is not recorded in his diary. There he notes in the briefest form his moves, his lectures, and very occasional meetings, with only an incidental remark in addition. His official lecture schedule was punishing. He had two subjects in his portfolio, the first being the background to the discovery and the discovery itself, the second being the discoveries of the recent season. His

6 Letter of 21 April in O.I. Director's Office Corr. 1924.

first two talks in New York were arranged specially for invited audiences in the Metropolitan Museum – 'bread-and-butter' talks, given in gratitude for all that the Museum had done. Lindsley Hall who attended the first (on 21 April) reported: 'This eve he talked informally at the Museum and I heard him. Slides and movies good, but he is hard to understand.' A nervous performance at the very least might have been expected for this initiatory dip into the waters of the American lecture circuit. Hall's comment was to be made by others at this early stage; his diction, said in later life to have been precise, clipped and sub-Upper Class, did not impress all his listeners. His serious public series began on 23 April with an afternoon lecture in Carnegie Hall; he was introduced by Edward Robinson, Director of the Metropolitan Museum, and there were 2500 people in the audience. The *New York Times* reported this and his second lecture in the same hall (on 25 April in the evening) with good, but wholly uncritical, accounts.[7] He spoke in Carnegie Hall four times before the end of April, and supplemented these appearances with one lecture in the Natural History Museum and two in the Brooklyn Academy of Music.

His tour away from New York began with visits to Philadelphia, New Haven (for Yale), Washington and Baltimore. On 8 May he was invited to meet the US President, Mr Calvin Coolidge, in the White House. Noting this private audience on the next day, the *New York Times* reported that Carter 'was both amazed and flattered by the President's familiarity with his work in Egypt and that he was greatly pleased with Mr. Coolidge's commendation of the work.' There was so much interest in the White House that Carter was invited back to give a private talk to Mr and Mrs Coolidge and guests on the next day. Carter puts it down as having happened in his diary, but in fact the Coolidges had not been there. On the following day Mrs Coolidge's secretary wrote to him apologizing for their absence, because 'of the great sorrow that had come so suddenly to a member of their official family.'[8]

New England came next: first to Boston on 10 May. A side-trip to Worcester, Massachusetts, was followed by two lectures in the Boston Opera House, and then one in Hartford, Connecticut. The pace quickened somewhat. He left Hartford on 18 May for Pittsburgh, arrived at 9.30 on the morning of the 19th, lectured at 8.30 in the evening and took the train for Chicago at midnight. After New York, Chicago was his most important place of engagement, for here waited James Henry Breasted, eager to see how his reluctant lecture pupil would perform, and avid to exploit the occasion for his own purposes. He had persuaded Carter to give a private lecture for the University of Chicago, and had hope that it might be in a large hall, enabling the University to invite many friends and benefactors. Breasted left it rather late to fix the arrangements with Lee Keedick, and

7 *New York Times* for 24 April 1924, p. 21, and for 26 April, p. 18.
8 Letter in the possession of John Carter.

a night letter requesting 'Besides faculty and students would you be willing to have us invite a small list of prominent people like trustees and special friends of the University' received the brief reply, 'Please limit invitations to trustees.'[9] Carter was to give two lectures in Orchestra Hall, and his agent naturally did not want to have large numbers of possible ticket-buyers siphoned off to the free presentation at the University.

In other respects Breasted was very solicitous on Carter's behalf, and went out of his way to give him helpful advice, and to commiserate with him on the strains of social engagements and the importunities of the Press. His letter of 13 May alerted Carter to what was in store for him:[10]

> Mrs. Rockefeller McCormick . . . is anxious to give you a tea and a reception. I can quite understand that you are 'fed up' with this kind of thing. We should be delighted to show you all kinds of hospitality at the University but I know how tired you must be, and I do not want to overload you with such social responsibilities before you arrive.

Still, perhaps a luncheon could be arranged. Breasted then took a swipe at the Press:

> I have been very much vexed with the absurd things the newspapers have reported me as saying, especially that I brought back a bed from the tomb of Tutenkhamon. Of course I never said anything of the kind. The bed in question is the one you probably saw in the hands of Mohammed Mohasseb, which anyone would recognize at once as enormously older than anything in the tomb. I suppose you are getting very 'fed up' with the absurdities of the American Press. It is one of the things we Americans deplore, but cannot alter.

In the event things went well in Chicago, and Carter passed the Breasted test with flying colours. After four days of busy activity he left the city on the midnight train for Cincinnati on the next stage of his circuit in the USA, before an excursion into Canada. Breasted waited until 3 June, ten days later, before writing his letter of thanks:[11]

> I have heard the most gratifying expressions of appreciation on all hands, which I am sure, if you could hear them, would afford you pleasure. I have been asked also by the President to assure you of our sense of indebtedness, and our conviction of the great value of the service you have rendered. The leading men of the University have spoken to me about it as of the greatest value in the further development of our subject both in this University and throughout America.

9 Both letters in the O.I. Director's Office Corr. 1924.
10 Copy in O.I. Director's Office Corr. 1924.
11 Copy as last.

That the thanks conveyed in this letter were not just those of the conventional letter of appreciation is confirmed by what Breasted had to say to Alan Gardiner a few days later:[12]

Carter has recently left us having lectured in the city twice to crowded houses, and a third time at the University exclusively to invited guests – a donation on his part which was greatly appreciated. I must say his lecture did him credit. He had dropped the note of high tragedy to which you referred in commenting on his London lecture. He talked evenly and familiarly and in a pleasing vein. I have heard numerous appreciative comments. I think the universal kindness which had been shown him in America has contributed to soothe his ruffled spirits and sweeten up many bitter memories.

The final comments here may represent a total misjudgement of Carter's true state of mind at this point in the American tour. News from Egypt, which will shortly be considered, could scarcely have contributed towards a general equanimity. But Carter was, by his solitary nature, adept, it seems, at controlling his inner feelings when circumstances did not lead to a public outburst of temper. Yet Breasted was surely right in claiming that the treatment Carter was receiving in America was therapeutic to some extent. How could he have failed to respond positively to such generous hospitality?

Breasted's 'thank-you' letter also contained a suggestion for the investing of the substantial sums of money that Carter could expect to collect from his tour:

Don't take your financial returns from this lecture tour to England and put it into pounds sterling, which are bound to come down every time the British Government makes an interest payment to the United States. Do take your balance to some well known investment banker in New York and buy public service securities of some kind on which you can get from five to six percent interest – very much better I am confident than you can do at home.

I might mention that Petrie followed the above suggested policy with the £8000 which he received for the Illahun Jewelry. Forgive me for 'butting in' on another man's private business, but I am sure you will understand that it is kindly meant.

Breasted, it seems, always knew best; but there is no evidence that Carter followed his advice in this matter. Indeed, had he done so, he might well have regretted his decision when the American market collapsed in 1929. In money matters Carter always behaved prudently, and on this occasion he may, after his return to Great Britain, have taken steps which secured

12 G.I. Gardiner Corr. AHG/42.37.13 of 12 June 1924.

for him a reasonably stable financial future. His diary for 9 July notes 'Saw Victor Walker re. annuity'; and under 14 July he wrote 'For 1000 per annum pay 13394 .1. 1 = 9%'. It is known that at least by 1928 he received an annuity of £1000 from the Standard Life Assurance Co., in half-yearly instalments of £500. A letter written to him by his solicitor J. R. Molony in 1932, answering an enquiry Carter had made (possibly on behalf of Axel Munthe), stated that Sun of Canada would require something over £ .000 to secure £1000 a year, and the Norwich Union would be about £ 9 more.[13] These figures do suggest that he considered the possibility of an annuity of £1000 per annum immediately after his return from his American trip, and may well have purchased one at that time. It would have been an eminently sensible way of using a large sum of money without exposing it to the hazards of the stock market.

The time-table of the lecture tour, as arranged by Mr Lee Keedick, contained bursts of flurried movement and activity, followed by short periods when some peace might be found. Chicago had been a point for a little rest, and the next would be Cleveland, Ohio, where Carter would find people in the Museum of Art with whom he had corresponded over purchases of antiquities since 1917. Strangely, the Museum has no record of a visit by Carter at this time, or of any entertainment connected with his visit; the brief entries in Carter's diary mention only the Masonic Hall where he lectured on 2 and 3 June. The two preceding days were possibly spent visiting the Museum, and in recuperating from the marathon progress since Chicago: 24 May, midnight train to Cincinnati; 25 May, arrive Cincinnati 9.20 a.m.; 26 May, lecture 8.30 p.m., leave for Detroit, 11.15 p.m.; 27 May, arrive Detroit 7.30 a.m.; 28 May, saw Henry Ford a.m., lecture 8.30 p.m.; 29 May, still in Detroit, lecture 8.30 p.m.; 30 May, to Cleveland. And so it would continue after Cleveland, with visits to Columbus, Ohio, and Buffalo.

On 7 June Carter reached Toronto and for the next 9 days he remained in Canada, giving lectures in Toronto, Montreal and Ottawa. In Toronto his point of contact was C. T. Currelly, Director of the Royal Ontario Museum, who had been an active archaeologist; he had worked in Egypt with Naville at Deir el-Bahri in the days when Carter was in his period of 'retirement' after the unfortunate events of 1905. To all outward appearances Carter was now a man enjoying the success he had earned by his discoveries, and he could occasionally write of his apparent satisfaction. From Chicago he had written to Winlock in New York, thanking him for all that he had done on his behalf in Egypt; he added:[14]

I had a delightful time with your family at Boston and regretted that

---

13 Letters on the annuity enquiries are in the possession of John Carter.
14 Letter of 24 May in M.M.A., Department of Egyptian Art, Carter files.

I had to quit so soon – the machinations of Reisner and Co there were most amusing – I think they have made asses of themselves. . . .

This lecturing tour is strenuous work but am enjoying seeing the country and kind people.

Winlock had indeed earned Carter's gratitude. The weeks he had spent in Egypt acting as Carter's proxy had not been easy, and had included in the early stages an event that had promised to develop into a major crisis. At the beginning of April the committee appointed by the Egyptian government to review matters in the Valley set about listing the material in the various tombs in the Valley used by Carter. In tomb no. 4, that of King Ramesses XI, they found a Fortnum and Mason box containing a wooden head, plastered and painted, of a young boy, emerging from a lotus flower – an exceptionally fine and sensitive sculpture. The suspicions of the Egyptian members of the commission were aroused, and Winlock cabled Carter on 2 April:[15]

send all information you can relating to origin STOP Advise us by letter if any inquiry is made we shall be prepared STOP Made a bad impression on Egyptian members it was announced by telegram to Zaghlul immediately and sent by express Cairo STOP Lacau and Engelbach have suggested to them you have bought for account of Earl last year from Amarna do not know whether they believe that actually.

On the following day, Winlock again cabled:

Edgar Engelbach called today and have suggested Carter confirm purchase of head thus can give great assistance to Lacau who has great confidence in him and desires if possible to prevent an attempt made by press to misrepresent Carter STOP. . . . Have been informed by servant voluntarily he made a mistake in storing empties. Code very difficult.

The last remark presumably refers to the problem of conveying adequate messages when a form of code, used for confidential cables by members of the Metropolitan Museum staff, was employed. Carter replied by cable from London on 3 April:

The piece mentioned belongs like all other pieces belonging tomb in number four to material found in filling of passage STOP They are noted on plan in group numbers but not yet fully registered in index STOP

15 Cables and letters on this head are reprinted in the last appendix to *The Tomb of Tut.ank.Amen. Statement with Documents as to the Events which occurred in Egypt in the Winter of 1923–24, leading to the ultimate breach with the Egyptian Government* (London, 1924, 'for private circulation only'). Carter's letter of 7 April is in M.M.A., Department of Egyptian Art, Carter files.

Quoting all three cables, Carter wrote a more detailed account of the circumstances of the finding of the head in a letter to Winlock on 7 April, pointing out how he had used tomb no. 4 as 'the only magazine for the safe keeping of antiquities I had up to that stage', and that before the opening of the Antechamber 'all objects pertaining to the excavation' were stored in that tomb. He was very annoyed at the action taken by the commission:

> This actual piece in question, the most important object found at that stage of the work, was discovered in a very perishable condition, and it took Mr. Callender and myself some little time to salvage it as well as fallen fragments of its painted decoration from the rubble and dust. It was carefully packed and immediately stored in tomb No. 4, with the fragments belonging to it in a separate parcel, and left there 'till the opportunity came for its correct handling.
>
> I am at a loss to understand such a procedure on the part of the Department as sending it 'by express Cairo' before it had received the proper treatment for transport, and I must sincerely trust that the fragments salvaged by us have received proper care. It would be deplorable if this wonderful and unique portrait head of the young king has suffered damage through such extraordinary action.

In the meanwhile Winlock had written to Carter from Cairo to say that Lacau was 'perfectly delighted' with the explanation in Carter's cable.[16] To Winlock the incident seemed closed. And so indeed it remained, until in recent years, unfortunately, it has been seized on and given prominence as if to prove that Carter had been concealing the piece for later improper removal.[17] It is indeed strange that the head had been apparently overlooked, even temporarily forgotten, in its box in tomb no. 4, and it is noticeable that, in spite of its artistic and historical value, it was not mentioned in the first volume of *The Tomb of Tut.ankh.Amen*.[18] Still it is perhaps not surprising that a piece, even one of outstanding importance, might have remained neglected, when every day brought new wonders of discovery in the tomb. Furthermore, if Carter had intended to remove it surreptitiously, he could have done so on many occasions between November 1922 and February 1924. It is not known what happened to the head and the fragments immediately after they were sent to Cairo; but an inspection of the piece today shows that many pieces of gesso-plaster are missing. Carter's comments on the dangers implicit in its premature removal before conservation had been carried out were only too pertinent.

Winlock did not find that progress in solving the problems of Tutankhamun's tomb had greatly improved with Carter away from Egypt.

16 Letter of 5 April in M.M.A., Department of Egyptian Art, Carter files.
17 See T. Hoving, *Tutankhamun. The Untold Story* (New York, 1978), p. 318.
18 It is illustrated as Plate 1 in volume III.

The legacy of Breasted's vacillation and the inefficiency of Morton Howell, the American Minister, offered serious impediments to progress. On the very day when he could write encouragingly to Carter about the wooden head, he sent an exasperated letter to Lythgoe about Howell and the irresponsible behaviour of the newspaper-man Bradstreet.[19] The latter had written an article criticising Howell as being too much on Carter's side, and laying himself open to insults from the Egyptians. Although Howell was grossly misrepresented (ineffective though he might have been), he incurred an unjustified reprimand from the State Department. The position therefore remained unpromising:

> The way things look to me Lacau's reforms stand an excellent chance of going through before next season. You can put no dependence on what they told Howell – any more than in this Tut affair.

On Tutankhamun matters Winlock was rather more positive in writing to Carter. He continued his Carter letter of 5 April with a comment that everyone in the Antiquities Service wanted Carter back, even though he would have only two rights: to take the blame if anything goes wrong, and to pay the bills. For the moment he recommends Carter to accept any offered concession, at least formally:

> A blank refusal now would add fuel to the fire. If we just quietly pass the word to Howell and let him pass it to the government and it only comes out publicly much later, it will not cause so much excitement. You can say later 'Oh yes there was something offered but it was not workable'.

Winlock could now perhaps see some possibility of settlement, although the Carter affair might be more susceptible of a favourable outcome than the business of general archaeological concessions in Egypt. He wrote regularly to Carter during the weeks when he acted on his behalf. He was undoubtedly more pragmatic in terms of field practicalities than Breasted had been, and he was now helped by a new lawyer, Georges Merzbach, who was in the process of taking over from F. M. Maxwell on the latter's retirement to England. Merzbach, unencumbered by the memory of the Morcos Hanna treason trial, and very accustomed to dealing with local issues in the Egyptian courts, was equally free from the set positions that had developed in Carter's case since January. He was all on the side of negotiation rather than litigation, and although Carter feared at first that he might be 'double'[20] – possibly meaning 'two-faced' – he would prove to be a sterling guide and support in future negotiations. So useful did he become that he continued to act for Carter in later years in matters in

19 Letter in M.M.A., Department of Egyptian Art, Carter files.
20 In a letter of 24 May to H. E. Winlock in M.M.A., Department of Egyptian Art, Carter files.

contention in the Egyptian courts. At the present early stage it was Merzbach who could detect in Lacau a distinct willingness to be 'friendly and
liberal'.[21]

After Winlock had returned to New York in mid-May, he wrote a long
letter bringing Carter up to date with recent developments.[22] There had
been much discussion over new possible wordings of an agreement for the
reopening of work on the Tomb of Tutankhamun; there were to be some
concessions. Unfortunately the Carnarvon side now dug in its heels, and
General Sir John Maxwell particularly showed his opposition, suggesting
to Merzbach that the renunciation of claims for objects from the discovery
should be withdrawn. 'Carter', he said, 'may have been not far wrong.'
Something had to be done to placate Sir John, but Winlock and Merzbach
were convinced that they should persist with the modified agreement they
had prepared. Winlock saw Lacau on 25 April and found three 'amusing
points' in the interview. First, Morcos Hanna had shown Lacau Carter's
letter disclaiming the use of the word 'bandits', and they agreed it was
satisfactory. Morcos then, subsequently and without Lacau's knowledge,
demanded changes in the text; Lacau regarded the changes as 'merely
pretexts'. Second, Lacau strongly opposed the suggestion that five Egyptian
students should be attached to Carter's work; he claimed to have discovered that they would be spies. Third, Lacau thought Sir John Maxwell
a reasonable man. When he learned from Winlock that Sir John was now
opposed to renunciation, Lacau called the whole affair tragic.

Lacau and Winlock agreed that Carter need not offer a disavowal of the
use of 'bandits', and that he should not write a letter promising to be
good. Winlock claimed that he told Lacau 'I would gladly murder you, if
you weren't good, but that was as far as I would agree to go'. He and
Merzbach pressed the negotiations fitfully forward. The end of the month
of April was fixed for his return to New York, but it became clear that
no end could be brought to the matter before further discussions with the
Carnarvon side took place. Winlock was, as he reported, able to have 'one
last fling' at Lacau. He told him that he sincerely believed that Lacau had
the best interests of archaeology at heart, but was dominated by the
Egyptian politicians:

> Likewise on the question of concessions in general I find you hold
> the sincerest desire for the continuation of archaeological work in
> Egypt but that you think it necessary to give way on every side to
> the desires of Egyptian politicians for the sake of peace.

Lacau replied that he thought Winlock's summing up was rather naïve;
all he wanted to do was to avoid further conflict.

At the end of his long letter of 22 May, and on the point of bowing out

21 Letter of 10 April in M.M.A., Department of Egyptian Art, Carter files.
22 Letter of 22 May in M.M.A., as last.

of his office of Carter-proxy, Winlock urges a willingness to be conciliatory and to accept Lacau's apparent eagerness to have him back. But:

> There is no use mincing words or trying to fool ourselves. In Cairo you have the reputation of being difficult. Some of this goes back to the old days and a long series of incidents in which you have not been sparing of the knocks.

So he concludes,

> In short I believe you stand about as follows:
> 1 They want you and your collaborators back.
> 2 They will give a concession which is after all workable.
> 3 You must get the Carnarvons' renunciation.
> 4 You must convince them that they are totally wrong in their childish idea that you like to quarrel for the fun of insulting the Egyptian nation.

Finally, he offers to return his power of attorney,

> Otherwise I shall keep it as a souvenir of a very strenuous six weeks with Tutankhamon. You may be sure, however, that I have no desire ever to use it or to hear of the old fellow again.

Winlock could not so easily let himself off the hook, for Carter was still in America, weighed down with guilt at the burdens he had laid on his friends, and as ever finding it difficult to bend. A few days after receiving Winlock's letter, Carter had one from Lythgoe with unsatisfactory news about the terms of future concessions likely to be offered to institutions like the Metropolitan Museum.[23] Carter clearly felt that he was in large part responsible for what was happening. He was in Detroit, obliged to perform almost daily to adulatory audiences, he had nobody to talk to who understood the circumstances. He had to be guarded in his statements to the newspapers. How miserable he must have been! And so he wrote in return:[24]

> Thank you indeed for yours of May 26th – All the news therein is very sorrowful, in fact, too sad for contemplation. The more so as I have been for some unfortunate reason an upsetting element in the general cause – It was but an endeavour to carry out a duty.
>
> I cannot agree to any action on my part that would in any way prejudice the rights of others. I shall therefore retire – renouncing any claim whatsoever to the Tut.ankh.Amen discovery, and also from future archaeological research – with a broken heart to find after

23 Letter of 26 May in M.M.A., as last.
24 Letter of 30 May in M.M.A., as last.

many years work that all our alleged faults are dashed upon the scales without one possible good dead used to counterbalance them.

The debt of gratitude that I owe to your Trustees, your Director, and yourselves, I fear I can never properly fulfil. So kind colleagues take this as a farewell from a retiring fellow archaeologist, who remains an everlasting grateful friend.

Winlock, who was shown this letter by Lythgoe, was much upset: 'It has knocked all of the spirit out of me for I feel that my long report to you must have discouraged you and made you sceptical even of one of your best wishers.'[25] There can be little doubt that he was right in thinking that his very long letter had overwhelmed Carter, even though its tenor had not been wholly depressing. One can visualize a tired Carter, lonely in a hotel room, recovering from one lecture, contemplating another, sorting his slides, trying to avoid going over once again his future lecture plans with Mr Keedick, and leafing through Winlock's multi-page letter, confused, expecting the worst, not looking for the hopeful. Still, it did not deter Winlock from writing another letter – a four-pager only – to assure Carter that he had not, in argument with Lacau and others, admitted 'the government's contention that you personally are a difficulty.' But he did admit, on his own part, that any mistakes he might have committed, 'I fear my biggest has been in that last letter to you.' He then sets about convincing Howard Carter that he must go back to Egypt next season:[26]

> It's hard to write to you convincingly about some sort of an indefinite 'duty to science' after the way you have been treated in Egypt. . . . That job needs you and it's a bigger job than any single personality involved in it. No one out of Cairo knows who Lacau and Marcos Hanna are, and ten years hence they will be forgotten even in Cairo. It is Tutankhamon's name that will remain, and with it yours and Carnarvon's – and yours shall be with it to the end.

Unconsciously, no doubt, in making this stirring appeal, Winlock echoed the ancient Egyptian claim, so often made by a son or a successor, of having made a father's or predecessor's name live (for ever).

Winlock then commends Merzbach to Carter and urges him to write to Maxwell or Merzbach to see what their views are 'if you have an hesitation in following what I suggest.' He points out that in acting for Carter he had his interests at heart: 'I took it up as your friend – not as a member of this Museum – and I want to see you get all that is practically possible – but I believe I have no illusions on what is impossible.' Winlock truly believed that a settlement was negotiable. He was not trying to lull Carter

25 In a letter to Howard Carter of 3 June, in M.M.A., Department of Egyptian Art, Carter files.
26 In same letter as last.

into a sense of false confidence for the future. His position is made clear in a letter he wrote to Alan Gardiner on 2 June in which he moans about the malign influence of the tomb and briefly outlines his efforts on Carter's behalf in Cairo.[27] He concludes:

> I left Egypt without a definite settlement, but I feel perfectly confident that Carter will be back in the tomb next year. . . . I believe that everything is susceptible of settlement.

Letters from Columbus, Ohio, and Buffalo, New York, renewed Carter's thanks for all Winlock had done.[28] He does not agree to go on trying for a settlement, but, as a pointer for the future, he does report that he had cabled to Maxwell, releasing him from the case and asking him to hand over all documents to Merzbach. Still he continues his breast-beating for his behaviour, for having put his colleagues in difficult positions, for jeopardizing the future of other expeditions, and lamenting the uncharitable attitude of the Egyptians. It is difficult to understand how he could continue with his tour, especially as he says in his Columbus letter, 'I have been having a rotten time lately – tired and bad heads – but am now much better again.' He could have done with a good friend like Percy White to cheer him up. It is scarcely surprising that his behaviour often left much to be desired. Lee Keedick found him 'the most quarrelsome and cantankerous of men.' He enlarges:[29]

> He was never enjoying himself unless he was in argument over the most insignificant matter, and even children did not escape him. Cab drivers, hotel door men, railroad conductors, Pullman Dining Car conductors, and even little flower girls all came in for his invective and acrimonious and irritating comments. . . . The above indicates his normal mood.

Howard Carter's normal mood, as Lee Keedick saw it, was kept nicely in tune by the stresses of the lecture tour. He did not have to do anything to attract annoyance. The morning after he arrived in Toronto, his first point of call in Canada, he was surprised to find in the *Toronto Star Weekly* for 7 June a report of an interview supposedly given, if not the night before, then recently. In answer to the question, 'Is there any likelihood of Canada ever seeing any of the treasures from the tomb of King Tut?' he is said to have answered, 'I think so. When the distribution is finally made Canada should get some of the archaeological specimens.' In vexation Carter sent a cutting to Lythgoe, commenting:[30] 'I arrived in Toronto last night (Sat. 10.45 pm) – went straight to bed without seeing a single

27 G.I. Gardiner Corr. AHG/42, 375.41.
28 Letters of 4 and 6 June in M.M.A., Department of Egyptian Art, Carter files.
29 See n. 5 above.
30 Letter of 8 June in M.M.A., Department of Egyptian Art, Carter files.

news correspondent, and yet see what they say regarding a supposed interview and division of antiquities – for which I suppose I get the blame!'

Three days in Toronto were followed by three in Montreal and two in Ottawa. He arrived in Ottawa in time to take lunch with the Governor-General, Viscount Byng, a very distinguished First World War general, who had taken the precaution of sending his invitation to Toronto a week in advance.[31] Lee Keedick's notes of reminiscences of the Carter tour states that it was on the train from Montreal to Ottawa that Carter took great delight in writing critical remarks all over the dining car menu. If it so happened, and there is little reason to question the memory, Carter may have thought his behaviour a harmless form of letting off steam; the sending of the annotated card to the Superintendent of the Dining Car Service of the Canadian Pacific Railway offered a suitable, if juvenile, way of expressing his spleen.

By good planning – it might be called split-second timing – the lecture tour ended on 15 July, and Carter was back in New York on the 16th, with just a day to recover before travelling to Yale to accept the one academic honour he received in his whole career. It may have been Ludlow Bull who was the initiator of this honour. He was a graduate of Yale, and for many years was the honorary curator of the Egyptian Collection in the Peabody Museum in the University, and from 1925 an Assistant Professor in the Department of Near-Eastern Studies. He had recently been recruited to work with Breasted and Gardiner on the Coffin Text project of the Chicago Oriental Institute; he was therefore well acquainted with recent Carter events from the side most sympathetic to his cause. The presentation for the degree was made by William Lyon Phelps, a Professor of English, said to have been Yale's most inspiring teacher over many years.[32] Having outlined Carter's career in terms slightly reminiscent of Carter's *Who's Who* entry, Professor Phelps sums up:

By imagination, perseverance, courage, indomitable resolution and scientific skill, Howard Carter succeeded in making persons who had been dead thousands of years monopolize the first page of newspapers as the most important news of the day, thus making mummies more interesting than living man.

Provost Graves then declared:

In recognition of your preeminent achievements as a scientist and explorer, and more particularly of your work in Egypt that after long years of patient and courageous effort has revealed to the world the accurate story of an ancient civilization, we confer upon you the

31 The letter of invitation in John Carter's possession.
32 I am grateful to Dr Gerry D. Scott III for sending me photocopies of the relevant pages from the *Yale Alumni Weekly*, vol. 33, no. 40 of 4 July 1924.

degree of Doctor of Science and admit you to all its rights and privileges.

So he now became Dr Howard Carter. He would never be similarly honoured by an British university, but he could have no reason to be other than proud to be able to boast an honorary degree from one of America's premier institutions of higher learning.

The end of the tour left Howard Carter with almost two full weeks to rest and be entertained in New York and on Long Island (by the Harknesses, among others). It had been a long haul of two months of rail travel, meeting many eager and hospitable people, lecturing, being lionized, and the whole coloured, or perhaps tainted, by the news from Egypt and his future. He had, it seems, borne the strain unusually well, and the cantankerous behaviour remembered by Lee Keedick was particular, and perhaps even aimed obliquely at him. Two months of shepherding a sensitive personality was bound to generate stress, even antagonism. Carter had, in any case, done well; his lectures had been enthusiastically received, and he had been excellently rewarded. Precise figures of his 'profit' have not been recorded; the Keedick Lecture Bureau archives, which might have contained interesting details, were unfortunately destroyed in a warehouse fire in 1939.[33]

Now that he was back in New York, Carter had matters to discuss with Winlock, who earnestly believed that the basis for an agreement satisfactory to all sides was at last possible. Following their discussions, Winlock drew up for Carter a letter addressed to Lacau[34] which was conciliatory without being obsequious, in which Carter agreed to the renunciation of claims for objects from the tomb, although pointing out that it might still be difficult to persuade General Sir John Maxwell to reissue the renunciation of behalf of the Carnarvon estate. With the suggested articles of the newly proposed permit generally accepted, incidental but troublesome problems concerning the Press, visitors, lists of collaborators, and the inclusion of Tutankhamun objects in the Cairo Museum *Guide*, ceased to offer difficulty. It is not certain that Carter ever sent this letter, or a further revised version, to Lacau, but when he left New York on the SS *Mauretania* on 2 July he had good reasons for feeling confident that he would return to Egypt later in the year.

With characteristically bad timing, copies of the *Statement* containing the documentation on the troubles with the Cairo authorities in the winter of 1923–4 arrive in the Metropolitan Museum a few days before Carter took ship for Europe.[35] Winlock may or may not have believed that the idea of such a publication – which was limited and confidential – was good; it

33 Information provided by Mr Robert Keedick.
34 Copy of the text in M. M. A., Department of Egyptian Art, Carter files.
35 See p. 274 above.

did set out starkly the unhappy course of negotiations, showing Howard Carter, understandably, as the reasonable victim of unreasonable bureaucrats; but its issue at this moment seemed unfortunate, to say the least. It would be good if it were not sent to Lacau or to His Excellency Morcos Hanna. But what especially annoyed Winlock was a final appendix in which Carter printed his long letter to Winlock about the discovery of the painted wooden head of the young king emerging from a lotus flower. It included the exchange of cables, of which Winlock's had been marked confidential, and which he now seemed to think would in some way compromise him. A letter from Lythgoe to Winlock, written after Lythgoe had been apprised by Winlock of the contents of the *Statement*, and had seen a copy, makes it quite clear that the inclusion of the cables constituted not only Winlock's but also the Museum's objection to the dossier:[36]

> Unless I am much mistaken the contents of that pamphlet will soon leak out, and I feel it is a matter of urgent necessity that we should *stop* the appearance of those confidential cablegrams by a cablegram to Carter to catch him on his arrival in London next Tuesday ... at the same time you should cable Mr. Robinson informing him of the step you have taken.

In answer Winlock suggested a cautious approach to Carter,[37] using perhaps the mediation of Edward Robinson, who happened to be a fellow passenger on the *Mauretania* with Carter.

It must be presumed that Winlock or Lythgoe got in touch with Robinson, who had the opportunity during the Atlantic crossing to read through the *Statement*. Subsequently he wrote two letters to Lythgoe, outlining his thoughts on the matter and the results of his talks with Carter.[38] The impression he formed from the dossier was of 'a good case badly handled from start to finish'. He had been reluctant to tackle Carter head on, but was spared the task of finding the right moment by Carter's own raising of the matter. He had suggested to Carter that things had not been handled very adroitly, and he found that he was in receptive mood and agreed with almost everything he said. So he advised him not to circulate the *Statement*, and to be more accommodating to the Egyptian Government. It is perhaps not surprising that Carter and Robinson got on well together. Robinson was not an Egyptologist; he could observe the Egyptian problem from an independent although not unsympathetic position; he had wide artistic interests. Carter certainly felt no resentment at Robinson's intervention, and was happy to join Robinson and his wife on a visit to Bath very shortly after they arrived in England.

36 Written on 3 July from his home in Woodstock, Connecticut; in M.M.A., Department of Egyptian Art, Carter files.
37 A telegram to Lythgoe, a copy of the text of which, undated is in M.M.A., as last.
38 Letters of 15 and 18 July in M.M.A., as last.

As for the *Statement*, it is not known if excisions were made in any copies. The one sent to Breasted cannot be found; that sent to President Coolidge has not been examined;[39] Newberry's copy in the Griffith Institute, Oxford, retains the appendix, as does the copy in the Metropolitan Museum. Recorded reactions are few. Breasted wrote:[40] 'The summary will always be a monument in the history of research in the Near East.' No comment from Gardiner or the Carnarvons has survived. Repercussions seem to have been negligible until the copy kept in the Egyptian Department of the Metropolitan Museum was used rather freely as a documentary source by Thomas Hoving in 1978.[41] Carter's dramatic act of catharsis lay in the preparation and publication of the record, not in reading what its recipients thought about it.

Although there remained things to be done in order to ensure that his return to Egypt would be accompanied by a reissuing of Lady Carnarvon's excavation permit, Carter faced the summer in England in a much more relaxed frame of mind than he might have expected a month or two earlier. If the notes in his diary, already mentioned, truly indicated that he invested the bulk of the proceeds of his lecture tour in an annuity of £1000 a year, then he had good reason to feel that his financial future was reasonably secure. Still, with his dangerous tendency to punish himself unnecessarily, his first recorded excursion after his return was to Wembley on 14 July to view the travesty of his Theban tomb. No comment in his diary! Presumably he had been persuaded, by the withdrawal of his writ against the Directors of the British Empire Exhibition, that there was nothing to be done. If a catalogue had been available he could have amused himself by annotating it even more freely than the dining-car menu on the Montreal-Ottawa train. More agreeable, surely, was the visit he made to Bath with the Robinsons.

It was during this summer that Carter developed a taste for motoring. The car that Carnarvon had purchased for the Theban expedition had demonstrated the convenience and comfort of independent transport rather faster than the donkey, and travel by car was distinctly the best way to get about the countryside in Britain, especially when visiting friends in country houses. Carter never learned to drive. He certainly employed a driver in Egypt; a letter to Newberry on 12 March 1924 had asked him 'to tell my cook at my house and also my chauffeur to arrange for the car and donkeys on the river Sunday morning.'[42] With his new-found affluence he could afford to hire a car with a driver, and his diary notes a trip to the Welsh borders, to Tewkesbury, Gloucester, Worcester, Stratford and

---

39 A letter from the White House of 22 July acknowledging the receipt of the *Statement*, with John Carter.
40 Copy of the letter of 29 September in O.I. Director's Office Corr. 1924.
41 See Hoving, *Tutankhamun. The Untold Story*, chapters 25–32.
42 G.I. Newberry Corr. 8/80.

Malvern with Mary Carter[43] (5–13 August), another to Buxton in Derby-shire and then to Monmouth and Malvern (16–21 August), and a third with William Carter, again to Malvern (26 August – 2 September), includ-ing a visit to the Maces at Painswick in Gloucestershire. Just a few days later he motored to Tetton House near Taunton, to visit Mervyn Herbert, and he returned there (by train) on 19 September for two nights and some shooting. In between all these excursions well out of Town he also visited the Newberrys at Ightham in Kent. It was not all relaxation, however; with Mervyn Herbert he needed to discuss the position of the executors of the Earl of Carnarvon's estate, including the matter of the renunciation as a condition for a new permit. But mostly it was a time to unwind, to get out of London and away from the many demands on his time. He could admit to Lady Carnarvon,[44] 'I have just completed as good a holiday as the weather permitted in central England. . . . What a beautiful part of England for scenery – abbeys and cathedrals combined with most lovely air on both the Malvern and Cotswolds hills.' She was in Scotland at the time, but Carter needed to see her to pull together his plans and confirm his strategy for his return to Egypt. He also had it in mind – if she still wished it – to bring the Carnarvon collection from Highclere to Seamore Place in London.

His meeting with Lady Carnarvon did not take place until 6 November.[45] She then felt that the way forward was by accepting the terms that had been offered by Cairo earlier in the summer, although they would involve the sacrifice of her other interests in some favourable settlement over the contents of the tomb. She also then asked Carter to go down to Highclere and pack up the collection, not for transference to Seamore Place, but for deposit in the Bank of England. This packing he carried out between 11 and 18 November. The cases were sent to London on 17 November. The consignment contained all the antiquities considered to be 'the Carnarvon Collection'. As Carter noted on the list he drew up at the time. 'A few unimportant antiquities not belonging to the above series I left at High-clere'. These last were the objects which were rediscovered in Highclere in 1987 and subsequently. But as far as the main collection was concerned, Lady Carnarvon had decided to sell.[46]

In October Carter fulfilled a number of outstanding lecture engagements, and undertook others that might be classified as duty obligations.[47] He

43 This could have been Samuel's or William's wife, the latter being perhaps the more likely. She was to die later in the year on 30 November, the day Howard Carter returned from Madrid.
44 Copy of letter of 18 September in M.M.A., Department of Egyptian Art, Carter files.
45 Noted in a letter of 17 November which had never been sent on to Lady Carnarvon by his solicitors; in M.M.A., Department of Egyptian Art, Carter files.
46 See p. 355 below for the text of Carter's summary of the history of the collection after Carnarvon's death. On the discoveries at Highclere, see N. Reeves, *Ancient Egypt at Highclere Castle* (Highclere, 1989), pp. 17f.
47 Noted in his Pocket Diary for 1924 in G.I. Carter Papers.

spoke in Norwich, and was entertained by the Colmans, of mustard fame, at their great nineteenth-century mansion Crown Point Hall in Trowse Newton, a few miles out of the city. He went twice to Swaffham and lectured in the town cinema on 29 October. He spoke at Rugby School and Newbury Grammar School (while at Highclere), and at Eton College and Westminster School; he noted that it took him 50 minutes to motor to Eton. Soon there followed a long-planned visit to Spain as the guest of the Duke of Alba.[48] This distinguished Spanish nobleman, patron of the arts and President of the Comité Hispano-Inglès, had made several visits to Egypt and had developed a respect and liking for Carter which would continue right up until Carter's death. Alba first raised the question of a lecture in Madrid at the time when Carter was in Cairo attending Carnarvon in his last days, and the formal invitation was issued in December 1923; all expenses paid and a fee of £80. Finally November 1924 was fixed. Carter met the Duke of Alba in London on 5 November and arranged for his films to be sent to Madrid by the Spanish Ambassador's bag. Then on the 22nd he spent the night at the Ritz in Paris with the Duke, and together they travelled by train to Madrid. His first lecture on the 24th in the Salon of the Residencia de Estudiantes was so well attended that the second, on the following day, was transferred to the Teatro Fontalba. Such was the enthusiasm that followed these lectures that the Comité Hispano-Inglès endeavoured to satisfy public demand by organizing a third lecture with an exhibition of Tutankhamun photographs in the Real Cinema, with a text prepared by the well-known writer Manuel Machado from Carter's presentations. Shortly after Carter's departure he was elected a corresponding member of the Royal Academy of History of Madrid. In sending him the document of appointment and a medal,[49] the Duke of Alba wrote to say that the King Alfonso XIII had signed Carter's nomination for a royal decoration, 'but as usual your Government has refused the placet; this is a general rule since King Edward, because he always allowed British subjects to wear foreign decorations. I am sorry we could not do more and it is not our fault.' Carter would return to lecture again in Madrid in May 1928.

Back in London on 30 November, Carter had ten days only to settle matters and determine his programme for the coming season. He had booked his passage to Egypt for 10 December, but remained in some doubt about the advisability of going back. Uncertainty pervaded all discussions. He had talked the matter over with Lady Carnarvon before going to Madrid; her view was to accept what had been offered. It would involve a great sacrifice on her part, as Carter pointed out in his letter of 19

48 Details in the Pocket Diary, and in documents in the possession of John Carter. I am also grateful to Jaromir Malek for providing additional information about Carter's two visits to Spain.
49 Letter of 12 December with John Carter.

November which was not sent on by his solicitors, although he believed such a course would be 'most dignified and best'.[50] General Sir John Maxwell was unwilling to surrender the claims of the Carnarvon estate on partage or compensation.

Carter therefore wrote rather confusedly to Mervyn Herbert on 3 December, seeking advice on what he should do.[51] He pointed out that according to the concession that was on offer, 'the Estate is to bear all risks and costs past and future without any compensation whatsoever, the Eg. Gov. allowing the right of scientific publication only to the estate at our cost.' He felt that Lady Carnarvon should be allowed time to consider the question. He also wondered whether he should return to Egypt as planned 'under the present conditions'. He was much bothered about the future of excavation in the country following the introduction of new restrictions on expeditions, and he stated that scientific bodies in American, England and elsewhere were being obliged to stop work in Egypt. As some kind of testimonial of himself he also included the text of a statement put out by the Joint Archaeological Committee which was made up of representatives of the British Academy and the principal archaeological societies of England. It contained a strong statement of appreciation of Carter's work, it deplored the current controversies which imperilled the work, and it concluded:

> they are strongly of opinion that the interests of science demand that the exploration should remain in the hands of Mr. Howard Carter and his colleagues, with the independence which it is customary to allow to excavators of proved competence.

In this letter, and indeed in all the few documents surviving from the days before his return to Egypt, the only hint that there had been political changes in Egypt lies in those words 'under the present conditions'. At this very time significant developments were taking place, the outcome of which could not be reasonably predicted in early December. The administration led by Saad Zaghlul Pasha had run increasingly into difficulties with the British government, and had steadily wasted such goodwill as it retained with Lord Allenby in Cairo. Zaghlul had failed during the summer of 1924 to advance his treaty negotiations with Ramsay Macdonald in London, and had subsequently encouraged popular agitation in Egypt beyond the limits thought permissible for a constitutionally elected Prime Minister. His political demise was precipitated by the murder in Cairo on 19 November of Sir Lee Stack, Sirdar (Commander-in-Chief) of the Egyptian Army and Governor-General of the Sudan. Allenby was outraged at this act, and although Zaghlul was quick to express his regrets at what had happened, he could not avoid the High Commissioner's wrath, the

50 See n. 45.
51 Copy in M.M.A., Department of Egyptian Art, Carter files.

delivery of a severe ultimatum, and consequently the submission of his own resignation to the King on 22 November.

The political future of Egypt was very uncertain, particularly as the Wafd remained the strongest single party, and likely to obtain a majority in any election. For the moment, however, Zaghlul was replaced as Prime Minister by Ziwar Pasha, 'a Turkish-Egyptian of the old school who formed a Ministry of non-entities who were quite prepared to make up for their own impotence by sheltering behind the ample resources of the British High Commission.'[52] In this situation of political instability Howard Carter returned to Egypt, arriving in Cairo on 15 December. He could scarcely have chosen a more favourable moment to reopen negotiations. He had known Ziwar Pasha for some time and reckoned him to be very friendly. On the day after his arrival, and by extraordinary chance, he ran into Ziwar in the Continental Hotel where he was staying. What happened from that moment until late January 1925, when he was once again allowed to work in the Valley, is set out in some detail in a long report he sent to Molony, the solicitor in London. He also sent a copy, omitting a few confidential communications, to Edward Robinson with whom he now seemed to be on unusually good terms. In his covering letter to Robinson he spoke of his hopes for the future in Egypt, mentioned enthusiastically his visit to Spain – 'The pictures wonderful' – and looked forward to seeing the Robinsons in England again: 'I have discovered lots of really nice excursions . . . the next time you come.'[53]

Ziwar, as Carter reports, raised the question of the tomb of Tutankhamun as soon as they met, and they both agreed that it was important to settle outstanding problems, for the good not only of archaeology but also of tourism. They should meet officially to discuss the matter. Carter noticed that everyone wanted him back and the work to resume:

> Thus once again Tut-ankh.amen has become the centre of political intrigue, fortunately this time rather in favour of our interests than against them, and obviously a world wide advertisement for the Egyptian tourist and hotel Companies.

On the same day he saw his new lawyer in Egypt, Georges Merzbach, who also happened to be on good terms with Ziwar Pasha and other members of his administration. Merzbach had already been preparing his dispositions, seeking support from the High Commission for the renewal of Lady Carnarvon's permit on the basis of the terms already offered by the Government during the summer. The question of a gift of duplicate objects could be left to the discretion of the Egyptian Government. Carter

---

52 For the historical background, see J. Marlowe, *Anglo-Egyptian Relations 1800–1953* (London, 1954), p. 271.
53 A copy of the report to Molony in G.I. Carter Papers VI, 13A; Carter's letter to Robinson of 24 January 1925 in M.M.A., Department of Egyptian Art, Carter files.

then took the matter to Robert Furness, the Oriental Secretary at the High Commission, who promised to follow it up. As soon as Carter heard from Furness that Allenby would be willing to open negotiations, he felt that prospects for a reopening of work were so good that he telegraphed to Molony the promising news, requesting from the Carnarvon estate a small credit of £500–£1000 in expectation of the recommencement. Inevitably, things did not move forward as quickly as initial indications had promised.

Not until 28 December was Carter able to obtain an audience with Ziwar Pasha. It was the occasion when, as mentioned earlier, he shared the meeting with Georges Foucart, the Director of the French Institute in Cairo, who took the opportunity to intrigue against Lacau, and to speak strongly against the new regulations for excavators which were shortly to be introduced. Carter made some suggestions for the resolution of the dispute and proposed that Ziwar should arrange a meeting between Carter, Merzbach and the new Minister for Public Works. Ziwar asked Carter to put his request in writing, and this he did later in a letter drafted by Merzbach. Nothing much happened until 4 January 1925, when Merzbach set about organizing a meeting with Sidky Pasha, the Minister of the Interior, Lacau and Abd el-Hamid Bedawy Pasha. The last was the Conseiller Royal to the administration, who, on the basis of his style of negotiating in the spring of 1924, was not thought to be particularly well disposed to the British case. It was apparent that the new administration, in spite of being in principle favourable to Carter, had so little knowledge of earlier negotiations that they were obliged to fall back on those like Lacau and Bedawy Pasha, who had the affair at their fingertips. Carter had, however, again by chance, met Ziwar Pasha informally on the evening of the 4th, and had been told that there should be no difficulty over achieving a settlement on the basis of his letter, apart from the question of division. It was important that a claim for a division be renounced, but that 'the Egyptian Government would in the end be generous towards Almina, Countess Carnarvon, in the matter of duplicates which would not interfere with "le grand ensemble".'

The meeting arranged by Merzbach took place on 7 January and went badly at first, but was turned round by Merzbach himself who 'brilliantly carried through many points'. It was agreed that the British side would renounce its rights to a division, and a letter along the lines of the proposal made by Ziwar would be issued separately, committing the Egyptian Government to the granting of duplicates. Carter again cabled Molony, looking forward expectantly to a further meeting of the negotiating parties on the 11th. Unfortunately Merzbach and Carter found Bedawy Pasha and Lacau reluctant to follow the instructions they had certainly received from their superiors to show 'every latitude' in discussion. Once more Merzbach played the right cards, and satisfactory texts of a new concession and the letter on duplicates were received on the same day from the

Ministry of Public Works. The negotiations were finally concluded on the 12th, and Merzbach and Carter called on the minister, Mahmoud Bey Sidky, who received them very cordially, requesting Carter to return to Luxor as soon as possible to begin work again. Carter and Merzbach cabled Molony:

> To Almina and all concerned STOP Will sign tomorrow Wednesday new concession wherein Government is willing to give at his discretion Almina a choice of duplicates as representative as possible of discovery wherever such duplicates can be separated from whole without damage to science STOP This maximum reasonable in my opinion STOP Please request Almina and executors to at once renounce any claim whatsoever against Government STOP Please send credit National Bank Luxor work to proceed at once STOP Our heartiest congratulations.

Very little now remained in the way of Carter's return to Luxor. There were the inevitable dottings of i's and crossings of t's – the exchange of confirmatory letters between Carter and the Minister,[54] the settling of some problems over the unpacking of cases in the Cairo Museum, courtesy visits to the Prime Minister, and an audience with King Fuad on 14 January – 'His Majesty was most cordial. Our conversation was only very superficial.' A cable from Molony on 14 January clinched the agreement:

> Proposals approved by Lady Carnarvon and executors renunciation signed and posted you today cabling five hundred pounds.

Carter concluded his long letter to Molony with a handsome expression of thanks to Georges Merzbach: '. . . I believe I am right in mentioning that on one occasion in particular he saved a very grave situation. To his wise counsel I am deeply indebted.' Indeed it must be wondered whether the whole sorry affair might not have been concluded satisfactorily in the spring of 1924 if Merzbach had been in charge rather than Maxwell. Merzbach undoubtedly profited from his life-long experience of living in Egypt; from his instinctive understanding of how to negotiate with Egyptians, and from not being British. It is questionable whether he would have fared very much better than Maxwell at the time when so many people were involved in the negotiations – Breasted, Gardiner, Sir John Maxwell, Winlock, Carter himself. Nevertheless, in the less crowded circumstances that prevailed after May 1924 he was able to proceed quietly and efficiently, advising always negotiation not litigation. When Carter returned and the climate seemed perfect for settlement, it was again Merzbach who succeeded in preventing the resumption of bitter recriminatory skirmishing

---

54 The texts of the letters by Howard Carter and by Sidky Pasha, Minister of Public Works, are printed in H. Carter, *The Tomb of Tut.ankh.Amen*, II, p. xv.

between Carter on the one hand and Lacau and Abd el-Hamid Bedawy Pasha on the other. Carter and his side had every reason to be grateful.

Howard Carter was back in Luxor on 19 January and ready to set about a short campaign in which he expected to confine his activities to a general tidying up of things in the tomb and the laboratory in readiness for a full season to begin in September or October later in the year. On the following day he was joined by Callender from Armant. Their differences of the previous spring were, as it seems, placed in abeyance for the time being. Carter also had the pleasure – for so it may be hoped it was – of entertaining Georges Merzbach and his wife, who had come to Luxor for a holiday. They had never, presumably, seen the tomb of Tutankhamun, and the present moment offered a unique opportunity to be in at the reopening.

Carter and the Merzbachs first went to the Valley of the Kings on 22 January to inspect the state of the various places used by the excavators. The tomb itself was covered by a layer of rubbish about half a metre deep. The entrance to the tomb of Sethos II, the laboratory, was closed 'with a construction of a kind of lattice-work completely plastered over with white plaster.' Before the entrance of the tomb was a sorry sight:

> We found that beautiful linen pall that covered the King's grave, and for which I brought out Dr. Alexander Scott, Mr. and Mrs. Newberry from England especially to preserve it and had made a special lining for it, left out in the open unprotected from the Sun and wind. It is ruined! They had removed the carpenter's kiosk and placed it on the pall.

The magazine and lunch tomb (no. 4) 'from all outward appearances seems to be alright.'

And so, according to plan, the three tombs were handed back to Carter on 25 January 'with great pomp', as he reported to Lady Carnarvon:[55]

> by the Government Commission comprising: The Conseiller Royale [sic] Abd el Hamid Pasha Bedawi, The Mudir of Keneh, The Bey the Marmour [sic] of Luxor, two representatives of the Police, The Insp. in Chief of the Antiquity Depart., The Insp. of Luxor, Mr. Quibell, M. Lefebvre, and M. Baraize a sort of foreman to the S. des A. [Service des Antiquités].[56] Lacau was not present. It would seem that he was ashamed to show his face.

Merzbach and Callender were also in the party, and the portentous occasion was completed with an official dinner given by the Mudir of Qena (Keneh). Howard Carter was reinstalled in the Valley of the Kings. All seemed to be sweetness and light. The omens were promising. But

55 Copy in M.M.A., Department of Egyptian Art, Carter files.
56 Émile Baraize was Director of Works for the Antiquities Service, employed in the restoration and conservation of ancient buildings.

internal politics could easily change the prospect. On the day before the official hand-over, Carter wrote to Edward Robinson:[57]

> If the coming elections here go well, as I believe they will, and this new Government remains in power, I should not be surprised to see the Lacaunian plans derided. It will not be my fault it they are not. People in Egypt are beginning to find out where the real trouble lies, and the sooner the better.

For the moment Howard Carter could contemplate the future with a degree of equanimity which would surely have surprised his supporters of the previous spring.

57 Letter of 24 January, see n. 53 above.

14

THE ROYAL BODY, WITH REVERENCE

Howard Carter's return to Luxor in January 1925 was somewhat muted, as, no doubt, he would have wished. The excitement and drama of the preceding two seasons in the Valley of the Kings had more than adequately demonstrated that good archaeology could not easily be pursued when the lives of the archaeologists were bedevilled by the demands of publicity and the requirements of social life. The complication of legal proceedings, springing from ground fertilized and nourished by Press intrigues and political resentments, provided unexpected additional burdens which Carter in particular was ill-equipped to handle. For the moment, as far as the world at large was concerned, he seemed to be on his own, backed by the wise and energetic Merzbach. In the work of the tomb he still had Lucas and Burton, and also Callender who sadly had become less committed and more self-seeking, as events would show. Most of the influential supporters who had both helped and hindered his affairs in the spring of 1924, were mercifully out of Egypt; in the case of his colleagues in the Metropolitan House there was a distinct wariness of further involvement. He was not abandoned, but left to get on with his work – an outcome which scarcely displeased him. His colleagues at Luxor and elsewhere were yet very divided in mind about the future and their attitude to Carter and his tomb. Feelings of loyalty, revulsion and responsibility were mixed with a fascination for the great discovery. There was much more to be revealed, and it would be a shame to take up a position which might preclude future involvement.

In some respects Carter's most loyal supporter at this time remained Alan Gardiner. As ever he looked to the Egyptological importance of Tutankhamun's tomb, and the need for Carter to complete the job. The axe he ground was that of archaeological necessity, certainly the most disinterested of the many axes that had been ground and would be ground by others. Gardiner's own future involvement was uncertain. Carter had always thought of him (as Carnarvon had done) as the man best able to deal with the tomb's texts. But in early 1925 these texts were not high in Carter's priorities, and Gardiner, who was not without important pieces of work to engross his time, was left in doubt about what calls might be made on him in the future. He remained bitterly opposed to the regime of Pierre Lacau as Director-General of the Antiquities Service, and was not at all sanguine about Carter's prospects. Before Carter had quite returned to Luxor, Gardiner wrote to Albert Lythgoe:[1]

> I doubt whether any satisfactory arrangement will be reached so long as Lacau is at the head of the Service. . . . I read in the paper this morning that the difference with regard to the tomb has been settled, at which I am delighted, but Lacau has behaved so badly that I still feel that I should be unwilling to bolster up his position . . . the blame for all that has occurred, both as regards the tomb and as regards the new law, seems to me to rest almost wholly on Lacau's shoulders.

Almost one month later he wrote to Breasted:[2]

> What exactly my plan will be in 1926 I don't quite know. Carter has not written to me a single word and I don't know to what extent, or even whether, I shall be wanted to deal with the texts in the tomb.

It is possible that Carter had become shy of asking Gardiner to resume work in the tomb, aware of the latter's other commitments, not least of which was the completion of his great *Egyptian Grammar*, a monumental and abidingly important work which would transform the approach to the teaching of the Egyptian language. It would be published in 1927, and has remained, even in the face of significant advances in the understanding of ancient Egyptian, the most influential work both for scholars and for interested amateurs. The thought may well have struck Carter that he would be wise to have someone else in reserve, preferably someone on his own doorstep in Luxor. An excellent candidate would be Dr Harold H. Nelson, a pupil of James Henry Breasted, who had in the autumn of 1924 arrived in Luxor to become the first Director of the Epigraphic and Architectural Survey of the Oriental Institute of the University of Chicago – Breasted's very special baby. The new expedition's permanent home, Chicago House, had recently been built at Medinet Habu, near the temple of Ramesses III on which the expedition would be working. The design of the house had been conceived by Breasted, encouraged and financed by John D. Rockefeller Jr, and executed by Arthur Callender during the spring and summer of 1924. It would become a new and welcome addition to the centres of scholarship and hospitality in Western Thebes, most notably represented up until that time by the Metropolitan House. Chicago House would be and would increasingly become a true beacon for Egyptol-

1 Copy in G.I. Gardiner Corr. AHG/42.193.4, dated 3 January 1925.
2 O.I. Director's Office Corr. 1925, of 8 February.

ogists, especially when new premises were built in Luxor itself in the 1930s. The hospitality to be found there would not be as expansive as that offered by the New Yorkers, but it would always be ready and, in its own way, generous.

On his return to Luxor in January 1925 Howard Carter met Dr Nelson for the first time. Before Carter arrived Nelson had, possibly taking his stance from Breasted, been prepared to keep his distance. Writing on 26 January to T. G. Allen, a Chicago colleague destined to become a distinguished, although inadequately recognized Egyptological scholar, he commented:[3] 'Everyone about here is talking of the opening of Tut's tomb. I am not in the least interested myself nor shall I make any effort to get into the tomb.' This somewhat grand and dismissive attitude would be modified as time passed. On 17 February he reported to Breasted a visit by Carter and Lucas to Chicago House:[4]

> When leaving, Carter asked me to come up and see the tomb and his work and bring Mrs. Nelson along. I felt very embarassed [sic] as he did not ask Mrs. Breasted, who was present at the time. I presume, however, that it would be best for us to go some day, as this will be the best way to relieve you of any trouble about asking for us. I would like very much to go with you, but we shall see about that when you return. Carter was most pleasant today.

The Nelsons made their visit in early March and were suitably impressed. Harold Nelson's brief account to George Allen provides a fresh impression from a knowledgeable scholar at a time when Carter was engaged in the unspectacular work of conservation and study, the kind of work which would take up his time during the short 1925 season and also future seasons until the tomb and its contents could be finally declared cleared in 1932:[5]

> Carter gave us about two hours and showed us everything he could in the tomb and the laboratory. Carter is working only on the stuff that he had already taken out of the tomb last season. He does not intend to take out anything this season, reserving that till next year. He was working on one of the statues which stood beside the door of the tomb chamber. He showed us the alabaster vase made in two parts with painted figures between the parts of which Breasted has doubtless told you. It is a most extraordinary object. To me one of the most interesting objects was the reed staff, an ordinary reed such as grows besides the canals, tipped with gold at either end, and bearing an inscription stating that it had been cut by the king's own

3 Same source.
4 Same source.
5 Same source.

hand beside his favorate [sic] pleasure lake. It gives a real human touch to the object. The collection of staves of various kinds, of gold and silver, solid, of wood overlaid with irridescent green and red beetles wings, etc. was marvelous and must have been gorgeous, if barbaric, when they were new.

He goes on to write of the silver trumpet which Carter described as a hunting horn. It bore on its bell figures of the gods Amon-Re, Re-Herakhty and Ptah, and Nelson suggested that as these deities were connected with the divisions of the Egyptian army during the Nineteenth Dynasty, the instrument was probably a military trumpet. Carter, ever ready to spot a winning idea, 'fell for that suggestion readily, though I hope he does not make too much of it.' Nelson was worried that his idea might get into the papers. In the event, Carter did use the suggestion in the second volume of his popular publication,[6] but without acknowledging its author; for which lack of courtesy Nelson was probably profoundly grateful.

In his published note on the trumpet Carter stated 'were it blown would still fill the Valley with a resounding blast.' He had in fact tried it himself; in a letter to Lady Carnarvon on 17 February he reported: 'though I am no expert with such musical instruments, I managed to get a good blast out of it which broke the silence of the Valley.'[7] Memorable recordings of this silver and the bronze trumpets from the tomb were made by the BBC in April 1939.[8] The trumpeter was Bandsman James Tappern of the 11th Prince Albert's Own Hussars, and sadly his use of a modern mouthpiece inserted into the silver trumpet shattered the instrument. It was later so well repaired by Lucas that it could be blown by Philip Jones, the distinguished brass instrumentalist, in the Cairo Museum in January 1975. He subsequently wrote,[9] 'Its sound was not exactly melodious, as the bore in relation to its length is quite out of proportion, but it was probably the most thrilling experience I shall have as a trumpet-player.' The use of a mouth-piece enabled Bandsman Tappern to obtain a wider range of notes than would have been possible otherwise; as a martial instrument in antiquity it would commonly have been played on a single pitch.

It may have been as a result of Nelson's helpful comments on the silver trumpet that Carter began to consider him as a possible collaborator to work on texts in the tomb. In several letters written towards the end of the season Nelson referred distastefully to the prospect of being drawn into this association:[10]

[2 April to Breasted] Carter again intimated yesterday that he might

6 H. Carter, *The Tomb of Tut.ankh.Amen*, II (London, 1927), pp. 19, 30ff., and pl. II (b).
7 Letter in M.M.A., Department of Egyptian Art, Carter files.
8 See N. Reeves, *The Complete Tutankhamun* (London, 1990), pp. 164f.
9 Letter of 9 April 1975 in Department of Egyptian Antiquities, British Museum.
10 O.I. Director's Office Corr. Nelson 1925.

need me at the tomb next fall. I am not anxious to get involved in that enterprise, but if he can find no one else, I suppose I ought to do what I can.

[22 April to Breasted] I am not anxious to be in Gurnah [Qurna] when Carter returns, for he again suggested my presence at the tomb when he opened the mummy case in the fall. The more I think of his suggestion, the less I like it.

Nelson never specifies any particular reason for his unwillingness to be involved, but it may have been the result of what he had heard from others who had been persuaded to work with Carter since the discovery of the tomb of Tutankhamun. Something of his poor reputation in this respect comes out in a letter written to Breasted from Beirut on 6 July 1925. Even away from Egypt and on holiday, Nelson brooded on the matter:

Callender had a talk with me just before I left in which he warned me against having anything to do with Carter's suggestion. Of course, Callender has a special grievance against Carter, but I am afraid there is only too much ground for his warning. However, I can tell Carter that I am too busy at the House to take on any obligation elsewhere.

Subsequently, when the coffins were opened late in 1925, Nelson was inexorably drawn into an involvement with Carter, as will be seen. The experience did not, apparently, prove to be as disagreeable as he had feared.

The Callender grievance mentioned by Nelson concerned his supposed loss of income through the shortness of the 1923–4 season(already mentioned), and the late start in January 1925. The matter came to a head in June–July 1925 when a letter from Callender to Alan Gardiner, passed on to General Sir John Marshall and then back to Carter, led to an exchange of letters between Carter and Callender.[11] Carter invoked friendship and common sense; Callender pressed his case vigorously but ineffectively. Lawyers were consulted. The outcome seems to have been wholly unsatisfactory for Callender, who never again worked with Carter in the Valley of the Kings. It was a sad and disappointing end to an old and friendly association which extended to times before the discovery of Tutankhamun's tomb. Callender may have been expecting more than he could justify from what seems to have been a verbal proposal by Carter for the length of his employment each season, and he seems to have made no allowance for the external circumstances which had curtailed the work in the second and third seasons. On the other hand, it seems extraordinarily

11 In M.M.A., Department of Egyptian Art, Carter files.

insensitive and ungenerous on Carter's part to behave so intractably towards one to whom he described himself as being 'among your very best friends'. Some accommodation should surely have been found to satisfy Callender and avoid a complete break. For the whole of the time from January 1925 until the end of the season in early April Carter and Callender were in daily contact, the latter even living for most of the time in Carter's house. Some other specific coolness must have modified the warmth of their old friendship, as had apparently happened in January 1924, when Callender for unknown reasons submitted his resignation to Carter. It may be thought that Carter was the more culpable in this rift, but the possibility must be allowed that the time had come for his association with Callender to end, and he felt no necessity to prolong it by some form of sympathetic arrangement. As it was, in 1925 Callender was working with Carter from 25 January until the first week in April, a total of about eleven weeks, for which he received a full four months' salary, as Callender himself conceded.

A bare two months of this time was available for work on the objects removed from the tomb in the preceding year. It was, nevertheless, a satisfactory period with much being accomplished, and with little interference from bureaucracy. Carter could report to Lady Carnarvon[12] 'that things are running very smoothly here and that I am gradually getting the preservation work of the material in the laboratory done. It should be through by the end of March, when I hope to have everything packed ready for transport to the Cairo Museum.' In the same letter he comments, 'Quite a number of people came professin [sic] to be great friends of yours, saying that it was your express wish that I show them the Tomb.' Without a letter they got short shrift. His diary notes that there were many government visitors, and that on 27 February the Prime Minister, Ziwar Pasha, came to the Valley: 'He seemed very pleased with the discovery and the results of our discovery in general.' He could also note on 10 February: 'Up to the present no newspaper correspondents have shown any interest nor demanded any news.' Conservation happily did not make headlines. One satisfied private visitor was Dr Axel Munthe, the Swedish doctor, physician of the Queen of Sweden, a highly successful society practitioner whose evocative book on his life and house on Capri, *The Story of San Michele*, became a continuing best-selling work. He had been introduced to Carter in 1923 as a friend of Lord Carnarvon by Lord Allenby and James Rennell Rodd.[13] An intermittent friendship developed subsequently, and Munthe kept in touch with Carter for many years. He may have been instrumental in initiating a profitable visit by Carter to

12 Copy of letter of 17 February in M.M.A., Department of Egyptian Art, Carter files.
13 The letters of introduction are in M.M.A., Department of Egyptian Art, Carter files. James Rennell Rodd was a diplomat with Near-Eastern service, created Baron Rennell in 1923.

Sweden in 1930 in the course of which he got to know the Crown Prince, later King Gustav VI Adolf, a keen and knowledgeable amateur archaeologist.[14]

As often, with no surviving comments from Carter it is impossible to say how welcoming he was to visitors like Axel Munthe, whose demands (subsequently, at least) went beyond a simple desire to see work in progress.[15] Carter could, without deliberate intention, offend by failing to recognize an undeclared desire from an occasional acquaintance. Such happened with Welles Bosworth, an American architect who was engaged with James Henry Breasted in preparing plans for a new museum in Cairo to be funded by John D. Rockefeller Jr. Bosworth was in Luxor in February 1925 collecting ideas for his project, and came across Carter 'in front of his tomb. He was cordial but he didn't invite me in and I didn't propose it – won't he be sorry some day? Perhaps he "missed a trick" and then again perhaps he didn't.'[16] Bosworth writes as if he had come across Carter sitting on the perch of his house and had not been asked in for a drink. He clearly did not appreciate that an unexpected visit represented for Carter an unplanned loss of time in the work he had to do. In fact he seems to have retained good relations with Welles Bosworth, and even engaged with him in tortuous antiquities dealings in the 1930s.[17]

The early 1925 season came to an end in the last days of March, and nineteen cases of antiquities were sent down to Cairo on the 31st by steamer, with Carter and Callender following a few days later to supervise the unpacking in the Cairo Museum. For the time being relations with Lacau and the Museum seemed to be good if not cordial, and, as had been the case with the work of the season, few obstacles were placed in Carter's way. Lacau had not become a 'reformed character', if that were to be what his adversaries of the previous year would have wanted. Gardiner's view has been mentioned; Breasted was equally cautious. In a letter to Carter from Cairo, written on 28 March, he says:[18]

> I suppose you have heard that Lacau has cancelled 3 concessions, those of Mond, Benedite and Foucart; there is much discussion about it down here.

At least in this action Lacau could not be accused of being particularly anti-British. While Robert Mond certainly might have thought so, Georges Bénédite, Curator of the Egyptian Department in the Louvre, and Georges Foucart, Director of the French Institute in Cairo, could hardly have done the same.

14 See p. 378 below.
15 See p. 401 below.
16 Letter in O.I. Director's Office Corr. 1925.
17 See p. 390 below.
18 O.I. Director's Office Corr. 1925.

Breasted himself could not resist the lure of the tomb, or the pursuit of possibilities which might advance his own work. As ever he knew what was best, and he had written to Carter on 19 March a long didactic letter explaining the three distinct book-buying publics of America: people who buy books in book-shops, people who buy from house-to-house salesmen, and pupils in schools.[19] Finally he advised Carter to make a contract with a good subscription-sale publisher who would market his first volume and subsequent ones, dividing them into smaller units to promote sales. For school purposes, he wanted to write a text-book himself, but would need to have photographs of the objects already published; an arrangement with Carter would be made. 'What financial return would you expect?' It seems that Carter may in conversation have indicated some interest in the idea, but he did nothing to pursue the matter. But after he had returned to England Breasted pressed him again and asked especially for five photographs for publication; he also reminded Carter of the complete set of tomb photographs for the Oriental Institute which Carter had said was in preparation. Things did not work out well for Breasted. On a copy of the letter he wrote on 2 July inviting Carter to tea at the Connaught Hotel, he set out bluntly what had happened:[20]

On Monday July 6 Carter called on me at this hotel and after expressing some irritation at my request (a request wh[ich] he had formerly accepted) and said I c'd have anything I wanted, he gave me a memorandum signed by him authorising his photographer Sinclair to furnish me with the desired 5 prints at a charge of £10 – 0 – 0. It was understood *orally* that in view of this charge I had permission to publish the photographs.

Although Carter always wrote politely to Breasted, it is easy to detect how tired he was with the great historian's regular and rather patronising approaches. The differences between the two were partly matters of style and nationality, but it may be recalled that Breasted had from earlier days been in doubt about Carter's reliability, and had been distinctly upset over the loss of the sculpture to the Cleveland Museum. Carter was acceptable as the discoverer of Tutankhamun's tomb, as a source of useful information and helpful publicity; he could be supported and defended against forces which were generally hostile to archaeology in Egypt. But in other respects doubts remained, and this photographic charge seemed to snap Breasted's forbearance. later in the same year he could write to his wife 'to come into contact with Carter since my last interview with him in London is very distasteful to me.'[21]

There is some evidence to suggest that Howard Carter struck a particu-

19 Same source.
20 Same source.
21 Letter of 17 November 1925, O.I. same source.

341

larly low point in personal morale during the summer of 1925. Although he was re-established in Luxor and had completed a good, if not spectacular, season's work, he had become increasingly isolated. He had alienated Breasted and lost Callender. His Metropolitan Museum friends had been less in evidence during his months in Egypt than in previous seasons. He may even have kept away from them deliberately. Minnie Burton's diary entries, punctilious in their recording of who came to luncheon, tea and dinner at the Metropolitan House, contain only occasional mentions of Carter until the very last days of his season. He may also have been unwell and particularly irritable, which might have accounted for a letter written by Somers Clarke, his old architectural mentor of Deir el-Bahri days, to H. R. H. Hall, Keèper of Egyptian and Assyrian Antiquities in the British Museum.[22] It apparently answered one from Hall in which Carter's moods had been mentioned. Clarke did not mince matters:

> Poor old Carter. I fear for him. He has a liver of the first magnitude and consequently a temper. The great ones will soon be tired of him and drop him – Then the vitriol will drop from his lips, no more honey. I am in agreement with your views about the bearers of stiff collars and shirtfronts. Happily up here [Mahamid by Elkab] and at the present temp. I have no clothes at all.

There was further for Carter the distinct worry about the coming season when he would tackle what could be the most difficult and certainly the most sensitive part of his whole work on the tomb, the opening of the coffins and the exposure and exploration, archaeologically and anatomically, of the mummy of the first royal body to have survived unviolated since antiquity. Here was a task that would call on his very best skills, and demand a reverential approach which did not normally enter into archaeological activities. Could he handle the expected stresses and conflicting requirements that would be expected of him? In the event, he succeeded beyond all expectations; but the tasks in advance must surely have seemed daunting. And he could not expect this time to have such sympathetic support as had sustained him at the opening of the tomb, the breaching of the Burial Chamber, and even the raising of the great sarcophagus lid. Still he could hope to have at his side Alfred Lucas and Harry Burton, and for the mummy, Dr Douglas Derry and Dr Saleh Bey Hamdi, his chosen collaborators.

One matter that was set up satisfactorily during the summer of 1925 was the preparation of volume two of *The Tomb of Tut.ankh.Amen*. Howard Carter put its shaping into the reliable hands of his old friend Percy White, who had exercised some function in the writing of volume one. White had now necessarily retired from his professorship in the Egyptian University,

22 Letter of 30 August 1925 in Department of Western Asiatic Antiquities, British Museum.

for that institution had closed down in 1925. He was 73 and living in England.[23] According to plan, the new volume would continue the general narrative from the first volume, dealing principally with the Burial Chamber, and covering what might be revealed by the exploration of the coffins in the coming season. White wrote up the notes provided by Carter, and made suggestions about the form and additional content of the volume generally. Letters written from the Savile Club in November indicate something of the process in action:[24]

> [16 Nov.] The whole of your daily record I've now turned into narrative form and am now about to study it to avoid repetition and to give it a natural sweep if I can.

> [20 Nov.] I think it would be well, in framing official descriptions to lay as much stress as possible on the *light* thrown by your discovery on Egyptian burial ceremonial.

This suggestion was adopted by Carter and an appropriate chapter, 'Points of Interest in Egyptian Burial Customs', was included in the volume. It is not a particularly comprehensive essay on funerary procedures, but it derives special interest from the incorporation of references to work carried out by Carter in the Valley of the Kings and elsewhere before his discovery of Tutankhamun's tomb. He was indeed fortunate in having such a friend as Percy White, who could in so many ways take up the telling of the Tutankhamun story after the sad withdrawal of Arthur Mace.

Leaving London on 23 September, Carter travelled by way of Trieste and Alexandria to arrive in Cairo, where he found that the management of the Continental Hotel had put him into 'the same room as poor Ld. C. used to have'. The fact that he mentioned it in his diary suggests that he was specially touched by this sensitive gesture.[25] It might have been upsetting to some, but Carter probably appreciated the recognition of his position. His intention now was to get to work as soon as possible, and to this end he went to see Edgar on 1 October and arranged to start operations on 11 October. There were, however, problems. How should he proceed? His intention was that 'the scientific examinations should be carried out as reverently as possible, but that I should delay rewrapping the mummy until I knew whether the Ministers would like to inspect the royal remains.' He suspected that Lacau would want to be present during the examination of the mummy, and Lacau did not plan to return to Egypt from France until November. There were also worrying signs that the Press might be difficult this season. The opening of the coffins and inspection of the mummy provided sufficient bait to attract the familiar sharks.

---

23 In a letter of 13 April 1930, in John Carter's possession; White mentions his age as 78.
24 Letters with John Carter.
25 In Carter's 'Egyptian', i.e. working diary, G.I. Carter Notebook 1.

Lacau indicated that he would expect to be at the unwrapping of the mummy, and that he would be in Luxor by 10 November. Carter was vexed at the prospect of delay, but he realized that there would be much to do before the delicate work on the body could begin. But even he had not divined what difficulties he would encounter in the following weeks. The opening and separation of the various coffins and the removal of the body were to test all his ingenuity and the scientific skills of Lucas. The unwrapping of the mummy would be an exercise in stratigraphic excavation as the various layers of bodily protection and jewellery were investigated and unravelled. The tiresome delay would in the end provide just about enough time to have everything ready for Lacau's arrival in Luxor. Prudently Carter put off the arrival of Derry and Hamdi Bey until 10 November.

There was no time to waste. On 12 October the tomb and laboratory were opened and found to be in excellent condition. Carter describes in the published account[26] how 'familiarity can never entirely dissipate the feeling of mystery', and how his first renewed viewing of the outer gilded coffin in the sarcophagus provided an even more powerful impression than before: 'With the shadows of the ancient gods there can be no vulgar intimacy.' Whether composed by Carter or White, the comment was most apposite; it has the flavour of a true Carter sentiment.

Procedures for lifting the lid of the outermost coffin had been worked out in the preceding season, so a minimum of time was spent in starting with the removal of the ten silver pins that secured the silver tongues which held the lid in place on the shell of the coffin. The lid was lifted on the 13th, to reveal a further gilded wooden coffin within; a badly decayed and discoloured linen shroud covered this second coffin, and the pathetic remains of floral garlands provided distinct links with the human hands that had attended the burial so many centuries before. As ever, Carter displayed his restraint and strict adherence to the good practices he had established earlier by halting the work until Harry Burton's expected arrival in Luxor. On the 15th Burton was able to photograph the second, shrouded coffin. Already Carter was disturbed by the condition of the linen, which suggested that some form of dampness had penetrated the burial and might have affected the mummy itself.

The next stage concerned the removal of the whole of the coffin assemblage from the sarcophagus so that investigation would proceed more easily than if the coffins were unpacked while still lying in the sarcophagus. It turned out to be a relatively easy operation using lifting tackle attached to steel pins passed through the holes which had been used for the silver pins securing the outer lid to the shell. Wooden planks placed across the sarcophagus provided a base on which the assemblage could rest while

26 *The Tomb of Tut.ankh.Amen*, II, pp. 69ff.

the next stages were considered. The second coffin fitted the outer coffin so snugly that only about one centimetre of space existed between the two. Here it was only possible to withdraw the pins securing the lid to the shell far enough to allow stout copper wire to be attached to them. So supported the second coffin was separated from the outermost coffin, which itself was lowered back into the sarcophagus. The fragile nature of the gilded and inlaid gesso decoration on the second coffin required the least handling possible, and it was again with great ingenuity that the lid was removed on 23 October, revealing within its shell the third and most magnificent coffin. A reddish shroud and garlands covered this third coffin, and it was not until after the whole had been photographed and the coverings removed that the excavators realized that this innermost coffin was of solid gold. The weight of the whole assemblage was now explained. Even so, the very idea of a solid gold coffin was almost beyond belief, and certainly beyond Breasted's belief. He foolishly wrote to his wife:[27]

> Carter and Lacau seem to be on better terms. They have shut the newspapers out and issue brief bulletins at long intervals. Some of these bulletins contain arrant nonsense like the statement that the innermost coffin is of 'solid gold' in a bulletin signed by both Carter and Lacau. Of course we are all familiar with the fact that Carter does not know the meaning of the English language. There can be no doubt that the coffin is wood overlaid with gold. This probably heavy sheet gold and by itself it is solid, but this is far from justifying the statement that the *coffin* is of 'solid gold'.

It was as well that Breasted did not commit himself to print on the matter; at least no such published comment has been traced.

The second coffin shell with its contents was then taken out of the Burial Chamber into the Antechamber for easier examination. They found that substantial quantities of a black viscid substance, probably sacred unguent, had been poured over the innermost coffin, fixing it solidly in place, and when the lid had been removed, the same treatment was found to have been given to the mummy within. Carter reckoned that 'something like two bucketsful of the liquid unguents had been poured over the golden coffin, and a similar amount over the body inside.'[28] At this moment, and with the advice of Lucas, Carter realized that only by the application of heat could the black viscid mass be melted and the various components separated. He decided, therefore, that the examination of the mummy should be carried out as it lay in the gold coffin, itself still lying within the shell of the second coffin. It took place as planned on 11 November.

The solemn but expectant party which gathered in the tomb of Sethos II at 9.45 a.m. differed markedly from those that had attended the earlier

27 Letter in O.I. Director's Office Corr. 1925, dated 27 November.
28 *The Tomb of Tut.ankh.Amen*, II, p. 89.

'openings' in the tomb. There were no representatives of international Egyptology – no Breasted, no Gardiner – no member of the Carnarvon family, nobody from the Metropolitan Museum Egyptian Expedition, if Harry Burton be excepted; there were no distinguished British archaeological grandees, or representatives from the High Commission in Cairo. The party consisted wholly of Egyptian government servants and local officials, members of the Antiquities Service and Carter's staff.[29] Carter lists H. E. Salah Enan Pasha, Under-Secretary of State in the Ministry of Public Works, H. E. Sayid Fuad Bey el-Kholi, Governor of Qena Province, Pierre Lacau, Tewfik Effendi Boulos, Chief Inspector of Upper Egypt, and Mohammed Effendi Shabaan, Assistant Curator in the Cairo Museum; with Carter himself, Lucas, Burton, Derry and Saleh Bey Hamdi. It may have seemed a modest turn-out for such an important occasion, but it was as well that there was no crush of spectators to view one of the most delicate archaeological operations that had ever been undertaken.

Lucas and Carter together undertook the opening up of the mummy bandages. It was a frustrating job because of the friability of the linen and the pervasive remains of the unguents. But gradually over four days the work moved forward. The account given by Carter in *The Tomb of Tut.ankh.- Amen*, vol. II, pp. 107ff, is authoritative and clear, although it is sometimes difficult to visualize the positions of some of the jewellery and other objects contained within the wrappings and on the body of the king. As the work progressed, Carter made careful notes of what was found, and from these, and with the help of Burton's photographs, he subsequently made clear, informative sketches of the various levels as the unwrappings revealed the stages in reverse.[30] These sketches are now to be found among the Carter papers in the Griffith Institute in Oxford. It was a painstaking and wonderfully rewarding task, with the revelation of splendid and unparallelled pieces at almost every stage of the work: jewellery, ritual objects, pectorals, insignia, remarkable daggers. Every technique of the ancient craftsman was exemplified, every fine and precious material available to the ancient Egyptians employed. The damage caused by the unguents – a kind of slow combustion – and the consequent deterioration of the bandages and the threadings of the jewellery, demanded slow progress, and determined the need for many photographs as well as Carter's notes. To clean and reconstitute the material found on the body would provide work enough for many months in the laboratory.

The pitiable remains of the body were removed piecemeal from the coffin, and the head in particular caused special difficulties as it was trapped within the great golden mask, itself held firm in the coffin by the congealed ungents. Everything took time; and yet in a matter of days

29 *Ibid.*, p. 106.
30 See also N. Reeves, *The Complete Tutankhamun*, pp. 116ff; the sketches are reproduced on p. 113.

Carter and Lucas succeeded in separating all the components of the nest of coffins, using heating techniques which are terrifying to read about[31] but certainly achieved the desired results. On 31 December Carter was able to take to Cairo the solid gold innermost coffin and the mask – the two most precious and perhaps the most splendid objects in the burial equipment. Minnie Burton noted on the day:

> Said goodbye to Mr. Lucas. He and Mr. Carter going to Cairo by tonight's train in service car with armed guard, taking the gold coffin and mask down to the Museum.

In the weeks following the investigation of the coffins and the body, Carter took advantage of the more relaxed relationship with the Egyptian administration and the Antiquities Service to welcome groups of resident scholars and their families to inspect the spectacular results of the season's work so far. He presumably cleared the visits with Tewfik Boulos, the Chief Inspector, according to the agreement that had been reached in the previous season. As Carter recorded in his diary entry for 28 January 1925,

> It was decided that no visitors should be allowed to enter or visit the tomb, whether Government invitees or otherwise, except on Tuesdays, unless there be some exceptional reason or exceptional case, when I am to refer it to the Chief Inspector who will refuse entry if he has not received special instructions from the Government.

It was on 3 December, a Tuesday, that Minnie Burton noted a visit by members of the Metropolitan Museum Expedition:

> We all (Winlocks, Frances and Barbara, Miss Perry, Miss Bowditch, Davieses, Mr. Meyer and Mr. Hauser and Mr. Wilkinson) went over to the Valley to No. 15 [the laboratory] and Mr. Carter showed us the Tutankhamen jewels – masses and masses of them, most exquisite inlaid things, and rings, gold plaques in the shape of spread-winged vultures, inlaid bracelets and amulets. A lovely perfume box in gold and inlay on polished iron base [in fact, silver], and gorgeous daggers in sheaths, one with crystal stopper handle and polished iron blade, very sharp. Also the gold and inlaid mask, so like Akhnaton, in the gold coffin. Also the wonderful coffin lid, and the inlaid second coffin, as well as the first we had already seen. We saw a hand of the mummy with the ring on and gold finger stalls, and the head of the king, very small and well-preserved, lacking nose. After a lengthy stay in No. 15 we went to the Tomb and saw the sarcophagus again, and Mr. C. opened the door of the store chamber so that we could look in and see the Anubis and the Canopic chest.

---

31 *The Tomb of Tut.ankh.Amen*, II, pp. 86ff.

Shortly afterwards it was the turn of Chicago House, and Harold Nelson included a mention in a letter of 16 December to Breasted. He was more concerned, however, by Carter's specific request for help:[32]

Carter told me that he wanted me to help him arrange in order the inscribed pieces of the bands of inlaid hieroglyphics that run down the front and back and around the sides of the mummy. Of course they are mortuary texts but I am not familiar with them having read next to nothing of such texts. I presume these are all more or less alike on the mummies of any given period. Can you tell me off hand of any publication I might secure from Cairo which would furnish me with examples of such inscriptions that I may read up on them a little before Carter calls on me for help? I do not want to fall down on such a job.

Breasted, who was in Cairo, recommended Maspero's *Momies Royales*, an important work on the Deir el-Bahri cache of royal mummies found in 1881, and he arranged for a copy to be sent to Nelson.[33] He encouraged Nelson to give Carter the help he needed: 'I should be glad . . . to have our expedition of use in the work of T's tomb.' He warned Nelson that he could expect to be dropped by Carter as soon as he had what he wanted and added, perhaps a little gratuitously, 'I have just received from confidential sources in New York, the statement that Carter's treatment of the Metropolitan Museum has been "simply outrageous". These are the words of the man who has from the first been most loyal to him.' He then says that he could apply the same words to the treatment he had received 'when I paid him $10 apiece for prints of *already published* photographs, which I needed for my *History of Egypt*; the transaction being accompanied by insolence on his part which I should be glad to forget.' Nelson should therefore be forewarned, but ought to help, even as the Metropolitan continued to do. Nelson, in acknowledging Breasted's letter,[34] confessed that he had already received warnings from others about Carter's cavalier treatment of his helpers; but 'as we accepted Carter's invitation to visit the Tomb both last year and this year, I did not feel that I could do anything else than comply when he asked me to look over his arrangement of the mummy bands after he had cleaned them up properly.'

Carter's complexity of character seemingly both antagonized people and attracted them. There was also, of course, the draw of the tomb; to be associated in the work was for most Egyptologists more than they could reject, and it was worth putting up with a fair amount of boorishness from Carter to be allowed to participate in the study of such remarkable material. The guarded remarks about Carter's outrageous behaviour can

32 O.I. Director's Office Corr. 1925.
33 Same source, letter of 27 December.
34 Same source, letter of 31 December.

only be treated with caution. The man who had been 'most loyal' to Carter might have been Albert Lythgoe or Herbert Winlock, more probably the former. For Winlock's view of the time it seems proper to invoke the letter which he wrote to Edward Harkness, an influential member of the board of trustees of the Metropolitan Museum, on 15 April 1926.[35] Its background was set by a long, busy winter and spring during which, since December, Carter had been wholly taken up with the cleaning, restringing and restoring of the objects found on the mummy of Tutankhamun. To begin he says, 'We are just drawing to the end of the season, in which one of the pleasantest things – among many pleasant things – has been my relations with our friend H. C. I know that will interest you.' He continues by describing how things began 'clumsily', and how the old H. C. appeared under the strains of unwrapping the mummy. Carter had, however, not been pestered by the government; but he had missed Callender. He couldn't understand how Callender could take his irritability so seriously; although he did call it his 'worse disease'. On the recovery of the jewellery, Winlock had this to say:

> Burton took a great many photographs of the things in position, and Carter, I believe, took adequate notes. From the photographs and notes he has made a most ingenious series of diagrams showing the position of each object on the body. They are wonderfully clear, and I believe that no one will be able to complain of any lack of information in his record.
>
> The winter has gone, really, in the restoration of the jewelery, and at that, Carter is really incomparable. He is a wonderfully neat worker, and with his fingers of an artist there is no better person to whom this stuff could have been entrusted.

Winlock then describes some pieces of jewellery and comments on the mummy and the view, which he shares with Carter, that Tutankhamun was the son of Akhenaten by one of the lesser ladies of the harem. Returning to Carter and his behaviour during the season, he concludes:

> All together, the way I sum it up he has been better off alone – or rather with only Lucas – this winter. Most of the work has been cleaning and restoring the minute details in the jewellery, and, as I wrote above, there is no one who can touch him on that.

Winlock's opinion at this point represents an important testimony of Carter's professional competence, especially as it came after a time of difficulties between the two. Further it was made when Winlock surely still had in mind the quite special abilities of Arthur Mace, who had first been offered to Carter for precisely the kind of intricate work which Carter was now executing so supremely well. It would be impossible – and indeed

35 M.M.A., Department of Egyptian Art, Carter files.

very unfair – to try to place Carter and Mace in an order of competence; but it is fair to believe that Winlock reckoned that Carter's abilities measured up well against those that Mace had displayed so miraculously in the reconstitution of the material from Senebtisi's tomb before the Great War.

Carter had not been quite as alone during the season as Winlock stated in his letter. Apart from Lucas and Burton, he had with him for some weeks Dr Harold Plenderleith, the assistant of Dr Alexander Scott of the British Museum, who subsequently succeeded Scott as Keeper of the Research Laboratory, and in 1959 became the first Director of the International Centre for the Study of the Preservation and Restoration of Cultural Property, in Rome. He came to Thebes to continue the work started by Scott in 1924, and he collected samples of many materials for later examination and analysis in the laboratory of the British Museum and elsewhere. He remains a living link with the days of active work in the laboratory of tomb No. 15, and some of his memories of working with Carter both in Egypt and in London are drawn on later in this volume.[36] He worked closely with Lucas, who was responsible for the systematic examination of the objects from a scientific point of view, and Carter was, as he remembers, very kind to him. This attitude he does not attribute to Carter's natural benevolence, but to his desire to extract as much information as possible from Plenderleith without Lucas's knowing, so that he could confound Lucas with what might appear to be his own percipience.

At that time, when the scientific and archaeological study of the objects from the tomb began to assume great importance in the scheme of Carter's work, he spared no pains to obtain the best advice on a wide range of materials and techniques. The second and third volumes of *The Tomb of Tut.ankh.Amen* include valuable appendices containing some of the results of the scientific studies made during the clearance of the tomb. They represent only a small part of the work that was carried out in many laboratories and research institutes both at that time and during the 1930s. Samplings of the rich organic and metal materials in the tomb in particular were made available on a generous level. Alexander Scott, for example, mentions a quantity of about 450 grams of a cosmetic substance in one alabaster vase, which allowed ample sampling for experimental purposes.[37] Carter himself was assiduous is seeking competent researchers, and many of the findings resulting from their work are to be found in the voluminous notes he gathered in readiness for the final scholarly report on the tomb, which he planned to prepare when the clearance of all the chambers was completed. Lucas in due course incorporated much of his own work in the later revisions of his *Ancient Egyptian Materials and Industries*; but the scientific material remaining unpublished, including work that could still be carried

36 I was able to talk at length with Dr Plenderleith in the autumn of 1989.
37 *The Tomb of Tut.ankh.Amen*, II, p. 207.

out on the objects from the tomb, could generate studies of major importance.[38]

The great disappointment of the tomb was the state of the royal body.
As a result of the corrosive and apparently combustible effects of the
unguents which were poured so lavishly over the body, there was far less
left for Derry and Saleh Hamdi to examine than had been hoped for. They
had based their expectations on the condition of the royal bodies found in
the Deir el-Bahri cache, which were in very much better condition than
that of Tutankhamun. As Carter pointed out, the bodies from the cache
had been desecrated, rescued, cleaned and rebandaged within a relatively
short time after their original burials, and before the unguents had been
able to cause the damage found on Tutankhamun's body after the 3000
years of undisturbed burial.

From their initial investigations, Derry and Saleh Hamdi 'declared the
age of the young king to be about eighteen years'. So Carter reported in
his diary entry for 15 November. On the following day, after the relatively
well preserved head had, with considerable difficulty, been partly extracted
from its awkward position within the mask, he commented,

> Sufficient of the head was exposed today to show us that Tut-ankh-
> Amen was of a type exceedingly refined and cultured. The face has
> beautiful and well formed features.

Derry further concluded that at the time of his death Tutankhamun was
about 1.676m tall (5ft 6in.) and that the body showed no indications of
cause of death. Subsequent examinations and studies of the body have
substantially confirmed the findings of the specialists, except that Professor
R. G. Harrison's investigations of 1968 revealed a small fragment of skull
bone within the cranial cavity.[39] On the basis of this apparently ante-
mortem damage it has been suggested that the king was killed by a blow
to the head – a conclusion which should perhaps be taken with suitable
caution. Derry's final report on the autopsy of the body, rather more
scientifically expressed and considerably fuller than the more general
account in Appendix I of Carter's second volume, was finally published
in 1972.[40]

The strain which Winlock noted had threatened to upset the new and
welcome equanimity displayed by Carter during the 1925–6 season led to
a deterioration in his health in the New Year. In February he decided to
run up to Aswan for a rest. Breasted remarked in a letter to his son
Charles that 'He is in very bad health.'[41] This was written on 17 February,
and on the 23rd he wrote to Mrs John D. Rockefeller Jr that he had taken

38 E.g. Nigel Hepper, *Pharaoh's Flowers* (London, 1990).
39 R. G. Harrison and A. G. Abdalla, in *Antiquity* 46 (1972), pp. 8ff.
40 F. F. Leek, *The Human Remains from the Tomb of Tut'ankhamūn* (Oxford, 1972).
41 O.I. Director's Office Corr. 1926.

the Misses Aldrich and McFadden to see the royal tombs, including that of Tutankhamun.[42] Did he arrange it while Carter was away? Or did he swallow his pride and ask permission from Carter in order to gratify his guests? It is unlikely that they queued to see the tomb along with the general public. Carter is not mentioned as being about. Yet they were able to enter the tomb and 'stand looking down into the deep monolithic sarcophagus of Tutenkhamon and to see lying within, the golden figure of the King stretched out full length and forming the lid of the coffin.' It is just possible that he was romancing a little, as he certainly was later in the same letter. He comments imaginatively on the burial, and on the third 'solid gold coffin' (as he now conceded) and the golden mask, which for him showed 'clearly the face of a sensitive youth, a Hamlet totally unequal to the crushing responsibilities he was called upon to bear.'

Howard Carter was not one to complain openly about his health. His inclination if he were not well was to withdraw from public gaze like a wounded animal. A small reflection of the strain he was under during this long and exhausting season comes out in a letter he wrote on 26 February to his uncle, Henry William Carter, who was six years younger than Howard Carter's father, and 85 in 1926. Howard's letter is preserved as a copy included in another letter written on 9 March by Henry to his slightly older brother James (Jim) and his wife Margaret (Mag).[43] Henry mentions a recent visit by William Carter, Howard's brother, who was 'very cut up by Polly's [his wife Mary] death, been married 42 years.' The various small errors in the transcript may be evenly attributed to Howard and Henry. A family letter of this kind by Howard Carter is exceptionally rare at this period:

My dear Uncle,
Thank you indeed for your kind and appreciative letter.
I was *lucky* to get such fine results, the jewelry, some 200 pieces, that were enclosed with the wrappings of the young King is also very magnificent as well as being very interesting, showing the origin of much of earlier Mediterranean material. Unfortunately due to decomposition of the consecration oils that were poured over the mummy by producing fatty acids much discolorisation was set up with the result the jewelly require much careful cleaning which will take us into the late spring and will prevent further investigations for some time in the two remaining chambers hitherto untouched. Again the mass of visitors that are now inundating Luxor allow one little time for work. Still next month I hope to be quiet and get back to real work again.

42 Same source.
43 A copy with John Carter.

To have one's workshop a sort of prowl and pilgrimage is certainly a bore and one would like to escape.

There have been over 9,000 people to see the Tomb since Jan.ʸ 2nd (Dxxxx !!!)

Best wishes to all and again sincere thanks for your kind thoughts.

> Yrs
>
> Howard

Work on the jewellery and coffins continued until early May. Then followed a few days packing the objects for Cairo, and on the 7th Carter was able to hand over the tombs in the Valley to the care of Tewfik Boulos. He left for Cairo on the 8th and spent the following two weeks supervising the unpacking in the Cairo Museum and in winding down with friends and making official visits. Back in England on 28 May, he was soon faced with the difficult problem of the sale of the Carnarvon collection.

Before dealing with that awkward issue he made a special visit to see Arthur Mace, whose health remained seriously impaired. There was surely some wistful envy in the words Mace wrote on 3 July to Alfred Lythgoe in the Metropolitan Museum:[44]

> Carter came down a few days after he got back looking extremely fit and well. How does he do it? He has extraordinary recuperative powers, and I realize now how unnecessary it is for anyone to try and shoulder his worries for him.

This may have been the last occasion on which Carter saw Mace. They were both closely linked by the experience of Tutankhamun, and also by early apprenticeships with Flinders Petrie (of whom Mace was a cousin). They would have had much to talk about, although there is little indication that there was great warmth of feeling in their relationship.

As for the Carnarvon collection, it may be recalled that a codicil to Lord Carnarvon's will specified:

> Should she [Lady Carnarvon] find it necessary to sell the collection, I suggest that the nation – i.e. the British Museum – be given the first refusal at £20,000, far below its value. . . . Otherwise, I would suggest that the collection be offered to the Metropolitan, New York, Mr. Carter to have charge of the negotiations and to fix the price.
>
> Should my wife decide to keep the collection, I leave it absolutely to her whether she leaves it to my son or to the nation, or to Evelyn Herbert. I suggest, however, that she consult Dr. Gardiner and Mr. Carter on the subject.

44 M.M.A., Department of Egyptian Art, Carter files. This reference was pointed out to me by Christopher Lee.

From the wording of this codicil it is clear that the Countess of Carnar-von had ultimately a free hand in the disposal of the collection if she decided not to keep it. It is difficult to determine what Howard Carter's own position was towards the fate of the collection which he had been instrumental in putting together. He had no strong attachment to the British Museum. He was on good terms with H. R. H. Hall who had succeeded Sir Wallis Budge as Keeper of Egyptian and Assyrian Antiqui-ties in 1924; but the relationship was not as close as that between Carnar-von and Budge had been. The case with the Metropolitan Museum was very different. Since long before the Great War, Carter had worked in Thebes as an archaeological neighbour of that museum's Egyptian Expedition in Deir el-Bahri; he was nearly always welcome at their hospit-able headquarters house in Thebes; and he had become since the discovery of Tutankhamun's tomb indebted to a major extent to the Metropolitan Museum for invaluable aid. The direct contributions of the members of the Egyptian Expedition to his work had transformed his scientific capa-bility; the friendship of most of the large staff and their families had sustained him through some very difficult times; Herbert Winlock had done as much as anyone (except perhaps Georges Merzbach) to help resolve his difficulties in 1924; he was on very friendly terms with several of the museum's trustees, particularly Edward Harkness; he could count Edward Robinson, the museum's director, as a personal friend. It would not have been surprising, therefore, if Carter had nursed a predilection for the sale of the Carnarvon collection to the Metropolitan Museum. He could further have argued that its acquisition by New York would form a handsome compensation for all that had been so readily done for the Carnarvon expedition; particularly as the original expectation of the museum's acquiring objects from Tutankhamun's tomb had by 1926 faded to a possible – but by no means certain – share in the promised gift of duplicates to Lady Carnarvon.

The attitude of Almina, Countess of Carnarvon, to the collection was archaeologically and artistically indifferent; she may also have seen it as a constant reminder of her husband's work in Egypt and possibly contami-nated in some way with the supposed curse of Tutankhamun, to which his death was ascribed by the superstitious and the imaginative. It will be remembered that Carter had in 1924 packed up the collection rather unceremoniously and deposited it in the Bank of England. There can be no doubt that the immediate Carnarvon family had very uncertain feelings about Tutankhamun, and the 6th Earl would not have his name uttered at Highclere for many years. It was not surprising, therefore, that Lady Carnarvon decided to sell the collection, and called on a reluctant Howard Carter to help. In August 1926 he prepared a document setting out the history of the collection after Carnarvon's death, and he sent a copy to his old friend Percy Newberry. It was, as it seems, a document explaining and justifying Carter's involvement, but it also contains quite forthright statements about his own feelings concerning what happened in the end.[45] The stages are set out annually:

1924

Contrary to my advice, and I believe the wish of the present Lord Carnarvon the collection was removed (packed by me, in accordance with instructions from Almina, Countess of Carnarvon) from High-clere Castle where it was housed in glass cases.

Special cases were designed and made at large expense behind the oak panelling at 1, Seamore Place, to receive the collection. ·

When the collection was transported by motor from Highclere to London, it was placed in the Bank of England (Burlington Gardens), instead of in the glass cases prepared for it in Seamore Place.

1925

When I returned from Egypt (Spring 1925), I found that it had been arranged to sell the collection at Sotheby's, and that dates had been allotted for that season for the sale.

I took immediate steps to prevent this sale, and with Almina, Countess of Carnarvon's sanction I instructed Sotheby's representatives to cancel any arrangements made in this connection.

1926

Notwithstanding my advice, and my earnest appeal, soon after my return from Egypt (May 1926), I was requested by Almina, Countess of Carnarvon, and by her lawyers, to sell the collection to Sir Joseph Duveen, failing this I was instructed to place the collection for sale at Sotheby's as early as possible in July (1926). I was also told that if I did not act, Almina would do so herself.

With regard to sale at Sotheby's, I represented that to put a collection of that kind up to auction at so short a notice would be out of the question. With reference to its sale to Sir Joseph Duveen, though I opened negotiations with Sir Joseph, I was careful that those negotiations failed. And as all my representations to Almina, Countess of Carnarvon were of no avail, she not allowing me to offer the collection to the British Museum, I urged her to allow me to offer it in its entirety to the Metropolitan Museum of Art, New York, – to this Almina acquiesced.

H.C. August 1926

From this document it would seem that no approach was made to the British Museum in accordance with the Earl of Carnarvon's suggestion in his will. It is, however, generally thought that some member of the firm

45 G.I. Newberry Corr. 8/82.

Frere Cholmeley and Co., the Carnarvon (and Carter) solicitors, called at short notice on Sir Frederick Kenyon, the Director of the British Museum, to offer the collection for purchase; a decision would be required later the same day. No documentary evidence has been traced in the museum archives to support this visit and offer, and it might be questioned whether, as stated here simply, the visit ever took place. A decision on a substantial purchase could not have been made at short notice without the approval of the Trustees, and it may be doubted whether funds on a sufficient scale would have been available. The summer months represented, generally speaking, a period of inactivity as far as museum purchases were concerned, for the trustees did not meet between July and late September. An approach at short notice, therefore, would certainly have been a calculated move to ensure that the British Museum would not buy, while satisfying in small degree the suggestion in Lord Carnarvon's will. Even so, it would surely have seemed to be in the circumstances a very crude tactic, designed not just to avoid such a sale to the 'nation', but to ensure that a better price could be obtained from America.

That the Museum might have been interested in acquiring the Carnarvon collection should not be in doubt. Alan Gardiner later claimed that 'Almina . . . promised me faithfully to present the Carnarvon collection to the B.M.'[46] Gardiner had, after all been recommended as one of the advisers in the matter by Lord Carnarvon. Further, S. R. K. Glanville, an Assistant Keeper in the Department of Egyptian and Assyrian Antiquities, wrote to Percy Newberry about the Museum's position:[47] 'Hall thinks there is little he could do as the annual grant is practically absorbed in anticipation ahead, for the next three years'. Nevertheless he would like very much to talk to Newberry about it. Such expressions of hope could have had no effect, and in fact there was little that could be done at departmental level in the Museum. And so, for $145,000 – more, but not greatly more, than the £20,000 suggested by Carnarvon – the collection went to the Metropolitan Museum, forming an acquisition which over the years has been seen as one of increasing value and interest, not least for the large numbers of excavated pieces of fine quality that it contains.

Much has been made of the handful of objects in the Carnarvon collection which may have been taken from Tutankhamun's tomb. The matter of removals from the tomb will be discussed briefly later in this book. At this point it may be noted that no object bearing Tutankhamun's name was included in the collection that went to New York. If Carnarvon had taken objects 'on account' from the tomb, it would have been surprising if they had not included some inscribed pieces. It seems possible to suggest that if there were objects inscribed with the king's name in the Carnarvon collection, they were extracted by Carter before the collection was packed

46 Letter to Newberry of 3 November 1943, G.I. Newberry Corr. 18/118.
47 Letter of 14 June 1926, in G.I. Newberry Corr. 17/39.

and sent to the Bank of England in 1924. At that point, and indeed in 1926, the possibility still existed that some of the pieces from the tomb might be given to Lady Carnarvon. But the presence of objects quite clearly traceable to the tomb would have been an embarrassment to the Metropolitan Museum (or, indeed, the British Museum) had they been included in the purchase of the Carnarvon collection. The fate of the inscribed Tutankhamun objects in Carter's possession at the time of his death will be dealt with later.[48]

48 See p. 407 below.

15

A LONG AND STEADY PLOD

After the first opening of the tomb of Tutankhamun it had been evident to Howard Carter that its clearance could not be rushed and that the task would be spread over several seasons. Initially he may have thought in terms of three full campaigns and indeed, after the prompt and efficient clearing of the Antechamber in a few months, his early estimations might not have appeared too optimistic. But after the rapid progress during the first season, problems arose which made any speedy completion impossible. Even without the difficulties with the Government and the Antiquities Service, the death of Lord Carnarvon and the withdrawal of Arthur Mace, the complexities of the work demanded delays and a slow pace. The dismantling of the shrines in the Burial Chamber turned out to be far more awkward than expected; the archaeology of the nest of coffins and the mummy was fraught with difficulties, and was far more complicated than anyone could have conceived. Furthermore, the condition of many objects removed from the tomb, while being in most cases remarkable after 3000 years of burial, required individual attention, including cleaning, conservation and repair to an unparalleled degree. No stage of the work in the tomb could proceed while the back-log of pieces waiting for attention in tomb No. 15 remained large. Nevertheless, Carter could hope, when he returned to Egypt in late September 1926, that perhaps no more than two full seasons would see the end of his labours.

A pattern of work in the tomb and the laboratory was established in the season of 1925–6 – although certainly not seen as such at the time – which was followed in subsequent seasons. It represented an arrangement which suited both the requirements of the excavators and the needs of the visitors to Luxor. At that time the tourist season did not seriously start until after Christmas, so that the months of autumn and early winter were available for concentrated work free from the need to consider others apart from official and professional visitors. So by arriving in September Carter could hope for three clear months to work uninterruptedly in the tomb. The time after the turn of the year could then be spent on intensive work in the tomb of Sethos II, the laboratory tomb No. 15, where Alfred Lucas would already be deep into his season's labours. On 29 September Carter arranged his plan for the coming months with Edgar in the Cairo Museum.[1] He would begin with the *déblaiement*, 'clearance' (as he now liked to describe his work, as opposed to *fouilles*, 'excavation') of the room opening off the Burial Chamber. He still called this room the Store Chamber, but he was soon to realize that its purpose was less prosaic than simple storage, and he renamed it the Innermost Treasury, or more commonly the Treasury. The tomb, it was agreed, would be opened to the public on 1 January 1927, and would remain available for visitors on three days a week until mid-March.

Back in Luxor with Lucas, Carter opened up the laboratory tomb on 7 October and was horrified to discover that rats had burrowed under the entrance. 'A little sand placed at the base [of the gate] would have prevented this. Luckily very little harm had been done by the rats, which is fortunate, as it might have been far worse.' Indeed it might well have been so, for much ancient material was stored in the tomb, including gilded wooden coffins and the royal body. The first task was to prepare the outermost coffin and the body for replacement in the tomb. This was accomplished on 23 October, and the king lay again, denuded of his treasures but respectfully treated, in a coffin within the great quartzite sarcophagus, where he still lies today, the only king to occupy his own coffin in his original burial place in the Valley of the Kings. The ceremony was carried out by Carter and Lucas, just with the help of their workmen, and with the minimum of formality. Carter was inclined to write solemnly of the feelings of awe and respect which struck him at moments in his excavation of the tomb which seemed to require solemnity. But the practicalities of moving and replacing objects needed to be carried out in as efficient a manner as possible, without the attendance of a lector-priest reading out the appropriate spells of the ancient rituals.

On the following day, the 24th, he would at last turn his attention to the Treasury, which had effectively been closed since the opening of the Burial Chamber. It is certain that Carter had from time to time opened up this room and shown it to visitors, but he had, with immense restraint, held back from disturbing the contents until he could deal with them as systematically as those in the Antechamber and the Burial Chamber. These two first rooms were not wholly clear at this time; parts of the dismantled shrines that had surrounded the sarcophagus remained stacked against the walls, waiting for removal and treatment when all else had been taken from the tomb. Priority now rested with the objects in the Treasury and those in the so-called Annexe, the room leading out of the Antechamber. It was the beginning of a slow and tedious operation which would extend until the spring of 1928 – a long and steady plod, which would then be

1 The details of the successive seasons' work are taken from Carter's excavation diary, G.I. Carter Notebook 1.

extended even further until the tomb was finally cleared and the last object conserved and sent down to Cairo in 1932.

There would, however, be huge rewards for the patient workers as objects of unique and particular beauty and grandeur were brought out – objects previously glimpsed in some cases, but in others yet to be revealed by the opening of shrines and boxes. First to come out was the portable shrine topped by the great black Anubis jackal shrouded in linen, the deity of the Necropolis, guarding the precious contents of the Treasury, a figure that had made such an impression on the first visitors to the tomb after the opening of the Burial Chamber. Carter was fascinated by this figure. He was well acquainted with the local Theban jackals, and recalled in his diary note for 27 October the pair of jackals he had seen in May, earlier in the year. The note he wrote reveals clearly his abiding interest in natural history, and his excellent powers of observation:

> In the hills above my house at Elwat e'Diban, Western Thebes, I saw a pair of jackals about 6 pm making their way towards the cultivated land. They probably had cubs in the hills as otherwise it was early for them to descend to inhabited and cultivated quarters. But the great interest was, while one of them was of normal size and colouring, the other – I was unable to tell whether dog or bitch, as they did not approach nearer than 250 yds – was totally black, much taller and attenuated, resembling, though tail not quite so bushy, the type inpw [the ancient Egyptian word for Anubis] as found upon the monuments. This is the first example of this colouring and of that line of jackal I have seen in Egypt over 35 years experience in the desert, and it suggested to me, unless the black jackal is known, a sport of the old and original Egyptian jackal only now known to us as Anubis. 𓃥 is what it appeared like through my Zeiss glasses, while the other was a much stouter and smaller animal of normal colouring – a grisly grey brown.

He then reports the opinion he had been able to discover from asking local people. Individual black specimens were known to them 'always more slender, of the slughi (greyhound) type, as compared with the *grizzly* or *red* species.' His fascination with the possibility that a 'sport' or 'throw-back' of jackal, the original of the Anubis-creature, still survived was fuelled by a further sighting he made on 22 October 1928:

> I had an interesting experience. When driving up the Valley (8 am), I saw, quite near the car (not more than twenty yards away) a seven to ten month old jackal. Quite black (perhaps a few grey hairs under the abdomen); long muzzle; large pointed ears; and of the attenuated form of the Ancient Egyptian Anubis-animal. But the tail though drooping was shorter than that represented by the God.

360

His mention of the sightings of black jackals in the third volume of *The Tomb of Tut.ankh.Amen* (pp. 43f.), inspires a few general comments, but it may be supposed that, had he been able to proceed to a full publication of the tomb's contents, a much fuller zoological treatment would have been included.

It was good, but quite characteristic of him, that he could be diverted in his work by considerations of this kind. His notes on the objects brought from the tomb chambers are frequently enlivened by 'immediate' comments, not all by any means apposite or even correct, but revealing a lively mind stocked with much material, particularly ornithological and zoological as well as archaeological. Some of these comments were incorporated into the narrative of his three-volume popular publication. The second volume was published in early 1927, very much formed by Percy White's authorial and editorial skills. It took the story of the excavation up to the end of the clearance of the Burial Chamber, and the work on the coffins and the body. The third and final volume would not appear until 1933.

Although the Treasury was a small chamber, barely 15½ by 12½ ft and 7½ ft high (more precisely 4.75 m by 3.8 m by 2.33 m), it contained a huge quantity of mostly funerary material, arranged by Carter into 75 groups and comprising well over 500 important pieces, as well as many small and fragmentary things. There was a far greater sense of order in the arrangement of the various boxes, baskets and individual items, even though the room had been worked through by the thieves who had made such a confusion in the Antechamber and the Annexe. It is just possible that in the Burial Chamber and Treasury, in the presence of the royal burial itself and so much intimately associated material, an element of awe affected the thieves and inhibited a general rifling of the funerary equipment. Many of the boxes had been opened and their most intrinsically valuable objects removed, but the Necropolis guards in their perfunctory repacking had restored at least a kind of order.

The dominating object in the Treasury was the magnificent Canopic shrine with its four exquisite figures of Isis, Nephthys, Neith and Selkis. Simple inspection had given no hint of what it might contain, and its careful investigation would be delayed for the time being. After the removal of the jackal-shrine there were objects enough to keep Carter and Lucas busy for many months. Their labours were relieved to some extent by the arrival on 31 October of Henri Landauer, a young assistant possibly introduced by Pierre Lacau, who would have seen the advantage of having someone learn from watching and helping the Carter-Lucas team in the work in the laboratory. Carter gives no indication of Landauer's character or abilities, but he may have welcomed his help. From Carter's diaries it is clear that the young assistant stayed until mid-April 1927 and returned for the following season, staying from late November 1927 until mid-April again.

The steady clearance of individual items and boxes from the Treasury continued until the end of the year which was notably marked on 31 December by the visit of King Fuad to inspect the tomb and the objects in the laboratory. Carter had seen the King in audience in January 1925 before he concluded his negotiations with the government of Ziwar Pasha for his return to the Valley. On that occasion he noted that his conversation with the King 'was only very superficial', although 'His Majesty was most cordial'. Now Carter reported that the King 'seemed well pleased with results.' On the following day the tomb was opened for tourists, who were able to visit on Tuesdays, Thursdays and Saturdays from 9 o'clock to noon, and so until 31 March. For Carter, Lucas and Landauer, the tomb of Sethos II would be their primary place of work until mid-April. They would be joined, whenever necessary, by Harry Burton, who had now returned to work principally with the Metropolitan Museum team in Deir el-Bahri. This was the new arrangement, which suited the requirements of both expeditions.

On 16 April the antiquities which had been conserved were sent down to Cairo, and Carter followed on the 24th, staying in the Residency until he left for England on the 29th. This was the first occasion for him to enjoy such official hospitality from the High Commission. Lord Allenby had been succeeded by Lord Lloyd in 1925. He had served in Egypt in the Arab Bureau during the Great War, and had known High Commission staff like Ronald Storrs. At this time he might have got to know Carter during his period of employment with the Intelligence Service. An old acquaintanceship of this kind may have led to Carter's invitation to stay at the Residency. It was also the case that his position was now better established than in the earlier days of the Tutankhamun excavation; he was then Carnarvon's man and, after the latter's death, the man who caused so much trouble with the new Egyptian government. By 1927 with his work in Thebes based on a less controversial footing, Carter was a man of more accepted status in the British community in Egypt. He was indeed quite respectable, and was seen as someone who could be trusted to maintain good standards of behaviour in the presence of important and distinguished people. Throughout his career he had been accustomed to mix with members of high society, but almost always in a rather subservient role. Now things were rather different, and he would be seen as someone quite suitable to attend Her Royal Highness Princess Mary, the Princess Royal, when she came to Luxor with her husband for a four-day visit in late March 1928. She subsequently sent Carter a signed photograph in gratitude for his services.[2]

2 With John Carter.

It may have been during his stay in the Residency that Carter was able to engage the High Commissioner's interest in the question of some form of compensation for Lady Carnarvon, either in the form of a gift of duplicate objects – as promised by the Ziwar administration – or a financial settlement. The politics of Egypt were excessively tortuous at the time, and while civil disturbance did not form part of the pattern, it looked inevitable that the Wafd party would remain the most powerful and popular element in Egyptian political life for the foreseeable future. At that moment there was no evident threat to the continuation of Carter's work on the lines of the agreement of early 1925, but he himself sensibly refrained from raising the matter of a settlement. There is evidence, however, that moves were beginning to be made on the diplomatic level to see whether some accommodation could be reached by which a selection of objects from the tomb might be presented, or even given in exchange for some financial consideration, to the British Museum.[3] Unfortunately, the path of the negotiations is not clear, and Carter's own surviving papers give no concrete information about the various moves that were being made in the later 1920s before the ultimate financial settlement of 1930 was reached.

By mid-September 1927 Howard Carter was back in Cairo, apparently eager to continue his work of *déblaiement* as expeditiously as possible. He was by nature not a man to hasten his work without proper preparation and care; he possessed unlimited determination, and the task of clearance was one which suited his temperament. Progress might be slow, but it was appreciable, and the excavators were encouraged by the regular revelation of objects of beauty and interest as they emerged from the boxes and black-painted shrines of the Treasury. Carter could now see a terminus to his labours, and an early start would move things forward. Harold Nelson ran into Carter in Cairo, and reported to Breasted:[4]

Carter and Lucas are going up on the same train as us. Carter tells me he hopes to finish the removal of the remaining objects from the tomb this season, with the exception of the shrine.

With this intention in mind Carter arranged his programme and signed his concession for the season with Henri Gauthier, the new Secretary-General of the Antiquities Service, on 15 September, and on the 24th he inspected the laboratory tomb which, happily, was this year 'free from dust, insects and rats'.

The tomb of Tutankhamun itself was opened on 6 October, and it took only two days to complete the clearance of the Treasury with the exception of the Canopic shrine and three boats. A week passed before Harry Burton arrived in Luxor and was able to catch up on photographing what had been removed already to the laboratory. It was a suitable moment to pause

3 E.g. file FO 141, 619/121 in the Public Records Office.
4 Letter of 19 September in O.I. Director's Office Corr. 1927.

and dispose of as much work as possible before the clearance of the Annexe was started.

Problems and mysteries were not uncommon in the tomb of Tutankhamun, and two connected with objects in the Treasury may be specially mentioned. The first was presented by a simple wooden box which contained two miniature anthropoid coffins, each of which contained smaller coffins holding mummified foetuses; one, probably female, was about five months into gestation; the other, also probably female, was at about the seventh-month stage of gestation. The care that had been lavished on these two tiny premature babies – homunculae is the word that springs to mind – makes it most probable that they were the ill-timed offspring of Tutankhamun and his wife Ankhesenamun, possibly the last direct, but tenuous, links with the family of King Amenophis III. What hopes died with these pathetic still-born infants! And yet it was felt right that they should be given proper post-mortem treatment for children of royal birth, and buried close to the body of their father, the divine King Tutankhamun.[5]

The second mystery was revealed when the Canopic shrine was dismantled. Inside there was a splendid monolithic chest of Egyptian alabaster with a characteristic sloping lid, the whole covered by a fine linen shroud. When the lid was removed, four cylindrical depressions were found, each stoppered with a sensitively carved royal head, and each containing a miniature coffin of gold inlaid with glass and semi-precious stones. These coffins held the embalmed internal organs of the king; they were the equivalents of the Canopic jars commonly found in contemporary burials. The stoppers are now generally thought, on stylistic grounds, not to represent Tutankhamun, while the small Canopic coffins are similarly inconsistent stylistically, and also show traces of changes in their inscriptions, with alterations to the royal names in the cartouches. These discrepancies were not at first noticed by Carter, but subsequent examination revealed these problems of identification, which extend in fact to other objects in the funeral provision. These facts suggested that certain second-hand items or, more precisely, unused pieces from earlier projected burials, were included in the equipment, perhaps because the king's death had been unexpected and there was insufficient time to make all the necessary pieces.[6]

In some respects the Annexe presented the archaeologists – or should they now be called *déblayeurs*? – with greater difficulties than they had previously experienced. The problems were caused not just by the depredations of the tomb-robbers and the failure of the Necropolis guards to

5 See H. Carter, *The Tomb of Tut.ankh.Amen*, III (London, 1933), Appx I; F. F. Leek, *The Human Remains from the Tomb of Tut'ankhamūn* (Oxford, 1972), pp. 21ff.; N. Reeves, *The Complete Tutankhamun* (London, 1990), pp. 123f.
6 Generally, see N. Reeves, *The Complete Tutankhamun*, p. 122.

do more than very superficial tidying-up. It became clear in due course, when the room had been cleared and Carter had the opportunity to study the positions of the object and their order of placing in the room, that its primary purpose had been modified when the tomb was being stocked at the time of the king's burial.[7] Carter, knowing the general plan of the royal tombs in the Valley of the Kings, attempted to reconcile the unusual lay-out of Tutankhamun's tomb with the common, if not standard, scheme. Any solution of the question was necessarily tentative, especially as the tomb in question was not designed for Tutankhamun, and probably not for a royal person. In a more conventionally designed royal tomb the approach corridor ends in a pillared hall, beyond which, at lower level, is the burial chamber with sarcophagus. Side rooms open on each side of the hall and of the sarcophagus area. In Tutankhamun's tomb, the entrance corridor leads to the Antechamber (using Carter's terminology), representing the pillared hall, beyond which, at lower level, is the Burial Chamber. The Annexe and the Treasury take the place of the rooms opening off the pillared hall and sarcophagus area.

The rooms opening off the pillared hall were conventionally used to hold the materials required for the daily well-being of the dead king – food and drink and oils in particular. Such, therefore, should have made up the contents of the Annexe. As it was found, however, the room contained a huge quantity of what might be termed extraneous objects, many of which were similar to objects found principally in the Antechamber. There were beds and other pieces of furniture, some of them quite splendid in their decoration and workmanship, like the one Carter called the king's 'Ecclesiastical Throne', a ceremonial object in the form of a folding chair, although of fixed construction, with a seat simulating an animal skin and an intricately decorated back. There were many smaller pieces of furniture, boxes containing confusing collections of personal objects, all rifled and summarily repacked. There were even *shabti*-figures, the small mummiform figures which would act for the king in the after-life, and belonging properly to the equipment in the Treasury. The objects which could strictly be regarded as right for the store-room were at the bottom of the pile, and listed by Carter as 'nearly forty pottery wine-jars . . . on the floor at the northern end of this Annexe; next to these . . . at least thirty-five heavy alabaster vessels containing oils and unguents; stacked beside them, some even on top . . . one hundred and sixteen baskets of fruits.'[8]

The disordered piles of furniture and other objects on top of the food, drink and oils, rose to a height of almost two metres, and many pieces were balanced precariously. The experience gained in the earlier stages of the tomb's clearance proved invaluable for the Annexe. Numbers were assigned to objects and groups of objects, and photographs were taken of

7 On the Annex and its clearance, see *The Tomb of Tut.ankh.Amen*, III, pp. 98ff.
8 *Ibid.*, p. 104.

the contents with and without their numbers before any attempt was made to take anything away. Again experience ensured success; and it was now allied with the supreme skill that Carter and Lucas had developed over the preceding five years in handling delicate material. To begin was the most difficult part because the entrance was small and deep, and the floor of the Annexe was almost a metre below the level of the Antechamber; it was impossible at first to find space on which to stand. Consequently, whoever worked to remove the initial objects had to bend low and lean forward with outstretched arms over the heaped-up contents, and he was supported in this unnatural position by a rope sling passed around the body under the arm-pits.[9] So the clearance began in the last days of November, and continued uninterruptedly until it was completed, according to Carter's excavation diary, on 15 December. There were 283 groups of objects made up of over 2000 separate pieces, numerically constituting more than half the contents of the tomb.

Once more, in the established rhythm of the post-1924 seasons, the pendulum of concentration swung from the tomb to the laboratory, where the harvest of objects from the autumn months could be worked on – description, careful measurements, notes on particular details, including points of construction, drawing of special features, then cleaning, restoration and general conservation. When enough objects were ready for transfer to the Cairo Museum, they were carefully packed in made-to-measure cases, constructed under Carter's supervision in the Valley. Consignments were commonly sent at the end of the season, and were closely followed by Carter and one of his collaborators, at first Mace and then Callender, to see the cases unpacked in the Museum and the objects, where appropriate, put on display. In the 1927-8 season so much material had accumulated that an early dispatch was made on 25 January, containing objects recovered from the tomb in 1925 and 1926. Carter followed the next day, as was his practice.

On this occasion Carter had an additional reason to take him to Cairo. He was to meet Lady Burghclere, the sister of his late patron, who had written such a sensitive memoir of her brother for the first volume of *The Tomb of Tut.ankh.Amen*. He brought her back to Luxor on 31 January, and she spent a week there before being escorted to Aswan for a three-week stay. Carter was a friend of long standing, and he made her visit an opportunity for perhaps the longest holiday he had allowed himself in Egypt during his time of working on the tomb of Tutankhamun. He was not particularly well at the time – indeed he was rarely in a state of good health for the rest of his life – and the strain of working in confined circumstances in the tomb and the laboratory for months on end had taken its toll. It was not surprising that his patience was at times stretched

9 *Ibid.*, p. 102.

beyond endurance, and from his brief diary notes few things seemed to try his forbearance more than the official demands to show special visitors the tomb and the laboratory. His attitude was undoubtedly ambivalent, because vexation could be set beside possible advantage. He was not averse from the honour of receiving specially important visitors, and he carefully kept letters of thanks which followed up such visits. The two pans of the balance contained on one side self-esteem and on the other irritability; but in general an impression is gained that he was more honoured than upset by the great.

A good example of his equivocal attitude is provided by the visit of the Crown prince of Sweden in November 1930. When the occasion is dealt with later, it will be seen that Carter did his best to accommodate Prince Gustav Adolf for the whole of this visit, even to the extent of changing his own travel arrangements so that they could travel together to Egypt.[10] Yet his diary entry is somewhat testy:

> Our work was temporarily stopped owing to the arrival of the Crown Prince of Sweden, whom I was obliged to attend during his three days visit to Luxor. *On Monday the third of Nov.* At the request of the Crown Prince I opened one of the niches containing the magical figures in the burial chamber of the tomb.

It is difficult to believe that Carter did not arrange this visit in detail, and even volunteered to show the Prince the Osiris figure in unbaked clay which occupied the niche. But he could affect mild annoyance in his diary notes.

In the 1927–8 season the tally of the great was considerable. At the end of December the King of Afghanistan visited Luxor and the tomb as part of a state visit to Egypt. On 3 February Umberto, the Crown Prince of Italy, was conducted around the Valley by Carter, in the middle of Lady Burghclere's visit. In late March the expected visit of the Princess Royal took place. She was accompanied by her husband, Viscount Lascelles, and Carter again was expected to act the dragoman for the four days of their stay. There were also visits from the Egyptian Queen Mother, the Sultana Malek, who had a house at Luxor and took occasional advantage of Carter's readiness to oblige her very real interest in his work. He kept several letters of thanks from her secretary.[11]

Not long before the end of the season the news reached Luxor that Arthur Mace had died. It happened on 6 April, and on the 9th Carter cabled to Winifred Mace in Haywards Heath, Sussex, what seems at first glance to have been a very inadequate expression of regret:[12] 'Please accept since[re] condolences for sad loss he was a man for whom I had great

10 See p. 378 below.
11 In the possession of John Carter.
12 With Margaret Orr, in the Mace Papers.

respect Carter.' Under the circumstances it may have been the most he could do, bearing in mind his tendency to conceal his feelings. At least, one could say, it was a prompt response. He would certainly have recalled the excellent but all too brief partnership which had set the Tutankhamun juggernaut rolling along the right lines and in the right direction. Mace could temperamentally accommodate himself to Carter's uncertain moods. His great common sense would save Carter from making many a mistake. His staunch support would sustain Carter in times of exasperation and fury. His experience in dealing with intricate antiquities would prove invaluable in the days when the excavation procedures in the tomb were being established. His advice on documentation was crucial for the written record of the excavation. His literary abilities ensured the success of the first popular volume on the tomb, in which very properly his name was linked with that of Carter. All such considerations were surely appreciated by Carter, but he was probably incapable of writing a suitable letter of sympathy to Winifred Mace, especially as he may have felt a little guilty at not having kept in regular touch with Mace in recent years.

When he had returned to England in late April, Carter seems to have made an excursion to see Winifred Mace in Sussex. The visit can be inferred from a letter written by Mrs Mace on 7 July to Albert Lythgoe in New York, in which she says,[13] 'Mr. Carter had his tonsils out on Monday and has done very well. He was in a terribly nervy state, so it is a good thing he was not upset by the operation.' These words suggest that she had seen him before he went into hospital, and had heard subsequently how he had fared. The severe cold he had suffered in the early spring had no doubt obliged him to take medical advice on his return. Egyptian colds can be vicious, long-lasting, inclined to renewal, and have a tendency to settle in throat and chest.[14] In his time Howard Carter had enjoyed his fair share of such ills, and the removal of his tonsils was surely a wise move, as it would have been seen medically at that time.

The summer break of 1928 lasted a little longer than had been the case in recent years. From late April until 20 September Carter remained in England, presumably making the visits to friends and relatives which at that time formed the course of his life away from Egypt. No general diaries have survived after 1925, so that details of his movements and activities can be learned only from occasional letters and similar documents. He undoubtedly was engaged in matters of business connected with the work in Egypt, and he spent some time in the sale-rooms and the shops of dealers in works of art, particularly carpets. Records of some of his transactions are dealt with later in the volume.

Throughout most of the 1920s his London home was at 19 Collingham Gardens where his brother Samuel lived. It was, as has already been

13 In M.M.A., Department of Egyptian Art, Carter files.
14 See p. 107 above.

noted, in Chelsea, close to the Old Brompton Road and the site of Rich Terrace where he had been born. Letters of the time more regularly give his address as 19B Collingham Gardens, and there is evidence to suggest that he rented part of Samuel's home as a London *pied-à-terre*. Cables to Samuel in the early 1920s requesting him to open up (and air) his quarters certainly indicate separate accommodation, and a note in the possession of John Carter shows that for 1930–1 Howard rented 19B Collingham Gardens for a sum of £300. This rent seems quite excessive for the period, and it may be supposed that it actually represented an inflated payment for charitable purposes. Samuel was not, it seems, a man who had made a success of his life – he too was an artist – and there is reason to think that Howard became increasingly tired of Samuel's shortcomings, particularly what used to be called a fondness for the bottle. Letters in August 1930 indicate that the differences between the brothers had come to a head. It seems that Samuel had written to Howard while he was out of Town to tell him that a crisis had occurred one night when his wife Mary had an attack of her intermittent heart trouble. Having nothing suitable to give her in his house, Samuel had entered Howard's rooms and tried to open his drinks cabinet to get some brandy. Unfortunately the key jammed and he had been obliged to break the door open. Howard was not impressed, and told Samuel quite clearly that he should not try to mislead him.[15] Very shortly afterwards Howard moved to 2 Prince's Gate Court in Kensington Gore, beside the Albert Hall, a distinctly more fashionable address.[16] Photographs of his rooms at Collingham Gardens and his later London flats show comfortable, well appointed apartments, tastefully equipped with paintings, good furniture and rugs. Relations between Samuel and Howard were not completely broken off. In June 1931 Samuel wrote to say that he and Mary were about to move into a new flat and hoped that Howard could drop in for a bite to eat before they left Collingham Gardens.[17]

The new season in Egypt that began at the end of September 1928 looked set to see steady inroads being made on the material in the laboratory, and the removal of the parts of the shrines still stored in Tutankhamun's tomb itself. The fates, however, were not on Carter's side. He needed no problems to impede the flow of work, especially as he would not have the assistance of Henri Landauer. The tombs were opened up with everything in good order. Lucas arrived on 8 October with a cold and a fever which steadily developed until by the 18th paratyphoid was diagnosed, and Carter packed him off to Cairo and the Anglo-American Hospital. It would be some time before he could return, although reports suggested that he was

15 Letters on this incident are with John Carter.
16 Letter to Caroline Ransom Williams of 19 November 1930 signals his recent change of address; copy of letter with John Carter.
17 Letter of 16 June, with John Carter.

responding well to treatment. Carter found it difficult working on his own after so many years of having Lucas's company in the tomb of Sethos II. So he looked forward to the arrival of Harry Burton who would at least provide support and company as well as get on with much needed photography. There would be no relief. No sooner had Burton arrived than he went down with dengue fever, thought to have been contracted in Cairo. It was a distressing and painful illness, but responded to good nursing and was not considered to be fatal. But there was no chance of getting any work or company out of him and he was confined to bed at the Metropolitan House for several weeks. Unfortunately Minnie Burton's surviving diary ceased in October 1926, so posterity has been denied her account of the progress of the disease.

Nothing seemed to go right for Carter this season; he himself developed a bad cold, his car broke down, he became annoyed with his workmen. This last difficulty was unusual for him. He had always maintained excellent relations with his Egyptian foremen and workmen, and seemed to have an understanding of them which was comprehended and greatly appreciated by them in turn. In his late sketches he makes out how comfortable he always felt in the company of the inhabitants of Western Thebes, indeed of Egyptian countrymen in general. But in the autumn of 1928 with so much going wrong, whom else could he vent his wrath upon? 'Having a lot of stupidity on the part of the Reises and men, It seems that they get more stupid as they get older – and slacker having been, perhaps too long with me.' It was good, therefore, to get his regular collaborators back, Burton on 24 November and Lucas on 4 December.

Carter's excavation diary contains no information on the work undertaken during the rest of the season; there are, however, clear signs that a page has been cut out of the volume. One may presume that the work in the laboratory continued according to regular practice, that the tomb of Tutankhamun was opened to the public in the New Year, and that the season came to an end in April or early May. It had been a season in which expectations had not been fulfilled. It had been affected by a run of bad luck which some would attribute to the curse which was supposed to dog those who had been closely involved with the excavation.[18] The recent death of Mace only fuelled the imaginations of those who were disposed to believe in such a blight. The origin of the curse may have been due to a casual remark made by Arthur Weigall in a moment of vexation when he was denied the liberty of the tomb and could not endure the apparent lack of reverence shown to the shade of the dead king. But the idea of a curse suited the popular image of ancient Egypt, and the death of Lord Carnarvon provided the initial tragedy which established the idea of a baleful influence. To counter the excesses of such melodram-

18 A sober statement on the so-called curse in N. Reeves, *The Complete Tutankhamun*, pp. 62f.

atic beliefs by the invocation of common sense and the production of contrary evidence is a hopeless procedure. The idea of a curse is in a sense needed by many people to satisfy a kind of deep-seated expectation of supernatural evil. It does no good to point out the survivors among those most intimately connected with the discovery: Alan Gardiner died in 1963 aged 84; James Henry Breasted in 1935 aged 70; Evelyn Herbert (Lady Beauchamp) in 1980 aged 79; Harry Burton in 1940 aged 61; Alfred Lucas in 1945 aged 78. Even Carter – the arch-target surely – survived, even if in poor health, until 1939 when he was 65. People have to die, and many people die young, either by illness or accident.

Carter may have said that some kind of spell had affected his season in 1928–9; but he would have said it lightly. He was one to reject utterly the idea of the curse. His considered opinion on the subject, which no doubt he voiced on many occasions, is set out in a piece he wrote but apparently never published. Talking of Egyptian religion and cults, he says:[19]

> The sentiment of the Egyptologist, however, is not one of fear but of respect and awe. It is entirely opposed to the foolish superstitions which are far too prevalent among emotional people in search of 'psychic' excitement.
>
> It is not my intention to repeat the ridiculous stories which have been invented about the dangers lurking in ambush, as it were, in the Tomb, to destroy the intruder. Similar tales have been a common feature of fiction for many years, they are mostly variants of the ordinary ghost story, and may be accepted as a legitimate form of literary amusement. But there is another and a serious side to this question which calls for protest. It has been stated in various quarters that there are actual physical dangers hidden in Tut-ankh-Amen's Tomb – mysterious forces, called into being by some malefic power, to take vengeance on whomsoever should dare to pass its portals. There was probably no place in the world freer from risks than the Tomb. Scientific research had proved it to be sterile. Whatever foreign germs there may be within it today have been introduced from without, yet mischievous people have attributed many deaths, illnesses, and disasters to alleged mysterious and noxious influences in the tomb. Unpardonable and mendacious statements of this nature have been published and repeated in various quarters with a sort of malicious satisfaction. It is indeed difficult to speak of this form of 'ghostly' calumny with calm. If it be not actually libellous it points in that spiteful direction, and all sane people should dismiss such inventions with contempt. So far as the living are concerned curses of this nature have no part in the Egyptian Ritual.

19 In the possession of John Carter.

Breasted put the matter less ponderously in an interview he gave on the RMS *Laconia* in 1934, as reported by Reuters:[20]

'All tommyrot!' was the professor's comment on the superstition that those who worked on the king's tomb were doomed as victims of a curse.

'If anyone was "exposed" to it I was. For two weeks I slept in the tomb of King Tutankhamen and took my meals there. I never felt better in my life! And the tomb is a gorgeous place.'

Breasted never slept in the tomb, or took his meals there, and he was sometimes unwell when he was in Luxor to work on the tomb. But his reported comments were aimed at the right level of unconcern.

After he had returned to England in the late spring of 1929, Howard Carter had a meeting – the date is uncertain, but probably in late July – with William Valentiner, the Director of the Detroit Institute of Arts, and from it developed another association with an important American museum not unlike that established in 1917 between him and the Cleveland Museum of Arts.[21] William Valentiner, who had been appointed Director in 1924, was in the active process of building up the collections of the Institute of Arts; among his priorities was the creation of an Egyptian collection based on excavation, which might rival in due time the Egyptian collection at the Metropolitan Museum. By chance he was the grandson of the great nineteenth-century German Egyptologist, Karl Richard Lepsius, but as far as is known he had no experience of Egypt, and only marginal knowledge of Egyptian antiquities. His first enquiries with Albert Lythgoe in the Metropolitan Museum and with Breasted, through their mutual friend Mrs John D. Rockefeller Jr, led to the conclusion that excavation might not be the right road to follow. Valentiner's meeting with Carter was, therefore, timely, as he saw it, and the arrangement he rapidly made with Carter in the following weeks met with enthusiastic support from Lythgoe, who wrote:

There is no one more familiar with the Egyptian market or more closely in touch with all its best possibilities, and I need only to point to our own 'Carnarvon collection', which he formed for Carnarvon over a long period of years, to illustrate his excellence of judgement and sense of the beautiful.

Writing to Carter on 31 July 1929 Valentiner proposed that he should be given a free hand to purchase for the Institute pieces in categories favoured by the Institute within a fixed sum year by year. 'What we need

20 Reported in the *Cunard Atlantic News*. Special cruise edition. RMS *Laconia*, Wed. 4 April 1934, p. 3. I am gratetful to John Larson for drawing this item to my attention.
21 See W. H. Peck in *J.S.S.E.A.* 11 (1981), pp. 65ff. He outlines the course of Carter's dealings with Detroit from start to finish. The documentation is all in Detroit.

most would be a few important pieces, especially of the early periods, and
besides perhaps a number of smaller object which can be placed in the
cases and give a certain idea of the development of decorative arts in
Egypt.' He would recommend that the Detroit City Arts Commission make
available $25,000 for the first year. Carter agreed to act as agent and
suggested a commission of 10 per cent, which was 5 per cent less than he
had required in his dealings with Cleveland. Matters were quickly settled
and the first purchases were made in the spring of 1930 from two well
known Cairo antiquities dealers, Khawam Bros. and Nahman – two Old-
Kingdom mastaba reliefs, a Middle-Kingdom bust and a large scarab of
Amenophis III. The pieces from Khawam were paid for directly from
Detroit; the Nahman scarab and Carter's commission ($1800) came out
of a sum of $5000 which had been placed in Carter's bank account in
Egypt.

Unfortunately the good relationship which had thus begun so promis-
ingly was curtailed in 1930 because of the state of the Detroit city finances.
And so the arrangement was shelved for the time being, although Valentiner hoped that it would be only a passing condition, and 'that in spite
of it if you find anything which you think would be necessary for us, you
would kindly let us know, since the Arts Commission have the greatest
confidence in your excellent judgement.' There still remained in the
National Bank of Egypt $2700 out of the $5000 sent to Carter earlier in
1930, and there it remained until he was reminded of it by William
Valentiner in 1936. Carter then took the opportunity of suggesting the
purchase of 'a wonderful specimen of the XIV Cent. (B.C.) Egyptian blue
faience that has just appeared on the market.' This was an outstanding
sphinx figure of Amenophis III which he claimed rightly to be 'unmatched
– there being nothing of its kind in any Museum.' It could then be
purchased for about $25000 (i.e. £5000). There was no response on this
matter from Valentiner and the $2700 remained in Cairo and the sphinx
in Carter's possession. To complete this Detroit story, it can be added that
at Carter's death the debt was settled by the sending to Detroit of two
Late-Period heads and a faience cinerary urn of the Roman Period, all
from Carter's private collection. By a kind of strange and ironical chance
the sphinx of Amenophis III, which was also still in Carter's possession
at his death, was sold to the Cranbrook Academy of Art in Bloomfield
Hills, Michigan, just a few miles from Detroit. It is now a treasured
possession of the Metropolitan Museum, but for some years before its sale
by Cranbrook it was placed on display in the Detroit Institute of Arts –
a temporary fulfilment of what Carter had vainly tried to arrange in 1936.

Vexation and frustration may have characterized the 1928–9 season, but
the problems of the illness-ridden time were nothing compared with the
exasperation of the 1929–30 season. Carter returned to Egypt in the
autumn in the expectation of continuing and possibly completing work on

the dismantled shrines which were still stacked in the tomb. His diary record for the season is contained in a single entry:

> No work was done during this season. Negociations [*sic*] with the Eg. Gov. with regard to some favourable settlement for the Carnarvon Estate and heirs for work rendered. Also with regard to favourable conditions for the completion of the remaining work to be done on behalf of the Eg. Gov., took the greater part of the season. . . . It was not until late in Sept, (1930) that the Eg. Gov. saw its way to pay over to the Carnarvon heirs the sum of 35971£E covering the Carnarvon expenses for work rendered commencing from the discovery to the completion of their part of the works in April 1929. The question of the recompense for the Met. Mus. Art of N.Y. for the assistance at their own sacrifice given during the whole of the operations has yet to be considered by the Eg. Gov., they taking over the responsibility from us.

The circumstances revealed by this entry remain uncertain in detail. The Countess of Carnarvon had decided, probably on Carter's advice, not to renew her concession for the work on the tomb after it ran out in October 1929. The clearance of the tomb was now completed and what remained to be done to satisfy the formal requirements of the concession (apart from publication) was the removal of the shrines from the tomb – a formal though difficult operation and not part of the *déblaiement*, strictly speaking, followed by their conservation and transport to Cairo. Presumably Carter thought that these final activities could best be carried out under an arrangement between himself and the Antiquities Service, which in fact was negotiated later, in February 1930. He had not, however, allowed for complications caused by the surrendering of the concession, and by the changed political situation in Egypt. After 31 October he had no formal status *vis-à-vis* the tomb, and would find that he might not even be able to hold the keys to enter it. He could not conceive how the Antiquities Service could be so crass. His appeal to the Service had elicited an unsatisfactory answer from Henri Gauthier, the Secretary-General, asking him to organize his work in the laboratory-tomb, but pointing out that the chief *ghaffir* (guard) could not hold the keys.[22] The local Inspector of Antiquities could hold them and open up for Carter. Regular hours should be kept, so that time would not be lost. In some desperation Carter appealed to Percy Newberry to intercede on his behalf. Newberry had in 1929 taken up an appointment as Professor of Ancient History and Archaeology in Cairo University, and he did what he could; but to no avail. He wrote to Carter on 15 January 1930 explaining his efforts on his behalf and reporting that His Excellency Neguib el-Halaly had pointed out that

22 This letter with John Carter.

374

it was against the law to hand over the key of any government property to an individual who was not on the permanent staff of the Egyptian government. He could, however, arrange to have a permanent official sent to Luxor who would hold the keys and be entirely at Carter's disposal.[23]

Howard Carter was well aware how inefficiently such an arrangement would work, and his reply of 18 January pointed out that the keys, locks, the portcullis and steel gate were all 'our property', that is belonged to the Carnarvon expedition, and equally everything in the laboratory except the antiquities. The keys had always been in his custody. Lady Carnarvon had not renewed her concession, but, he continued,[24]

> Last April I offered to complete the technical work that still remains to be done in the laboratory at my cost, and further to help the Antiquities Department in the very intricate undertaking of removing those large shrines from the tomb of Tutankhamen. Under such circumstances I fail to understand why in the eleventh hour should exception be made in my case with regard to the custody of the keys of the laboratory.

Politically things had changed in a number of disadvantageous ways. At the Residency Lord Lloyd had been succeeded by Sir Percy Loraine, a career diplomat – the first to occupy this important position. Meanwhile, after a confused and troublesome period of domestic politics, the Wafd were reestablished in government with Nahas Pasha as Prime Minister. A less sympathetic attitude towards any settlement for the Carnarvon family than had been offered five years earlier by Ziwar Pasha could now be expected. No account of the course of the negotiations has – perhaps happily – been preserved, but it was a trying time for Carter. Winlock wrote to Gardiner on 9 December; having described Newberry, in his new position, as being 'as happy as a child with a new toy', he continued:[25]

> Carter arrived here from Cairo day before yesterday, in quite the opposite mood. He hasn't been able to make any headway at all with his affairs and up to the present hasn't even been able to get into his own laboratory.

In the face of the tiresome attitude to keys – one which would come up again in the following year – Carter seems to have given up all hope for work in the tomb and the laboratory for the season, and he concentrated on trying to conclude the matter of the Carnarvon compensation. Eventually in the spring the Nahas government decided to revoke the promise of duplicates; the question of financial recompense remained, and would in fact be settled during the summer. The negotiations on the Carnarvon

23 With John Carter.
24 G.I. Newberry Corr. 8/76.
25 G.I. Gardiner Corr. AGH/42.375.41.

side had been principally conducted by Sir Robert Hutchinson, who had on the whole secured a satisfactory outcome.[26]

Troubles did not come singly to Carter; he found himself during the season also engaged in litigation. The trouble which led to the action is not made clear in the minimal documentation preserved.[27] What is known is that it involved someone named A. Galani, that it was handled for Carter by Georges Merzbach, and that it was settled in Carter's favour in March 1930. Carter's inclination to engage in legal action has been noted before. He jealously guarded his 'rights', as he conceived them, and was particularly sensitive about his reputation. Rarely did matters come to court, except over the tomb troubles in 1924; settlements were made out of court, as happened with the business over the Tutankhamun tomb replica at the British Empire Exhibition, also in 1924. Recourse to law was an unnecessary expense for someone in Carter's position, and there is little evidence to show that his reputation was either damaged seriously by the incidents which prompted litigation, or particularly enhanced by any success in this respect. A good example of unnecessary recourse to law came in 1932 when Mr James R. Ogden seemed to have doubted Carter's part in the discovery of the tomb of Tutankhamun.[28] James Ogden was a Harrogate jeweller and a well known enthusiast in Egyptological matters and a member of the committee of the Egypt Exploration Society during the early 1930s.

In the *Cambridge Daily News* of 21 October 1932 James Ogden was reported as saying in a public lecture that when the discovery of the steps leading down to the tomb was made, Carter had gone to Cairo for a week and had left a foreman to supervise the clearance of debris. This foreman, acting contrary to instructions, removed debris in a southward instead of a northward direction, and the tomb, therefore, was discovered by chance. On having this statement drawn to his attention, Carter instructed his solicitors to extract an apology from Mr Ogden, and to secure the publication of a retraction in *The Times* and the *Cambridge Daily News*. As soon as he was approached James Ogden readily agreed to do what was requested, explaining that he had read the statement about the discovery in an English or an Egyptian newspaper, and had quoted it to show that what was said in the report was not in accordance with the facts. He had been badly reported, something about which Carter might well have sympathised with him. His retraction was sent to the two specified newspapers on 9 December, and he paid all the expenses involved in the matter. He also expressed to the solicitors his gratitude at the way the affair had been handled. One may well feel, however, that the satisfactory outcome could

26 Mentioned in a letter of Carter's to Newberry of 18 January 1930, G.I. Newberry Corr. 8/76.
27 With John Carter.
28 The papers are with John Carter.

have been just as easily achieved by Carter's addressing a private letter to Ogden. For someone who favoured the light touch in his professional work, he was too inclined to resort to the sledge-hammer in settling disputes in his private affairs.

The final settlement of the Carnarvon compensation claim was made in the early summer of 1930. J. R. H. Molony of Frere Cholmeley wrote to Carter on 25 June announcing the acceptance of the sum of £35,867 13s. 8d.[29] Lady Carnarvon had promised to give Carter one quarter of the total, a figure that Moloney worked out as £8966 18s. 5d. Carter in the end was not to receive the full amount. In September Lady Carnarvon's solicitor, Alfred W. Freyser of Arundel Street off the Strand, sent Carter a cheque for £8012, writing in explanation:

> I am to add that her ladyship has paid to the Trustees of the late Earl of Carnarvon's estate so much of the money received by her from Egypt as is referable to the amount expended by the late Lord Carnarvon on the work in his lifetime, and it is her intention, when as she anticipates she receives from the Trustees in her capacity of beneficiary under her late Husband's will, the net amount remaining from the sum after payment of duties, and expenses, to allocate 25% of this to you.

Later in the year Lady Carnarvon's solicitor wrote again to say that there was a refund on estate and legacy duty amounting to £2184 10s. 11d., of which Carter was being sent £546 2s. 9d. His total share of the compensation, therefore, amounted to £8558 2s. 9d. So was this long-lasting dispute over compensation brought to an end with some satisfaction for the Carnarvon Estate and Howard Carter. Nothing was ever done to recompense the Metropolitan Museum for its expenditure over the years, estimated at £8000.

In the course of the summer Carter celebrated his good fortune by taking a long holiday in July and August, a sentimental return-journey to the country of the West Midlands which he felt he had discovered in 1924. This time he took with him as travelling companion his old friend Percy White, who had been 78 on 14 April 1930. He owed White much for the work he had done on the second volume of *The Tomb of Tut.ankh.Amen*, and he may, during this tour, have discussed the form of the final volume in which, however, no mention of White occurs. The 1930 tour began in the Cotswolds with a visit to Fairford Park, where Carter and White were guests of Colonel A. J. Palmer; then they went to the Wye Valley, to Tintern and Chepstow; back to Tewkesbury, and north to Ludlow in Shropshire; back to Malvern, which held specially fond memories for

29 In *The Tomb of Tut.ankh.Amen*, III, p. vii, Carter gives the figure received by Lady Carnarvon as 'a sum equivalent to £36,000 sterling'. The figures given in this volume come from solicitors' letters in the possession of John Carter.

Carter; a return to Lydbrook-on-Wye, and then some days again in the Cotswolds (Stanway and Stow-on-the-Wold) and to Bishop's Frome and Bosbury in Herefordshire. The itinerary of such a visit might not seem very well planned, if the map and economy of driving are considerations, but Carter and White had time, and the inclination to travel gently through unspoilt countryside, visiting picturesque villages and fine churches. White particularly remembered Tewkesbury Abbey. It was all surely balm to Carter after the frustrations of the recent season in Egypt.[30]

Not long after his return to England in the late spring of 1930 Carter had undertaken a very busy programme of lectures in Sweden: two in Stockholm, and others in Malmö, Uppsala, Västerås and Gothenburg; he also gave several talks on the radio. It was during this visit that he met the Crown Prince, Gustav Adolf, with whom he seems to have established a very friendly relationship.[31] Subsequently the Prince wrote in his own hand to Carter to tell him of his projected visit to Egypt later in the year. He hoped to meet Carter again, and clearly expected to be shown Tutankhamun's tomb. A flurry of letters passed between them. The Prince suggested that they might travel to Egypt together; Carter had already made his own plans, but might be able to change them. In the end they did travel together on the SS *Ausonia*, leaving England on 24 September and arriving in Cairo on the 29th. Carter's diary notes 'accompanying H. R. H. Crown Prince of Sweden'. Before he went down to Luxor the Prince went to Cyprus, presumably to visit the Swedish-Cyprus archaeological expedition. His antiquarian interests were far from being casual. His visit to Luxor had already been mentioned.

Initially Carter had better success with his work. He opened up the laboratory tomb on 8 October, and the tomb itself on the 11th. He was joined by Arthur Lucas on the 13th. There remained objects to be worked on as well as the sections of the shrines. He was still not allowed to hold the keys, and was obliged each day to wait for the arrival of an inspector to open up. The possibility of delay was not the only disadvantage of having this new supervision – an arrangement arising from the conditions for work which he had negotiated in the spring of the year. On 10 October, working on the elaborate faldstool, he noted, 'Find work very trying when having an Inspector watching one and asking questions as to one's actions the whole time!' The next day, as if in small part to moderate this criticism, he writes:

Getting along very well with Tewfik Effendi and Edward Effendi notwithstanding they kept me waiting (they being late) and both told

30 The details of the tour are taken from the order of the photographs taken by Carter and mounted in an album now in the possession of John Carter. White's letter of thanks is also with John Carter.
31 Letters on the visit to Sweden and correspondence with the Crown Prince are in the possession of John Carter.

me how to do my work – reparation of chair 351 and the removal
of the shrines from the Tomb!!!

The removal of the shrine sections needed careful preparation and took
some time because the operation required the enlarging of the entrance
passage to allow the withdrawal of the sections in a partly packed state,
which was necessary for their protection. From the tomb they were taken
to the laboratory for detailed conservation and study. The emptying of the
tomb of the last piece by the end of the year led to another dispute over
keys. Carter did not want to be encumbered with a fixed arrangement
with the local inspector. He could not see why the chief *ghaffir* could not
hold the keys, and complained bitterly to Lacau on 6 January 1931, in
answer to what must have been a rather negative letter – as he would
have read it.[32] He claimed that what Lacau wanted was contrary to the
arrangement made in February 1930; he also pointed out that 'the operations upon which I shall be engaged as well as those which I have
already carried out this autumn are for your advantage and scarcely can be
considered to be for my personal benefit.' He hoped that a delegate of the
Service could be made available to be at his disposal 'at any time that is
most convenient for the particular work upon which I am engaged in lab.
No. 15.' He was about to go south to Wadi Halfa, upstream from Abu
Simbel and just within the Sudan – presumably taking some important,
but unspecified, visitor.

When Carter returned he found an answer from Lacau which was as
reasonable as he could have hoped for, although the Director-General was
quite firm about not allowing the chief *ghaffir* to hold the keys. He still
urged Carter to fix regular hours so as not to oblige the Service's delegate
– one of the Inspectors – to hang about all day in the Valley waiting for
Carter to turn up. He could always indicate in the morning what his plans
were for the day. Lacau ends on a most accomodating note: 'Cela me
semble facile et nous rendrait service. C'est cela seulement dont il est
question. Faites au mieux sur ce point' (That seems easy to me, and would
do us a favour. That alone is the point at issue. Do your best in this
matter). It must be presumed that the arrangement worked, for there have
survived no further indications of dispute over Carter's working practices.
Although his own diary of work contains no entries after November 1930,
mentions of his activities in Lindsley Hall's diary allow some track to be
kept of his progress. Hall had returned to work with the Metropolitan
Egyptian Expedition in Luxor in November 1930, bringing with him Elizabeth, his newly married bride. This was the first time he had been back
in Luxor since 1923 when he had been engaged on the plan of the Antechamber of Tutankhamun's tomb along with Walter Hauser. Hall made

32 Carter's letter to Lacau and Lacau's answer are with John Carter.

several visits during the 1930–1 season to his old haunts in the Valley of the Kings, and to see Carter.

1930
[20 Nov.] After tea Walter [Hauser] drove me to Carter's. He is still at work on Tut-ankh-Amūn. He sent me home in his car.

1931
[29 Jan.] After tea E [Elizabeth] and I walked down to Carter's, where we had ½ hr's pleasant visit with the gentleman.

[10 Feb.] This A.M. Hayes drove Mrs. W. [Winlock], Miss Kay, Elizabeth and me to the Valley of the Kings. We visited Tut-ʿankh-Amūn, the gold coffin lying in quartzite sarcophagus. The wall paintings are ugly.

[10 March] Yesterday I rose early and after 7:15 breakfast went to the Valley of the Kings and took pictures of great wagon being man-pulled to river with Tut-ʿankh-Amūn objects leaving for Cairo.

[26 March] Carter came to tea. He leaves Luxor tomorrow.

Lindsley Hall did not return to Luxor for the next season, and was, therefore, not about to see the departure from the Valley of the last sections of the shrines. Howard Carter's mammoth task came to an end in February 1932. He had been in Egypt since early October[33] and had been moving to a conclusion, slowly and steadily, but almost as if he now could scarcely bring himself to finish. It had all taken so much longer than anyone could have foreseen. As he himself pointed out in the Preface to the third volume of *The Tomb of Tut.ankh.Amen*, one whole season had been spent on dismantling the great shrines, and the last two seasons on consolidating them fit for transport to Cairo. The task from beginning to end had needed determination, patience and skill. And in recognizing Carter's achievement, it must not be forgotten that he had never been deserted by Arthur Lucas, whose contribution was enormous and can never be overpraised. Recall what Petrie told Newberry in 1923: 'We can only say how lucky it is all in the hands of Carter and Lucas.'[34]

33 In a letter of 17 September 1931 to Newberry, Carter mentions that he expects to arrive in Cairo on 6 October, G.I. Newberry Corr. 8/78. The completion of his work on Tutankhamun's tomb in February 1932 is stated in *The Tomb of Tut.ankh.Amen*, III, p. vii.
34 See p. 228 above.

16

NON-FULFILMENT AND DECLINE

Lacau's letter to Howard Carter in January 1931, in which he proposed the accommodation over keys, contained the supposition that Carter by now would be eager to complete his work in tomb No. 15 so that he might begin his publication. There can be little doubt that Carter indeed had the great scholarly publication of Tutankhamun's tomb in mind, but first his intention in that direction would be the production of the third volume of his popular work. He may also have had an understandable surfeit as far as the tomb was concerned. The years of search, excavation, *déblaiement*, had been intensive and exhausting, and excessively trying for a man whose natural inclination was to work alone, to watch birds, and to paint water-colours. The immense success was there; he was the best known archaeologist in the world; he could, had he wished, have spent all his time being fêted and entertained. The thought may have occurred to him that he had had enough of the tomb and the Valley of the Kings for the time being. It is not surprising, therefore, that when he was asked by newspaper reporters in 1930 what his plans were now that Tutankhamun was virtually finished, he told them that he intended to search for and excavate the tomb of Alexander the Great.

The site of the tomb, presumed from classical indications to be in Alexandria, had been sought, but without serious effort, for many years, and without success. Carter claimed to have a very good idea of where it was; but it may be suggested that he was pulling the legs of his old friends, the gentlemen of the Press.[1] As far as can be judged from knowledge of his movements over the years in Egypt, he never spent more than a few hours in Alexandria at the start and finish of each season, with one certain exception, during the summer of 1918 when he took a holiday there with a friend from the Residency. Nevertheless, Alexander's tomb was to be his next task, and the idea not only convinced the newspapers, but stimulated a number of people, mostly a little cranky, to write to him with offers of

---

1 He talked to colleagues about this idea, as Charles Wilkinson confirmed; but he was reluctant to reveal any plans. See T. Hoving, *Tutankhamun. The Untold Story* (New York, 1978), p. 58.

help and 'good' advice. An emigré Russian professor wrote from Paris suggesting the use of a torsion balance, which would draw attention to 'any buried cavity beneath the surface of the earth', and establish its exact situation, depth and dimensions. He would, of course, be happy to put his experience 'as a specialist in subsoil research with the torsion balance' at Carter's disposal.[2]

Carter may well have toyed with the idea of starting some new project, without perhaps having a clear idea of what it should be. Some credence to the possibility may be given by a strange episode involving the young Cyril Aldred,[3] subsequently the Keeper of Art and Archaeology in the Royal Scottish Museum, a distinguished Egyptologist, who was 18 when he met Carter in 1932. Aldred had been introduced to Carter's brother William at the Chelsea Arts Club by one of his schoolmasters, and having already an interest in Egypt, he was sent to see Howard Carter at 2 Prince's Gate Court. On that occasion – it was at teatime – he was surprised at finding himself being tested to provide dates for a number of small Egyptian objects which were in the flat. It was a testing experience indeed, for Aldred's knowledge of Egyptian antiquities was very rudimentary. He remembered being asked about a small vessel for *kohl* (eye-paint), and saying 'Middle Kingdom'. Carter then asked whether it was early or late in the period, and again Aldred guessed, saying it was late. He claimed that he used some invented criterion for this date, perhaps the particular shape of the curve of the vessel. Carter, it seems, was impressed and said that he had never considered that criterion. There were several subsequent meetings, and in June 1933 Carter gave Aldred a written certificate:

To all that may be concerned

I have examined Mr. Cyril Aldred and have found him to have a very fair knowledge of Egyptological subjects especially that of Ancient Egyptian Art.

About this time he also proposed that Aldred should spend a season with him in Egypt to obtain practical experience in the field. His letter explaining this opportunity sets out what seemed to be a remarkably generous offer:

I myself am a great believer of practical experience. With a good educational foundation it is, without doubt, the finest instruction of all. You see other worlds, you see other people. And one must never

2 This and other letters on Alexandria are in the possession of John Carter. The torsion balance, an invention of R. von Eötvös, a Hungarian geophysicist, is an instrument devised to estimate the gravitational deceleration of the surface of the Earth.

3 Information on this episode and other remembrances of Howard Carter were given to the author by Cyril Aldred in a series of informal talks 1988–90. The letters quoted are in the possession of his widow.

forget that in moulding our future our greatest enemy or friend is ourselves.

Now, with regard to my proposal – a season in Egypt, roughly speaking six months, say from the end of Oct. to the end of April 1933 [sic] – financially that should cost you nothing. Your fares there and back would be paid. You would have no travelling exs. [expenses] in Egypt. You would naturally live with me, and I should be willing to cover your necessary outfit plus a little pocket money.

But remember this. Your future lies in your hands as before.

Cyril Aldred did not, in the event, take up this offer, but followed parental and school advice and undertook a conventional university education. He himself had no reason to believe that Carter had any motive other than wishing to help a young and promising potential Egyptologist. He had begun his own career by patronage, and he was now in a position to act the patron himself. Aldred could not recall that Carter had any particular piece of work in prospect with which he could provide his young protégé with experience. He might not have had excavation in mind, but some other kind of archaeological work, even epigraphy, the skill in which he was possibly best equipped to instruct. The Theban Necropolis could provide a host of possible and profitable tasks through which a young man with artistic interests could gain valuable experience. After completing his degree in 1936 Aldred contacted Carter again, and was invited to visit him to tell how he was getting on. That, it seems, was their last contact. Carter would surely have been pleased had he been able to follow Aldred's career in which he made himself the leading Egyptological art historian in Great Britain, and an acknowledged expert in subjects which were close to Carter's heart – the reign of King Amenophis III, the Amarna Period and Tutankhamun.

Lacau, however, was right in thinking that publication would be the proper priority for Carter once the 1931–2 season was finished. It was a daunting prospect. Throughout the years of work on the tomb, in the laboratory and in England, when possible, during the summers, a remarkable documentation had been painstakingly been built up. It grew as material arrived, through the personal work of Carter and Lucas, the laboratory studies of Scott and Plenderleith, the textual commentaries of Breasted and Gardiner, the botanical notes of Newberry and L.A. Boodle of the Jodrell Laboratory at Kew, and the anatomical examinations of Derry and Saleh Hamdi. There were many others who were seen or written to by Carter for advice on special technical matters, and their remarks and opinions were carefully filed away against the time when work would start on the final report. For the moment, however, this great mass of material, although superficially organized, was in no way digested or put into any convenient shape by which a publication could easily advance.

Carter had recently been asked to contribute a section on the material from Tutankhamun's tomb to a rather general conspectus, *The Art of Egypt through the Ages* (1931), conceived and edited by E. Denison Ross, the Director of the School of Oriental Studies. It was not a notably good book, although Carter was in rather good company; it was marred in parts by poor photographs. Carter's own contribution was unexciting and somewhat ordinary, but the preparation of it had been a useful exercise which possibly helped him in the completion of the third volume of *The Tomb of Tut.ankh.-Amen*. In his Preface to this volume he acknowledges help in the writing from no specific person, but thanks generally 'the numerous colleagues who have been so good as to help me whenever called upon.' He singles out Alan Gardiner for his aid with translating the inscriptions, and the Metropolitan Museum for allowing him to have the 'advantage of Mr. Harry Burton's unremitting labours.' But neither Gardner nor Burton seems to have had a hand in the text of the volume, and it must be concluded that it was principally Howard Carter's own work. As has been suggested earlier, he may have discussed its form with Percy White, particularly during their long tour of the West Midlands in 1930. Apart from reasonably straightforward accounts of the clearance of the Treasury and the Annexe, the volume contained an essay on the historical background to the reign of Tutankhamun, in which Carter gave a very reasonable summary of contemporary thinking on the Amarna Period. He also included a very interesting chapter on the reasons for the poor condition of much of the material found in the tomb, based not only on the work of Lucas, but also on Carter's own experiences and observations over nearly forty years working in the Theban area. He had always written with a fair sense of style and in a lively manner, but he had a tendency to over-egg the pudding of his composition with purplish patches and dramatic, sentimental comments and judgements. He showed himself remarkably restrained in the writing of this volume III, and it must be thought that there was another hand at work, if only that of a very good editor. As ever the book was illustrated with a splendid series of Harry Burton's photographs.

Carter expected that in preparing the final report he would have help from Gardiner. It is very probable that they had talked about it in general terms from time to time. They had worked together well in the past and Carter knew how much skill and knowledge in matters of scholarly publication Gardiner would bring to the enterprise. He took the matter up in a letter written in the summer after the completion of his work on the tomb:[4]

I want much to see you to discuss the layout of the final publication 'Report upon the tomb of Tut'ankhamun' (for which you have kindly

4 Copy of the letter of 30 August 1932 with John Carter.

accepted to do certain parts) so that we may have some idea and now know what lines to work upon.

In making a sort of synopsis of the subjects and material to be dealt with it looks very much like 6 vols. to be brought out separately one by one. It is upon their make up that I should like your views and collaboration.

It is interesting to note that in this letter Carter uses for the first time the spelling of the Egyptian king's name that was favoured by Gardiner – here in the title of the proposed publication. It is the form still used mostly by British Egyptologists, but it should be said that all forms of spelling of ancient Egyptian names are governed by conventions, and are of doubtful authenticity. Some conventions are, however, better based than others, and it would be a foolhardy Egyptologist who claimed that his own chosen convention was right beyond all doubt. So there remains room for many different spellings of ancient names, and particularly of Tutankhamun, as readers of this book will have noticed. In the writing favoured by Gardiner, it is now common to omit the indication of a guttural sound (ʿ) in non-specialist works.

Carter was surely not bothered particularly by the way the royal name was spelled, but he did seem eager to get on with the publication. No positive reply from Gardiner has survived, but almost a year later he wrote to congratulate Carter on the appearance of volume III of *The Tomb of Tut.ankh.Amen*, and added:[5]

And now you will soon be starting on the larger publication. I shall be most happy to help you to the full extent of my power. We will have a talk about it very soon, if you will.

Again it is not known if Carter and Gardiner had further discussions, although there is evidence for at least one meeting from the correspondence over a very unfortunate incident which happened in the autumn of 1934. It would not have been like Gardiner to prevaricate over a matter in which he had great interest, and on which he would certainly have had strong views. The cause of what resulted in a complete rupture of relations between the two was a small amulet of glazed composition (more generally called faience), in the form of an animal leg ( ) – the Egyptian sign with a phonetic value *whm* (usually pronounced *wehem*), and meaning 'repeat'. During the summer of 1934 Carter gave such an amulet to Gardiner, assuring him that it did not come from the tomb of Tutankhamun. Subsequently Gardiner showed it to Rex Engelbach, who was by that time the Chief Keeper of the Cairo Museum; he asserted that it did come from the tomb, because there were others like it in the tomb-material in the Cairo Museum. Gardiner thereupon sent the amulet back to Cairo, and tactlessly sent copies

5 Card of 12 June 1933 with John Carter.

of the correspondence with Engelbach to Carter. Understandably, Carter was very annoyed, especially as he had first heard of the return of the amulet from Lacau in Cairo. He wrote a stiff letter back to Gardiner reiterating his belief that the amulet did not come from the tomb. He said that he found the contents of Gardiner's letter 'staggering', and concluded:[6]

> I think, Gardiner, that on second thoughts, you will agree that it would perhaps have been kinder had you advised me upon the matter before actually taking the steps you did. Especially as I see by your letter to Engelbach dated 23rd Oct., that I was in London at the time. However I take it that what you did was done with the best intentions, and remain
>
> Yours sincerely,
> Howard Carter

Carter was surely right in the sentiment of his last sentence. Gardiner's conscience could easily get the better of him, and he was ever inclined to act in a hasty manner. In that case, sadly, his impetuosity led to an end in their association over the publication, and consequently sounded the death knell of the project for Carter as well. After Carter's death Gardiner said somewhat wistfully in a letter to Newberry,[7] 'I was not on good terms with Carter during the last years of his life'; and some years later he did his very best to initiate plans for a full publication of Carter's great achievement. In 1951 it looked as if funds for a splendid multi-volume work would be found in Egypt itself. A commitment by the Egyptian Council of Ministers seemed to crown Gardiner's efforts, but the chance was lost with the Egyptian Revolution of 1952.[8]

There is not a great deal of evidence that Carter did anything to begin even a first volume of his grand scheme, although he did from time to time add snippets of information to his voluminous files. He did, however, write a series of sketches on his early life, and on special incidents and episodes in his working life, during his last years. They exist in several copies, in differing stages of completion and revision, and some have been drawn upon in the writing of the present volume. They vary considerably in accuracy, the account of his early days in particular being flawed by many small errors. But they are lively, colourful and imaginative. He certainly had an intention to publish, but he could never bring himself to complete them. After his death his niece Phyllis Walker wrote to Percy Newberry asking him to help her with the sketches, which she said Carter had planned to publish with her help. Newberry agreed to help, but nothing further seems to have happened.[9]

6 Copy of the letter of 27 November 1934 with John Carter.
7 G.I. Newberry Corr. 18/7, of 25 July 1939.
8 See his late account of his efforts in *My Working Years* (privately published, 1963), p. 39.
9 Letters of 9 and 14 June 1939 in G.I. Newberry Corr. 44/60.

Among the sketches now in the Carter papers in the Griffith Institute in Oxford[10] is one which deals with the robbery of the tomb of King Amenophis II in the Valley of the Kings in 1901; in a sequel to his principal account, Carter adds remarks which set out his own views on the ethics of excavation. From internal evidence this section was written in about 1937. It is a kind if *apologia pro vita sua*:

I have noticed from time to time letters written to the editors of the daily newspapers commenting upon the so-called 'profanation' on the part of archaeologists; some of these letters specially aimed at myself. Those that make such complaints seem unaware that the profanation they allude to is really applicable to the tomb-plunderers of the past and the present day. They seem to forget that what the archaeologist is doing in Egypt and elsewhere, for the sake of the history of man, is to endeavour to rescue these remains of the past from the destructive vandalism of the grave-robbers. In such letters referring to archaeological activities I have noticed even terms used of a kind which verge on libel by their very false and defamatory suggestions. For example: 'It is monstrous that the Tombs of the dead should thus be rifled, their contents scattered far and wide, and the bodies un-wrapped and exposed to the public gaze, not only from the religious point of view is the profanation abominable, but also from a national. . . . Public opinion both in this country (England) and in Egypt should rise up against and stop this sort of thing.' Ignorance is always abusive; the man who does not know is full of violent affirmations and malign interpretations.

The suggestion of 'profanation' on the part of a properly trained archaeologist is, I repeat, nothing less than libellous by its very reflection. I therefore think it right for me to solemnly affirm – not arrogantly or defiantly – that profanation is the very last idea of a true archaeologist. In his research work his one and sole idea is to rescue remains of the past from destruction, and that when in the course of his work he passes inviolate thresholds, he feels not only an awe and wonder distilled from their tremendous past, but the sense of a sacred obligation. I would add, everything goes to prove that if scientific research of this kind ended tomorrow, greater would be the number of unauthorized persons sacking graves that would yield gold and precious objects who sold and 's[c]attered far and wide'; and, for all practical purposes, that would be the end of them.

With regard to legitimate discovery of such treasures, the words of His Holiness the Pope, Pius XII,[11] invites reminiscence. Referring

10 In Carter Notebook 17, pp. 189ff.
11 Probably Pius XI, who died in February 1939, to be succeeded by Pius XII.

to the Tut.ankh.Amun discovery, he said to Lady Burghclere: 'It is
not an exhumation, it is a resurrection.'

There will be many who, while accepting in general Carter's justification
for excavation of burials, will detect a strong scent of hypocrisy in what
he says about the robbing of tombs, the selling of objects and the scattering
of the ancient legacy far and wide. Carter himself never disguised his
interest in and love for fine and beautiful antiquities, and he was only
conventionally secretive about his activities as a gentleman dealer. He
would have claimed, almost certainly, that he did not sell objects he had
himself excavated. Objects acquired in a division with the Antiquities
Service were in his day legitimately the property of the excavating authority
or individual, and, as has been pointed out, it did sometimes happen that
objects might be sold by excavators to finance further work, or to cover
other costs. Objects which turned up on the market could in some cases
be assigned with certainty to particular sources, even particular excavations, and Carter had a good record of trying from time to time to alert
excavators when he came across pieces in dealers' shops which could be
retrieved for the archaeological record. But most objects in the shops were
not easily assignable, and they were, he surely felt, fair game for purchase.
He had in his possession at the time of his death a small collection of
Egyptian antiquities, including a few important pieces like the faience
sphinx of Amenophis III. Such were the objects on which he had tested
Cyril Aldred, who did not remember that sphinx, but did recall one
identifiable piece from Tutankhamun's tomb, a small *shabti*-figure which
Carter kept on his desk. Aldred believed that Carter may have been
allowed to take this piece, one only of many similar in the tomb, as a
token 'keep-sake' of his long endeavours, which had enriched the Cairo
Museum so magnificently.

The same was less likely to have been the case with a group of objects
inscribed with Tutankhamun's names, and therefore almost certainly from
the tomb. It cannot be proved that Carter himself took them from the
tomb; it seems, on the contrary, more likely that he withdrew them from
the Carnarvon collection, as has already been suggested, at the time when
it was packed up and sent to the Bank of England. The ultimate fate of
these objects will be described later. For the present discussion it is important to state that there is no evidence that Carter ever sold Tutankhamun
objects in his lifetime. He may have given some small pieces to friends
and others to whom he felt particularly indebted, but it is impossible now
to determine the circumstances of any particular gift. Nearly all the pieces
thought to have been given by him were what may be termed 'odds and
ends', parts of larger pieces of jewellery, for example, the debris of the
early depredations by robbers in the tomb. The matter may be capable of
elucidation by further enquiry, but any result is very unlikely to show that

Carter was criminally profligate in the distribution of Tutankhamun pieces to others. He was like Petrie and other archaeologists of his time, being in the habit of handing out archaeological trifles to visitors. It was no uncommon experience to have visitors to the British Museum bring in antiquities presented by Carter to parents or relatives, and inevitably carrying by implication the cachet of Tutankhamun's tomb. These gifts were always genuine but very ordinary pieces which could at that time be almost trawled on the surface of the Theban Necropolis. Carter presumably had a boxful of such 'going-home' presents.

The one Tutankhamun piece in his possession of real importance (although almost duplicated by another in Cairo) was a glass head-rest or 'pillow' with a gold band and an identifying text. Carter may at one point have been tempted to sell it through Messrs Spink and Son of King Street, St James's, once one of the foremost dealers in Egyptian antiquities in London. A letter from the firm to Carter, dated 7 May 1930,[12] refers to a possible client for the 'pillow' and contains the words, 'knowing that you will rely on me to see that the secrecy of the transaction, should it come off, will be observed – my man I think can be described as a real sportsman – and hoping that you will let me show it to him.' Nothing came of this suggestion, and a further letter from Spink's, dated 21 May 1930, refers to Carter's having taken away the 'pillow' and another piece.[13] Nothing in this correspondence confirms that Carter was actually contemplating a sale. He scarcely needed the money at that time. Possibly he had deposited the pieces with Spinks for safe-keeping while he was in Egypt for the winter, as he valued the head-rest very highly (at that time £15,000 according to Spink's). Spink's had then been tempted to test the possibility of a sale when a suitable client presented himself. There is no convincing evidence that Carter had suggested the sale, and none that he ever put the piece up for sale during the next nine years. It was still in his possession when he died. Newberry claimed in a letter to Gardiner that he had no idea that Carter had taken objects from the tomb until a few months before he died.[14] He said that according to Carter's own inventory he valued the head-rest at £10,000. Valuation is one thing, sale is another. The position remains sadly compromised as far as Carter was concerned, although not as badly as has sometimes been thought.

A further comment on this sensitive subject is that the antiquities in his possession at death, after the extraction of the Tutankhamun objects, were valued for probate by Messrs Spink at £1093.[15] This was certainly a low

12 G.I. Carter Papers 227.
13 With John Carter.
14 G.I. Gardiner Corr. AHG/42. 222. 54.
15 A copy of the probate valuation is in the library of the Department of Egyptian Antiquities, British Museum. For a study of the objects see N. Reeves 'Howard Carter's Collection of Egyptian and Classical Antiquities', in A. B. Lloyd (ed.), *Greatest of Seers* (London, 1992?).

valuation, as was not uncommon for probate purposes, but it does give some indication of the relatively modest nature of his private collection. And finally, it may be said that any fine small object of Eighteenth-Dynasty date which turned up in a private collection or on the market in the 1920s and 1930s was almost without fail attributed to Tutankhamun's tomb. Attribution by inference or association is a very uncertain method of determining provenance, or of ascribing improper behaviour to an excavator.

The dealing activities which Carter pursued for a great part of his career continued in his later years, but with less intensity and with greater concentration, as far as Egyptian antiquities were concerned, on what might be called targetted sales. The records are not substantial, but correspondence survives with dealers like Khawam Bros, with outlets in Cairo and Paris (from whom he purchased pieces for the Detroit Institute of Arts), and another Paris dealer, Eustache de Lorey.[16] The transaction concerning a pair of pieces, a fine head of Ramesses II and a figure of a falcon (hawk), indicate the scale, intricacy and leisurely progress of the business. The first mention of the two pieces in the surviving documentation occurs in a letter from Herbert Winlock to Carter on 8 September 1930:[17] 'If you have not already gotten rid of your hawk and your head of Ramses II, could you let me have photographs of them? I think I may know someone who might be interested in them.' Carter answered promptly: 'Alas, the National Art Fund are buying the two pieces for the B.M. – that is they have the option up to the Midsummer 1931, to purchase them for 10,000£.' H.R.H. Hall, the Keeper of Egyptian and Assyrian Antiquities at the British Museum, was eager to secure the acquisition through this organization devoted to obtaining important works of art for national and local museums and galleries in Great Britain. Unfortunately Hall died in the following October and in the end the Fund was not able to help. What then happened to the pieces is uncertain. Sale negotiations went underground, and when they became evident again in 1934 Carter had acquired a partner in the form of Welles Bosworth, architect of John D. Rockefeller Jr, who lived in Paris. Together they used as an intermediary Eustache de Lorey, who with Bosworth 'worked out a scheme of strategy by which he alone is visible . . . We are angling for two or three different fish, but feel confident that we shall be able to accomplish something.'[18] Eventually in June 1934 de Lorey concluded a sale to the Metropolitan Museum of Art for £7000, considerably less than Carter had

16 With John Carter.
17 In M.M.A., Department of Egyptian Art, Carter files, also Carter's reply.
18 Letter to Carter of 23 March 1934 in the possession of John Carter. The falcon now carries the Metropolitan Museum number 34.2.1, and the head 34.2.2. The latter has recently been identified as a head of Amenmesse, a king of the late Nineteenth Dynasty; see P. Cardon in *Metropolitan Museum Journal* 14 (1979), pp. 5f.

originally expected; but a price reflecting the financial problems of the time.

The cloak-and-dagger means by which this sale was accomplished suggests that Carter, and probably Bosworth, were trying to minimize their declared income. Carter in particular was having problems with the Income Tax authorities in Britain now that he was spending longer summers in the country, and no doubt wished to conceal his profits on dealing. His declared income for 1928 was £1666 10s. 6d., and for 1929 £2264 18s. 1d.; the 1929 figure was made up of annuity (£1000), dividends (£413), interest on deposit account (£129), and earnings from newspapers (£721).[19] These figures did not include what he may have earned in Egypt by way of dealing and of income from Egyptian government stocks and interest on bank deposits. It was a very satisfactory financial situation for a man whose expectations had been rather modest up to the Great War.

Inevitably the Inland Revenue began probing his situation and challenging his status, on which he could base the allowance of certain expenses. A characteristically perverse correspondence was conducted between the Inland Revenue and Frere Cholmeley on Carter's behalf in 1931 as to whether Carter was liable to pay Income Tax in Great Britain. One may enjoy at this distance the statement in a letter from the Inspector of Taxes of 11 September 1931: 'It is not clear that Mr. Howard Carter is assessable as an Archaeologist.' And even more teasing are the comments in a letter of 27 May 1932:

It is not in dispute that Mr. Carter has been engaged as an archaeologist during the past three years. On the facts available, however, I am unable to agree that his activities in this direction have constituted the carrying on of a trade or profession.

Unfortunately the outcome of the negotiation is not known, but Carter may well have been obliged to pay some tax. He would therefore have appreciated the surreptitious sale of the falcon and head of Ramesses II in 1934.

Throughout his life Howard Carter had been careful in money matters, that is in the management of his own affairs, even if he allowed himself to become accustomed to a style of life which needed a substantial income to support it. He was prudent in negotiating his agency agreements with museums, and took sensible steps to ensure that his major lecture tour in America was accomplished to his financial advantage. One of the most sensible arrangements he made was the purchase of his annuity of £1000 from the Standard Life Assurance Co., probably in 1924 after returning from America. It was certainly being paid by 1928 in twice-yearly instalments into his account in the National Bank of Egypt. He later made

19 Papers including the figures of his earnings, letters to his solicitors and correspondence with the Tax Inspector, all with John Carter.

enquiries about an annuity for his brother William from Standard Life in August 1932. William was then 69, and for an annuity of £160, Howard Carter would have had to pay £1707 1s. 4d.[20] It is not sure whether he completed the transaction. Such an apparently small sum, amounting to about £3 per week, would have been at the time a very useful supplement to William's uncertain income from portrait painting. His friends clearly thought that Carter had been very sensible in securing his financial future in this way, and sought his advice on the subject. One who considered the matter seriously was Axel Munthe, who asked Carter to find out what a £1000 annuity would cost him in 1931, at the age of 75. His solicitors looked into the matter and obtained a quotation of £11,000 from Sun of Canada, and another of about £11,500 from the Norwich Union. Again it is not known if Munthe followed up the advice. As he lived for another eighteen years, it would have been a wise arrangement at that time.

Carter's life, after the completion of the work on the tomb of Tutankhamun and in the laboratory, was divided as before, between London and Luxor. Its content, however, changed dramatically. No longer had he to gird himself annually for the seemingly inevitable confrontation with the Antiquities Service after his return to Cairo in the early autumn. He could now contemplate a much less aggravated existence, living quietly in his house on the hill of Elwat el-Diban. How he spent his time is scarcely known. Dr Harold Plenderleith recalls his life in Thebes in the mid–1920s as being very comfortable, with memories of a house much above the standard for field bases, and of frequent champagne.[21] He entertained guests from time to time. Professor Magdi Wahba of Cairo University remembered being taken to lunch in Carter's house with his parents in about 1936; he recollected a good meal, Carter an excellent host but given to nervous giggling. On occasion Carter had visitors to stay. In 1931 his niece Phyllis Walker spent much of the season with him. He appreciated her presence, and wrote to Winlock,[22] 'I have brought my niece out this season so have good company.' She was the daughter of his favourite sister Amy, and at the end became his principal legatee. While she was in Luxor Phyllis annotated a picture postcard of the house – what she called *La Maison Cartaire*. Having indicated the use of various rooms, she adds, 'The rest is desert! All in mud colour – I play "sister Anne" at the window sometimes to watch the sunset.' In 1934 Harry Burton wrote to Percy Newberry:[23]

We've only seen Carter once, or rather twice, since we came. He had

20 Letters on the annuities of A. Munthe and William Carter are with John Carter.
21 These remarks are based on personal reminiscences of Dr H. Plenderleith and the late Professor Magdi Wahba.
22 Letter of 13 November 1931, in M.M.A., Department of Egyptian Art, Carter files. The Phyllis Walker postcard is with John Carter.
23 G.I. Newberry Corr. 6/109.

a man named Carter, no relation, staying with him and they went down to Cairo by boat a few days after we got here. H. was in great form.

From all his last years there have survived scarcely any documents, or even signs in letters, that he was doing any serious work on his publication. His own collection of reference books was not extensive, but there were local resources in Luxor that he could have used. There was an excellent library in the Metropolitan House, and another growing rapidly in Chicago House. He would have been welcome in both places. For a person with not enough to do, compared with his old intensive existence, life in Luxor could become enervating. There was always the possibility of wasting time, and the danger of a relaxation of values in day-to-day behaviour. In general Carter seems to have kept up appearances. The picture remains one of a very conventional Englishman abroad, carefully dressed in a three-piece suit, wearing a bow-tie, sporting a Homburg hat and carrying a walking stick. He is said to have taken his style of dress from Lord Carnarvon and to have used the same tailor and other tradesmen in London. It was a casually formal style, elegant and distinguished, but not too precise. How then should one interpret an incident reported by Dr Harold Nelson to Charles Breasted in October, 1928?[24]

Carter, I understand, came down to call the other afternoon, clad in his pyjamas, but when he reached the corner of our house he discovered Mrs. Nelson and Mrs. Edgerton on the porch and beat a hasty retreat. Why this sudden modesty?

This encounter may have formed the one memorable visit of the season for Chicago House. Charles Breasted commented in reply: 'While I am surprised that he beat a hasty retreat, I am still more surprised that he bothered to bring pyjamas!' Nelson next wrote in November, 'This letter was interrupted by a call from Carter, this time clothed.' The whole episode seems so out of character for Carter, and undoubtedly made a deep impression on Harold Nelson.

The common remembrance of Carter in Luxor in the later 1930s was one of a man who had to a great extent given up on the work which had determined his life for such a long time; who, as his health deteriorated over the decade, spent his time increasingly across the river in Luxor town, in the dealers' shops and the Winter Palace Hotel, where he had been made very welcome over many years by Anton Badrutt, the general manager. Professor Charles Nims of the Oriental Institute of the University of Chicago was on the staff of Chicago House before the Second World War, and wrote many years later of Carter's way of life at the time:[25]

24 Letters in O.I. Director's Office Corr. Nelson 1928.
25 Letter of 1 July 1981 to Dr William Peck in the Detroit Institute of Arts, who kindly sent me a copy.

Carter did almost nothing after the closing of the Tutankhamun concession in 1931. In 1937–38 I used to meet him in the morning on the west side of the Nile as I was going to spend the day at Medinet Habu and he was on his way to spend the day on the veranda of the Winter Palace. He talked of further explorations but this was, apparently only his pipe dreams.

This disappointing vignette of Carter idling his days at the Winter Palace is supported by another provided by Sir Evelyn Wrench who wrote an occasional piece about a visit to Egypt for the *Spectator* for 6 September, 1935. It was entitled 'Egypt Calls':

No one should go to Upper Egypt unless he has steeped himself in the wonders of the Cairo Museum – surely one of the most interesting buildings in the world. A few days later I was hearing from the lips of Mr. Howard Carter in the welcome cool of the vestibule of the Winter Palace at Luxor the story of the Tutankhamen discovery.

Others have remembered seeing him sitting by himself in the entrance hall of the same hotel, sunk in thought, and solitary – a doleful sight. It is pitiful to think of him in his sad isolation, waiting like the Ancient Mariner to trap some visitor to whom he might talk. He was not by any means poor and so cannot have been hoping to be bought a drink; he was just destitute of spirit, and a seriously ill person. Throughout his life he had suffered from indifferent health, and, as has been suggested earlier, many of his moods were surely the result of feeling miserably sick. His most recent operation, to remove his tonsils in 1928, had, however, done him a little good, as some would think. Axel Munthe remarked in a letter written afterwards:[26] 'The removal of your tonsils seems to have had an invigorating effect upon your memory for your far away and forgotten friends – so glad.' His condition deteriorated seriously from the mid-1930s, the trouble being a glandular affliction which would be diagnosed as Hodgkin's disease. His few letters of the period contain little of complaint, indeed little of any specific information. But one draft letter preserved in a notebook in the Metropolitan Museum gives some indication of what he may have endured. It is of uncertain date, but must have been written during the 1930s because of his mentioning leaving London not until mid-December. In the days when he was hard at work in the Valley he usually arrived in Egypt in the early autumn. The addressee of the letter has not been identified:

Dear Princess,
    Very many thanks for your letter and enquiries. I am sorry that your stay in R ... [? Romania, Russia] should be marred by the

26 Undated letter with John Carter.

cold. We too are suffering from dry cutting winds peculiar to January in these regions. However, with them we are recompensed with brilliant sun.

I did not leave London until the second week in December. In November my ills took a turn for the bad, but happily I found an excellent doctor who seemed to understand my trouble. He dosed me with arsenic and gave me deep-ray (a form of X-ray), and in the course of a month I became another being. The misfortune was that the ray treatment brought on a temporary form of acute nausia [*sic*] and loss of the sense of taste, which was certainly a bore.

If such were his condition, then there would have been little that he would have wanted to exert himself to do. His former pleasures of observing the wild-life of the Theban area and of painting seemed no longer to distract him as in the past. In his late sketches he writes with enthusiasm, but vicariously, of the birds he used to watch in his early days, and the memory of what he saw could still delight him. So, recalling his time at El-Bersha, he writes of the wild-life shown on the tomb walls, and to be seen in the neighbourhood:[27]

The birds and animals depicted on those walls were alone enough to keep me interested. And to my delight, upon the rock shelves of the precipitous cliffs of that ravine a colony of griffon vultures retired for the night – after these I loved to sneak. Nearby there was a congregation of ravens, their high-pitched croaks when soaring overhead were our music during the day; and in the evening, skipping about like tiny kangaroos were jerboas; most delightful little rodents with silky coats harmonizing with the desert, large black eyes like boot-buttons, and long tufted tails. These little denizens of the desert, whose burrows were but a stone's throw from the camp, came, I suppose, seeking food. They hunted here and there; yet they drew a continual pleasure from their toil for a subsistence.

Such passages may be consciously composed, the memories conjured from more than simple recollection, but they are vivid and convey a spirit of true excitement and enthusiasm. To this quoted passage he adds a footnote in which he lists, with full Latin names, the species he claims to have noted down, presumably at the time of observation. In a sense the footnote spoils the effect of the text, because it reinforces the suspicion that the whole of the writing is contrived. Nevertheless, his passion for the natural phenomena of Egypt persisted, even if he did not actively engage in observation. And similarly, he apparently abandoned painting in these last years. His last watercolour box was retrieved from his house by Harry Burton after Carter's death, and later passed into the hands of Charles

27 G.I. Carter Notebook 15, p. 28.

Wilkinson of the Metropolitan Museum, an old friend of Carter's and a very good artist himself. It is tragic to think of Carter in his last years, when he could have spent so much time painting and sketching, but was bereft of the spirit to engage in what had so often been his consolation and delight.

Carter's life in London during his last years was very different from his winter existence. He effected the transition for a number of years by travelling from Egypt to Switzerland, staying in St Moritz at the Kulm Hotel where Anton Badrutt had become a director, if not the manager. He had finally left Egypt after spending sixteen years as general manager of the Upper Egyptian hotels in Luxor and Aswan. He wrote a touching letter addressed to 'the family of Howard Carter' after Carter's death, saying that 'my friend Howard used to spend every summer 5–6 weeks with me at St. Moritz. Unfortunately he was not very well last summer [1938] and my wife and I visited him in London in November last.'[28] It is known that Carter took a cruise in the Greek islands in the summer of 1933, but usually he passed most of the summer months in London, probably making short visits to see friends in the country. The centre of his life in Town was his flat. Cyril Aldred knew 2 Prince's Gate Court, to which Carter had moved in 1930 from 19B Collingham Gardens. According to Aldred's memory it was well appointed, with some fine pieces of furniture, excellent carpets, interesting pictures and some good silver. Carter had the time and the inclination to haunt the sale-rooms and the dealers' shops, and had an eye for a good bargain and for quality. He developed a more than ordinary competence in the judging of oriental carpets, and was from time to time consulted by private owners.[29] Aldred remembers his showing him his most recent good purchases, and formed the impression that he supplemented his income by selling what he did not want to keep himself.

Carter's voice is remembered as being rather plummy, which is confirmed by existing recordings in the archives of the BBC. He had, it seems, modelled himself in this respect on members of the upper class with whom he had spent much time; but Dr Harold Plenderleith states that Carter took elocution lessons to improve his speaking voice for lecturing. Aldred thought that his shortness with others, especially servants and people like head-waiters (or stewards on Canadian Pacific railway trains) was a form of mannerism characteristic of 'grand' people of his period. It was thought to be right and proper to be abrupt and dismissive to such 'underlings'. On this aspect of his character it can only be said that his natural inclination to irascibility needed little instruction from others, whether they were highborn or not.

In 1932 Carter moved house again, travelling a few yards only from

28 Dated 10 March 1939 with John Carter.
29 Letters in the possession of John Carter outline some transactions and consultations.

Prince's Gate Court to 49 Albert Court, a flat in another fine late Victorian mansion block in the precincts of the Albert Hall. The move seems strange, for he was not improving his address. Possibly he had only a short lease on the Prince's Gate Court flat; perhaps the outlook was better; perhaps the service facilities were more reliable. The accommodation in the new flat was certainly spacious for a single gentleman. From the information in Spink's detailed valuation of its contents, it can be deduced that it consisted of an entrance hall, drawing room, dining-room, study, serving room, bedroom, housekeeper's sitting room, kitchen, bathroom, lavatory, box-room, and additional storage space 'upstairs'. There was no guest bedroom, and it may be supposed that if he ever had visitors to stay he put them up elsewhere. When he was not out in London, being entertained, or away in the country, he lived a fairly solitary life – the kind of life he used to claim suited him admirably. He dined out frequently, and took guests to one of the many local hotels with grill-rooms of the kind favoured in the 1930s. Aldred remembers being taken to one such grill-room about five minutes' distance away, where Carter appeared to be a regular diner. Dr Harold Plenderleith, whose acquaintance with Carter covered the late 1920s and early 1930s, said that he had a rather grand style of living in London, his own memories, however, being coloured by expensive lunches to which Carter entertained him after, as he put it, 'picking my brains'.

Carter also spent time and entertained at the Savile Club which had recently migrated from Piccadilly to Brook Street. He had been introduced to the club as a member by Percy White. He was also a member of the Burlington Fine Arts Club in Savile Row, a haunt of members of the artistic community with which Carter had always kept in touch through his brother William. By the time Carter had settled more permanently in London, Percy White seems no longer to be part of his small circle of friends. White was 82 in 1932, and may have spent much of the year in Roquebrune in Alpes-Maritimes in the South of France. He had been a good friend and invaluable literary adviser to Carter since before the Great War; one of the few people whom Carter could count as a real friend, bridging his two lives in Egypt and in London. It is not easy to build up a picture of Carter's intimate acquaintanceship; it is even possible that one did not exist. In his early days in London, before he achieved some status and grand companions, he spent much of his time in the company of his London-based brothers and his sister Amy, mixing with the artistic community in Chelsea. The evidence is slight, but it does suggest that he was particularly close to Amy. She had married a John Walker at about the turn of the century, and there is a photographic record in existence showing Howard Carter on holiday with the Walker family in July-September 1901.[30] Phyllis, who was Amy's only

30 Formerly in the possession of Miss Ivy Wilson. Now in the Swaffham Museum.

child, became undoubtedly Howard's favourite relation, especially after Amy's early death.

After his departure from 19 Collingham Gardens in 1930 and his difference with his brother Samuel, the only other member of his large family he kept in regular touch with was William. He had become a reasonably successful portrait painter, with a long list of influential clients to his credit. In his earlier years he had done a very stylish painting of the Earl of Carnarvon and, in 1924, the well-known, 'standard', full-length portrait of Howard. William never achieved conventional recognition by the British art establishment, but he was on intimate terms with many who had become Royal Academicians and Associates. When he died his executor was Sir Henry Rushbury, a most distinguished architectural artist and Keeper of the Royal Academy from 1949 to 1964.[31] Through William, Howard could keep in touch with at least some of the artistic circles in the capital. William, who was eleven years Howard's senior, survived his young brother by only a few months, although he was fit enough to attend Howard's funeral.

It would be a mistake to claim that Carter lost all contact with other members of his family during his last years. The evidence just does not exist to support the other conclusion. It will be seen that he may have set up his brother Vernet's widow, Audrey, in a cottage in Norfolk, but again there are no substantive details of the regularity of his visits to see her. There is also no evidence that he returned to Swaffham during the 1930s. His two maiden aunts who had been partly responsible for his early upbringing were dead, Fanny in 1913, and Catherine in 1929. There were plenty of other Carter relations in and around Swaffham, but he felt no closes ties to them, and may even have feared exploitation. Miss Ivy Wilson, who still lives in Swaffham, and who as a little girl lived near the Sporle Road Cottage, and ran errands for the Carter family recalls visits by Howard Carter during the summers in the 1920s. She remembers him wearing cream-coloured suits and looking very tanned; she thought he was Egyptian. Her memories are now dimmed, but she believes his visits were eagerly expected as occasions for presents all round. Of her own contacts with him, she can only remember cold 'thank you's' as she handed him the post which she had brought to the cottage from Swaffham.

If it is difficult to discover even in general outline the course of Howard Carter's professional activities in Egypt on occasion, it is practically impossible to determine the order of his private life in London. No diaries of his last years can be traced, and few letters have survived. There is no reason to believe, however, that he cleared the record before he died, for many trivial letters have survived which would surely not have been spared in any general clear-out. More is known about his grand, occasional friends

31 I am grateful to Julia Rushbury for information about William Carter.

than his regular acquaintances. One must suppose that he knew many people, and that he was until his very last year or two always welcome at the dinner-tables of London hostesses – many invitations have survived; but such occasions do not represent indications of true friendship.[32] Throughout his life, the signs suggest that he did not make close friendships, but was content to maintain good relations with a wide range of people whom he was pleased to see intermittently and to stay with from time to time.

Carter did not seek out Egyptological colleagues as companions, and Percy Newberry was the only one whom he saw regularly in England. Newberry remained a staunch supporter of Carter, and he and his wife regularly entertained Carter at their various houses in the country throughout his life. He seems to have formed a warm friendship with Mrs. Newberry, taking a great interest in her own speciality, needlework, and seemingly escaping from Egyptology in her company. In spite of his manifest success as an archaeologist, he retained a kind of inferiority complex over his general skills as an academic Egyptologist; he seemed almost to avoid the company of professional colleagues, as if he might suffer some form of exposure of ignorance. He was essentially an artist and a man of practical abilities, to whom scholarship in the strictest sense did not come naturally. He would not commonly have sought out colleagues to discuss Egyptological interests and problems in a general way, although he would readily talk to them about particular matters connected with his work in hand. When he came to draw up his will in 1931 he chose as executors, from among his friends and colleagues, Harry Burton and Bruce Ingram, a strangely assorted pair but yet representative of different sides of his life. From the Egyptological side, Burton was perhaps an obvious choice. He was not exactly a bosom friend, but he had worked closely with Howard Carter for ten years; he knew the Egyptian half of Carter's life, and the Luxor scene in particular; he would probably be on hand in Egypt to handle the winding-up of Carter's estate there. Bruce Ingram, the editor of the *Illustrated London News*, represented the London side of Carter's life. It is some indication of how little is known of Carter's private life that Ingram appears almost from nowhere in the position of executor.[33] His association, even friendship, with Carter must have developed in the late 1920s. There was an historic connection between the Carter family and the *Illustrated London News*. Carter's father had been the agricultural illustrator for the magazine for many years before his death in 1892, long before Bruce Ingram took over the editorship of what was an Ingram family publication. His own Carter involvement began in December 1922,

---

32 A large number of invitations with John Carter.
33 Unfortunately all *Illustrated London News* records pre-Second World War were destroyed by bombing.

with a letter starting 'My dear Sir'.[34] Ingram was of course eager to publish photographs of the Tutankhamun discovery, and he succeeded in negotiating a special agreement with Carnarvon and *The Times* to have exceptional facilities, including the sole rights to publication in colour. The quality of the photographic reproductions in the *Illustrated London News* far exceeded what was possible for daily newspapers to accomplish, and the special issues put out by Ingram made a huge impact on the public. They also did no harm to the success of the periodical, and during the summer of 1923 Ingram cemented a relationship with Howard Carter, through a number of meetings and social entertainments.[35] In the course of these meetings he would certainly have been told of Carter's father's association with the publication; he also discovered Carter's own graphic talent. In the issue of 17 November 1923 he published a most sensitive drawing by Carter of a figure of Khaemhet, a vizir of King Amenophis III, from his tomb at Thebes. It was executed in Carter's best epigraphic style, and Ingram rightly characterized Carter as a 'first-class artist'. It was the first of a number of Carter drawings and watercolours published in the *Illustrated London News* over the years, in addition to regular helpings of material from Tutankhamun's tomb. Carter did not always respond as promptly as Bruce Ingram would have wished. In November 1925, after the revelation of the rich accoutrements on the royal body, Ingram wrote to Percy Newberry:[36]

Carter's discoveries are enough to make anyone's mouth water and mine is positively dribbling. If only he can square the authorities, I will make such a number that will never be forgotten, but what the hopes are I don't know as Carter seems even worse than I am about letter writing.

The feudal character of the ownership of the *Illustrated London News*, and the almost heriditary nature of the Carter family connection through Samuel and Howard, probably encouraged a closer association between Ingram and Carter than might have been expected. The two must have developed a good, if occasional, friendship over the years, but the surviving record totally lacks details of how this friendship was maintained. The same is the case for other friends and acquaintanceships which, one may suspect, Carter revived or allowed to lie fallow as time and circumstances permitted. What, for example, happened to Louis Steele? A letter of 5 August 1920, written by Steele to Carter from H.M. Dockyard Portsmouth, starts 'My dear old Carter', and is couched in familiar and friendly terms;[37] it was about the chemical technology of glass-making, a subject of particu-

34 Letter of 29 December 1922 in M.M.A., Department of Egyptian Art, Carter files.
35 Notes in Carter's Pocket Diary for 1923 in Griffith Institute, Carter Papers.
36 G.I. Newberry Corr. 26/21.
37 M.M.A., Department of Egyptian Art, Carter files.

lar interest to Carter and Lord Carnarvon at that time. Who could this old friend be? By chance a collection of photographs taken by Louis John Steele was presented to the Swaffham Museum in 1987; they illustrated many objects, and scenes of excavation from the Carnarvon-Carter explorations in the Theban Necropolis before the Great War, and point to a fairly long stay, or more than one stay, by Louis Steele while the excavators were at work. Nothing further is known of Steele; it may be that he was only a passing acquaintance, who happened to be in Luxor at a suitable time to be helpful; who could then be approached on a particular matter – glass – many years later. A slight impression is gained that Carter probably had a talent for making himself friendly to new acquaintances, but very little ability, or inclination, to keep them.

The friendships about which a little is known are with important people, whose letters Carter sometimes kept, like the Crown Prince of Sweden, the Duke of Alba, Axel Munthe. The Duke of Alba, perhaps more than the others, maintained contact over a longer period of time. After Carter's visits to Madrid in 1924 and 1928, the Duke continued to see Carter when he came to London, and they may also have met in Switzerland during Carter's annual visits to the Kulm Hotel in St Moritz. He last tried to see Carter on 13 February 1939, and wrote to him afterwards having heard 'you are laid up and have a nurse in attendance. I hope it is nothing very serious, and I shall be glad to have news of you.'[38] The Axel Munthe relationship may have been more one-sided. Cyril Aldred said that Carter did not care for him very much. It may be suspected, from the tone of Munthe's surviving letters, that he was too persistent in exploiting Carter's willingness to be helpful in matters like visits to the tomb of Tutankhamun, especially when there were difficulties. It was for this purpose that he had first got to know Carter through the recommendations of Lord Allenby and Rennell Rodd.

To be a long-term friend of Howard Carter one surely needed to be a pretty tolerant person or a connoisseur of astringent and testy behaviour, someone always ready to make allowances for moods and furies. Cyril Aldred formed the opinion that he did not spare whatever company he was in if he felt inclined to disagree with what might have been said. He recalled having heard of an occasion when Carter was distinctly short to Lauritz Melchior, the famous Swedish Wagnerian *Heldentenor*. Melchior, it seems, had made some fatuous general statement, and Carter answered, 'That is spherical and in the plural.' The story may be apocryphal, but it probably well represents the style of repartee Carter made use of. In spite of having mixed in grand company over many years Carter seemed to have remained rather uncertain of himself, exhibiting a kind of irascible shyness, uneasy and yet rather pompous. Carter may not often have been

38 Surviving Alba letters and later Munthe letters are with John Carter. Some early Munthe letters in M.M.A., Department of Egyptian Art, Carter files.

invited twice by the same hostess; but there were many who were eager to take the risk. Carter might enliven a dull gathering.

Welles Bosworth, the American partner in Carter's somewhat clandestine dealing venture in 1934, wrote enthusiastically to James Henry Breasted about a brief visit Carter made to Paris in May of that year:[39]

> Howard Carter passed through last week on his way to London, and came over for coffee with us, as he had an hour to go from one station to the other. He is in fine form these days and, with his wonderful sense of humor, is a most enjoyable person. Some lady expressed disappointment at his not remembering her, and reminded him of how she had met him in 1924 (or was it 1923?) and he said 'My dear lady, you really can't blame me if I don't remember you. I met just 78,642 people that winter, and showed the tomb to most of them.'

Not the kind of humour that everyone would appreciate.

Warmth in friendship did not come easily to Carter, and there is very little evidence that even the kind of enthusiasm shown by Welles Bosworth was commonly expressed by Carter's acquaintances. To that extent his life was indeed lonely; he could find companionship, but rarely the kind of intimacy which true friendship brings. He may have found it with Percy White, but the signs suggest only that they enjoyed each others' company while they were together, but that little contact was maintained by correspondence. Carter's companionship was that of the club; one that ended after dinner, and a post-dinner chat over a drink. There is no sign of any closer attachment, male or female, throughout his life. Cyril Aldred reported a suggestion by Charles Wilkinson, who knew Carter well at Thebes for many years, that he had a French mistress; but sadly Wilkinson, with the coy restraint of his generation, would not enlarge on what he had hinted at. A rumour from rural Norfolk that Carter had a cottage in North Creake where a French lady kept a welcoming establishment for his occasional visits turned out to be equally disappointing. The cottage, possibly purchased by Carter himself, was occupied by Vernet Carter's widow Audrey. The search for more substantial liaisons has yielded nothing. The one claim for greater consideration is the attachment between himself and Lady Evelyn Herbert, which supposedly blossomed into something more serious during the time when Tutankhamun's tomb was first excavated. The evidence for such an 'affair' is said to be found in the circumstances of the falling-out between Carnarvon and Carter in the spring of 1923, which has already been discussed as being differently based;[40] and also a letter written to Carter by Lady Evelyn on Boxing Day (the day after Christmas Day) 1922. This letter has also been partly quoted

39 in O.I. Director's Office Corr. 1934.
40 See p. 255 above.

in support of the claim that entrance was made into the Burial Chamber of the tomb by Carter and the Carnarvon party shortly after the, tomb was first entered. In view of the alleged amorous implications of the letter, it seems proper to quote it *in extenso*:[41]

Dearest Howard,

I would like to think this letter would reach you on New Year's Day, but alas it won't though it will get to you quicker than if I posted it. My dear I wish you just the very best of *everything*. May you be as happy as you are successful and for many, many years – bless you – you deserve it. By now you are world-renowned and your name dear will be added to the famous men in the annals of history. It is wonderful and I wish you could have flown to England if only for a few hours, for the genuine, universal interest and excitement that your Discovery has created would have thrilled you with pleasure and would have justly rewarded the many years of labour and disappointment that you have had.

Of course one is pestered, morning, noon and night, and I know you are too. There was no place or hour that one was not met by a 'reporter' when we first returned. Pups really has had a lot of work to do and was somewhat fatigued when we came down here Sat.[urday]. However, he revels in it all, and when slightly weary calls me in to tell him again and again of the 'Holy of Holies', which always acts like a magnum of champagne! I can never thank you sufficiently for allowing me to enter its precincts. It was the *Great Moment* of my life. More I cannot say, except that I am panting to return to you.

Bless you. My best love

Yrs truly grateful and affect.

Eve.

That this letter is no more than an effusive expression of thanks and good wishes from a young and affectionate lady, a product of her times – the post-War 1920s – becomes apparent when set beside other letters written to Howard Carter at the same time, and from Highclere Castle. Lady Carnarvon, also on Boxing Day, writes, 'My dear Howard, This line is to send you my love and every blessing in the coming year.' After four pages of news and congratulations, she ends, 'With much love and every good wish for the New Year. Yrs affly [affectionately], Almina Carnarvon.' Someone else, who signs herself Dorothy D., writes on Christmas Day, 'Dearest Howard. This, my Dear, to tell you, how just *wonderful* it all is, and *how How* pleased I am for you.' She ends, '*All the best of* everything to you in the New Year *and all happiness* and my love.' Carter was clearly

---

41 The Christmas letters of 1922 are in M.M.A., Department of Egyptian Art, Carter files. Hoving, *Tutankhamun. The Untold Story*, pp. 107, 222, seems to overestimate the significance of the Evelyn Herbert letter.

very much in favour at Highclere Castle at Christmas 1922. Apart from anything else, he had at last more than fulfilled the hopes of Lord Carnarvon, and for that he deserved everyone's gratitude.

In view of his outstanding success, Carter received little in the way of formal honours. His professional achievement was recognized by his Yale doctorate, and Corresponding Membership of the Royal Academy of History, Madrid. Yet he was denied the Spanish decoration, organized by the Duke of Alba.[42] In 1926 he received a decoration from the King of Egypt, and permission from the Residency in Cairo to wear it. He was also decorated by the King of the Belgians, presumably a late recognition of his courtesy to the Queen of the Belgians (if not of his exasperation with Jean Capart). Its award was attended by an odd intervention by Carter's friend Anton Badrutt, the General Manager of the Winter Palace Hotel. He wrote to Carter on 16 December 1931 expressing his indignation at the delay in his receiving this decoration from the King of the Belgians, and he said that he had written to someone to find out why. It is not clear what reason Badrutt, a Swiss, had for acting in this way, unless he was acting as the honorary consul of Belgium in Luxor at that time. Eventually Carter was informed that on 6 May 1932 the King had conferred on him the decoration of Commandeur de l'ordre de Léopold II. On 20 May he received a letter from Buckingham Palace instructing him that he had restricted permission to wear the insignia of the Order but, in effect, only in Belgium and on occasions elsewhere, including Britain, when Belgium was involved.

He was never honoured by the British monarch, or by a British university, and surprise has often been expressed at this neglect. To take Academe first, it must be said that Carter, having no formal educational background, and displaying in his published work no remarkable command of a scholarly apparatus or outstanding intellectual capacity, was not superficially a candidate for formal academic honours. He had no active supporters in the British Egyptological field (which was remarkably rich in talent in the 1920s), who were so placed as to be able to promote his claims. Newberry, his greatest advocate, had left his chair in Liverpool in 1919, and his successor, T. E. Peet, had no particular reason to put Carter's name forward for an honorary degree. In Oxford, Francis Ll. Griffith may never have considered the matter, being himself unconcerned with worldly honours. Flinders Petrie in University College London would not have put himself out in such a cause. The British Academy in its representation on the Joint Archaeological Committee of Britain, was institutionally a signatory of the statement of support for Carter issued in 1924; but Carter would not have been thought a suitable candidate for Fellowship. In fact, Carter did not fit into any of the categories which commonly take someone

42 Documents concerning his various decorations are with John Carter.

forward, almost inexorably, to academic honours when the circumstances are right.

A similar reason may be adduced for his failure to receive any royal honour in Britain. It is necessary for someone or some institution to put forward a name and a recommendation; each application is considered, and accepted or rejected. There is little doubt that the Earl of Carnarvon would have pressed Carter's case hard, had he lived. The next likely source for action would probably have been the Residency in Cairo. Unfortunately, the problems over the work in the tomb in 1923–4 put Carter in an unfavourable position for recommendation and presumably his name, even if brought up, was passed over or set on one side for future consideration. There were others among his friends and supporters who might have initiated an award, and his name could have been considered from the very top; for it is known that King George V was very interested in the work at Thebes. But without proper promotion nothing normally will happen, and it must be supposed that in the end it was Carter's contrary behaviour that spoilt his chances. It has been suggested that he may have been offered some relatively modest honour, for example, one of the lower classes of the Order of the British Empire, and that in disgust he refused to allow his name to go forward; there is no evidence to support such a suggestion. It nevertheless remains strange that the man who had made such a wonderful discovery and become so fêted and favoured in other ways should have been, as seems certainly to have been the case, passed over for formal honours.

In view of the extraordinary interest taken in the tomb of Tutankhamun since the late 1960s when great exhibitions were organized out of Egypt, coupled with the vast increase in tourism in Egypt one focus of which has been the Cairo Museum with its Tutankhamun galleries, it is surprising to consider the relatively low level of interest shown generally in the 1930s. The spectacular publicity which greeted the original discovery and every important stage of revelation subsequently seemed to have exhausted the public passion for news. Carter himself had in a sense worked the tomb and its treasures out of his system. Illness and the lack of support and encouragement from someone like Alan Gardiner, who rarely passed a day without spending many hours on his Egyptological researches, drained Carter's enthusiasm and sense of purpose. Even if he could not vigorously tackle the writing of his final six-volume report, he might have maintained public interest and his own resolve by giving public lectures. He would certainly have found ready audiences even in Britain which, in this century at least, has never exhibited the kind of enthusiasm found in America for serious presentations. Carter did speak occasionally in the early 1930s, for example to the Institute of Public Hygiene in September 1932 on 'The Contribution of Ancient Egypt to the Progress of the World' – the surviving notes do not suggest an inspiring text – and to an unspecified audience at

the Victoria and Albert Museum in October 1934 on 'Colour'.[43] This
second lecture had the merit of including some personal and original
thoughts on colour in general, and on its use by ancient Egyptian artists;
but the preamble with which he began was poorly judged, at least by later
twentieth-century standards. Carter's arch attempt at a light touch seems
badly pitched:

> I see before me an array of ladies who, from their childhood, have
> studied the pleasurable emotions of attractiveness – the art of agree-
> ment of pattern and style, matching ribbons, and discovering that
> which is most fitted for .both character and dress – in which the
> function of colour is foremost.
>
> In fact, I feel about as impertinent were I to advise a drake upon
> his Spring plumage.

Otherwise, his life apparently fell away into inactivity and loss of interest;
there is very little surviving documentation to support a view that his daily
regime was other than one of unadventurous existence. The progress of
his life, made increasingly burdensome by illness, passed into a steady
decline in his last years, which brought him by early 1939 to a condition
which required a nurse in attendance. At this time his regular, if not
constant, companion was his niece, Phyllis Walker. She was the secretary
of Lady Dawson of Penn,[44] and lived across the Park in Nutford Place
near Marble Arch. She kept a general eye on his condition and on the
attention he received, but there was little that could be done to prevent
the inevitable end. His death certificate gives two causes of death, cardiac
failure and lymphadenoma, the former being the immediate cause, and the
latter the effective cause. Carter's condition would now be described as
malignant lymphoma, or, less technically, Hodgkin's disease. It is marked
by an enlargement of the lymphatic tissues and spleen, and considered to
be a cancerous condition. For Howard Carter it was surely a seriously
debilitating condition, leading to a painful and miserable death. But at
least he died in his own bed at 49 Albert Court; Phyllis was present at
the conclusion of his long struggle, on 2 March 1939.

His burial in Putney Vale Cemetery has been described in the opening
pages of this book. The smallness of the company attending gives some
indication of his circle of friends and relatives. The 'floral tributes', which
were listed by the undertaker, enlarge their numbers, but not substantially:[45] Mr and Mrs Ernest Duveen, Almina, Countess of Carnarvon, Lady
Pinching and Adrienne and John Dunn-Yarker, Bruce and Amy Ingram,
Major and Mrs H. E. Bradley, Mai Mond, Edgar Carter and family (in

43 Notes on both lectures are in the possession of John Carter.
44 Lord Dawson of Penn was Physician in Ordinary to King George V and Queen Mary.
45 The details are in the possession of John Carter, who also has the letter from Carter's
   servants.

Birmingham), Mr and Mrs Maurice Silverston, the Earl of Carnarvon, Mr and Mrs O. Gutekunst, Mrs Emile Mond, Lady Selsdon and family, A. M. Parsons and family, Lady Evelyn Beauchamp, Phyllis Walker, Averil Ingram, and his nurse. The list contains no Egyptologist, although Gerald Wainwright, a former Inspector in the Antiquities Service and something of an outsider in British Egyptological circles, attended in person. His brother William and his nephew Samuel John were also there as family representatives. For the rest, his departure was noted and attended by society friends. It was indeed an unrepresentative and muted farewell to one whose name, Evelyn Herbert had said, 'will be added to the famous men in the annals of history'. There were others who mourned his death, of whom his house servants at Elwat el-Diban provided the most touching tribute. It is addressed to 'Sir Miss Phyllis Walker Nutfield House Nutfield Place Marble Arch London':

> Respectifully we have heard with illness by the death of our Head Dr. H. Carter we and our famillies and all the native of our country and Egypt. ill. I have sarved Dr. H. Carter 42 years pass well. This notice ill us much spacially about us your most obedient servants. Sir Mr. Bartin [Burton] gave us this notice we are ill and uncontent we are write this letter hoping that you Miss shall be well and in a good health and you shall be in the service of the Dr. H. Carter. We hope that you shall be well and good health – we are waiting your notice and about health and All.
> We remain.
> Your most obbedient servants
> Abd-El-Aal Ahmad Sayed and Hosein Ibraheem Sayed
> El-Korna Luxor Upper Egypt. Egypt   19/3/1939

By his will, made in London on 14 July 1931 and without amendment or codicil, Howard Carter left £E150 to Abd el-Aal Ahmed 'if still in my service at my death in appreciation of his many years service.' To his two executors and trustees, Harry Burton and Bruce Ingram, he left £250 each. His house and contents in Thebes he left to the Metropolitan Museum. Everything else went to Phyllis Walker, 'and I strongly recommend to her that she consult my Executors as to the advisability of selling any Egyptian or other antiquities included in this bequest.'

The force of the advice about selling antiquities was soon brought home to Phyllis Walker and the executors when the contents of the flat were examined. Among the antiquities was a small number of pieces which could without question be identified as having come from the tomb of Tutankhamun. Their presence in Carter's possession has been discussed. The problem facing the executors was to decide what to do with them. Taking advice from others, particularly Percy Newberry, the executors removed them from the rest of the estate and decided, with Phyllis Walker's approval, that they should be returned to Egypt and the Cairo Museum. This return might have been managed without too much difficulty but for the outbreak of war, and also for the unhelpful attitude of Rex Engelbach in the Cairo Museum, who had never been on easy terms with Carter. At first it was thought that they could be sent back in the Diplomatic Bag, but the Foreign Office would not countenance the suggestion.[46] The best that Harry Burton could obtain in the way of official co-operation was an undertaking from Sir Miles Lampson, the British High Commissioner in Egypt, that he would help to arrange that if they were imported in the ordinary way, it would be handled without publicity. Sadly, Burton himself died in June 1940, but not before he had made over Carter's house in Thebes to the Metropolitan Museum; its contents were moved into the Metropolitan House for the duration of the war. The house is now used as an Inspector's house by the Antiquities Service.

Phyllis Walker, on advice, wrote to Monsieur Étienne Drioton, who was then the Director-General of the Antiquities Service, on 22 March 1940, making the formal offer of the objects, about which he had already been advised by Harry Burton. Realising the sensitive nature of the matter, he wrote a graceful reply on 30 April.[47] He praised Miss Walker's generosity, and expressed his understanding that the gift should not be held against the memory of her uncle, and assured her that there would be no adverse press campaign. He had consulted His Majesty King Farouk who had spontaneously offered to act as the intermediary in the transfer to the Egyptian Museum. 'Nobody will dare to make inappropriate insinuations in the case of a matter in which His Majesty is himself interested.' He finally suggested that the objects be handed over under seal (a very Egyptian touch) to the Egyptian Consulate in London, who would be instructed to pass them on to the King. The objects were then sent to the Egyptian Consulate (or Embassy) in London, and there they remained until the end of the Second World War. Finally, on 12 October 1946, Phyllis Walker could report to Newberry that the 'objects', as she called them discreetly, had been returned at last by air to Egypt and the King.[48] In due course they were passed to the Cairo Museum as a presentation by the King. In concluding this ostensibly embarrassing episode, attention may be drawn to a remark by Alan Gardiner to Newberry in a postscript to a letter of 21 March 1945:[49]

Oh yes, of course I knew everything about the handing over of the objects from the tomb to the Egyptian Embassy. I had counselled this all along to Carter himself.

46 Letters on the negotiations are in the possession of John Carter.
47 A copy of Drioton's letter is filed with one from Phyllis Walker to Newberry of 15 May 1940, G.I. Newberry Corr. 44/74.
48 G.I. Newberry Corr. 44/81.
49 G.I. Newberry Corr. 49/10.

The implication of this remark surely is that Carter, in letting Gardiner see the objects, had expressed his own disquiet at having them in his possession – possibly because they had come from Carnarvon's collection. He might, perhaps, have done something about them if he could have talked the matter over with Engelbach. He would have found that difficult to do without bringing discredit on himself or on the person who had taken them in the first place. Ultimately, it must be presumed, to do anything with them became too difficult, and the problem was left for his executors to deal with.

The bulk of Carter's professional records, including those left by him in Egypt, were eventually presented to the Griffith Institute in Oxford by Phyllis Walker in 1945. There the Carter papers form an important research archive, much consulted by scholars, and used as the basis for a series of monographs on the material from Tutankhamun's tomb. But there is much more in the archives than Tutankhamun records. They contain the remarkable Deir el-Bahri drawings, which established Carter's reputation as a draughtsman-artist, and the even finer drawings of the Opet Festival scenes in the Luxor Temple, executed for Alan Gardiner in the fallow years of the Great War; also most of the notes and other documents which make up the archaeological record of Carter's work in Thebes and in the Delta, when he was Chief Inspector in the early years of the century, and when he first worked for the Earl of Carnarvon. These last show the beginnings of a career as an excavator in which the going was somewhat hesitant, but was already informed with excellent observation and an instinct for proper practice in the conducting of field work. The overwhelming Tutankhamun documentation may greatly exceed the rest in bulk and quality, but it surely represents the final harvest of the ploughing and sowing that had filled the first thirty years of Howard Carter's career in Egypt. The whole formed the path to Tutankhamun, and the success of a life devoted to Egypt and archaeology; but it was in the end a life of sad success.

APPENDIX I

Letter of 9 January from Monsieur A. Jouveau to Monsieur Gaston Maspero, concerning the fracas at Saqqara on 8 January 1905.
This text is taken from Howard Carter's own transcription now in the Griffith Institute, Oxford, Carter Papers V 108.

J'ai l'honneur de porter à votre connaissance les faites suivants:

Hier nous arrivions aux Pyramides de Sakkareh, 14 personnes, dont deux dames et deux enfants.

Nous nous faisions délivrer des tickets pour visiter le Sérapéum, à l'entrée de ce monument nous constations que sans lumière il était impossible d'y pénétrer: les bédouins attachés au Service des Antiquités nous déclarant qu'ils n'avaient pas de bougies à nous fournir, nous demandâmes le remboursement du prix de chaque ticket, Le surveillant en Chef, un Effendi, nous dit qu'il devait en référer à son Chef Mr. Ward Carter, Inspecteur en Chef, (Anglais) qui se trouvait non loin de là. Dans l'attente la dispute s'aggrava et une vingtaine de bédouins se trouvaient réunis dans la maison de Mariette. L'inspecteur Anglais arriva suivi d'une quinzaine de bédouins munis de nabouts.

Nos révendications lui furent expliquées en Anglais; il nous répondit par un refus catégorique. Nous déclarâmes alors que nous quitterions pas la terrasse, sans avoir été remboursés.

Cet inspecteur donna l'ordre immediatement à son subordonné, en Anglais (de chasser ces sales Français et de nous frapper), les bédouins ne saissant pas bien cet ordre il leur répéta en Arabe. De suite la mélée devint générale. Les dames et les enfants furent entraînés par deux des nôtres et nous demeurions sept à nous défendre, dépourvus de tout objet, tandis qu'une quarantaine d'individus nous tombaient dessus à coup de nabout.

Un quartier de pierre me fendait la tête et je tombai baigné dans mong sang.

Peu après, Mr Georges Fabre, comptable à la Compagnie du Gaz, tombait à son tour, le front ouvert d'un coup de nabout.

Mr Baudry, décorateur chez le Prince Halim Pacha Helmy, était renversé d'un coup de nabout sur le dos. Et les autres plus ou moins contusionnés.

Mis hors de l'enceinte nous fûmes poursuivis à coup de pierres, et ce fut à grand peine que nous regagnâmes Bedrechein en pleine nuit.

Au carocol nous fûmes dresser procès verbal, un agent nous accompagna au Caire, où procès verbal fut dressé au caracol de la gare. Nous fûmes conduits au Gouvernorat où 1 medecin de service nous donna les premiers soins.

A noter qu'aucun agent du police ne se trouvait dans les parages de l'incident.

Je vous laisse le soin, Monsieur le Directeur Général, de tirer la conclusion d'un tel acte commandé par un fonctionnaire Anglais.

Veuillez agréer, Monsieur le Directeur Général l'assurance de ma parfaite considération.

A. Jouveau
Chef comptable
de la Compagnie du Gaz
Au Caire

APPENDIX II

The text of the Earl of Carnavon's permit to excavate in the Valley of the Kings.

It is taken from Howard Carter's dossier of documents dealing with the troubles between himself and the Egyptian Government during the winter of 1923–24, referred to as the Statement in this volume. The copy used is in the Griffith Institute, Oxford, Carter Papers VI 13.

Ministry of Public Works
Antiquities Service

AUTHORIZATION TO EXCAVATE

I, the undersigned, Director-General of the Antiquities Service, acting in virtue of the powers delegated to me, hereby authorize the Right Honourable Earl of Carnarvon, residing at Highclere Castle, to carry out scientific excavations in the Valley of the Kings, on lands belonging to the State, free, unbuilt upon, uncultivated, not included within the Military Zone, nor comprising any cemeteries, quarries, etc., and, in general, not devoted to any public use, and this on the following conditions:-

1. The work of excavation shall be carried out at the expense, risk and peril of the Earl of Carnarvon by Mr. Howard Carter; the latter should be constantly present during excavation.

2. Work shall be executed under the control of the Antiquities Service, who shall have the right not only to supervise the work, but also to alter the manner of the execution if they so deem proper for the success of the undertaking.

3. If a tomb, or any other monument, happens to be discovered, the Permitted or his representative is bound to give notice at once to the Chief Inspector of Upper Egypt, at Luxor.

4. To the Permittee himself shall be reserved the privilege of opening the tomb or monument discovered, and of being the first to enter therein.

5. At the moment of the opening the Chief Inspector of the Antiquities

Service shall, if he considers necessary, place on the spot the number of guardians he shall deem to be required.

6. The Permittee, or his representative, after examining the said tomb or monument, and having taken such notes as he may judge necessary, shall, if so desired, hand it over to the Inspector of Antiquities Service or to any other agent to be appointed by the said Service.

7. The Permittee, or his representative, is bound to draw up forthwith a 'Procès-verbal' showing the particularities observed at the moment of the opening and the place occupied by each object, subjoining thereto as many photographs and drawings as possible.

8. Mummies of the Kings, of Princes, and of High Priests, together with their coffins and sarcophagi, shall remain the property of the Antiquities Service.

9. Tombs which are discovered intact, together with all objects they may contain, shall be handed over to the Museum whole and without division.

10. In the case of tombs which have already been searched, the Antiquities Service shall, over and above the mummies and sarcophagi intended in Article 8, reserve for themselves all objects of capital importance from the point of view of history and archaeology, and shall share the remainder with the Permittee.

As it is probable that the majority of such tombs as may be discovered will fall within the category of the present article, it is agreed that the Permittee's share will sufficiently recompense him for the pains and labour of the undertaking.

11. Once the excavations are completed, the Permittee is bound to leave the site of his operations in a satisfactory condition of levelling.

12. The Permittee further engages:–

A. Not to take squeezes of coloured monuments by means of wet paper.

B. To deposit at the Museum and, if possible, at the Sultanian Library copies of such books, memoirs, pamphlets, or collections of engravings as may be published by him on the objects discovered in the course of his excavations.

C. To deliver to the Antiquities Service, within two years from the day on which the works have been completed: (1) a sketch or, if necessary in the opinion of the Service, a plan of the field of excavations, ready for publication in the Annals of the Museum; (2) a summary list referring to the plan and showing the position of the objects forming a whole, such as sarchophagi, boats, funerary statues, glassware, or amulets, etc., belonging to the same sarcophagus.

13. Any infraction, on the part of the Permittee or his agents, of the conditions above stated shall entail the cancellation of the present authorization, without any notice being given or any formality being taken.

In such case the Antiquities Service, acting departmentally, shall at once stop all work and shall take such steps as it may deem necessary in its own interests and for the safe-guarding of the monuments or objects already discovered at the moment of the stoppage of the excavations, and this without the Permittee, or any agent of his, having any right to claim any indemnity or compensation whatsoever or for any reason.

The present authorization holds good for one year, to run from April 18th, 1915, subject to renewal at the discretion of the Service.

Done, in duplicate, at Cairo,
April 18th, 1915.
Acting Director-General Antiquities Service,
Signed: Daressy.

Seen and accepted the present authorization for the Earl of Carnarvon.
Signed: Howard Carter.

APPENDIX III

The Earl of Carnvarvon's account of the opening of Tutankhamun's tomb.
This fragment, unsigned and undated, is preserved in the Metropolitan Museum of Art, Department of Egyptian Art, Carter files.

At last this passage was cleared. We again reached a sealed door or wall bearing the same seals as in the case of the former one. We wondered if we should find another staircase, probably blocked behind this wall, or whether we should get into a chamber. I asked Mr. Carter to take out a few stones and have a look in. After a few minutes this was done. He pushed his head partly into the aperture. With the help of a candle, he could dimly discern what was inside. A long silence followed, until I said, I fear in somewhat trembling tones, 'Well, what is it!' 'There are some marvellous objects here', was the welcome reply.

Having given up my place to my daughter, I myself went to the hole, and I could with difficulty restrain my excitement. At the first sight, with the inadequate light, all that one could see was what appeared to be gold bars. On getting a little more accustomed to the light, it became apparent that there were colossal gilt couches with extraordinary heads, boxes here and boxes there. We enlarged the hole and Mr. Carter managed to scramble in – the chamber is sunk two feet below the bottom passage – and then, as he moved around with a candle, we knew we had found something absolutely unique and unprecedented.

Even with the poor light of the candle one could see a marvellous collection of furniture and other objects in the chamber. There were two life-sized statues of the king, beds, chariots, boxes of all sizes and shapes – some with every sort of inlay whilst others were painted – walking sticks, marvellous alabaster vases, and so on. After slightly enlarging the hole we went in, and this time we realized in a fuller degree the extent of the discovery, for we had managed to tap the electric light from the tomb above, which gave us far better illumination for our examination.

416

The King's Throne

One of the finest objects is the chair or throne of the King. It is in wood. The back panel is of surpassing beauty, and portrays the King and his Queen protected by Aton rays. All the figures, &c., in this scene are built up by means of semi-precious carved stones, inlaid into wood. The delicacy and grace of this work of art are indescribable, and it is, indeed, fortunate that we have struck a period when Egyptian art reached one of its culminating points. I kept on wondering why we had found no coffins; nothing of the shape of one was visible. A few minutes later, beneath one of the beds of state, we came on a small opening, giving into another chamber. There the confusion was beyond conception. It was impossible to enter, as the room was packed with chairs, beds, boxes, statuettes, alabasters, and every other conceivable object to the height of five feet. As far as could be seen, however, no coffin had been placed there.

But on examining the first chamber again we discovered, between the two life-sized statues of the King, a walled-up portion of the northern end of the first chamber. This was also covered with seals, but on the level of the floor, in the centre of this wall, there were traces of a very small break having been made, large enough to admit a small man. This had been subsequently resealed, probably by Rameside inspectors.

Lastly, the absence of mummies was explained. There is little doubt that behind this wall there exists a chamber or chambers, and in one of these probably reposes, in his coffins and sarcophagus, the body of King Tutankhamen.

APPENDIX IV

THE *TIMES* AGREEMENT

MEMORANDUM OF AGREEMENT made the ninth day of January One thousand nine hundred and twenty-three *BETWEEN* THE RIGHT HONOURABLE GEORGE EDWARD STANHOPE MOLYNEUX HERBERT EARL OF CARNARVON (hereafter referred to as 'the Earl') of the one part and THE TIMES PUBLISHING COMPANY LIMITED (hereinafter referred to as 'the Times') of the other part WHEREAS the Earl is now conducting exploration work in the Valley of the Tombs of the Kings Luxor Egypt and has made interesting investigations which may lead to the discovery of the tomb of Tutankhamen AND WHEREAS the Earl has agreed to appoint the Times sole agents for the sale throughout the World to newspapers magazines and other publications of news articles interviews and the photographs (other than cinematograph and coloured photographs) relating thereto on the terms and conditions hereinafter contained NOW THESE PRESENTS WITNESS AND IT IS HEREBY AGREED by and between the parties hereto as follows:–

1. The Earl hereby appoints the Times as sole agents for the sale throughout the world to newspapers magazines and other publications of all news articles interviews and photographs (other than cinematograph and coloured photographs both of which are excluded from this Agreement) relating to the present and future exploration work conducted by the Earl and his agents in the Valley of the Tombs of the Kings Luxor Egypt so far as they relate to the excavation of the several chambers already opened and yet to be opened of the tomb of Tutankhamen and the Earl hereby agrees that neither he nor his staff nor any persons authorised by him or them will knowingly communicate or permit to be communicated any such news articles interviews or photographs relating to any such exploration work as aforesaid to any person or persons company or companies other than the Times and the special representative of the Times to be attached to the staff of the Earl except as hereinafter provided and further that neither the Earl nor his agents will authorise or permit any personal friends acquaintances or other persons whatsoever to be present at any such exploration work or to inspect any of the results thereof unless such persons

shall (where it is possible to obtain a pledge) first pledge themselves to grant no interviews to and to make no communication and give no information whatsoever as to what such persons shall have seen or heard whether to representatives of the Press in any part of the world or to any other persons whatsoever and the Earl and his agents shall take all such steps such as shall be reasonably possible to prevent any leakage of news or photographs articles or interviews and to give to the Times the full benefit of this Agreement.

2. The Times shall place at the disposal of the Earl the services of one or more members of the staff of the Times as the Times shall think fit (to be previously approved by the Earl) but such member or members of the Times staff (hereinafter referred to as 'the Times representative') shall be attached to the Earl's party and be subject to his directions and control and if arrangements can be made shall accompany the Earl's party from England to Egypt and shall be deemed to be a permanent member of the Earl's staff but unless otherwise requested by the Earl he shall confine himself entirely to the newspaper publicity and the Times shall pay the salary of the Times representative and all expenses connected with his journey and his work it being the intention that no expense incurred by or through the Times representative shall fall upon the Earl. The whole of the photographs other than cinematograph or coloured photographs which may be taken by or on behalf of the Earl Mr Howard Carter his agent Dr Allen Gardner or by any other member of the staff of the Earl or anyone duly authorised by him or them shall be supplied to the Times representative and the Times representative shall be supplied by Mr Howard Carter or any other person authorised by him or by the Earl in Egypt as soon as possible after any exploration or discoveries with all material which the Times representative may think desirable or necessary for publication and which the Earl can reasonably give including all news of discoveries special articles interviews in addition to photographs for the purpose of the same being forthwith transmitted by the Times representative to the Times in London either by telegraph or by mail at the sole discretion of the Times representative and while the material of any such news interviews and special articles shall be approved by Mr Howard Carter as agent for the Earl or by any other person authorised by him the Times representative shall be solely responsible for the language or actual wording of the message or messages by which that material shall be conveyed to the Times. The Times undertakes to place all such news articles interviews and photographs that it may receive from the Times representative as aforesaid at the disposal of the Press of the world that is to say:–

(a) All other London newspapers (except that in the case of evening newspapers only after publication in the morning newspapers)

(b) The British Provincial newspapers (including Scotland Ireland The Channel Isles and the Isle of Man) through the Press Association or otherwise

(c) The newspapers of the United States and Canada

(d) Newspapers of the British Dominions

(e) Newspapers of Continental Europe and

(f) Newspapers of Egypt

(g) And Newspapers published in all other parts of the world,

on terms and conditions hereinafter specified and so as to insure simultaneous publication so far as possible (except in the case of photographs) and that the Times shall obtain no preference over any other newspapers taking the service in time for publication or otherwise except as hereinafter mentioned.

3. The Times shall fix the price which shall be charged to any such newspapers magazines and other publications for the sale to them of all such news articles interviews and photographs as aforesaid and the Times shall have the entire conduct of all the negotiations with regard to such sale and the Times shall be at liberty to make such sale on the best possible terms and to impose any reasonable conditions on any such newspapers magazines and other publications who shall take any such news articles interviews and photographs as the Times may think proper and necessary but so that no preference shall be given to any particular newspapers magazines or other publications over any other such newspapers magazines and other publications but so far as possible the same terms and conditions shall apply to all as hereinafter mentioned All newspapers magazines and other publications throughout the world who are prepared to take the news articles interviews and photographs upon the terms and conditions imposed by the Times shall have placed at their disposal all the available news articles interviews and photographs which shall be received by the Times save and except newspapers and magazines and other publications which shall be published in Great Britain and Ireland the Channel Islands and the Isle of Man. But as regards all such newspapers magazines and other publications published in Great Britain Ireland the Channel Islands and the Isle of Man in consideration of the heavy expenses and liabilities which the Times is undertaking under these presents the Times shall not be bound to offer more than half of any such news messages special articles or interviews nor more than 50% of all photographs provided nevertheless and the Times hereby agrees that so far as it is reasonably possible the portion of all such news messages special articles or interviews which the Times shall supply to newspapers magazines and other publications in Great Britain Ireland the Channel Islands or the Isle of Man shall contain all essential information but as to what is the essential information in any such news messages special

articles or interviews the Times shall be the sole judge the Earl being satisfied that the Times will act with the utmost fairness towards the whole of the press of the country and as regards the Egyptian native newspapers the Times shall supply all available material news articles interviews and photographs to such Egyptian native newspapers who may desire to take and publish the same free of all charge including Egyptian telegraph fees where necessary.

4. All news matter and photographs which shall be published by the Times or any other newspaper magazines or other publications shall be published together with the following Acknowledgment 'The Times World Copyright by arrangement with the Earl of Carnarvon.'

5. The copyright in all such news interviews and special articles and photographs which shall be supplied to the Times or the Times representative under the terms of this Agreement shall belong to the Times and the Earl will at the expense of the Times do or procure to be done all such other acts matters and things as may be necessary for effectually vesting in the Times all such copyright save and except that the Earl reserves all film rights coloured photography rights books rights or lecture rights but the Earl and his agents and persons authorised by him shall not release for any purpose any film which may be taken and shall not publish or permit any of his agents to publish a book and shall not himself lecture or authorise any of his agents or other persons to engage in any lecture relating to any matters the subject of this agreement before certain specified dates but in no event later than two months after supplying the subject matter thereof to the Times and all films when taken shall be forthwith deposited in some bank or other safe institution to be mutually agreed upon by the parties hereto and shall remain there pending the decision by agreement between the parties hereto as to the date for the release of such film whether for private or public exhibition but in no event later than two months unless by consent of the Earl.

6. In consideration of the appointment of the Times by the Earl as his sole agents for the sale throughout the world to newspapers magazines and other publications of all such news special articles interviews and photographs as aforesaid the Times shall pay to the Earl the sum of Five thousand pounds on the signing of this agreement and shall further pay to the Earl Seventy-five per cent of the net profits over and above the said sum of Five thousand pounds which the Times may receive from the sale of the said news interviews special articles and photographs for publication in all other newspapers magazines and other publications throughout the world but in arriving at such net profits no charge shall be debited to the Times for the publication in the Times newspaper the weekly edition of the Times or any other newspaper or publication belonging to the Times of any such news special articles interviews or photographs and the Times shall be entitled to charge all expenses of every kind which shall be

incurred by the Times in connection with the obtaining by the Times of the said material and the transmission and sale thereof to other newspapers magazines and publications including the remuneration paid to and the expenses of the Times representative and all cable and other fees and expenses properly incurred in carrying this agreement into effect and the net sum only which shall remain after deducting all such expenses and after deducting the said sum of Five thousand pounds hereinbefore agreed to be paid by the Times to the Earl on the signing of these presents shall be paid to the Earl as soon as may be after such net profits (if any) shall be ascertained and if there shall be any dispute between the parties hereto as to the amount of such net profits (if any) the certificate of the auditor or auditors for the time being of the Times shall be conclusive as to the amount of such net profits. In the event of the net profits which shall be received by the Times from the sale to such other newspapers magazines or publications as aforesaid not amounting to the said sum of Five thousand pounds paid by the Times to the Earl on the signing of this Agreement then the Times shall be entitled to keep all such profits as it shall have received but shall not in any event be entitled to claim any refund from the Earl of any part of the said sum of Five thousand pounds paid to the Earl on the signing of these presents.

7. Notwithstanding anything herein contained the Earl shall have the right at all future times to make use of any of the Times articles published on the subject matter of this Agreement or of any of the photographs supplied to them for the purpose of any lecture film caption or any book or books which he may hereafter deliver write publish produce or cause or authorise to be delivered written published or produced.

8. The Times shall have no authority or control relating to the present and future excavation work hereinbefore referred to which shall be carried out solely under the direction of and at the time when the Earl and his representative or representatives shall decide.

9. While the Earl has confidence in the result of his discoveries and believes them to have an important bearing on the history of Egypt it is understood and agreed by the Times that he is not to be held responsible for any failure or disappointment in the result of his investigation and that he makes no warranty or guarantee that his anticipations will be fulfilled and that in no circumstances is the Earl liable or to be liable to refund the money paid or payable hereunder.

10. If any dispute shall arise between the parties hereto concerning any matter arising under or in respect of this Agreement or the construction thereof the same shall be referred to arbitration pursuant to the provisions of the Arbitration Act 1889.

IN WITNESS WHEREOF the Earl of Carnarvon and William Lints Smith Manager of the Times Publishing Company Limited have hereunto set their hands the day and year first above written.

SOURCES AND BIBLIOGRAPHY

1 ABBREVIATIONS

A.J.S.L.L.	*American Journal of Semitic Languages and Literature* (Chicago)
A.S.A.E.	*Annales du Service des Antiquités de l'Égypte* (Cairo)
B.M.M.A.	*Bulletin of the Metropolitan Museum of Art* (New York)
E.E.F.	Egypt Exploration Fund
E.E.S.	Egypt Exploration Society
E.E.F. Arch. Rep.	*Egypt Exploration Fund. Archaeological Reports* (London)
G.I.	Griffith Institute, Ashmolean Museum, Oxford
J.A.R.C.E.	*Journal of the American Research Center in Egypt* (New York)
J.E.A.	*Journal of Egyptian Archaeology* (London)
J.S.S.E.A.	*Journal of the Society for the Study of Egyptian Antiquities* (Toronto)
K.M.T	*K.M.T. A modern journal of Ancient Egypt* (San Francisco)
M.M.A.	Metropolitan Museum of Art
O.I.	Oriental Institute, the University of Chicago
P.S.B.A	*Proceedings of the Society of Biblical Archaeology* (London)
Rev. d'Eg.	*Revue d'Égyptologie* (Paris)

2 MANUSCRIPT SOURCES

The principal collection of original sources used in this volume is housed in the Griffith Institute in the Ashmolean Museum, Oxford, comprising the bulk of surviving Carter papers dealing with his excavations, including Tutankhamun (with a set of the Harry Burton photographs), and much documentary material associated with his early career: cited as G. I. Carter Papers. The Newberry Papers contain the large collection of letters to Newberry which cover the whole of Carter's working life (G. I. Newberry Corr.). Important material is also to be found in the Gardiner Papers (G. I. Gardiner Corr.), and in the archive of F. Ll. Griffith. The original drawings of the Deir el-Bahri temple of Hatshepsut are in the Carter Papers, and his Luxor Temple drawings are in the Gardiner Papers.

Substantial documentary material mostly from the Tutankhamun years, and much representing the residue of papers from Carter's Theban house, is in the Metropolitan Museum of Art, New York; referred to as M. M. A. Department of Egyptian Art, Carter files. The Department of Egyptian Art also contains a transcript of the Emma Andrews diary, covering the annual visits she made to Egypt with Theodore Davis on his *dahabiya Bedawin* from 1899 to 1912.

The letters and documents surviving from Carter's London flat are in the possession of John Carter, a grandson of Howard Carter's brother Edgar. This collec-

423

tion contains interesting early letters, a set of the late sketches, and most of the surviving personal docummentation for Carter's last years.

For Carter's earliest years of work in Egypt, there is a useful body of material in the archives of the Egypt Exploration Society. Letters from this time of working with Naville are preserved in the Bibliothèque publique et universitaire of the city of Geneva.

A group of letters from and to members of the Amherst family, dealing mostly with Carter's years as Chief Inspector, are in the possession of Terry J. Eva (cited as The Amherst Papers, T. J. Eva Egyptian Collection). Some of Lady Amherst's (earlier Lady William Cecil) journals, including those covering her archaeological work at Aswan, are in the archive of the Biltmore Estate, at Biltmore House, Ashville, North Carolina. Two volumes of Alicia Amherst's journal of the Amherst family Nile tour of 1894–5 are in the possession of Mrs Stanley Chattey.

Parts of the journal of Mervyn Herbert, half-brother of the 5th Earl of Carnarvon, are kept in the library of the Middle East Centre in St Antony's College, Oxford. Minnie Burton's diary covering the years of the excavation of the tomb of Tutankhamun, up to 1926, are in the possession of Mrs Rosalind Berwald. The diaries of Lindsley Hall are in the archives of the Oregon Historical Society, Portland, Oregon.

The family letters and other papers of Arthur Cruttenden Mace, especially important for the first two years of the Tutankhamun excavation, are in the possession of Mrs Margaret Orr, Mace's daughter. His professional papers are in the Department of Egyptian Art, the Metropolitan Museum; some papers are in the Carter archive in the Griffith Institute.

Very considerable papers covering the relations between Carter and James Henry Breasted are housed in the archives of the Oriental Institute of the University of Chicago and are quoted Courtesy of the Oriental Institute. Correspondence on Carter's agency dealings with the Cleveland Museum of Art and the Detroit Institute of Arts are to be found in the archives of these two institutions.

Letters from a variety of correspondents on Carter matters are in the Central Archive of the British Museum, and in the Departments of Egyptian Antiquities, and Western Asiatic Antiquities (formerly together forming the Department of Egyptian and Assyrian Antiquities). Private letters from Sir Alan Gardiner to his wife and daughter are in the possession of Margaret Gardiner.

At Swaffham, Norfolk, there is some photographic and other material in the Swaffham Museum, and also with Mr Benjamin Ripper, a grandson of Robert Carter, a brother of Howard Carter's father, Samuel John Carter.

3 BIBLIOGRAPHY

Note: Comprehensive bibliographies on the Valley of the Kings and on the excavation, contents and subsequent studies of the tomb of Tutankhamun can be found in C. N. Reeves, *The Valley of the Kings*, and (as N. Reeves) *The Complete Tutankhamun;* both listed below.

Aldred, Cyril, *Jewels of the Pharaohs* (London, 1971).
Aldred, Cyril, *Akhenaten and Nefertiti* (London, 1973).
Aldred, Cyril, *Akhenaten, King of Egypt* (London, 1988).
Amherst, Margaret, Lady, of Hackney, *A Sketch of Egyptian History, from the earliest times to the present day* (London, 1904).
Anson, Lady Clodagh, *Victorian Days* (2nd ed., London, 1957).
Baines, John and Jaromir Malek, *Atlas of Ancient Egypt* (Oxford, 1984).
Bateman, Donald, *Berkeley Moynihan, Surgeon* (London, 1940).

Bell, Martha, 'An armchair excavation of KV 55', in *J.A.R.C.E.* 27 (New York, 1990), pp. 97–137.

Belzoni, Giovanni-Battista, *Narrative of the Operations and Recent Discoveries within the Pyramids, Temples, Tombs and Excavations in Egypt and Nubia; and of a Journey to the Coast of the Red Sea, in search of the ancient Berenice; and another to the Oasis of Jupiter Ammon*, 2 vols (London, 1820).

Bissing, Friederich W., Freiherr von, *Ein thebanischer Grabfund aus dem Anfang des neuen Reichs* (Berlin, 1900).

Blackman, Aylward, M., *The Rock Tombs of Meir*, 6 vols (London, 1914–53).

Bouriant, Urbain, Georges Legrain and Gustave Jéquier, *Monuments pour servir à l'étude du culte d'Atounou en Égypte*, I, *Les tombes de Khouitatonou* (Cairo, 1903).

Breasted, Charles, *Pioneer of the Past. The Story of James H. Breasted* (London, 1948).

The Brooklyn Museum, *Egyptian Sculpture of the Late Period 700 B.C. to A.D. 100* (New York, 1960).

Brunton, Guy, 'Howard Carter', in *A.S.A.E.* 39 (Cairo, 1939), pp. 49–53.

Budge, Ernest A. W., *By Nile and Tigris*, 2 vols (London, 1920).

Budge, Ernest A. W., *Tutankhamen, Amenism, Atenism and Egyptian Monotheism* (London, 1923).

Burlington Fine Arts Club, *Catalogue of an Exhibition of Ancient Egyptian Art* (London, 1921).

Butters, David, *In the Pedlar's Foosteps* (North Walsham, 1990).

Buttles, Janet, *The Queens of Egypt* (London, 1908).

Caminos, Ricardo A. and Henry G. Fischer, *Ancient Egyptian Epigraphy and Palaeography* (New York, 1976).

Capart, Jean, *The Tomb of Tutankhamen* (London, 1923).

Carnarvon, the Earl of and Howard Carter, *Five Years' Explorations at Thebes. A record of work done 1907–1911* (Oxford, 1912).

Carter, Howard, 'Report on a tomb-pit opened on the 26th January 1901, in the valley of the tombs of the kings between no. 4 and no. 28', in *A.S.A.E.* 2 (Cairo, 1901), pp. 144–5.

Carter, Howard, 'Report on the work done at the Ramesseum during the years 1900–1901', in *A.S.A.E.* 2 (Cairo, 1901), pp. 193–5.

Carter, Howard, 'Report upon the tomb of Sen-nefer found at Biban el-Molouk near that of Thotmes III, no 34', in *A.S.A.E.* 2 (Cairo, 1901), pp. 196–200.

Carter, Howard, 'Report on the tomb of Mentuhotep 1st at Deir el-Bahari, known as Bab el-Hoçan', in *A.S.A.E.* 2 (Cairo, 1901), pp. 201–5.

Carter, Howard, 'Report on the robbery of the tomb of Amenothes II, Biban el Moluk', in *A.S.A.E.* 3 (Cairo, 1902), pp. 115–21.

Carter, Howard, 'Report on general work done in the southern inspectorate', in *A.S.A.E.* 4 (Cairo, 1903), pp. 43–50.

Carter, Howard, 'Report of work done in Upper Egypt (1902–1903)', in *A.S.A.E.* 4 (Cairo, 1903), pp. 171–80.

Carter, Howard, *Six Portraits of the Thothmes Family* (possibly London, 1907–1909).

Carter, Howard, 'Report on the tomb of Zeser-ka-ra Amenhotep I, discovered by the Earl of Carnarvon in 1914', in *J.E.A.* 3 (London, 1917), pp. 147–54.

Carter, Howard, 'A tomb prepared for Queen Hatshepsuit and other recent discoveries at Thebes', in *J.E.A.* 4 (London, 1917), pp. 107–18.

Carter, Howard, 'A tomb prepared for Queen Hatshepsuit discovered by the Earl of Carnarvon (October, 1916)', in *A.S.A.E.* 16 (Cairo, 1917), pp. 179–82.

Carter, Howard, 'An ostracon depicting a red jungle-fowl (the earliest known drawing of the domestic cock)', in *J.E.A.* 9 (London, 1923), pp. 1–4.

Carter, Howard, *The Tomb of Tut.ankh.Amen. Statement with Documents, as to the Events which occurred in Egypt in the Winter of 1923–24, leading to the ultimate break with the Egyptian Government* (London, 1924, 'For private circulation only').

Carter, Howard and Alan H. Gardiner, 'The tomb of Ramesses IV and the Turin plan of a royal tomb', in *J.E.A.* 4 (London, 1917), pp. 130–58.

Carter, Howard and Georges Legrain, 'Report of work done in Upper Egypt (1903–1904)', in *A.S.A.E.* 6 (Cairo, 1905), pp. 112–29.

Carter, Howard and Arthur C. Mace, *The Tomb of Tut.ankh.Amen*, 3 vols (London, 1923–33).

Carter, Howard and Percy E. Newberry, *The Tomb of Thoutmôsis IV* (London, 1904).

Carter, Howard and Percy E. Newberry, *The Tomb of Thoutmosis IV. Catalogue générale des antiquités égyptiennes du Musée du Caire nos. 46001–46529* (London, 1904).

Cecil, Lady William, 'Report on the work done at Aswan', in *A.S.A.E.* 4 (Cairo, 1903), pp. 51–73.

Cecil, Lady William, 'Report of work done at Aswan during the first months of 1904 by Lady William Cecil', in *A.S.A.E.* 6 (Cairo, 1905), pp. 273–83.

Davies, Nina M. and Alan H. Gardiner, *Tutankhamun's Painted Box* (Oxford, 1962).

Davies, Norman de G., *The Rock Tombs of el Amarna*, 6 vols, (London, 1903–8).

Davis, Theodore and others, *The Tomb of Hâtshopsîtû* (London, 1906).

Davis, Theodore and others, *The Tomb of Iouiya and Touiyou* (London, 1907).

Davis, Theodore and others, *The Tomb of Queen Tîyi* (London, 1910).

Davis, Theodore and others, *The Tombs of Harmhabi and Toutânkhamanou* (London, 1912).

Dawson, Warren R. and Eric P. Uphill, *Who Was Who in Egyptology* (2nd ed., London, 1972).

De Meulenaere, Herman and Pierre MacKay, *Mendes*, II (Warminster, 1976).

Desroches-Noblecourt, Christiane, *Tutankhamen. Life and Death of a Pharaoh* (London, 1963).

Drower, Margaret S., *Flinders Petrie. A Life in Archaeology* (London, 1985).

Edgar, Campbell, C., 'The Treasure of Toukh el-Qarmous', in *Le Musée Égyptien*, II (Cairo, 1907), pp. 49–52.

Edwards, Iorwerth, E. S., *Treasures of Tutankhamun* Exhibition Catalogue (London, 1972).

Edwards, Iorwerth, E. S., *The Pyramids of Egypt* (rev. ed., Harmondsworth, 1985).

Engelbach, Reginald (Rex), *A Supplement to the Topographical Catalogue of the Private Tombs of Thebes (Nos. 253 to 334). With some notes on the Necropolis from 1913 to 1924* (Cairo, 1924).

Evelyn-White, Hugh G., *The Sayings of Jesus from Oxyrhynchus* (Cambridge, 1920).

Gardiner, Alan H., 'Three engraved plaques in the collection of the Earl of Carnarvon', in *J.E.A.* 3 (1916), pp. 73–5.

Gardiner, Alan H., 'The Defeat of the Hyksos by Kamôse: the Carnarvon Tablet, no. 1', in *J.E.A.* 3 (London, 1916), pp. 95–110.

Gardiner, Alan H. 'A stela of the early Eighteenth Dynasty from Thebes', in *J.E.A.* 3 (London, 1916), p. 256.

Gardiner, Alan H., 'The tomb of a much-travelled Theban official', in *J.E.A.* 4 (London, 1917), pp. 28–38.

Gardiner, Alan H, and Arthur E. P. B. Weigall, *A Topographical Catalogue of the Private Tombs at Thebes* (London, 1913).

Gardiner, Alan H., *My Working Years* (privately published, 1963).

Gardiner, Margaret, *A Scatter of Memories* (London, 1988).

Habachi, Labib, *The Second Stela of Kamose, and his struggle against the Hyksos ruler and his capital* (Glückstadt, 1972).

Harris, James E. and Edward F. Wente, *An X-ray Atlas of the Royal Mummies* (Chicago, 1980).

Harrison, R. G. and A. G. Abdalla, 'The remains of Tutankhamun', in *Antiquity* 46 (Cambridge, 1972), pp. 8–14.

Hayes, William C., *The Scepter of Egypt*, 2 vols (New York, 1953, 1959).

Helck, Wolfgang, Eberhard Otto and Wolfhart Westendorf, *Lexikon der Ägyptologie*, 7 vols (Wiesbaden, 1975-).

Hepper, F. Nigel, *Pharaoh's Flowers. Plants of Tutankhamun's Tomb* (London, 1990).

Hoving, Thomas, *Tutankhamun. The Untold Story* (New York, 1978).

James, Thomas G. H., *The British Museum and Ancient Egypt* (London, 1981).

James, Thomas G. H. ed., *Excavating in Egypt. The Egypt Exploration Society 1882–1982* (London, 1982).

James, Thomas, G. H., *Ancient Egypt. The Land and its Legacy* (London, 1988).

James, Thomas, G. H. 'The discovery and identification of the Alabaster Quarries of Hatnub', in *Cahier de recherches de l'Institut de Papyrologie et d'Égyptologie de Lille* 13. *Mélanges Jacques Jean Clère* (Lille, 1991), pp. 79–84.

James, Thomas G. H., 'Howard Carter and the Cleveland Museum of Art', in Evan H. Turner, ed., *Object Lessons. Cleveland creates an Art Museum* (Cleveland, 1991), pp. 66–77.

James, Thomas G. H., 'The very best artist', contribution to the Cyril Aldred memorial volume, Lloyd, A. B. (ed.), *Greatest of Seers* (London, 1992?).

Keynes, Geoffrey, *The Gates of Memory* (Oxford, 1981).

Knight, Donald R. and Alan D. Sobey, *The Lion roars at Wembley* (London, 1984).

Lange, Kurt and Max Hirmer, *Egypt. Architecture, Sculpture, Painting* (4th ed., London 1968).

Lee Christopher, C., . . . *the Grand Piano came by Camel. The Story of Arthur C. Mace, Egyptologist and his family c. 1890–1928* (Renfrew, 1990).

Leek, Frank, F., *The Human Remains from the Tomb of Tut'ankhamún* (Oxford, 1972).

Lichtheim, Miriam, *Ancient Egyptian Literature*, 3 vols (Berkeley, Los Angeles, London, 1973, 1976, 1980).

Lloyd, A. B. (ed.), *Greatest of Seers* (London, 1992?).

Lucas, Alfred, 'Notes on some of the objects from the tomb of Tut-ankhamun', in *A.S.A.E.* 41 (Cairo, 1942), pp. 135–47.

Lucas, Alfred, 'Notes on some of the objects from the tomb of Tut-ankhamun', in *A.S.A.E.* 45 (Cairo, 1947), pp. 133–4.

Lucas, Alfred and John R. Harris, *Ancient Egyptian Materials and Industries* (4th ed. London, 1962).

Mace, Arthur, C., 'Work at the tomb of Tutenkhamen', in *B.M.M.A.* Dec. 1922, Part II, *The Egyptian Expedition 1922–23* (New York, 1923), pp. 5–11.

McPherson, Joseph W., *The Moulids of Egypt* (Cairo, 1941).

Malek, Jaromir, 'Paiuenamun, Sambehdet, and Howard Carter's survey of Tell el-Balamun in 1913', in *Rev.d'Ég.* 36 (Paris, 1985), pp. 181–5.

Marlowe, John, *Anglo-Egyptian Relations 1800–1953*, (London, 1954).

Martin, Geoffrey T., *The Royal Tomb at El-'Amarna*, 2 vols (London, 1974, 1989).

Mekhitarian, Arpag, 'La Fondation Égyptologique Reine Élisabeth', in *Liber Memorialis 1835–1985* (Brussels, 1985), pp. 187–9.

Montagu, Jeremy, 'One of Tut'ankhamūn's trumpets', in *J.E.A.* 64 (London, 1978), pp. 133–4.

Naville, Édouard, *The Temple of Deir el Bahari*, introductory memoir and 6 vols (London, 1894–1908).

Newberry, Percy E., *El Bersheh*, 2 vols (London, 1895).

Newberry, Percy E., 'Howard Carter', in *J.E.A.* 25 (London, 1939), pp. 67–9.

Newberry, Percy E. and others, *Beni Hasan*, 4 vols (London, 1893–1900).

Northampton, William G. S. Compton, 5th Marquis and others, *Report on some excavations in the Theban Necropolis during the winter of 1898–9* (London, 1908).

Peck, William H., 'The discoverer of the tomb of Tutankhamun and the Detroit Institute of Arts', in *J.S.S.E.A.* 11 (Toronto, 1981), pp. 65–7.

Petrie, William M. F., *Tell el Amarna* (London, 1894).

Petrie, William M. F., *Seventy Years in Archaeology* (London, 1931).

Pier, Garrett C., 'A new historical stela of the Intefs', in *A.J.S.L.L.* 21 (Chicago, 1904–5), pp. 159–62.

Rapports sur la marche du Service des Antiquités de 1899 à 1910 (Cairo, 1912).

Reeves, Nicholas, *Ancient Egypt at Highclere Castle* (Highclere, 1989).

Reeves, Nicholas, *The Complete Tutankhamun* (London, 1990).

Reeves, Nicholas, 'Howard Carter's Collection of Egyptian and Classical Antiquities', in A. B. Lloyd (ed.), *Greatest of Seers* (London, 1992?).

Reeves, (Carl) Nicholas, *The Valley of the Kings. The Decline of a Royal Necropolis* (London, 1990).

Ripper, Benjamin, *Ribbons from the Pedlar's Pack* (Swaffham, 1979).

Romer, John 'Tuthmosis I and the Bibân el-Molûk: some problems of attribution', in *J.E.A.* 60 (London, 1974), pp. 119–33.

Romer, John, *Valley of the Kings* (London, 1981).

Ross, E. Denison, *The Art of Egypt through the Ages* (London, 1931).

Ryan, Donald P., 'Who is buried in KV 60?', in *K.M.T.* 1 (San Francisco, Spring, 1990), pp. 34f.

Sayce, Archibald H., *Reminiscences* (Oxford, 1923).

Sayce, Reginald H. and Arthur E. Cowley, *Aramaic Papyri discovered at Assuan* (London, 1906).

Smith, Grafton Elliot, *Tutankhamen and the Discovery of his Tomb by the late Earl of Carnarvon and Mr. Howard Carter* (London, 1923).

Storrs, Ronald, *Orientations* (London, 1937).

Tillett, Selwyn, *Egypt Itself. The Career of Robert Hay Esquire, of Linplum and Nunraw, 1799–1863* (London, 1984).

Weigall, Arthur E. P., *A Guide to the Antiquities of Upper Egypt from Abydos to the Sudan frontier* (London, 1910).

Weigall, Arthur E. P., 'Miscellaneous notes', in *A.S.A.E.* 11 (Cairo, 1911), pp. 170–76.

Weigall, Arthur E. P., *The Life and Times of Akhnaton, Pharaoh of Egypt*, 2nd edn, (London, 1922).

Weigall, Arthur E. P., *Tutankhamen and other essays* (London, 1923).

Wheeler-Holohan, V., *The History of the King's Messengers* (London, 1935).

Williams, Valentine, *The World of Action* (London, 1938).

Winlock, Herbert E., 'An Egyptian Flower Bowl', in *Metropolitan Museum Studies* 5, pt 2 (New York, Sept, 1936), pp. 147f.

Winlock, Herbert E., *Materials used at the Embalming of King Tut-ʿankh-Amūn* (New York, 1941).

Winlock, Herbert E., *Excavations at Deir el Bahri 1911–1931* (New York, 1942).

Winlock, Herbert E., *The Treasure of Three Egyptian Princesses* (New York, 1948)

Winstone, H. V. F., *Howard Carter and the Discovery of the Tomb of Tutankhamun* (London, 1991).

INDEX

The definite and indefinite articles, including the Arabic El, are ignored in the ordering of entries.

137, 144, 148, 150, 152, 155–7, 162, 164, 167, 172, 180, 197f, 207, 211f, 228, 268, 270, 284, 292, 300, 302, 304, 325f, 354, 356, 374f, 380, 383, 386, 389, 392, 400, 404, 407f; recruits Carter for work in Egypt 10f, 14–16, 19; works with Carter in Egypt 19–33, 40–2, 49–52; excavates for T. Davis 76, 87; difference with Carter over MacGregor sale 209f, 257; joins controversy with Lacau 287, 292, 295–7; works on pall from tomb 332; friendship with Carter 399
Newbury Grammar School 327
Newbury Museum 154, 207
New Haven, *see* Yale
Newport, R.I. 134
New Oxford Theatre 268
New York 309ff, 314, 322ff, 354
New York Times 243, 309ff
News International plc xiii
Nims, Charles F. 393
Northampton, Earl of 135, 137f, 267
North Creake 402
Norwich 3, 208, 327
Norwich School of Artists 4
Norwich Union 314, 392
Nubia 80, 102, 106, 137, 173

obelisk 55, 253
Ogden, James R. 376f
Opet Festival 182f, 409
Orchestra Hall, Chicago 312
Oregon Historical Society xii, 214
Oriental Institute, Chicago xii, 130, 199f, 210, 236, 264f, 270, 322, 335, 341, 393
Orr, Margaret xi, 237, 263, 282f; *see also* Mace, M.
Oryx nome 21
Osiris 84
ostraca 184, 192
Ottawa 314, 322
Oxyrhynchus Papyri 43

Paget, Rosalind 59f
Painswick 326
Pa-iu-en-Amun 164
Pa-khen-n-Amen 164
Palestine 196
papyrus 43f, 82–4, 123, 150, 181, 200, 209, 259

Paris 124, 161, 264f, 327, 390, 402
partage of antiquities 75f, 154, 156, 172, 192, 194f, 213ff, 231, 234, 256, 273, 284, 318, 328, 330, 388
Paterson, Emily 41, 46f, 56
pavement, painted, at El-Amarna 34
Peabody Museum 322
Peck, William H. xii, 372, 393
Pedlar of Swaffham 4
Peet, T.E. 296, 404
Pemberton, Anne xi, 177, 298
Pemberton, Jeremy xi
Petrie, Hilda 99, 109
Petrie, (Sir) William M.F. 2, 7, 11–13, 20, 24f, 28–41, 43, 45, 50f, 54, 56, 59f, 67, 69, 90, 98, 104, 118, 143, 146f, 154, 172, 194, 201, 209, 228, 233, 268, 297, 313, 353, 380, 389, 404
Pevsner, Sir Nikolaus 4
Le Phare d'Alexandrie 76–8
Phelps, William Lyon 322
Philadelphia 311
Philae 80
Piccione, Peter xiv, 159
Pier, G.C. 78
Pittsburgh 311
Pius XI, Pope 387
Pius XII, Pope 387
Plenderleith, Harold xii, 350, 383, 392, 396f
Polish Centre of Mediterranean Archaeology 58
Poole, Reginald S. 46, 58
Porchester (Porch), Lord, *see* Carnarvon, 5th Earl, 6th Earl
Portman Square 15
Prince's Gate Court 369, 382, 396f
Proceedings of the Society of Biblical Archaeology 17, 27, 117
Psamtik (Psammetichus II) 83
Ptah 337
Ptahhotpe, Instruction of 148
Public Works, Ministry of 113ff, 194, 230, 277f, 289, 293, 331; Minister of 281, 284, 288, 292, 294, 307, 330
Punt 54, 60
Putney Vale Cemetery 1, 406
Puyemre 150

Qau 297
Qena 69, 226, 332, 246
Qubbet el-Hawa 81ff, 253